Worlds of History

A Comparative Reader

Volume Two: Since 1400

Worlds of History

A Comparative Reader

Volume Two: Since 1400

Third Edition

Kevin Reilly
Raritan Valley College

Bedford/St. Martin's
Boston • New York

To those who taught me to think historically: Eugene Meehan, Donald Weinstein, and Peter Stearns; and to the memory of Warren Susman and Traian Stoianovich

For Bedford/St. Martin's

Publisher for History: Mary V. Dougherty
Executive Editor for History: Katherine Meisenheimer
Director of Development for History: Jane Knetzger
Senior Developmental Editor: Louise Townsend
Editorial Assistant: Holly Dye
Senior Production Supervisor: Joe Ford
Senior Marketing Manager: Jenna Bookin Barry
Project Management: Books By Design, Inc.
Cover Design: Billy Boardman
Cover Art: J. H. Wilner, *Rice Harvest*. Haitian (20th c.) Coll. Manu Sassoonian, New York, N.Y., U.S.A. © Manu Sassoonian/Art Resource, N.Y. Qing Dynasty (1644–1912). *Harvesting Tea Leaves*. From a series of paintings depicting tea curing. Qing dynasty, 19th c. © Scala/Art Resource, N.Y.
Composition: Pine Tree Composition, Inc.
Printing and Binding: RR Donnelley & Sons Company

President: Joan E. Feinberg
Editorial Director: Denise B. Wydra
Director of Marketing: Karen Melton Soeltz
Director of Editing, Design, and Production: Marcia Cohen
Manager, Publishing Services: Emily Berleth

Library of Congress Control Number: 2006927524

For information, write: Bedford/St. Martin's, 75 Arlington Street, Boston, MA 02116   (617-399-4000)

ISBN-10: 0-312-44686-1
ISBN-13: 978-0-312-44686-4

Acknowledgments
Acknowledgments and copyrights are continued at the back of the book on pages 543–47, which constitutes a continuation of the copyright page.

Preface

Teaching introductory world history to college students for more than thirty-five years has helped me appreciate three enduring truths that provide the framework for this book. The first is that any introductory history course must begin by engaging with the students, as they sit before us in their remarkable diversity. The second is that world history requires a wide lens; it embraces all, the entire past, the whole world. The third is that students need to learn to think historically, critically, and independently, and realize that the subject matter of history can teach them how. With these truths in mind, I have constructed chapters in *Worlds of History* that pique student interest, teach broad trends and comparative experiences, and develop what today we call "critical thinking skills" and the Romans used to call "habits of mind."

The primary and secondary source selections in this reader address specific topics that I believe can imbue a general understanding of world history while helping students develop critical thinking skills. The reader's format helps students (and instructors) make sense of the overwhelming richness and complexity of world history. First, the reader has a **topical organization** that is also chronological, with each chapter focusing on an engaging topic within a particular time period. I am convinced that students are generally more interested in topics than eras, and that an appreciation of period and process can be taught by concentrating on topics. Into these topical chapters I've woven a **comparative approach,** examining two or more cultures at a time. In some chapters students can trace parallel developments in separate regions, such as the role of women in ancient China, India, and the Greco-Roman world in Volume One, or the rise of capitalism and industrialization in Latin America, India, Europe, and Japan in Volume Two. In other cases students examine the enduring effects of contact and exchange between cultures, as in Volume One's chapter on Mongol and Viking raiding and settlements from the tenth to the fourteenth centuries or Volume Two's chapter on the scientific revolution in Europe, the Americas, and Asia.

A wealth of **pedagogical tools** helps students unlock the readings and hone their critical thinking skills. Each chapter begins with **"Historical Context,"** an introduction to the chapter's topic that sets the stage for directed comparisons among the readings. A separate **"Thinking Historically"** section follows, exploring a particular critical thinking skill — reading primary and secondary sources or distinguishing causes of change — that ties to the chapter's selections. These skills build students' capacity to analyze, synthesize, and interpret one step at a time. A set of **"Reflections"** that both summarizes and extends the chapter's lessons concludes each chapter.

Each volume's fourteen chapters should correspond to general survey texts and to most instructors' syllabi. Understanding that some variation might exist, I have included a correlation chart in the **Instructor's Resource Manual** that matches each reading in this text with related chapters in more than a dozen of the most widely used survey texts. The manual, available at **bedfordstmartins.com/reilly** as well as in a one-volume print version, provides the rationale for the selection and organization of the readings, suggestions for teaching with the documents, and information about additional resources, including films and Internet sites.

NEW TO THIS EDITION

While I am continually testing selections in my own classroom, I appreciate input from readers and adopters, and I want to thank them for their many suggestions. Having incorporated some of this feedback, I think those who have used the reader previously will find the third edition even more geographically and topically comprehensive, interesting, and accessible to students. Twenty-five to 30 percent new documents on regions and topics from Latin America to Polynesia and from genocide to women in politics in the twentieth century have allowed me to introduce fresh material into each volume. In addition, I have included one new chapter in each volume, coincidentally, both Chapter 12: "The Black Death" in Volume One offers an in-depth look at this momentous event in Afro-Eurasian history; in Volume Two, "Religion and Politics: Israel, Palestine, and the West" provides a compelling and troubling look at contemporary conflict in the Middle East and its historic antecedents. Finally, I have also included five new "Thinking Historically" exercises across the volumes: "Distinguishing Historical Understanding from Moral Judgments," "Considering Cause and Effect," "Understanding and Explaining the Unforgivable," "Evaluating Grand Theories," and "Making Use of the Unexpected."

Another exciting substantive change to this edition is the inclusion of more visuals as documents and increased emphasis on their importance as historical evidence. Four chapters in each volume incorporate visual evidence, including Egyptian wall paintings, Fayum portraits of women, images of the Black Death, and illustrations of humans and the environment in Volume One; and contrasting views of Amerindians, Japanese images of Westernization, World War I propaganda posters, and "Global Snapshots" of the world's energy use, population, and wealth distribution in Volume Two.

Two more changes to this edition of *Worlds of History* I hope have made the reader even more accessible. Improved and new maps in almost every chapter — for example, "The Expansion of Islam to 750" in Volume One, Chapter 7, and "U.S. Involvement in Central America" in Volume

Two, Chapter 11 — will help students locate the regions and cultures under consideration. A running pronunciation guide at the base of the page that sounds out difficult-to-pronounce terms and names for readers should help students discuss the sources with greater confidence.

I am not a believer in change for its own sake; when I have a successful way of teaching a subject, I am not disposed to jettison it for something new. Consequently, many of my most satisfying changes are incremental: a better translation of a document or the addition of a newly discovered source. In some cases I have been able to further edit a useful source, retaining its muscle, but providing room for a precious new find. I begin each round of revision with the conviction that the book is already as good as it can get. And I end each round with the surprising discovery that it is much better than it was.

ACKNOWLEDGMENTS

A book like this cannot be written without the help and advice, even if sometimes unheeded, of a vast army of colleagues and friends. I consider myself enormously fortunate to have met and known such a large group of gifted and generous scholars and teachers during my years with the World History Association. Some were especially helpful in the preparation of this new edition. They include Jean Berger, *University of Wisconsin–Fox Valley*; Fred Bilenkis, *John Jay College, CUNY*; John Bohstedt, *University of Tennessee, Knoxville*; Jason Freitag, *Ithaca College*; Jesse Hingson, *Georgia College*; Theodore Kallman, *San Joaquin Delta College*; Andrew J. Kirkendall, *Texas A&M University*; Leonora Neville, *The Catholic University of America*; Lauren Ristvet, *Georgia State University*; Fulian Patrick Shan, *Grand Valley State University*; Anthony J. Steinhoff, *University of Tennessee-Chattanooga*; and Stephen Tallackson, *Purdue University Calumet*.

Over the years I have benefited from the suggestions of innumerable friends and fellow world historians. Among them: Michael Adas, *Rutgers University*; Jerry Bentley, *University of Hawaii*; David Berry, *Essex County Community College*; Edmund (Terry) Burke III, *UC Santa Cruz*; Catherine Clay, *Shippensburg University*; Philip Curtin, *Johns Hopkins University*; S. Ross Doughty, *Ursinus College*; Ross Dunn, *San Diego State University*; Marc Gilbert, *North Georgia College*; Steve Gosch, *University of Wisconsin at Eau Claire*; Gregory Guzman, *Bradley University*; Brock Haussamen, *Raritan Valley College*; Allen Howard, *Rutgers University*; Sarah Hughes, *Shippensburg University*; Stephen Kaufman, *Raritan Valley College*; Karen Jolly, *University of Hawaii*; Maghan Keita, *Villanova University*; Pat Manning, *University of Pittsburgh*; John McNeill, *Georgetown University*; William

H. McNeill, *University of Chicago*; Gyan Prakash, *Princeton University*; Robert Rosen, *UCLA*; Heidi Roupp, *Aspen High School*; John Russell-Wood, *Johns Hopkins University*; Lynda Shaffer, *Tufts University*; Robert Strayer, *UC Santa Cruz*; Robert Tignor, *Princeton University*; and John Voll, *Georgetown University*.

I also want to thank the people at Bedford/St. Martin's. Joan Feinberg and Denise Wydra remained involved and helpful throughout, as did Mary Dougherty, Katherine Meisenheimer, and Jane Knetzger. Amy Leathe provided invaluable help in reviewing the previous edition, and Holly Dye developed the instructor's manual and companion Web site for the book. I want to thank my production managers, Nancy Benjamin, for her project management, and Emily Berleth, for overseeing the entire production process (some thirty-five years after she first made me an author). I would also like to thank Mary Sanger for copyediting, Billy Boardman and Donna Dennison for the cover design, and Jenna Bookin Barry for advertising and promotion. Finally, it was a pleasure to work with senior developmental editor Louise Townsend. Rarely is an editor so knowledgeable in a field as vast as world history, so vigorous and insightful in her comments and suggestions, and so ready and able to do more.

While writing this book, memories of my own introduction to history and critical thinking came flooding back to me. I was blessed at Rutgers in the 1960s with teachers I still aspire to emulate. Eugene Meehan taught me how to think and showed me that I could. Traian Stoianovich introduced me to the world and an endless range of historical inquiry. Warren Susman lit up a room with more life than I ever knew existed. Donald Weinstein guided me as a young teaching assistant to listen to students and talk with them rather than at them. And Peter Stearns showed me how important and exciting it could be to understand history by making comparisons. I dedicate this book to them.

Finally, I want to thank my own institution, Raritan Valley College, for nurturing my career, allowing me to teach whatever I wanted, and entrusting me with some of the best students one could encounter anywhere. I could not ask for anything more. Except, of course, a loving wife like Pearl.

                                                        Kevin Reilly

Introduction

You have here fourteen lessons in world history, each of which deals with a particular historical period and topic since the fifteenth century. (A companion volume addresses human history to 1550.) Some of the topics are narrow and specific, covering events such as overseas expansion in the Early Modern period or the Arab-Israeli crisis in detail, while others are broad and general, such as state and religion or westernization and nationalism in the modern world.

As you learn about historical periods and topics, you will also be learning to explore history by analyzing primary and secondary sources systematically. The "Thinking Historically" exercises in each chapter encourage habits of mind that I associate with my own study of history. They are not necessarily intended to turn you into historians but, rather, to give you skills that will help you in all of your college courses and throughout your life. For example, the first chapter distinguishes primary sources (eyewitness accounts) from secondary sources (historical interpretations) — certainly something that historians do. But the true value of this exercise, and of the others that build on it in the reader, is in helping you to differentiate between fact and opinion and otherwise to build critical thinking, clearly abilities as necessary at work, on a jury, in the voting booth, and in discussions with friends as they are in the study of history.

World history is nothing less than everything ever done or imagined, so we cannot possibly cover it all. In his famous novel *Ulysses*, James Joyce imagines the thoughts and actions of a few friends on a single day in Dublin, June 16, 1904. The book runs almost a thousand pages. Obviously, there were many more than a few people in Dublin on that particular day, countless other cities in the world, and infinitely more days than that one particular day in world history. So we are forced to choose among different places and times in our study of the global past.

In this volume our choices do include some particular moments in time, like Lakota Indian Luther Standing Bear's experience in the 1880s of being "civilized" at a white-run boarding school, but our attention will be directed toward much longer periods as well. And while we will visit particular places in time like this boarding school in the late nineteenth century, typically we will study more than one place at a time by using a comparative approach.

Comparisons can be enormously useful in studying world history. When we compare the Enlightenment in Europe and the Americas, capitalism in England and in Japan, or genocide in Guatemala and Rwanda, we learn about the general and the specific at the same time. My hope is that by comparing some of the various *worlds* of history, a deeper and more nuanced understanding of our global past will emerge. With that understanding, we are better equipped to make sense of the world today and to confront whatever the future holds.

Contents

3. State and Religion

Asian, Islamic, and Christian States, 1500–1800   88

*In this chapter, we view the relationship between religion and political author-
ity through the prism of Chinese, Japanese, South Asian, and Western experience in the early modern period. By examining the competing and sometimes
cooperating dynamics between church and state in the past, we explore the history of an issue much debated in our own time and gain new insights into
church-state relations today.*

HISTORICAL CONTEXT   88

THINKING HISTORICALLY
Relating Past and Present   89

4. Gender and Family

China, Southeast Asia, Europe,
and "New Spain," 1600–1750   122

With the blinds drawn on the domestic lives of our ancestors, one might as-
sume their private worlds were uneventful and everywhere the same. By com-
paring different cultures we see historical variety in family and economic life
and the roles of both men and women.

5. The Scientific Revolution

Europe, the Ottoman Empire, China, Japan,
and the Americas, 1600–1800   *159*

The scientific revolution of the seventeenth and eighteenth centuries occurred
in Europe, but had important roots in Asia, and its consequences reverberated
throughout the world. In this chapter we seek to understand what changed and
how. How "revolutionary" was the scientific revolution and how do we distin-
guish between mere change and "revolutionary" change?

6. Enlightenment and Revolution
Europe and the Americas, 1650–1850　193

The eighteenth-century Enlightenment applied scientific reason to politics, but reason meant different things to different people and societies. What were the goals of the political revolutions produced by the Enlightenment? A close reading of the period texts reveals disagreement and shared dreams.

HISTORICAL CONTEXT　193

THINKING HISTORICALLY
Close Reading and Interpretation of Texts　194

7. Capitalism and the Industrial Revolution
Europe and the World, 1750–1900　227

Modern society has been shaped dramatically by capitalism and the industrial revolution, but these two forces are not the same. Which one is principally responsible for the creation of our modern world: the economic system of the market or the technology of the industrial revolution? Distinguishing different "causes" allows us to gauge their relative effects and legacies.

HISTORICAL CONTEXT　227

THINKING HISTORICALLY
Distinguishing Causes of Change　228

8. Colonized and Colonizers
Europeans in Africa and Asia, 1850–1930 273

Colonialism resulted in a world divided between the colonized and the coloniz-ers, a world in which people's identities were defined by their power relation-ships with others who looked and often spoke differently. The meeting of strangers and their forced adjustment to predefined roles inspired a number of great literary works that we look to in this chapter for historical guidance.

HISTORICAL CONTEXT 273

THINKING HISTORICALLY
Using Literature in History 275

9. Nationalism and Westernization
Japan, India, and the Americas, 1880–1930 308

Western colonialism elicited two often conflicting responses among the colo-nized — the assertion of national independence and the desire to imitate West-ern power or culture. Exploring these sometimes contradictory movements through the visual and written sources in this chapter reveals much about the historical process and helps us appreciate the struggles of peoples torn between different ideals.

Contents

10. World War I and Its Consequences

Europe and the Soviet Union, 1914–1920   346

The First World War brutally ended an era — the world would never be the same after such death and destruction. We read historical accounts and analyze images from the era so that we can begin to understand the war's far-reaching chain of causes and consequences.

11. World War II and Genocide
Europe, Japan, China, Rwanda, and Guatemala, 1931–1994   383

The rise of fascism in Europe and Asia led to world war and genocide. Although we hope another world war will not occur, the legacy of World War II's genocide and of the mass killings that preceded it earlier in the century lives on in contemporary genocides around the globe. How could (how can) people allow their governments, armies, families, and friends to commit such unspeakable acts? How does the unforgivable happen?

HISTORICAL CONTEXT   *383*

THINKING HISTORICALLY
Understanding and Explaining the Unforgivable   *385*

Reflections   *419*

12. Religion and Politics
Israel, Palestine, and the West, 1896 to the Present   421

The conflict between Israel and Palestine allows us to study the role of religion and politics in a particular place at a particular time, but the conflict is one whose impact can be felt not just across the Middle East but throughout the world. Learning to make use of new and unexpected information and ideas found in historical documents can provide a fresh take on seemingly intractable conflicts.

HISTORICAL CONTEXT   *421*

THINKING HISTORICALLY
Making Use of the Unexpected   *422*

13. Women's World
1950 to the Present   469

The lives of women in the modern world are as diverse as those of men. Can you find any patterns in these personal accounts and stories? Can you develop any theories about women's lives in the modern world?

HISTORICAL CONTEXT   469

THINKING HISTORICALLY
Constructing Theory   470

14. Globalization and Planetary Health
1960 to the Present   506

Globalization is a word with many meanings and a process with many causes. What are the forces most responsible for the shrinking of the world into one global community? Do the forces of globalization unite or divide us? What are the environmental effects of these forces? We undertake the study of process to answer these questions.

HISTORICAL CONTEXT   506

THINKING HISTORICALLY
Understanding Process   508

List of Maps

Worlds of History

A Comparative Reader

Volume Two: To 1400

Overseas Expansion
in the Early Modern Period

China and Europe, 1400–1600

HISTORICAL CONTEXT

Between 1400 and 1500, the balance between Chinese and European sea power changed drastically. Before 1434, Chinese shipbuilding was the envy of the world. Chinese ships were larger, more numerous, safer, and better outfitted than European ships. The Chinese navy made frequent trips through the South China Sea to the Spice Islands, through the Indian Ocean, and as far as East Africa and the Persian Gulf (see Map 1.1). Every island, port, and kingdom along the route was integrated into the Chinese system of tributaries. Goods were exchanged, marriages arranged, and princes taken to visit the Chinese emperor.

In the second half of the fifteenth century, the Chinese navy virtually disappeared. At the same time, the Portuguese began a series of explorations down the coast of Africa and into the Atlantic Ocean. In 1434, Portuguese ships rounded the treacherous Cape Bojador, just south of Morocco. In 1488, Bartolomeu Dias rounded the Cape of Good Hope. Vasco da Gama sailed into the Indian Ocean, arriving in Calicut the following year. And in 1500 a fortuitous landfall in Brazil by Pedro Cabral gave the Portuguese a claim from the western Atlantic to the Indian Ocean. By 1512, Portuguese ships had reached the Bandas and Moluccas — the Spice Islands of what is today eastern Indonesia.

Beginning in 1492, after the defeat of the Moors (Muslims) and the voyages of Columbus, the Spanish claimed most of the Western Hemisphere until challenged by the Dutch, English, and French. European control in the Americas penetrated far deeper than in Asia, where it was limited to enclaves on the coast, and where European nations were in an almost perpetual state of war with each other. Taken together, the nations of Western Europe dominated the seas of the world after 1500 (see Map 1.2).

1

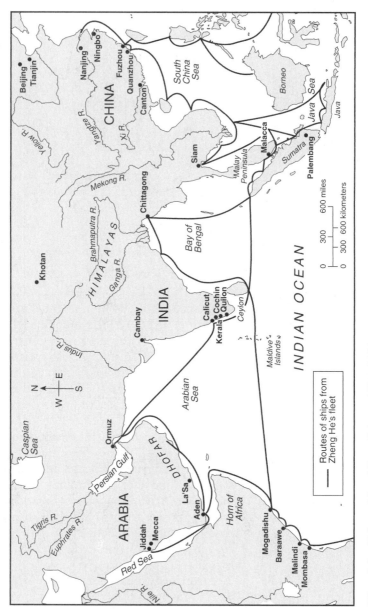

Map 1.1 Chinese Naval Expeditions, 1405–1433.

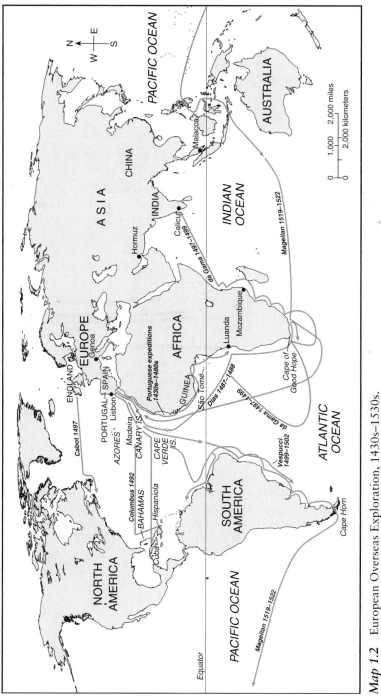

Map 1.2 European Overseas Exploration, 1430s–1530s.

What accounts for the different fortunes of China and Europe in the fifteenth century? Were the decline of China and the rise of Europe inevitable? Probably no objective observer of the time would have thought so. In what ways were the expansions of China and Europe similar? In what ways were they different? Think about these questions as you reflect on the readings in this chapter.

THINKING HISTORICALLY
Reading Primary and Secondary Sources

This chapter contains both primary and secondary sources. *Primary sources* are actual pieces of the past and include anything — art, letters, essays, and so on — from the historical period being studied. If a future historian were to study and research students in American colleges at the beginning of the twenty-first century, some primary sources might include diaries, letters, cartoons, music videos, posters, paintings, e-mail messages, blogs and Web sites, class notes, school newspapers, tests, and official and unofficial records. *Secondary sources* are usually books and articles *about* the past — interpretations of the past. These sources are "secondary" because they must be based on primary sources; therefore, a history written after an event occurs is a secondary source.

In your studies, you will be expected to distinguish primary from secondary sources. A quick glance at the introductions to this chapter's selections tells you that the first article is written by a modern journalist and the third and fifth are written by an amateur historian and an environmentalist, taken from books published in 2003 and 1991, respectively. In contrast, the second selection, an inscription ordered by Admiral Zheng He* that dates from the fifteenth century, and the fourth selection, a letter penned by Christopher Columbus more than five hundred years ago, are firsthand accounts of worlds long past.

Having determined whether selections are primary or secondary sources, we also explore some of the subtle complexities that are overlooked by such designations.

Note: Pronunciations of difficult-to-pronounce terms will be given throughout the chapter. The emphasis goes on the syllable appearing in all capital letters. [Ed.]
   *jung HUH

JOSEPH KAHN

"China Has an Ancient Mariner to Tell You About"

In this 2005 *New York Times* article journalist Joseph Kahn, currently Beijing bureau chief for the *Times,* combines a brief history of the life of Zheng He with a critical view of recent Chinese government efforts at reviving the reputation of the fifteenth-century admiral. Who was Zheng He? Why, according to Kahn, is China focusing attention on him?

Thinking Historically

Newspaper stories are not primary sources — unless the subject is the newspaper itself, the reporter of the story, or the way in which newspapers presented the particular story. Some historians would say that a newspaper story as brief as this one is hardly even a secondary source because it tells us very little of what modern historians know about Zheng He. For an understanding of the great Chinese admiral, this might better be called a third level, or tertiary, source. Still, even a news story must rely on sources. What primary and secondary sources does this article refer to?

The captivating tale of Zheng He, a Chinese eunuch who explored the Pacific and Indian Oceans with a mighty armada almost a century before Columbus discovered America, has long languished as a tantalizing footnote in China's imperial history.

Zheng He (pronounced jung huh) fell into disfavor before he completed the last of his early 15th-century voyages, and most historical records were destroyed. Authorities protected his old family home in Nanjing, but it was often shuttered, its rooms used to store unrelated relics.

Joseph Kahn, "Letter from Asia: China Has an Ancient Mariner to Tell You About," *New York Times,* July 20, 2005, Section A, p. 4.

Now, on the 600th anniversary of Zheng He's first mission in 1405, all that is changing. Zheng He's legacy is being burnished — some critics say glossed over — to give rising China a new image on the world stage.

Books and television shows, replicas of Zheng He's ships and a new $50 million museum in Nanjing promote Zheng He as a maritime cultural ambassador for a powerful but ardently peaceful nation.

Officials have even endorsed the theory, so far unproven, that one of Zheng He's ships foundered on the rocks near Lamu island, off the coast of today's Kenya, with survivors swimming ashore, marrying locals and creating a family of Chinese-Africans that is now being reunited with the Chinese motherland.

The message is that Zheng He foreshadowed China's 21st-century emergence as a world power, though one that differs in crucial respects from Spain, Britain, France, Germany, Japan, and, most pointedly, the United States.

"In the heyday of the Ming Dynasty, China did not seek hegemony," says Wan Ming, a leading scholar of the era. "Today, we are once again growing stronger all the time, and China's style of peaceful development has been welcomed all over the world."

The Communist Party hopes to signal to its own people that it has recaptured past glory, while reassuring foreign countries that China can be strong and non-threatening at the same time.

Even within China, though, the use of poorly documented history as a modern propaganda prop has generated a backlash.

Several scholars have publicly criticized the campaign as a distortion, saying Zheng He treated foreigners as barbarians and most foreign countries as vassal states. His voyages amounted to a wasteful tribute to a maniacal emperor, some argue.

Zheng He resonates, favorably or not, in Asia. Arguably for the first time since his final voyage in 1433, China is vying to become a major maritime power.

Beijing has upgraded its navy with Russian-built Sovremenny-class guided missile destroyers, Kilo-class diesel submarines, and a new nuclear submarine equipped to carry intercontinental ballistic missiles. It has flirted with the idea of building an aircraft carrier, according to conflicting reports in state media.

Sustained double-digit increases in defense spending have helped make China one of the largest military powers in the world, though still well behind the United States. China says it aims only to defend itself. But others are skeptical.

"Since no nation threatens China, one wonders: why this growing investment?" Defense Secretary Donald H. Rumsfeld asked recently in a speech on China's buildup during a visit to Singapore last month.

Beijing clearly hopes history will help answer the question.

Zheng He was a Chinese Muslim who, following the custom of the day, was castrated so he could serve in the household of a prince, Zhu Di.*

Zhu Di later toppled the emperor, his brother, and took the throne for himself. He rewarded Zheng He, his co-conspirator, with command of the greatest naval expedition that the world had ever seen. Beginning in July 1405, Zheng He made port calls all around Southeast Asia, rounded India, explored the Middle East and reached the eastern coast of Africa.

The three ships Columbus guided across the Atlantic 87 years later, the Niña, Pinta, and Santa María, could fit inside a single large vessel in Zheng He's armada, which at its peak had up to 300 ships and 30,000 sailors. Some of China's maritime innovations at the time, including watertight compartments, did not show up on European vessels for hundreds of years.

Zheng He was China's first big ocean trader, presenting gifts from the emperor to leaders in foreign ports and hauling back crabapples, myrrh, mastic gum, and even a giraffe.

In time, though, the emperor turned against seafaring, partly because of the exorbitant cost, partly because of China's religious certitude that it had nothing to learn from the outside world. By the latter part of the 15th century the country had entered a prolonged period of self-imposed isolation that lasted into the 20th century, leaving European powers to rule the seas.

For Chinese officials today, the sudden end of China's maritime ambitions 600 years ago conveniently signals something else: that China is a gentle giant with enduring good will.

Zheng He represents China's commitment to "good neighborliness, peaceful coexistence, and scientific navigation," government-run China Central Television said during an hour-long documentary on the explorer last week.

Earlier this month, authorities opened a $50 million memorial to Zheng He. Tributes to him fill courtyard-style exhibition halls, painted in stately vermillion and imperial yellow. A hulking statue of Zheng He, his chest flung forward as in many Communist-era likenesses of Mao, decorates the main hall.

As the Zheng He anniversary approached, delegations of Chinese diplomats and scholars also traveled to Kenya to investigate the claims that islanders there could trace their roots to sailors on Zheng He's fleet.

On one remote island, called Siyu, the Chinese found a 19-year-old high school student, Mwamaka Sharifu, who claimed Chinese ancestry.

*zhoo DEE

Beijing's embassy in Nairobi arranged for her to visit China to attend Zheng He celebrations. Beijing has invited her back to study in China, tuition-free, this fall.

"My family members have round faces, small eyes, and black hair, so we long believed we are Chinese," Ms. Sharifu said in a telephone interview. "Now we have a direct link to China itself."

The outreach effort has generated positive publicity for China in Kenya and some other African countries, as well as around Southeast Asia, where Zheng He is widely admired.

But Zheng He has been more coolly received by some scholars in China and abroad.

Geoff Wade, a China specialist at the National University of Singapore, argued in an academic essay that Zheng He helped the Ming state colonize neighboring countries. His far-flung expeditions aimed at enforcing a "pax Ming" through Southeast Asia, allowing China to wrest control of trade routes dominated at that time by Arabs, he wrote.

Several Chinese experts also questioned whether Zheng He's legacy is as salutary as government officials hope.

Ye Jun, a Beijing historian, said the official contention that Zheng He was a good-will ambassador is a "one-sided interpretation that blindly ignores the objective fact that Zheng He engaged in military suppression" to achieve the emperor's goals.

"These matters should be left to scholars," Mr. Ye said.

2

ZHENG HE

Inscription to the Goddess

This inscription was carved on a stone erected to the Chinese Daoist goddess called the Celestial Spouse at Changle in Fujian Province of China in 1431. Zheng He left other inscriptions to other deities on his travels so it would be a mistake to read much of a religious motive in this act by the admiral who had been raised a Muslim. In fact, in

Zheng He, "Inscription to the Goddess," in *China and Africa in the Middle Ages*, ed. Teobaldo Filesi, trans. David L. Morrison (London: Frank Cass, 1972), 57–61. Americanized and slightly simplified.

1411, Zheng He erected a monument in Sri Lanka dedicated to three deities in three languages. The Chinese portion praised Buddha, a section in Tamil was dedicated to the god Tenavarai-Nayanar, and a third section in Persian was inscribed to Allah.

This selection conveys some idea of how Zheng He must have perceived his mission or wanted it to be understood. Judging from this inscription, would you call Zheng He, to use Joseph Kahn's terms, a good-will ambassador or a military oppressor?

Thinking Historically

Primary sources like this one can be difficult for a modern reader to interpret because they were not written for us, but for another audience in a different time. A modern journalist like Joseph Kahn speaks directly to us; the fifteenth-century mariner does not. This lack of "fit" between ancient source and modern ear can actually be a benefit, however, because it better enables us to distinguish fact from propaganda, truth from spin. As you read this selection, ask yourself what the author wants the reader to believe and what in his writing he could not have crafted for the purpose of persuading or fooling the audience. Your answer to the latter part of this question provides us with historical knowledge of a high degree of certainty.

For an example of how this works, look at the first sentence, the title that declares the nature of the inscription: "Record of the miraculous answer (to prayer) of the goddess the Celestial Spouse." We *do not* learn from this that the author received a miraculous answer to his prayer. We cannot even be sure that he thought he did (since he may not be telling the truth). But we do learn some things beyond doubt. We learn from this sentence that some Chinese believed in a goddess called "the Celestial Spouse." We learn that some Chinese prayed to the goddess and that some believed she could provide "miraculous answers." We learn all of these things because the inscription would make no sense otherwise. These are the assumptions rather than the arguments of the inscription. We learn from primary sources by asking about the things they *assume*. Try this exercise with the rest of the selection.

Record of the miraculous answer (to prayer) of the goddess the Celestial Spouse.

The Imperial Ming Dynasty unifying seas and continents, surpassing the three dynasties even goes beyond the Han and Tang dynasties. The countries beyond the horizon and from the ends of the earth have all become subjects and to the most western of the western or the most northern of the northern countries, however far they may be, the distance and the routes may be calculated. Thus the barbarians from beyond the seas, though their countries are truly distant, have come to audience bearing precious objects and presents.

The Emperor, approving of their loyalty and sincerity, has ordered Zheng He and others at the head of several tens of thousands of officers and flag-troops to ascend more than one hundred large ships to go and confer presents on them in order to make manifest the transforming power of the imperial virtue and to treat distant people with kindness. From the third year of Yongle (1405) till now we have seven times received the commission of ambassadors to countries of the western ocean. The barbarian countries which we have visited are: by way of Zhancheng (Champa), Zhaowa (Java), Sanfoqi (Palembang) and Xianle (Siam) crossing straight over to Xilanshan (Ceylon) in South India, Guli (Calicut), and Kezhi (Cochin), we have gone to the western regions Hulumosi (Hormuz), Adan (Aden), Mugudushu (Mogadishu), altogether more than thirty countries large and small. We have traversed more than one hundred thousand li[1] of immense water spaces and have beheld in the ocean huge waves like mountains rising sky-high, and we have set eyes on barbarian regions far away hidden in a blue transparency of light vapors, while our sails loftily unfurled like clouds day and night continued their course rapid like a star, traversing those savage waves as if we were treading a public thoroughfare. Truly this was due to the majesty and the good fortune of the Court and moreover we owe it to the protecting virtue of the divine Celestial Spouse.

The power of the goddess having indeed been manifested in previous times has been abundantly revealed in the present generation. In the midst of the rushing waters it happened that, when there was a hurricane, suddenly there was a divine lantern shining in the mast, and as soon as this miraculous light appeared the danger was appeased, so that even in the danger of capsizing one felt reassured that there was no cause for fear. When we arrived in the distant countries we captured alive those of the native kings who were not respectful and exterminated those barbarian robbers who were engaged in piracy, so that consequently the sea route was cleansed and pacified and the natives put their trust in it. All this is due to the favors of the goddess.

It is not easy to enumerate completely all the cases where the goddess has answered prayers. Previously in a memorial to the Court we have requested that her virtue be registered in the Court of Sacrificial Worship and a temple be built at Nanking on the bank of the dragon river where regular sacrifices should be transmitted forever. We have respectfully received an Imperial commemorative composition exalting the miraculous favors, which is the highest recompense and praise in-

---

[1]A li = ⅓ mile. [Ed.]

deed. However, the miraculous power of the goddess resides wherever one goes. As for the temporary palace on the southern mountain at Changle, I have, at the head of the fleet, frequently resided there awaiting the favorable wind to set sail for the ocean.

We, Zheng He and others, on the one hand have received the high favor of a gracious commission of our Sacred Lord, and on the other hand carry to the distant barbarians the benefits of respect and good faith. Commanding the multitudes on the fleet and being responsible for a quantity of money and valuables, in the face of the violence of the winds and the nights, our one fear is not to be able to succeed; how should we then dare not to serve our dynasty with exertion of all our loyalty and the gods with the utmost sincerity? How would it be possible not to realize what is the source of the tranquility of the fleet and the troops and the salvation on the voyage both going and returning? Therefore we have made manifest the virtue of the goddess on stone and have moreover recorded the years and months of the voyages to the barbarian countries and the return in order to leave the memory for ever.

I. In the third year of Yongle (1405) commanding the fleet we went to Guli (Calicut) and other countries. At that time the pirate Chen Zuyi had gathered his followers in the country of Sanfoqi (Palembang), where he plundered the native merchants. When he also advanced to resist our fleet, supernatural soldiers secretly came to the rescue so that after one beating of the drum he was annihilated. In the fifth year (1407) we returned.

II. In the fifth year of Yongle (1407) commanding the fleet we went to Zhaowa (Java), Guli (Calicut), Kezhi (Cochin), and Xianle (Siam). The kings of these countries all sent as tribute precious objects, precious birds, and rare animals. In the seventh year (1409) we returned.

III. In the seventh year of Yongle (1409) commanding the fleet we went to the countries visited before and took our route by the country of Xilanshan (Ceylon). Its king Yaliekunaier (Alagakkonara) was guilty of a gross lack of respect and plotted against the fleet. Owing to the manifest answer to prayer of the goddess the plot was discovered and thereupon that king was captured alive. In the ninth year (1411) on our return the king was presented to the throne as a prisoner; subsequently he received the Imperial favor of returning to his own country.

IV. In the eleventh year of Yongle (1413) commanding the fleet we went to Hulumosi (Ormuz) and other countries. In the country of Sumendala (Samudra)[2] there was a false king Suganla (Sekandar) who was marauding and invading his country. Its king Cainu-liabiding

---

[2]Kerala, India. [Ed.]

(Zaynu-'l-Abidin) had sent an envoy to the Palace Gates in order to lodge a complaint. We went thither with the official troops under our command and exterminated some and arrested other rebels, and owing to the silent aid of the goddess we captured the false king alive. In the thirteenth year (1415) on our return he was presented to the Emperor as a prisoner. In that year the king of the country of Manlajia (Malacca) came in person with his wife and son to present tribute.

V. In the fifteenth year of Yongle (1417) commanding the fleet we visited the western regions. The country of Hulumosi (Ormuz) presented lions, leopards with gold spots, and large western horses. The country of Adan (Aden) presented qilin of which the native name is culafa (giraffe), as well as the long-horned animal maha (oryx). The country of Mugudushu (Mogadishu) presented huafu lu ("striped" zebras) as well as lions. The country of Bulawa (Brava)[3] presented camels which run one thousand li as well as camel-birds (ostriches). The countries of Zhaowa (Java) and Guli (Calicut) presented the animal miligao. They all vied in presenting the marvelous objects preserved in the mountains or hidden in the seas and the beautiful treasures buried in the sand or deposited on the shores. Some sent a maternal uncle of the king, others a paternal uncle or a younger brother of the king in order to present a letter of homage written on gold leaf as well as tribute.

VI. In the nineteenth year of Yongle (1421) commanding the fleet we conducted the ambassadors from Hulumosi (Ormuz) and the other countries that had been in attendance at the capital for a long time back to their countries. The kings of all these countries prepared even more tribute than previously.

VII. In the sixth year of Xuande (1431) once more commanding the fleet we have left for the barbarian countries in order to read to them (an Imperial edict) and to confer presents.

We have anchored in this port awaiting a north wind to take the sea, and recalling how previously we have on several occasions received the benefits of the protection of the divine intelligence we have thus recorded an inscription in stone.

---

[3]Baraawe, Somalia. [Ed.]

GAVIN MENZIES

From 1421: The Year China Discovered America

Writer Gavin Menzies has recently caused a stir among historians by arguing in his book *1421: The Year China Discovered America* that Zheng He's ships actually reached America. This selection from that same work contains the author's more reliable discussion of the preparations for the great Chinese naval expedition of 1421, Zheng He's sixth, setting events in the broader context of Chinese imperial history and its tribute system.

As Zheng He indicated in the "Inscription to the Goddess" (selection 2), the 1421 voyage was intended to return a number of foreign ambassadors to their home countries after they had participated in the inauguration of the emperor Zhu Di's new capital city at Beijing. How was such a voyage part of the Chinese system of trade and diplomacy? What did the Chinese stand to gain by such a system? What did those tribute-paying countries gain? Does Menzies's description support the Chinese government claim that the tribute system was peaceful, or does it seem to be the "military suppression" charged by at least one historian (see selection 1)?

Thinking Historically

This is clearly a secondary source. It depends on many primary and other secondary sources. As indicated in the first selection of this chapter, the gathering of primary sources about the Chinese treasure ships suffers from severe limitations. Most of the imperial archives as well as the ships were destroyed by the successor Ming emperors after 1435. Persuaded by the traditional Confucian bureaucracy to abandon the naval ventures favored by palace eunuchs, later emperors even banned Chinese habitation along the coastal corridor of the China Sea.

For this selection, however, on the preparations for the voyage of 1421, Gavin Menzies is able to use available primary and secondary sources on various aspects of Ming Chinese society and culture. Notice also how he uses information from other cultures and other periods to

Gavin Menzies, *1421: The Year China Discovered America* (New York: HarperCollins, 2003), 60–71.

help the reader understand the scale of these Ming treasure ships. The ordinary reader cannot distinguish Menzies's assumptions from his arguments as easily as with a primary source. One tends to read a secondary source less critically than a primary source. Nevertheless, what are the advantages of a secondary source like this? Without checking the footnotes (and Menzies provides very few), which of the details or interpretations in this selection are you most inclined to question? Why?

Chinese foreign policy was quite different from that of the Europeans who followed them to the Indian Ocean many years later. The Chinese preferred to pursue their aims by trade, influence, and bribery rather than by open conflict and direct colonization. Zhu Di's policy was to despatch huge armadas every few years throughout the known world, bearing gifts and trade goods; the massive treasure ships carrying a huge array of guns and a travelling army of soldiers were also a potent reminder of his imperial might: China alone had the necessary firepower to protect friendly countries from invasion and quash insurrections against their rulers. The treasure ships returned to China with all manner of exotic items: "dragon saliva [ambergris], incense and golden amber" and "lions, gold spotted leopards and camel-birds [ostriches] which are six or seven feet tall" from Africa; gold cloth from Calicut in south-west India, studded with pearls and precious stones; elephants, parrots, sandalwood, peacocks, hardwood, incense, tin, and cardamom from Siam (modern Thailand).

Those rulers who accepted the emperor's overlordship were rewarded with titles, protection, and trade missions. In south-east Asia, Malacca was rewarded for its loyalty by being promoted as a trading port at the expense of Java and Sumatra; the emperor even personally composed a poem for the Malaccan sultan, and can be said to have been the founder of Malaysia. The subservient Siamese were also extended trading privileges to the detriment of the truculent Cambodians. Korea was especially important to China. Zhu Di lost no time in despatching an envoy to the King of Korea, Yi Pang-Won, granting him an honorary Chinese title. The Koreans needed Chinese medicine, books, and astronomical instruments, and in return they agreed to set up an observatory to co-operate with Zhu Di in charting the world. They traded leopards, seals, gold, silver and horses — one thousand of them in 1403, ten thousand the next year. Despite some reluctance, they also found it expedient to comply with Chinese requests to fill Zhu Di's harem with virgins. Many Korean ships were to join the Chinese fleets when they left to sail the world.

As soon as he had expelled the last Mongols from China in 1382, Zhu Di had despatched his eunuch Isiha to the perennially troublesome region of Manchuria in the far north-east, and in 1413 the Jurchen people of Manchuria responded by sending a prestigious mission to Beijing, where its members were showered with titles, gifts, and trading rights. Japan was also assiduously courted. The third Ashikaga Shogun Yoshimitsu was a Sinophile[1]; he lost no time in kow-towing as "your subject, the King of Japan." His reward was a string of special ports opened to promote trade with Japan, at Ningbo, Quanzhou, and Guangdong (Canton). Like Korea, Japan also set up an observatory to aid Zhu Di's astronomical research, and Japanese ships also joined the globetrotting Chinese convoys.

Having pacified Manchuria and brought Korea and Japan into the Chinese tribute system, Zhu Di next turned his attention to Tibet. Another court eunuch, Hau-Xian, led a mission to court the famous holy man the Karmapa, leader of one of the four sects of Tibetan Buddhism, and bring him to China. When he arrived, a procession of Buddhist monks met him outside the city and Zhu Di bestowed upon him the title "Divine Son of India Below the Sky and Upon the Earth, Inventor of the Alphabet, Incarnated Buddha, Maintainer of the Kingdom's Prosperity, Source of Rhetoric." The emperor then presented the Karmapa with a square black hat bearing a diamond-studded emblem. It has been worn by successive incarnations of the Karmapa ever since.

Joining China's tribute system also gave rulers and their envoys the opportunity to visit the capital of the oldest and finest civilization in the world. The traditional imperial capital of Nanjing had received dignitaries from around the world, and now the new capital of Beijing began to welcome the latest arrivals. Although the emperor's main concern was to awe all countries into becoming tribute-bearing states, great efforts were also made to learn about their history, geography, manners, and customs. Beijing was to be not only the world's greatest city but its intellectual capital, with encyclopedias and libraries covering every subject known to man. In December 1404, Zhu Di had appointed two long-time advisers, Yao Guang Xiao and Lui Chi'ih, assisted by 2,180 scholars, to take charge of a project, the Yong-le-Dadian, to preserve all known literature and knowledge. It was the largest scholarly enterprise ever undertaken. The result, a massive encyclopedia of four thousand volumes containing some fifty million characters, was completed just before the Forbidden City was inaugurated.

In parallel with this great endeavour, Zhu Di ordered the opinions of 120 philosophers and sages of the Song dynasty to be collated and stored in the Forbidden City together with the complete commentaries of thinkers from the eleventh to the thirteenth centuries. In addition to this wealth of academic knowledge, hundreds of printed novels could be bought from Beijing market stalls. There was nothing remotely

---

[1]A lover of China and things Chinese. [Ed.]

comparable anywhere in the world. Printing was unknown in Europe — Gutenberg did not complete his printed Bible for another thirty years — and though Europe was on the eve of the Renaissance that was to transform its culture and scientific knowledge, it lagged far behind China. The library of Henry V (1387–1422) comprised six handwritten books, three of which were on loan to him from a nunnery, and the Florentine Francesco Datini, the wealthiest European merchant of the same era, possessed twelve books, eight of which were on religious subjects.

The voyage to the intellectual paradise of Beijing also offered foreign potentates and envoys many earthly delights. Carried in sumptuous comfort aboard the leviathan ships, they consumed the finest foods and wines, and pleasured themselves with the concubines whose only role was to please these foreign dignitaries. The formal inauguration of the Forbidden City was followed by a sumptuous banquet. Its scale and opulence emphasized China's position at the summit of the civilized world. In comparison, Europe was backward, crude, and barbaric. Henry V's marriage to Catherine of Valois took place in London just three weeks after the inauguration of the Forbidden City. Twenty-six thousand guests were entertained in Beijing, where they ate a ten-course banquet served on dishes of the finest porcelain; a mere six hundred guests attended Henry's nuptials and they were served stockfish (salted cod) on rounds of stale bread that acted as plates. Catherine de Valois wore neither knickers nor stockings at her wedding; Zhu Di's favourite concubine was clad in the finest silks and her jewellery included cornelians from Persia, rubies from Sri Lanka, Indian diamonds and jade from Kotan (in Chinese Turkestan). Her perfume contained ambergris from the Pacific, myrrh from Arabia, and sandalwood from the Spice Islands. China's army numbered one million men, armed with guns; Henry V could put five thousand men in the field, armed only with longbows, swords, and pikes. The fleet that would carry Zhu Di's guests home numbered over a hundred ships with a complement of thirty thousand men; when Henry went to war against France in June of that year, he ferried his army across the Channel in four fishing boats, carrying a hundred men on each crossing and sailing only in daylight hours.

For a further month after the inauguration of the Forbidden City, the rulers and envoys in Beijing were provided with lavish imperial hospitality — the finest foods and wines, the most splendid entertainments and the most beautiful concubines, skilled in the arts of love. Finally, on 3 March 1421, a great ceremony was mounted to commemorate the departure of the envoys for their native lands. A vast honour guard was assembled: "First came commanders of ten thousands, next commanders of thousands, all numbering about one hundred thousand men. . . . Behind them stood troops in serried ranks, two hundred thousand strong. . . . The whole body . . . stood so silent it seemed there was not a breathing soul there." At noon precisely, cymbals clashed, elephants lowered their trunks, and clouds of smoke wafted from incense-holders in the shape of tortoises and cranes. The emperor appeared, striding through the smoke to present the departing ambassadors with their farewell gifts — crates of blue and white porcelain, rolls of silk, bundles of cotton cloth, and bamboo cases of jade. His great fleets stood ready to carry them back to Hormuz, Aden, La'Sa, and Dhofar in Arabia; to Mogadishu, Brava, Malindi, and Mombasa in Africa; to Sri Lanka, Calicut, Cochin, and Cambay in India; to Japan, Vietnam, Java, Sumatra, Malacca, and Borneo in south-east Asia, and elsewhere.

Admiral Zheng He, dressed in his formal uniform — a long red robe and a tall black hat — presented the emperor with his compliments and reported that an armada comprising four of the emperor's great fleets was ready to set sail; the fifth, commanded by Grand Eunuch Yang Qing, had put to sea the previous month. The return of the envoys to their homelands was only the first part of this armada's overall mission. It was then to "proceed all the way to the end of the earth to collect tribute from the barbarians beyond the seas . . . to attract all under heaven to be civilised in Confucian harmony." Zheng He's reward for his lifelong, devoted service to his emperor had been the command of five previous treasure fleets tasked with promoting Chinese trade and influence in Asia, India, Africa, and the Middle East. Now he was to lead one of the largest armadas the world had ever seen. Zhu Di had also rewarded other eunuchs for their part in helping him to liberate China. Many of the army commanders in the war against the Mongols were now admirals and captains of his treasure fleets. Zheng He had become a master of delegation. By the fourth voyage fleets were sailing separately. On this great sixth voyage loyal eunuchs would command separate fleets. Zheng He would lead them to the Indian Ocean then re-turn home confident that they would handle their fleets as he had taught them.

The envoys' parting gifts were packed into their carriages, the emperor made a short speech, and then, after kow-towing one last time, the envoys embarked and the procession moved off. Servants ran behind the carriages as they rumbled down to the Grand Canal a mile to the east of the city. There, a fleet of barges decked with silk awnings awaited them. Teams of horses, ten to twelve for each barge, stood on the banks, bamboo poles tied to their harnesses. When the envoys were aboard, whips cracked and the sturdy animals began to drag the barges on their slow journey down to the coast.

Two days and thirty-six locks later, they arrived at Tanggu (near the modern city of Tianjin) on the Yellow Sea. The sight that greeted the envoys at Tanggu was one that must have lingered long in their minds. More than one hundred huge junks rode at anchor, towering above the watchers on the quayside — the ships were taller by far than the thatched houses lining the bay. Surrounding them was a fleet of smaller merchant ships. Each capital ship was about 480 feet in length (444 *chi*, the standard Chinese unit of measurement, equivalent to about 12.5 inches or 32 centimetres) and 180 feet across — big enough to swallow fifty fishing boats. On the prow, glaring serpents' eyes served to frighten away evil spirits. Pennants streamed from the tips of a forest of a thousand masts; below them great sails of red silk, light but immensely strong, were furled on each ship's nine masts. "When their sails are spread, they are like great clouds in the sky."

The armada was composed very much like a Second World War convoy. At the centre were the great leviathan flagships, surrounded by a host of merchant junks, most 90 feet long and 30 feet wide. Around the perimeters were squadrons of fast, manoeuvrable warships. As the voyage progressed, trading ships of several other nations, especially Japan, Korea, Burma, Vietnam, and India, joined the convoy, taking advantage of the protection afforded by the warships and the opportunities offered as the magnificent armada, almost a trading country in its own right, swept over the oceans. By the time it reached Calicut, it comprised more than eight hundred vessels whose combined population exceeded that of any city between China and India. Each treasure ship had sixteen internal watertight compartments, any two of which could be flooded without sinking the ship. Some internal compartments could also be partially flooded to act as tanks for the trained sea-otters used in fishing, or for use by divers entering and leaving the sea. The otters, held on long cords, were employed to herd shoals of fish into nets, a method still practised in parts of China, Malaysia, and Bengal today. The admiral's sea cabin was above the stern of his flagship. Below were sixty staterooms for foreign ambassadors, envoys and their entourages. Their concubines were housed in adjacent cabins and most had balconies overlooking the sea. Chinese ambassadors, one for each country to be visited, were housed in less grand but nonetheless spacious apartments. Each ambassador had ten assistants as *chefs de protocol* and a further fifty-two eunuchs served as secretaries. The crewmen's quarters were on the lower decks.

In 1407, Zheng He had established a language school in Nanjing, the Ssu-i-Quan (Si Yi Guan), to train interpreters, and sixteen of its finest graduates travelled with the fleets, enabling the admirals to communicate with rulers from India to Africa in Arabic, Persian, Swahili, Hindi, Tamil, and many other languages. Zhu Di and Zheng He also actively sought out foreign navigators and cartographers; the diaries of one of them, an Indonesian by the name of Master Bentun, have survived. Religious tolerance was one of Zhu Di's great virtues, and the junks also habitually carried Islamic, Hindu, and Buddhist savants to provide advice and guidance. Buddhism, with its teachings of universal compassion and tolerance, had been the religion of the majority of the Chinese people for centuries. Buddhism in no way conflicted with Confucianism, which could be said to be a code of civic values rather than a religion. On this sixth and final voyage of the treasure fleets which would last until 1423, the Buddhist monk Sheng Hui and the religious leaders Ha San and Pu He Ri were aboard. After the inauguration of the Forbidden City and the dedication of the awesome encyclopedia the Yong-le-Dadian, thousands of scholars found themselves without an obvious role. It would have been natural for Zhu Di to send them overseas on the great voyages of exploration. Through interpreters, Chinese mathematicians, astronomers, navigators, engineers, and architects would have been able to converse with and learn from their counterparts throughout the Indian Ocean. Once the ambassadors and their entourages had disembarked, the vast ships with their labyrinths of cabins would have been well suited to use as laboratories for scientific experiments. Metallurgists could prospect for minerals in the countries the Chinese visited, physicians could search out new healing plants, medicines, and treatments that might help to combat plagues and epidemics, and botanists could propagate valuable food plants. Chinese agricultural scientists and farmers had millennia of experience of developing and propagating hybrids.

The native Chinese flora is perhaps the richest in the world: "In wealth of its endemic species and in the extent of the genus and species potential of its cultivated plants, China is conspicuous among other centres of origin of plant forms. Moreover the species are usually represented by enormous numbers of botanical varieties and hereditary forms." In Europe, a long period of economic and agricultural decline followed the fall of the Roman Empire. The plant forms known to the Western world from Theophrastus to the German fathers of botany show that European knowledge had slumped, but there was no corresponding "dark age" in Chinese scientific history. Botanical knowledge, and the number of plant species recorded by the Chinese, grew steadily as the centuries passed. The contrast between the voyages of discovery of the Chinese and those of the Europeans cannot be overestimated. The only interest of the Spanish and Portuguese was in gathering sustenance, gold, and spices, while warding off attacks from the natives. The great Chinese fleets undertook scientific expeditions the Europeans could not even begin to equal in scale or scope until Captain Cook set sail three and a half centuries later.

As the admirals and envoys embarked, and the armada was readied for sea, the water around the great ships was still black with smaller craft shuttling from ship to shore. For days the port had been in turmoil as cartloads of vegetables and dried fish and hundreds of tons of water were hauled aboard to provision this armada of thirty thousand men for their voyage. Even at this late hour, barges were still bringing final supplies of fresh water and rice. The great armada's ships could remain at sea for over three months and cover at least 4,500 miles without making landfall to replenish food or water, for separate grain ships and water tankers sailed with them. The grain ships also carried an array of flora the Chinese intended to plant in foreign lands, some as further benefits of the tribute system and others to provide food for the Chinese colonies that would be created in new lands. Dogs were also taken aboard as pets, others to be bred for food and to hunt rats, and there were coops of Asiatic chickens as valuable presents for foreign dignitaries. The larger ships even kept sties of Chinese pigs. Separate horse-ships carried the mounts for the cavalry.

The staggering size of the individual ships, not to mention the armada itself, can best be understood by comparison with other navies of the same era. In 1421, the next most powerful fleet afloat was that of Venice. The Venetians possessed around three hundred galleys — fast, light, thin-skinned ships built with soft-wood planking, rowed by oarsmen and only suitable for island-hopping in the calm of a Mediterranean summer. The biggest Venetian galleys were some 150 feet long and 20 feet wide and carried at best 50 tons of cargo. In comparison, Zhu Di's treasure ships were ocean-going monsters built of teak. The rudder of one of these great ships stood 36 feet high — almost as long as the whole of the flagship the *Niña* in which Columbus was later to set sail for the New World. Each treasure ship could carry more than two thousand tons of cargo and reach Malacca in five weeks, Hormuz in the Persian Gulf in twelve. They were capable of sailing the wildest oceans of the world, in voyages lasting years at a time. That so many ships were lost on the Chinese voyages of discovery testifies not to any lack of strength in their construction but rather to the perilous, uncharted waters they explored and the hurricanes and tsunami they encountered along rocky coasts and razor-sharp coral reefs to the ice-strewn oceans of the far north and far south. Venetian galleys were protected by archers; Chinese ships were armed with gunpowder weapons, brass and iron cannon, mortars, flaming arrows, and exploding shells that sprayed excrement over their adversaries. In every single respect — construction, cargo capacity, damage control, armament, range, communications, the ability to navigate in the trackless ocean and to repair and maintain their ships at sea for months on end — the Chinese were centuries ahead of Europe. Admiral Zheng He would have had no difficulty in destroying any fleet that crossed his path. A battle between this Chinese armada and the other navies of the world combined would have resembled one between a pack of sharks and a shoal of sprats.

By the end of the middle watch — four in the morning — the last provisions had been lashed down and the armada weighed anchor. A prayer was said to Ma Tsu, Taoist goddess of the sea, and then, as their red silk sails slowly filled, the ships, resembling great houses, gathered way before the winds of the north-east monsoon. As they sailed out across the Yellow Sea, the last flickering lights of Tanggu faded into the darkness while the sailors clustered at the rails, straining for a last sight of their homeland. In the long months they would spend travelling the oceans, their only remaining links to the land would be memories, keepsakes, and the scented roses many brought with them, growing them in pots and even sharing their water rations with them. The majority of those seamen at the rails would never see China again. Many would die, many others would be shipwrecked or left behind to set up colonies on foreign shores. Those who eventually returned after two and a half years at sea would find their country convulsed and transformed beyond all recognition.

4

CHRISTOPHER COLUMBUS

Letter to King Ferdinand and Queen Isabella

Christopher Columbus sent this letter to his royal backers, King Ferdinand and Queen Isabella of Spain, on his return in March 1493 from his first voyage across the Atlantic. (See Map 1.3.)

An Italian sailor from Genoa, Columbus, in 1483–1484, tried to convince King John II of Portugal to underwrite his plan to sail across the western ocean to the spice-rich East Indies. Relying on a Florentine map that used Marco Polo's overstated distance from Venice to Japan across Asia and an understated estimate of the circumference of the globe, Columbus believed that Japan lay only 2,500 miles west of the Portuguese Azores. King John II rejected the proposal because more accurate estimates indicated that sailing around Africa was the shorter route, a feat achieved in 1488 by Portuguese navigator Bartolomeu Dias.

Less knowledgeable about navigation, the new Spanish monarchs, Ferdinand and Isabella, supported Columbus and financed his plan to sail west to Asia. In four voyages, Columbus touched a number of Caribbean islands and the coast of Central America, settled Spaniards on Hispaniola (Española), and began to create one of the largest

---

"First Voyage of Columbus," in *The Four Voyages of Columbus*, ed. Cecil Jane (New York: Dover, 1988), 1–18.

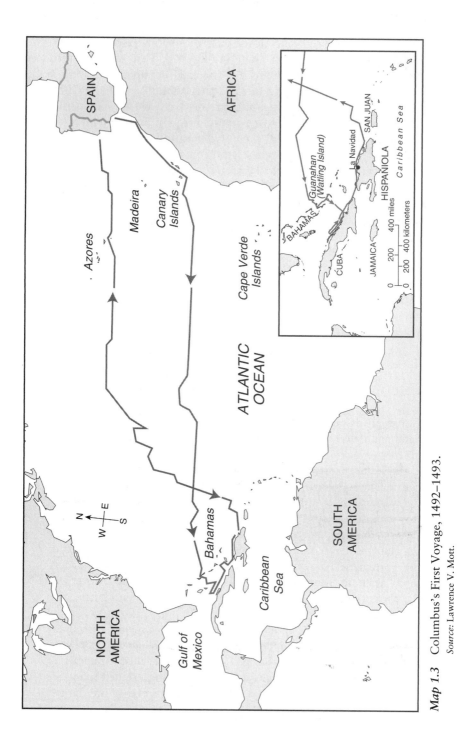

Map 1.3 Columbus's First Voyage, 1492–1493.
Source: Lawrence V. Mott.

empires in world history for Spain — all the while thinking he was near China and Japan, in the realm of the Great Khan whom Marco Polo had met and who had died hundreds of years earlier.

In what ways was the voyage of Columbus similar to that of Zheng He? In what ways was it different? How were the relationships of the explorers with their kings similar and different? Were the motives driving Chinese and European expansion more alike or different?

Thinking Historically

Because this document comes from the period we are studying and is written by Columbus himself, it is a primary source. Primary sources, like this letter and Zheng He's inscription, have a great sense of immediacy and can often "transport" us to the past intellectually. However, involvement when reading does not always lead to understanding, so it is important to think critically about the source and the writer's intended audience as you read. First we must determine the source of the document. Where does it come from? Is it original? If not, is it a copy or a translation? Next, we must determine who wrote it, when it was written, and for what purpose. After answering these questions, we are able to read the document with a critical eye, which leads to greater understanding.

The original letter by Columbus has been lost. This selection is an English translation based on three different printed Spanish versions of the letter. So this text is a reconstruction, not an original, though it is believed to be quite close to the original.

The original letter was probably composed during a relaxed time on the return voyage before its date of February 15, 1493 — possibly as early as the middle of January — and sent to the Spanish monarchs from Lisbon in order to reach them by the time Columbus arrived in Barcelona.

What does Columbus want to impart to Ferdinand and Isabella? First and foremost, he wants them to know that he reached the Indies, that the voyage was a success. And so, the letter's opening sentence tells us something that Columbus certainly did not intend or know. We learn that on his return in 1493, Columbus thought he had been to the Indies when in fact he had not. (It is due to Columbus's confusion that we call the islands he visited the West Indies and Native Americans "Indians.")

Knowing what the author wants a reader to believe is useful information because it serves as a point of reference for other statements the author makes. The success of Columbus's voyage is a case in point. Columbus does not admit to the loss of one of his ships in his letter, nor does he explain fully why he had to build a fort at Navidad and leave some of his crew there, returning home without them. Clearly, Columbus had reason to worry that his voyage would be viewed as a failure. He had not found the gold mines he sought or the Asian cities described by Marco Polo. He thought he had discovered many spices, though only the chili peppers were new. Notice, as you read this letter, how Columbus presents his voyage in the best light.

Aside from what Columbus intends, what facts do you learn from the letter about Columbus, his first voyage, and his encounter with the New World? What seems to drive Columbus to do what he does? What is Columbus's attitude toward the "Indians"? What does Columbus's letter tell us about the society and culture of the Taino* — the people he met in the Caribbean?

Sir, As I know that you will be pleased at the great victory with which Our Lord has crowned my voyage, I write this to you, from which you will learn how in thirty-three days, I passed from the Canary Islands to the Indies with the fleet which the most illustrious king and queen, our sovereigns, gave to me. And there I found very many islands filled with people innumerable, and of them all I have taken possession for their highnesses, by proclamation made and with the royal standard unfurled, and no opposition was offered to me. To the first island which I found, I gave the name *San Salvador,* in remembrance of the Divine Majesty, Who has marvellously bestowed all this; the Indians call it "Guanahani."† To the second, I gave the name *Isla de Santa María de Concepción*; to the third, *Fernandina*; to the fourth, *Isabella*; to the fifth, *Isla Juana*, and so to each one I gave a new name.

When I reached Juana, I followed its coast to the westward, and I found it to be so extensive that I thought that it must be the mainland, the province of Catayo. And since there were neither towns nor villages on the seashore, but only small hamlets, with the people which I could not have speech, because they all fled immediately, I went forward on the same course, thinking that I should not fail to find great cities and towns. And, at the end of many leagues, seeing that there was no change and that the coast was bearing me northwards, which I wished to avoid, since winter was already beginning and I proposed to make from it to the south, and as moreover the wind was carrying me forward, I determined not to wait for a change in the weather and retraced my path as far as a certain harbour known to me. And from that point, I sent two men inland to learn if there were a king or great cities. They travelled three days' journey and found an infinity of small hamlets and people without number, but nothing of importance. For this reason, they returned.

I understood sufficiently from other Indians, whom I had already taken, that this land was nothing but an island. And therefore I fol-

*TY noh
†gwah nah HAH nee

lowed its coast eastwards for one hundred and seven leagues to the point where it ended. And from that cape, I saw another island, distant eighteen leagues from the former, to the east, to which I at once gave the name "Española." And I went there and followed its northern coast, as I had in the case of Juana, to the eastward for one hundred and eighty-eight great leagues in a straight line. This island and all the others are very fertile to a limitless degree, and this island is extremely so. In it there are many harbours on the coast of the sea, beyond comparison with others which I know in Christendom, and many rivers, good and large, which is marvellous. Its lands are high, and there are in it very many sierras and very lofty mountains, beyond comparison with the island of Teneriffe. All are most beautiful, of a thousand shapes, and all are accessible and filled with trees of a thousand kinds and tall, and they seem to touch the sky. And I am told that they never lose their foliage, as I can understand, for I saw them as green and as lovely as they are in Spain in May, and some of them were flowering, some bearing fruit, and some in another stage, according to their nature. And the nightingale was singing and other birds of a thousand kinds in the month of November there where I went. There are six or eight kinds of palm, which are a wonder to behold on account of their beautiful variety, but so are the other trees and fruits and plants. In it are marvellous pine groves, and there are very large tracts of cultivatable lands, and there is honey, and there are birds of many kinds and fruits in great diversity. In the interior are mines of metals, and the population is without number. Española is a marvel.

The sierras and mountains, the plains and arable lands and pastures, are so lovely and rich for planting and sowing, for breeding cattle of every kind, for building towns and villages. The harbours of the sea here are such as cannot be believed to exist unless they have been seen, and so with the rivers, many and great, and good waters, the majority of which contain gold. In the trees and fruits and plants, there is a great difference from those of Juana. In this island, there are many spices and great mines of gold and of other metals.

The people of this island, and of all the other islands which I have found and of which I have information, all go naked, men and women, as their mothers bore them, although some women cover a single place with the leaf of a plant or with a net of cotton which they make for the purpose. They have no iron or steel or weapons, nor are they fitted to use them, not because they are not well built men and of handsome stature, but because they are very marvellously timorous. They have no other arms than weapons made of canes, cut in seeding time, to the ends of which they fix a small sharpened stick. And they do not dare to make use of these, for many times it has happened that I have sent ashore two or three men to some town to have speech, and countless people have come out to them, and as soon as they have seen my men approaching they have fled, even a father not waiting for his son. And this, not because ill has been done to anyone; on the contrary, at every point where I have been and have been able to have speech, I have given to them of all that I had, such as cloth and many other things, without receiving anything for it; but so they are, incurably timid. It is true that, after they have been reassured and have lost their fear, they are so guileless and so generous with all they possess, that no one would believe it who has not seen it. They never refuse anything which they possess, if it be asked of them; on the contrary, they invite anyone to share it, and display as much love as if they would give their hearts, and whether the thing be of value or whether it be of small price, at once with whatever trifle of whatever kind it may be that is given to them, with that they are content. I forbade that they should be given things so worthless as fragments of broken crockery and scraps of broken glass, and ends of straps, although when they were able to get them, they fancied that they possessed the best jewel in the world. So it was found that a sailor for a strap received gold to the weight of two and a half *castellanos*, and others much more for other things which were worth much less. As for new *blancas*, for them they would give everything which they had, although it might be two or three *castellanos'* weight of gold or an *arroba* or two of spun cotton. . . . They took even the pieces of the broken hoops of the wine barrels and, like savages, gave what they had, so that it seemed to me to be wrong and I forbade it. And I gave a thousand handsome good things, which I had brought, in order that they might conceive affection, and more than that, might become Christians and be inclined to the love and service of their highnesses and of the whole Castilian nation, and strive to aid us and to give us of the things which they have in abundance and which are necessary to us. And they do not know any creed and are not idolaters; only they all believe that power and good are in the heavens, and they are very firmly convinced that I, with these ships and men, came from the heavens, and in this belief they everywhere received me, after they had overcome their fear. And this does not come because they are ignorant; on the contrary, they are of a very acute intelligence and are men who navigate all those seas, so that it is amazing how good an account they give of everything, but it is because they have never seen people clothed or ships of such a kind.

And as soon as I arrived in the Indies, in the first island which I found, I took by force some of them, in order that they might learn and give me information of that which there is in those parts, and so it was that they soon understood us, and we them, either by speech or signs, and they have been very serviceable. I still take them with me, and they are always assured that I come from Heaven, for all the intercourse which they have had with me; and they were the first to announce this wherever I went, and the others went running from house to house and to the neighbouring towns, with loud cries of, "Come! Come to see the people from Heaven!" So all, men and women alike, when their minds were set at rest concerning us, came, so that not one, great or small, remained behind, and all brought something to eat and drink, which they gave with extraordinary affection. In all the island, they have very many canoes, like rowing *fustas*, some larger, some smaller, and some are larger than a *fusta* of eighteen benches. They are not so broad, because they are made of a single log of wood, but a *fusta* would not keep up with them in rowing, since their speed is a thing incredible. And in these they navigate among all those islands, which are innumerable, and carry their goods. One of these canoes I have seen with seventy and eighty men in her, and each one with his oar.

In all these islands, I saw no great diversity in the appearance of the people or in their manners and language. On the contrary, they all understand one another, which is a very curious thing, on account of which I hope that their highnesses will determine upon their conversion to our holy faith, towards which they are very inclined.

I have already said how I have gone one hundred and seven leagues in a straight line from west to east along the seashore of the island Juana, and as a result of that voyage, I can say that this island is larger than England and Scotland together, for, beyond these one hundred and seven leagues, there remain to the westward two provinces to which I have not gone. One of these provinces they call "Avan," and there the people are born with tails; and these provinces cannot have a length of less than fifty or sixty leagues, as I could understand from those Indians whom I have and who know all the islands.

The other, Española, has a circumference greater than all Spain, from Colibre, by the sea-coast, to Fuenterabia in Vizcaya, since I voyaged along one side one hundred and eighty-eight great leagues in a straight line from west to east. It is a land to be desired and, seen, it is never to be left. And in it, although of all I have taken possession for their highnesses and all are more richly endowed than I know how, or am able, to say, and I hold them all for their highnesses, so that they may dispose of them as, and as absolutely as, of the kingdoms of Castile, in this Española, in the situation most convenient and in the best position for the mines of gold and for all intercourse as well with the mainland here as with that there, belonging to the Grand Khan, where will be great trade and gain, I have taken possession of a large town, to which I gave the name *Villa de Navidad*, and in it I have made fortifications and a fort, which now will by this time be entirely finished, and I have left in it sufficient men for such a purpose with arms and artillery and provisions for more than a year, and a *fusta*, and one, a master of all seacraft, to build others, and great friendship with the king of that land, so much so, that he was proud to call me, and to treat me as, a brother. And even if he were to change his attitude to one of hostility towards these men, he and his do not know what arms are and they go naked, as I have already said, and are the most timorous people that there are in the world, so that the men whom I have left there alone would suffice to destroy all that land, and the island is without danger for their persons, if they know how to govern themselves.

In all these islands, it seems to me that all men are content with one woman, and to their chief or king they give as many as twenty. It appears to me that the women work more than the men. And I have not been able to learn if they hold private property; what seemed to me to appear was that, in that which one had, all took a share, especially of eatable things.

In these islands I have so far found no human monstrosities, as many expected, but on the contrary the whole population is very well-formed, nor are they negros as in Guinea, but their hair is flowing, and they are not born where there is intense force in the rays of the sun; it is true that the sun has there great power, although it is distant from the equinoctial line twenty-six degrees. In these islands, where there are high mountains, the cold was severe this winter, but they endure it, being used to it and with the help of meats which they eat with many and extremely hot spices. As I have found no monsters, so I have had no report of any, except in an island "Quaris," the second at the coming into the Indies, which is inhabited by a people who are regarded in all the islands as very fierce and who eat human flesh. They have many canoes with which they range through all the islands of India and pillage and take as many as they can. They are no more malformed than the others, except that they have the custom of wearing their hair long like women, and they use bows and arrows of the same cane stems, with a small piece of wood at the end, owing to lack of iron which they do not possess. They are ferocious among these other people who are cowardly to an excessive degree, but I make no more account of them than of the rest. These are those who have intercourse with the women of "Matinino," which is the first island met on the way from Spain to the Indies, in which there is not a man. These women engage in no feminine occupation, but use bows and arrows of cane, like those already mentioned, and they arm and protect themselves with plates of copper, of which they have much.

In another island, which they assure me is larger than Española, the people have no hair. In it, there is gold incalculable, and from it and from the other islands, I bring with me Indians as evidence.

In conclusion, to speak only of that which has been accomplished on this voyage, which was so hasty, their highnesses can see that I will give them as much gold as they may need, if their highnesses will render me very slight assistance; moreover, spice and cotton, as much as their highnesses shall command; and mastic, as much as they shall order to be shipped and which, up to now, has been found only in Greece, in the island of Chios, and the Seignory sells it for what it pleases; and aloe wood, as much as they shall order to be shipped, and slaves, as many as they shall order to be shipped and who will be from the idolaters. And I believe that I have found rhubarb and cinnamon, and I shall find a thousand other things of value, which the people whom I have left there will have discovered, for I have not delayed at any point, so far as the wind allowed me to sail, except in the town of Navidad, in order to leave it secured and well established, and in truth, I should have done much more, if the ships had served me, as reason demanded.

This is enough . . . and the eternal God, our Lord, Who gives to all those who walk in His way triumph over things which appear to be impossible, and this was notably one; for, although men have talked or have written of these lands, all was conjectural, without suggestion of ocular evidence, but amounted only to this, that those who heard for the most part listened and judged it to be rather a fable than as having any vestige of truth. So that, since Our Redeemer has given this victory to our most illustrious king and queen, and to their renowned kingdoms, in so great a matter, for this all Christendom ought to feel delight and make great feasts and give solemn thanks to the Holy Trinity with many solemn prayers for the great exaltation which they shall have, in the turning of so many peoples to our holy faith, and afterwards for temporal benefits, for not only Spain but all Christians will have hence refreshment and gain.

This, in accordance with that which has been accomplished, thus briefly.

Done in the caravel,[1] off the Canary Islands, on the fifteenth of February, in the year one thousand four hundred and ninety-three.

At your orders.   El Almirante.

After having written this, and being in the sea of Castile, there came on me so great a south-south-west wind, that I was obliged to lighten ship. But I ran here to-day into this port of Lisbon, which was the greatest marvel in the world, whence I decided to write to their highnesses. In all the Indies, I have always found weather like May; where I went in thirty-three days and I had returned in twenty-eight, save for these storms which have detained me for fourteen days, beating about in this sea. Here all the sailors say that never has there been so bad a winter nor so many ships lost.

Done on the fourth day of March.

---

[1]Sailing ship, in this case the *Santa María*. [Ed.]

KIRKPATRICK SALE

From The Conquest of Paradise

In this selection from his popular study of Columbus, Sale is concerned with Columbus's attitude toward nature in the New World. Do you think Sale's comments are accurate? Are they insightful? Do they help us understand Columbus?

Sale regards Columbus as a symbol of European expansion. Let us for the moment grant him that. If Columbus is distinctly European, what is Sale saying about European expansion? How and what does Sale add to your understanding of the similarities and differences between Chinese and European expansion?

Was Columbus much different from Zheng He? Or were the areas and peoples they visited causes for different responses?

Thinking Historically

Clearly, this selection is a secondary source; Sale is a modern writer, not a fifteenth-century contemporary of Columbus. Still, you will not have to read very far into the selection to realize that Sale has a distinct point of view. Secondary sources, like primary ones, should be analyzed for bias and perspective and should identify the author's interpretation.

Sale is an environmentalist and a cultural critic. Do his beliefs and values hinder his understanding of Columbus, or do they inform and illuminate aspects of Columbus that might otherwise be missed? Does Sale help you recognize things you would not have seen on your own, or does he persuade you to see things that might not truly be there?

Notice how Sale uses primary sources in his text. He quotes from Columbus's journal and his letter to King Ferdinand and Queen Isabella. Do these quotes help you understand Columbus, or do they simply support Sale's argument? What do you think about Sale's use of the Spanish "Colón"* for "Columbus"? Does Sale "take possession" of Columbus by, in effect, "renaming" him for modern readers? Is the effect humanizing or debunking?

*koh LOHN

Kirkpatrick Sale, *The Conquest of Paradise* (New York: Penguin, 1991), 92–104.

Notice how Sale sometimes calls attention to what the primary source did *not* say rather than what it did say. Is this a legitimate way to understand someone, or is Sale projecting a twentieth-century perspective on Columbus to make a point?

Toward the end of the selection, Sale extends his criticism beyond Columbus to include others. Who are the others? What is the effect of this larger criticism?

Admiral Colón spent a total of ninety-six days exploring the lands he encountered on the far side of the Ocean Sea — four rather small coralline islands in the Bahamian chain and two substantial coastlines of what he finally acknowledged were larger islands — every one of which he "took possession of" in the name of his Sovereigns.

The first he named San Salvador, no doubt as much in thanksgiving for its welcome presence after more than a month at sea as for the Son of God whom it honored; the second he called Santa María de la Concepcíon, after the Virgin whose name his flagship bore; and the third and fourth he called Fernandina and Isabela, for his patrons, honoring Aragon before Castile for reasons never explained (possibly protocol, possibly in recognition of the chief sources of backing for the voyage). The first of the two large and very fertile islands he called Juana, which Fernando [Columbus's son] says was done in honor of Prince Juan, heir to the Castilian throne, but just as plausibly might have been done in recognition of Princess Juana, the unstable child who eventually carried on the line; the second he named la Ysla Española, the "Spanish Island," because it resembled (though he felt it surpassed in beauty) the lands of Castile.

It was not that the islands were in need of names, mind you, nor indeed that Colón was ignorant of the names that native peoples had already given them, for he frequently used those original names before endowing them with his own. Rather, the process of bestowing new names went along with "taking possession of" those parts of the world he deemed suitable for Spanish ownership, showing the royal banners, erecting various crosses, and pronouncing certain oaths and pledges. If this was presumption, it had an honored heritage: It was Adam who was charged by his Creator with the task of naming "every living creature," including the product of his own rib, in the course of establishing "dominion over" them.

Colón went on to assign no fewer than sixty-two other names on the geography of the islands — capes, points, mountains, ports — with a blithe assurance suggesting that in his (and Europe's) perception the act of name-giving was in some sense a talisman of conquest, a rite that changed raw neutral stretches of far-off earth into extensions of

Europe. The process began slowly, even haltingly — he forgot to record, for example, until four days afterward that he named the landfall island San Salvador — but by the time he came to Española at the end he went on a naming spree, using more than two-thirds of all the titles he concocted on that one coastline. On certain days it became almost a frenzy: on December 6 he named six places, on the nineteenth six more, and on January 11 no fewer than ten — eight capes, a point, and a mountain. It is almost as if, as he sailed along the last of the islands, he was determined to leave his mark on it the only way he knew how, and thus to establish his authority — and by extension Spain's — even, as with baptism, to make it thus sanctified, and real, and official. . . .

This business of naming and "possessing" foreign islands was by no means casual. The Admiral took it very seriously, pointing out that "it was my wish to bypass no island without taking possession" (October 15) and that "in all regions [I] always left a cross standing" (November 16) as a mark of Christian dominance. There even seem to have been certain prescriptions for it (the instructions from the Sovereigns speak of "the administering of the oath and the performing of the rites prescribed in such cases"), and Rodrigo de Escobedo was sent along as secretary of the fleet explicitly to witness and record these events in detail.

But consider the implications of this act and the questions it raises again about what was in the Sovereigns' minds, what in Colón's. Why would the Admiral assume that these territories were in some way unpossessed — even by those clearly inhabiting them — and thus available for Spain to claim? Why would he not think twice about the possibility that some considerable potentate — the Grand Khan of China, for example, whom he later acknowledged (November 6) "must be" the ruler of Española — might descend upon him at any moment with a greater military force than his three vessels commanded and punish him for his territorial presumption? Why would he make the ceremony of possession his very first act on shore, even before meeting the inhabitants or exploring the environs, or finding out if anybody there objected to being thus possessed — particularly if they actually owned the great treasures he hoped would be there? No European would have imagined that anyone — three small boatloads of Indians, say — could come up to a European shore or island and "take possession" of it, nor would a European imagine marching up to some part of North Africa or the Middle East and claiming sovereignty there with impunity. Why were these lands thought to be different?

Could there be any reason for the Admiral to assume he had reached "unclaimed" shores, new lands that lay far from the domains of any of the potentates of the East? Can that really have been in his mind — or can it all be explained as simple Eurocentrism, or Eurosuperiority, mixed with cupidity and naiveté? . . .

Once safely "possessed,"[1] San Salvador was open for inspection. Now the Admiral turned his attention for the first time to the "naked people" staring at him on the beach—he did not automatically give them a name, interestingly enough, and it would be another six days before he decided what he might call them—and tried to win their favor with his trinkets.

> They all go around as naked as their mothers bore them; and also the women, although I didn't see more than one really young girl. All that I saw were young people [*mancebos*], none of them more than 30 years old. They are very well built, with very handsome bodies and very good faces; their hair [is] coarse, almost like the silk of a horse's tail, and short. They wear their hair over their eyebrows, except for a little in the back that they wear long and never cut. Some of them paint themselves black (and they are the color of the Canary Islanders, neither black nor white), and some paint themselves white, and some red, and some with what they find. And some paint their faces, and some of them the whole body, and some the eyes only, and some of them only the nose.

It may fairly be called the birth of American anthropology.

A crude anthropology, of course, as superficial as Colón's descriptions always were when his interest was limited, but simple and straightforward enough, with none of the fable and fantasy that characterized many earlier (and even some later) accounts of new-found peoples. There was no pretense to objectivity, or any sense that these people might be representatives of a culture equal to, or in any way a model for, Europe's. Colón immediately presumed the inferiority of the natives, not merely because (a sure enough sign) they were naked, but because (his society could have no surer measure) they seemed so technologically backward. "It appeared to me that these people were very poor in everything," he wrote on that first day, and, worse still, "they have no iron." And they went on to prove their inferiority to the Admiral by being ignorant of even such a basic artifact of European life as a sword: "They bear no arms, nor are they acquainted with them," he wrote, "for I showed them swords and they grasped them by the blade and cut themselves through ignorance." Thus did European arms spill the first drops of native blood on the sands of the New World, accompanied not with a gasp of compassion but with a smirk of superiority.

Then, just six sentences further on, Colón clarified what this inferiority meant in his eyes:

---

[1]Given Spanish names. [Ed.]

They ought to be good servants and of good intelligence [*ingenio*]. . . .
I believe that they would easily be made Christians, because it seemed
to me that they had no religion. Our Lord pleasing, I will carry off six
of them at my departure to Your Highnesses, in order that they may
learn to speak.

No clothes, no arms, no possessions, no iron, and now no religion —
not even speech: hence they were fit to be servants, and captives. It may
fairly be called the birth of American slavery.

Whether or not the idea of slavery was in Colón's mind all along is
uncertain, although he did suggest he had had experience as a slave
trader in Africa (November 12) and he certainly knew of Portuguese
plantation slavery in the Madeiras and Spanish slavery of Guanches in
the Canaries. But it seems to have taken shape early and grown ever
firmer as the weeks went on and as he captured more and more of the
helpless natives. At one point he even sent his crew ashore to kidnap
"seven head of women, young ones and adults, and three small children"; the expression of such callousness led the Spanish historian Salvador de Madariaga to remark, "It would be difficult to find a starker
utterance of utilitarian subjection of man by man than this passage
[whose] form is no less devoid of human feeling than its substance."

To be sure, Colón knew nothing about these people he encountered
and considered enslaving, and he was hardly trained to find out very
much, even if he was moved to care. But they were in fact members of
an extensive, populous, and successful people whom Europe, using its
own peculiar taxonomy, subsequently called "Taino" (or "Taíno"),
their own word for "good" or "noble," and their response when asked
who they were. They were related distantly by both language and culture to the Arawak people of the South American mainland, but it is
misleading (and needlessly imprecise) to call them Arawaks, as historians are wont to do, when the term "Taino" better establishes their ethnic and historical distinctiveness. They had migrated to the islands from
the mainland at about the time of the birth of Christ, occupying the
three large islands we now call the Greater Antilles and arriving at
Guanahani (Colón's San Salvador) and the end of the Bahamian chain
probably sometime around A.D. 900. There they displaced an earlier
people, the Guanahacabibes (sometimes called Guanahatabeys), who
by the time of the European discovery occupied only the western third
of Cuba and possibly remote corners of Española; and there, probably
in the early fifteenth century, they eventually confronted another people
moving up the islands from the mainland, the Caribs, whose culture
eventually occupied a dozen small islands of what are called the Lesser
Antilles.

The Tainos were not nearly so backward as Colón assumed from
their lack of dress. (It might be said that it was the Europeans, who

generally kept clothed head to foot during the day despite temperatures regularly in the eighties, who were the more unsophisticated in garmenture — especially since the Tainos, as Colón later noted, also used their body paint to prevent sunburn.) Indeed, they had achieved a means of living in a balanced and fruitful harmony with their natural surroundings that any society might well have envied. They had, to begin with, a not unsophisticated technology that made exact use of their available resources, two parts of which were so impressive that they were picked up and adopted by the European invaders: *canoa* (canoes) that were carved and fire-burned from large silk-cotton trees, "all in one piece, and wonderfully made" (October 13), some of which were capable of carrying up to 150 passengers; and *hamaca* (hammocks) that were "like nets of cotton" (October 17) and may have been a staple item of trade with Indian tribes as far away as the Florida mainland. Their houses were not only spacious and clean — as the Europeans noted with surprise and appreciation, used as they were to the generally crowded and slovenly hovels and huts of south European peasantry — but more apropos, remarkably resistant to hurricanes; the circular walls were made of strong cane poles set deep and close together ("as close as the fingers of a hand," Colón noted), the conical roofs of branches and vines tightly interwoven on a frame of smaller poles and covered with heavy palm leaves. Their artifacts and jewelry, with the exception of a few gold trinkets and ornaments, were based largely on renewable materials, including bracelets and necklaces of coral, shells, bone, and stone, embroidered cotton belts, woven baskets, carved statues and chairs, wooden and shell utensils, and pottery of variously intricate decoration depending on period and place.

Perhaps the most sophisticated, and most carefully integrated, part of their technology was their agricultural system, extraordinarily productive and perfectly adapted to the conditions of the island environment. It was based primarily on fields of knee-high mounds, called *conucos*, planted with yuca (sometimes called manioc), *batata* (sweet potato), and various squashes and beans grown all together in multicrop harmony: The root crops were excellent in resisting erosion and producing minerals and potash, the leaf crops effective in providing shade and moisture, and the mound configurations largely resistant to erosion and flooding and adaptable to almost all topographic conditions including steep hillsides. Not only was the *conuco* system environmentally appropriate — "conuco agriculture seems to have provided an exceptionally ecologically well-balanced and protective form of land use," according to David Watts's recent and authoritative *West Indies* — but it was also highly productive, surpassing in yields anything known in Europe at the time, with labor that amounted to hardly more than two or three hours a week, and in continuous yearlong harvest. The pioneering American geographical scholar Carl Sauer calls

Taino agriculture "productive as few parts of the world," giving the "highest returns of food in continuous supply by the simplest methods and modest labor," and adds, with a touch of regret, "The white man never fully appreciated the excellent combination of plants that were grown in conucos."

In their arts of government the Tainos seem to have achieved a parallel sort of harmony. Most villages were small (ten to fifteen families) and autonomous, although many apparently recognized loose allegiances with neighboring villages, and they were governed by a hereditary official called a *kaseke* (*cacique*,* in the Spanish form), something of a cross between an arbiter and a prolocutor, supported by advisers and elders. So little a part did violence play in their system that they seem, remarkably, to have been a society without war (at least we know of no war music or signals or artifacts, and no evidence of intertribal combats) and even without overt conflict (Las Casas reports that no Spaniard ever saw two Tainos fighting). And here we come to what was obviously the Tainos' outstanding cultural achievement, a proficiency in the social arts that led those who first met them to comment unfailingly on their friendliness, their warmth, their openness, and above all — so striking to those of an acquisitive culture — their generosity.

"They are the best people in the world and above all the gentlest," Colón recorded in his *Journal* (December 16), and from first to last he was astonished at their kindness:

They became so much our friends that it was a marvel. . . . They traded and gave everything they had, with good will [October 12].

I sent the ship's boat ashore for water, and they very willingly showed my people where the water was, and they themselves carried the full barrels to the boat, and took great delight in pleasing us [October 16].

They are very gentle and without knowledge of what is evil; nor do they murder or steal [November 12].

Your Highnesses may believe that in all the world there can be no better or gentler people . . . for neither better people nor land can there be. . . . All the people show the most singular loving behavior and they speak pleasantly [December 24].

I assure Your Highnesses that I believe that in all the world there is no better people nor better country. They love their neighbors as themselves; and they have the sweetest talk in the world, and are gentle and always laughing [December 25].

Even if one allows for some exaggeration — Colón was clearly trying to convince Ferdinand and Isabella that his Indians could be easily

*kah SEEK

conquered and converted, should that be the Sovereigns' wish — it is obvious that the Tainos exhibited a manner of social discourse that quite impressed the rough Europeans. But that was not high among the traits of "civilized" nations, as Colón and Europe understood it, and it counted for little in the Admiral's assessment of these people. However struck he was with such behavior, he would not have thought that it was the mark of a benign and harmonious society, or that from it another culture might learn. For him it was something like the wondrous behavior of children, the naive guilelessness of prelapsarian[2] creatures who knew no better how to bargain and chaffer and cheat than they did to dress themselves: "For a lacepoint they gave good pieces of gold the size of two fingers" (January 6), and "They even took pieces of the broken hoops of the wine casks and, like beasts [*como besti*], gave what they had" (Santangel Letter)[3]. Like beasts; such innocence was not human.

It is to be regretted that the Admiral, unable to see past their nakedness, as it were, knew not the real virtues of the people he confronted. For the Tainos' lives were in many ways as idyllic as their surroundings, into which they fit with such skill and comfort. They were well fed and well housed, without poverty or serious disease. They enjoyed considerable leisure, given over to dancing, singing, ballgames, and sex, and expressed themselves artistically in basketry, woodworking, pottery, and jewelry. They lived in general harmony and peace, without greed or covetousness or theft. . . .

It is perhaps only natural that Colón should devote his initial attention to the handsome, naked, naive islanders, but it does seem peculiar that he pays almost no attention, especially in the early days, to the spectacular scenery around them. Here he was, in the middle of an old-growth tropical forest the likes of which he could not have imagined before, its trees reaching sixty or seventy feet into the sky, more varieties than he knew how to count much less name, exhibiting a lushness that stood in sharp contrast to the sparse and denuded lands he had known in the Mediterranean, hearing a melodious multiplicity of bird songs and parrot calls — why was it not an occasion of wonder, excitement, and the sheer joy at nature in its full, arrogant abundance? But there is not a word of that: He actually said nothing about the physical surroundings on the first day, aside from a single phrase about "very green trees" and "many streams," and on the second managed only that short sentence about a big island with a big lake and green trees. Indeed, for the whole two weeks of the first leg of his voyage through the Bahamas to Cuba, he devoted only a third of the lines of descrip-

---

[2]Before the Fall. In other words, before the time, according to the Old Testament, when Adam and Eve sinned and were banished by God from the Garden of Eden. [Ed.]

[3]Santangel was the minister of Ferdinand and Isabella who received the letter (see selection 4).

tion to the phenomena around him. And there are some natural sights he seems not to have noticed at all: He did not mention (except in terms of navigation) the nighttime heavens, the sharp, glorious configurations of stars that he must have seen virtually every night of his journey, many for the first time.

Eventually Colón succumbed to the islands' natural charms as he sailed on — how could he not? — and began to wax warmly about how "these islands are very green and fertile and the air very sweet" (October 15), with "trees which were more beautiful to see than any other thing that has ever been seen" (October 17), and "so good and sweet a smell of flowers or trees from the land" (October 19). But his descriptions are curiously vapid and vague, the language opaque and lifeless:

> The other island, which is very big [October 15] . . . this island is very large [October 16] . . . these islands are very green and fertile [October 15] . . . this land is the best and most fertile [October 17] . . . in it many plants and trees . . . if the others are very beautiful, this is more so [October 19] . . . here are some great lagoons . . . big and little birds of all sorts . . . if the others already seen are very beautiful and green and fertile, this one is much more so [October 21] . . . full of very good harbors and deep rivers [October 28].

You begin to see the Admiral's problem: He cares little about the features of nature, at least the ones he doesn't use for sailing, and even when he admires them he has little experience in assessing them and less acquaintance with a vocabulary to describe them. To convey the lush density and stately grandeur of those tropical forests, for example, he had little more than the modifiers "green" and "very": "very green trees" (October 12), "trees very green" (October 13), "trees . . . so green and with leaves like those of Castile" (October 14), "very green and very big trees" (October 19), "large groves are very green" (October 21), "trees . . . beautiful and green" (October 28). And when he began to be aware of the diversity among those trees, he was still unable to make meaningful distinctions: "All the trees are as different from ours as day from night" (October 17), "trees of a thousand kinds" (October 21), "a thousand sorts of trees" (October 23), "trees . . . different from ours" (October 28), "trees of a thousand sorts" (November 14), "trees of a thousand kinds" (December 6).

Such was his ignorance — a failing he repeatedly bemoaned ("I don't recognize them, which gives me great grief," October 19) — that when he did stop to examine a species he often had no idea what he was looking at. "I saw many trees very different from ours," he wrote on October 16, "and many of them have branches of many kinds, and all on one trunk, and one twig is of one kind and another of another, and so different that it is the greatest wonder in the world how much diversity there is of one kind from the other. That is to say, one branch has leaves like a cane, and another like mastic, and thus on one tree five or six kinds, and all so different." There is no such tree in existence, much less "many of them," and never was: Why would anyone imagine, or so contrive, such a thing to be?

Colón's attempts to identify species were likewise frequently wrongheaded, usually imputing to them commercial worth that they did not have, as with the worthless "aloes" he loaded such quantities of. The "amaranth" he identified on October 28 and the "oaks" and "arbutus" of November 25 are species that do not grow in the Caribbean; the "mastic" he found on November 5 and loaded on board to sell in Spain was gumbo-limbo, commercially worthless. (On the other hand, one of the species of flora he deemed of no marketable interest — "weeds [*tizon*] in their hands to drink in the fragrant smoke" [November 6] — was tobacco.) Similarly, the "whales" he spotted on October 16 must have been simply large fish, the "geese" he saw on November 6 and again on December 22 were ducks, the "nightingales" that kept delighting him (November 6; December 7, 13) do not exist in the Americas, and the skulls of "cows" he identified on October 29 were probably not those of land animals but of manatees.

This all seems a little sad, revealing a man rather lost in a world that he cannot come to know, a man with a "geographic and naturalistic knowledge that doesn't turn out to be very deep or nearly complete," and "a limited imagination and a capacity for comparisons conditioned by a not very broad geographic culture," in the words of Gaetano Ferro, a Columbus scholar and professor of geography at the University of Genoa. One could not of course have expected that an adventurer and sailor of this era would also be a naturalist, or necessarily even have some genuine interest in or curiosity about the natural world, but it is a disappointment nonetheless that the Discoverer of the New World turns out to be quite so simple, quite so inexperienced, in the ways of discovering his environment.

Colón's limitations, I hasten to say, were not his alone; they were of his culture, and they would be found in the descriptions of many others — Vespucci, Cortés, Hawkins, Juet, Cartier, Champlain, Ralegh — in the century of discovery to follow. They are the source of what the distinguished English historian J. H. Elliott has called "the problem of description" faced by Europeans confronting the uniqueness of the New World: "So often the physical appearance of the New World is either totally ignored or else described in the flattest and most conventional phraseology. This off-hand treatment of nature contrasts strikingly with the many precise and acute descriptions of the native inhabitants. It is as if the American landscape is seen as no more than a backcloth against which the strange and perennially fascinating peoples of the New World are dutifully grouped." The reason, Elliott thinks, and this is telling, may be "a lack of interest among sixteenth-century

Europeans, and especially those of the Mediterranean world, in land-scape and in nature." This lack of interest was reflected in the lack of vocabulary, the lack of that facility common to nature-based peoples whose cultures are steeped in natural imagery. Oviedo, for example, setting out to write descriptions for his *Historia general* in the next century, continually threw his hands up in the air: "Of all the things I have seen," he said at one point, "this is the one which has most left me without hope of being able to describe it in words"; or at another, "It needs to be painted by the hand of a Berruguete or some other excellent painter like him, or by Leonardo da Vinci or Andrea Mantegna, famous painters whom I knew in Italy." Like Colón, visitor after visitor to the New World seemed mind-boggled and tongue-tied trying to convey the wonders before them, and about the only color they seem to have eyes for is green — and not very many shades of that, either. . . .

REFLECTIONS

It is difficult to ignore moral issues when considering explorations and explorers. The prefix *great* is used liberally, and words like *discovery* and *courage* readily fit when describing "firsts" and "unknowns." However, celebratory images, national myths, and heroic biographies inevitably engender the reverse. Ye Jun and a new breed of Beijing historians condemn Zheng He for military suppression. Kirkpatrick Sale charges Columbus with arrogance, ignorance, and insufficient curiosity.

On the matter of preparation, the difference between the Chinese and Columbian voyages is especially striking. The floating Chinese scientific laboratories, traveling experts, sages, and interpreters contrast starkly with the lack of a single artist or naturalist on board Columbus's ships. But the inability to distinguish shades of green is not a moral failure. We might say that Columbus's voyage was premature, Zheng He's meticulously planned and prepared. Like the designers of a modern aircraft, the Chinese built in redundancies: separate compartments that could fill with water without sinking the ship, more rice and fresh water than they would need, experts to find plants that might cure diseases yet unknown. By contrast, Columbus seems like a loose cannon, unaware of where he was going or where he had been, capable of lighting a match inside a dark powder shed.

These were, and in many ways still are, the differences between Chinese and European (now Western) scientific innovation. No European could (or can) organize an enterprise on the scale of Zhu Di. No Chinese emperor had reason to sanction an experimental voyage into the unknown. In the same book from which we excerpted a noncontroversial section, Gavin Menzies argues that Zheng He's voyage of 1421 led eventually around Africa and across the Atlantic to the Americas. But in addition to the weakness of the evidence that Zheng He reached the Americas, this would have been out of character for Chinese imperial tribute missions. There were, no doubt, Chinese sailors who came upon unknown lands, possibly even across the great Pacific Ocean; but the domain of the emperor was the known world, of which he was the center. In the Europe of closely competing princes, a Columbus could hatch a personal scheme with minimal supervision and barely sufficient funding and the consequences could still be — indeed, were — momentous. (See Chapter 2.) Was such a system irresponsible? Today, as we begin to probe the heavens around us, even as we tamper with technologies that change the balance of natural forces on earth, we might consider whether the Confucian scholars of six hundred years ago were on to something when they burned the ships and destroyed all of the records of their age of great discovery.

Primary sources are not limited to written records, however. When the Chinese recently revived the memory of Zheng He, Joseph Kahn tells us, they drew on an unlikely record of Chinese settlement in east Africa: the young woman from Kenya, Mwamaka Sharifu, who claimed Chinese ancestry. Chinese-African faces on the coast of East Africa are evidence of contact, but not of contact in 1421. Combined, however, with family stories, DNA tests, local histories, archaeological finds, a single living primary source may become the basis for a new interpretation of a broader history. In the case of Mwamaka Sharifu, members of her family, and other residents of coastal Somalia and Kenya, the evidence has proved convincing.

Lawyers are fond of saying that the absence of evidence is not the same as the evidence of absence. Still, the absence of primary evidence, despite Gavin Menzies's Herculean but ultimately fruitless efforts at finding evidence of Chinese settlement in the Americas, seriously challenges his secondary interpretation. The absence of any fifteenth-century Chinese remains in the Western Hemisphere contrasts starkly with the archaeological and genetic record of the Indian Ocean. Primary sources, then, reveal by their silences as well as their inclusions. As Menzies himself notes, Zheng He's account of his voyages dots the Indian Ocean ports from Ceylon to India to Arabia to East Africa, as far as the Somali ports of Mogadishu and Brava — but no further (see Map 1.1). Sometimes primary sources are more reliable than secondary ones, if the Zheng He and Menzies selections are any indication. But both kinds of sources are necessary to develop the historical sensibility required to engage the difficult moral issues that the past and, of course, the future confront us with.

2

Atlantic World Encounters

Europeans, Americans,
and Africans, 1500–1750

HISTORICAL CONTEXT

European expansion in the Atlantic that began with Portuguese voyages along the African coast in the 1440s and Columbus's discovery of the Americas in 1492 had by 1750 created a new Atlantic zone of human contact and communication that embraced four continents and one ocean. Until this point, nothing — neither the Chinese contacts with Africa in the early fifteenth century, nor the expansion of Islam throughout Eurasia in the almost thousand years since the Prophet Muhammad's death in 632 — had so thoroughly and so permanently changed the human and ecological balance of the world.

Sub-Saharan Africa had already been integrated into the world of Eurasia by 1450. African populations became more mixed, as peoples from the Niger River area migrated east and south throughout the continent during the fifteen hundred years before the arrival of the Portuguese. Muslims from North Africa and the Middle East had aided or established Muslim states and trading ports south of the Sahara in East and West Africa after 1000. Cultural and technical innovations of the Middle East, like the literacy that came with Islam, penetrated slowly, and the spread of the many plants and animals of the northern hemisphere was slowed by the Sahara and equator. However, microbes traveled swiftly and easily from Eurasia to Africa, creating a single set of diseases and immunities for the peoples of the Afro-Eurasian Old World.

The peoples of the Americas, having been isolated ecologically for more than a thousand years, were not so fortunate. The arrival of Europeans and Africans in the Americas after 1492 had devastating consequences for Native American populations. Old World diseases like smallpox were responsible for millions of Native American deaths — a tragedy far worse in scope than the casualties caused by wars. To work the mines and plantations of the New World, Europeans used Indian labor, but increasingly, especially for lowland plantations, they used African slaves (see Map 2.1). By 1750, the combination of Indian "die off" and African and European migration resulted in vastly different populations in the Americas. On some Caribbean islands and in plantation areas like northeastern Brazil, Indian populations were entirely replaced by Africans. At the same time, European animals (for example, goats, cattle, horses) multiplied in the absence of natural predators.

The new Atlantic ecological system was not a uniform zone, however. Coastal regions in Western Europe and towns on the eastern seaboard of the Americas prospered, while American interiors and African populations in Africa stagnated or declined. The Atlantic Ocean became a vast lake that united port cities and plantations with sailing ships that carried African slaves to the Caribbean, Caribbean sugar and rum to North American and European industrial ports, and guns, pots, and liquor to the African "Slave Coast."

Thus, the Atlantic world was integrated with the Old World. Trade routes that began in Boston or Bahia, Brazil, stretched across Eurasia and around southern Africa into the Indian Ocean and the China Sea. Crops that had previously been known only to Native Americans — corn, potatoes, and tomatoes — fueled population explosions from Ireland to China and graced the tables of peasants and princes in between. What began as an effort by European merchants to import Asian spices directly became after 1650 (as European tastes for pepper and Asian spices moderated) a new global pantry of possibilities.

In this chapter, we will read selections that describe some of the first contacts that led to this new global dynamic. We will read of Europeans in Mexico, North America, and West Africa and examine European depictions of natives from both North and South America. We will also explore some of the African and American responses to this European expansion. When studying these accounts and images, notice how these individuals at the frontier of a new age understand and treat each other. Consider how these initial exchanges, so apparently fortuitous and transitory at the time, changed the face of the world.

THINKING HISTORICALLY
Comparing Primary Sources

By comparing and contrasting one thing with another, we learn more about each, and by examining related works in their proper context, we learn more about the whole of which they are part. In the first chapter we compared China and Europe or Chinese and European (mainly

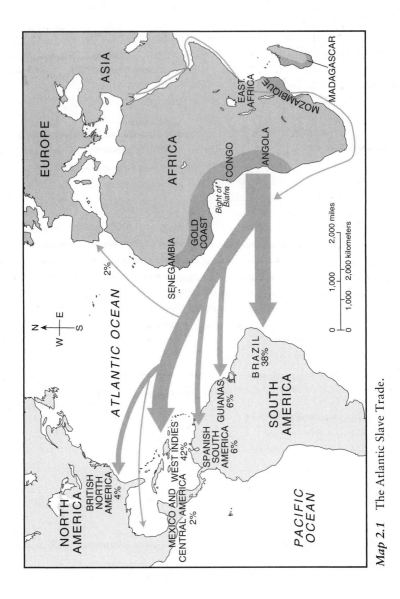

Map 2.1 The Atlantic Slave Trade.

Spanish) expansion in the fifteenth century. In this chapter we look at the Atlantic world, specifically at Europeans in Africa and the Americas. We begin with three views of the Spanish conquest of Mexico — separate accounts by the Spanish conquistadors, by the Mexicans, and by a Dominican friar. The fourth selection juxtaposes two European depictions of Native Americans. The fifth selection recounts the Dutch conquest of the Algonquin nation in North America (in what is today New York City), and allows us to compare Dutch and Spanish colonial policies.

The final three readings examine encounters between Europeans and Africans and the development of the Atlantic slave trade. Did Europeans treat Native Americans and Africans differently? If so, why?

6

BERNAL DÍAZ

From The Conquest of New Spain

Bernal Díaz del Castillo was born in Spain in 1492, the year Columbus sailed to America. After participating in two explorations of the Mexican coast, Díaz joined the expedition of Hernán Cortés to Mexico City in 1519. He wrote this history of the conquest much later, when he was in his seventies; he died circa 1580, a municipal official with a small estate in Guatemala.

The conquest of Mexico did not automatically follow from the first Spanish settlements in Santo Domingo, Hispaniola, and then Cuba in the West Indies. The Spanish crown had given permission for trade and exploration, not colonization. But many Spaniards, from fortune-seeking peasant-soldiers to minor nobility, were eager to conquer their own lands and exploit the populations of dependent Indians.

Cortés, of minor noble descent, sailed to the Indies at the age of nineteen, where he established a sizeable estate on the island of Hispaniola. When he heard stories of Montezuma's gold, he was determined to find the fabled capital of the Aztec empire, Tenochtitlán*

*teh nohch teet LAHN

Bernal Díaz, *The Conquest of New Spain*, trans. J. M. Cohen (Baltimore: Penguin Books, 1963), 217–19, 221–25, 228–38, 241–43.

(modern Mexico City). He gathered more than five hundred amateur soldiers, eleven ships, sixteen horses, and several pieces of artillery, then sailed across the Caribbean and Gulf of Mexico and there began the long march from the coast up to the high central plateau of Mexico.

The Aztecs were new to central Mexico, arriving from the North American desert only about two hundred years before the Spanish, around 1325. By 1500 they had established dominion over almost all other city-states of Mexico, ruling an empire that stretched as far south as Guatemala and as far east as the Mayan lands of the Yucatan Peninsula.

Aztec power relied on a combination of old and new religious ideas and a military system that conquered through terror. The older religious tradition that the Aztecs adopted from Toltec culture centered on Quetzalcoatl* — the feathered serpent, god of creation and brotherhood, whose nurturing forces continued in Aztec society in a system of universal education and in festivals dedicated to life, creativity, and procreation. But the Aztecs also worshipped Huitzilopochtli,[†] a warrior god primed for death and sacrifice, who was given dominant status in the Aztec pantheon. Huitzilopochtli (rendered "Huichilobos"[‡] in this selection) was a force for building a powerful Aztec empire. Drawing on the god's need for human sacrifice — a need not unknown among religions of central Mexico (or Christians) — Montezuma's predecessors built altars to Huitzilopochtli at Tenochtitlán, Cholula, and other sites. The war god required a neverending supply of human hearts, a need that prompted armies to evermore remote sections of Central America in search of sacrificial victims and creating an endless supply of enemies of the Aztecs, among these, the Tlaxcalans.

With the help of his Indian captive and companion Doña Marina — called La Malinche[§] by some of the Indians (thus, Montezuma sometimes calls Cortés "Lord Malinche" in the selection) — Cortés was able to communicate with the Tlaxcalans and other Indians who were tired of Aztec domination. On his march toward Tenochtitlán, Cortés stopped to join forces with the Tlaxcalans, perhaps cementing the relationship and demonstrating his resolve through a brutal massacre of the people of Cholula, an Aztec ally and arch enemy of the Tlaxcalans. By the time Cortés arrived at Tenochtitlán, Montezuma knew of the defeat of his allies at Cholula.

This selection from Bernal Díaz begins with the Spanish entry into Tenochtitlán. What impresses Díaz, and presumably other Spanish

---

*keht zahl koh AH tuhl
[†]wheat zee loh poácht lee
[‡]wee chee LOH bohs
[§]La Malinche (lah   mah LEEN cheh). A variation on "Marina." In contemporary Mexico a traitor is often called a "Malinchisto."

conquistadors, about the Mexican capital city? What parts of the city attract his attention the most? What conclusions does he draw about Mexican (or Aztec) civilization? Does he think Spanish civilization is equal, inferior, or superior to that of Mexico?

Thinking Historically

Díaz gives us a dramatic account of the meeting of Cortés and Montezuma. What do you think each is thinking and feeling? Do you see any signs of tension in their elaborate greetings? Why are both behaving so politely? What do they want from each other?

Notice how the initial hospitality turns tense. What causes this? Is either side more to blame for what happens next? Was conflict inevitable? Could the encounter have ended in some sort of peaceful resolution?

Remember, we are going to compare Díaz's view with a Mexican view of these events. From your reading of Díaz, does he seem able to understand the Mexican point of view? Would you call him a sympathetic observer?

When Cortes saw, heard, and was told that the great Montezuma was approaching, he dismounted from his horse, and when he came near to Montezuma each bowed deeply to the other. Montezuma welcomed our Captain, and Cortes, speaking through Doña Marina, answered by wishing him very good health. Cortes, I think, offered Montezuma his right hand, but Montezuma refused it and extended his own. Then Cortes brought out a necklace which he had been holding. It was made of those elaborately worked and coloured glass beads called *margaritas*, . . . and was strung on a gold cord and dipped in musk to give it a good odour. This he hung round the great Montezuma's neck, and as he did so attempted to embrace him. But the great princes who stood round Montezuma grasped Cortes' arm to prevent him, for they considered this an indignity.

Then Cortes told Montezuma that it rejoiced his heart to have seen such a great prince, and that he took his coming in person to receive him and the repeated favours he had done him as a high honour. After this Montezuma made him another complimentary speech, and ordered two of his nephews who were supporting him, the lords of Texcoco and Coyoacan, to go with us and show us our quarters. Montezuma returned to the city with the other two kinsmen of his escort, the lords of Cuitlahuac and Tacuba; and all those grand companies of *Caciques*[1] and dignitaries who had come with him returned also in his train. . . .

---

[1] Chiefs. Kah SEEK [Ed.]

On our arrival we entered the large court, where the great Montezuma was awaiting our Captain. Taking him by the hand, the prince led him to his apartment in the hall where he was to lodge, which was very richly furnished in their manner. Montezuma had ready for him a very rich necklace, made of golden crabs, a marvellous piece of work, which he hung round Cortes' neck. His captains were greatly astonished at this sign of honour.

After this ceremony, for which Cortes thanked him through our interpreters, Montezuma said: "Malinche, you and your brothers are in your own house. Rest awhile." He then returned to his palace, which was not far off.

We divided our lodgings by companies, and placed our artillery in a convenient spot. Then the order we were to keep was clearly explained to us, and we were warned to be very much on the alert, both the horsemen and the rest of us soldiers. We then ate a sumptuous dinner which they had prepared for us in their native style.

So, with luck on our side, we boldly entered the city of Tenochtitlán or Mexico on 8 November in the year of our Lord 1519.

The Stay in Mexico

. . . Montezuma had ordered his stewards to provide us with everything we needed for our way of living: maize, grindstones, women to make our bread, fowls, fruit, and plenty of fodder for the horses. He then took leave of us all with the greatest courtesy, and we accompanied him to the street. However, Cortes ordered us not to go far from our quarters for the present until we knew better what conduct to observe.

Next day Cortes decided to go to Montezuma's palace. But first he sent to know whether the prince was busy and to inform him of our coming. He took four captains with him: Pedro de Alvarado, Juan Velazquez de Leon, Diego de Ordaz, and Gonzalo de Sandoval, and five of us soldiers.

When Montezuma was informed of our coming, he advanced into the middle of the hall to receive us, closely surrounded by his nephews, for no other chiefs were allowed to enter his palace or communicate with him except upon important business. Cortes and Montezuma exchanged bows, and clasped hands. Then Montezuma led Cortes to his own dais, and setting him down on his right, called for more seats, on which he ordered us all to sit also.

Cortes began to make a speech through our interpreters, saying that we were all now rested, and that in coming to see and speak with such a great prince we had fulfilled the purpose of our voyage and the orders of our lord the King. The principal things he had come to say on behalf of our Lord God had already been communicated to Montezuma through his three ambassadors, on that occasion in the sand-hills when he did us the favour of sending us the golden moon and sun. We had then told him that we were Christians and worshipped one God alone, named Jesus Christ, who had suffered His passion and death to save us; and that what they worshipped as gods were not gods but devils, which were evil things, and if they were ugly to look at, their deeds were uglier. But he had proved to them how evil and ineffectual their gods were, as both the prince and his people would observe in the course of time, since, where we had put up crosses such as their ambassadors had seen, they had been too frightened to appear before them.

The favour he now begged of the great Montezuma was that he should listen to the words he now wished to speak. Then he very carefully expounded the creation of the world, how we are all brothers, the children of one mother and father called Adam and Eve; and how such a brother as our great Emperor, grieving for the perdition of so many souls as their idols were leading to hell, where they burnt in living flame, had sent us to tell him this, so that he might put a stop to it, and so that they might give up the worship of idols and make no more human sacrifices — for all men are brothers — and commit no more robbery or sodomy. He also promised that in the course of time the King would send some men who lead holy lives among us, much better than our own, to explain this more fully, for we had only come to give them warning. Therefore he begged Montezuma to do as he was asked.

As Montezuma seemed about to reply, Cortes broke off his speech, saying to those of us who were with him: "Since this is only the first attempt, we have now done our duty."

"My lord Malinche," Montezuma replied, "these arguments of yours have been familiar to me for some time. I understand what you said to my ambassadors on the sandhills about the three gods and the cross, also what you preached in the various towns through which you passed. We have given you no answer, since we have worshipped our own gods here from the beginning and know them to be good. No doubt yours are good also, but do not trouble to tell us any more about them at present. Regarding the creation of the world, we have held the same belief for many ages, and for this reason are certain that you are those who our ancestors predicted would come from the direction of the sunrise. As for your great King, I am in his debt and will give him of what I possess. For, as I have already said, two years ago I had news of the Captains who came in ships, by the road that you came, and said they were servants of this great king of yours. I should like to know if you are all the same people."

Cortes answered that we were all brothers and servants of the Emperor, and that they had come to discover a route and explore the seas and ports, so that when they knew them well we could follow, as we had done. Montezuma was referring to the expeditions of Francisco

Hernandez de Cordoba and of Grijalva, the first voyages of discovery. He said that ever since that time he had wanted to invite some of these men to visit the cities of his kingdom, where he would receive them and do them honour, and that now his gods had fulfilled his desire, for we were in his house, which we might call our own. Here we might rest and enjoy ourselves, for we should receive good treatment. If on other occasions he had sent to forbid our entrance into his city, it was not of his own free will, but because his vassals were afraid. For they told him we shot out flashes of lightning, and killed many Indians with our horses, and that we were angry *Teules*, and other such childish stories. But now that he had seen us, he knew that we were of flesh and blood and very intelligent, also very brave. Therefore he had a far greater esteem for us than these reports had given him, and would share with us what he had.

We all thanked him heartily for his . . . good will, and Montezuma replied with a laugh, because in his princely manner he spoke very gaily: "Malinche, I know that these people of Tlascala with whom you are so friendly have told you that I am a sort of god or *Teule*, and keep nothing in any of my houses that is not made of silver and gold and precious stones. But I know very well that you are too intelligent to believe this and will take it as a joke. See now, Malinche, my body is made of flesh and blood like yours, and my houses and palaces are of stone, wood, and plaster. It is true that I am a great king, and have inherited the riches of my ancestors, but the lies and nonsense you have heard of us are not true. You must take them as a joke, as I take the story of your thunders and lightnings."

Cortes answered also with a laugh that enemies always speak evil and tell lies about the people they hate, but he knew he could not hope to find a more magnificent prince in that land, and there was good reason why his fame should have reached our Emperor.

While this conversation was going on, Montezuma quietly sent one of his nephews, a great *Cacique*, to order his stewards to bring certain pieces of gold, which had apparently been set aside as a gift for Cortes, and ten loads of fine cloaks which he divided: the gold and cloaks between Cortes and the four captains, and for each of us soldiers two gold necklaces, each worth ten pesos, and two loads of cloaks. The gold that he then gave us was worth in all more than a thousand pesos, and he gave it all cheerfully, like a great and valiant prince.

As it was now past midday and he did not wish to be importunate, Cortes said to Montezuma: "My lord, the favours you do us increase, load by load, every day, and it is now the hour of your dinner." Montezuma answered that he thanked us for visiting him. We then took our leave with the greatest courtesy, and returned to our quarters, talking as we went of the prince's fine breeding and manners and deciding to show him the greatest respect in every way, and to remove our quilted caps in his presence, which we always did.

The great Montezuma was about forty years old, of good height, well proportioned, spare and slight, and not very dark, though of the usual Indian complexion. He did not wear his hair long but just over his ears, and he had a short black beard, well-shaped and thin. His face was rather long and cheerful, he had fine eyes, and in his appearance and manner could express geniality or, when necessary, a serious composure. He was very neat and clean, and took a bath every afternoon. He had many women as his mistresses, the daughters of chieftains, but two legitimate wives who were *Caciques* in their own right, and when he had intercourse with any of them it was so secret that only some of his servants knew of it. He was quite free from sodomy. The clothes he wore one day he did not wear again till three or four days later. He had a guard of two hundred chieftains lodged in rooms beside his own, only some of whom were permitted to speak to him. When they entered his presence they were compelled to take off their rich cloaks and put on others of little value. They had to be clean and walk barefoot, with their eyes downcast, for they were not allowed to look him in the face, and as they approached they had to make three obeisances, saying as they did so, "Lord, my lord, my great lord!" Then, when they had said what they had come to say, he would dismiss them with a few words. They did not turn their backs on him as they went out, but kept their faces towards him and their eyes downcast, only turning round when they had left the room. Another thing I noticed was that when other great chiefs came from distant lands about disputes or on business, they too had to take off their shoes and put on poor cloaks before entering Montezuma's apartments; and they were not allowed to enter the palace immediately but had to linger for a while near the door, since to enter hurriedly was considered disrespectful. . . .

Montezuma had two houses stocked with every sort of weapon; many of them were richly adorned with gold and precious stones. There were shields large and small, and a sort of broadsword, and two-handed swords set with flint blades that cut much better than our swords, and lances longer than ours, with five-foot blades consisting of many knives. Even when these are driven at a buckler or a shield they are not deflected. In fact they cut like razors, and the Indians can shave their heads with them. They had very good bows and arrows, and double and single-pointed javelins as well as their throwing-sticks and many slings and round stones shaped by hand, and another sort of shield that can be rolled up when they are not fighting, so that it does not get in the way, but which can be opened when they need it in battle and covers their bodies from head to foot. There was also a great deal of cotton armour richly worked on the outside with different coloured feathers, which they used as devices and distinguishing marks, and they had casques and helmets made of wood and bone which were also highly decorated with feathers on the outside. They had other arms of different kinds which I will not mention through fear of prolixity, and workmen skilled in the manufacture of such things, and stewards who were in charge of these arms. . . .

I have already described the manner of their sacrifices. They strike open the wretched Indian's chest with flint knives and hastily tear out the palpitating heart which, with the blood, they present to the idols in whose name they have performed the sacrifice. Then they cut off the arms, thighs, and head, eating the arms and thighs at their ceremonial banquets. The head they hang up on a beam, and the body of the sacrificed man is not eaten but given to the beasts of prey. They also had many vipers in this accursed house, and poisonous snakes which have something that sounds like a bell in their tails. These, which are the deadliest snakes of all, they kept in jars and great pottery vessels full of feathers, in which they laid their eggs and reared their young. They were fed on the bodies of sacrificed Indians and the flesh of the dogs that they bred. We know for certain, too, that when they drove us out of Mexico and killed over eight hundred and fifty of our soldiers, they fed those beasts and snakes on their bodies for many days, as I shall relate in due course. These snakes and wild beasts were dedicated to their fierce idols, and kept them company. As for the horrible noise when the lions and tigers roared, and the jackals and foxes howled, and the serpents hissed, it was so appalling that one seemed to be in hell. . . .

When our Captain and the Mercedarian friar realized that Montezuma would not allow us to set up a cross at Huichilobos' *cue*[2] or build a church there, it was decided that we should ask his stewards for masons so that we could put up a church in our own quarters. For every time we had said mass since entering the city of Mexico we had had to erect an altar on tables and dismantle it again.

The stewards promised to tell Montezuma of our wishes, and Cortes also sent our interpreters to ask him in person. Montezuma granted our request and ordered that we should be supplied with all the necessary material. We had our church finished in two days, and a cross erected in front of our lodgings, and mass was said there each day until the wine gave out. For as Cortes and some other captains and a friar had been ill during the Tlascalan campaign, there had been a run on the wine that we kept for mass. Still, though it was finished, we still went to church every day and prayed on our knees before the altar and images, firstly because it was our obligation as Christians and a good habit, and secondly so that Montezuma and all his captains should observe us and, seeing us worshipping on our knees before the cross — especially when we intoned the Ave Maria — might be inclined to imitate us.

[2]The temple of the sun god who demanded human sacrifice. [Ed.]

It being our habit to examine and inquire into everything, when we were all assembled in our lodging and considering which was the best place for an altar, two of our men, one of whom was the carpenter Alonso Yañez, called attention to some marks on one of the walls which showed that there had once been a door, though it had been well plastered up and painted. Now as we had heard that Montezuma kept his father's treasure in this building, we immediately suspected that it must be in this room, which had been closed up only a few days before. Yañez made the suggestion to Juan Velazquez de Leon and Francisco de Lugo, both relatives of mine, to whom he had attached himself as a servant; and they mentioned the matter to Cortes. So the door was secretly opened, and Cortes went in first with certain captains. When they saw the quantity of golden objects — jewels and plates and ingots — which lay in that chamber they were quite transported. They did not know what to think of such riches. The news soon spread to the other captains and soldiers, and very secretly we all went in to see. The sight of all that wealth dumbfounded me. Being only a youth at the time and never having seen such riches before, I felt certain that there could not be a store like it in the whole world. We unanimously decided that we could not think of touching a particle of it, and that the stones should immediately be replaced in the doorway, which should be blocked again and cemented just as we had found it. We resolved also that not a word should be said about this until times changed, for fear Montezuma might hear of our discovery.

Let us leave this subject of the treasure and tell how four of our most valiant captains took Cortes aside in the church, with a dozen soldiers who were in his trust and confidence, myself among them, and asked him to consider the net or trap in which we were caught, to look at the great strength of the city and observe the causeways and bridges, and remember the warnings we had received in every town we had passed through that Huichilobos had counselled Montezuma to let us into the city and kill us there. We reminded him that the hearts of men are very fickle, especially among the Indians, and begged him not to trust the good will and affection that Montezuma was showing us, because from one hour to another it might change. If he should take it into his head to attack us, we said, the stoppage of our supplies of food and water, or the raising of any of the bridges, would render us helpless. Then, considering the vast army of warriors he possessed, we should be incapable of attacking or defending ourselves. And since all the houses stood in the water, how could our Tlascalan allies come in to help us? We asked him to think over all that we had said, for if we wanted to preserve our lives we must seize Montezuma immediately, without even a day's delay. We pointed out that all the gold Montezuma had given us, and all that we had seen in the treasury of his father Axayacatl, and all the food we ate was turning to poison in our bodies, for we could not sleep by night or day or take any rest while these thoughts were in our minds. If any of our soldiers gave him less drastic advice, we concluded, they would be senseless beasts charmed by the gold and incapable of looking death in the eye.

When he had heard our opinion, Cortes answered: "Do not imagine, gentlemen, that I am asleep or that I do not share your anxiety. You must have seen that I do. But what strength have we got for so bold a course as to take this great lord in his own palace, surrounded as he is by warriors and guards? What scheme or trick can we devise to prevent him from summoning his soldiers to attack us at once?"

Our captains (Juan Velazquez de Leon, Diego de Ordaz, Gonzalo de Sandoval, and Pedro de Alvarado) replied that Montezuma must be got out of his palace by smooth words and brought to our quarters. Once there, he must be told that he must remain as a prisoner, and that if he called out or made any disturbance he would pay for it with his life. If Cortes was unwilling to take this course at once, they begged him for permission to do it themselves. With two very dangerous alternatives before us, the better and more profitable thing, they said, would be to seize Montezuma rather than wait for him to attack us. Once he did so, what chance would we have? Some of us soldiers also remarked that Montezuma's stewards who brought us our food seemed to be growing insolent, and did not serve us as politely as they had at first. Two of our Tlascalan allies had, moreover, secretly observed to Jeronimo de Aguilar that for the last two days the Mexicans had appeared less well disposed to us. We spent a good hour discussing whether or not to take Montezuma prisoner, and how it should be done. But our final advice, that at all costs we should take him prisoner, was approved by our Captain, and we then left the matter till next day. All night we prayed God to direct events in the interests of His holy service. . . .

From The Broken Spears:
The Aztec Account of
the Conquest of Mexico

This Aztec account of the encounter between the Spanish and the Indians of Mexico was written some years after the events described.
Spanish Christian monks helped a postconquest generation of Aztec
Nahuatl* speakers translate the illustrated manuscripts of the conquest period. According to this account, how did Montezuma respond
to Cortés? Was Montezuma's attitude toward the Spanish shared by
other Aztecs? How reliable is this account, do you think, in describing
Montezuma's thoughts, motives, and behavior?

Thinking Historically

How does the Aztec account of the conquest differ from that of the
Spanish, written by Díaz? Is this difference merely a matter of perspective, or do the authors disagree about what happened? To the extent
to which there are differences, how do you decide which account to
believe and accept?

Speeches of Motecuhzoma and Cortes

When Motecuhzoma[1] had given necklaces to each one, Cortes asked
him: "Are you Motecuhzoma? Are you the king? Is it true that you are
the king Motecuhzoma?"

And the king said: "Yes, I am Motecuhzoma." Then he stood up to
welcome Cortes; he came forward, bowed his head low and addressed
him in these words: "Our lord, you are weary. The journey has tired
you, but now you have arrived on the earth. You have come to your
city, Mexico. You have come here to sit on your throne, to sit under its
canopy.

"The kings who have gone before, your representatives, guarded it
and preserved it for your coming. The kings Itzcoatl, Motecuhzoma the
Elder, Axayacatl, Tizoc, and Ahuitzol ruled for you in the City of

*nah WAH tuhl
[1]Original Indian spelling of Montezuma. [Ed.]

The Broken Spears: The Aztec Account of the Conquest of Mexico, ed. Miguel Leon-Portilla
(Boston: Beacon Press, 1990), 64–76.

Mexico. The people were protected by their swords and sheltered by their shields.

"Do the kings know the destiny of those they left behind, their posterity? If only they are watching! If only they can see what I see!

"No, it is not a dream. I am not walking in my sleep. I am not seeing you in my dreams. . . . I have seen you at last! I have met you face to face! I was in agony for five days, for ten days, with my eyes fixed on the Region of the Mystery. And now you have come out of the clouds and mists to sit on your throne again.

"This was foretold by the kings who governed your city, and now it has taken place. You have come back to us; you have come down from the sky. Rest now, and take possession of your royal houses. Welcome to your land, my lords!"

When Motecuhzoma had finished, La Malinche translated his address into Spanish so that the Captain could understand it. Cortes replied in his strange and savage tongue, speaking first to La Malinche: "Tell Motecuhzoma that we are his friends. There is nothing to fear. We have wanted to see him for a long time, and now we have seen his face and heard his words. Tell him that we love him well and that our hearts are contented."

Then he said to Motecuhzoma: "We have come to your house in Mexico as friends. There is nothing to fear."

La Malinche translated this speech and the Spaniards grasped Motecuhzoma's hands and patted his back to show their affection for him.

Attitudes of the Spaniards
and the Native Lords

The Spaniards examined everything they saw. They dismounted from their horses, and mounted them again, and dismounted again, so as not to miss anything of interest.

The chiefs who accompanied Motecuhzoma were: Cacama, king of Tezcoco; Tetlepanquetzaltzin, king of Tlacopan; Itzcuauhtzin the Tlacochcalcatl, lord of Tlatelolco; and Topantemoc, Motecuhzoma's treasurer in Tlatelolco. These four chiefs were standing in a file.

The other princes were: Atlixcatzin [chief who has taken captives];[2] Tepeoatzin, the Tlacochcalcatl; Quetzalaztatzin, the keeper of the chalk; Totomotzin; Hecateupatiltzin; and Cuappiatzin.

When Motecuhzoma was imprisoned, they all went into hiding. They ran away to hide and treacherously abandoned him!

---

[2]Military title given to a warrior who had captured four enemies.

The Spaniards Take Possession of the City

When the Spaniards entered the Royal House, they placed Motecuhzoma under guard and kept him under their vigilance. They also placed a guard over Itzcuauhtzin, but the other lords were permitted to depart.

Then the Spaniards fired one of their cannons, and this caused great confusion in the city. The people scattered in every direction; they fled without rhyme or reason; they ran off as if they were being pursued. It was as if they had eaten the mushrooms that confuse the mind, or had seen some dreadful apparition. They were all overcome by terror, as if their hearts had fainted. And when night fell, the panic spread through the city and their fears would not let them sleep.

In the morning the Spaniards told Motecuhzoma what they needed in the way of supplies: tortillas, fried chickens, hens' eggs, pure water, firewood, and charcoal. Also: large, clean cooking pots, water jars, pitchers, dishes, and other pottery. Motecuhzoma ordered that it be sent to them. The chiefs who received this order were angry with the king and no longer revered or respected him. But they furnished the Spaniards with all the provisions they needed — food, beverages, and water, and fodder for the horses.

The Spaniards Reveal Their Greed

When the Spaniards were installed in the palace, they asked Motecuhzoma about the city's resources and reserves and about the warriors' ensigns and shields. They questioned him closely and then demanded gold.

Motecuhzoma guided them to it. They surrounded him and crowded close with their weapons. He walked in the center, while they formed a circle around him.

When they arrived at the treasure house called Teucalco, the riches of gold and feathers were brought out to them: ornaments made of quetzal feathers, richly worked shields, disks of gold, the necklaces of the idols, gold nose plugs, gold greaves, and bracelets and crowns.

The Spaniards immediately stripped the feathers from the gold shields and ensigns. They gathered all the gold into a great mound and set fire to everything else, regardless of its value. Then they melted down the gold into ingots. As for the precious green stones, they took only the best of them; the rest were snatched up by the Tlaxcaltecas. The Spaniards searched through the whole treasure house, questioning and quarreling, and seized every object they thought was beautiful.

The Seizure of Motecuhzoma's Treasures

Next they went to Motecuhzoma's storehouse, in the place called Toto-calco [Place of the Palace of the Birds],[3] where his personal treasures were kept. The Spaniards grinned like little beasts and patted each other with delight.

When they entered the hall of treasures, it was as if they had arrived in Paradise. They searched everywhere and coveted everything; they were slaves to their own greed. All of Motecuhzoma's possessions were brought out: fine bracelets, necklaces with large stones, ankle rings with little gold bells, the royal crowns, and all the royal finery — everything that belonged to the king and was reserved to him only. They seized these treasures as if they were their own, as if this plunder were merely a stroke of good luck. And when they had taken all the gold, they heaped up everything else in the middle of the patio.

La Malinche called the nobles together. She climbed up to the palace roof and cried: "Mexicanos, come forward! The Spaniards need your help! Bring them food and pure water. They are tired and hungry; they are almost fainting from exhaustion! Why do you not come forward? Are you angry with them?"

The Mexicans were too frightened to approach. They were crushed by terror and would not risk coming forward. They shied away as if the Spaniards were wild beasts, as if the hour were midnight on the blackest night of the year. Yet they did not abandon the Spaniards to hunger and thirst. They brought them whatever they needed, but shook with fear as they did so. They delivered the supplies to the Spaniards with trembling hands, then turned and hurried away.

The Preparations for the Fiesta

The Aztecs begged permission of their king to hold the fiesta of Huitzilopochtli.[3] The Spaniards wanted to see this fiesta to learn how it was celebrated. A delegation of the celebrants came to the palace where Motecuhzoma was a prisoner, and when their spokesman asked his permission, he granted it to them.

As soon as the delegation returned, the women began to grind seeds of the *chicalote*.[4] These women had fasted for a whole year. They ground the seeds in the patio of the temple.

The Spaniards came out of the palace together, dressed in armor and carrying their weapons with them. They stalked among the women

---

[3]The zoological garden attached to the royal palaces.
[4]Edible plants also used in medicines.

and looked at them one by one; they stared into the faces of the women who were grinding seeds. After this cold inspection, they went back into the palace. It is said that they planned to kill the celebrants if the men entered the patio.

The Statue of Huitzilopochtli

On the evening before the fiesta of Toxcatl, the celebrants began to model a statue of Huitzilopochtli. They gave it such a human appearance that it seemed the body of a living man. Yet they made the statue with nothing but a paste made of the ground seeds of the chicalote, which they shaped over an armature of sticks.

When the statue was finished, they dressed it in rich feathers, and they painted crossbars over and under its eyes. They also clipped on its earrings of turquoise mosaic; these were in the shape of serpents, with gold rings hanging from them. Its nose plug, in the shape of an arrow, was made of gold and was inlaid with fine stones.

They placed the magic headdress of hummingbird feathers on its head. They also adorned it with an *anecuyotl*, which was a belt made of feathers, with a cone at the back. Then they hung around its neck an ornament of yellow parrot feathers, fringed like the locks of a young boy. Over this they put its nettle-leaf cape, which was painted black and decorated with five clusters of eagle feathers.

Next they wrapped it in its cloak, which was painted with skull and bones, and over this they fastened its vest. The vest was painted with dismembered human parts: skulls, ears, hearts, intestines, torsos, breasts, hands, and feet. They also put on its *maxtlatl*, or loincloth, which was decorated with images of dissevered limbs and fringed with amate paper. This *maxtlatl* was painted with vertical stripes of bright blue.

They fastened a red paper flag at its shoulder and placed on its head what looked like a sacrificial flint knife. This too was made of red paper; it seemed to have been steeped in blood.

The statue carried a *tehuehuelli*, a bamboo shield decorated with four clusters of fine eagle feathers. The pendant of this shield was blood-red, like the knife and the shoulder flag. The statue also carried four arrows.

Finally, they put the wristbands on its arms. These bands, made of coyote skin, were fringed with paper cut into little strips.

The Beginning of the Fiesta

Early the next morning, the statue's face was uncovered by those who had been chosen for that ceremony. They gathered in front of the idol in single file and offered it gifts of food, such as round seedcakes or perhaps human flesh. But they did not carry it up to its temple on top of the pyramid.

All the young warriors were eager for the fiesta to begin. They had sworn to dance and sing with all their hearts, so that the Spaniards would marvel at the beauty of the rituals.

The procession began, and the celebrants filed into the temple patio to dance the Dance of the Serpent. When they were all together in the patio, the songs and the dance began. Those who had fasted for twenty days and those who had fasted for a year were in command of the others; they kept the dancers in file with their pine wands. (If anyone wished to urinate, he did not stop dancing, but simply opened his clothing at the hips and separated his clusters of heron feathers.)

If anyone disobeyed the leaders or was not in his proper place they struck him on the hips and shoulders. Then they drove him out of the patio, beating him and shoving him from behind. They pushed him so hard that he sprawled to the ground, and they dragged him outside by the ears. No one dared to say a word about this punishment, for those who had fasted during the year were feared and venerated; they had earned the exclusive title "Brothers of Huitzilopochtli."

The great captains, the bravest warriors, danced at the head of the files to guide the others. The youths followed at a slight distance. Some of the youths wore their hair gathered into large locks, a sign that they had never taken any captives. Others carried their headdresses on their shoulders; they had taken captives, but only with help.

Then came the recruits, who were called "the young warriors." They had each captured an enemy or two. The others called to them: "Come, comrades, show us how brave you are! Dance with all your hearts!"

The Spaniards Attack the Celebrants

At this moment in the fiesta, when the dance was loveliest and when song was linked to song, the Spaniards were seized with an urge to kill the celebrants. They all ran forward, armed as if for battle. They closed the entrances and passageways, all the gates of the patio: the Eagle Gate in the lesser palace, the Gate of the Canestalk and the Gate of the Serpent of Mirrors. They posted guards so that no one could escape, and then rushed into the Sacred Patio to slaughter the celebrants. They came on foot, carrying their swords and their wooden or metal shields.

They ran in among the dancers, forcing their way to the place where the drums were played. They attacked the man who was drumming and cut off his arms. Then they cut off his head, and it rolled across the floor.

They attacked all the celebrants, stabbing them, spearing them, striking them with their swords. They attacked some of them from behind, and these fell instantly to the ground with their entrails hanging out. Others they beheaded: they cut off their heads, or split their heads to pieces.

They struck others in the shoulders, and their arms were torn from their bodies. They wounded some in the thigh and some in the calf. They slashed others in the abdomen, and their entrails all spilled to the ground. Some attempted to run away, but their intestines dragged as they ran; they seemed to tangle their feet in their own entrails. No matter how they tried to save themselves, they could find no escape.

Some attempted to force their way out, but the Spaniards murdered them at the gates. Others climbed the walls, but they could not save themselves. Those who ran into the communal houses were safe there for a while; so were those who lay down among the victims and pretended to be dead. But if they stood up again, the Spaniards saw them and killed them.

The blood of the warriors flowed like water and gathered into pools. The pools widened, and the stench of blood and entrails filled the air. The Spaniards ran into the communal houses to kill those who were hiding. They ran everywhere and searched everywhere; they invaded every room, hunting and killing.

8

BARTOLOMEO DE LAS CASAS

From The Devastation of the Indies

Las Casas (1484–1566) emigrated with his father from Spain to the island of Hispaniola in 1502. Eight years later he became a priest, served as a missionary to the Taino of Cuba (1512), attempted to create a utopian society for the Indians of Venezuela, and became a Dominican friar in 1522. Repelled by his early experience among the conquistadors, Las Casas the priest and friar devoted his adult life to aiding the Indians in the Americas and defending their rights in the Spanish court. This selection is drawn from his brief history, *The Devastation of the Indies*, published in 1555. The work for this book and

Bartolomeo de Las Casas, *The Devastation of the Indies: A Brief Account*, trans. Herma Briffault (Baltimore: Johns Hopkins University Press, 1992), 32–35, 40–41.

a larger volume, *In Defense of the Indians,* presented his case against Indian slavery in the great debate at the Spanish court at Valladolid in 1550. Along with his monumental *History of the Indies,* published after his death, the writings of Las Casas constituted such an indictment of Spanish colonialism that Protestant enemies were able to argue that Catholic slavery and exploitation of the "New World" was worse than their own, a dubious proposition that became known as "the Black Legend." What do you make of this account by Las Casas? Does he exaggerate, or is it likely that these events happened?

Thinking Historically

Compare this account with the two previous selections. Do you think the Spanish treated the people of Hispaniola and Mexico differently? Do these three readings offer different interpretations of the role of Christianity in the Americas?

This [Hispaniola][1] was the first land in the New World to be destroyed and depopulated by the Christians, and here they began their subjection of the women and children, taking them away from the Indians to use them and ill use them, eating the food they provided with their sweat and toil. The Spaniards did not content themselves with what the Indians gave them of their own free will, according to their ability, which was always too little to satisfy enormous appetites, for a Christian eats and consumes in one day an amount of food that would suffice to feed three houses inhabited by ten Indians for one month. And they committed other acts of force and violence and oppression which made the Indians realize that these men had not come from Heaven. And some of the Indians concealed their foods while others concealed their wives and children and still others fled to the mountains to avoid the terrible transactions of the Christians.

And the Christians attacked them with buffets and beatings, until finally they laid hands on the nobles of the villages. Then they behaved with such temerity and shamelessness that the most powerful ruler of the islands had to see his own wife raped by a Christian officer.

From that time onward the Indians began to seek ways to throw the Christians out of their lands. They took up arms, but their weapons were very weak and of little service in offense and still less in defense. (Because of this, the wars of the Indians against each other are little more than games played by children.) And the Christians, with their horses and swords and pikes began to carry out massacres and strange

---

[1]The island that today includes the Dominican Republic and Haiti. [Ed.]

cruelties against them. They attacked the towns and spared neither the children nor the aged nor pregnant women nor women in childbed, not only stabbing them and dismembering them but cutting them to pieces as if dealing with sheep in the slaughter house. They laid bets as to who, with one stroke of the sword, could split a man in two or could cut off his head or spill out his entrails with a single stroke of the pike. They took infants from their mothers' breasts, snatching them by the legs and pitching them headfirst against the crags or snatched them by the arms and threw them into the rivers, roaring with laughter and saying as the babies fell into the water, "Boil there, you offspring of the devil!" Other infants they put to the sword along with their mothers and anyone else who happened to be nearby. They made some low wide gallows on which the hanged victim's feet almost touched the ground, stringing up their victims in lots of thirteen, in memory of Our Redeemer and His twelve Apostles, then set burning wood at their feet and thus burned them alive. To others they attached straw or wrapped their whole bodies in straw and set them afire. With still others, all those they wanted to capture alive, they cut off their hands and hung them round the victim's neck, saying, "Go now, carry the message," meaning, Take the news to the Indians who have fled to the mountains. They usually dealt with the chieftains and nobles in the following way: they made a grid of rods which they placed on forked sticks, then lashed the victims to the grid and lighted a smoldering fire underneath, so that little by little, as those captives screamed in despair and torment, their souls would leave them.

I once saw this, when there were four or five nobles lashed on grids and burning; I seem even to recall that there were two or three pairs of grids where others were burning, and because they uttered such loud screams that they disturbed the captain's sleep, he ordered them to be strangled. And the constable, who was worse than an executioner, did not want to obey that order (and I know the name of that constable and know his relatives in Seville), but instead put a stick over the victims' tongues, so they could not make a sound, and he stirred up the fire, but not too much, so that they roasted slowly, as he liked. I saw all these things I have described, and countless others.

And because all the people who could do so fled to the mountains to escape these inhuman, ruthless, and ferocious acts, the Spanish captains, enemies of the human race, pursued them with the fierce dogs they kept which attacked the Indians, tearing them to pieces and devouring them. And because on few and far between occasions, the Indians justifiably killed some Christians, the Spaniards made a rule among themselves that for every Christian slain by the Indians, they would slay a hundred Indians. . . .

Because the particulars that enter into these outrages are so numerous they could not be contained in the scope of much writing, for in

truth I believe that in the great deal I have set down here I have not revealed the thousandth part of the sufferings endured by the Indians, I
now want only to add that, in the matter of these unprovoked and destructive wars, and God is my witness, all these acts of wickedness I
have described, as well as those I have omitted, were perpetrated
against the Indians without cause, without any more cause than could
give a community of good monks living together in a monastery. And
still more strongly I affirm that until the multitude of people on this island of Hispaniola were killed and their lands devastated, they committed no sin against the Christians that would be punishable by man's
laws, and as to those sins punishable by God's law, such as vengeful
feelings against such powerful enemies as the Christians have been,
those sins would be committed by the very few Indians who are hard-
hearted and impetuous. And I can say this from my great experience
with them: their hardness and impetuosity would be that of children, of
boys ten or twelve years old. I know by certain infallible signs that the
wars waged by the Indians against the Christians have been justifiable
wars and that all the wars waged by the Christians against the Indians
have been unjust wars, more diabolical than any wars ever waged anywhere in the world. This I declare to be so of all the many wars they
have waged against the peoples throughout the Indies.

After the wars and the killings had ended, when usually there survived only some boys, some women, and children, these survivors were
distributed among the Christians to be slaves. The *repartimiento* or distribution was made according to the rank and importance of the Christian to whom the Indians were allocated, one of them being given
thirty, another forty, still another, one or two hundred, and besides the
rank of the Christian there was also to be considered in what favor he
stood with the tyrant they called Governor. The pretext was that these
allocated Indians were to be instructed in the articles of the Christian
Faith. As if those Christians who were as a rule foolish and cruel and
greedy and vicious could be caretakers of souls! And the care they took
was to send the men to the mines to dig for gold, which is intolerable
labor, and to send the women into the fields of the big ranches to hoe
and till the land, work suitable for strong men. Nor to either the men
or the women did they give any food except herbs and legumes, things
of little substance. The milk in the breasts of the women with infants
dried up and thus in a short while the infants perished.

9

Two European Views of Native Americans

Las Casas's sympathetic view of the Indians was hardly one shared by the average Frenchman, Italian, or Scot. Indeed, many Europeans harbored fantastical and negative notions about the inhabitants of the "New World," envisioning them as wild and cannibalistic, savage and ruthless toward their enemies. Reinforcing this impression were images that circulated throughout Europe during the sixteenth and seventeenth centuries, such as this engraving from the 1590s, part of a series by Flemish engraver Theodore de Bry, based on paintings by an artist who had accompanied a French expedition to Florida a few decades earlier. Figure 2.1 shows the cannibalistic practices by natives supposedly witnessed by the explorers. What is going on in this picture? It is likely that de Bry made adjustments to his engravings from the originals to please potential buyers. If so, what does this tell us about the expectations of European audiences about the Americas and their inhabitants?

Almost seventy-five years later, a very different set of no less remarkable images emerged from a Dutch colony in northeastern Brazil. Count Johan Maurits, the humanist governor general of the colony from 1636 to 1644, brought several artists and scientists with him to observe and record the region's flora and fauna as well as its inhabitants. Johan Maurits, who was fascinated by the local peoples and their cultures, commissioned from artist Albert Eckhout a number of still-lifes and group and individual portraits, including one showing a female Tapuya Indian (see Figure 2.2). According to Dutch accounts, the Tapuya were more warlike and less "civilized" than some of the other local peoples — for example, they sometimes consumed their dead instead of burying them. Aside from the body parts this woman carries in her hand and in her bag, what other signs of this warlike tendency do you see in Figure 2.2? Look closely at the many interesting details in this painting. What does the artist seem to be interested in showing?

Thinking Historically

What are the differences in style and content between Figures 2.1 and 2.2, and how do you account for them? Which of the following factors do you think is most important in explaining their differences: chronology, agenda of the artist, the potential audience for the image, the setting in which they were produced? What might be the pitfalls for students of history in comparing these two images? How do you reconcile Las Casas's account in the previous source with the scene

Figure 2.1   Cannibalism, Engraving by Theodore de Bry.

Source: Service Historique de la Marine, Vincennes, France, Giraudon/The Bridgeman Art
Library International.

portrayed in Figure 2.1? Which source would you consider more reliable and why? Which source would a sixteenth-century Spaniard have
considered more reliable and why? Consider how women (or woman)
are depicted in these works. What differences and similarities do you
see? What might that tell us about European notions of women and
gender in the New World?

Figure 2.2   Tapuya Indian, by Albert Eckhout.
Source: National Museum of Denmark.

10

DAVID PIETERZEN DeVRIES

A Dutch Massacre of the Algonquins

David Pieterzen DeVries was a ship's captain who became a landlord or "patroonship" holder in the Dutch colony of New Amsterdam (now New York). After a disastrous venture to establish a farming and whaling colony, Swanendael on the Delaware River (near modern Philadelphia), he was granted the first patroonship on Staten Island. There he had frequent contact with the Algonquin and Raritan Indians. He was a member of the Board of Directors (the Twelve Men), responsible to the Dutch West India Company for the governance of New Amsterdam. When in 1642, a new governor, Dutch merchant Willem Kieft, urged increased settlement and Indian removal, DeVries urged caution. He described what happened in February 1643 in his book, *Voyages from Holland to America*.

Why did DeVries oppose the governor's plan to attack the Algonquins? What does his story suggest about Dutch-Indian relations before 1643? What were the consequences of the massacre?

Thinking Historically

How is the Dutch treatment of the Algonquins different from the Spanish treatment of the Native Americans? What accounts for these differences? Consider this source in light of the images in the previous document. How might seventeenth-century Europeans reconcile the scene in Figure 2.1 with what DeVries describes in his account?

Do you think an Algonquin account of this encounter would be significantly different from that of DeVries? How might it differ?

The 24th of February, sitting at a table with the Governor, he began to state his intentions, that he had a mind to *wipe the mouths* of the savages; that he had been dining at the house of Jan Claesen Damen, where Maryn Adriaensen and Jan Claesen Damen, together with Jacob Planck, had presented a petition to him to begin this work. I answered him that they were not wise to request this; that such work could not

David Pieterzen DeVries, *Voyages from Holland to America*, A.D. *1632–1644*, trans. H. C. Murphy (New York: Billing Brothers, 1853), 114–17.

be done without the approbation of the Twelve Men; that it could not take place without my assent, who was one of the Twelve Men; that moreover I was the first patroon, and no one else hitherto had risked there so many thousands, and also his person, as I was the first to come from Holland or Zeeland to plant a colony; and that he should consider what profit he could derive from this business, as he well knew that on account of trifling with the Indians we had lost our colony in the South River at Swanendael, in the Hoere-kil, with thirty-two men, who were murdered in the year 1630; and that in the year 1640, the cause of my people being murdered on Staten Island was a difficulty which he had brought on with the Raritan Indians, where his soldiers had for some trifling thing killed some savages. . . . But it appeared that my speaking was of no avail. He had, with his comurderers, determined to commit the murder, deeming it a Roman deed, and to do it without warning the inhabitants in the open lands that each one might take care of himself against the retaliation of the savages, for he could not kill all the Indians. When I had expressed all these things in full, sitting at the table, and the meal was over, he told me he wished me to go to the large hall, which he had been lately adding to his house. Coming to it, there stood all his soldiers ready to cross the river to Pavonia to commit the murder. Then spoke I again to Governor Willem Kieft: "Let this work alone; you wish to break the mouths of the Indians, but you will also murder our own nation, for there are none of the settlers in the open country who are aware of it. My own dwelling, my people, cattle, corn, and tobacco will be lost." He answered me, assuring me that there would be no danger; that some soldiers should go to my house to protect it. But that was not done. So was this business begun between the 25th and 26th of February in the year 1643. I remained that night at the Governor's, sitting up. I went and sat by the kitchen fire, when about midnight I heard a great shrieking, and I ran to the ramparts of the fort, and looked over to Pavonia. Saw nothing but firing, and heard the shrieks of the savages murdered in their sleep. I returned again to the house by the fire. Having sat there awhile, there came an Indian with his squaw, whom I knew well, and who lived about an hour's walk from my house, and told me that they two had fled in a small skiff, which they had taken from the shore at Pavonia; that the Indians from Fort Orange had surprised them; and that they had come to conceal themselves in the fort. I told them that they must go away immediately; that this was no time for them to come to the fort to conceal themselves; that they who had killed their people at Pavonia were not Indians, but the Swannekens, as they call the Dutch, had done it. They then asked me how they should get out of the fort. I took them to the door, and there was no sentry there, and so they betook themselves to the woods. When it was day the soldiers returned to the fort, having massacred or murdered eighty Indians, and considering they had done a deed of Roman valor, in murdering so many in their sleep; where infants were torn from their mothers' breasts, and hacked to pieces in the presence of the parents, and the pieces thrown into the fire and in the water, and other sucklings, being bound to small boards, were cut, stuck, and pierced, and miserably massacred in a manner to move a heart of stone. Some were thrown into the river, and when the fathers and mothers endeavored to save them, the soldiers would not let them come on land but made both parents and children drown — children from five to six years of age, and also some old and decrepit persons. Those who fled from this onslaught, and concealed themselves in the neighboring sedge, and when it was morning, came out to beg a piece of bread, and to be permitted to warm themselves, were murdered in cold blood and tossed into the fire or the water. Some came to our people in the country with their hands, some with their legs cut off, and some holding their entrails in their arms, and others had such horrible cuts and gashes, that worse than they were could never happen. And these poor simple creatures, as also many of our own people, did not know any better than that they had been attacked by a party of other Indians — the Maquas. After this exploit, the soldiers were rewarded for their services, and Director Kieft thanked them by taking them by the hand and congratulating them. At another place, on the same night, on Corler's Hook near Corler's plantation, forty Indians were in the same manner attacked in their sleep, and massacred there in the same manner. Did the Duke of Alva[1] in the Netherlands ever do anything more cruel? This is indeed a disgrace to our nation, who have so generous a governor in our Fatherland as the Prince of Orange, who has always endeavored in his wars to spill as little blood as possible. As soon as the savages understood that the Swannekens had so treated them, all the men whom they could surprise on the farmlands, they killed; but we have never heard that they have ever permitted women or children to be killed. They burned all the houses, farms, barns, grain, haystacks, and destroyed everything they could get hold of. So there was an open destructive war begun. They also burnt my farm, cattle, corn, barn, tobacco-house, and all the tobacco. My people saved themselves in the house where I alone lived, which was made with embrasures, through which they defended themselves. Whilst my people were in alarm the savage whom I had aided to escape from the fort in the night came there, and told the other Indians that I was a good chief, that I had helped him out of the fort, and that the killing of the Indians took place

---

[1]Spanish tyrant who ruled over the Netherlands before the Dutch gained their independence in 1581. [Ed.]

contrary to my wish. Then they all cried out together to my people that they would not shoot them; that if they had not destroyed my cattle they would not do it, nor burn my house; that they would let my little brewery stand, though they wished to get the copper kettle, in order to make darts for their arrows; but hearing now that it had been done contrary to my wish, they all went away, and left my house unbesieged. When now the Indians had destroyed so many farms and men in revenge for their people, I went to Governor Willem Kieft, and asked him if it was not as I had said it would be, that he would only effect the spilling of Christian blood. Who would now compensate us for our losses? But he gave me no answer. He said he wondered that no Indians came to the fort. I told him that I did not wonder at it; "why should the Indians come here where you have so treated them?"

11

NZINGA MBEMBA

Appeal to the King of Portugal

Europeans were unable to conquer Africa as they did the Americas until the end of the nineteenth century. Rivers that fell steeply to the sea, military defenses, and diseases like malaria proved insurmountable to Europeans before the age of the steamship, the machine gun, and quinine pills. Before the last half of the nineteenth century, Europeans had to be content with alliances with African kings and rulers. The Portuguese had been the first to meet Africans in the towns and villages along the Atlantic coast, and they became the first European missionaries and trading partners.

Nzinga Mbemba, whose Christian name was Affonso, was king of the west African state of Congo (comprising what is today parts of Angola as well as the two Congo states) from about 1506 to 1543. He succeeded his father, King Nzinga a Kuwu who, shortly after their first Portuguese contact in 1483, sent officials to Lisbon to learn European ways. In 1491 father and son were baptized, and Portuguese

Basil Davidson, *The African Past* (Boston: Little, Brown, and Company, 1964), 191–94.

priests, merchants, artisans, and soldiers were provided with a coastal settlement.

What exactly is the complaint of the King of Congo? What seems to be the impact of Portuguese traders (factors) in the Congo? What does King Affonso want the King of Portugal to do?

Thinking Historically

This selection offers an opportunity to compare European expansion in the Americas and Africa. Portuguese contact with Nzinga Mbemba of the Congo was roughly contemporaneous with Spanish colonialism in the Americas. What differences do you see between these two cases of early European expansion? Can you think of any reasons that Congo kings converted to Christianity while Mexican kings did not?

Compare the European treatment of Africans with their treatment of Native Americans. Why did Europeans enslave Africans and not, for the most part, American Indians?

Sir, Your Highness [of Portugal] should know how our Kingdom is being lost in so many ways that it is convenient to provide for the necessary remedy, since this is caused by the excessive freedom given by your factors and officials to the men and merchants who are allowed to come to this Kingdom to set up shops with goods and many things which have been prohibited by us, and which they spread throughout our Kingdoms and Domains in such an abundance that many of our vassals, whom we had in obedience, do not comply because they have the things in greater abundance than we ourselves; and it was with these things that we had them content and subjected under our vassalage and jurisdiction, so it is doing a great harm not only to the service of God, but to the security and peace of our Kingdoms and State as well.

And we cannot reckon how great the damage is, since the mentioned merchants are taking every day our natives, sons of the land and the sons of our noblemen and vassals and our relatives, because the thieves and men of bad conscience grab them wishing to have the things and wares of this Kingdom which they are ambitious of; they grab them and get them to be sold; and so great, Sir, is the corruption and licentiousness that our country is being completely depopulated, and Your Highness should not agree with this nor accept it as in your service. And to avoid it we need from those [your] Kingdoms no more than some priests and a few people to teach in schools, and no other goods except wine and flour for the holy sacrament. That is why we beg of Your Highness to help and assist us in this matter, commanding your factors that they should not send here either merchants or wares, because it is *our will that in these Kingdoms there should not be any trade of slaves nor outlet for them.*[1] Concerning what is referred above, again we beg of Your Highness to agree with it, since otherwise we cannot remedy such an obvious damage. Pray Our Lord in His mercy to have Your Highness under His guard and let you do for ever the things of His service. I kiss your hands many times.

At our town of Congo, written on the sixth day of July.
João Teixeira did it in 1526.
The King. Dom Affonso.
[On the back of this letter the following can be read:
To the most powerful and excellent prince Dom João, King our Brother.]

Moreover, Sir, in our Kingdoms there is another great inconvenience which is of little service to God, and this is that many of our people [*naturaes*], keenly desirous as they are of the wares and things of your Kingdoms, which are brought here by your people, and in order to satisfy their voracious appetite, seize many of our people, freed and exempt men; and very often it happens that they kidnap even noblemen and the sons of noblemen, and our relatives, and take them to be sold to the white men who are in our Kingdoms; and for this purpose they have concealed them; and others are brought during the night so that they might not be recognized.

And as soon as they are taken by the white men they are immediately ironed and branded with fire, and when they are carried to be embarked, if they are caught by our guards' men the whites allege that they have bought them but they cannot say from whom, so that it is our duty to do justice and to restore to the freemen their freedom, but it cannot be done if your subjects feel offended, as they claim to be.

And to avoid such a great evil we passed a law so that any white man living in our Kingdoms and wanting to purchase goods in any way should first inform three of our noblemen and officials of our court whom we rely upon in this matter, and these are Dom Pedro Manipanza and Dom Manuel Manissaba, our chief usher, and Gonçalo Pires our chief freighter, who should investigate if the mentioned goods are captives or free men, and if cleared by them there will be no further doubt nor embargo for them to be taken and embarked. But if the white men do not comply with it they will lose the aforementioned goods. And if we do them this favor and concession it is for the part Your Highness has in it, since we know that it is in your service too that these goods are taken from our Kingdom, otherwise we should not consent to this. . . .

---

[1]Emphasis in the original.

Sir, Your Highness has been kind enough to write to us saying that we should ask in our letters for anything we need, and that we shall be provided with everything, and as the peace and the health of our Kingdom depend on us, and as there are among us old folks and people who have lived for many days, it happens that we have continuously many and different diseases which put us very often in such a weakness that we reach almost the last extreme; and the same happens to our children, relatives, and natives owing to the lack in this country of physicians and surgeons who might know how to cure properly such diseases. And as we have got neither dispensaries nor drugs which might help us in this forlornness, many of those who had been already confirmed and instructed in the holy faith of Our Lord Jesus Christ perish and die; and the rest of the people in their majority cure themselves with herbs and breads and other ancient methods, so that they put all their faith in the mentioned herbs and ceremonies if they live, and believe that they are saved if they die; and this is not much in the service of God.

And to avoid such a great error and inconvenience, since it is from God in the first place and then from your Kingdoms and from Your Highness that all the goods and drugs and medicines have come to save us, we beg of you to be agreeable and kind enough to send us two physicians and two apothecaries and one surgeon, so that they may come with their drug-stores and all the necessary things to stay in our kingdoms, because we are in extreme need of them all and each of them. We shall do them all good and shall benefit them by all means, since they are sent by Your Highness, whom we thank for your work in their coming. We beg of Your Highness as a great favor to do this for us, because besides being good in itself it is in the service of God as we have said above.

12

WILLIAM BOSMAN

Slave Trader

William Bosman was the chief agent of the Dutch West India Company on the African coast where he lived from 1686 to 1702. Here he explains how slaves were brought to Whydah, an English fort on the coast of Dahomey (between the Gold Coast of Ghana and the slave coast of Nigeria). Bosman discusses various ways in which he received slaves. What were these ways? Which does he seem to prefer?

Thinking Historically

Compare Bosman's description of the slave trade with that of Nzinga Mbemba in the preceding selection. How do you account for the differences? Are they due to Dutch and Portuguese practice, to policies of the Congo and Dahomey, or to the passage of time between 1526 and 1700?

The author, a Dutchman, makes certain comparisons between Dutch slave ships and those of other Europeans. Do you see any evidence for his claims?

The first business of one of our factors [agents] when he comes to Fida [Whydah], is to satisfy the customs of the king and the great men, which amounts to about a hundred pounds in Guinea value, as the goods must yield there. After which we have free license to trade, which is published throughout the whole land by the crier.

But yet before we can deal with any person, we are obliged to buy the king's whole stock of slaves at a set price, which is commonly one third or one fourth higher than ordinary; after which, we obtain free leave to deal with all his subjects, of what rank soever. But if there happen to be no stock of slaves, the factor must then resolve to run the risk of trusting the inhabitants with goods to the value of one or two hundred slaves; which commodities they send into the inland country, in

William Bosman, *A New and Accurate Description of the Coast of Guinea, Divided into the Gold, the Slave, and the Ivory Coasts,* 2nd ed., trans. from Dutch (London: 1721), Barnes & Noble, 1967, pp. 363a–365a.

order to buy with them slaves at all markets, and that sometimes two hundred miles deep in the country. For you ought to be informed, that markets of men are here kept in the same manner as those of beasts with us.

Not a few in our country fondly imagine that parents here sell their children, men their wives, and one brother the other. But those who think so, do deceive themselves; for this never happens on any other account but that of necessity, or some great crime; but most of the slaves that are offered to us, are prisoners of war, which are sold by the victors as their booty.

When these slaves come to Fida, they are put in prison all together; and when we treat concerning buying them, they are all brought out together in a large plain; where, by our surgeons, whose province it is, they are thoroughly examined, even to the smallest member, and that naked, both men and women, without the least distinction or modesty. Those that are approved as good, are set on one side; and the lame or faulty are set by as invalids, which are here called *mackrons*: these are such as are above five and thirty years old, or are maimed in the arms, legs, or feet; have lost a tooth, are grey-haired, or have films over their eyes; as well as all those which are affected with any venereal distemper, or several other diseases.

The invalids and the maimed being thrown out, as I have told you, the remainder are numbered, and it is entered who delivered them. In the meanwhile, a burning iron, with the arms or name of the companies, lies in the fire, with which ours are marked on the breast. This is done that we may distinguish them from the slaves of the English, French, or others (which are also marked with their mark), and to prevent the Negroes exchanging them for worse, at which they have a good hand. I doubt not but this trade seems very barbarous to you, but since it is followed by mere necessity, it must go on; but we yet take all possible care that they are not burned too hard, especially the women, who are more tender than the men.

We are seldom long detained in the buying of these slaves, because their price is established, the women being one fourth or fifth part cheaper than the men. The disputes which we generally have with the owners of these slaves are, that we will not give them such goods as they ask for them, especially the *boesies* [cowry shells] (as I have told you, the money of this country) of which they are very fond, though we generally make a division on this head, in order to make one part of the goods help off another; because those slaves which are paid for in *boesies*, cost the company one half more than those bought with other goods. . . .

When we have agreed with the owners of the slaves, they are returned to their prison; where, from that time forwards, they are kept at our charge, cost us two pence a day a slave; which serves to subsist them, like our criminals, on bread and water: so that to save charges, we send them on board our ships with the very first opportunity, before which their masters strip them of all they have on their backs; so that they come to us stark-naked, as well women as men: in which condition they are obliged to continue, if the master of the ship is not so charitable (which he commonly is) as to bestow something on them to cover their nakedness.

You would really wonder to see how these slaves live on board; for though their number sometimes amounts to six or seven hundred, yet by the careful management of our masters of ships, they are so [well] regulated, that it seems incredible. And in this particular our nation exceeds all other Europeans; for as the French, Portuguese, and English slave-ships are always foul and stinking; on the contrary, ours are for the most part clean and neat.

The slaves are fed three times a day with indifferent good victuals, and much better than they eat in their own country. Their lodging place is divided into two parts; one of which is appointed for the men, the other for the women, each sex being kept apart. Here they lie as close together as it is possible for them to be crowded.

We are sometimes sufficiently plagued with a parcel of slaves which come from a far inland country, who very innocently persuade one another, that we buy them only to fatten, and afterwards eat them as a delicacy. When we are so unhappy as to be pestered with many of this sort, they resolve and agree together (and bring over the rest of their party) to run away from the ship, kill the Europeans, and set the vessel ashore; by which means they design to free themselves from being our food.

I have twice met with this misfortune; and the first time proved very unlucky to me, I not in the least suspecting it; but the uproar was timely quashed by the master of the ship and myself, by causing the abettor to be shot through the head, after which all was quiet.

But the second time it fell heavier on another ship, and that chiefly by the carelessness of the master, who having fished up the anchor of a departed English ship, had laid it in the hold where the male slaves were lodged, who, unknown to any of the ship's crew, possessed themselves of a hammer, with which, in a short time they broke all their fetters in pieces upon the anchor: After this, they came above deck, and fell upon our men, some of whom they grievously wounded, and would certainly have mastered the ship, if a French and English ship had not very fortunately happened to lie by us; who perceiving by our firing a distressed-gun, that something was in disorder on board, immediately came to our assistance with shallops and men, and drove the slaves under deck: notwithstanding which, before all was appeased, about twenty of them were killed.

The Portuguese have been more unlucky in this particular than we; for in four years time they lost four ships in this manner.

13

OLAUDAH EQUIANO
Enslaved Captive

The Interesting Narrative of the Life of Olaudah Equiano,* or *Gustavus Vassa the African, written by himself* was published in 1789. It tells the story of a young boy sold into slavery in Africa and transported to the Americas, who after winning his freedom became a spokesman for the abolition of slavery in England and America. Recent research suggests that the author, Equiano, may have actually been born a slave in South Carolina and that his tale of earlier African slavery may be a composite of the stories of others. If *The Interesting Narrative* is less autobiographical than once believed, it is no less interesting, and still conveys a wealth of useful information about African experiences of slavery. How was slavery in Africa different from slavery in America? What were the worst aspects of the Atlantic slave trades according to the author? Why does Equiano address his audience as "nominal Christians"?

Thinking Historically

Compare Equiano's attitude toward slavery with that of another author in this chapter. Is Equiano opposed to all forms of slavery or only to certain kinds of slavery? How does Equiano's attitude towards Europeans compare with that of other authors in this chapter?

I hope the reader will not think I have trespassed on his patience in introducing myself to him with some account of the manners and customs of my country. They had been implanted in me with great care, and made an impression on my mind, which time could not erase, and which all the adversity and variety of fortune I have since experienced, served only to rivet and record: for, whether the love of one's country be real or imaginary, or a lesson of reason, or an instinct of nature, I still look back with pleasure on the first scenes of my life, though that pleasure has been for the most part mingled with sorrow.

*oh law OO dah   eh kwee AH noh

"Olaudah Equiano of the Niger Ibo," ed. G. I. Jones, in *Africa Remembered,* ed. Philip D. Curtin (Madison: University of Wisconsin Press, 1967), 60–98.

I have already acquainted the reader with the time and place of my birth. My father, besides many slaves, had a numerous family, of which seven lived to grow up, including myself and sister, who was the only daughter. As I was the youngest of the sons, I became, of course, the greatest favorite with my mother, and was always with her; and she used to take particular pains to form my mind. I was trained up from my earliest years in the art of war: my daily exercise was shooting and throwing javelins, and my mother adorned me with emblems, after the manner of our greatest warriors. In this way I grew up till I had turned the age of eleven, when an end was put to my happiness in the following manner: Generally, when the grown people in the neighborhood were gone far in the fields to labor, the children assembled together in some of the neighboring premises to play; and commonly some of us used to get up a tree to look out for any assailant, or kidnapper, that might come upon us — for they sometimes took those opportunities of our parents' absence, to attack and carry off as many as they could seize. . . . Alas! ere long it was my fate to be thus attacked, and to be carried off, when none of the grown people were nigh.

One day, when all our people were gone out to their works as usual, and only I and my dear sister were left to mind the house, two men and a woman got over our walls, and in a moment seized us both, and, without giving us time to cry out, or make resistance, they stopped our mouths, and ran off with us into the nearest wood. Here they tied our hands, and continued to carry us as far as they could, till night came on, when we reached a small house, where the robbers halted for refreshment, and spent the night. We were then unbound, but were unable to take any food; and, being quite overpowered by fatigue and grief, our only relief was some sleep, which allayed our misfortune for a short time. The next morning we left the house, and continued travelling all the day. For a long time we had kept the woods, but at last we came into a road which I believed I knew. I had now some hopes of being delivered; for we had advanced but a little way before I discovered some people at a distance, on which I began to cry out for their assistance; but my cries had no other effect than to make them tie me faster and stop my mouth, and then they put me into a large sack. They also stopped my sister's mouth, and tied her hands; and in this manner we proceeded till we were out of sight of these people. When we went to rest the following night, they offered us some victuals, but we refused it; and the only comfort we had was in being in one another's arms all that night, and bathing each other with our tears. But alas! we were soon deprived of even the small comfort of weeping together.

The next day proved a day of greater sorrow than I had yet experienced; for my sister and I were then separated, while we lay clasped in each other's arms. It was in vain that we besought them not to part us; she was torn from me, and immediately carried away, while I was left in a state of distraction not to be described. I cried and grieved continually; and for several days did not eat anything but what they forced into my mouth. At length, after many days' travelling, during which I had often changed masters, I got into the hands of a chieftain, in a very pleasant country. This man had two wives and some children, and they all used me extremely well, and did all they could do to comfort me; particularly the first wife, who was something like my mother. Although I was a great many days' journey from my father's house, yet these people spoke exactly the same language with us. This first master of mine, as I may call him, was a smith, and my principal employment was working his bellows, which were the same kind as I had seen in my vicinity. They were in some respects not unlike the stoves here in gentlemen's kitchens, and were covered over with leather; and in the middle of that leather a stick was fixed, and a person stood up, and worked it in the same manner as is done to pump water out of a cask with a hand pump. I believe it was gold he worked, for it was of a lovely bright yellow color, and was worn by the women on their wrists and ankles. . . .

Soon after this, my master's only daughter, and child by his first wife, sickened and died, which affected him so much that for some time he was almost frantic, and really would have killed himself, had he not been watched and prevented. However, in a short time afterwards he recovered, and I was again sold. I was now carried to the left of the sun's rising, through many dreary wastes and dismal woods, amidst the hideous roarings of wild beasts. The people I was sold to used to carry me very often, when I was tired, either on their shoulders or on their backs. I saw many convenient well-built sheds along the road, at proper distances, to accommodate the merchants and travellers, who lay in those buildings along with their wives, who often accompany them; and they always go well armed. . . .

After travelling a considerable time. I came to a town called Tinmah, in the most beautiful country I had yet seen in Africa. It was extremely rich, and there were many rivulets which flowed through it, and supplied a large pond in the centre of the town, where the people washed. Here I saw for the first time cocoanuts, which I thought superior to any nuts I had ever tasted before; and the trees, which were loaded, were also interspersed among the houses, which had commodious shades adjoining, and were in the same manner as ours, the insides being neatly plastered and whitewashed. Here I also saw and tasted for the first time, sugar-cane. Their money consisted of little white shells, the size of the fingernail. I was sold here for one hundred and seventy-two of them, by a merchant who lived and brought me there.

I had been about two or three days at his house, when a wealthy widow, a neighbor of his, came there one evening, and brought with her an only son, a young gentleman about my own age and size. Here they saw me; and, having taken a fancy to me, I was bought of the merchant, and went home with them. Her house and premises were situated close to one of those rivulets I have mentioned, and were the finest I ever saw in Africa: they were very extensive, and she had a number of slaves to attend her. The next day I was washed and perfumed, and when meal time came, I was led into the presence of my mistress, and ate and drank before her with her son. This filled me with astonishment; and I could scarce help expressing my surprise that the young gentleman should suffer me, who was bound, to eat with him who was free; and not only so, but that he would not at any time either eat or drink till I had taken first, because I was the eldest, which was agreeable to our custom. Indeed, every thing here, and all their treatment of me, made me forget that I was a slave. The language of these people resembled ours so nearly, that we understood each other perfectly. They had also the very same customs as we. There were likewise slaves daily to attend us, while my young master and I, with other boys, sported with our darts and bows and arrows, as I had been used to do at home. In this resemblance to my former happy state, I passed about two months; and I now began to think I was to be adopted into the family, and was beginning to be reconciled to my situation, and to forget by degrees my misfortunes, when all at once the delusion vanished; for, without the least previous knowledge, one morning early, while my dear master and companion was still asleep, I was awakened out of my reverie to fresh sorrow, and hurried away. . . .

Thus, at the very moment I dreamed of the greatest happiness, I found myself most miserable; and it seemed as if fortune wished to give me this taste of joy only to render the reverse more poignant. The change I now experienced was as painful as it was sudden and unexpected. It was a change indeed, from a state of bliss to a scene which is inexpressible by me, as it discovered to me an element I had never before beheld, and till then had no idea of, and wherein such instances of hardship and cruelty continually occurred, as I can never reflect on but with horror. . . .

Thus I continued to travel, sometimes by land, sometimes by water, through different countries and various nations, till, at the end of six or seven months after I had been kidnapped, I arrived at the sea coast. . . .

The first object which saluted my eyes when I arrived on the coast was the sea, and a slave ship, which was then riding at anchor, and waiting for its cargo. These filled me with astonishment, which was soon converted into terror, when I was carried on board. I was immediately handled, and tossed up to see if I were sound, by some of the crew; and I was now persuaded that I had gotten into a world of bad spirits, and that they were going to kill me. Their complexions, too, differing so much from ours, their long hair, and the language they spoke (which was very different from any I had ever heard), united to confirm me in this belief. . . . When I looked round the ship too, and saw a large furnace of copper boiling, and a multitude of black people of every description chained together, every one of their countenances expressing dejection and sorrow, I no longer doubted of my fate; and, quite overpowered with horror and anguish, I fell motionless on the deck and fainted. . . .

I now saw myself deprived of all chance of returning to my native country, or even the least glimpse of hope of gaining the shore, which I now considered as friendly; and I even wished for my former slavery in preference to my present situation, which was filled with horrors of every kind, still heightened by my ignorance of what I was to undergo. I was not long suffered to indulge my grief; I was soon put down under the decks, and there I received such a salutation in my nostrils as I had never experienced in my life: so that, with the loathsomeness of the stench, and crying together, I became so sick and low that I was not able to eat, nor had I the least desire to taste anything. I now wished for the last friend, death, to relieve me; but soon, to my grief, two of the white men offered me eatables; and, on my refusing to eat, one of them held me fast by the hands, and laid me across, I think, the windlass, and tied my feet, while the other flogged me severely. I had never experienced anything of this kind before, and, although not being used to the water, I naturally feared that element the first time I saw it, yet, nevertheless, could I have got over the nettings, I would have jumped over the side, but I could not; and besides, the crew used to watch us very closely who were not chained down to the decks, lest we should leap into the water; and I have seen some of these poor African prisoners most severely cut for attempting to do so, and hourly whipped for not eating. This indeed was often the case with myself.

In a little time after, amongst the poor chained men, I found some of my own nation, which in a small degree gave ease to my mind. I inquired of them what was to be done with us? They gave me to understand we were to be carried to these white people's country to work for them. I then was a little revived, and thought, if it were no worse than working, my situation was not so desperate: but still I feared I should be put to death, the white people looked and acted, as I thought, in so savage a manner; for I had never seen among any people such instances of brutal cruelty; and this not only shown towards us blacks, but also to some of the whites themselves. One white man in particular I saw, when we were permitted to be on deck, flogged so unmercifully with a large rope near the foremast, that he died in consequence of it; and they tossed him over the side as they would have done a brute. This made me fear these people the more; and I expected nothing less than to be treated in the same manner. I could not help expressing my fears and apprehensions to some of my countrymen: I asked them if these people had no country, but lived in this hollow place the ship? They told me they did not, but came from a distant one. "Then," said I, "how comes it in all our country we never heard of them?" They told me, because they lived so very far off. I then asked, where were their women? Had they any like themselves? I was told they had. "And why," said I, "do we not see them?" They answered, because they were left behind. I asked how the vessel could go? They told me they could not tell; but that there were cloth put upon the masts by the help of the ropes I saw, and then the vessel went on; and the white men had some spell or magic they put in the water when they liked in order to stop the vessel. I was exceedingly amazed at this account, and really thought they were spirits. I therefore wished much to be from amongst them, for I expected they would sacrifice me: but my wishes were vain — for we were so quartered that it was impossible for any of us to make our escape. . . .

At last, when the ship we were in had got in all her cargo, they made ready with many fearful noises, and we were all put under deck, so that we could not see how they managed the vessel. But this disappointment was the least of my sorrow. The stench of the hold while we were on the coast was so intolerably loathsome, that it was dangerous to remain there for any time, and some of us had been permitted to stay on the deck for the fresh air; but now that the whole ship's cargo were confined together, it became absolutely pestilential. The closeness of the place, and the heat of the climate, added to the number in the ship, which was so crowded that each had scarcely room to turn himself, almost suffocated us. This produced copious perspirations, so that the air soon became unfit for respiration, from a variety of loathsome smells, and brought on a sickness amongst the slaves, of which many died — thus falling victims to the improvident avarice, as I may call it, of their purchasers. This wretched situation was again aggravated by the galling of the chains, now become insupportable; and the filth of the necessary tubs, into which the children often fell, and were almost suffocated. The shrieks of the women, and the groans of the dying, rendered the whole a scene of horror almost inconceivable. Happily perhaps for myself I was soon reduced so low here that it was thought necessary to keep me almost always on deck; and from my extreme youth I was not put in fetters. In this situation I expected every hour to share the fate of my companions, some of whom were almost daily brought upon deck at the point of death, which I began to hope would soon put an end to my miseries. Often did I think many of the inhabitants of the deep much more happy than myself; I envied them the freedom they enjoyed, and as often wished I could change my condition for theirs. Every circumstance I met with served only to render my state more painful, and heighten my apprehensions and my opinion of the cruelty of the whites.

One day they had taken a number of fishes; and when they had killed and satisfied themselves with as many as they thought fit, to our astonishment who were on the deck, rather than give any of them to us to eat, as we expected, they tossed the remaining fish into the sea again, although we begged and prayed for some as well as we could, but in vain; and some of my countrymen, being pressed by hunger, took an opportunity, when they thought no one saw them, of trying to get a little privately; but they were discovered, and the attempt procured them some very severe floggings.

One day, when we had a smooth sea, and moderate wind, two of my wearied countrymen, who were chained together (I was near them at the time), preferring death to such a life of misery, somehow made through the nettings, and jumped into the sea; immediately another quite dejected fellow, who, on account of his illness, was suffered to be out of irons, also followed their example; and I believe many more would very soon have done the same, if they had not been prevented by the ship's crew, who were instantly alarmed. Those of us that were the most active were in a moment put down under the deck; and there was such a noise and confusion amongst the people of the ship as I never heard before, to stop her, and get the boat out to go after the slaves. However, two of the wretches were drowned, but they got the other, and afterwards flogged him unmercifully, for thus attempting to prefer death to slavery. In this manner we continued to undergo more hardships than I can now relate; hardships which are inseparable from this accursed trade. Many a time we were near suffocation, from the want of fresh air, which we were often without for whole days together. This, and the stench of the necessary tubs, carried off many.

During our passage I first saw flying fishes, which surprised me very much: They used frequently to fly across the ship, and many of them fell on the deck. I also now first saw the use of the quadrant. I had often with astonishment seen the mariners make observations with it, and I could not think what it meant. They at last took notice of my surprise; and one of them, willing to increase it, as well as to gratify my curiosity, made me one day look through it. The clouds appeared to me to be land, which disappeared as they passed along. This heightened my wonder, and I was now more persuaded than ever that I was in another world, and that every thing about me was magic.

At last, we came in sight of the island of Barbadoes, at which the whites on board gave a great shout, and made many signs of joy to us. We did not know what to think of this; but, as the vessel drew nearer, we plainly saw the harbour, and other ships of different kinds and sizes; and we soon anchored amongst them off Bridge Town. Many merchants and planters now come on board, though it was in the evening. They put us in separate parcels, and examined us attentively.

They also made us jump, and pointed to the land, signifying we were to go there. We thought by this we should be eaten by these ugly men, as they appeared to us; and when, soon after we were all put down under the deck again, there was much dread and trembling among us, and nothing but bitter cries to be heard all the night from these apprehensions, insomuch that at last the white people got some old slaves from the land to pacify us. They told us we were not to be eaten, but to work, and were soon to go on land where we should see many of our country people. This report eased us much; and sure enough, soon after we landed, there came to us Africans of all languages.

We were conducted immediately to the merchant's yard, where we were all pent up together like so many sheep in a fold, without regard to sex or age. As every object was new to me, everything I saw filled me with surprise. What struck me first was, that the houses were built with bricks, in stories, and in every other respect different from those I have seen in Africa; but I was still more astonished on seeing people on horseback. I did not know what this could mean; and indeed I thought these people were full of nothing but magical arts. . . .

We were not many days in the merchant's custody, before we were sold after their usual manner, which is this: On a signal given (as the beat of a drum), the buyers rush at once into the yard where the slaves are confined, and make choice of that parcel they like best. The noise and clamor with which this is attended, and the eagerness visible in the countenances of the buyers, serve not a little to increase the apprehension of the terrified Africans, who may well be supposed to consider them as the ministers of that destruction to which they think themselves devoted. In this manner, without scruple, are relations and friends separated, most of them never to see each other again.

I remember in the vessel in which I was brought over, in the men's apartment, there were several brothers who, in the sale, were sold in different lots; and it was very moving on this occasion to see and hear their cries at parting. O, ye nominal Christians! Might not an African ask you — learned you this from your God, who says unto you, Do unto all men as you would men should do unto you. Is it not enough that we are torn from our country and friends to toil for your luxury and lust of gain? Must every tender feeling be likewise sacrificed to your avarice? Are the dearest friends and relations, now rendered more dear by their separation from their kindred, still to be parted from each other, and thus preventing from cheering the gloom of slavery with the small comfort of being together, and mingling their sufferings and sorrows? Why are parents to love their children, brothers their sisters, or husbands their wives? Surely this is a new refinement in cruelty, which, while it has no advantage to atone for it, thus aggravates distress, and adds fresh horrors even to the wretchedness of slavery.

REFLECTIONS

This chapter asks you to compare European encounters with Native Americans and Africans. Why did Europeans enslave Africans and not, for the most part, American Indians? Because so many Africans were brought to the Americas to work on plantations, this topic is especially compelling.

Initially, of course, Indians *were* enslaved. Recall the letter of Columbus (selection 4). Part of the reason this enslavement did not continue was the high mortality of Native Americans exposed to smallpox and other Old World diseases. In addition, Native Americans who survived the bacterial onslaught had the "local knowledge" and support needed to escape from slavery.

Above and beyond this were the humanitarian objections of Spanish priests like Bartolomeo de Las Casas and the concerns of the Spanish monarchy that slavery would increase the power of the conquistadors at the expense of the crown. In 1542, the enslavement of Indians was outlawed in Spanish dominions of the New World. Clearly, these "New Laws" were not always obeyed by Spaniards in the Americas or by the Portuguese subjects of the unified Spanish-Portuguese crown between 1580 and 1640. Still, the different legal positions of Africans and Indians in the minds of Europeans require further explanation.

Some scholars have suggested that the difference in treatment lies in the differing needs of the main European powers involved in the encounter. The anthropologist Marvin Harris makes the argument this way:

> The most plausible explanation of the New Laws [of 1542] is that they represented the intersection of the interests of three power groups: the Church, the Crown, and the colonists. All three of these interests sought to maximize their respective control over the aboriginal populations. Outright enslavement of the Indians was the method preferred by the colonists. But neither the Crown nor the Church could permit this to happen without surrendering their own vested and potential interests in the greatest resource of the New World — its manpower.

Why then did they permit and even encourage the enslavement of Africans? In this matter all three power groups stood to gain. Africans who remained in Africa were of no use to anybody, since effective military and political domination of that continent by Europeans was not achieved until the middle of the nineteenth century. To make use of African manpower, Africans had to be removed from their homelands. The only way to accomplish this was to buy them as slaves from dealers on the coast. For both the Crown and the Church, it was better to have Africans under the control of the New World colonists than to leave Africans under the control of Africans.[1]

But of course the Atlantic world slave trade was just one of the lasting outcomes of Atlantic world encounters. Towards the end of his dramatic account of the Spanish conquest of Mexico (selection 6), Bernal Díaz describes a grizzly discovery made by the victorious conquistadors:

> I solemnly swear that all the houses and stockades in the lake were full of heads and corpses. I do not know how to describe it but it was the same in the streets and courts of Tlatelolco. We could not walk without treading on the bodies and heads of dead Indians. (Díaz, 1963, 405)

After two years of continual and heavy warfare, the fortunes of the Spanish turned in their favor and they seized a ravaged city where, according to Bernal Díaz, "the stench was so bad, no one could endure it." Díaz assumed that the Mexicans had been starved and denied fresh water, but we now know that at least part of the cause was the spread of smallpox, a disease which the Spanish carried from the Old World and for which the Native Americans had no immunities. Because of thousands of years of contact, Africans shared many of the same immunities as Europeans, but Native Americans, having inhabited a separate biological realm for over ten thousand years, were completely vulnerable to the new diseases and perished in droves.

Ultimately, slavery came to an end, even if in some cases — the work of Italians on Brazilian sugar plantations, Chinese rail workers, or free African day laborers — it was hard to tell the difference. In any case, the long-term impact of the "Columbian exchange" was more ecological than economic. The potatoes of South America and the corn of Mexico fed more families in Afro-Eurasia than had ever existed in the Americas. The flora and fauna of the New World became new again, through the introduction of the grasses, trees, fruits, grains, horses, cattle, pigs, and chickens that the Old World had known for centuries.

---

[1] Marvin Harris, *Patterns of Race in the Americas* (New York: W. W. Norton, 1964), 17.

3

State and Religion

Asian, Islamic, and Christian States, 1500–1800

HISTORICAL CONTEXT

The relationship between state and religion is a matter of concern and debate almost everywhere in the modern world. In the United States, the issue of the separation of church and state engenders conflicts about the legality of abortion, prayer in the schools, government vouchers for religious schools, and the public display of religious symbols like the Ten Commandments, Nativity scenes, and Chanukah menorahs. Governments in countries as diverse as France and Turkey have recently debated the wearing of headscarves and the display of religious symbols in public schools and other public spaces.

Few states in the world today are dedicated to a single religion as are Saudi Arabia, Israel, and the Vatican. Yet even such places where religious devotion is extreme allow citizenship, residence, and rights in some measure for people of other religions. A few other states have official religions: Brazil is officially Roman Catholic, as was Italy until 1984; Iran is officially Muslim. But, with some notable exceptions, these designations often have little effect on what people believe or how they behave.

While the role of religion in public life and the relationship between church and state are important current issues, from the long-term historical view, the state has only become more important in peoples' lives while religion has become less influential. In the period before 1500, with the notable exception of China, many religious organizations were more important in people's lives than political entities. But, in much of the world, the story of the last five hundred years has been the replacement of religious authority by that of the state.

From the shortened perspective of the last fifty years, such changes may seem negligible. In some places in the world — the United States

88

and the Middle East — religious commitment and fundamentalism have been on the rise in recent decades, becoming more pervasive than fifty years ago, if not more than five hundred years ago. In this chapter, we look at religion and the state in three parts of the world two to five hundred years ago to see how different things were but also to locate the roots of present church-state conflicts. We look first at China where state formation began over two thousand years ago and official Confucianism supported the authority of the emperor. Japan, by contrast, emerged from feudalism to begin state formation only after 1600. Both East Asian societies struggled with the claims of Buddhists, Christians, Muslims, and popular religious sects. Next we look at India, conquered by the Muslim Mughals after 1500, many of whom were remarkably tolerant of Hindus and Hinduism. We conclude with the West, Europe, and colonial America to understand how Christian states struggled with some of the challenges posed by religion. Ultimately, we will be looking for the roots of religious toleration.

Kings and political leaders are almost all more comfortable with some kind of orthodoxy (conventional belief and practice) than with heterodoxy (dissident or heretical belief and practice). But one person's orthodox belief is another's heterodoxy. Most Muslim states, for instance, see Iran's Shi'ism as heterodox, but for most Iranian governments Shi'ism has been the orthodox norm and Sunni Islam more heretical. Orthodoxy frequently undermines religious toleration, but toleration is not the same as heterodoxy. In modern society, we see toleration as a product of secularism. In fact, its history suggests something very different.

THINKING HISTORICALLY
Relating Past and Present

"The past," novelist L. P. Hartley famously wrote, "is a foreign country. They do things differently there." Understanding the past can be like learning a foreign language or exercising muscles gone slack from the daily grind of the commonplace and predictable. These are the muscles that help us imagine and tolerate differences, accept the strange as a possible norm, and allow us to hold conflicting ideas together without forcing agreement or rushing to judgment.

The issue of "state and religion" or "church and state" is a very modern one. We are invoking that modern concern in framing our study of the period between 1500 and 1800. But we should be wary of how past ideas of state and religion may differ from our own. Even the words we use reflect our modern vocabulary and understanding. For the most part, before the sixteenth century, the world's people did not make a distinction between state and religion. Not only were states few and far between, but religious life was not separated from politics or other aspects of life.

In this chapter we ask questions about the history of religious toleration. This too is a modern question. Toleration is a modern idea, but, as we shall see, that does not mean that emperors or governments did not practice it. Various empires throughout history have allowed a variety of beliefs and practices among their subjects, not because they believed it was morally the right thing to do, but because it made good practical political sense.

As you read the following selections, you will be asked to flex your imaginative muscles and reflect on how our modern conceptions of an apparently familiar topic are often different from those of our "foreign" predecessors. Then we can ask how those differences affect our ability to use the past to understand the present.

JONATHAN SPENCE
The Ming Chinese State and Religion

In this brief introduction to China of the Ming dynasty (1368–1644), a leading modern historian of China paints a picture of an advanced civilization where a confident government need not "tolerate other centers of authority." What were the elements of Chinese state authority? What religious authorities might have challenged these? Why was the Chinese state able to control these challenges?

Thinking Historically

Spence uses architectural imagery to describe China in 1600. Architecture can tell us much about a society's priorities and values, if only because building represents such a large investment in resources and labor. What does Ming architecture tell us about state and religion in China? What priorities and values might you deduce from our own society's architecture?

Jonathan D. Spence, *The Search for Modern China* (New York: W. W. Norton, 1990), 7–9.

Architectural monuments and buildings offer a constant reminder of the past. But because construction continues from one generation to the next and some buildings last longer than others, we rarely see a single period of the past on a city street or even a single building. We must "read" the architectural styles and details to separate the various layers of the past found in any city or complex settlement.

Oddly, our interest in imagining the past is evoked more by ruins. We cannot help imagining how people might have lived in an ancient city ruin, its building blocks askew, like the Roman Forum or the Mayan remains at Tulum on the Yucatán Peninsula. We are less likely to imagine what a place that has been rebuilt over the generations, such as a modern city, was like in past ages. In such "living museums" the past is drowned out by current distractions. The study of history is based on evidence and facts, but it is nourished by imagination. Look around. Imagine what your surroundings looked like fifty years ago and five hundred years ago.

In the year A.D. 1600, the empire of China was the largest and most sophisticated of all the unified realms on earth. The extent of its territorial domains was unparalleled at a time when Russia was only just beginning to coalesce as a country, India was fragmented between Mughal and Hindu rulers, and a grim combination of infectious disease and Spanish conquerors had laid low the once great empires of Mexico and Peru. And China's population of some 120 million was far larger than that of all the European countries combined.

There was certainly pomp and stately ritual in capitals from Kyoto to Prague, from Delhi to Paris, but none of these cities could boast of a palace complex like that in Peking, where, nestled behind immense walls, the gleaming yellow roofs and spacious marble courts of the Forbidden City symbolized the majesty of the Chinese emperor. Laid out in a meticulous geometrical order, the grand stairways and mighty doors of each successive palace building and throne hall were precisely aligned with the arches leading out of Peking to the south, speaking to all comers of the connectedness of things personified in this man the Chinese termed the Son of Heaven.

Rulers in Europe, India, Japan, Russia, and the Ottoman Empire were all struggling to develop systematic bureaucracies that would expand their tax base and manage their swelling territories effectively, as well as draw to new royal power centers the resources of agriculture and trade. But China's massive bureaucracy was already firmly in place, harmonized by a millennium of tradition and bonded by an immense body of statutory laws and provisions that, in theory at least, could offer pertinent advice on any problem that might arise in the daily life of China's people.

One segment of this bureaucracy lived in Peking, serving the emperor in an elaborate hierarchy that divided the country's business among six ministries dealing respectively with finance and personnel, rituals and laws, military affairs and public works. Also in Peking were the senior scholars and academicians who advised the emperor on ritual matters, wrote the official histories, and supervised the education of the imperial children. This concourse of official functionaries worked in uneasy proximity with the enormous palace staff who attended to the emperor's more personal needs: the court women and their eunuch watchmen, the imperial children and their nurses, the elite bodyguards, the banquet-hall and kitchen staffs, the grooms, the sweepers, and the water carriers.

The other segment of the Chinese bureaucracy consisted of those assigned to posts in the fifteen major provinces into which China was divided during the Ming dynasty. These posts also were arranged in elaborate hierarchies, running from the provincial governor at the top, down through the prefects in major cities to the magistrates in the countries. Below the magistrates were the police, couriers, militiamen, and tax gatherers who extracted a regular flow of revenue from China's farmers. A group of officials known as censors kept watch over the integrity of the bureaucracy both in Peking and in the provinces.

The towns and cities of China did not, in most cases, display the imposing solidity in stone and brick of the larger urban centers in post-Renaissance Europe. Nor, with the exception of a few famous pagodas, were Chinese skylines pierced by towers as soaring as those of the greatest Christian cathedrals or the minarets of Muslim cities. But this low architectural profile did not signify an absence of wealth or religion. There were many prosperous Buddhist temples in China, just as there were Daoist temples dedicated to the natural forces of the cosmos, ancestral meeting halls, and shrines to Confucius, the founding father of China's ethical system who had lived in the fifth century B.C. A scattering of mosques dotted some eastern cities and the far western areas, where most of China's Muslims lived. There were also some synagogues, where descendants of early Jewish travelers still congregated, and dispersed small groups with hazy memories of the teachings of Nestorian Christianity, which had reached China a millennium earlier. The lesser grandeur of China's city architecture and religious centers represented not any absence of civic pride or disesteem of religion, but rather a political fact: The Chinese state was more effectively centralized than those elsewhere in the world; its religions were more effectively controlled; and the growth of powerful, independent cities was prevented by a watchful government that would not tolerate rival centers of authority.

15

MATTEO RICCI

Jesuit Missionaries in Ming China

Matteo Ricci (1555–1610) was born in Italy, studied law and mathematics, entered the Jesuit monastic order (founded by the Spaniard Ignatius Loyola in 1540), and sailed to Portuguese Goa in India where he was ordained into the priesthood, learned Chinese, and directed a Jesuit expedition to China. After living in the southern capital of Nanking, Ricci was expelled and set up a mission in the secondary city of Nanchang (referred to in the following document as "Nancian"), where the events described in this selection took place in 1606 and 1607. Ricci went on to live in the northern capital of Peking for the rest of his life. There he gained the attention of the emperor with his fluent Chinese, his incomparable memory, and his work in astronomy and mathematics. He published a remarkably accurate map of the world, translated the books of Euclid, the Greek mathematician, into Chinese, and published a number of other books in Chinese.

The following selection is excerpted from Ricci's journals, published posthumously by one of his fellow Jesuits in 1615. What does this selection tell you about Jesuit missionary life in China at this time? How would you describe Chinese attitudes toward Christianity? What does this selection tell you about Chinese ideas regarding religion and the state?

Thinking Historically

Parts of this story evoke the feeling that "some things never change." Consider for instance, the envy generated by the Jesuit purchase of a larger house, or the conflict between two intellectual elites: the new Bachelors (Confucian literati who have passed their exams) and the foreign Jesuit community. What other elements in the story strike you as fairly universal or constant throughout history? Are there elements of the story that strike you as foreign or strange, suggesting a very different way of doing things in the Chinese Ming dynasty?

When we get to the point where we can feel somewhat "at home" in a particular past, we may also find elements in a primary source that surprise us because they run counter to our expectations. In this story do any elements that you would have expected to be very different turn

China in the Sixteenth Century: The Journals of Matthew Ricci: 1583–1610, trans. Louis J. Gallagher, S.J. (New York: Random House, 1953), 522–30.

out to be very similar to modern ways of doing things? How do you account for that "strange familiarity"?

During 1606 and the year following, the progress of Christianity in Nancian was in no wise retarded, . . .

Through the efforts of Father Emanuele Dias another and a larger house was purchased, in August of 1607, at a price of a thousand gold pieces. This change was necessary, because the house he had was too small for his needs and was situated in a flood area. Just as the community was about to change from one house to the other, a sudden uprising broke out against them. It happened that some of the pedants among the lettered Bachelors[1] had become dissatisfied with the growing popularity of the Christian faith. So they wrote out a complaint against the Fathers and took it to the governing Pimpithau, the Mayor, who had charge of all city affairs. They were neither well received nor patiently listened to, and he answered them saying, "If this Christian law, against which you are complaining, does not seem good to you, then do not accept it. I have not as yet heard that anyone has been forced into it. If the house which they have bought happens to be large, you are not the ones who are paying for it, and they will never interfere with your property." This answer only aroused their anger, and they went to the Governor of the metropolitan district. It happened that this man, whose name was Lu, was a friend of Father Ricci, with whom he had become acquainted, some years before, in Pekin. He accepted their complaint and then disregarded it, and the lawyers who presented it could not persuade him to give them an answer. This second rebuff also had its effect on their impatience.

At the beginning of each month, the Magistrates hold a public assembly, together with the Bachelors in Philosophy, in the temple of their great Philosopher.[2] When the rites of the new-moon were completed in the temple, and these are civil rather than religious rites, one of those present took advantage of the occasion to speak on behalf of the others, and to address the highest Magistrate present, the Pucinsu. "We wish to warn you," he said, "that there are certain foreign priests in this royal city, who are preaching a law, hitherto unheard of in this kingdom, and who are holding large gatherings of people in their house." Having said this, he referred them to their local Magistrate, called Ticho, who was also head of the school to which the speaker was attached, and he in turn ordered the plaintiffs to present their case in

---

[1]The Confucian literati. [Ed.]
[2]Confucius. [Ed.]

writing, assuring them that he would support it with all his authority, in an effort to have the foreign priests expelled. The complaint was written out that same day and signed with twenty-seven signatures. They gave one copy to the Director of the school and one to the Supreme Magistrate. The content of the document was somewhat as follows.

"Matthew Ricci, Giovanni Soeiro, Emanuele Dias, and certain other foreigners from western kingdoms, men who are guilty of high treason against the throne, are scattered amongst us, in five different provinces. They are continually communicating with each other and are here and there practicing brigandage on the rivers, collecting money, and then distributing it to the people, in order to curry favor with the multitudes. They are frequently visited by the Magistrates, by the high nobility and by the Military Prefects, with whom they have entered into a secret pact, binding unto death.

"These men teach that we should pay no respect to the images of our ancestors, a doctrine which is destined to extinguish the love of future generations for their forebears. Some of them break up the idols, leaving the temples empty and the gods to be pitied, without any patronage. In the beginning they lived in small houses, but by this time they have bought up large and magnificent residences. The doctrine they teach is something infernal. It attracts the ignorant into its fraudulent meshes, and great crowds of this class are continually assembled at their houses. Their doctrine gets beyond the city walls and spreads itself through the neighboring towns and villages and into the open country, and the people become so wrapt up in its falsity, that students are not following their courses, laborers are neglecting their work, farmers are not cultivating their acres, and even the women have no interest in their housework. The whole city has become disturbed, and, whereas in the beginning there were only a hundred or so professing their faith, now there are more than twenty thousand. These priests distribute pictures of some Tartar or Saracen, who they say is God, who came down from heaven to redeem and to instruct all of humanity, and who alone according to their doctrine, can give wealth and happiness; a doctrine by which the simple people are very easily deceived. These men are an abomination on the face of the earth, and there is just ground for fear that once they have erected their own temples, they will start a rebellion, as they did in recent years, according to report, in the provinces of Fuchian and Nankin. Wherefore, moved by their interest in the maintenance of the public good, in the conservation of the realm, and in the preservation, whole and entire, of their ancient laws, the petitioners are presenting this complaint and demanding, in the name of the entire province, that a rescript of it be forwarded to the King, asking that these foreigners be sentenced to death, or banished from the realm, to some deserted island in the sea."

Such, in brief, was the content of the complaint, eloquently worded, with alleged proofs and testimony, and couched in a persuasive style, at which the quasi-literati are very adept. Each of the Magistrates to whom the indictment was presented asserted that the spread of Christianity should be prohibited, and that the foreign priests should be expelled from the city, if the Mayor saw fit, after hearing the case, and notifying the foreigners. All those who knew nothing about the method of conducting affairs in the Chinese kingdom, were fairly well persuaded that the Fathers would at least be chased out of the metropolitan city, and as a result their many friends hesitated to come to their assistance, in what looked like a hopeless case. But the Fathers, themselves, were not too greatly disturbed, placing their confidence in Divine Providence, which had always been present to assist them on other such dangerous occasions. Their first problem was to decide upon the initial step to be taken in a matter of so grave importance.

Many of their friends thought they should seek out an intercessor, who might be induced for a consideration to have the sentence of the Magistrates revoked, as a favor to him. Instead, Father Emanuele, in his own defense, wrote out a request for justice, which he began with an instant petition to the Magistrates to make an exact inquiry into the crimes of which they had been accused, and if they were found guilty, to punish them to the full extent of the law. The Mayor and the same Magistrate, Director of the Schools, received copies of this document, and after the Chief Justice had heard the Fathers and kept them a long time on their knees, clad as criminals, he broke forth with the following questions: "Why is it that you have not left the city, after arousing the hatred of the Baccalaureates? What is this law that you are promulgating? What is this crime you have committed? Why do you forbid the people to honor their ancestors? What infernal image is this that you honor? Where did you get the money to buy these houses?" These and more questions were hurled at them, with little show of civility. Father Emanuele undertook to answer these questions with one of his Lay Brothers acting as an interpreter. First he gave a brief outline of the Christian doctrine. Then he showed that according to the divine law, the first to be honored, after God, were a man's parents. But the judge had no mind to hear or to accept any of this and he made it known that he thought it was all false. After that repulse, with things going from bad to worse, it looked as if they were on the verge of desperation, so much so, indeed, that they increased their prayers, their sacrifices and their bodily penances, in petition for a favorable solution of their difficulty. Their adversaries appeared to be triumphantly victorious. They were already wrangling about the division of the furniture of the Mission residences, and to make results doubly certain, they stirred up the flames anew with added accusations and indictments. They persuaded the civil leaders to urge on the Magistrates. One of the minor Magistrates to whom a copy of the new indictment was given, in order to flatter their zeal, said there was no need to inquire, as to whether or not the Christian law was true. The fact that it was being preached by foreigners was sufficient reason for suppressing it, adding that he himself would exterminate such men, if the complaint had not been handed on to the higher court.

The Mayor, who was somewhat friendly with the Fathers, realizing that there was much in the accusation that was patently false, asked the Magistrate Director of the Schools, if he knew whether or not this man Emanuele was a companion of Matthew Ricci, who was so highly respected at the royal court, and who was granted a subsidy from the royal treasury, because of the gifts he had presented to the King. Did he realize that the Fathers had lived in Nankin for twelve years, and that no true complaint had ever been entered against them for having violated the laws. Then he asked him if he had really given full consideration as to what was to be proven in the present indictment. To this the Director of the Schools replied that he wished the Mayor to make a detailed investigation of the case and then to confer with him. The Chief Justice then ordered the same thing to be done. Fortunately, it was this same Justice who was in charge of city affairs when Father Ricci first arrived in Nancian. It was he who first gave the Fathers permission, with the authority of the Viceroy, to open a house there. After that, through a series of promotions he returned to Nancian, to occupy the highest position in this metropolis. He exercised great prudence in handling the public rebuff the Fathers had received, being careful not to favor either side in the case. He was set on making the truth appear, and yet he did not wish to throw out the case of the quasi-literati because he himself was at one time the Director of their schools.

At that time, some of the accusing element, feeling certain that they had gained a victory, went into the houses of the neophytes looking for pictures of the Saviour, two or three of which they tore to pieces. Father Emanuele then advised the new Christians to hide the pictures from these bandits and, for the time being, not to hang them in their living rooms. He told them that in so doing they were not denying their faith but just preventing further sacrilege. He told them also that they could carry their rosaries in public if they wished to, but that there was no obligation to do so.

After the Mayor had examined the charges of the plaintiffs and the reply of the defendants, he subjected the quasi-literati to an examination in open court, and taking the Fathers under his patronage, he took it upon himself to refute the calumnies of their accusers. He said he was fully convinced that these strangers were honest men, and that he knew that there were only two of them in their local residence and not twenty, as had been asserted. To this they replied that the Chinese were becoming their disciples. To which the Justice in turn replied: "What of it? Why should we be afraid of our own people? Perhaps you are unaware of the fact that Matthew Ricci's company is cultivated by everyone in Pekin, and that he is being subsidized by the royal treasury. How dare the Magistrates who are living outside of the royal city, expel men who have permission to live at the royal court? These men here have lived peacefully in Nankin for twelve years. I command," he added, "that they buy no more large houses, and that the people are not to follow their law." Then in the presence of the court he addressed the Fathers, very kindly, saying that there were some in the city who were angry because they had bought the larger house, when the smaller one would have served their needs.

Relative to the Christian law, he told Father Emanuele that he had no objection whatsoever to its observance by him and by his own people, but that he should not teach it to the people of this country, because in this respect they are not trustworthy. He warned him, that even if the people did accept his religion, in the beginning, they would afterwards turn against it. All this he told them, calmly, and more of a similar nature, and what he said was accepted by all as being quite favorable. Afterwards, while speaking with one of his associates, in open court, he told them that the law which this man professed was quite in keeping with right reason, and that Father Emanuele was a good example of a man who lived according to what he preached. He explained that the Baccalaureates were bold enough to enter charges against Father Emanuele because he was a foreigner and, as they thought, unprotected by any patronage. The Chief Justice then told the Director of the Schools not to make any trouble for the Father, because it was evident that the general charges made by the Baccalaureates were fictitious and trumped up for the purpose of securing bribe money. He said the people of Nancian were a hard lot to please, and that he would give Father Emanuele permission to buy the house because, formerly, when he was Mayor, he gave Father Ricci permission to buy whatever house he wished.

16

Japanese Edicts Regulating Religion

The history of the state in Japan was very different from that of China. Between 1200 and 1600 Japan went through a period in which the state was eclipsed by aristocratic, warrior, and religious groups. When the Tokugawa Shogunate reasserted the authority of a central state in 1600, the memory of monk-soldiers and numerous independent armies called for a series of measures directed at controlling religious institutions and other independent powers. In one measure, all farmers were forbidden to have swords. Another regulated all religious temples. Between 1633 and 1639 the Tokugawa government took the further step of closing the country to all foreign religions, a move directed mainly at the influence previously enjoyed by Portuguese Catholic missionaries.

The first of the two documents in this selection is a vow by which Japanese Christians renounced their faith in 1645. The second document is a government edict regulating temples, mainly Buddhist temples, in 1665. What do these documents tell you about the relationship between the state and religion in Tokugawa Japan?

Thinking Historically

We tend to think of religions as fixed phenomena: eternal and unchanging. In fact, religious ideas and behavior change over time. Religious change is particularly striking in cases where missionaries convert people from a foreign culture. Inevitably, the religion that the convert accepts is different from the religion the missionary preaches. Can you identify some of the changes Christianity underwent in Japan?

Similarly, the regulation of Buddhist temples by the new centralizing Tokugawa government brought changes in Buddhism. How would you expect the edict of 1665 to have changed Japanese Buddhism?

Much in these documents will strike the modern reader as very foreign, even to the extent of requiring an imaginative leap to understand how people might have thought. Choose one of these passages and explain how and why it is so strange to you. Try also to explain how you might understand it.

Yosaburo Takekoshi, *The Economic Aspects of the History of the Civilization of Japan*, vol. 2 (New York: Macmillan, 1930), 88–89. Reprinted in *Japan: A Documentary History*, vol. I, ed. David J. Lu (Armonk, N.Y.: M. E. Sharpe, 2005), 224–25.
Japan: A Documentary History, vol. I, ed. David J. Lu (Armonk, N.Y.: M. E. Sharpe, 2005), 219–20.

Renouncing the Kirishitan Faith, 1645

Vow of Namban (Southern Barbarians): We have been Kirishitans for many years. But the more we learn of the Kirishitan doctrines the greater becomes our conviction that they are evil. In the first place, we who received instructions from the padre regarding the future life were threatened with excommunication which would keep us away from association with the rest of humanity in all things in the present world, and would cast us into hell in the next world. We were also taught that, unless a person committing a sin confesses it to the padre and secures his pardon, he shall not be saved in the world beyond. In that way the people were led into believing in the padres. All that was for the purpose of taking the lands of others.

When we learned of it, we "shifted" from Kirishitan and became adherents of Hokkekyō while our wives became adherents of Ikkōshō. We hereby present a statement in writing to you, worshipful Magistrate, as a testimony.

Hereafter we shall not harbor any thought of the Kirishitan in our heart. Should we entertain any thought of it at all, we shall be punished by Deus Paternus (God the Father), Jesus (His Son), Spirito Santo (the Holy Ghost), as well as by Santa Maria (St. Mary), various angels, and saints.

The grace of God will be lost altogether. Like Judas Iscariot, we shall be without hope, and shall be mere objects of ridicule to the people. We shall never rise. The foregoing is our Kirishitan vow.

Japanese Pledge: We have no thought of the Kirishitan in our hearts. We have certainly "shifted" our faith. If any falsehood be noted in our declaration now or in the future, we shall be subject to divine punishment by Bonten, Taishaku, the four deva kings, the great or little gods in all the sixty or more provinces of Japan, especially the Mishima Daimyōjin, the representatives of the god of Izu and Hakone, Hachiman Daibosatsu, Temman Daijizai Tenjin, especially our own family gods, Suwa Daimyōjin, the village people, and our relatives. This is to certify to the foregoing.

The second year of Shōhō [1645]
Endorsement.

Regulations for Buddhist Temples, 1665

1. The doctrines and rituals established for different sects must not be mixed and disarranged. If there is anyone who does not behave in accordance with this injunction, an appropriate measure must be taken expeditiously.

2. No one who does not understand the basic doctrines or rituals of a given sect is permitted to become the chief priest of a temple. Addendum: If a new rite is established, it must not preach strange doctrines.

3. The regulations which govern relationships between the main temple and branch temples must not be violated. However, even the main temple cannot take measures against branch temples in an unreasonable manner.

4. Parishioners of the temples can choose to which temple they wish to belong and make contributions. Therefore priests must not compete against one another for parishioners.

5. Priests are enjoined from engaging in activities unbecoming of priests, such as forming groups or planning to fight one another.

6. If there is anyone who has violated the law of the land, and that fact is communicated to a temple, it must turn him away without question.

7. When making repairs to a temple or a monastery, do not make them ostentatiously. Addendum: Temples must be kept clean without fail.

8. The estate belonging to a temple is not subject to sale, nor can it be mortgaged.

9. Do not allow anyone who has expressed a desire to become a disciple but is not of good lineage to enter the priesthood freely. If there is a particular candidate who has an improper and questionable background, the judgment of the domanial lord or magistrate of his domicile must be sought and then act accordingly.

The above articles must be strictly observed by all the sects. . . .

Fifth year of Kanbun [1665], seventh month, 11th day.

17

BADA'UNI
Akbar and Religion

At the same time the Chinese and Japanese confronted Christian missionaries, the descendents of Muslim Turkic and Mongol peoples of central Asia were conquering the Hindu kingdoms of northern India. Babur (1483–1530), the first of these Mughal rulers, swept into India from Afghanistan in 1525. Successive Mughal emperors enlarged the empire so that by the time of Akbar (r. 1556–1605) it included all of northern India. Like his contemporaries Philip II of Spain (r. 1556–1598) and Elizabeth of England (r. 1558–1603), Akbar created an elaborate and enduring administrative bureaucracy. But unlike Philip and Elizabeth, who waged religious wars against each other and forcibly converted their domestic subjects and newly conquered peoples, Akbar reached out to his Hindu subjects in ways that would have astonished his European contemporaries. In fact, he angered many of his own Muslim advisors, including Bada'uni, the author of the following memoir. What bothered Bada'uni about Akbar? What does this selection tell you about Akbar's rule? What factors might have motivated his toleration of heterodoxy?

Thinking Historically

What strikes the modern reader here is Akbar's evident curiosity about religious ideas and his lack of doctrinal rigidity. These are not qualities most people expect from a Muslim ruler, perhaps especially a premodern one. Why are we modern readers surprised by this? How might our ideas about Islam and Hinduism in the modern world influence our understanding of these religious traditions in the past?

We know from other sources that Akbar made special efforts to include Hindus in his administration. About a third of his governing bureaucracy were Hindus and he gave Hindu-governed territories a large degree of self-rule — allowing them to retain their own law and courts. Various taxes normally paid by non-Muslims were abolished. Among Akbar's five thousand wives his favorite was the mother of his

Bada'uni, 'Abdul Qadir. *Muntakhab ut-Tawarikh*, vol. 2, trans. G. S. A. Ranking and W. H. Lowe (Calcutta: Asiatic Society of Bengal 1895–1925), 200–201, 255–61 *passim*, 324. Edited and reprinted in *Sources of Indian Tradition*, ed. Ainslie T. Embree (New York: Columbia University Press, 1988), 465–68.

successor, Jahangir (r. 1605–1628). Akbar's policy of toleration continued under his son and grandson, Jahangir and Shah Jahan (r. 1628–1658), but was largely reversed by his great grandson, Aurangzeb (r. 1658–1707). How does this understanding of a particular past affect our ideas about the present? Does it make conflict seem less inevitable?

In the year nine hundred and eighty-three [1605] the buildings of the 'Ibādatkhāna[1] were completed. The cause was this. For many years previously the emperor had gained in succession remarkable and decisive victories. The empire had grown in extent from day to day; everything turned out well, and no opponent was left in the whole world. His Majesty had thus leisure to come into nearer contact with ascetics and the disciples of his reverence [the late] Mu'īn, and passed much of his time in discussing the word of God and the word of the Prophet. Questions of Sufism,[2] scientific discussions, inquiries into philosophy and law, were the order of the day.

And later that day the emperor came to Fatehpur. There he used to spend much time in the Hall of Worship in the company of learned men and shaikhs and especially on Friday nights, when he would sit up there the whole night continually occupied in discussing questions of religion, whether fundamental or collateral. The learned men used to draw the sword of the tongue on the battlefield of mutual contradiction and opposition, and the antagonism of the sects reached such a pitch that they would call one another fools and heretics. The controversies used to pass beyond the differences of Sunni, and Shī'a, of Hanafī and Shāfi'ī, of lawyer and divine, and they would attack the very bases of belief. And Makhdūm-ul-Mulk wrote a treatise to the effect that Shaikh 'Abd-al-Nabī had unjustly killed Khizr Khān Sarwānī, who had been suspected of blaspheming the Prophet [peace be upon him!], and Mīr Habsh, who had been suspected of being a Shī'a, and saying that it was not right to repeat the prayers after him, because he was undutiful toward his father, and was himself afflicted with hemorrhoids. Shaikh 'Abd-al-Nabī replied to him that he was a fool and a heretic. Then the mullās [Muslim theologians] became divided into two parties, and one party took one side and one the other, and became very Jews and Egyptians for hatred of each other. And persons of

[1]Hall of Religious Discussions. [Ed.]
[2]Mystical, poetic Islamic tradition. [Ed.]

novel and whimsical opinions, in accordance with their pernicious ideas and vain doubts, coming out of ambush, decked the false in the garb of the true, and wrong in the dress of right, and cast the emperor, who was possessed of an excellent disposition, and was an earnest searcher after truth, but very ignorant and a mere tyro, and used to the company of infidels and base persons, into perplexity, till doubt was heaped upon doubt, and he lost all definite aim, and the straight wall of the clear law and of firm religion was broken down, so that after five or six years not a trace of Islam was left in him: and everything was turned topsy-turvy. . . .

And samanas [Hindu or Buddhist ascetics] and brāhmans (who as far as the matter of private interviews is concerned gained the advantage over everyone in attaining the honor of interviews with His Majesty, and in associating with him, and were in every way superior in reputation to all learned and trained men for their treatises on morals, and on physical and religious sciences, and in religious ecstasies, and stages of spiritual progress and human perfections) brought forward proofs, based on reason and traditional testimony, for the truth of their own, and the fallacy of our religion, and inculcated their doctrine with such firmness and assurance, that they affirmed mere imaginations as though they were self-evident facts, the truth of which the doubts of the sceptic could no more shake "Than the mountains crumble, and the heavens be cleft!" And the Resurrection, and Judgment, and other details and traditions, of which the Prophet was the repository, he laid all aside. And he made his courtiers continually listen to those revilings and attacks against our pure and easy, bright and holy faith. . . .

Some time before this a brāhman, named Puruk'hotam, who had written a commentary on the Book, *Increase of Wisdom* (Khirad-afzā), had had private interviews with him, and he had asked him to invent particular Sanskrit names for all things in existence. And at one time a brāhman, named Debi, who was one of the interpreters of the *Mahābhārata*, was pulled up the wall of the castle sitting on a bedstead till he arrived near a balcony, which the emperor had made his bedchamber. Whilst thus suspended he instructed His Majesty in the secrets and legends of Hinduism, in the manner of worshiping idols, the fire, the sun and stars, and of revering the chief gods of these unbelievers, such as Brahma, Mahadev [Shiva], Bishn [Vishnu], Kishn [Krishna], Ram, and Mahama (whose existence as sons of the human race is a supposition, but whose nonexistence is a certainty, though in their idle belief they look on some of them as gods, and some as angels). His Majesty, on hearing further how much the people of the country prized their institutions, began to look upon them with affection. . . .

Sometimes again it was Shaikh Tāj ud-dīn whom he sent for. This shaikh was son of Shaikh Zakarīya of Ajodhan. . . . He had been a pupil of Rashīd Shaikh Zamān of Panipat, author of a commentary on the *Paths* (*Lawā'ih*), and of other excellent works, was most excellent in Sufism, and in the knowledge of theology second only to Shaikh Ibn 'Arabī and had written a comprehensive commentary on the *Joy of the Souls* (*Nuzhat ul-Arwāh*). Like the preceding he was drawn up the wall of the castle in a blanket, and His Majesty listened the whole night to his Sufic obscenities and follies. The shaikh, since he did not in any great degree feel himself bound by the injunctions of the law, introduced arguments concerning the unity of existence, such as idle Sufis discuss, and which eventually lead to license and open heresy. . . .

Learned monks also from Europe, who are called *Padre*, and have an infallible head, called *Papa*,[3] who is able to change religious ordinances as he may deem advisable for the moment, and to whose authority kings must submit, brought the Gospel, and advanced proofs for the Trinity. His Majesty firmly believed in the truth of the Christian religion, and wishing to spread the doctrines of Jesus, ordered Prince Murād to take a few lessons in Christianity under good auspices, and charged Abū'l Fazl to translate the Gospel. . . .

Fire worshipers also came from Nousarī in Gujarat, proclaimed the religion of Zardusht [Zarathustra] as the true one, and declared reverence to fire to be superior to every other kind of worship. They also attracted the emperor's regard, and taught him the peculiar terms, the ordinances, the rites and ceremonies of the Kaianians [a pre-Muslim Persian dynasty]. At last he ordered that the sacred fire should be made over to the charge of Abū'l Fazl, and that after the manner of the kings of Persia, in whose temples blazed perpetual fires, he should take care it was never extinguished night or day, for that it is one of the signs of God, and one light from His lights. . . .

His Majesty also called some of the yogis, and gave them at night private interviews, inquiring into abstract truths; their articles of faith; their occupation; the influence of pensiveness; their several practices and usages; the power of being absent from the body; or into alchemy, physiognomy, and the power of omnipresence of the soul.

[3]The Roman Catholic Pope. [Ed.]

18

DONALD QUATAERT

Ottoman Inter-communal Relations

Between 1500 and 1922 the Ottoman Empire, centered in Turkey, embraced a greater variety of religious and ethnic groups than any other state in world history. Many of these peoples, like the Jews expelled from Spain in 1492, came as exiles. According to this history of the empire by modern historian Donald Quataert, Ottoman administration of this incredibly diverse empire was remarkably tolerant. The degree of intercommunal peace and cooperation declined in later centuries, however. What evidence does the author offer of a generally cooperative interchange in the early centuries? Why, according to the author, did this situation change after 1800?

Thinking Historically

As the author points out in the beginning of this selection, the number of recent conflicts occurring in the territory of the old Ottoman Empire has engendered much interest in this topic. It is common to imagine that intractable contemporary conflicts have an ancient history. Often the participants in a conflict have a stake in overemphasizing the longevity of the conflict. But in this selection, the author argues that the roots of these conflicts are not nearly so deep. The causes are more recent than ancient. If he is right, how does that change our present understanding of these conflicts? How might it change our ability to deal with these conflicts?

The subject of historical intergroup relations in the Ottoman empire looms large because of the many conflicts that currently plague the lands it once occupied. Recall, for example, the Palestinian-Israeli struggle, the Kurdish issue, the Armenian question, as well as the horrific events that have befallen Bosnia and Kossovo. All rage in lands once Ottoman. What then, is the connection between these struggles of today and the inter-communal experiences of the Ottoman past?

Donald Quataert, *The Ottoman Empire, 1700–1922* (Cambridge: Cambridge University Press, 2000), 172–77.

There was nothing inevitable about these conflicts — all were historically conditioned. Other outcomes historically were possible but did not happen because of a particular unfolding of events. Nor are any of these struggles ancient ones reflecting millennia-old hatreds. Rather, each of them can be explained with reference to the nineteenth and twentieth centuries, through the unfolding of specific events rather than racial animosities. But because these contemporary struggles loom so large and because we assume that present-day hostilities have ancient and general rather than recent and specific causes, our understanding of the Ottoman inter-communal record has been profoundly obscured.

Despite all stereotypes and preconceptions to the contrary, intergroup relations during most of Ottoman history were rather good relative to the standards of the age. For many centuries, persons who were of minority status enjoyed fuller rights and more legal protection in the Ottoman lands than, for example, did minorities in the realm of the French king or of the Habsburg emperor. It is also true that Ottoman inter-communal relations worsened in the eighteenth and nineteenth centuries. In large part, this chapter argues, the deterioration derives directly from the explosive mixture of Western capital, Great Power interference in internal Ottoman affairs, and the transitional nature of an Ottoman polity struggling to establish broader political rights. Such an assessment does *not* aim to idealize the Ottoman record of inter-communal relations, which was hardly unblemished, or explain away the major injustices and atrocities inflicted on Ottoman subjects.

Nonetheless, the goal is to replace the stereotypes that too long have prevailed regarding relations among the religious and ethnic Ottoman communities. One's religion — as Muslim, Christian, or Jew — was an important means of differentiation in the Ottoman world. Indeed, ethnic terms confusingly often described what actually were religious differences. In the Balkan and Anatolian lands, Ottoman Christians informally spoke of "Turks" when in fact they meant Muslims. "Turk" was a kind of shorthand for referring to Muslims of every sort, whether Kurds, Turks, or Albanians (but not Arabs). Today's Bosnian Muslims are called Turks by the Serbian Christians even though they actually have a common Slavic ethnicity. In the Arab world, Muslim Arabs used "Turk" when sometimes they meant Albanian or Circassian Muslim, one who had come from outside the region.

Stereotypes present distorted pictures of Ottoman subjects living apart, in sharply divided, mutually impenetrable religious communities called *millets* that date back to the fifteenth century. In this incorrect view, each community lived in isolation from one another, adjacent but separate. And supposedly implacable hatreds prevailed: Muslims hated Christians who hated Jews who hated Christians who hated Muslims. Recent scholarship shows this view to be fundamentally wrong on almost every score. To begin with, the term *millet* as a designator for

Ottoman non-Muslims is not ancient but dates from the reign of Sultan Mahmut II, in the early nineteenth century. Before then, *millet* in fact meant Muslims within the empire and Christians *outside* it.

Let us continue this exploration of inter-communal relations with two different versions of the past in Ottoman Bulgaria during the 1700–1922 era. In the first version, we hear the voices of Father Paissiy (1722–1773) and S. Vrachanski (1739–1813) calling their Ottoman overlords "ferocious and savage infidels," "Ishmaelites," "sons of infidels," "wild beasts," and "loathsome barbarians." Somewhat later, another Bulgarian Christian writer Khristo Botev (1848–1876) wrote of the Ottoman administration:

> And the tyrant rages
> and ravages our native home:
> impales, hangs, flogs, curses
> and fines the people thus enslaved.

In the first quotation are the words of Bulgarian emigré intelligentsia who were seeking to promote a Bulgarian nation state and break from Ottoman rule.[1] To justify this separation, they invented a new past in which the Ottomans had brought an abrupt end to the Bulgarian cultural renaissance of the medieval era, destroying its ties to the West and preventing Bulgaria from participating in and contributing to western civilization.

And yet, hear two other Bulgarian Christian voices speaking about Bulgarian Muslims, the first during the period just before formal independence in 1908 and the other a few years later:

> Turks and Bulgarians lived together and were good neighbors. On holidays they exchanged pleasantries. We sent the Turks *kozunak* and red eggs at Easter, and they sent us baklava at Bayram. And on these occasions we visited each other.[2]
>
> In Khaskovo, our neighbors were Turks. They were good neighbors. They got on well together. They even had a little gate between their gardens. Both my parents knew Turkish well. My father was away fighting [during the Balkan Wars]. My mother was alone with four children. And the neighbors said: "You're not going anywhere. You'll stay with us. . . ." So Mama stayed with the Turks. . . . What I'm trying to tell you is that we lived well with these people."[3]

---

[1] The quotations provided from the oral interviews conducted in Bulgaria by Barbara Reeves-Ellington, Binghamton University.

[2] Interview with Simeon Radev, 1879–1967, describing his childhood before 1900, provided by Barbara Reeves-Ellington.

[3] Interview with Iveta Gospodarova, personal narrative, Sofia, January 19, 1995, provided by Barbara Reeves-Ellington.

Concepts of the "other" abound in history. The ancient Greeks divided the world into that of the civilized Greek and of the barbarian others. Barbarians could be brave and courageous but they did not possess civilization. For Jews, there are the *goyim* — the non-Jew, the other — whose lack of certain characteristics keeps them outside the chosen, Jewish, community. For Muslims, the notion of the *dhimmi* is another way of talking about difference. In this case, Muslims regard Christians and Jews as "the People of the Book" (*dhimmi*), who received God's revelation before Muhammad and therefore only incompletely. Thus, *dhimmi* have religion, civilization, and God's message. But since they received only part of that message, they are inherently different from and inferior to Muslims.

In the Ottoman world, people were acutely aware of differences between Muslims and non-Muslims. Muslims, as such, shared their religious beliefs with the dynasty and most members of the Ottoman state apparatus. The state itself, among its many attributes, called itself an Islamic one and many sultans included the term "*gazi*," warrior for the Islamic faith, among their titles. Later on, as seen, they revived the title of caliph, one with deep roots in the early Islamic past. Further, for many centuries military service primarily was carried out as a Muslim duty, although there were always some non-Muslims in the military service such as Christian Greeks serving as sailors in the navy during the 1840s. Yet, in a real sense, the military obligation had become a Muslim one. Even when an 1856 law required Ottoman Christian military service, the purchase of exemption quickly became institutionalized as a special tax. A 1909 law ended this loophole but then hundreds of thousands of Ottoman Christians fled the empire rather than serve. Thus, subjects understood that Muslims needed to fight but non-Muslims did not.

A variety of mechanisms maintained difference and distinction. Clothing laws . . . distinguished among the various religious communities, delineating the religious allegiance of passersby. They reassured maintenance of the differences not simply as instruments of discipline but useful markers of community boundaries, immediately identifying outsiders and insiders. Apparel gave a sense of group identity to members of the specific community.

Until the nineteenth century, the legal system was predicated on religious distinctions. Each religious community maintained its own courts, judges, and legal principles for the use of coreligionists. Since Muslims theologically were superior, so too, in principle, was their court system. Muslim courts thus held sway in cases between Muslims and non-Muslims. The latter, moreover, simply did not possess the necessary authority (*velayet*) and so, with a few exceptions, could not testify against Muslims. The state used the religious authorities and courts to announce decrees and taxes and, more generally, as instruments of imperial control. The ranking government official of an area, for example, the governor, received an imperial order and summoned the various religious authorities. They in turn informed their communities which negotiated within themselves over enforcement of the order or distribution of the taxes being imposed.

Muslim courts often provided rights to Christians and Jews that were unavailable in their own courts. And so non-Muslims routinely sought out Muslim courts when they were under no obligation to do so. Once they appeared before the Islamic court, its decisions took precedence. They often appealed to Muslim courts to gain access to the provisions of Islamic inheritance laws which absolutely guaranteed certain shares of estates to relatives — daughters, fathers, uncles, sisters. Thus, persons who feared disinheritance or a smaller share in the will of a Christian or Jew placed themselves under Islamic law. Christian widows frequently registered in the Islamic courts because these provided a greater share to the wife of the deceased than did ecclesiastical law. Or, take the case of *dhimmi* girls being forced into arranged marriages by fellow Christians or Jews. Since Islamic law required the female's consent to the marriage contract, the young woman in question could go to the Muslim court that took her side, thus preventing the unwanted arranged marriage.

With the Tanzimat reforms,[4] the old system of differentiation and distinction and of Muslim legal superiority formally disappeared. Equality of status meant equality of obligation and military service for all. The clothing laws disappeared and, while the religious courts remained, many of their functions vanished. New courts appeared: so-called mixed courts at first heard commercial, criminal, and then civil cases involving persons of different religious communities. Then, beginning in 1869, secular courts (*nizamiye*) presided over civil and criminal cases involving Muslim and non-Muslim. Whether or not these changes automatically and always improved the rights and status of individuals — Christian, Jew, or Muslim — currently is being debated by scholars. Some, for example, argue that women's legal rights overall declined with the replacement of Islamic by secular law, but others disagree.

So, how equal were Ottoman subjects and how well were non-Muslims treated? Quite arbitrarily, I offer the testimony of the Jewish community of Ottoman Salonica, as recorded in the "Annual Report of the Jews of Turkey" of the *Bulletin de l'Alliance Israélite Universelle* in 1893. French Jews had founded the Alliance Israélite Universelle in 1860 to work for Jewish emancipation and combat discrimination all over the world. The organization placed great stress on schools and education as a liberating device, establishing its first Ottoman school in 1867 and within a few decades, some fifty more. It published a journal,

---

[4]1839–1876. [Ed.]

the *Bulletin*, in Paris, to which Jewish communities from all over the world sent letters reporting on local conditions. Here then is the statement which the Jewish community of Salonica sent to the *Bulletin* in 1893:

> There are but few countries, even among those which are considered the most enlightened and the most civilized, where Jews enjoy a more complete equality than in Turkey [the Ottoman Empire]. H. M. the sultan and the government of the Porte display towards Jews a spirit of largest toleration and liberalism.

To place these words in context, we need to consider several points. First of all, the statement likely can be read at face value since it was not prepared for circulation within the empire. Second, Ottoman Jewish-Muslim relations were better than Muslim-Christian (or Jewish-Christian) relations. Nonetheless, this statement likely represents the sentiments of large numbers of Ottoman non-Muslim subjects, Christian and Jewish alike during the eighteenth and nineteenth centuries.

$$\boxed{19}$$

MARTIN LUTHER

Law and the Gospel: Princes and Turks

Martin Luther (1483–1546) launched the Protestant Reformation when he published his "95 Theses" in 1517, challenging the domination of Christianity by Rome and the Papacy. Luther's immediate complaint centered on the authority of the Pope and his agents to sell indulgences, which promised lessened time in purgatory for deceased loved ones on receipt of a contribution to a building fund for St. Peter's Cathedral. As Luther's criticism of papal practices reached the point of a breach, Luther turned to the German princes to support churches independent of Rome.

The issue of religious and political authority has long been debated and negotiated in Christian Europe. Unlike Islam, which was founded

---

The Table-Talk of Martin Luther, trans. William Hazlitt, Esq. (Philadelphia: The Lutheran Publication Society, 1997).

by a prophet who also governed, Christianity was founded and grew in an anti-Roman and even antipolitical environment. Typically, Christianity settled on an ambiguous or dualistic relationship between government and God. "Render to Caesar the things that are Caesar's, and to God the things that are God's," Jesus declared according to Mark (12:17) and Matthew (22:21). St. Augustine distinguished between the two cities: the city of God and the city of Man. In the Middle Ages, the doctrine of the two swords, temporal and spiritual, suggested a similar duality. Periodically one force asserted superiority over the other. In 800 Charlemagne took the coronation crown from the hands of the Pope. In 1054, the Holy Roman Emperor was said to crawl through the snow on his hands and knees to beg forgiveness from the Pope. The popes of the Italian Renaissance lived like kings, but in the sixteenth century, secular princes increased the power of the state.

Martin Luther's initial break with Rome encouraged other protests against both secular and religious authorities. His stress on individual interpretation of scripture and the power of following one's own conscience inspired more radical groups like the German Anabaptists to defy all worldly authority. In the wake of a peasant's revolt throughout Germany in 1523–1525, Luther joined forces with the German princes and voiced approval of the authority of the state.

This selection is drawn from a collection of conversational statements by Luther that were recorded by his followers and published under the title *Table-Talk* in 1566, after Luther's death.

What was Luther's attitude toward law and the state? What role did he think princes or governments ought to have in enforcing religious doctrine or behavior? What did he think of the Ottoman Turks?

Thinking Historically

Luther's ideas live on today in the minds of modern Protestants, especially Lutherans. Even the words Luther used — *law, conscience, government* — are as familiar now as they were in the sixteenth century. But Luther's ideas are also the product of a sixteenth-century thinker in sixteenth-century circumstances. Consequently, we can never assume that when we use these words or express these ideas we mean what Luther meant.

Notice, for instance, how Martin Luther dealt with the laws of the state and the call of conscience or the Gospel in the selections on "Law and the Gospel." What did "law" mean for the first Protestant? How did "conscience" or "the Gospel" provide better footing for Luther's challenge of the church? How do people compare or contrast law and conscience today? Would Luther have understood a modern appeal to conscience that led to civil disobedience?

In the selections on "Princes and Potentates" Luther turns his attention to the laws that would be enforced by his allies, the German princes. What vision of religion and politics is implied in these selections? What role did Luther leave for conscience or nonconformity? Would we want to allow a greater freedom of conscience today? Do we?

In what ways are Luther's ideas of the Ottoman Turks similar to European ideas of Muslim countries today? Was Luther poorly informed or prejudiced? Are we?

Of the Law and the Gospel

CCLXXI

We must reject those who so highly boast of Moses' laws, as to temporal affairs, for we have our written imperial and country laws, under which we live, and unto which we are sworn. Neither Naaman the Assyrian, nor Job, nor Joseph, nor Daniel, nor many other good and godly Jews, observed Moses' laws out of their country, but those of the Gentiles among whom they lived. Moses' law bound and obliged only the Jews in that place which God made choice of. Now they are free. If we should keep and observe the laws and rites of Moses, we must also be circumcised, and keep the mosaical ceremonies; for there is no difference; he that holds one to be necessary, must hold the rest so too. Therefore let us leave Moses to his laws, excepting only the *Moralia*,[1] which God has planted in nature, as the ten commandments, which concern God's true worshipping and service, and a civil life. . . .

CCLXXXVIII

In what darkness, unbelief, traditions, and ordinances of men have we lived, and in how many conflicts of the conscience we have been ensnared, confounded, and captivated under popedom, is testified by the books of the papists, and by many people now living. From all which snares and horrors we are now delivered and freed by Jesus Christ and his Gospel, and are called to the true righteousness of faith; insomuch that with good and peaceable consciences we now believe in God the Father, we trust in him, and have just cause to boast that we have sure and certain remission of our sins through the death of Christ Jesus, dearly bought and purchased. Who can sufficiently extol these treasures of the conscience, which everywhere are spread abroad, offered, and presented merely by grace? We are now conquerors of sin, of the

---

[1]Moral code. [Ed.]

law, of death, and of the devil; freed and delivered from all human traditions. If we would but consider the tyranny of auricular confession,[2] one of the least things we have escaped from, we could not show ourselves sufficiently thankful to God for loosing us out of that one snare. When popedom stood and flourished among us, then every king would willingly have given ten hundred thousand guilders, a prince one hundred thousand, a nobleman one thousand, a gentleman one hundred, a citizen or countryman twenty or ten, to have been freed from that tyranny. But now seeing that such freedom is obtained for nothing, by grace, it is not much regarded, neither give we thanks to God for it.

CCLXXXIX

. . . We must make a clear distinction; we must place the Gospel in heaven, and leave the law on earth; we must receive of the Gospel a heavenly and a divine righteousness; while we value the law as an earthly and human righteousness, and thus directly and diligently separate the righteousness of the gospel from the righteousness of the law, even as God has separated and distinguished heaven from earth, light from darkness, day from night, etc., so that the righteousness of the Gospel be the light and the day, but the righteousness of the law, darkness and night. Therefore all Christians should learn rightly to discern the law and grace in their hearts, and know how to keep one from the other, in deed and in truth, not merely in words, as the pope and other heretics do, who mingle them together, and, as it were, make thereout a cake not fit to eat. . . .

Of Princes and Potentates

DCCXI

Government is a sign of the divine grace, of the mercy of God, who has no pleasure in murdering, killing, and strangling. If God left all things to go where they would, as among the Turks and other nations, without good government, we should quickly dispatch one another out of this world.

DCCXII

Parents keep their children with greater diligence and care than rulers and governors keep their subjects. Fathers and mothers are masters naturally and willingly; it is a self-grown dominion; but rulers and magis-

---

[2]Catholic confession to a priest. [Ed.]

trates have a compulsory mastery; they act by force, with a prepared dominion; when father and mother can rule no more, the public police must take the matter in hand. Rulers and magistrates must watch over the sixth commandment.

DCCXIII

The temporal magistrate is even like a fish net, set before the fish in a pond or a lake, but God is the plunger, who drives the fish into it. For when a thief, robber, adulterer, murderer, is ripe, he hunts him into the net, that is, causes him to be taken by the magistrate, and punished; for it is written: "God is judge upon earth." Therefore repent, or thou must be punished.

DCCXIV

Princes and rulers should maintain the laws and statues, or they will be condemned. They should, above all, hold the Gospel in honor, and bear it ever in their hands, for it aids and preserves them, and ennobles the state and office of magistracy, so that they know where their vocation and calling is, and that with good and safe conscience they may execute the works of their office. At Rome, the executioner always craved pardon of the condemned malefactor, when he was to execute his office, as though he were doing wrong, or sinning in executing the criminal; whereas 'tis his proper office, which God has set.

St. Paul says: "He beareth not the sword in vain"; he is God's minister, a revenger, to execute wrath upon him that does evil. When the magistrate punishes, God himself punishes.

On the Turks

DCCCXXVII

The power of the Turk is very great; he keeps in his pay, all the year through, hundreds of thousands of soldiers. He must have more than two millions of florins annual revenue. We are far less strong in our bodies, and are divided out among different masters, all opposed the one to the other, yet we might conquer these infidels with only the Lord's prayer, if our own people did not spill so much blood in religious quarrels, and in persecuting the truths contained in that prayer. God will punish us as he punished Sodom and Gomorrah, but I would fain 'twere by the hand of some pious potentate, and not by that of the accursed Turk. . . .

DCCCXXX

News came from Torgau that the Turks had led out into the great square at Constantinople twenty-three Christian prisoners, who, on their refusing to apostatize, were beheaded. Dr. Luther said: Their blood will cry up to heaven against the Turks, as that of John Huss[3] did against the papists. 'Tis certain, tyranny and persecution will not avail to stifle the Word of Jesus Christ. It flourishes and grows in blood. Where one Christian is slaughtered, a host of others arise. 'Tis not on our walls or our arquebusses[4] I rely for resisting the Turk, but upon the *Pater Noster*. 'Tis that will triumph. The Decalogue is not, of itself, sufficient. I said to the engineers at Wittenberg: Why strengthen your walls — they are trash; the walls with which a Christian should fortify himself are made, not of stone and mortar, but of prayer and faith. . . .

DCCCXXXV

. . . The Turks pretend, despite the Holy Scriptures, that they are the chosen people of God, as descendants of Ishmael. They say that Ishmael was the true son of the promise, for that when Issac was about to be sacrificed, he fled from his father, and from the slaughter knife, and, meanwhile, Ishmael came and truly offered himself to be sacrificed, whence he became the child of the promise; as gross a lie as that of the papists concerning one kind in the sacrament. The Turks make a boast of being very religious, and treat all other nations as idolaters. They slanderously accuse the Christians of worshipping three gods. They swear by one only God, creator of heaven and earth, by his angels, by the four evangelists, and by the eighty heaven-descended prophets, of whom Mohammed is the greatest. They reject all images and pictures, and render homage to God alone. They pay the most honorable testimony to Jesus Christ, saying that he was a prophet of preeminent sanctity, born of the Virgin Mary, and an envoy from God, but that Mohammed succeeded him, and that while Mohammed sits, in heaven, on the right hand of the Father, Jesus Christ is seated on his left. The Turks have retained many features of the law of Moses, but, inflated with the insolence of victory, they have adopted a new worship; for the glory of warlike triumphs is, in the opinion of the world, the greatest of all.

Luther complained of the emperor Charles's[5] negligence, who, taken up with other wars, suffered the Turk to capture one place after

---

[3]In Czech, known as Jan Hus. Hus (1369–1415) was a Czech forerunner of the Protestant Reformation. [Ed.]

[4]Primitive firearms used from the fifteenth to the seventeenth centuries. [Ed.]

[5]Charles V (1500–1558), the Habsburg Emperor, fought the French as well as the Ottomans. [Ed.]

another. 'Tis with the Turks as heretofore with the Romans, every subject is a soldier, as long as he is able to bear arms, so they have always a
disciplined army ready for the field; whereas we gather together
ephemeral bodies of vagabonds, untried wretches, upon whom is no
dependence. My fear is, that the papists will unite with the Turks to exterminate us. Please God, my anticipation come not true, but certain it
is, that the desperate creatures will do their best to deliver us over to
the Turks.

20

ROGER WILLIAMS

The Bloody Tenent of Persecution for Cause of Conscience

Roger Williams (1603–1683), a minister of the Church of England
sympathetic to its puritan reformist wing, sailed from England in
1630 to join the newly founded Massachusetts Bay Colony. But for
Williams the colony remained too close to the Church of England, especially in its continuing legacies of Catholicism: bishops, infant baptism, ritual kneeling, and making the sign of the cross. Williams
moved on to the more separatist Pilgrim colony in Plymouth and to a
church in Salem in 1633. There he became engaged in a series of conflicts with the General Court of Massachusetts for defaming the
churches and the civil authority of the colony. For his "dangerous
opinions" he was given six weeks to leave. In the howling winter of
1635, he brought his small band of followers south to Narragansett
Bay where he bought a tract of land from the Indians which he called
Providence and which would later become Rhode Island.

   The Bloody Tenent, written sometime between 1636 and 1644
when it was finally published (and then burned) in London, summarized the disagreements that Williams had with the Massachusetts authorities, the Church of England, and, one might add, the long history
of Catholicism. What did Williams mean by the "bloody tenent"

Roger Williams, *The Bloody Tenent of Persecution for Cause of Conscience, Discussed in a
Conference between Truth and Peace,* ed. Richard Groves (Macon, Ga.: Mercer University
Press, 2001)

(tenet or doctrine) of persecution for conscience? Why does he call this doctrine bloody? According to Williams, what should be the relationship between church and state? Why? How is Williams's idea of this relationship different from Luther's? How do you account for that difference?

Thinking Historically

In Protestant America of the 1630s the more fervent advocates of religious purity rallied around symbols and signs that more mainstream Protestants dismissed as unimportant. But the religious purists and the mainstreamers of the American seventeenth century argued the exact opposite of what we might expect to hear today. Roger Williams and his Separatist followers objected to the display of the most sacred Christian symbol, the cross, on the English flag. For them the cross on the flag was a sacrilegious confusion of nation and church, politics and faith. Some of the Separatists of Salem got into trouble with the Massachusetts government for desecrating the flag by cutting out the cross. Williams and the Separatists also objected to political officials taking an oath of office saying "so help me God." The judges and officials of the state should not presume to act for God, Williams argued, and nonbelievers should not be forced to take the name of "the Lord thy God" in vain. Nothing good could come from governments policing faith or from communities of the faithful mucking about in worldly affairs. What do you think Roger Williams would have thought of prayer in the public schools, the idea that America was a "Christian nation," or politicians saying "God Bless America"?

In this selection, Williams makes reference to a number of different historical periods. First he refers to the religious wars between Catholics and Protestants that had ravaged Europe. Like Luther, he also refers to two of the most important historical markers for Christians: Ancient Israel of the Old Testament and the coming of Christ. Why does he say what he says about ancient Israel? What is his attitude toward Jews and non-Christians alike after the coming of Christ? Christian theology was (and is) highly historical. It envisions a timeline that stretches into the future as well. What future developments does Williams envision?

First, that the blood of so many hundred thousand souls of Protestants and papists, spilled in the wars of present and former ages for their respective consciences, is not required nor accepted by Jesus Christ the Prince of Peace.

Secondly, pregnant scriptures and arguments are throughout the work proposed against the doctrine of persecution for cause of conscience.

Thirdly, satisfactory answers are given to scriptures and objections produced by Mr. Calvin, Beza,[1] Mr. Cotton, and the ministers of the New English churches, and others former and later, tending to prove the doctrine of persecution for cause of conscience.

Fourthly, the doctrine of persecution for cause of conscience is proved guilty of all the blood of the souls crying for vengeance under the altar.

Fifthly, all civil states, with their officers of justice, in their respective constitutions and administrations, are proved essentially civil, and therefore not judges, governors, or defenders of the spiritual, or Christian, state and worship.

Sixthly, it is the will and command of God that, since the coming of his Son the Lord Jesus, a permission of the most paganish, Jewish, Turkish, or anti-Christian consciences and worships be granted to all men in all nations and countries, and they are only to be fought against with that sword which is only, in soul matters, able to conquer, to wit, the sword of God's Spirit, the word of God.

Seventhly, the state of the land of Israel, the kings and people thereof, in peace and war, is proved figurative and ceremonial, and no pattern nor precedent for any kingdom or civil state in the world to follow.

Eighthly, God requires not a uniformity of religion to be enacted and enforced in any civil state; which enforced uniformity, sooner or later, is the greatest occasion of civil war, ravishing of conscience, persecution of Christ Jesus in his servants, and of the hypocrisy and destruction of millions of souls.

Ninthly, in holding an enforced uniformity of religion in a civil state, we must necessarily disclaim our desires and hopes of the Jews' conversion to Christ.

Tenthly, an enforced uniformity of religion throughout a nation or civil state confounds the civil and religious, denies the principles of Christianity and civility, and that Jesus Christ is come in the flesh.

Eleventhly, the permission of other consciences and worships that a state professes only can, according to God, procure a firm and lasting peace; good assurance being taken, according to the wisdom of the civil state, for uniformity of civil obedience from all sorts.

Twelfthly, lastly, true civility and Christianity may both flourish in a state or kingdom, notwithstanding the permission of divers and contrary consciences, either of Jew or Gentile.

---

[1]Theodore Beza (1519–1605), John Calvin's successor. [Ed.]

REFLECTIONS

School prayer, abortion, the public display of religious symbols — what is the proper relationship of government and religion? Roger Williams reminds us that the principle of the separation of church and state, a pillar of modern civic society, originated not as a secular humanist denigration of religion but as an effort by the most fervent Protestant Separatists to preserve their religion's purity and independence.

Luther's discussion of government and religion strikes a more expected tone. The great reformer was able to dismiss thousands of years of law from ancient Israel and the Roman papacy, but he gave German princes far greater authority over religious matters than most Christians would allow today. How do we account for the differences between Martin Luther and Roger Williams on this issue? Is it simply a matter of each preaching the politics of their position — the privileged versus the persecuted?

The Christian debate was unique. Muslims also quarreled about who had the truth, but they lacked a tradition of separating religious and secular authority. In the Ottoman Empire the sultan issued edicts on matters that were not covered in the Koran, but this body of secular law merely supplemented Koranic law, and both were administered by the same judges and officials. There was neither the theoretical possibility that the two systems would disagree nor that separate judicial institutions might come into conflict. Nevertheless, the Ottomans developed a tolerance for differences that would have struck many Catholics and Protestants, in their less accommodating moods, as sheer folly. In the Ottoman Empire, non-Muslims were subject to the religious law of their own communities, and when they violated the secular law of the states, Muslims often suffered more severe punishment on the principle that Muslims should set a better example.

Like Christians, however, Muslims held religious truths that they believed applied to all people. As a consequence both Christian and Muslim society gave rise to religious zealots who wanted the state to enshrine God's Truth. In that way, Christians and Muslims were very different from the rulers, subjects, and thinkers of China and Japan.

Neither the Chinese nor Japanese traditions held religious orthodoxies. But both required proper observance of certain social and political proprieties. Strong governments, as in most of Chinese history, turned principles like Confucian filial piety into virtual religions but they had the force of law and made little appeal to conscience or individual choice. Daoism and Buddhism appealed to the inner lives of Chinese and Japanese devotees, but posed no conflict to state power. Only in periods of unrest, feudalism, or the breakdown of the state did Buddhist or Daoist priests and monks exercise political power. Even then, however, they did not challenge the state as much as they filled the vacuum left by its disappearance. In both Japan and Europe, the post-feudal age was one in which the state's rise depended, in part, on the reclamation and monopolization of powers previously exercised by religious institutions.

Three pasts, but increasingly one present. As cultural differences meld with the force of rockets and the speed of the Internet, one might well ask what separate histories matter to a common present. Increasingly principles of toleration are enshrined by international organizations in declarations of human rights and the proceedings of international tribunals. Whether we see the roots of modern principles of tolerance in Confucian secularism, Christian separation of church and state, or Muslim cosmopolitanism, we live in a world where intolerance is widely condemned and legitimately prosecuted.

And yet, fanaticism and intolerance have not disappeared. Religious fundamentalists of various stripes declare their missions to take over governments, convert populations, and bring about the rule of God. History has shown that tolerance need not be secular. Indeed even the aggressively secular regimes of the twentieth and twenty-first centuries have demonstrated and continue to demonstrate a capacity for brutal persecution of dissidents, religious and otherwise.

The study of the past may be more proficient at telling us what we want than how we can achieve it. But the knowledge of how to get there from here begins with the knowledge of where we are and where we have been. At the very least, the knowledge of how things have changed from the past to the present holds the key to unlocking the future.

4

Gender and Family

China, Southeast Asia, Europe, and "New Spain," 1600–1750

HISTORICAL CONTEXT

Women are half of humanity. The family is the oldest and most important social institution. Marriage is one of the most important passages in one's life. Yet up until the last few decades these subjects rarely registered as important topics in world history. There were at least two reasons for this: One was the tendency to think of history as the story of public events only — the actions of political officials, governments, and their representatives — instead of the private and domestic sphere. The second was the assumption that the private or domestic sphere had no history, and that it had always been the same. As the documents in this chapter will show, nothing could be further from the truth.

Since the urban revolution five thousand years ago most societies have been patriarchal. The laws, social codes, and dominant ideas have enshrined the power and prestige of men over women, husbands over wives, fathers over children, gods over goddesses, even brothers over sisters. Double standards for adultery, inheritance laws that favor sons, and laws that deny women property or political rights all attest to the power of patriarchal culture and norms. Almost everywhere patriarchies have limited women to the domestic sphere while granting men public and political power. Nevertheless, we will see in this chapter that not all patriarchies were alike. Some were less stringent than others, and in many societies during this period, women, individually, in families, and even in larger groups, discovered ways both large and small to assert their social, cultural, and economic independence. As you read about women in China, Southeast Asia, Europe, and the Americas, consider how women's lives varied from one patriarchal society to another and how women found openings to express themselves and create their own worlds.

THINKING HISTORICALLY
Making Comparisons

We learn by making comparisons. Every new piece of knowledge we acquire leads to a comparison with what we already know. For example, we arrive in a new town and we are struck by something that we have not seen before. The town has odd street lamps, flowerpots on the sidewalks, or lots of trucks on the street. We start to formulate a theory about the differences between what we observe in the new town and what we already know about our old town. We think we're on to something, but our theory falls apart when we make more observations by staying in the new town another day, or traveling on to the next town, or going halfway across the world. As we gain more experience and make more observations, our original theory explaining an observed difference is supplanted by a much more complex theory about *types* of towns.

History is very much like travel. We learn by comparison, one step at a time, and the journey is never ending. On this trip we begin in China and then move on to other regions of the world. We begin with primary sources, but make comparisons based on secondary sources as well. In fact, we conclude with a secondary source that will allow us to draw upon our previous readings to make increasingly informed and complex comparisons. Welcome aboard. Next stop, China.

$$\boxed{21}$$

Family Instructions for the Miu Lineage

Chinese families in Ming times (1368–1644) often organized themselves into groups by male lineage. These groups often shared common land, built ancestral halls, published genealogies, honored their common ancestors, and ensured the success and well-being of future generations. To accomplish the last of these, lineage groups frequently compiled lists of family rules or instructions. This particular example, from the various lines of the Miu family of the Guangdong province

"Family Instructions for the Miu Lineage, Late Sixteenth Century," trans. Clara Yu, in *Chinese Civilization: A Sourcebook*, 2nd ed., ed. Patricia Ebrey (New York: Free Press, 1993), 238–40, 241–43.

in the south, shows how extensive these instructions could be. What values did these family instructions encourage? What activities did the Miu lineage regulate? What kind of families, and what kind of individuals, were these rules intended to produce? How would these rules have had a different impact on women and men?

Thinking Historically

It is difficult to read this selection without thinking of one's own family and of families in one's own society. How many of the Miu lineage's concerns are concerns of families you know? Family instructions and lineage organizations are not common features of modern American society, even among Chinese Americans who may have a sense of their lineage and family identity. What institutions in modern American society regulate the activities addressed by these family instructions? Or are these activities allowed to regulate themselves or to go unregulated? From reading this document, what do you think are some of the differences between Ming-era Chinese families and modern American families?

Work Hard at One of the Principal Occupations

1. To be filial to one's parents, to be loving to one's brothers, to be diligent and frugal — these are the first tenets of a person of good character. They must be thoroughly understood and faithfully carried out.

One's conscience should be followed like a strict teacher and insight should be sought through introspection. One should study the words and deeds of the ancients to find out their ultimate meanings. One should always remember the principles followed by the ancients, and should not become overwhelmed by current customs. For if one gives in to cruelty, pride, or extravagance, all virtues will be undermined, and nothing will be achieved.

Parents have special responsibilities. *The Book of Changes*[1] says: "The members of a family have strict sovereigns." The "sovereigns" are the parents. Their position in a family is one of unique authority, and they should utilize their authority to dictate matters to maintain order, and to inspire respect, so that the members of the family will all be obedient. If the parents are lenient and indulgent, there will be many troubles which in turn will give rise to even more troubles. Who is to blame for all this? The elders in a family must demand discipline of themselves, following all rules and regulations to the letter, so that the younger members emulate their good behavior and exhort each other

---

[1]The *I Ching*, a Chinese classic. [Ed.]

to abide by the teachings of the ancient sages. Only in this way can the family hope to last for generations. If, however, the elders of a family should find it difficult to abide by these regulations, the virtuous youngsters of the family should help them along. Because the purpose of my work is to make such work easier, I am not afraid of giving many small details. . . .

2. Those youngsters who have taken Confucian scholarship as their hereditary occupation should be sincere and hard-working, and try to achieve learning naturally while studying under a teacher. Confucianism is the only thing to follow if they wish to bring glory to their family. Those who know how to keep what they have but do not study are as useless as puppets made of clay or wood. Those who study, even if they do not succeed in the examinations, can hope to become teachers or to gain personal benefit. However, there are people who study not for learning's sake, but as a vulgar means of gaining profit. These people are better off doing nothing.

Youngsters who are incapable of concentrating on studying should devote themselves to farming; they should personally grasp the ploughs and eat the fruit of their own labor. In this way they will be able to support their families. If they fold their hands and do nothing, they will soon have to worry about hunger and cold. If, however, they realize that their forefathers also worked hard and that farming is a difficult way of life, they will not be inferior to anyone. In earlier dynasties, officials were all selected because they were filial sons, loving brothers, and diligent farmers. This was to set an example for all people to devote themselves to their professions, and to ensure that the officials were familiar with the hardships of the common people, thereby preventing them from exploiting the commoners for their own profit.

3. Farmers should personally attend to the inspection, measurement, and management of the fields, noting the soil as well as the terrain. The early harvest as well as the grain taxes and the labor service obligations should be carefully calculated. Anyone who indulges in indolence and entrusts these matters to others will not be able to distinguish one kind of crop from another and will certainly be cheated by others. I do not believe such a person could escape bankruptcy.

4. The usual occupations of the people are farming and commerce. If one tries by every possible means to make a great profit from these occupations, it usually leads to loss of capital. Therefore it is more profitable to put one's energy into farming the land; only when the fields are too far away to be tilled by oneself should they be leased to others. One should solicit advice from old farmers as to one's own capacity in farming.

Those who do not follow the usual occupations of farming or business should be taught a skill. Being an artisan is a good way of life and will also shelter a person from hunger and cold. All in all, it is important to remember that one should work hard when young, for when youth expires one can no longer achieve anything. Many people learn this lesson only after it is too late. We should guard against this mistake.

5. Fish can be raised in ponds by supplying them with grass and manure. Vegetables need water. In empty plots one can plant fruit trees such as the pear, persimmon, peach, prune, and plum, and also beans, wheat, hemp, peas, potatoes, and melons. When harvested, these vegetables and fruits can sustain life. During their growth, one should give them constant care, nourishing them and weeding them. In this way, no labor is wasted and no fertile land is left uncultivated. On the contrary, to purchase everything needed for the morning and evening meals means the members of the family will merely sit and eat. Is this the way things should be?

6. Housewives should take full charge of the kitchen. They should make sure that the store of firewood is sufficient, so that even if it rains several days in succession, they will not be forced to use silver or rice to pay for firewood, thereby impoverishing the family. Housewives should also closely calculate the daily grocery expenses, and make sure there is no undue extravagance. Those who simply sit and wait to be fed only are treating themselves like pigs and dogs, but also are leading their whole households to ruin. . . .

Exercise Restraint

1. Our young people should know their place and observe correct manners. They are not permitted to gamble, to fight, to engage in lawsuits, or to deal in salt[2] privately. Such unlawful acts will only lead to their own downfall.

2. If land or property is not obtained by righteous means, descendants will not be able to enjoy it. When the ancients invented characters, they put gold next to two spears to mean "money," indicating that the danger of plunder or robbery is associated with it. If money is not accumulated by good means, it will disperse like overflowing water; how could it be put to any good? The result is misfortune for oneself as well as for one's posterity. This is the meaning of the saying: "The way of Heaven detests fullness, and only the humble gain." Therefore, accumulation of great wealth inevitably leads to great loss. How true are the words of Laozi![3]

---

[2]Get involved in the salt trade, a state monopoly. Salt was used as a preservative for fish, meat, and other foods. [Ed.]

[3]Lao Tzu, legendary Chinese philosopher and author of the *Dao de Jing*, the Daoist classic. [Ed.]

A person's fortune and rank are predestined. One can only do one's best according to propriety and one's own ability; the rest is up to Heaven. If one is easily contented, then a diet of vegetables and soups provides a lifetime of joy. If one does not know one's limitations and tries to accumulate wealth by immoral and dishonest means, how can one avoid disaster? To be able to support oneself through life and not leave one's sons and grandsons in hunger and cold is enough; why should one toil so much?

3. Pride is a dangerous trait. Those who pride themselves on wealth, rank, or learning are inviting evil consequences. Even if one's accomplishments are indeed unique, there is no need to press them on anyone else. "The way of Heaven detests fullness, and only the humble gain." I have seen the truth of this saying many times.

4. Taking concubines in order to beget heirs should be a last resort, for the sons of the legal wife and the sons of the concubine are never of one mind, causing innumerable conflicts between half brothers. If the parents are in the least partial, problems will multiply, creating misfortune in later generations. Since families have been ruined because of this, it should not be taken lightly.

5. Just as diseases are caused by what goes into one's mouth, misfortunes are caused by what comes out of one's mouth. Those who are immoderate in eating and unrestrained in speaking have no one else to blame for their own ruin.

6. Most men lack resolve and listen to what their women say. As a result, blood relatives become estranged and competitiveness, suspicion, and distance arise between them. Therefore, when a wife first comes into a family, it should be made clear to her that such things are prohibited. "Start teaching one's son when he is a baby; start teaching one's daughter-in-law when she first arrives." That is to say, preventive measures should be taken early.

7. "A family's fortune can be foretold from whether its members are early risers" is a maxim of our ancient sages. Everyone, male and female, should rise before dawn and should not go to bed until after the first drum. Never should they indulge themselves in a false sense of security and leisure, for such behavior will eventually lead them to poverty.

8. Young family members who deliberately violate family regulations should be taken to the family temple, have their offenses reported to the ancestors, and be severely punished. They should then be taught to improve themselves. Those who do not accept punishment or persist in their wrongdoings will bring harm to themselves.

9. As a preventive measure against the unpredictable, the gates should be closed at dusk, and no one should be allowed to go out. Even when there are visitors, dinner parties should end early, so that there will be no need for lighting lamps and candles. On very hot or very cold days, one should be especially considerate of the kitchen servants.

10. For generations this family had dwelt in the country, and everyone has had a set profession; therefore, our descendants should not be allowed to change their place of residence. After living in the city for three years, a person forgets everything about farming; after ten years, he does not even know his lineage. Extravagance and leisure transform people, and it is hard for anyone to remain unaffected. I once remarked that the only legitimate excuse to live in a city temporarily is to flee from bandits.

11. The inner and outer rooms, halls, doorways, and furniture should be swept and dusted every morning at dawn. Dirty doorways and courtyards and haphazardly placed furniture are sure signs of a declining family. Therefore, a schedule should be followed for cleaning them, with no excuses allowed.

12. Those in charge of cooking and kitchen work should make sure that breakfast is served before nine o'clock in the morning and dinner before five o'clock in the afternoon. Every evening the iron wok and other utensils should be washed and put away, so that the next morning, after rising at dawn, one can expect tea and breakfast to be prepared immediately and served on time. In the kitchen no lamps are allowed in the morning or at night. This is not only to save the expense, but also to avoid harmful contamination of food. Although this is a small matter, it has a great effect on health. Furthermore, since all members of the family have their regular work to do, letting them toil all day without giving them meals at regular hours is no way to provide comfort and relief for them. If these rules are deliberately violated, the person in charge will be punished as an example to the rest.

13. On the tenth and twenty-fifth days of every month, all the members of this branch, from the honored aged members to the youngsters, should gather at dusk for a meeting. Each will give an account of what he has learned, by either calling attention to examples of good and evil, or encouraging diligence, or expounding his obligations, or pointing out tasks to be completed. Each member will take turns presenting his own opinions and listening attentively to others. He should examine himself in the matters being discussed and make efforts to improve himself. The purpose of these meetings is to encourage one another in virtue and to correct each other's mistakes.

The members of the family will take turns being the chairman of these meetings, according to schedule. If someone is unable to chair a meeting on a certain day, he should ask the next person in line to take his place. The chairman should provide tea, but never wine. The meetings may be canceled on days of ancestor worship, parties, or other such occasions, or if the weather is severe. Those who are absent from these meetings for no reason are only doing themselves harm.

There are no set rules for where the meeting should be held, but the place should be convenient for group discussions. The time of the meeting should always be early evening, for this is when people have free time. As a general precaution the meeting should never last until late at night.

14. Women from lower-class families who stop at our houses tend to gossip, create conflicts, peek into the kitchens, or induce our women to believe in prayer and fortune-telling, thereby cheating them out of their money and possessions. Consequently, one should question these women often and punish those who come for no reason, so as to put a stop to the traffic.

15. Blood relatives are as close as the branches of a tree, yet their relationships can still be differentiated according to importance and priority: Parents should be considered before brothers, and brothers should be considered before wives and children. Each person should fulfill his own duties and share with others profit and loss, joy and sorrow, life and death. In this way, the family will get along well and be blessed by Heaven. Should family members fight over property or end up treating each other like enemies, then when death or misfortune strikes they will be of even less use than strangers. If our ancestors have consciousness, they will not tolerate these unprincipled descendants who are but animals in man's clothing. Heaven responds to human vices with punishments as surely as an echo follows a sound. I hope my sons and grandsons take my words seriously.

16. To get along with patrilineal relatives, fellow villages, and relatives through marriage, one should be gentle in speech and mild in manners. When one is opposed by others, one may remonstrate with them; but when others fall short because of their limitations, one should be tolerant. If one's youngsters or servants get into fights with others, one should look into oneself to find the blame. It is better to be wronged than to wrong others. Those who take affront and become enraged, who conceal their own shortcomings and seek to defeat others, are courting immediate misfortune. Even if the other party is unbearably unreasonable, one should contemplate the fact that the ancient sages had to endure much more. If one remains tolerant and forgiving, one will be able to curb the other party's violence.

22

MAO XIANG

How Dong Xiaowan Became My Concubine

Mao Xiang* (1611–1693) was one of the great poets, artists, and calligraphers of the late Ming dynasty and, after its demise in 1644, a persistent critic of the succeeding Manchu or Ching dynasty. He was also known for his love of beautiful women, especially three famous courtesans who were also talented artists: Dong Xiaowan† (1625–1651), Cai Han (1647–1686), and Qin Yue (c. 1660–1690). (Note what these dates reveal.) Whether or not this is a reliable account of how Dong Xiaowan became his concubine, what does this piece from Mao Xiang's memoir tell you about his society's attitudes towards women, marriage, and family?

Thinking Historically

If comparisons originate in our recognition of institutions and ideas that are foreign to our own, certainly the acceptance of concubines in seventeenth-century Chinese society is a sharp contrast to modern American family values. Concubines were mainly an indulgence of upper-class Chinese men, but concubinage was an institution that touched all classes of Chinese society. Poor peasants knew that they could sell their daughters into the trade, if need be. And even middle-class wives worried that a concubine might be waiting in the wings should they prove to be infertile, unable to bear a son, or otherwise displeasing to their husband or mother-in-law.

We might also compare this selection with the previous one. How does the blatant acceptance of concubinage in this selection compare to the emphasis on family stability in the Miu lineage rules? Are these documents from two different Chinas, or are they compatible? Does this selection force you to modify the contrast you drew between Ming China and modern America from the previous selection?

*mow   zhee ANG
†dong   zhow AHN

"How Dong Xiaowan Became My Concubine," in *Chinese Civilization: A Sourcebook*, 2nd ed., ed. Patricia Ebrey (New York: Free Press, 1993), 246–49.

I was rather depressed that evening, so I got a boat and went with a friend on an excursion to Tiger Hill. My plan was to send a messenger to Xiangyang the next morning and then set out for home. As our boat passed under a bridge, I saw a small building by the bank. When I asked who lived there, my friend told me that this was [the singing girl] Dong's home. I was wildly happy with memories of three years before. I insisted on the boat's stopping, wanting to see Xiaowan at once. My friend, however, restrained me, saying, "Xiaowan has been terrified by the threat of being kidnapped by a powerful man and has been seriously ill for eighteen days. Since her mother's death,[1] she is said to have locked her door and refrained from receiving any guests." I nevertheless insisted on going ashore.

Not until I had knocked two or three times did the door open. I found no light in the house and had to grope my way upstairs. There I discovered medicine all over the table and bed.

Xiaowan, moaning, asked where I had come from and I told her I was the man she once saw beside a winding balustrade, intoxicated.

"Well, Sir," she said, recalling the incident, "I remember years ago you called at my house several times. Even though she only saw you once, my mother often spoke highly of you and considered it a great pity that I never had the chance to wait on you. Three years have passed. Mother died recently, but on seeing you now, I can hear her words in my ears. Where are you coming from this time?"

With an effort, she rose to draw aside the curtains and inspected me closely. She moved the lamp and asked me to sit on her bed. After talking awhile, I said I would go, not wanting to tire her. She, however, begged me to remain, saying, "During the past eighteen days I have had no appetite for food, nor have I been able to sleep well. My soul has been restless, dreaming almost all the time. But on seeing you, I feel as if my spirit has revived and my vigor returned." She then had her servant serve wine and food at her bedside, and kept refilling my cup herself.

Several times I expressed my desire to leave, but each time she urged me to stay. . . . The following morning, I was eager to set off on the trip home, but my friend and my servant both asked me not to be ungrateful for Xiaowan's kindness as she had had only a brief chance to talk with me the previous night. Accordingly I went to say goodbye to her. I found her, fresh from her toilet, leaning against a window upstairs quite composed. On seeing my boat approaching the bank, she hurried aboard to greet me. I told her that I had to leave immediately,

---

[1]The "mother" here may well be the woman who managed her, rather than her natural mother.

but she said that she had packed up her belongings and would accompany me. I felt unable to refuse her.

We went from Hushuguan to Wuxi, and from there to Changzhou, Yixing, and Jiangyin, finally arriving at Jinjiang. All this took twenty-seven days, and twenty-seven times I asked her to go back, but she was firm in her desire to follow me. On climbing Golden Hill, she pointed to the river and swore, "My body is as constant as the direction of the Yangzi River. I am determined never to go back to Suzhou!"

On hearing her words, I turned red and reiterated my refusal, "The provincial examination is coming up soon. Because my father's recent posts have been dangerous ones, I have failed to attend to family affairs and have not been able to look after my mother on a daily basis. This is my first chance to go back and take care of things. Moreover, you have so many creditors in Suzhou and it will take a lot to redeem your singing-girl's contract in Nanjing. So please go back to Suzhou for the time being. After I have taken the examination at the end of summer, I will send word and meet you in Nanjing. At any rate, I must await the result of the examination before I even think about these matters. Insisting on it now will do neither of us any good."

She, however, still hesitated. There were dice on the table, and one of my friends said to her jokingly, "If you are ever going to get your wish [to become his concubine], they will land with the same side up." She then bowed toward the window, said a prayer, and tossed the dice. They all landed on six. All on board expressed their amazement, and I said to her, "Should Heaven really be on our side, I'm afraid we might bungle the whole thing if we proceed too hurriedly. You had better leave me temporarily, and we'll see what we can do by and by." Thus against her wishes she said goodbye, concealing her tearstained face with her hands.

I had pity for her plight but at the same time once I was on my own felt relieved of a heavy burden. Upon arrival at Taizhou, I sat for the examination. When I got home in the sixth month, my wife said to me, "Xiaowan sent her father to bring word that since her return to Suzhou, she has kept to a vegetarian diet and confined herself to her home, waiting on tiptoe for you to bring her to Nanjing as you promised. I felt awkward and gave her father ten taels[2] of silver, asking him to tell her that I am in sympathy with her and consent to her request, but she must wait till you finish the examination."

I appreciated the way my wife had handled Xiaowan's request. I then directly proceeded to Nanjing without keeping my promise to send someone to fetch her, planning to write to her after I had finished the examination. However, scarcely had I come out of the examination hall

---

[2]A tael is equivalent to about 1¼ ounce. [Ed.]

on the morning of the 15th of the eighth month when she suddenly called at my lodgings at Peach Leaf Ferry. It turned out that after waiting in vain for news from me, she had hired a boat, setting out from Suzhou and proceeding along the river with an old woman as her companion. She met with robbers on the way, and her boat had to hide among reeds and rushes. With the rudder broken, the boat could not proceed, and she had had practically nothing to eat for three days. She arrived at Sanshan Gate of Nanjing on the 8th, but not wanting to disturb my thoughts during the examination, she delayed entering the city for two days.

Though delighted to see me, she looked and sounded rather sad as she vividly described what had happened during the hundred days of our separation, including her confinement at home on vegetarian fare, her encounter with robbers on the river, and her other experiences of a voyage fraught with danger. Now she was more insistent than ever on getting her wish. The men in my literary society from Kashan, Sungjiang, Fujian, and Henan all admired her farsightedness and sincerity and encouraged her with their verses and paintings.

When the examination was over, I thought I might pass it, so hoped I would soon be able to settle my affairs and gratify her desire to become my concubine. Unexpectedly, on the 17th I was informed that my father had arrived by boat. . . . I had not seen him for two years and was overjoyed that he had returned alive from the battlefront. Without delaying to tell Xiaowan, I immediately went to meet him. . . . Before long she set out by boat in pursuit of me from the lodging house at Peach Leaf Ferry. A storm at Swallow's Ledge nearly cost her her life. At Shierhui she came on board and stayed with me again for seven days.

When the results of the examination were announced, I found my name on the list of the not quite successful candidates. I then traveled day and night to get home, while she followed weeping, unwilling to part. I was, however, well aware that I could not by myself settle her affairs in Suzhou and that her creditors would, on discovering her departure, increase their demands. Moreover, my father's recent return and my disappointment in the exams had made it all the more difficult to gratify her desire at once. On arrival at Puchao on the outskirts of my native city, I had to put on a cold face and turn ironhearted to part from her, telling her to go back to Suzhou to set her creditors at ease and thus pave the way for our future plans.

In the tenth month, while passing Jinjiang, I went to visit Mr. Zheng, the man who had been my examiner. At that time, Liu Daxing of Fujian had arrived from the capital. During a drinking party in his boat with General Chen, my friend Prefect Liu, and myself, my servant returned from seeing Xiaowan home. He reported that on arrival at Suzhou she did not change out of her autumn clothing, saying that she intended to die of cold if I did not see my way to settle her affairs promptly. On hearing this, Liu Daxing pointed to me and said, "Pijiang, you are well known as a man of honor. Could you really betray a girl like this?"

"Surely scholars are not capable of the gallant deeds of Huang Shanke and Gu Yaya," I replied.

The prefect raised his cup, and with a gesture of excitement exclaimed, "Well, if I were given a thousand taels of silver to pay my expenses, I'd start right away today!"

General Chen at once lent me several hundred taels, and Liu Daxing helped with a present of several catties[3] of ginseng. But how could it have been anticipated that the prefect, on arrival at Suzhou, failed to carry out his mission, and that when the creditors had kicked up a row and the matter had been brought to a deadlock, he fled to Wujiang? I had no chance to make further inquiries, as I returned home shortly afterwards.

Xiaowan was left in an awkward position, with little she could do. On hearing of her trouble, Qian Qianyi of Changshu went to Bantang himself and brought her to his boat. He approached her creditors, from the gentry to the townsmen, and within three days managed to clear every single debt of hers, the bills redeemed piling up a foot in height. This done, he arranged a farewell banquet on a pleasure boat and entertained her at the foot of Tiger Hill. He then hired a boat and sent someone to see her to Rugao.

On the evening of the 15th of the eleventh month when I was drinking wine with my father in our Zhuocun Hall, I was suddenly informed that Xiaowan had arrived at the jetty. After reading Qian's long interesting letter, I learned how she had gotten here. I also learned that Qian had written to a pupil of his, Zhang of the ministry of rites, asking him to redeem her singing girl's contract at once. Her minor problems at Suzhou were later settled by Mr. Zhou of the bureau of ceremonies while Mr. Li, formerly attached to that bureau, had also rendered her great assistance in Nanjing.

Ten months thereafter, her desire was gratified [and she became my concubine]. After the endless tangle of troubles and emotional pain, we had what we wanted.

[3]One catty is equivalent to 16 taels, 20 ounces, or a British pound. [Ed.]

23

KENNETH POMERANZ

How the Other Half Traded

The "other half" of this recent essay, written by historian Kenneth Pomeranz, refers not only to women, but to the women who were the Southeast Asian trading partners of Portuguese and then Dutch merchants in the sixteenth and seventeenth centuries. Why did these women play such an important role in European trade with Southeast Asia? How did both Europeans and Southeast Asians benefit socially and economically from these alliances?

Thinking Historically

Pomeranz enables us to make a number of comparisons about gender and family. How, for instance, was the role of women in Southeast Asia different from that of their sisters in China? How did the role and rights of women in Europe differ from those in Southeast Asia? Were gender relations more alike in Europe and Southeast Asia, or in Europe and China? How would you expect European trade with China to be different from European trade with Southeast Asia?

Even today, companies often find that keeping up the morale of employees sent overseas is difficult. But consider an earlier multinational: the Dutch East India Company (VOC) of the seventeenth and eighteenth centuries. Its outposts in India, Southeast Asia, Japan, and Taiwan were places where few Dutchwomen were willing to live; and while most men working for the company were quite willing to seek mates among indigenous women, this brought complications of its own. Given the cultural gulf separating these couples, it may be no great surprise that the private letters of these men are full of references to how hard it was to "tame" these women into the kinds of wives they expected. What may be more surprising is how hard the VOC, the Dutch Reformed Church, and other Europeans in Southeast Asia found it to break the *commercial* power of these women, many of whom were substantial traders in their own right.

Kenneth Pomeranz, "How the Other Half Traded," in Kenneth Pomeranz and Steven Topik, eds., *The World That Trade Created* (Armonk, N.Y.: M. E. Sharpe, 2006), 27–30.

Long before Europeans arrived, maritime Southeast Asia (including present-day Malaysia, Indonesia, and the Philippines) carried on a substantial long-distance trade. Many of the merchants were women — in some cases because commerce was thought too base an occupation for upper-class men, but too lucrative for elite families to abstain from completely. (Some elites carried this snobbery a step further, and held that noble women were also too lofty to barter in the marketplace or to visit the Chinese settlements where much long-distance trading was arranged; they were not, however, too noble to supervise a team of servants who carried out these businesses.) Malay proverbs of the 1500s spoke of the importance of teaching daughters how to calculate and make a profit.

More generally, these societies typically allowed women to control their own property, gave them considerable voice in the choice of husbands, and were often quite tolerant of other liaisons. The long journeys away from home that some of these women took even made it necessary to allow them, within the crude limits of available technology, to control their own fertility. (Herbal medicines, jumping from rocks to induce miscarriages, and even occasional infanticides were among the methods used.) Both the Islamic missionaries who swept through the area in the 1400s and the Christians who followed a hundred years later were appalled, and hoped to bring such women to heel.

But despite these qualms, the Portuguese, the first Europeans to establish themselves in this world, had found intermarrying with such women to be an indispensable part of creating profitable and defensible colonies. When the VOC gave up on importing Dutchwomen — having sometimes found "willing" candidates only in the orphanages or even brothels of Holland, and facing discontent among the intended husbands of these women — it turned to the daughters of these earlier Portuguese-Asian unions: they at least spoke a Western language, and were at least nominally Christian. Many had also learned from their mothers how useful a European husband could be for protecting their business interests in an increasingly multinational and often violent trading world. Councillors of the Dutch court in Batavia (present-day Jakarta), who were rarely rich themselves, but were very well placed to prevent the VOC's rules and monopoly claims from interfering with their wives' trade, were often particularly good matches for the richest of these women. Thus, arranging elite interracial marriages proved relatively easy: but making the resulting families conform to visions hatched in Amsterdam proved harder.

The VOC's principal goal, of course, was profit, and profit was best secured by monopolizing the export of all sorts of Asian goods — from pepper to porcelain — back to Europe. In theory, the Company also claimed — at least intermittently — the right to license and tax (or sink) all the ships participating in the much larger intra-Asian trade, including those of Southeast Asia's women traders. But the realities of huge oceans and numerous rivals made enforcing such a system impossible, and the VOC also faced powerful enemies within. Most Company servants soon discovered that while smuggling goods back to Holland was risky and difficult, they could earn sums by trading illegally (or semi-legally) within Asia that dwarfed their official salaries. Here their wives were a perfect vehicle for making a fortune: they were well connected in and knowledgeable about local markets, often possessed of considerable capital, and able to manage the family business continuously without being susceptible to sudden transfer by the Company.

And for some particularly unscrupulous Dutchmen there was the possibility of a kind of lucrative cultural arbitrage: after profiting from the relatively high status of Southeast Asian women, one might take advantage of their low status in Dutch law to gain sole control of the family fortune, and then perhaps even return to the Netherlands to settle down with a "proper" wife. (Though even with the law on the man's side, such a process could be very complex if the woman used her informal influence cleverly and hid her assets — in one such case the man eventually won control of most of his wife's profits, but the legal proceedings took nineteen years.)

But if men had powerful allies in the Dutch law and church, women had the climate on their side. Foreigners tended to die young in India and Southeast Asia, leaving behind wealthy widows. Such women were often eagerly sought after by the next wave of incoming European adventurers, enabling them to strike marriage bargains that safeguarded at least some of their independence; many wed and survived three or four husbands. The rare Dutchman who did live a long life in Batavia was likely to rise quite high in the VOC, become very wealthy, and marry more than once himself; but since such men (not needing a particularly well-connected or rich spouse once they'd risen this high) often chose a last wife much younger than themselves, they tended to leave behind a small circle of very wealthy widows, whose behavior often scandalized those Dutchmen who took their Calvinism seriously.

From the founding of Batavia in 1619 until the late 1800s, Dutch moralists and monopolists waged an endless battle to "tame" these women, and at least partially succeeded; later generations, for instance, seem to have conformed much more than earlier ones to European sexual mores. And as the scale of capital and international contacts needed to succeed in long-distance trade grew larger, European companies and their Chinese or Indian merchant allies — all of them male — did increasingly shrink the sphere in which these women operated.

Eventually, when late nineteenth-century innovations — the Suez Canal, telegraphs, refrigerated shipping, vaccinations, and so on — made it more and more possible to live a truly European life-style in Southeast Asia, a new generation of Dutch officials chose to bring wives with them, or to assume they would quickly return to Holland and marry there.

Even so, trade managed by Eurasian women remained a crucial part of local and regional economies: many, for instance, managed commercial real estate and money-lending operations through which they funneled profits from their husbands' activities into local development around the fringes of Southeast Asian trading cities. (Ironically, this niche may have been kept for them in part through the racism of many of their husbands, who preferred to deal with the locals as little as possible.)

As late as the turn of the twentieth century, this sphere and those who managed it refused to disappear — the Indonesian novelist Pramoedaya Toer has painted a powerful portrait of one such woman, who waged a running battle to hold on to the businesses (and children) she had handled for years against her half-mad Dutch consort and his "legal" family back in Holland. Along with most of her real-life counterparts, this fictional woman was ultimately defeated; but for three centuries, women like her had built and sustained much of the world their husbands claimed was theirs.

24

JOHN E. WILLS JR.

Sor Juana Inés de la Cruz

After the conquest of the Aztecs, the Spanish attempted to govern Mexico by converting the surviving Indians to Roman Catholicism and exploiting their labor. In addition, they encouraged fellow Spaniards to settle in the colony and imported African slaves, creating a mixed society of Europeans, Indians, and Africans. As in the rest of North America, the dividing line between slave and free was the most important social distinction. But unlike their English counterparts to the north, New Spain's colonists also distinguished between *Peninsulares*, colonists who were born in Spain, and Creoles, colonists who were born of Spanish parents in the Americas.

In the following selection a modern historian evokes the life of Sor Juana Inés de la Cruz* (1651–1695), a poet, artist, and nun who lived

*sohr hoo AH nah   ee NEZ   duh lah CROOZ

John E. Wills Jr., "Sor Juana Inés de la Cruz," in *1688: A Global History* (New York: W. W. Norton, 2001), 13–19.

in Mexico City in "New Spain." Sister Juana was a Creole woman and the author argues she was distinctly a product of Mexican Creole society. In what ways was she Spanish? In what ways was she Mexican? How do you think the life of a Creole woman, born and raised in the colony, would be different from that of a woman born in Spain?

Thinking Historically

The previous selection reminds us that some societies, like Southeast Asia, were less patriarchal than others. The arrival of Europeans sometimes enhanced the wealth and influence of women traders in Southeast Asia. The widows and daughters of mixed marriages often benefited from both worlds.

The daughters of Spanish settlers in the Americas had fewer opportunities for financial advancement than did the daughters of Dutch settlers in Java, and the Spanish patriarchy was as unyielding as any in Europe. Nevertheless, the culture that the Old World imported into the New provided alternatives for women that were absent in the East Indies. What were these alternatives? Were they a product of Europe, America, or the intermixture of the two?

On April 28, 1688, a long procession moved out of Mexico City, along the causeways that crossed the nearby lakes, and through the small towns and farms of the plateau, on its way toward the pass between the two volcanoes Iztaccihuatl and Popocatépetl, both more than sixteen thousand feet high, and down to the tropical port of Vera Cruz. The farmers in their villages and fields were used to a good deal of such coming and going, but this time they stopped their work to look and to call out to each other in Nahuatl, the main indigenous language, for this was no ordinary procession. Cavalry outriders and a huge coach were followed by many baggage wagons and a long line of fine coaches. The marquis of Laguna had served as viceroy of New Spain from 1680 to 1686. With their wealth, powerful connections in Madrid, and a taste for elegance and the arts, he and his wife had given the viceregal court a few years of splendor and sophistication comparable, if not to Madrid, certainly to many of the lesser courts of Europe. Now their wealthy Spanish friends were riding in their coaches as far as the Villa de Guadalupe, seeing the marquis and marchioness off on their voyage home to Spain.

> A child born of a slave shall be received,
> according to our Law, as property
> of the owner to whom fealty
> is rendered by the mother who conceived.

The harvest from a grateful land retrieved,
the finest fruit, offered obediently,
is for the lord, for its fecundity
is owing to the care it has received.
   So too, Lysis divine, these my poor lines:
as children of my soul, born of my heart,
they must in justice be to you returned;
   Let not their defects cause them to be spurned,
for of your rightful due they are a part,
as concepts of a soul to yours consigned.

These lines were written sometime later in 1688 and sent off from
Mexico to the marchioness of Laguna in Spain. They make use of
metaphors and classical conceits to express and conceal the feelings of
the author, who had lost, with the marchioness's departure, the object
of the nearest thing she had ever known to true love and, with the marquis's departure, her ultimate protection from those who found her
opinions and her way of life scandalous. The trouble was not that the
author was lesbian — although her feelings toward men and women
were unusually complicated and unconventional, anything approaching
a physical relation or even passion is most unlikely — but that she was
a cloistered Hieronymite nun, who read and studied a wide range of
secular books, held long intellectual conversations with many friends,
wrote constantly in a variety of religious and secular styles, and betrayed in her writings sympathy for Hermetic and Neoplatonic views
that were on the edge of heresy if not beyond it. Her name in religion
was Sor Juana Inés de la Cruz. She is recognized today as one of the
great poets in the history of the Spanish language.
   Mexico in the 1680s was a society of dramatic contradictions. The
elegant viceregal court and the opulent ecclesiastical hierarchy looked
toward Europe for style and ideas. The vast majority of the population
sought to preserve as much as possible of the language, beliefs, and
ways of life that had guided them before the coming of the Spaniards;
the worship of the Virgin of Guadalupe, for example, owed much to
the shrine of an Aztec goddess that had been the setting of the original
appearance of the Virgin to a Mexican peasant. In between the "peninsular" elite and the "Indians," the native-born "creoles" of Spanish
language and culture managed huge cattle ranches and sought constantly new veins of profitable silver ore and new techniques to exploit
old ones. Neither "Spanish" nor "Indian," they experienced the full
force of the contradictions of Mexican society and culture.
   The literary world in which Sor Juana was such an anomalous eminence thrived on these contradictions of society and culture. This was a
baroque culture. The word *baroque*, originating as a Portuguese term

for the peculiar beauty of a deformed, uneven pearl, suggests a range of artistic styles in which the balance and harmony of the Renaissance styles are abandoned for imbalance, free elaboration of form, playful gesture, and surprising allusion, through which the most intense of emotions and the darkest of realities may be glimpsed, their power enhanced by the glittering surface that partially conceals them. Contradiction and its partial, playful reconciliation are the stuff of the baroque style. So is the layering of illusion on illusion, meaning upon meaning. And what more baroque conceit could be imagined than the literary eminence of a cloistered nun in a rough frontier society, with a church and state of the strongest and narrowest male supremacist prejudices? Look again at the poem quoted earlier: The chaste nun refers to her poem as her child or the harvest from a grateful land. She declares her love once again to the departed marchioness.

Sor Juana was a product of Mexican creole society, born on a ranch on the shoulder of the great volcano Popocatépetl. Her mother was illiterate and very probably had not been married to her father. But some of the family branches lived in the city, with good books and advantageous connections. As soon as she discovered the books in her grandfather's library, she was consumed with a thirst for solitude and reading. Her extraordinary talents for literature and learning were recognized. When she was fifteen, in 1664, she was taken into the household of a newly arrived viceroy, as his wife's favorite and constant companion. She must have enjoyed the attention, the luxury, the admiration of her cleverness. She no doubt participated in the highly stylized exchange of "gallantries" between young men and young women. But she had no dowry. Solitude was her natural habitat. As a wife and mother, what chance would she have to read, to write, to be alone? In 1668 she took her vows in the Hieronymite convent of an order named after Saint Jerome, cloistered and meditative by rule.

This was a big decision, but less drastic than one might think. Certainly she was a believing Catholic. Her new status did not require total devotion to prayer and extinction of self. It did not imply that she was abandoning all the friendships and secular learning that meant so much to her. The nuns had a daily round of collective devotions; but many rules were not fully honored, and the regimen left her much free time for reading and writing. Each of the nuns had comfortable private quarters, with a kitchen, room for a bathtub, and sleeping space for a servant and a dependent or two; Sor Juana usually had one slave and one or two nieces or other junior dependents living in her quarters. The nuns visited back and forth in their quarters to the point that Sor Juana complained of the interruptions to her reading and writing, but outsiders spoke to the nuns only in the locutory especially provided for that purpose. From the beginning she turned the locutory into an elegant salon, as the viceroy and his lady and other fashionable people came to visit her and they passed hours in learned debate, literary improvisation, and gossip.

One of Sor Juana's most constant friends and supporters was Carlos de Sigüenza y Góngora, professor of mathematics at the University of Mexico, an eminently learned creole scholar whose position was almost as anomalous as hers. He had been educated by the Jesuits and had longed to be one of them but had been expelled from their college. He had managed to obtain his position, without a university degree, by demonstrating his superior knowledge of his subject. He had added Góngora to his name to emphasize his distant kinship, through his mother's family, with the most famous of Spain's baroque poets. But he always felt insecure among the European-born professors, churchmen, and high officials. He wrote a great deal, much of it about the history of Mexico. He was in no way Sor Juana's equal as a writer, but he probably was responsible for most of her smattering of knowledge of modern science and recent philosophy.

There was a rule of poverty among the Hieronymites, but it was generally ignored. Sor Juana received many gifts, some of them substantial enough to enable the former dowerless girl to invest money at interest. By gift and purchase she built up a library of about four thousand volumes and a small collection of scientific instruments, probably provided by Sigüenza. Her reading was broad but not very systematic, contributing to the stock of ideas and allusions she drew on constantly in her writings but giving her little sense of the intellectual tensions and transformations that were building up in Europe. She wrote constantly, in a wide variety of complex and exacting forms. Voluntarily or upon commission or request, she wrote occasional poems of all kinds for her friends and patrons. A celebration might call for a *loa*, a brief theatrical piece in praise of a dignitary. In one of hers, for example, a character "clad in sunrays" declares:

I am a reflection
of that blazing sun
who, among shining rays
numbers brilliant sons:
when his illustrious rays
strike a speculum,
on it is portrayed
the likeness of his form.

Sor Juana's standing in society reached a new height with the arrival in 1680 of the marquis and marchioness of Laguana. Even in the public festivities celebrating their arrival, she outdid herself in baroque elaborations of texts and conceits for a temporary triumphal arch erected at the cathedral. It was an allegory on Neptune, in which the deeds of the Greek god were compared to the real or imaginary deeds of the marquis. Much was made of the echoes among the marquis's title of Laguna, meaning *lake*, Neptune's reign over the oceans, and the origins of Mexico City as the Aztec city of Tenochtitlán in the middle of its great lake: an elaborate union of sycophancy to a ruler, somewhat strained classical allusion, and a creole quest for a Mexican identity. In parts of the text the author even drew in Isis as an ancestor of Neptune, and in others of her works from this time she showed a great interest in Egyptian antiquity as it was then understood, including the belief that the god Hermes Trismegistus had revealed the most ancient and purest wisdom and anticipated the Mosaic and Christian revelations. These ideas, the accompanying quasi-Platonic separation of soul and body, and her use of them to imply that a female or androgynous condition was closer to the divine wisdom than the male took her to the edge of heresy or beyond and was turned against her in later years.

Sor Juana soon established a close friendship with the marchioness of Laguna. Some of the poems she sent her are among her very finest, and they are unmistakably love poems. Some of them accompanied a portrait of the author. Several portraits in which a very handsome woman gazes boldly at us, her black-and-white habit simply setting off her own strength and elegance, have come down to us. [See Figure 4.1.]

> And if it is that you should rue
> the absence of a soul in me [the portrait],
> you can confer one, easily,
> from the many rendered you:
> and as my soul I [Sor Juana] tendered you,
> and though my being yours obeyed,
> and though you look on me amazed
> in this insentient apathy,
> you are the soul of this body,
> and are the body of this shade.

The marquis of Laguna stepped down as viceroy in 1686 but remained in Mexico until 1688. In that year Sor Juana was very busy. The marchioness was taking texts of her poems back to Spain, where they soon would be published. She added to them a play, *The Divine Narcissus*, interweaving the legend of Narcissus and the life of Jesus, which probably was performed in Madrid in 1689 or 1690. Her niece took her vows in the convent in 1688. Late in the year, after her noble friends had left, she wrote the poem quoted earlier as well as a romantic comedy, *Love Is the Greater Labyrinth*, which was performed in Mexico City early in 1689.

A large collection of her poetry was published in Madrid in 1689. The next year in Mexico she published a letter taking abstruse issue with a sermon preached decades before by the famous Portuguese Jesuit

Figure 4.1 Portrait of Sor Juana Inés de la Cruz, 1750.
This portrait of Sor Juana was done by one of Mexico's most famous painters, Miguel Cabrera (1695–1768), the official painter of the Archbishop of Mexico. The nun sits surrounded by the emblems of her literary life, including quill pens, inkwell, and an open volume from her enormous library. In the original portrait, the viewer can discern a host of classical authors lining the shelves, including Hippocrates, Virgil, and Cicero.
Source: Schalkwijk/Art Resource, N.Y.

Antonio Vieira. Her casual way with the rules of the religious life, her flirtings with heresy, her many writings in secular forms with intimations of understanding of love inappropriate to her profession had made her many enemies, but they could do nothing while the marquis of Laguna and his lady were on hand to protect her. Now they closed in. In 1694 she was forced formally to renounce all writing and humane studies and to relinquish her library and collection of scientific instruments. In 1695 she devotedly cared for her sisters in the convent during an epidemic, caught the disease, and died.

$$\boxed{25}$$

ANNA BIJNS

"Unyoked Is Best! Happy the Woman without a Man"

Anna Bijns* (1494–1575) was a Flemish poet who lived in Antwerp, taught in a Catholic school in that city, wrote biting criticism of Martin Luther and the Protestant Reformation, and in her many works helped shape the Dutch language. The impact of Luther, and Protestantism more generally, on the lives of women has been the subject of much debate. Luther opposed nunneries and monasticism, believing that it was the natural duty of all women to marry and bear children. At the same time, he encouraged a level of reciprocal love and respect in marriage that was less emphasized in Catholicism. The Protestant translations of the Bible from Latin also opened a pathway for individuals, including educated women, to participate in the religious life, though not as nuns. Whether or not the sentiments of this poem are more Catholic than Protestant, are they more European than Chinese? Why or why not?

Thinking Historically

No one should imagine that the ideas conveyed in this poem were typical or representative of European thought in the sixteenth century. This was obviously an extreme view that ran counter to traditional and commonly accepted ideas. Note how some phrases of the poem convey the recognition that most people will disagree with the sentiments being expressed.

*bynz

Anna Bijns, "Unyoked Is Best," trans. Kristiaan P. G. Aercke, in *Women and Writers of the Renaissance and Reformation*, ed. Katharina M. Wilson (Athens: The University of Georgia Press, 1987), 382–83.

When we are comparing documents from different cultures, we must always try to understand how representative they are of the views of the larger population. The Miu family document (selection 21) expresses the views of a single family, but lineage regulations were common in sixteenth-century China, and their ubiquity reflected an even greater consensus on the importance of the family. Anna Bijns's poem is a personal view that expresses a minority opinion. But in what sense is this a European, rather than Chinese, minority view? What sort of extreme minority views might Southeast Asian or European-American cultures produce? Do you think Anna Bijns's view might appeal to more people today than it did in the sixteenth century? If so, why?

How good to be a woman, how much better to be a man!
Maidens and wenches, remember the lesson you're about to hear.
Don't hurtle yourself into marriage far too soon.
The saying goes: "Where's your spouse? Where's your honor?"
But one who earns her board and clothes
Shouldn't scurry to suffer a man's rod.
So much for my advice, because I suspect —
Nay, see it sadly proven day by day —
'T happens all the time!
However rich in goods a girl might be,
Her marriage ring will shackle her for life.
If however she stays single
With purity and spotlessness foremost,
Then she is lord as well as lady, Fantastic, not?
Though wedlock I do not decry:
Unyoked is best! Happy the woman without a man.

Fine girls turning into loathly hags —
'Tis true! Poor sluts! Poor tramps! Cruel marriage!
Which makes me deaf to wedding bells.
Huh! First they marry the guy, luckless dears,
Thinking their love just too hot to cool.
Well, they're sorry and sad within a single year.
Wedlock's burden is far too heavy.
They know best whom it harnessed.
So often is a wife distressed, afraid.
When after troubles hither and thither he goes
In search of dice and liquor, night and day,
She'll curse herself for that initial "yes."
So, beware ere you begin.
Just listen, don't get yourself into it.
Unyoked is best! Happy the woman without a man.

A man oft comes home all drunk and pissed
Just when his wife had worked her fingers to the bone
(So many chores to keep a decent house!),
But if she wants to get in a word or two,
She gets to taste his fist — no more.
And that besotted keg she is supposed to obey?
Why, yelling and scolding is all she gets,
Such are his ways — and hapless his victim.
And if the nymphs of Venus he chooses to frequent,
What hearty welcome will await him home.
Maidens, young ladies: learn from another's doom,
Ere you, too, end up in fetters and chains,
Please don't argue with me on this,
No matter who contradicts, I stick to it:
Unyoked is best! Happy the woman without a man.

A single lady has a single income,
But likewise, isn't bothered by another's whims.
And I think: that freedom is worth a lot.
Who'll scoff at her, regardless what she does,
And though every penny she makes herself,
Just think of how much less she spends!
An independent lady is an extraordinary prize —
All right, of a man's boon she is deprived,
But she's lord and lady of her very own hearth.
To do one's business and no explaining sure is lots of fun!
Go to bed when she list,[1] rise when she list, all as she will,
And no one to comment! Grab tight your independence then.
Freedom is such a blessed thing.
To all girls: though the right Guy might come along:
Unyoked is best! Happy the woman without a man.

Regardless of the fortune a woman might bring,
Many men consider her a slave, that's all.
Don't let a honeyed tongue catch you off guard,
Refrain from gulping it all down. Let them rave,
For, I guess, decent men resemble white ravens.
Abandon the airy castles they will build for you.
Once their tongue has limed[2] a bird:
Bye bye love — and love just flies away.
To women marriage comes to mean betrayal

[1]Wants. [Ed.]
[2]Caught. [Ed.]

And the condemnation to a very awful fate.
All her own is spent, her lord impossible to bear.
It's *peine forte et dure*[3] instead of fun and games.
Oft it was the money, and not the man
Which goaded so many into their fate.
Unyoked is best! Happy the woman without a man.

[3]Long and forceful punishment; a form of torture whereby the victim was slowly crushed by heaping rocks on a board laid over his or her body. [Ed.]

26

MARY JO MAYNES
AND ANN WALTNER

Women and Marriage in Europe and China

This article is the product of a rich collaboration between historians of China and Europe who show us how a study of women and marriage is anything but peripheral to a study of these areas. Rather it can help us answer a major historical question: How do we explain the dramatic rise of Western Europe after 1500, especially in the wake of prodigious Chinese growth that continued into the sixteenth century?

The authors begin by comparing the role of religion, the state, and the family in setting marriage patterns in both China and Europe. Did Christianity allow European women more independence than Confucianism allowed women in China? In which society was the patriarchal family more powerful, and what was the relative impact of patriarchy on women in both societies? How did the age and rate at which people married in each society compare? What was the importance of Chinese concubinage and Christian ideals of chastity?

Thinking Historically

The authors' questions about marriage in Europe and China lead finally to a consideration of one of the most frequently asked comparative questions: Why did Europe industrialize before China? Do the dif-

Mary Jo Maynes and Ann Waltner, "Childhood, Youth, and the Female Life Cycle: Women's Life-Cycle Transitions in a World-Historical Perspective: Comparing Marriage in China and Europe," *Journal of Women's History*, 12, no. 4 (Winter 2001), 11–19.

ferent European and Chinese marriage patterns answer this question? What other comparative questions would we have to ask to arrive at a full answer?

Comparing Marriage Cross-Culturally

A number of years ago, we were involved in organizing a comparative historical conference on gender and kinship (our areas of specialization are Chinese and European family and women's history). Conversations that began at the conference resulted in a collection of coedited articles, but they also spurred the two of us to collaboratively teach a world history course in which family and women's history play key roles. We introduce students in that course to historical comparison by talking about marriage. In particular, we begin with a pointed comparison between the history of marriage in China and Europe based on research presented at the kinship conference.

Beginning in the late 1500s, women in northern Italy began to appeal to legal courts run by the Catholic Church when they got into disputes with their families over arranged marriages. Within the early modern Italy family system the father held a great deal of authority over his children and it was usual for the parents to determine when and whom sons and daughters married. Women and children held little power in comparison with adult men. But the Catholic Church's insistence that both parties enter into the marriage willingly gave some women an out — namely, an appeal to the Church court, claiming that the marriage their family wanted was being forced upon them without their consent. Surprisingly, these young women often won their cases against their fathers. In early modern China, by way of contrast, state, religion, and family were bound together under the veil of Confucianism. Paternal authority echoed and reinforced the political and the moral order. Religious institutions could rarely be called upon to intervene in family disputes. Therefore, young women (or young men, for that matter) had no clearly established institutional recourse in situations of unwanted marriage. So, despite the fact that paternal power was very strong in both early modern Italy and early modern China, specific institutional differences put young women at the moment of marriage in somewhat different positions.

We began with the presumption that however different the institution of "marriage" was in Italy and China, it nevertheless offered enough similarities that it made sense to speak comparatively about a category called "marriage." Parallels in the two cultures between the institution of marriage and the moment in the woman's life course that it represented make comparison useful. Nevertheless, this particular comparison also isolates some of the variable features of marriage systems that are especially significant in addressing gender relations in a world-historical context. In China, the rules of family formation and family governance were generally enforced within the bounds of each extended family group. State and religious influences were felt only indirectly through family leaders as mediators or enforcers of state and religious law. Throughout Europe, beginning in the Middle Ages, the institution of marriage was altered first by the effort of the Catholic Church to wrest some control over marriage from the family by defining it as a sacrament, and then eventually by the struggle between churches and state authorities to regulate families.

This contest among church, state, and family authorities over marriage decisions turns out to have been a particular feature of European history that had consequences for many aspects of social life. A focus on the moment of marriage presents special opportunities for understanding connections between the operation of gender relations in everyday life and in the realm of broader political developments. Marriage is a familial institution, of course, but, to varying degrees, political authorities also have a stake in it because of its implications for property transfer, reproduction, religion, and morality — in short, significant aspects of the social order. In this essay, we compare one dimension of marriage — its timing in a woman's life cycle — in two contexts, Europe and China. We argue that variations in marriage timing have world-historical implications. We examine how a woman's status and situation shifted at marriage and then suggest some implications of comparative differences in the timing and circumstances of this change of status.

The Moment of Marriage in European History

One striking peculiarity of Central and Western European history between 1600 and 1850 was the relatively late age at first marriage for men and women compared with other regions of the world. The so-called "Western European marriage pattern" was marked by relatively late marriage — that is, relative to other regions of the world where some form of marriage usually occurred around the time of puberty. In much of Europe, in contrast, men did not typically marry until their late twenties and women their mid-twenties. This practice of relatively late marriage was closely connected with the custom of delaying marriage until the couple commanded sufficient resources to raise a family. For artisans this traditionally meant having a shop and master status. For merchants it entailed saving capital to begin a business. In the case of peasant couples, this meant having a house and land and basic farming equipment. It was the responsibility of the family and the community to oversee courtship, betrothal, and marriage to assure that these conditions were met. This phenomenon was also rooted in the common practice of neolocality — the expectation that a bride and groom would set up their own household at or soon after marriage. This "delayed" marriage has attracted the attention of European historical demographers. The delay of marriage meant, quite significantly, that most European women did not begin to have children until their twenties. But this marriage pattern also has significance in other realms as well. In particular, young people of both sexes experienced a relatively long hiatus between puberty and marriage.

Unmarried European youth played a distinctive role in economic, social, cultural, and political life through such institutions as guilds, village youth groups, and universities. For the most part, historians' attention to European youth has centered on young men. Major works on the history of youth in Europe, like theories of adolescent development, tend to center on the male experience as normative. Only when gender differences in youth are recognized and the history of young women is written will the broad historical significance of the European marriage pattern become clear. Contrast between European demographic history and that of other world regions suggests a comparative pattern of particular significance for girls: Delayed marriage and childbearing meant that teenage girls were available for employment outside the familial household (either natal or marital) to a degree uncommon elsewhere. Household divisions of labor according to age and gender created constant demand for servants on larger farms; typically, unmarried youth who could be hired in from neighboring farms as servants filled this role. A period of service in a farm household, as an apprentice, or as a domestic servant in an urban household characterized male and female European youth in the lifecycle phase preceding marriage. Historians have noted but never fully explored the role young women played in European economic development, and in particular their role in the early industrial labor force.

Late marriage had gender-specific cultural ramifications as well. Whereas it was considered normal and even appropriate for teenage men to be initiated into heterosexual intercourse at brothels, in most regions of Europe, young women were expected to remain chaste until marriage. Delay of marriage heightened anxiety over unmarried women's sexuality, especially the dangers to which young women were increasingly exposed as the locus of their labor shifted from home and village to factory and city. Premarital or extramarital sexuality was uncommon, and was rigorously policed especially in the period following the religious upheavals of the Reformation in the sixteenth century. In rural areas, church and community, in addition to the family, exerted control over sexuality. Moreover, the unmarried male youth cohort of many village communities often served, in effect, as "morals police," enforcing local customs. These young men regulated courtship rituals,

organized dances that young people went to, and oversaw the formation of couples. Sometimes, judging and public shaming by the youth
group was the fate of couples who were mismatched by age or wealth
or who violated sexual taboos. Some customs, at least symbolically,
punished young men from far away who married local women, removing them from the marriage pool. Often, such a bridegroom had to pay
for drinks in each village that the bridal couple passed through as they
moved from the bride's parish church to their new abode — the longer
the distance, the more expensive his bill.

Once married, a couple would usually begin having children immediately. Demographic evidence suggests that for most of Central and
Western Europe there was virtually no practice of contraception among
lower classes prior to the middle of the nineteenth century. Women had
babies about every two years (more or less frequently according to region and depending on such local customs as breast-feeding length and
intercourse taboos). Even though completed family sizes could be large
by modern standards, the number of children most women bore was
still less than if they had married in their teens. And prevailing high
mortality rates further reduced the number of children who survived to
adulthood.

The Moment of Marriage in Chinese History

The Chinese marriage system was traditionally characterized by early
age at marriage, nearly universal marriage for women, virilocal residence (a newly married couple resided with the groom's parents), concubinage for elite men, and norms that discouraged widow remarriage.
From the sixteenth through twentieth centuries, Chinese men and
women married much younger on average than did their European
counterparts — late teens or early twenties for women and a bit later
for men. A bride typically moved to her husband's family home, which
was often in a different village from her own. The moment of marriage
not only meant that a girl would leave her parents but that she would
also leave her network of kin and friends, all that was familiar. Families
chose marriage partners, and a matchmaker negotiated the arrangements. Nothing resembling courtship existed; the bride and groom
would often first meet on their wedding day.

Because a newly married Chinese couple would typically reside in
an already-existing household, it was not necessary for an artisan to become established, a merchant to accumulate capital, or a peasant to
own a farm before marrying. Newly married couples participated in
ongoing domestic and economic enterprises that already supported the
groom's family. New households were eventually established by a
process of household division, which typically happened at the death of

the father rather than the moment of marriage (although it could happen at other points in the family cycle as well).

Daughters were groomed from birth for marriage. They were taught skills appropriate to their social class or the social class into which their parents aspired to marry them. (In the ideal Chinese marriage, the groom was in fact supposed to be of slightly higher social status than the bride.) The feet of upper-class girls (and some who were not upper class) were bound, since Chinese men found this erotic. Bound feet also symbolically, if not actually, restricted upper-class women's movement. Thus bound feet simultaneously enhanced the sexual desirability of upper-class women and served to contain their sexuality within domestic bounds.

Virtually all Chinese girls became brides, though not all of them married as principal wives. (This contrasts with the European pattern where a substantial minority of women in most regions never married.) Upper-class men might take one or more concubines in addition to a principal wife. The relationship between a man and his concubine was recognized legally and ritually, and children born of these unions were legitimate. A wife had very secure status: divorce was almost nonexistent. A concubine's status, in contrast, was much more tenuous. She could be expelled at the whim of her "husband"; her only real protection was community sentiment. Although only a small percentage of Chinese marriages (no more than 5 percent) involved concubines, the practice remained an important structural feature of the Chinese marriage system until the twentieth century. Concubinage also provides a partial explanation of why, despite the fact that marriage was nearly universal for women, a substantial proportion of men (perhaps as high as 10 percent) never married. Also contributing to this apparent anomaly was the practice of sex-selective infanticide, a common practice that discriminated against girl babies and, ultimately, reduced the number of potential brides.

Once married, Chinese couples began to have children almost immediately, generally spacing births at longer intervals than did European couples. The reasons for this are not yet completely understood, although infanticide, extended breast-feeding, and the fairly large number of days on which sexual intercourse was forbidden all seem to have played a role in lowering Chinese family size.

Early marriage in China meant that the category of "youth," which has been so significant for European social and economic history, has no precise counterpart in Chinese history. Young Chinese women labored, to be sure, but the location of their work was domestic — either in the household of their father or husband. Female servants existed in China, but their servitude was normally of longer duration than the life-cycle servitude common in Europe. The domestic location of young women's labor in the Chinese context also had implications for the particular ways in which Chinese industries were organized, as we suggest below.

Patterns of Marriage in Europe and China

To sum up, then, there are differences of both timing of and residency before and after marriage that are particularly germane to the comparative history of young women. As demographic historians James Z. Lee and Wang Feng also have argued, "in China, females have always married universally and early . . . in contrast to female marriage in Western Europe, which occurred late or not at all." Whereas, in the nineteenth century, all but 20 percent of young Chinese women were married by age twenty, among European populations, between 60 and 80 percent of young women remained single at this age. In traditional China, only 1 or 2 percent of women remained unmarried at age thirty, whereas between 15 and 25 percent of thirty-year-old Western European women were still single. (For men, the differences though in the same direction are far less stark.) As for residence, in the Western European neolocal pattern, norms and practices in many regions resulted in a pattern whereby newly married couples moved into a separate household at marriage; but concomitant with this was their delaying marriage until they could afford a new household. In China, newly married couples generally resided in the groom's father's household. In Western Europe, the majority of postpubescent young men and many young women left home in their teenage years for a period of employment. In the early modern era, such employment was often as a servant or apprentice in either a craft or a farm household, but, over time, that employment was increasingly likely to be in a nondomestic work setting, such as a factory, store, or other urban enterprise. "Youth" was a distinctive phase in the life course of young men and increasingly of young women in Europe, although there were important gender distinctions. Such a period of postpubescent semiautonomy from parental households did not exist for Chinese youth, especially not for young women in traditional China. Young men more typically remained in their father's household and young women moved at marriage in their late teens from their own father's household to that of their husband's father.

Comparing the Moment of Marriage: Implications and Cautions

We would now like to discuss some of the world-historical implications of this important (if crude) comparison in the marriage systems of China and Western Europe. There are obviously many possible realms for investigation. For example, these patterns imply differences in young women's education, intergenerational relationships among women (especially between mothers and daughters and mothers-in-law and daughters-in-law), and household power relations. Here, we restrict our discussion to two areas of undoubted world-historical significance, namely economic development, on the one hand, and sexuality and reproduction, on the other.

The question of why the Industrial Revolution, or, alternatively, the emergence of industrial capitalism, occurred first in Europe, has been and remains salient for both European and world historians. R. Bin Wong explores this question in his innovative comparative study of economic development in Europe and China. Wong argues that there were rough parallels in the dynamics linking demographic expansion and economic growth in China and Europe until the nineteenth century. Both economies were expanding on the basis of growth of rural industrial enterprises in which peasant families supplemented agricultural work and income with part-time industrial production. What the Chinese case demonstrates, Wong argues, is that this so-called protoindustrial form of development may be viewed as an alternative route to industrialization rather than merely a precursor of factory production. Indeed, Charles Tilly has suggested that a prescient contemporary observer of the European economy in 1750 would likely have predicted such a future — that is "a countryside with a growing proletariat working in both agriculture and manufacturing."

While Wong's study is devoted to comparative examination of the economic roots and implications of varying paths to industrial development, he also connects economic and demographic growth. In particular, Wong mentions the link between marriage and economic opportunity: "in both China and Europe, rural industry supported lower age at marriage and higher proportions of ever married than would have been plausible in its absence. This does not mean that ages at marriage dropped in Europe when rural industry appeared, but the possibility was present. For China, the development of rural industry may not have lowered ages at marriage or raised proportions married as much as it allowed previous practices of relatively low ages at marriage and high proportions of women ever married to continue." What Wong does not explore is the way in which these "previous practices" that connected the low age at marriage with both virilocality and a relatively high commitment to the domestic containment of daughters and wives also had implications for patterns of economic development. In a comparative account of why Chinese industrial development relied heavily on domestic production, the fact that the young female labor force in China was to an extent far greater than that of Europe both married and "tied" to the male-headed household needs to be part of the story. This pattern of female marriage and residency held implications for entrepreneurial choice that helped to determine the different paths toward industrialization in Europe and China. World-historical comparison, taking into account aspects of gender relations and marriage and kinship systems, highlights their possible significance for economic development, a significance that has not been given proper attention by economic historians. Indeed, it is arguable that the family and marital status of the young women who played so significant a role in the workforce (especially those employed in the textile industry, which was key to early industrial development in both Europe and China) were major factors in the varying paths to development followed in China and Europe in the centuries of protoindustrial growth and industrialization.

A second set of implications concerns sexuality and reproduction. Again, we are aided by another recent study, which, in a fashion parallel to Wong's, uses Chinese historical evidence to call into question generalizations about historical development based on a European model. In their book on Chinese demographic history, Lee and Wang argue against the hegemonic Malthusian (mis)understandings according to which the family and population history to China has been seen as an example of a society's failure to curb population growth by any means other than recurrent disaster (by "positive" rather than "preventive" checks in Malthusian terms). They note the important difference in marriage systems that we have just described, but they dispute conclusions too often drawn from the Chinese historical pattern concerning overpopulation. Instead, according to Lee and Wang "persistently high nuptiality . . . did not inflate Chinese fertility, because of . . . the low level of fertility within marriage."

This second example points to another important realm for which the age at which women marry has great consequences. But the findings reported by Lee and Wang also caution scholars against leaping to comparative conclusions about one society on the basis of models established in another, even while their claims still suggest the value of comparison. We should not presume that since Chinese women were married universally and young, they therefore had more children or devoted a greater proportion of their time and energy to childbearing and child rearing than did their later married counterparts in Europe. Although the evidence is far from definitive, it nevertheless indicates that total marital fertility may have been somewhat lower in China than in Europe until the late nineteenth or early twentieth centuries. The factors in China that produced this pattern included relatively high rates of infanticide, especially of female infants, as well as different beliefs and practices about child care and sexuality. For example, babies were apparently breast-fed longer in China than in Europe (a pattern in turn related to the domestic location of women's work), which would have both increased infants' chances of survival and also lengthened the intervals between births. In the realm of sexuality, pertinent factors include both prescriptions for men against overly frequent intercourse, and coresidence with a parental generation whose vigilance included policing young couples' sexual behavior.

These two examples are meant to suggest how looking at women's life cycles comparatively both enhances our understanding of the implications of varying patterns for women's history and also suggests the very broad ramifications, indeed world-historical significance, of different ways of institutionalizing the female life cycle.

REFLECTIONS

Women's history has entered the mainstream during the last few decades. An older view, still pervasive in the academic world forty years ago, assumed women's history was adequately covered by general history, which was largely the story of the exploits of men. Political, military, and diplomatic history took precedence over historical fields seen as less resolutely masculine, such as social and cultural history.

Today, women's history not only stands independently in college and university curriculums, it has helped open doors to a wide range of new fields in social history — gender, family, childhood, sexuality, domesticity, and health, to name but a few. These new research fields have also contributed significantly to issues of general history, as the authors of the last reading show. In fact, the growth and development of new fields of research and teaching in social and cultural history have had the effect of relegating the study of presidents, wars, and treaties to the periphery of the profession. The 2006 meeting of the American Historical Association, where historians came together to talk about their work, had more sessions on women, gender, and sexuality than on politics, diplomacy, military, war, World War I, World War II, and the American Civil War, combined.

Some more traditional historians complain that this is a fad, and that sooner or later the profession will get back to the more "important" topics. But others respond that it is hard to think of anything more important than the history of half of humanity or the history of human health. This debate leads to questions about the importance of particular individuals in history. Who had a greater impact, for instance, thirtieth U.S. president Calvin Coolidge (1872–1933) or Marie Curie (1867–1934), who won the Nobel Prize for isolating radium for therapeutic purposes?

What role do individuals play on the historical canvas anyway? A president or Nobel laureate works according to social norms, available resources, supporting institutions, and the work of hundreds or thousands of others, living and dead. Forty years ago, historians put greater stress on institutions, movements, and perceived forces than they do today. In recent years, historians have looked for the "agency" of individuals and groups, perhaps in an effort to see how people can have an impact on their world. The power of slavery and the impact of imperialism have been balanced with the tales of slave revolts, the stories of successful collaborators, adapters, and resisters, and the voices of slaves and indigenous and colonized peoples. We see this in the study of women's history as well.

We began this chapter with the observation that we live in a patriarchy. Even if we are dismantling it in the twenty-first century, it was a powerful force between 1500 and 1800: a historical force, not natural, but a product of the urban revolution, perhaps, beginning about five thousand years ago. It is useful to understand its causes, describe its workings, and relate its history. But does doing so only hamper our capacity for change? Does it ignore the stories of women who have made a difference? Conversely, are women empowered, humanity enriched, by knowing how individual women were able to work within the system, secure their needs, engage, negotiate, compromise? Do the stories of a Sor Juana or the poems of an Anna Bijns inspire us? Or do they misrepresent the past and, by consequence, delude us?

Perhaps there are no easy answers to those questions, but our exercise in comparison might come in handy. The rich and varied detail of the human past should warn us against absolute declarations. We may emphasize patriarchy or emphasize women's power, but we would be foolish to deny either. In consequence, it may be most useful to ask more specific questions and to compare. Can women own property here? Is there more restriction on women's movement in this society or that? Only then can we begin to understand why here and not there, why then and not now. And only then can we use our understanding of the past to improve the present.

5

The Scientific Revolution

Europe, the Ottoman Empire, China, Japan, and the Americas, 1600–1800

HISTORICAL CONTEXT

Modern life is unthinkable apart from science. We surround ourselves with its products, from cars and computers to telephones and televisions; we are dependent on its institutions — hospitals, universities, and research laboratories; and we have internalized the methods and procedures of science in every aspect of our daily lives, from balancing checkbooks to counting calories. Even on social and humanitarian questions, the scientific method has become almost the exclusive model of knowledge in modern society.

We can trace the scientific focus of modern society to the "scientific revolution" of the seventeenth century. The seventeenth-century scientific revolution was a European phenomenon, with such notables as Nicolas Copernicus (1473–1543) in Poland, Galileo Galilei (1564–1642) in Tuscany, and Isaac Newton (1642–1727) in England. But it was also a global event, prompted initially by Europe's new knowledge of Asia, Africa, and the Americas, and ultimately spread as a universal method for understanding and manipulating the world.

What was the scientific revolution? How revolutionary was it? How similar, or different, was European science from that practiced elsewhere in the world? And how much did the European revolution affect scientific traditions elsewhere? These are some of the issues we will study in this chapter.

THINKING HISTORICALLY
Distinguishing Change from Revolution

The world is always changing; it always has been changing. Sometimes, however, the change seems so formidable, extensive, important, or quick that we use the term *revolution*. In fact, we will use the term in this and the next two chapters. In this chapter we will examine what historians call the scientific revolution. The next chapter will deal with political revolutions and the chapter following with the industrial revolution. In each of these cases there are some historians who object that the changes were not really revolutionary, that they were more gradual or limited. Thus, we ask the question, how do we distinguish between mere change and revolutionary change?

In this chapter you will be asked, how revolutionary were the changes that are often called the scientific revolution? The point, however, is not to get your vote, pro or con, but to get you to think about how you might answer such a question. Do we, for instance, compare "the before" with "the after" and then somehow divide by the time it took to get from one to the other? Do we look at what people said at the time about how things were changing? Are we gauging speed of change or extent of change? What makes things change at different speeds? What constitutes a revolution?

$$27$$

FRANKLIN LE VAN BAUMER
The Scientific Revolution in the West

In this selection, an intellectual historian of Europe summarizes the scientific revolution. Without enumerating the achievements of European science in the seventeenth century, Baumer finds evidence of the "revolutionary" nature of the transformation by referring to the popularity of scientific societies and the powerful appeal of the new scien-

Franklin Le Van Baumer, "The Scientific Revolution in the West," in *Main Currents of Western Thought*, ed. F. Le Van Baumer (New Haven: Yale University Press, 1978).

tific mentality. How does he define the scientific revolution? How does he date it? Why does he believe that it was a revolution?

Thinking Historically

What intellectual or cultural changes did the scientific revolution bring about, according to Baumer? What ideas did Europeans have about nature before the scientific revolution? Baumer suggests that we can see the scientific revolution in new intellectual institutions, educational reforms, and new careers. What were these changes? How rapid, extensive, or important were they?

In his book *The Origins of Modern Science* Professor [Herbert] Butterfield of Cambridge writes that the "scientific revolution" of the sixteenth and seventeenth centuries "outshines everything since the rise of Christianity and reduces the Renaissance and Reformation to the rank of mere episodes, mere internal displacements, within the system of medieval Christendom." "It looms so large as the real origin both of the modern world and of the modern mentality that our customary periodisation of European history has become an anachronism and an encumbrance." This view can no longer be seriously questioned. The scientific achievements of the century and a half between the publication of Copernicus's *De Revolutionibus Orbium Celestium* (1543) and Newton's *Principia* (1687) marked the opening of a new period of intellectual and cultural life in the West, which I shall call the Age of Science. What chiefly distinguished this age from its predecessor was that science — meaning by science a body of knowledge, a method, an attitude of mind, a metaphysic (to be described below) — became the directive force of Western civilization, displacing theology and antique letters. Science made the world of the spirit, of Platonic Ideas, seem unreliable and dim by comparison with the material world. In the seventeenth century it drove revealed Christianity out of the physical universe into the region of history and private morals; to an ever growing number of people in the two succeeding centuries it made religion seem outmoded even there. Science invaded the schools, imposed literary canons, altered the world-picture of the philosophers, suggested new techniques to the social theorists. It changed profoundly man's attitude toward custom and tradition, enabling him to declare his independence of the past, to look down condescendingly upon the "ancients," and to envisage a rosy future. The Age of Science made the intoxicating discovery that melioration depends, not upon "change from within" (St. Paul's birth of the new man), but upon "change from without" (scientific and social mechanics).

1

Some people will perhaps object that there was no such thing as "scientific revolution" in the sixteenth and seventeenth centuries. They will say that history does not work that way, that the new science was not "revolutionary," but the cumulative effect of centuries of trial and error among scientists. But if by "scientific revolution" is meant the occasion when science became a real intellectual and cultural force in the West, this objection must surely evaporate. The evidence is rather overwhelming that sometime between 1543 and 1687, certainly by the late seventeenth century, science captured the interest of the intellectuals and upper classes. Francis Bacon's ringing of a bell to call the wits of Europe together to advance scientific learning did not go unheeded. Note the creation of new intellectual institutions to provide a home for science — the *Academia del Cimento* at Florence (1661), the Royal Society at London (1662), the *Académie des Sciences* at Paris (1666), the Berlin Academy (1700), to mention only the most important. These scientific academies signified the advent of science as an organized activity. Note the appearance of a literature of popular science, of which Fontenelle's *Plurality of Worlds* is only one example, and of popular lectures on scientific subjects. Note the movement for educational reform sponsored by Bacon and the Czech John Amos Comenius, who denounced the traditional education for its exclusive emphasis upon "words rather than things" (literature rather than nature itself). Evidently, by the end of the seventeenth century the prejudice against "mechanical" studies as belonging to practical rather than high mental life had all but disappeared. Bacon complained in 1605 that "matters mechanical" were esteemed "a kind of dishonour unto learning to descend to inquiry or meditation upon." But the Royal Society included in its roster a number of ecclesiastics and men of fashion. The second marquis of Worcester maintained a laboratory and published a book of inventions in 1663. Not a few men appear to have been "converted" from an ecclesiastical to a scientific career, and, as Butterfield notes, to have carried the gospel into the byways, with all the zest of the early Christian missionaries.

To account historically for the scientific revolution is no easy task. The problem becomes somewhat more manageable, however, if we exclude from the discussion the specific discoveries of the scientists. Only the internal history of science can explain how Harvey, for example, discovered the circulation of the blood, or Newton the universal law of gravitation.

But certain extrascientific factors were plainly instrumental in causing so many people to be simultaneously interested in "nature," and, moreover, to think about nature in the way they did. Professor [Alfred North] Whitehead reminds us that one of these factors was medieval Christianity itself and medieval scholasticism. Medieval Christianity sponsored the Greek, as opposed to the primitive, idea of a rationally ordered universe which made the orderly investigation of nature seem possible. Scholasticism trained western intellectuals in exact thinking. The Renaissance and the Protestant Reformation also prepared the ground for the scientific revolution — not by design, but as an indirect consequence of their thinking. . . . [H]umanism and Protestantism represented a movement toward the concrete. Erasmus preferred ethics to the metaphysical debates of the philosophers and theologians. The Protestants reduced the miraculous element in institutional Christianity and emphasized labor in a worldly calling. Furthermore, by attacking scholastic theology with which Aristotle was bound up, they made it easier for scientists to think about physics and astronomy in un-Aristotelian terms. As [philosopher] E. A. Burtt has noted of Copernicus, these men lived in a mental climate in which people generally were seeking new centers of reference. Copernicus, the architect of the heliocentric theory of the universe, was a contemporary of Luther and Archbishop Cranmer, who moved the religious center from Rome to Wittenberg and Canterbury. In the sixteenth century the economic center of gravity was similarly shifting from the Mediterranean to the English Channel and the Atlantic Ocean. The revival of ancient philosophies and ancient texts at the Renaissance also sharpened the scientific appetite. The Platonic and Phythagorean revival in fifteenth-century Italy undoubtedly did a good deal to accustom scientists to think of the universe in mathematical, quantitative terms. The translation of Galen and Archimedes worked the last rich vein of ancient science, and made it abundantly clear that the ancients had frequently disagreed on fundamentals, thus necessitating independent investigation. By their enthusiasm for natural beauty, the humanists helped to remove from nature the medieval stigma of sin, and thus to make possible the confident pronouncement of the scientific movement that God's Word could be read not only in the Bible but in the great book of nature.

But no one of these factors, nor all of them together, could have produced the scientific revolution. One is instantly reminded of Bacon's statement that "by the distant voyages and travels which have become frequent in our times, many things in nature have been laid open and discovered which may let in new light upon philosophy." The expansion of Europe, and increased travel in Europe itself, not only stimulated interest in nature but opened up to the West the vision of a "Kingdom of Man" upon earth. Much of Bacon's imagery was borrowed from the geographical discoveries: He aspired to be the Columbus of a new intellectual world, to sail through the Pillars of Hercules (symbol of the old knowledge) into the Atlantic Ocean in search of new and more useful knowledge. Bacon, however, failed to detect the coincidence of the scientific revolution with commercial prosperity and the rise of the middle class. Doubtless, the Marxist Professor Hessen greatly oversimplified when he wrote that "Newton was the typical representative of the rising bourgeoisie, and in his philosophy he embodies the characteristic features of his class." The theoretical scientists had mixed motives. Along with a concern for technology, they pursued truth for its own sake, and they sought God in his great creation. All the same, it is not stretching the imagination too far to see a rough correspondence between the mechanical universe of the seventeenth-century philosophers and the bourgeois desire for rational, predictable order. Science and business were a two-way street. If science affected business, so did business affect science — by its businesslike temper and its quantitative thinking, by its interest in "matter" and the rational control of matter.

2

The scientific revolution gave birth to a new conception of knowledge, a new methodology, and a new worldview substantially different from the old Aristotelian-Christian worldview. . . .

Knowledge now meant exact knowledge: what you know for certain, and not what may possibly or even probably be. Knowledge is what can be clearly apprehended by the mind, or measured by mathematics, or demonstrated by experiment. Galileo came close to saying this when he declared that without mathematics "it is impossible to comprehend a single word of (the great book of the universe);" likewise Descartes when he wrote that "we ought never to allow ourselves to be persuaded of the truth of anything unless on the evidence of our Reason." The distinction between "primary" and "secondary qualities" in seventeenth-century metaphysics carried the same implication. To Galileo, Descartes, and Robert Boyle those mathematical qualities that inhered in objects (size, weight, position, etc.) were "primary," i.e., matters of real knowledge; whereas all the other qualities that our senses tell us are in objects (color, odor, taste, etc.) were "secondary," less real because less amenable to measurement. The inference of all this is plain: Knowledge pertains to "natural philosophy" and possibly social theory, but not to theology or the older philosophy or poetry which involve opinion, belief, faith, but not knowledge. The Royal Society actually undertook to renovate the English language, by excluding from it metaphors and pulpit eloquence which conveyed no precise meaning. The "enthusiasm" of the religious man became suspect as did the "sixth sense" of the poet who could convey pleasure but not knowledge.

The odd thing about the scientific revolution is that for all its avowed distrust of hypotheses and systems, it created its own system of nature, or worldview. "I perceive," says the "Countess" in Fontenelle's popular dialogue of 1686, "Philosophy is now become very Mechanical." "I value (this universe) the more since I know it resembles a Watch, and the whole order of Nature the more plain and easy it is, to me it appears the more admirable." Descartes and other philosophers of science in the seventeenth century constructed a mechanical universe which resembled the machines — watches, pendulum clocks, steam engines — currently being built by scientists and artisans. However, it was not the observation of actual machines but the new astronomy and physics that made it possible to picture the universe in this way. The "Copernican revolution" destroyed Aristotle's "celestial world" of planets and stars which, because they were formed of a subtle substance having no weight, behaved differently from bodies on earth and in the "sublunary world." The new laws of motion formulated by a succession of physicists from Kepler to Newton explained the movement of bodies, both celestial and terrestrial, entirely on mechanical and mathematical principles. According to the law of inertia, the "natural" motion of bodies was in a straight line out into Euclidean space. The planets were pulled into their curvilinear orbits by gravitation which could operate at tremendous distances, and which varied inversely as the square of the distance.

Thus, the universe pictured by Fontenelle's Countess was very different from that of Dante in the thirteenth, or Richard Hooker in the sixteenth century. Gone was the Aristotelian-Christian universe of purposes, forms, and final causes. Gone were the spirits and intelligences which had been required to push the skies daily around the earth. The fundamental features of the new universe were numbers (mathematical quantities) and invariable laws. It was an economical universe in which nature did nothing in vain and performed its daily tasks without waste. In such a universe the scientist could delight and the bourgeois could live happily ever after — or at least up to the time of Darwin. The fact that nature appeared to have no spiritual purpose — Descartes said that it would continue to exist regardless of whether there were any human beings to think it — was more than compensated for by its dependability. Philosophy had indeed become very mechanical. Descartes kept God to start his machine going, and Newton did what he could to save the doctrine of providence. But for all practical purposes, God had become the First Cause, "very well skilled in mechanics and geometry." And the rage for mechanical explanation soon spread beyond the confines of physics to encompass the biological and social sciences. Thus did Descartes regard animals as a piece of clockwork, Robert Boyle the human body as a "matchless engine."

Under the circumstances, one would logically expect there to have been warfare between science and religion in the seventeenth century. But such was not the case. To be sure, some theologians expressed dismay at the downfall of Aristotelianism, and the Roman Church took steps to suppress Copernicanism when Giordano Bruno interpreted it to mean an infinite universe and a plurality of worlds. But the majority of the scientists and popularizers of science were sincerely religious men — not a few were actually ecclesiastics — who either saw no conflict or else went to some lengths to resolve it. Science itself was commonly regarded as a religious enterprise. . . .

In the final analysis, however, the new thing in seventeenth-century thought was the dethronement of theology from its proud position as the sun of the intellectual universe. Bacon and Descartes and Newton lived in an age that was finding it increasingly difficult to reconcile science and religion. To save the best features of both they effected a shaky compromise. For all practical purposes they eliminated religious purpose from nature — thus allowing science to get on with its work, while leaving religion in control of private belief and morals. By their insistence that religious truth itself must pass the tests of reason and reliable evidence, John Locke and the rationalists further reduced theology's prerogatives. Bacon was prepared to believe the word of God "though our reason be shocked at it." But not Locke: "'I believe because it is impossible,' might," he says, "in a good man, pass for a sally of zeal, but would prove a very ill rule for men to choose their opinions or religion by." Good Christian though Locke might be, his teaching had the effect of playing down the supernatural aspects of religion, of equating religion with simple ethics. . . .

$$28$$

GALILEO GALILEI
Letter to the Grand Duchess Christina

One reason for thinking of European scientific developments in the seventeenth century as a revolution lies in their condemnation by established authority, particularly religious authority. Both Protestants and Catholics condemned the sun-centered model of the universe proposed by Copernicus and modified by Tycho Brahe (1546–1601) and Johannes Kepler (1571–1630). Giordano Bruno, a religious philosopher and Copernican, was burned at the stake in 1600 by the Catholic

Galileo's Letter to the Grand Duchess Christina (1615), in *The Galileo Affair: A Documentary History*, ed. and trans. Maurice A. Finocchiaro (Berkeley and Los Angeles: University of California Press, 1989), 87–90, 114–18.

Church. Galileo was investigated in 1615 and 1616 for work that gave added weight to Copernicus's theory. His use of the telescope revealed more stars than the fixed number seen by the naked eye or shown on the accepted model of the heavenly spheres of the ancient authority, Ptolemy. Galileo, by assuming that the Earth revolved around the sun (and the moon around the Earth), conceived orbits that were neater and closer to what had been observed.

This letter to the Grand Duchess Christina in 1615 shows Galileo already under siege. He had received a letter in 1613 from a supporter, Benedetto Castelli, who had been questioned by Christina (of Lorraine), the mother of the Grand Duke of Tuscany, Cosimo II de' Medici, about Galileo's views. Having left his twenty-year post at the University of Padua, Galileo was in 1613 philosopher and mathematician to the Duchy of Tuscany, and so he was in the delicate and precarious position of receiving notice of his employer's dissatisfaction with his views. This letter is his attempt to explain himself and to prevent the initiation of an inquisition. His efforts were unsuccessful. In 1633 Galileo was tried, condemned, forced to recant his views, and placed under house arrest. (The condemnation was retracted by the papacy in 1992.)

What seem to be Grand Duchess Christina's objections? How does Galileo try to answer them? How convincing would you find Galileo if you were the Grand Duchess?

Thinking Historically

What claims to new discoveries did Galileo make in this letter? In what respect did Galileo claim his work was not new? On balance, what did he perceive to be the differences between himself and his contemporaries? How is his argument "modern" or scientific? Does this letter support Baumer's interpretation of the scientific revolution?

To the Most Serene Ladyship the Grand Duchess Dowager:

As Your Most Serene Highness knows very well, a few years ago I discovered in the heavens many particulars which had been invisible until our time. Because of their novelty, and because of some consequences deriving from them which contradict certain physical propositions[1] commonly accepted in philosophical schools, they roused against

---

[1]In *The Starry Messenger* (Venice, 1610) Galileo had described his discovery, through telescopic observation, of lunar mountains, four satellites of Jupiter (which he named "Medicean planets"), the stellar composition of the Milky Way and of nebulas, and the existence of thousands of previously invisible fixed stars. Within a few years, Galileo added to these his observations of sunspots, the phases of Venus, and Saturn's rings.

me no small number of such professors, as if I had placed these things in heaven with my hands in order to confound nature and the sciences. These people seemed to forget that a multitude of truths contribute to inquiry and to the growth and strength of disciplines rather than to their diminution or destruction, and at the same time they showed greater affection for their own opinions than for the true ones; thus they proceeded to deny and to try to nullify those novelties, about which the senses themselves could have rendered them certain, if they had wanted to look at those novelties carefully. To this end they produced various matters, and they published some writings full of useless discussions and sprinkled with quotations from the Holy Scripture, taken from passages which they do not properly understand and which they inappropriately adduce.[2] . . .

These people are aware that in my astronomical and philosophical studies, on the question of the constitution of the world's parts, I hold that the sun is located at the center of the revolution of the heavenly orbs and does not change place, and that the earth rotates on itself and moves around it. Moreover, they hear how I confirm this view not only by refuting Ptolemy's and Aristotle's arguments, but also by producing many for the other side, especially some pertaining to physical effects whose causes perhaps cannot be determined in any other way, and other astronomical ones dependent on many features of the new celestial discoveries; these discoveries clearly confute the Ptolemaic system, and they agree admirably with this other position and confirm it. Now, these people are perhaps confounded by the known truth of the other

---

[2]Galileo has been notified that Cardinal Bellarmine finds the Copernican theory heretical because the sun must go around the Earth according to Psalm 19:

The heavens declare the glory of God;
. . . .
In them hath he set a tabernacle for the sun,
Which is as a bridegroom coming out of his chamber,
And rejoiceth as a strong man to run a race.
His going forth is from the end of the heaven,
And his circuit unto the ends of it:
And there is nothing hid from the heat thereof. (19:1, 4–6 King James Version)

The Grand Duchess mentioned to Castelli the passage in Joshua 10:12–13 (KJV):

Then spake Joshua to the Lord in the day when the Lord delivered the Amorites before the children of Israel, and he said in the sight of Israel, Sun, stand thou still upon Gibeon; and thou, Moon, in the valley of Ajalon. And the sun stood still, and the moon stayed, until the people had avenged themselves upon their enemies. Is not this written in the book of Jasher? So the sun stood still in the midst of heaven, and hastened not to go down about a whole day.

Thus, the Bible seemed to indicate that the sun revolved around the Earth. [Ed.]

propositions different from the ordinary which I hold, and so they may lack confidence to defend themselves as long as they remain in the philosophical field. Therefore, since they persist in their original self-appointed task of beating down me and my findings by every imaginable means, they have decided to try to shield the fallacies of their arguments with the cloak of simulated religiousness and with the authority of Holy Scripture, unintelligently using the latter for the confutation of arguments they neither understand nor have heard.

At first, they tried on their own to spread among common people the idea that such propositions are against Holy Scripture, and consequently damnable and heretical. Then they realized how by and large human nature is more inclined to join those ventures which result in the oppression of other people (even if unjustly) than those which result in their just improvement, and so it was not difficult for them to find someone who with unusual confidence did preach even from the pulpit that it is damnable and heretical; and this was done with little compassion and with little consideration of the injury not only to this doctrine and its followers, but also to mathematics and all mathematicians. Thus, having acquired more confidence, and with the vain hope that the seed which first took root in their insincere minds would grow into a tree and rise toward the sky, they are spreading among the people the rumor that it will shortly be declared heretical by the supreme authority. They also know that such a declaration not only would uproot these two conclusions, but also would render damnable all the other astronomical and physical observations and propositions which correspond and are necessarily connected with them; hence, they alleviate their task as much as they can by making it look, at least among common people, as if this opinion were new and especially mine, pretending not to know that Nicolaus Copernicus was its author or rather its reformer and confirmer. Now, Copernicus was not only a Catholic but also a clergyman and a canon, and he was so highly regarded that he was called to Rome from the remotest parts of Germany[3] when under Leo X the Lateran Council was discussing the reform of the ecclesiastical calendar; at that time this reform remained unfinished only because there was still no exact knowledge of the precise length of the year and the lunar month. Thus he was charged by the Bishop of Fossombrone,[4] who was then supervising this undertaking, to try by repeated studies and efforts to acquire more understanding and certainty about those celestial motions; and so he undertook this study, and, by truly Herculean labor and by his admirable mind, he made so much progress in this science and acquired such an exact knowledge of the periods of celestial

[3] Actually Poland.
[4] Paul of Middelburg (1445–1533).

motions that he earned the title of supreme astronomer; then in accordance with his doctrine not only was the calendar regularized,[5] but tables of all planetary motions were constructed. Having expounded this doctrine in six parts, he published it at the request of the Cardinal of Capua[6] and the Bishop of Kulm;[7] and since he had undertaken this task and these labors on orders from the Supreme Pontiff, he dedicated his book *On Heavenly Revolutions* to the successor of the latter, Paul III. Once printed this book was accepted by the Holy Church, and it was read and studied all over the world without anyone ever having had the least scruple about its doctrine.[8] Finally, now that one is discovering how well founded upon clear observations and necessary demonstrations this doctrine is, some persons come along who, without having even seen the book, give its author the reward of so much work by trying to have him declared a heretic; this they do only in order to satisfy their special animosity, groundlessly conceived against someone else who has no greater connection with Copernicus than the endorsement of his doctrine.

Now, in matters of religion and reputation I have the greatest regard for how common people judge and view me; so, because of the false aspersions my enemies so unjustly try to cast upon me, I have thought it necessary to justify myself by discussing the details of what they produce to detest and abolish this opinion, in short, to declare it not just false but heretical. They always shield themselves with a simulated religious zeal, and they also try to involve Holy Scripture and to make it somehow subservient to their insincere objectives; against the intention of Scripture and the Holy Fathers (if I am not mistaken), they want to extend, not to say abuse, its authority, so that even for purely physical conclusions which are not matters of faith one must totally abandon the senses and demonstrative arguments in favor of any scriptural passage whose apparent words may contain a different indication. . . .

---

[5]Though the Copernican system did play a role in the reform of the calendar, the new Gregorian calendar was constructed on the basis of non-Copernican ideas.

[6]Cardinal Nicolaus von Schoenberg (1472–1537), archbishop of Capua.

[7]Tiedemann Giese (1480–1550), Polish friend of Copernicus.

[8]Of course, Galileo had no way of knowing that one Giovanni Maria Tolosani had had quite a few scruples about it.

NATALIE ZEMON DAVIS
Metamorphoses: Maria Sibylla Merian

Davis, a modern historian, writes here of a woman scientist and artist, Maria Sibylla Merian* (1647–1717), whose work graphically illustrates the new approaches to nature in the seventeenth century. What did Merian accomplish? What do her accomplishments suggest about the history of science?

Thinking Historically

What aspects of Merian's work were radically new or revolutionary? What elements were continuations of traditional ideas? How might the idea of metamorphoses apply to her work and the scientific revolution?

In June 1699, . . . Maria Sibylla Merian and her daughter Dorothea were boarding a boat in Amsterdam, bound for America. Their destination was Suriname, where they intended to study and paint the insects, butterflies, and plants of that tropical land.

At age fifty-two, Maria Sibylla Merian was a person of some reputation. As early as 1675, when she was a young mother living with her husband in Nuremberg, the learned painter Joachim Sandrart had included her in his *German Academy,* as he called his history of German art. Not only was she skilled in watercolor and oils, in painting textiles and engraving copperplates; not only could she render flowers, plants, and insects with perfect naturalness; but she also was a knowing observer of the habits of caterpillars, flies, spiders, and other such creatures. A virtuous woman and a fine housekeeper (despite all the insects), Merian, said Sandrart, could be likened to the goddess Minerva. A few years later, when she published the two volumes of her *Wonderful Transformation and Singular Plant-Food of Caterpillars,* a Nuremberg luminary, Christopher Arnold, sang in verse of all the men who were being equaled by this ingenious woman. Her work was "*verwunderns*" — "amazing."

*ma REE ah   sih BIHL ah   meh ree AHN

Natalie Zemon Davis, *Women on the Margins: Three Seventeenth-Century Lives* (Cambridge: Harvard University Press, 1995), 140–41, 147–48, 149–50, 154–56, plate 23.

Then, in 1692, another kind of singularity was noted about Maria Sibylla Merian, for a different set of readers. Petrus Dittelbach, a disaffected member of the Labadists (a radical Protestant community in the Dutch province of Friesland) published an exposé of the conduct of his former coreligionists. Among them was "a woman of Frankfurt am Main" who had left her husband, the painter Johann Andreas Graff, in Germany to find peace among the Labadists of Wieuwerd. When Graff came to get her back, he was informed by the leading Brothers that a believer like Maria Sibylla was freed from marital obligations toward an unbeliever like him. Refused entry into the community, the husband stayed around for a time doing construction work outside its walls, and then left. Dittelbach had heard that he was going to break his matrimonial tie, and indeed, about the time *The Decline and Fall of the Labadists* appeared in print, Graff was asking the Nuremberg town council for a divorce from Maria Sibylla so that he could marry someone else.

These accounts suggest the turnings in the life of the artist-naturalist Maria Sibylla Merian. And there were more changes to come. She sailed back from America laden with specimens, published her great work *Metamorphosis of the Insects of Suriname*, amplified her *European Insects*, and was an important figure in the circle of Amsterdam botanists, scientists, and collectors till her death in 1717. . . .

. . . Her *Raupen* of 1679, or (to give the title in English) the *Wonderful Transformation and Singular Flower-Food of Caterpillars . . . Painted from Life and Engraved in Copper*, [was] followed by a second volume in 1683. In each of the hundred copperplates (fifty per volume, available in black and white or handcolored, depending on the buyer's wish and purse), one or more species of insect were depicted from life, in their various stages: caterpillar or larva; pupa with or without cocoon; and moth, butterfly, or fly, in flight or at rest (sometimes in both states). Many of the plates included the egg stage as well. Each picture was organized around a single plant, represented most often in the flowering stage and sometimes in the fruit stage; the plant was selected to show the leaves upon which the caterpillar fed and the places on the leaves or stem (or on the ground nearby) where the female laid its eggs. Each plant was identified by its German and Latin names, and a page or two of German text facing the picture gave Maria Sibylla's observations on how her insect specimen had looked and behaved at each stage, often with exact dates, and her reactions to its appearance. She did not give names to individual species of moths and butterflies — in fact, her contemporaries had names for only a small number of them — but her descriptions yielded individual life histories.

Here is what she said of an insect shown in its stages from egg to moth on a cherry plant (pictured in the illustrations in this volume):

Many years ago when I first saw this large moth, so prettily marked by nature, I could not marvel enough over its beautiful gradation of color and varying hue, and I made use of it often in my painting. Later, as through God's grace I discovered the metamorphosis of caterpillars, a long time went by until this beautiful moth appeared. When I caught sight of it, I was enveloped in such great joy and so gratified in my wishes that I can hardly describe it. Then for several years in a row I got hold of its caterpillars and maintained them until July on the leaves of sweet cherries, apples, pears, and plums. They have a beautiful green color, like the young grass of spring, and a lovely straight black stripe the length of the back, and across each segment also a black stripe out of which four little white round beads glisten like pearls. Among them is a yellow-gold oval spot and under them a white pearl. Underneath the first three segments they have three red claws on each side, then two empty segments, after which there are four little green feet of the same color as the caterpillars, and at the end again a foot on both sides. Sprouting out of each pearl are long black hairs, together with other, smaller ones, so stiff that one could almost be pricked by them. Strange to note, when they have no food, this variety of caterpillars devour each other, so great is their hunger; but so soon as they obtain [food], they leave off [eating each other].

When such a caterpillar attains its full size, as you can see [in my picture] on the green leaf and stem, then it makes a tough and lustrous cocoon, bright as silver and oval round, wherein it first sheds and expels its entire skin and changes itself into a liver-colored date stone [*Dattelkern*, her usual word for pupa], which stays together with the cast-off skin over the caterpillar. It remains thus motionless until the middle of August, when finally the moth of such laudable beauty comes out and takes flight. It is white and has gray spotted patches, two yellow eyes, and two brown feelers (Hörner). On each of the four wings are a few round circles in and about each other, which are black and white as well as yellow. The ends of the wings are brown, but near the tips (by which I mean only the ends of the moth's two outer wings) are two beautiful rose-colored spots. By day the moth is quiet, but at night very restless.

Her concern with beauty linked her to the still-life tradition in which she had been formed, and she herself acknowledged in her 1679 preface that her juxtaposition of plants and insects owed something to the artist's concern for adornment. She was also building on earlier efforts to achieve "naturalistic" or "mimetic" representations of flora and fauna. Detailed and lifelike pictures of insects and plants can be found in the margins of Netherlandish prayerbooks as early as the late fifteenth century, well before they surfaced in Dutch still-lifes in watercolor and oil. To give an example of the quest for precision close to home, Georg Flegel, Jacob Marrel's first teacher in Frankfurt, did small, careful studies of insects (one of them followed a silkworm from egg to moth); and flies, dragonflies, beetles, and butterflies appear among the foods, fruits, sugars, birds, and wines of Flegel's larger oil paintings.

But Maria Sibylla Merian had something else in mind when she did her insect studies from life. The moths and caterpillars of her *Raupen* did not just add to the "lively" (*"lebendig"*) quality of flower pictures, as in the bouquets and wreaths painted by her stepfather Marrel and his student Abraham Mignon. The insects were there for themselves. When necessary, Merian sacrificed verisimilitude (the way things might look to an observer) for a decorative portrayal of the stripes and spikes and legs the caterpillar actually had (what a nature lover must know about an insect).

Above all, her insects and plants were telling a life story. Time moved in her pictures not to suggest the general transience of things or the year's round of the most precious blossoms, but to evoke a particular and interconnected process of change. Her insects were not placed to convey metaphorical messages, as was the practice of many still-life painters and specifically of her step-father's Utrecht teacher, Jan Davidsz de Heem (the butterfly as the symbol of the resurrected soul, the fly as the symbol of sinfulness, and so on). The *Ignis* of Joris Hoefnagel, a remarkable collection of insect watercolors by an artist-naturalist of the late sixteenth century, was designed like an emblem book, each picture preceded by a biblical quote or adage and followed by a poem. Merian's work was infused with religious spirit, as we shall see, but, except for a nod at the goodness of the bee, there were no allegorical comments in her texts.

If Maria Sibylla recentered flower painting around the life cycle of moths and butterflies and the plant hosts of their caterpillars, how different were her volumes of 1679 and 1683 from the more narrowly scientific insect books of her day? The 1660s were important years for the history of entomology: sustained observation and improved magnification allowed much new understanding of the anatomy and molting of insects and laid to rest among naturalists the belief in abiogenesis (that is, spontaneous generation of certain insects from decaying matter). New systems of classification were tried out, quite different from those used in Renaissance encyclopedias such as the one the Merian brothers had illustrated and published in 1653. There Jan Jonston had followed Thomas Mouffet (and Aristotle) in making the possession of wings a major criterion for classification: wingless caterpillars were treated along with worms in chapters separate from butterflies and moths, and metamorphosis was accordingly slighted. . . .

Merian's goal was simply ill-served by boundary classifications. Her subject was a set of events — "you'll find in this volume more than a hundred transformations [*Verwandlungen*]," she said in 1683 — and to represent them properly meant crossing the line between orders and putting the plant and animal kingdoms in the same picture. Yet even while lacking the logic of classification, her sequence was not "tumultuous." Emerging from the sensibility of two artists, Merian and her publisher-husband Graff, the books moved the reader's eye through the transformations by a visually striking and pleasurable path. The "method" of the *Raupen* — highly particular pictures and accounts strung together by an aesthetic link — had scientific importance quite apart from the new species contained on its pages. It made the little-studied process of metamorphosis easy to visualize and remember, and insisted on nature's connections, a long-term contribution. It also fractured older classification systems by its particularism and surprising mixtures, and so cleared the ground for those like Swammerdam who were proposing a replacement.

Publishing the Raupen was "remarkable" for a woman, as Christopher Arnold told readers in his opening poem of 1679 — "remarkable that women also venture to write for you / with care / what has given flocks of scholars so much to do." Merian herself drew on her female status only once, perhaps disingenuously: in the midst of her description of the insects on the goose-foot plant, she imagined her readers asking whether the thousands of exceptionally large caterpillars during that year of 1679 would not lead to much damage. "Whereupon, following my womanly simplicity [*meiner Weiblichen Einfalt*] I give this answer: the damage is already evident in empty fruit trees and defective plants."

But can we go deeper than Arnold's "beyond-her-sex" topos and Maria Sibylla's modesty topos? Can we ask whether her experience or cultural habits as a seventeenth-century woman helped generate her ecological vision of nature and the crossing of boundaries in her particular narratives?

For the seventeenth century, Maria Sibylla Merian is a sample of one. Other women still-life painters of her day, such as Margaretha de Heer from Friesland, included insects in their pictures, but did not go so far as to breed and study them (Merian's daughters would do so under her influence, but only much later). Other women of her day collected butterflies, moths, and caterpillars, but did not write about or represent them. John Ray's four daughters all brought him specimens, but it was only he who wrote down the observations, naming each caterpillar after the daughter who had collected it. Moreover, Ray had been attentive to the habitat of insects in his early observations, even while making classification his most important goal, and continued to include metamorphoses in his descriptions of individual insects when he was aware of them.

Still Merian was a pioneer, crossing boundaries of education and gender to acquire learning on insects and nurturing daughters as she observed, painted, and wrote. Her focus on breeding, habitat, and metamorphosis fits nicely with the domestic practice of a seventeenth-century mother and housewife. We have here not a female mind uneasy with analysis or timelessly connected to the organic (images that have been thoroughly challenged in recent scholarship), but a woman perched for scientific enterprise on a creative margin — for her a buzzing ecosystem — between domestic workshop and learned academy.

More explicitly important to Maria Sibylla Merian than her gender was the legitimation, nay, the sanctification of her entomological task by religion: "These wondrous transformations," she wrote in her 1679 preface to the reader, "have happened so many times that one is full of praise for God's mysterious power and his wonderful attention to such insignificant little creatures and unworthy flying things . . . Thus I am moved to present God's miracles such as these to the world in a little book. But do not praise and honor me for it; praise God alone, glorifying Him as the creator of even the smallest and most insignificant of these worms.". . .

Maria Sibylla had not yet undergone her conversion experience when she began to publish the *Raupen*, but her stress on God's creativity in nature and her "enthusiasm" in talking about insects and their beauty surely prepared her ears for the prophetic and lyrical cadences that soon were to fill her world. As Jean de Labadie had said some years before: "Everything we hear or see announces God or figures him. The song of a bird, the bleating of a lamb, the voice of a man. The sight of heaven and its stars, the air and its birds, the sea and its fish, the land and its plants and animals . . . Everything tells of God, everything represents him, but few ears and eyes try to hear or see him." Maria Sibylla was one of those trying to see.

30

LADY MARY WORTLEY MONTAGUE

Letter on Turkish Smallpox Inoculation

Lady Mary Wortley Montague, an English aristocrat, came down with smallpox in 1715. She survived, but was badly scarred by the rash that accompanied the often-fatal disease. Her younger brother died from smallpox, one of the tens of thousands who succumbed in epidemics across Europe and around the world in the eighteenth and nineteenth centuries. Two years after her recovery Montague traveled to Istanbul with her husband, who was the British ambassador to the Ottoman Empire. There, she witnessed a new approach to warding off smallpox infections, as she described in the following letter to a friend in England. What process does Montague describe in her letter? What was her response to the events she witnessed in Turkey?

Thinking Historically

This letter provides a clear example of how scientific observation can change the material world in which we live. After observing the Turkish smallpox inoculation Montague had her son and daughter inoculated. In fact, she became an advocate for smallpox inoculation in England and played an important role in persuading the English medical profession to support the innovative procedure. Montague paved the way for a safer vaccine, developed by Edward Jenner in 1796, that would eventually eradicate the disease from the planet.

Despite her admirable efforts, it was difficult to convince Europeans to embrace smallpox inoculation, which had been practiced in Asia for centuries. Even though the effectiveness of this technology came to be recognized in England during Montague's lifetime, the French and other Europeans, according to Voltaire, thought that the English were "fools and madmen" for experimenting with inoculation. What does this suggest about the nature of scientific discovery? Besides lack of knowledge, what other obstacles need to be overcome?

Letters of Lady Mary Wortley Montague, written during her travels in Europe, Asia, and Africa, to which are added poems by the same author (Bordeaux, J. Pinard, 1805). The UCLA Louis M. Darling Biomedical Library, History and Special Collections Division.

To Mrs. S. C., Adrianople, April 1, O.S.

A Propos of distempers, I am going to tell you a thing, that will make you wish yourself here. The small pox, so fatal, and so general amongst us, is here entirely harmless, by the invention of ingrafting, which is the term they give it. There is a set of old women, who make it their business to perform the operation, every autumn, in the month of september, when the great heat is abated. People send to one another to know if any of their family has a mind to have the small-pox; they make parties for this purpose, and when they are met (commonly fifteen or sixteen together) the old woman comes with a nut-shell full of the matter of the best sort of small pox, and asks what vein you please to have opened. She immediately rips open than you offer to her, with a large needle (which gives you no more pain than a common scratch), and puts into the vein as much matter as can lie upon the head of her needle, and after that, binds up the little wound with a hollow bit of shell, and in this manner opens four or five veins. The Grecians have commonly the superstition of opening one in the middle of the forehead, one in each arm, and one in the breast, to mark the sign of the cross; but this has a very ill effect, all these wounds leaving little scars, and is not done by those that are not superstitious, who choose to have them in the legs, or that part of the arm that is concealed. The children or young patients play together all the rest of the day, and are in perfect health to the eighth.

Then the fever begins to seize them, and they keep their beds two days, very seldom three. They have very rarely above twenty or thirty in their faces, which never mark, and in eight days time they are as well as before their illness. Where they are wounded, there remains running sores during the distemper, which I don't doubt is a great relief to it. Every year thousands undergo this operation, and the French ambassador says pleasantly that they take the small-pox here by way of diversion, as they take the waters in other countries. There is no example of any one that has died in it, and you may believe I am well satisfied of the safety of this experiment, since I intend to try it on my dear little son. I am patriot enough to take pains to bring this useful invention into fashion in England, and I should not fail to write to some of our doctors very particularly about it, if I knew any one of them that I thought had virtue enough to destroy such a considerable branch of their revenue, for the good of mankind. But that distemper is too beneficial to them, not to expose to all their resentment the hardy wight[1] that should undertake to put an end to it. Perhaps if I live to return, I may, however have the courage to war with them. Upon this occasion, admire the heroism in the heart of

Your friend, etc. etc.

[1]Creature.

31

LYNDA NORENE SHAFFER

China, Technology, and Change

In this essay an important contemporary world historian asks us to compare the revolutionary consequences of scientific and technological changes that occurred in China and Europe before the seventeenth century. What is Shaffer's argument? In what ways was the European scientific revolution different from the changes in China she describes here?

Thinking Historically

What exactly was the impact of printing, the compass, and gunpowder in Europe? What was the "before" and "after" for each of these innovations? What, according to Shaffer, was the situation in China before and after each of these innovations? Were these innovations as revolutionary in China as they were in Europe?

Francis Bacon (1561–1626), an early advocate of the empirical method, upon which the scientific revolution was based, attributed Western Europe's early modern take-off to three things in particular: printing, the compass, and gunpowder. Bacon had no idea where these things had come from, but historians now know that all three were invented in China. Since, unlike Europe, China did not take off onto a path leading from the scientific to the Industrial Revolution, some historians are now asking why these inventions were so revolutionary in Western Europe and, apparently, so unrevolutionary in China.

In fact, the question has been posed by none other than Joseph Needham, the foremost English-language scholar of Chinese science and technology. It is only because of Needham's work that the Western academic community has become aware that until Europe's take-off, China was the unrivaled world leader in technological development. That is why it is so disturbing that Needham himself has posed this apparent puzzle. The English-speaking academic world relies upon him and repeats him; soon this question and the vision of China that it implies will become dogma. Traditional China will take on supersociety

Lynda Norene Shaffer, "China, Technology and Change," *World History Bulletin*, 4, no. 1 (Fall/Winter, 1986–1987), 1–6.

qualities — able to contain the power of printing, to rein in the potential of the compass, even to muffle the blast of gunpowder.

The impact of these inventions on Western Europe is well known. Printing not only eliminated much of the opportunity for human copying errors, it also encouraged the production of more copies of old books and an increasing number of new books. As written material became both cheaper and more easily available, intellectual activity increased. Printing would eventually be held responsible, at least in part, for the spread of classical humanism and other ideas from the Renaissance. It is also said to have stimulated the Protestant Reformation, which urged a return to the Bible as the primary religious authority.

The introduction of gunpowder in Europe made castles and other medieval fortifications obsolete (since it could be used to blow holes in their walls) and thus helped to liberate Western Europe from feudal aristocratic power. As an aid to navigation the compass facilitated the Portuguese- and Spanish-sponsored voyages that led to Atlantic Europe's sole possession of the Western Hemisphere, as well as the Portuguese circumnavigation of Africa, which opened up the first all-sea route from Western Europe to the long-established ports of East Africa and Asia.

Needham's question can thus be understood to mean, Why didn't China use gunpowder to destroy feudal walls? Why didn't China use the compass to cross the Pacific and discover America, or to find an all-sea route to Western Europe? Why didn't China undergo a Renaissance or Reformation? The implication is that even though China possessed these technologies, it did not change much. Essentially Needham's question is asking, What was wrong with China?

Actually, there was nothing wrong with China. China was changed fundamentally by these inventions. But in order to see the changes, one must abandon the search for peculiarly European events in Chinese history, and look instead at China itself before and after these breakthroughs.

To begin, one should note that China possessed all three of these technologies by the latter part of the Tang dynasty (618–906) — between four and six hundred years before they appeared in Europe. And it was during just that time, from about 850, when the Tang dynasty began to falter, until 960, when the Song dynasty (960–1279) was established, that China underwent fundamental changes in all spheres. In fact, historians are now beginning to use the term _revolution_ when referring to technological and commercial changes that culminated in the Song dynasty, in the same way that they refer to the changes in eighteenth- and nineteenth-century England as the Industrial Revolution. And the word might well be applied to other sorts of changes in China during this period.

For example, the Tang dynasty elite was aristocratic, but that of the Song was not. No one has ever considered whether the invention of

gunpowder contributed to the demise of China's aristocrats, which occurred between 750 and 960, shortly after its invention. Gunpowder
may, indeed, have been a factor although it is unlikely that its importance lay in blowing up feudal walls. Tang China enjoyed such internal
peace that its aristocratic lineages did not engage in castle-building of
the sort typical in Europe. Thus, China did not have many feudal fortifications to blow up.

The only wall of significance in this respect was the Great Wall,
which was designed to keep steppe nomads from invading China. In
fact, gunpowder may have played a role in blowing holes in this wall,
for the Chinese could not monopolize the terrible new weapon, and
their nomadic enemies to the north soon learned to use it against them.
The Song dynasty ultimately fell to the Mongols, the most formidable
force ever to emerge from the Eurasian steppe. Gunpowder may have
had a profound effect on China — exposing a united empire to foreign
invasion and terrible devastation — but an effect quite opposite to the
one it had on Western Europe.

On the other hand, the impact of printing on China was in some
ways very similar to its later impact on Europe. For example, printing
contributed to a rebirth of classical (that is, preceding the third century
A.D.) Confucian learning, helping to revive a fundamentally humanistic
outlook that had been pushed aside for several centuries.

After the fall of the Han dynasty (206 B.C. – A.D. 220), Confucianism had lost much of its credibility as a world view, and it eventually
lost its central place in the scholarly world. It was replaced by Buddhism, which had come from India. Buddhists believed that much
human pain and confusion resulted from the pursuit of illusory pleasures and dubious ambitions: Enlightenment and, ultimately, salvation
would come from a progressive disengagement from the real world,
which they also believed to be illusory. This point of view dominated
Chinese intellectual life until the ninth century. Thus the academic and
intellectual comeback of classical Confucianism was in essence a return
to a more optimistic literature that affirmed the world as humans had
made it.

The resurgence of Confucianism within the scholarly community
was due to many factors, but printing was certainly one of the most important. Although it was invented by Buddhist monks in China, and at
first benefited Buddhism, by the middle of the tenth century, printers
were turning out innumerable copies of the classical Confucian corpus.
This return of scholars to classical learning was part of a more general
movement that shared not only its humanistic features with the later
Western European Renaissance, but certain artistic trends as well.

Furthermore, the Protestant Reformation in Western Europe was in
some ways reminiscent of the emergence and eventual triumph of Neo-
Confucian philosophy. Although the roots of Neo-Confucianism can be

found in the ninth century, the man who created what would become its most orthodox synthesis was Zhu Xi (Chu Hsi, 1130–1200). Neo-Confucianism was significantly different from classical Confucianism, for it had undergone an intellectual (and political) confrontation with Buddhism and had emerged profoundly changed. It is of the utmost importance to understand that not only was Neo-Confucianism new, it was also heresy, even during Zhu Xi's lifetime. It did not triumph until the thirteenth century, and it was not until 1313 (when Mongol conquerors ruled China) that Zhu Xi's commentaries on the classics became the single authoritative text against which all academic opinion was judged.

In the same way that Protestantism emerged out of a confrontation with the Roman Catholic establishment and asserted the individual Christian's autonomy, Neo-Confucianism emerged as a critique of Buddhist ideas that had taken hold in China, and it asserted an individual moral capacity totally unrelated to the ascetic practices and prayers of the Buddhist priesthood. In the twelfth century Neo-Confucianists lifted the work of Mencius (Meng Zi, 370–290 B.C.) out of obscurity and assigned it a place in the corpus second only to that of the *Analects of Confucius*. Many facets of Mencius appealed to the Neo-Confucianists, but one of the most important was his argument that humans by nature are fundamentally good. Within the context of the Song dynasty, this was an assertion that morality could be pursued through an engagement in human affairs, and that the Buddhist monks' withdrawal from life's mainstream did not bestow upon them any special virtue.

The importance of these philosophical developments notwithstanding, printing probably had its greatest impact on the Chinese political system. The origin of the civil service examination system in China can be traced back to the Han dynasty, but in the Song dynasty government-administered examinations became the most important route to political power in China. For almost a thousand years (except the early period of Mongol rule), China was governed by men who had come to power simply because they had done exceedingly well in examinations on the Neo-Confucian canon. At any one time thousands of students were studying for the exams, and thousands of inexpensive books were required. Without printing such a system would not have been possible.

The development of this alternative to aristocratic rule was one of the most radical changes in world history. Since the examinations were ultimately open to 98 percent of all males (actors were one of the few groups excluded), it was the most democratic system in the world prior to the development of representative democracy and popular suffrage in Western Europe in the eighteenth and nineteenth centuries. (There were some small-scale systems, such as the classical Greek city-states, which might be considered more democratic, but nothing comparable in size to Song China or even the modern nation-states of Europe.)

Finally we come to the compass. Suffice it to say that during the Song dynasty, China developed the world's largest and most technologically sophisticated merchant marine and navy. By the fifteenth century its ships were sailing from the north Pacific to the east coast of Africa. They could have made the arduous journey around the tip of Africa and on into Portuguese ports; however, they had no reason to do so. Although the Western European economy was prospering, it offered nothing that China could not acquire much closer to home at much less cost. In particular, wool, Western Europe's most important export, could easily be obtained along China's northern frontier.

Certainly, the Portuguese and the Spanish did not make their unprecedented voyages out of idle curiosity. They were trying to go to the Spice Islands, in what is now Indonesia, in order to acquire the most valuable commercial items of the time. In the fifteenth century these islands were the world's sole suppliers of the fine spices, such as cloves, nutmeg, and mace, as well as a source for the more generally available pepper. It was this spice market that lured Columbus westward from Spain and drew Vasco Da Gama around Africa and across the Indian Ocean.

After the invention of the compass, China also wanted to go to the Spice Islands and, in fact, did go, regularly — but Chinese ships did not have to go around the world to get there. The Atlantic nations of Western Europe, on the other hand, had to buy spices from Venice (which controlled the Mediterranean trade routes) or from other Italian city-states; or they had to find a new way to the Spice Islands. It was necessity that mothered those revolutionary routes that ultimately changed the world.

Gunpowder, printing, the compass — clearly these three inventions changed China as much as they changed Europe. And it should come as no surprise that changes wrought in China between the eighth and tenth centuries were different from changes wrought in Western Europe between the thirteenth and fifteenth centuries. It would, of course, be unfair and ahistorical to imply that something was wrong with Western Europe because the technologies appeared there later. It is equally unfair to ask why the Chinese did not accidentally bump into the Western Hemisphere while sailing east across the Pacific to find the wool markets of Spain.

32

SUGITA GEMPAKU
A Dutch Anatomy Lesson in Japan

Sugita Gempaku* (1733–1817) was a Japanese physician who, as he tells us here in his memoir, suddenly discovered the value of Western medical science when he chanced to witness a dissection shortly after he obtained a Dutch anatomy book.

What was it that Sugita Gempaku learned on that day in 1771? What were the differences between the treatments of anatomy in the Chinese *Book of Medicine* and the Dutch medical book? What accounts for these differences?

Thinking Historically

How might the Dutch book have changed the way the author practiced medicine? How did it change his knowledge of the human body? How did it change the relevance of his knowledge of the human body to the medicine he practiced? How revolutionary was the new knowledge for Sugita Gempaku?

Whenever I met Hiraga Gennai (1729–1779), we talked to each other on this matter: "As we have learned, the Dutch method of scholarly investigation through field work and surveys is truly amazing. If we can directly understand books written by them, we will benefit greatly. However, it is pitiful that there has been no one who has set his mind on working in this field. Can we somehow blaze this trail? It is impossible to do it in Edo. Perhaps it is best if we ask translators in Nagasaki to make some translations. If one book can be completely translated, there will be an immeasurable benefit to the country." Every time we spoke in this manner, we deplored the impossibility of imple-

*SOO gee tah   gehm PAH koo

Sugita Gempaku, *Ranto Kotohajime* (The Beginning of Dutch Studies in the East), in David J. Lu, ed., *Japan: A Documentary History*, vol. I (Armonk, N.Y.: M. E. Sharpe, 2005), 264–66. Iwanami Shoten, *Nihon Koten Bunka Taikei* (Major Compilation of Japanese Classics), vol. 95 (Tokyo: Iwanami Shoten, 1969), 487–93.

menting our desires. However, we did not vainly lament the matter for long.

Somehow, miraculously I obtained a book on anatomy written in that country. It may well be that Dutch studies in this country began when I thought of comparing the illustrations in the book with real things. It was a strange and even miraculous happening that I was able to obtain that book in that particular spring of 1771. Then at the night of the third day of the third month, I received a letter from a man by the name of Tokuno Bambei, who was in the service of the then Town Commissioner, Magaribuchi Kai-no-kami. Tokuno stated in his letter that "A post-mortem examination of the body of a condemned criminal by a resident physician will be held tomorrow at Senjukotsukahara. You are welcome to witness it if you so desire." At one time my colleague by the name of Kosugi Genteki had an occasion to witness a post-mortem dissection of a body when he studied under Dr. Yamawaki Tōyō of Kyoto. After seeing the dissection firsthand, Kosugi remarked that what was said by the people of old was false and simply could not be trusted. "The people of old spoke of nine internal organs, and nowadays, people divide them into five viscera and six internal organs. That [perpetuates] inaccuracy," Kosugi once said. Around that time (1759) Dr. Tōyō published a book entitled *Zōshi* (*On Internal Organs*). Having read that book, I had hoped that some day I could witness a dissection. When I also acquired a Dutch book on anatomy, I wanted above all to compare the two to find out which one accurately described the truth. I rejoiced at this unusually fortunate circumstance, and my mind could not entertain any other thought. However, a thought occurred to me that I should not monopolize this good fortune, and decided to share it with those of my colleagues who were diligent in the pursuit of their medicine. . . . Among those I invited was one [Maeno] Ryōtaku (1723–1803). . . .

The next day, when we arrived at the location . . . Ryōtaku reached under his kimono to produce a Dutch book and showed it to us. "This is a Dutch book of anatomy called *Tabulae Anatomicae*. I bought this a few years ago when I went to Nagasaki, and kept it." As I examined it, it was the same book I had and was of the same edition. We held each other's hands and exclaimed: "What a coincidence!" Ryōtaku continued by saying: "When I went to Nagasaki, I learned and heard," and opened his book. "These are called *long* in Dutch, they are lungs," he taught us. "This is *hart*, or the heart. When it says *maag* it is the stomach, and when it says *milt* it is the spleen." However, they did not look like the heart given in the Chinese medical books, and none of us were sure until we could actually see the dissection.

Thereafter we went together to the place which was especially set for us to observe the dissection in Kotsukahara. . . . The regular man who performed the chore of dissection was ill, and his grandfather, who was ninety years of age, came in his place. He was a healthy old man. He had experienced many dissections since his youth, and boasted that he dissected a number of bodies. Those dissections were performed in those days by men of the *eta*[1] class. . . . That day, the old butcher pointed to this and that organ. After the heart, liver, gall bladder, and stomach were identified, he pointed to other parts for which there were no names. "I don't know their names. But I have dissected quite a few bodies from my youthful days. Inside of everyone's abdomen there were these parts and those parts." Later, after consulting the anatomy chart, it became clear to me that I saw an arterial tube, a vein, and the suprarenal gland. The old butcher again said, "Every time I had a dissection, I pointed out to those physicians many of these parts, but not a single one of them questioned 'what was this?' or 'what was that?'" We compared the body as dissected against the charts both Ryōtaku and I had, and could not find a single variance from the charts. The Chinese *Book of Medicine* (*Yi Jing*) says that the lungs are like the eight petals of the lotus flower, with three petals hanging in front, three in back, and two petals forming like two ears and that the liver has three petals to the left and four petals to the right. There were no such divisions, and the positions and shapes of intestines and gastric organs were all different from those taught by the old theories. The official physicians, Dr. Okada Yōsen and Dr. Fujimoto Rissen, have witnessed dissection seven or eight times. Whenever they witnessed the dissection, they found that the old theories contradicted reality. Each time they were perplexed and could not resolve their doubts. Every time they wrote down what they thought was strange. They wrote in their books. "The more we think of it, there must be fundamental differences in the bodies of Chinese and of the eastern barbarians [i.e., Japanese]." I could see why they wrote this way.

That day, after the dissection was over, we decided that we also should examine the shape of the skeletons left exposed on the execution ground. We collected the bones, and examined a number of them. Again, we were struck by the fact that they all differed from the old theories while conforming to the Dutch charts.

The three of us, Ryōtaku, [Nakagawa] Junan (1739–1786), and I went home together. On the way home we spoke to each other and felt the same way. "How marvelous was our actual experience today. It is a shame that we were ignorant of these things until now. As physicians who serve their masters through medicine, we performed our duties in complete ignorance of the true form of the human body. How disgraceful it is. Somehow, through this experience, let us investigate further the truth about the human body. If we practice medicine with this knowledge behind us, we can make contributions for people under heaven

---

[1] The eta were an untouchable caste in Japan, defined by their restriction to certain occupations associated with death — tanning or working with hides, cremating the dead, butchering meat, and, thus, doing autopsies. They could not be physicians. [Ed.]

and on this earth." Ryōtaku spoke to us. "Indeed, I agree with you wholeheartedly." Then I spoke to my two companions. "Somehow if we can translate anew this book called *Tabulae Anatomicae*, we can get a clear notion of the human body inside out. It will have great benefit in the treatment of our patients. Let us do our best to read it and understand it without the help of translators." Ryōtaku responded: "I have been wanting to read Dutch books for some time, but there has been no friend who would share my ambitions. I have spent days lamenting it. If both of you wish, I have been in Nagasaki before and have retained some Dutch. Let us use it as a beginning to tackle the book together." After hearing it, I answered, "This is simply wonderful. If we are to join our efforts, I shall also resolve to do my very best." . . .

The next day, we assembled at the house of Ryōtaku and recalled the happenings of the previous day. When we faced that *Tabulae Anatomicae*, we felt as if we were setting sail on a great ocean in a ship without oars or a rudder. With the magnitude of the work before us, we were dumbfounded by our own ignorance. However, Ryōtaku had been thinking of this for some time, and he had been in Nagasaki. He knew some Dutch through studying and hearing, and knew some sentence patterns and words. He was also ten years older than I, and we decided to make him head of our group and our teacher. At that time I did not know the twenty-five letters of the Dutch alphabet. I decided to study the language with firm determination, but I had to acquaint myself with letters and words gradually.

33

BENJAMIN FRANKLIN

Letter on a Balloon Experiment in 1783

Benjamin Franklin (1706–1790) was the preeminent statesman, diplomat, and spokesman for the British colonies that became the United States during his long lifetime. Trained as a candle maker and printer, he became a journalist, publisher, merchant, homespun philosopher, and inveterate inventor. He invented the lightning rod, the Franklin stove, bifocals, and the medical catheter, among other things. His

Nathan G. Goodman, ed., *The Ingenious Dr. Franklin, Selected Scientific Letters of Benjamin Franklin* (Philadelphia: University of Pennsylvania Press, 1931), 99–102.

inventions sprang from a gift of immense curiosity and an exhaustive reading in the science of his day.

Franklin, sometimes called "the first American," represented the fledging Republic in France during the Revolution, ensuring French participation against the British. In 1783 he signed the second Treaty of Paris, by which the British recognized the independence of the United States. Franklin was the only founding father to sign the Declaration of Independence (1776), the Treaty of Paris (1783), and the Constitution of the United States (1789). Throughout his life Franklin furthered his interest in scientific experiment and invention. In December of 1783, he wrote to a friend about a recent invention that fascinated him: an early experiment in air travel in a balloon. What did Franklin see and what did it mean to him?

Thinking Historically

What evidence do you see in this letter that the scientific revolution was a genuinely revolutionary change? What was revolutionary about it? What evidence do you see that the people of the time thought they were living in a revolutionary age? How would you compare their attitudes with those of people today toward modern technological innovations?

TO

Sir Joseph Banks

Passy, Dec. 1, 1783.

Dear Sir: —

In mine of yesterday I promised to give you an account of Messrs. Charles & Robert's experiment, which was to have been made this day, and at which I intended to be present. Being a little indisposed, and the air cool, and the ground damp, I declined going into the garden of the Tuileries, where the balloon was placed, not knowing how long I might be obliged to wait there before it was ready to depart, and chose to stay in my carriage near the statue of Louis XV, from whence I could well see it rise, and have an extensive view of the region of air through which, as the wind sat, it was likely to pass. The morning was foggy, but about one o'clock the air became tolerably clear, to the great satisfaction of the spectators, who were infinite, notice having been given of the intended experiment several days before in the papers, so that all Paris was out, either about the Tuileries, on the quays and bridges, in the fields, the streets, at the windows, or on the tops of houses, besides the inhabitants of all the towns and villages of the environs. Never before was a philosophical experiment so magnificently attended. Some guns were fired to give notice that the departure of the balloon was near, and a small one was discharged, which went to an amazing height, there being but little wind to make it deviate from its perpendicular course, and at length the sight of it was lost. Means were used, I am told, to prevent the great balloon's rising so high as might endanger its bursting. Several bags of sand were taken on board before the cord that held it down was cut, and the whole weight being then too much to be lifted, such a quantity was discharged as to permit its rising slowly. Thus it would sooner arrive at that region where it would be in equilibrio with the surrounding air, and by discharging more sand afterwards, it might go higher if desired. Between one and two o'clock, all eyes were gratified with seeing it rise majestically from among the trees, and ascend gradually above the buildings, a most beautiful spectacle. When it was about two hundred feet high, the brave adventurers held out and waved a little white pennant, on both sides [of] their car, to salute the spectators, who returned loud claps of applause. The wind was very little, so that the object though moving to the northward, continued long in view; and it was a great while before the admiring people began to disperse. The persons embarked were Mr. Charles, professor of experimental philosophy, and a zealous promoter of that science; and one of the Messieurs Robert, the very ingenious constructors of the machine. When it arrived at its height, which I suppose might be three or four hundred toises, it appeared to have only horizontal motion. I had a pocket-glass, with which I followed it, till I lost sight first of the men, then of the car, and when I last saw the balloon, it appeared no bigger than a walnut. I write this at seven in the evening. What became of them is not yet known here. I hope they descended by daylight, so as to see and avoid falling among trees or on houses, and that the experiment was completed without any mischievous accident, which the novelty of it and the want of experience might well occasion. I am the more anxious for the event, because I am not well informed of the means provided for letting themselves down, and the loss of these very ingenious men would not only be a discouragement to the progress of the art, but be a sensible loss to science and society.

I shall inclose one of the tickets of admission, on which the globe was represented, as originally intended, but is altered by the pen to show its real state when it went off. When the tickets were engraved the car was to have been hung to the neck of the globe, as represented by a little drawing I have made in the corner.

I suppose it may have been an apprehension of danger in straining too much the balloon or tearing the silk, that induced the constructors to throw a net over it, fixed to a hoop which went round its middle, and to hang the car to that hoop.

Tuesday morning, December 2d. — I am relieved from my anxiety by hearing that the adventurers descended well near L'Isle Adam before sunset. This place is near seven leagues from Paris. Had the wind blown fresh they might have gone much farther.

If I receive any further particulars of importance, I shall communicate them hereafter.

With great esteem, I am, dear sir, your most obedient and most humble servant,

FRANKLIN

P.S. *Tuesday evening.* — Since writing the above I have received the printed paper and the manuscript containing some particulars of the experiment, which I enclose. I hear further that the travellers had perfect command of their carriage, descending as they pleased by letting some of the inflammable air escape, and rising again by discharging some sand; that they descended over a field so low as to talk with the labourers in passing, and mounted again to pass a hill. The little balloon falling at Vincennes shows that mounting higher it met with a current of air in a contrary direction, an observation that may be of use to future aerial voyagers.

REFLECTIONS

Was there a scientific revolution in the seventeenth and eighteenth century? By most measures we would have to say "yes." There were new polished-glass instruments with which to observe and measure; books, theories, diagrams, debates, and discoveries emerged at a dizzying pace. Age-old authorities — Aristotle, Ptolemy, even the Bible — were called into question. The wisdom of the ages was interrogated for evidence and forced to submit to tests by experiment. But these changes would not have constituted a revolution if they occurred in a vacuum.

Maria Sibylla Merian's metaphor is perhaps most appropriate. There was a metamorphosis — a change from one way of looking at the world to another. We might even say it was a change from a medieval manner of wearing the world like a robe to a modern view of the world as a stage, as a reality seen through a window, something separate that could be touched, weighed, measured, even bought and sold.

However we choose to characterize the changes in scientific thinking during this period, it is important to emphasize the revolutionary impact of the European scientific revolution of the seventeenth century without slighting the scientific and technological achievements of other civilizations. Many of the scientific developments in Europe sprang from foreign innovations, and in some fields Europe was not as advanced as other societies. Yet the scientific revolution's unique combination of observation and generalization, experimentation and mathematics, induction and deduction established a body of knowledge and a method for research that proved lasting and irreversible.

Why was it that China, so scientifically and technologically adept during the Sung dynasty, pictured hearts and lungs as flower petals in the late-Ming and early-Ch'ing seventeenth century? Was it that Chinese science lost momentum or changed direction? Or does such a question, as Lynda Shaffer warns, judge China unfairly by Western standards? Do the petal hearts reflect a different set of interests rather than a failure of Chinese science?

Chinese scientists excelled in acupuncture, massage, and herbal medicine, while European scientists excelled in surgery. It turned out that the inner workings of the human body were better revealed in surgical dissection than in muscle manipulation or in oral remedies. And, as Sugita Gempaku reminds us, the Europeans not only cut and removed, they also named what they found and tried to understand how it worked. Perhaps the major difference between science in Europe and that in India, China, and Japan in the seventeenth century was one of perspective: Europeans were beginning to imagine the human body as a machine and asking how it worked. In some respects, the metaphor of man as a machine proved more fruitful than organic metaphors of humans as plants or animals.

Asking probing questions and testing the answers also changed our understanding of the heavens. If mathematical calculations indicated that a star would appear at a particular spot in the heavens and it did not, Galileo might just as soon have questioned the observation as the math. From the seventeenth century on, scientists would check one or the other on the assumption that observation and mathematics could be brought together to understand the same event, that they would have to be in agreement, and that such agreement could lead to laws that could then be tested and proved or disproved.

It is this method of inquiry, not the discoveries, that was new. For the scientific method that emerged during this period constituted a systematic means of inquiry based on agreed-upon rules of hypothesis, experimentation, theory testing, law, and dissemination. This scientific inquiry was a social process in two important ways: First, any scientific discovery had to be reproducible and recognized by other scientists to gain credence. Second, a community of scientists was needed to question, dismiss, or validate the work of its members.

Finally, we return to Baumer's emphasis on the societies of seventeenth-century science. The numerous organizations in Europe are testaments not only to a growing interest in science but to a continuing public conversation. Science in Europe thus became a matter of public concern, a popular endeavor. Compare the masses of Parisians Ben Franklin described who turned out to view the balloon experiment with the few physicians gathered around Sugita Gempaku who could learn from the expertise of outcast butchers.

Ultimately, then, the difference between European science and that of India or China in the seventeenth century may have had more to do with society than with culture. The development of modern scientific methods relied on the numerous debates and discussions of a self-conscious class of gentlemen scientists in a Europe where news traveled quickly and ideas could be translated and tested with confidence across numerous borders. To what extent does science everywhere today demonstrate the hallmarks of the seventeenth-century scientific revolution?

Enlightenment and Revolution

Europe and the Americas, 1650–1850

HISTORICAL CONTEXT

The modern world puts its faith in science, reason, and democracy. The seventeenth-century scientific revolution established reason as the key to understanding nature, and its application-directed thought, organized society, and measured governments during the eighteenth-century Enlightenment. Most — though, as we shall see, not all — people believed that reason would eventually lead to freedom. Freedom of thought, religion, and association, and political liberties and representative governments were hailed as hallmarks of the Age of Enlightenment.

For some, enlightened society meant a more controlled rather than a more democratic society. Philosophers like Immanuel Kant and Jean-Jacques Rousseau wanted people to become free but thought most people were incapable of achieving such a state. Rulers who were called "enlightened despots" believed that the application of reason to society would make people happier, not necessarily freer.

Ultimately, however, the Enlightenment's faith in reason led to calls for political revolution as well as for schemes of order. In England in the seventeenth century, in America and France at the end of the eighteenth century, and in Latin America shortly thereafter, revolutionary governments were created according to rational principles of liberty and equality that dispatched monarchs and enshrined the rule of the people. In this chapter we will concentrate on the heritage of the Enlightenment, examining competing tendencies toward order and revolution, stability and liberty, equality and freedom. We will also compare the American and the French Revolutions, and these with the later revolutions in Latin America. Finally, in reflection, we will briefly compare these distinctly European and American developments with processes in other parts of the world.

THINKING HISTORICALLY
Close Reading and
Interpretation of Texts

At the core of the Enlightenment was a trust in reasoned discussion, a belief that people could understand each other, even if they were not in agreement. Such understanding demanded clear and concise communication in a world where the masses were often swayed by fiery sermons and flamboyant rhetoric. But the Enlightenment also put its faith in the written word and a literate public. Ideas were debated face to face in the salons and coffeehouses of Europe and in the meeting halls of America, but it was through letters, diaries, the new world of newspapers, and the burgeoning spread of printed books that the people of the Enlightenment learned what they and their neighbors thought.

It is appropriate then for us to read the selections in this chapter — all primary sources — in the spirit in which they were written. We will pay special attention to the words and language that the authors use and will attempt to understand exactly what they meant, even why they chose the words they did. Such explication is a twofold process; we must understand the words first and foremost; then we must strive to understand the words in their proper context, as they were intended by the author. To achieve our first goal, we will paraphrase, a difficult task because the eighteenth-century writing style differs greatly from our own: Sentences are longer and arguments are often complex. Vocabularies were broad during this period, and we may encounter words that are used in ways unknown to us. As to our latter goal, we must try to make the vocabulary and perspective of the authors our own. Grappling with what makes the least sense to us and trying to understand why it was said is the challenge.

DAVID HUME
On Miracles

The European Enlightenment of the eighteenth century was the expression of a new class of intellectuals, independent of the clergy but allied with the rising middle class. Their favorite words were *reason*, *nature*, and *progress*. They applied the systematic doubt of René Descartes (1596–1650) and the reasoning method of the scientific revolution to human affairs, including religion and politics. With caustic wit and good humor, they asked new questions and popularized new points of view that would eventually revolutionize Western politics and culture. While the French *philosophes* and Voltaire (1694–1778) may be the best known, the Scottish philosopher David Hume (1711–1776) may have been the most brilliant. What does Hume argue in this selection? Does he prove his point to your satisfaction? How does he use reason and nature to make his case? Is reason incompatible with religion?

Thinking Historically

The first step in understanding what Hume means in this essay must come from a careful reading — a sentence-by-sentence exploration. Try to paraphrase each sentence, putting it into your own words. For example, you might paraphrase the first sentence like this: "I've found a way to disprove superstition; this method should be useful as long as superstition exists, which may be forever." Notice the content of such words as *just* and *check*. What does Hume mean by these words and by *prodigies*?

The second sentence is a concise definition of the scientific method. How would you paraphrase it? The second and third sentences summarize the method Hume has discovered to counter superstition. What is the meaning of the third sentence?

In the rest of the essay, Hume offers four proofs, or reasons, why miracles do not exist. How would you paraphrase each of these? Do you find these more or less convincing than his more general opening and closing arguments? What does Hume mean by *miracles*?

The Philosophical Works of David Hume (Edinburgh: A. Black and W. Tait, 1826).

I flatter myself that I have discovered an argument . . . , which, if just, will, with the wise and learned, be an everlasting check to all kinds of superstitious delusion, and consequently will be useful as long as the world endures; for so long, I presume, will the accounts of miracles and prodigies be found in all history, sacred and profane. . . .

A wise man proportions his belief to the evidence. . . .

A miracle is a violation of the laws of nature; and as a firm and unalterable experience has established these laws, the proof against a miracle, from the very nature of the fact, is as entire as any argument from experience can possibly be imagined. . . . Nothing is esteemed a miracle, if it ever happens in the common course of nature. It is no miracle that a man, seemingly in good health, should die on a sudden; because such a kind of death, though more unusual than any other, has yet been frequently observed to happen. But it is a miracle that a dead man should come to life; because that has never been observed in any age or country. There must, therefore, be an uniform experience against every miraculous event, otherwise the event would not merit that appellation. And as an uniform experience amounts to a proof, there is here a direct and full *proof*, from the nature of the fact, against the existence of any miracle. . . .

(Further) there is not to be found, in all history, any miracle attested by a sufficient number of men, of such unquestioned good sense, education, and learning, as to secure us against all delusion in themselves; of such undoubted integrity, as to place them beyond all suspicion of any design to deceive others; of such credit and reputation in the eyes of mankind, as to have a great deal to lose in case of their being detected in any falsehood. . . .

Secondly, We may observe in human nature a principle which, if strictly examined, will be found to diminish extremely the assurance, which we might, from human testimony, have in any kind of prodigy. . . . The passion of *surprise* and *wonder*, arising from miracles, being an agreeable emotion, gives a sensible tendency towards the belief of those events from which it is derived. . . .

With what greediness are the miraculous accounts of travellers received, their descriptions of sea and land monsters, their relations of wonderful adventures, strange men, and uncouth manners? But if the spirit of religion join itself to the love of wonder, there is an end of common sense; and human testimony, in these circumstances, loses all pretensions to authority. A religionist may be an enthusiast, and imagine he sees what has no reality: He may know his narrative to be false, and yet persevere in it, with the best intentions in the world, for the sake of promoting so holy a cause: Or even where this delusion has not place, vanity, excited by so strong a temptation, operates on him more powerfully than on the rest of mankind in any other circumstances; and self-interest with equal force. . . .

The many instances of forged miracles and prophecies and super-natural events, which, in all ages, have either been detected by contrary evidence, or which detect themselves by their absurdity, prove suffi-ciently the strong propensity of mankind to the extraordinary and mar-vellous, and ought reasonably to beget a suspicion against all relations of this kind.[1] . . .

Thirdly, It forms a strong presumption against all supernatural and miraculous relations, that they are observed chiefly to abound among ignorant and barbarous nations; or if a civilized people has ever given admission to any of them, that people will be found to have received them from ignorant and barbarous ancestors, who transmitted them with that inviolable sanction and authority which always attend re-ceived opinions. . . .

I may add, as a *fourth* reason, which diminishes the authority of prodigies, that there is no testimony for any, even those which have not been expressly detected, that is not opposed by any infinite number of witnesses; so that not only the miracle destroys the credit of testimony, but the testimony destroys itself. To make this the better understood, let us consider, that in matters of religion, whatever is different is contrary; and that it is impossible the religions of ancient Rome, of Turkey, of Siam, and of China, should all of them be established on any solid foun-dation. Every miracle, therefore, pretended to have been wrought in any of these religions (and all of them abound in miracles), as its direct scope is to establish the particular system to which it is attributed; so has it the same force, though more indirectly, to overthrow every other system. In destroying a rival system, it likewise destroys the credit of those miracles on which that system was established, so that all the prodigies of differ-ent religions are to be regarded as contrary facts, and the evidences of these prodigies, whether weak or strong, as opposite to each other. . . .

Upon the whole, then, it appears, that no testimony for any kind of miracle has ever amounted to a probability, much less to a proof; and that, even supposing it amounted to proof, it would be opposed by an-other proof, derived from the very nature of the fact which it would en-deavour to establish. It is experience only which gives authority to human testimony; and it is the same experience which assures us of the laws of nature. When, therefore, these two kinds of experience are con-trary, we have nothing to do but to subtract the one from the other, and embrace an opinion either on one side or the other, with that as-surance which arises from the remainder. But according to the principle here explained, this subtraction with regard to all popular religions amounts to an entire annihilation; and therefore we may establish it as a maxim, that no human testimony can have such force as to prove a miracle, and make it a just foundation for any such system of religion.

---

[1]Accounts of miracles. [Ed.]

35

DENIS DIDEROT

Supplement to the Voyage of Bougainville

French *philosophe* Denis Diderot* (1713–1784) personified the Enlightenment with his literary wit, faith in reason, passion for universal knowledge, and constant challenge to custom, convention, and censorship. He wrote his great *Encyclopedia* of seventeen volumes, a compendium of the wisdom of the eighteenth century, amidst a life of philosophical treatises, provocative popular essays, numerous marriages and affairs, and periods of imprisonment for his writings.

His *Supplement to the Voyage of Bougainville*† (1772) is a literary invention presented as if it were a recently discovered addition to the famous 1768 account of the voyage to Tahiti by the French explorer, Louis-Antoine de Bougainville. Bougainville's very popular *Voyage around the World* spread the idea of the South Sea Islanders as "noble savages," untarnished by civilization, free to lead a life in tune with nature. Such accounts became a literary model for European self-criticism.

In this passage, Diderot uses the departure of the French from Tahiti as an opportunity for an old Tahitian to wish them good riddance. What criticisms does Diderot's old Tahitian make of the French and their civilization?

Thinking Historically

The idea of presenting one's philosophical ideas in a "long-lost" book or in the voice of "the native" was an old technique in the eighteenth century, possibly initiated as early as 1516 in Thomas More's classic work in which a traveller describes an ideal world called *Utopia*. For both Diderot and More, the use of the foreigner's voice provided the author with a bit of distance for protection from the censor, or worse, the police and jailer. Under the guise of "only reporting what others said," the author could try out new and sometimes radical ideas. It is likely, however, that the speech Diderot put in the mouth of the old Tahitian in this section represented Diderot's own ideas about French civilization.

*dee duh ROH
†boo gan VEEL

Denis Diderot, *Supplement to the Voyage of Bougainville*, Part II, "The Old Man's Farewell" (Essex, U.K.: Project Gutenberg, University of Essex, 2006), http://courses.essex.ac.uk/cs/cs101/txframe.htm.

Bear in mind that Diderot is writing on the eve of the French Revolution, which broke out in 1789. While no one foresaw the future in 1772, the strains of the old regime were evident to many philosophers of the Enlightenment like Diderot: an indifferent monarchy; a depleted treasury to be worsened by aid to the American Revolution; a creakingly inequitable Parliament where the nobility and clergy each had as much representation as everyone else. What evidence do you see of Diderot's concern about these issues? In addition, thinkers like Voltaire and Diderot were critical of French colonialism and slavery. What evidence do you see of this critique in this document? What other criticisms does Diderot make of French civilization?

Part II, *"The Old Man's Farewell"*

He was the father of a large family. On the arrival of the Europeans, he cast looks of disdain at them, showing neither astonishment, fright, nor curiosity. [The presence of this old man and his attitude to the Europeans are mentioned by Bougainville.] They came up to him: he turned his back on them and retired into his cabin. His silence and his anxiety revealed his thoughts too well. He groaned within himself over the happy days of his country, now for ever eclipsed. On the departure of Bougainville, as the inhabitants rushed in a crowd on to the beach, attached themselves to his clothing, hugged his comrades in their arms and wept, this old man advanced, severe in mien, and said: "Weep, luckless Tahitiens weep, but for the arrival not for the departure of these ambitious and wicked men. One day you will know them better. One day they will return, holding in one hand the morsel of wood you see attached to this man's belt, in the other, the iron which hangs from that man's side: they will return to throw you into chains, to cut your throats, or to subject you to their extravagance and vices: one day you will serve under them, as corrupted, as vile, as luckless as they. One consolation I have. My life is drawing to its close. And the calamity I announce to you, *I* shall not see. O Tahitiens, my friends, there is one method which might save you from your tragic future. But I would rather die than advise it. Let them withdraw and live."

Then addressing Bougainville, he added:

"And thou, chief of the brigands who obey thee, quickly push off thy vessel from our shore. We are innocent; we are happy: and thou canst not but spoil our happiness. We follow the pure instinct of nature: thou hast sought to efface its character from our souls. Here all things belong to all men. Thou hast preached some strange distinction between thine and mine. Our daughters and our wives were held in common by us all: thou hast shared this privilege with us, and thou hast come and inflamed them with frenzies unknown before. They have lost their reason in thy arms. Thou hast become ferocious in theirs. They have come to hate each other. You have slaughtered each other for them: they have come back stained with your blood. We are free: and see thou hast planted in our earth the title of our future slavery. Thou art neither god nor demon. Who art thou then to make slaves? Orou! thou who understandest the language of these men, tell us all as thou hast told me, what they have written on this metal blade! *This country is ours*. This country is thine! And why? Because thou hast set foot there? If a Tahitien disembarked one day upon your shores, and graved upon one of your stones or on the bark of one of your trees: *This country belongs to the inhabitants of Tahiti*, what wouldst thou think of such a proceeding? Thou art the stronger! But what of that? When someone took from you one of those rubbishy trifles with which your hut is filled, thou didst cry out and take thy revenge. Yet at that moment thou wast projecting in the depth of thy heart the theft of a whole country. Thou art not a slave. Thou wouldst suffer death rather than become one, yet us thou wouldst enslave. Thinkest thou then that the Tahitien cannot defend his liberty and die? He, whom thou wishest to seize like an animal, the Tahitien, is thy brother. You are both children of nature. What right hast thou over him that he has not over thee? Thou art come. Did we fall upon thee? Did we pillage thy ship? Did we seize thee and expose thee to the arrows of our enemies? Did we yoke thee to our animals toiling in the fields? No. We have respected our image in thee. Leave us our customs. They are wiser and more honourable than thine. We have no wish to barter what thou callest our ignorance against thy useless knowledge. We possess all that is necessary and good for us. Do we deserve contempt because we have not known how to fabricate for ourselves wants in superfluity? When we are hungry we have enough to eat; when we are cold the means to clothe ourselves. Thou hast entered our cabins. What, in thy opinion, is lacking? Pursue as long as thou wilt what thou callest the commodities of life. But permit sensible beings to stop, when by continuing their painful labour they will gain but imaginary good. If thou persuadest us to cross the narrow limit of necessity, when shall we stop working? What time will be left over for enjoying ourselves? We have reduced to the smallest possible the sum of our annual and daily toil, because to us nothing seems better than repose. Go back to thine own country to trouble and torment thyself as much as thou wilt. Trouble us neither with thy artificial needs, nor thy imaginary virtues. Look at these men: how straight, healthy, and robust they are! Look at these women. How straight, healthy, fresh, and fair they are. Take this bow. It is mine. Call to help thee, one, two, three, four of thy comrades and try to bend it. I bend it myself alone. I plough the earth. I climb the mountain. I pierce the forest. I cover a league of the plain in less than an hour. Thy young companions can scarcely follow me, and I am ninety years old and more. Woe to this island! Woe to all Tahitiens present and to come for the day of this thy visit! We only know one illness that to which man, animal, and plant have been condemned, old age: and thou hast brought to us another. Thou hast infected our blood. Perhaps we shall have to exterminate with our own hands, our daughters, our wives, our children: the men who have approached thy women: the women who have approached thy men. Our fields will be damp with the impure blood which has passed from thy veins into ours: else our children will be condemned to nourish and perpetuate the ill thou hast given to their fathers and mothers and to transmit it for ever to their descendants. Wretch! thou wilt be guilty of the ravages that follow thy fatal embraces or of the murders we shall commit to check the poison! Thou speakest of crimes! Knowest thou a greater than thine own? What with thee is the punishment for the man who kills his neighbour? Death by iron. And what for the coward who poisons him? Death by fire. Compare thy crime to this latter one, and tell us, poisoner of nations, the punishment thou deservest. A moment ago the young Tahitien maiden abandoned herself with transport to the embraces of the Tahitien boy: she waited with impatience till her mother (authorized by her reaching the nubile age), raised her veil and bared her throat. She was proud to excite the desires or to fix the amorous gaze of the stranger, her parents or her brother. She accepted fearlessly and shamelessly, in our presence, midst a circle of innocent Tahitiens, to the sound of flutes, between the dances, the caresses of him her young heart and the secret voice of her senses had chosen. The idea of crime and the danger of disease have come with thee amongst us. Our pleasures, formerly so sweet, are accompanied by remorse and terror. That man in black, next you, who listens to me, has spoken to our boys. I know not what he has said to our girls. But our boys hesitate: our girls blush. Plunge if thou wilt into the dark forest with the perverse partner of thy pleasures, but allow the good and simple Tahitiens to reproduce without shame, in the face of heaven and the open day. What sentiment more honourable and greater couldst thou find to replace the one we have breathed into them and which animates their lives? They think the moment has come to enrich the nation and the family with a new citizen and they glory in it. They eat to live and grow. They grow to multiply, they find there neither vice nor shame. Listen to the succession of thy crimes. Scarcely hadst thou appeared among them, but they turn thieves. Scarcely hadst thou descended on our soil, but it smoked blood. That Tahitien who ran to meet thee, who greeted thee, who received thee crying *Taio, friend, friend*: you killed him. And why, did you kill him? Because he had been seduced by the glitter of thy little serpents' eggs. He gave thee his fruits: he offered thee his wife and daughter: he yielded thee his cabin. And thou hast killed him for a handful of these grains, which he took from thee without asking. And this people? At the sound of thy deadly firearms, terror seized them and they fled into the mountain. But understand they would have speedily come down again. Without me you may be sure you would all have perished in an instant. Why have I calmed, why have I restrained them? Why do I restrain them even now? I do not know. For thou deservest no sentiment of pity. Thou hast a ferocious soul which never felt it. Thou didst walk, thou and thine, in our island: thou hast been respected: thou hast enjoyed everything: thou hast found in thy way neither barrier nor refusal: thou wast invited in: thou sattest down: there was laid out before thee the abundance of the country. Didst thou wish for our young girls? Save for these, who have not yet the privilege of showing face and throat, their mothers presented thee them all quite naked. Thine the tender victim of hostly duty. For her and for thee the ground hast been scattered with leaves and flowers: the musicians have tuned their instruments: nothing has troubled the sweetness nor hindered the liberty of her caresses or thine. The hymn was chanted, the hymn which exhorted thee to be a man and our child to be a woman, a woman yielding and voluptuous. There was dancing round your bed, and it is on leaving the arms of this woman, after feeling on her breast the sweetest rapture, that thou hast killed her brother, her friend, her father perhaps. Thou hast done worse still. Look this way. See this enclosure stiff with arms: these arms which had only menaced our enemies, they are turned against our own children: see the wretched companions of our pleasures: see their sadness. See the grief of their fathers: the despair of their mothers. In that place they have been condemned to perish by our hands or by the ills that thou hast done them. Withdraw unless thy cruel eyes take pleasure in spectacles of death: withdraw, go, and may the guilty seas which have spared thee in thy voyage gain their own absolution and avenge us by swallowing thee up before thy return. And you, Tahitiens, return to your cabins every one of you and let these unworthy strangers hear on their departure but the moaning wave, and see but the foam whose fury whitens a deserted beach."

He had scarcely finished, but the crowd of inhabitants had disappeared. A vast silence reigned over all the island. Nothing was heard but the shrill whistle of the winds and the dull noise of the water along all the coast. One might have thought that air and water, responsive to the old man's voice, were happy to obey him.

36

The American Declaration of Independence

If anyone had taken a poll of Americans in the thirteen colonies as late as 1775, independence would not have won a majority vote anywhere. Massachusetts might have come close, perhaps, but nowhere in the land was there a definitive urge to separate from the British Empire. Still, three thousand miles was a long way for news, views, appointees, and petitions to travel and tensions between the colonies and Britain had been growing.

Of course, each side looked at the cost of colonial administration differently. The British believed that they had carried a large part of the costs of migration, administration of trade, and control of the sea, while the colonists resented the humiliation resulting from their lack of political representation and the often inept royal officials and punitive legislation imposed on them from afar by the Parliament and the king.

By the spring of 1775, events were rapidly pushing the colonies toward independence. In April, British troops engaged colonial forces at Lexington and Concord, instigating a land war that was to last until 1781. In the midst of other urgent business, most notably raising an army, the Continental Congress asked a committee that included Thomas Jefferson, Benjamin Franklin, and John Adams to compose a statement outlining these and other reasons for separation from Britain. Jefferson wrote the first draft, the bulk of which became the final version accepted by the Continental Congress on July 4, 1776.

The Declaration of Independence was preeminently a document of the Enlightenment. Its principal author, Thomas Jefferson, exemplified the Enlightenment intellectual. Conversant in European literature, law, and political thought, he made significant contributions to eighteenth-century knowledge in natural science and architecture. Benjamin Franklin and other delegates to the Congress in Philadelphia were similarly accomplished.

It is no wonder, then, that the Declaration and the establishment of an independent United States of America should strike the world as the realization of the Enlightenment's basic tenets. That a wholly new country could be created by people with intelligence and foresight, according to principles of reason, and to realize human liberty was heady stuff.

A Documentary History of the United States, ed. Richard D. Heffner (New York: Penguin Books, 1991), 15–18.

What were the goals of the authors of this document? In what ways was the Declaration a call for democracy? In what ways was it not?

Thinking Historically

Before interpreting any document, we must read it carefully and put it into context — that is, determine the what, where, and why. Some of this information may be available in the text itself. For instance, whom is the Declaration addressed to? What is the reason given for writing it?

We interpret or extract meaning from documents by asking questions that emerge from the reading. These questions may arise from passages we do not understand, from lack of clarity in the text, or from an incongruence between the text and our expectations. It may surprise some readers, for example, that the Declaration criticizes the king so sharply. To question this might lead us to explore the need for American colonists to defend their actions in terms of British legal tradition. For years, the American colonists blamed the king's ministers for their difficulties; in July 1776 they blamed the king — a traditional sign of revolutionary intent in England, which meant efforts toward independence were imminent.

Consider also the disparity between the lofty sentiments of liberty and independence and the existence of slavery in the Americas. How is it possible that Jefferson and some of the signers of the Declaration could own slaves while declaring it "self-evident that all men are created equal"? To whom did this statement apply?

In Congress, July 4, 1776, the Unanimous Declaration of the Thirteen United States of America

When in the course of human events, it becomes necessary for one people to dissolve the political bands which have connected them with another, and to assume among the powers of the earth, the separate and equal station to which the Laws of Nature and of Nature's God entitle them, a decent respect to the opinions of mankind requires that they should declare the causes which impel them to the separation.

We hold these truths to be self-evident, that all men are created equal, that they are endowed by their Creator with certain unalienable rights, that among these are life, liberty, and the pursuit of happiness. That to secure these rights, governments are instituted among men, deriving their just powers from the consent of the governed. That whenever any form of government becomes destructive of these ends, it is the right of the people to alter or to abolish it, and to institute new government, laying its foundation on such principles and organizing its powers in such form, as to them shall seem most likely to effect their safety and happiness. Prudence, indeed, will dictate that governments long established should not be changed for light and transient causes; and accordingly all experience hath shown, that mankind are more disposed to suffer, while evils are sufferable, than to right themselves by abolishing the forms to which they are accustomed. But when a long train of abuses and usurpations, pursuing invariably the same object evinces a design to reduce them under absolute despotism, it is their right, it is their duty, to throw off such government, and to provide new guards for their future security. Such has been the patient sufferance of these Colonies; and such is now the necessity which constrains them to alter their former systems of government. The history of the present King of Great Britain is a history of repeated injuries and usurpations, all having in direct object the establishment of an absolute tyranny over these States. To prove this, let facts be submitted to a candid world.

He has refused his assent to laws, the most wholesome and necessary for the public good.

He has forbidden his Governors to pass laws of immediate and pressing importance, unless suspended in their operation till his assent should be obtained; and when so suspended, he has utterly neglected to attend to them.

He has refused to pass other laws for the accommodation of large districts of people, unless those people would relinquish the right of representation in the Legislature, a right inestimable to them and formidable to tyrants only.

He has called together legislative bodies at places unusual, uncomfortable, and distant from the depository of their public records, for the sole purpose of fatiguing them into compliance with his measures.

He has dissolved representative houses repeatedly, for opposing with manly firmness his invasions on the rights of the people.

He has refused for a long time, after such dissolutions, to cause others to be elected; whereby the legislative powers, incapable of annihilation, have returned to the people at large for their exercise; the State remaining in the meantime exposed to all the dangers of invasion from without and convulsions within.

He has endeavoured to prevent the population of these states; for that purpose obstructing the laws of naturalization of foreigners; refusing to pass others to encourage their migration hither, and raising the conditions of new appropriations of lands.

He has obstructed the administration of justice, by refusing his assent to laws for establishing judiciary powers.

He has made judges dependent on his will alone, for the tenure of their offices, and the amount and payment of their salaries.

He has erected a multitude of new offices, and sent hither swarms of officers to harass our people, and eat out their substance.

He has kept among us, in times of peace, standing armies without the consent of our legislatures.

He has affected to render the military independent of and superior to the civil power.

He has combined with others to subject us to a jurisdiction foreign to our constitution, and unacknowledged by our laws; giving his assent to their acts of pretended legislation:

For quartering large bodies of armed troops among us:

For protecting them, by a mock trial, from punishment for any murders which they should commit on the inhabitants of these States:

For cutting off our trade with all parts of the world:

For imposing taxes on us without our consent:

For depriving us in many cases, of the benefits of trial by jury:

For transporting us beyond seas to be tried for pretended offences:

For abolishing the free system of English laws in a neighbouring Province, establishing therein an arbitrary government, and enlarging its boundaries so as to render it at once an example and fit instrument for introducing the same absolute rule into these Colonies:

For taking away our Charters, abolishing our most valuable laws, and altering fundamentally the forms of our governments:

For suspending our own Legislatures, and declaring themselves invested with power to legislate for us in all cases whatsoever.

He has abdicated government here, by declaring us out of his protection and waging war against us.

He has plundered our seas, ravaged our coasts, burnt our towns, and destroyed the lives of our people.

He is at this time transporting large armies of foreign mercenaries to complete the works of death, desolation, and tyranny, already begun with circumstances of cruelty and perfidy scarcely paralleled in the most barbarous ages, and totally unworthy the head of a civilized nation.

He has constrained our fellow citizens taken captive on the high seas to bear arms against their country, to become the executioners of their friends and brethren, or to fall themselves by their hands.

He has excited domestic insurrections amongst us, and has endeavoured to bring on the inhabitants of our frontiers, the merciless Indian savages, whose known rule of warfare, is an undistinguished destruction of all ages, sexes, and conditions.

In every state of these oppressions we have petitioned for redress in the most humble terms: our repeated petitions have been answered only by repeated injury. A prince whose character is thus marked by every act which may define a tyrant is unfit to be the ruler of a free people.

Nor have we been wanting in attention to our British brethren. We have warned them from time to time of attempts by their legislature to extend an unwarrantable jurisdiction over us. We have reminded them of the circumstances of our emigration and settlement here. We have appealed to their native justice and magnanimity, and we have conjured them by the ties of our common kindred to disavow these usurpations, which would inevitably interrupt our connections and correspondence. They too have been deaf to the voice of justice and of consanguinity. We must, therefore, acquiesce in the necessity, which denounces our separation, and hold them, as we hold the rest of mankind, enemies in war, in peace friends.

We, therefore, the Representatives of the United States of America, in General Congress assembled, appealing to the Supreme Judge of the world for the rectitude of our intentions, do, in the name, and by authority of the good people of these Colonies, solemnly publish and declare, That these United Colonies are, and of right ought to be Free and Independent States; that they are absolved from all allegiance to the British Crown, and that all political connection between them and the State of Great Britain, is and ought to be totally dissolved; and that as Free and Independent States, they have full power to levy war, conclude peace, contract alliances, establish commerce, and to do all other acts and things which Independent States may of right do. And for the support of this declaration, with a firm reliance on the protection of Divine Province, we mutually pledge to each other our lives, our fortunes, and our sacred honor.

$$\boxed{37}$$

The French Declaration of the Rights of Man and Citizen

The founding of the Republic of the United States of America provided a model for other peoples chafing under oppressive rule to emulate. Not surprisingly then, when the French movement to end political injustices turned to revolution in 1789 and the revolutionaries convened at the National Assembly, the Marquis de Lafayette (1757–1834), hero of the American Revolution, proposed a Declaration of the Rights of Man and Citizen. Lafayette had the American Declaration in

A Documentary History of the French Revolution, ed. John Hall Stewart (London: Macmillan, 1979).

mind, and he had the assistance of Thomas Jefferson, present in Paris as the first United States ambassador to France.

While the resulting document appealed to the French revolutionaries, the French were not able to start afresh as the Americans had done. In 1789 Louis XVI was still king of France: He could not be made to leave by a turn of phrase. Nor were men created equal in France in 1789. Those born into the nobility led lives different from those born into the Third Estate (the 99 percent of the population who were not nobility or clergy), and they had different legal rights as well. This disparity was precisely what the revolutionaries and the Declaration sought to change. Inevitably, though, such change would prove to be a more violent and revolutionary proposition than it had been in the American colonies.

In what ways did the Declaration of the Rights of Man and Citizen resemble the American Declaration of Independence? In what ways was it different? Which was more democratic?

Thinking Historically

The French Declaration is full of abstract, universal principles. But notice how such abstractions can claim our consent by their rationality without informing us as to how they will be implemented. What is meant by the first right, for instance? What does it mean to say that men are "born free"? Why is it necessary to distinguish between "born" and "remain"? What is meant by the phrase "general usefulness"? Do statements like these increase people's liberties, or are they intentionally vague so they can be interpreted at will?

The slogan of the French Revolution was "Liberty, Equality, Fraternity." Which of the rights in the French Declaration emphasize liberty, which equality? Can these two goals be opposed to each other? Explain how.

The representatives of the French people, organized in National Assembly, considering that ignorance, forgetfulness, or contempt of the rights of man are the sole causes of public misfortunes and of the corruption of governments, have resolved to set forth in a solemn declaration the natural, inalienable, and sacred rights of man, in order that such declaration, continually before all members of the social body, may be a perpetual reminder of their rights and duties; in order that the acts of the legislative power and those of the executive power may constantly be compared with the aim of every political institution and may accordingly be more respected; in order that the demands of the citizens, founded henceforth upon simple and incontestable principles, may always be directed towards the maintenance of the Constitution and the welfare of all.

Accordingly, the National Assembly recognizes and proclaims, in the presence and under the auspices of the Supreme Being, the following rights of man and citizen.

1. Men are born and remain free and equal in rights; social distinctions may be based only upon general usefulness.

2. The aim of every political association is the preservation of the natural and inalienable rights of man; these rights are liberty, property, security, and resistance to oppression.

3. The source of all sovereignty resides essentially in the nation; no group, no individual may exercise authority not emanating expressly therefrom.

4. Liberty consists of the power to do whatever is not injurious to others; thus the enjoyment of the natural rights of every man has for its limits only those that assure other members of society the enjoyment of those same rights; such limits may be determined only by law.

5. The law has the right to forbid only actions which are injurious to society. Whatever is not forbidden by law may not be prevented, and no one may be constrained to do what it does not prescribe.

6. Law is the expression of the general will; all citizens have the right to concur personally, or through their representatives, in its formation; it must be the same for all, whether it protects or punishes. All citizens, being equal before it, are equally admissible to all public offices, positions, and employments, according to their capacity, and without other distinction than that of virtues and talents.

7. No man may be accused, arrested, or detained except in the cases determined by law, and according to the forms prescribed thereby. Whoever solicit, expedite, or execute arbitrary orders, or have them executed, must be punished; but every citizen summoned or apprehended in pursuance of the law must obey immediately; he renders himself culpable by resistance.

8. The law is to establish only penalties that are absolutely and obviously necessary; and no one may be punished except by virtue of a law established and promulgated prior to the offence and legally applied.

9. Since every man is presumed innocent until declared guilty, if arrest be deemed indispensable, all unnecessary severity for securing the person of the accused must be severely repressed by law.

10. No one is to be disquieted because of his opinions, even religious, provided their manifestation does not disturb the public order established by law.

11. Free communication of ideas and opinions is one of the most precious of the rights of man. Consequently, every citizen may speak,

write, and print freely, subject to responsibility for the abuse of such liberty in the cases determined by law.

12. The guarantee of the rights of man and citizen necessitates a public force; therefore, is instituted for the advantage of all and not for the particular benefit of those to whom it is entrusted.

13. For the maintenance of the public force and for the expenses of administration a common tax is indispensable; it must be assessed equally on all citizens in proportion to their means.

14. Citizens have the right to ascertain, by themselves or through their representatives, the necessity of the public tax, to consent to it freely, to supervise its use, and to determine its quota, assessment, payment, and duration.

15. Society has the right to require of every public agent an accounting of his administration.

16. Every society in which the guarantee of rights is not assured or the separation of powers not determined has no constitution at all.

17. Since property is a sacred and inviolate right, no one may be deprived thereof unless a legally established public necessity obviously requires it, and upon condition of a just and previous indemnity.

38

MARY WOLLSTONECRAFT
A Vindication of the Rights of Woman

Mary Wollstonecraft (1759–1797) lived a short but influential life as a writer in England and France in the midst of the French Revolution. She wrote *A Vindication of the Rights of Woman* (1792) in response to the radical changes that were occurring in France. She also lent support to Thomas Paine's radical *Rights of Man* (1791) which challenged conservative Edmund Burke's critical *Reflections on the Revolution in France* (1790).

The American and French revolutions enshrined many of the ideas and much of the language of the eighteenth-century Enlightenment. The very success of these revolutions demonstrated the power of En-

Mary Wollstonecraft, *A Vindication of the Rights of Woman* (Boston: Peter Edes, 1792). Spelling Americanized.

lightenment ideas about freedom and equality and, thus, inspired other marginalized groups to wonder about their own rights. If all men were created equal, then what about slaves? If kings and their governments could be overthrown and replaced by the rule of "the people," why, then, did women have no power politically — they were people too, weren't they? Mary Wollstonecraft, sometimes called the first feminist, was one of those who wondered about this, and who took Enlightenment reasoning a step further.

The male thinkers of the Enlightenment had been content to declare the "rights of man" as sufficient protection for women, assuming that "man" stood for mankind. Wollstonecraft forced them to confront that when they declared that "all men" are created equal, they did not mean to include women. In fact, they believed that women did not have the same rational faculties as men, and that women were principally meant to attend to their appearance and the service of the naturally dominant sex. Wollstonecraft pointed out that women were trained by society to accept these insults as part of the "natural" state of things.

Modern feminists sometimes distinguish between two types of demands: political/legal and cultural. Generally political and legal demands are easier to identify and label — like the right to vote or the right to own property — and the only requirement for these rights to become available to women is that legislation be enacted. Cultural demands are often more subtle and complicated and require changes in the way people think. Which of Wollstonecraft's demands are political or legal? Which are cultural? Which of her demands have been realized since 1792? Which have not?

Thinking Historically

When Jefferson wrote that "all men are created equal," he was writing in the language of eighteenth-century enlightened universalism. But he did not imagine that any of his contemporaries would think the document included women or African slaves. Notice how Mary Wollstonecraft speaks of man in general in most of the first chapter and then turns to "men" in most of the rest of the selection. Why do you think she changes her focus from mankind to men?

In addition to the enormous differences between eighteenth-century and modern vocabulary and writing styles, both the questions and the answers of the eighteenth century were different from our own. Most people today would answer eighteenth-century questions very differently from the way they were answered then. If asked, few people today, for instance, would say that men alone should be educated. The idea that both men and women should be educated is an example of an idea that was new in 1792, but is now almost universally accepted. What other ideas does Wollstonecraft express that have since become fairly universal?

In addition, we no longer ask some of the questions that were asked in the eighteenth century. What examples do you see here of questions that are generally no longer asked? What other kinds of questions have we stopped asking? Why?

Chap. I. The Rights and Involved Duties of Mankind Considered

In the present state of society it appears necessary to go back to first principles in search of the most simple truths, and to dispute with some prevailing prejudice every inch of ground. To clear my way, I must be allowed to ask some plain questions, and the answers will probably appear as unequivocal as the axioms on which reasoning is built; though, when entangled with various motives of action, they are formally contradicted, either by the words or conduct of men.

In what does man's pre-eminence over the brute creation consist? The answer is as clear as that a half is less than the whole; in Reason.

What acquirement exalts one being above another? Virtue, we spontaneously reply.

For what purpose were the passions implanted? That man by struggling with them might attain a degree of knowledge denied to the brutes, whispers Experience.

Consequently the perfection of our nature and capability of happiness must be estimated by the degree of reason, virtue, and knowledge that distinguish the individual, and direct the laws which bind society: and that from the exercise of reason, knowledge and virtue naturally flow is equally undeniable, if mankind be viewed collectively.

The rights and duties of man thus simplified, it seems almost impertinent to attempt to illustrate truths that appear so incontrovertible; yet such deeply rooted prejudices have clouded reason, and such spurious qualities have assumed the name of virtues, that it is necessary to pursue the course of reason as it has been perplexed and involved in error, by various adventitious circumstances, comparing the simple axiom with casual deviations.

Men, in general, seem to employ their reason to justify prejudices, which they have imbibed, they cannot trace how, rather than to root them out. The mind must be strong that resolutely forms its own principles; for a kind of intellectual cowardice prevails which makes many men shrink from the task, or only do it by halves. Yet the imperfect conclusions thus drawn, are frequently very plausible, because they are built on partial experience, on just, though narrow, views. . . .

Chap. II. The Prevailing Opinion
of a Sexual Character Discussed

To account for, and excuse the tyranny of man, many ingenious arguments have been brought forward to prove, that the two sexes, in the acquirement of virtue, ought to aim at attaining a very different character: or, to speak explicitly, women are not allowed to have sufficient strength of mind to acquire what really deserves the name of virtue. Yet it should seem, allowing them to have souls, that there is but one way appointed by Providence to lead *mankind* to either virtue or happiness.

If then women are not a swarm of ephemeron triflers, why should they be kept in ignorance under the specious name of innocence? Men complain, and with reason, of the follies and caprices of our sex, when they do not keenly satirize our headstrong passions and groveling vices. Behold, I should answer, the natural effect of ignorance! The mind will ever be unstable that has only prejudices to rest on, and the current will run with destructive fury when there are no barriers to break its force. Women are told from their infancy, and taught by the example of their mothers, that a little knowledge of human weakness, justly termed cunning, softness of temper, *outward* obedience, and a scrupulous attention to a puerile kind of propriety, will obtain for them the protection of man; and should they be beautiful, every thing else is needless, for, at least, twenty years of their lives. . . .

How grossly do they insult us who thus advise us only to render ourselves gentle, domestic brutes! For instance, the winning softness so warmly, and frequently, recommended, that governs by obeying. What childish expressions, and how insignificant is the being — can it be an immortal one? who will condescend to govern by such sinister methods! "Certainly," says Lord Bacon,[1] "man is of kin to the beasts by his body; and if he be not of kin to God by his spirit, he is a base and ignoble creature!" Men, indeed, appear to me to act in a very unphilosophical manner when they try to secure the good conduct of women by attempting to keep them always in a state of childhood. . . .

Chap. IV. Observations on the State of Degradation
to Which Woman Is Reduced by Various Causes

. . . The power of generalizing ideas, of drawing comprehensive conclusions from individual observations, is the only acquirement, for an immortal being, that really deserves the name of knowledge. Merely to observe, without endeavoring to account for any thing, may (in a very

---

[1]Francis Bacon (1561–1626), English philosopher, writer, and statesman. [Ed.]

incomplete manner) serve as the common sense of life; but where is the store laid up that is to clothe the soul when it leaves the body?

This power has not only been denied to women; but writers have insisted that it is inconsistent, with a few exceptions, with their sexual character. Let men prove this, and I shall grant that woman only exists for man. I must, however, previously remark, that the power of generalizing ideas, to any great extent, is not very common amongst men or women. But this exercise is the true cultivation of the understanding; and every thing conspires to render the cultivation of the understanding more difficult in the female than the male world.

I am naturally led by this assertion to the main subject of the present chapter, and shall now attempt to point out some of the causes that degrade the sex, and prevent women from generalizing their observations. . . .

Ah! why do women, I write with affectionate solicitude, condescend to receive a degree of attention and respect from strangers, different from that reciprocation of civility which the dictates of humanity and the politeness of civilization authorize between man and man? And, why do they not discover, when "in the noon of beauty's power," that they are treated like queens only to be deluded by hollow respect, till they are led to resign, or not assume, their natural prerogatives? Confined then in cages like the feathered race, they have nothing to do but to plume themselves, and stalk with mock majesty from perch to perch. It is true they are provided with food and raiment, for which they neither toil nor spin; but health, liberty, and virtue, are given in exchange. But, where, amongst mankind has been found sufficient strength of mind to enable a being to resign these adventitious prerogatives; one who, rising with the calm dignity of reason above opinion, dared to be proud of the privileges inherent in man? And it is vain to expect it whilst hereditary power chokes the affections and nips reason in the bud. . . .

"I have endeavoured," says Lord Chesterfield,[2] "to gain the hearts of twenty women, whose persons I would not have given a fig for." . . .

I lament that women are systematically degraded by receiving the trivial attentions, which men think it manly to pay to the sex, when, in fact, they are insultingly supporting their own superiority. It is not condescension to bow to an inferior. So ludicrous, in fact, do these ceremonies appear to me, that I scarcely am able to govern my muscles, when I see a man start with eager, and serious solicitude to lift a handkerchief, or shut a door, when the *lady* could have done it herself, had she only moved a pace or two. . . .

---

[2]Philip Dormer Stanhope, fourth earl of Chesterfield (1694–1773), English statesman, diplomat, and wit. [Ed.]

Mankind, including every description, wish to be loved and respected for *something*; and the common herd will always take the nearest road to the completion of their wishes. The respect paid to wealth and beauty is the most certain, and unequivocal; and, of course, will always attract the vulgar eye of common minds. Abilities and virtues are absolutely necessary to raise men from the middle rank of life into notice; and the natural consequence is notorious; the middle rank contains most virtue and abilities. Men have thus, in one station, at least, an opportunity of exerting themselves with dignity, and of rising by the exertions which really improve a rational creature; but the whole female sex are, till their character is formed, in the same condition as the rich: for they are born, I now speak of a state of civilization, with certain sexual privileges, and whilst they are gratuitously granted them, few will ever think of works of supererogation,[3] to obtain the esteem of a small number of superior people. . . .

Women, commonly called Ladies, are not to be contradicted in company, are not allowed to exert any manual strength; and from them the negative virtues only are expected, when any virtues are expected, patience, docility, good-humor, and flexibility; virtues incompatible with any vigorous exertion of intellect. Besides, by living more with each other, and being seldom absolutely alone, they are more under the influence of sentiments than passions. Solitude and reflection are necessary to give to wishes the force of passions, and to enable the imagination to enlarge the object, and make it the most desirable. The same may be said of the rich; they do not sufficiently deal in general ideas, collected by impassioned thinking, or calm investigation, to acquire that strength of character on which great resolves are built.

Chap. XII. On National Education

The good effects resulting from attention to private education will ever be very confined, and the parent who really puts his own hand to the plow, will always, in some degree, be disappointed, till education becomes a grand national concern. A man cannot retire into a desert with his child, and if he did he could not bring himself back to childhood, and become the proper friend and play-fellow of an infant or youth. And when children are confined to the society of men and women, they very soon acquire that kind of premature manhood which stops the growth of every vigorous power of mind or body. In order to open their faculties they should be excited to think for themselves; and this

[3]More than is necessary. [Ed.]

can only be done by mixing a number of children together, and making them jointly pursue the same objects.

Let an enlightened nation then try what effect reason would have to bring them back to nature, and their duty; and allowing them to share the advantages of education and government with man, see whether they will become better, as they grow wiser and become free. They cannot be injured by the experiment; for it is not in the power of man to render them more insignificant than they are at present.

To render this practicable, day schools, for particular ages, should be established by government, in which boys and girls might be educated together. The school for the younger children, from five to nine years of age, ought to be absolutely free and open to all classes. . . .

After the age of nine, girls and boys, intended for domestic employments, or mechanical trades, ought to be removed to other schools, and receive instruction, in some measure appropriated to the destination of each individual, the two sexes being still together in the morning; but in the afternoon, the girls should attend a school, where plain-work, mantua-making, millinery, etc. would be their employment.

The young people of superior abilities, or fortune, might now be taught, in another school, the dead and living languages, the elements of science, and continue the study of history and politics, on a more extensive scale, which would not exclude polite literature.

Girls and boys still together? I hear some readers ask: yes. And I should not fear any other consequence than that some early attachment might take place; which, whilst it had the best effect on the moral character of the young people, might not perfectly agree with the views of the parents, for it will be a long time, I fear, before the world is so far enlightened that parents, only anxious to render their children virtuous, will let them choose companions for life themselves. . . .

In short, in whatever light I view the subject, reason and experience convince me that the only method of leading women to fulfill their peculiar duties, is to free them from all restraint by allowing them to participate in the inherent rights of mankind.

Make them free, and they will quickly become wise and virtuous, as men become more so; for the improvement must be mutual, or the injustice which one half of the human race are obliged to submit to, retorting on their oppressors, the virtue of man will be worm-eaten by the insect whom he keeps under his feet.

Let men take their choice, man and woman were made for each other, though not to become one being; and if they will not improve women, they will deprave them!

39

TOUSSAINT L'OUVERTURE
Letter to the Directory

When the French revolutionaries proclaimed the Declaration of the Rights of Man and Citizen in 1789, the French colony of Saint-Domingue[1] (now Haiti) contained a half million African slaves, most of whom worked on the sugar plantations that made France one of the richest countries in the world. Thus, the French were confronted with the difficult problem of reconciling their enlightened principles with the extremely profitable, but fundamentally unequal, institution of slavery.

French revolutionaries remained locked in debate about this issue when in 1791, the slaves of Saint-Domingue organized a revolt that culminated in establishing Haiti's national independence twelve years later. François Dominique Toussaint L'Ouverture,* a self-educated Haitian slave, led the revolt and the subsequent battles against the French planter class and French armies, as well as the Spanish forces of neighboring Santo Domingo, now the other half of the island known as the Dominican Republic and the antirevolutionary forces of Britain, all of whom vied for control of the island at the end of the eighteenth century.

At first Toussaint enjoyed the support of the revolutionary government in Paris; in the decree of 16 Pluviôse (1794) the National Convention abolished slavery in the colonies. But after 1795, the revolution turned on itself and Toussaint feared the new conservative government, called the Directory, might send troops to restore slavery on the island.

In 1797 he wrote the Directory the letter that follows. Notice how Toussaint negotiated a difficult situation. How did he try to reassure the government of his allegiance to France? At the same time, how did

---

[1]san doh MANG   Santo Domingo was the Spanish name for the eastern half of Hispaniola (now the Dominican Republic). Saint-Domingue was the French name for the western half of the island, now Haiti. San Domingo, which is used in the text, is a nineteenth-century abbreviation for Saint-Domingue. To further complicate matters, both the Spanish and French sometimes used their term for the whole island of Hispaniola. Spain controlled the entire island until 1697 when the Spanish recognized French control of the west. [Ed.]

*too SAN   loo vehr TUR

Toussaint L'Ouverture, "Letter to the Directory, November 5, 1797," in *The Black Jacobins*, ed. C. L. R. James (New York: Vintage Books, 1989), 195–97.

he attempt to convince the Directory that a return to slavery was unthinkable?

Thinking Historically

Notice how the author is torn between the ideals of the French Revolution and the interests of the people of Saint-Domingue. Where did Toussaint's true loyalty lie? At the time he wrote this letter events had not yet forced him to declare the independence of Saint-Domingue (Haiti); this would not happen until January 1, 1804. But, according to the letter, how and why did Toussaint regard the principles of the French Revolution as more important than his loyalty to France?

. . . The impolitic and incendiary discourse of Vaublanc has not affected the blacks nearly so much as their certainty of the projects which the proprietors of San Domingo are planning: insidious declarations should not have any effect in the eyes of wise legislators who have decreed liberty for the nations. But the attempts on that liberty which the colonists propose are all the more to be feared because it is with the veil of patriotism that they cover their detestable plans. We know that they seek to impose some of them on you by illusory and specious promises, in order to see renewed in this colony its former scenes of horror. Already perfidious emissaries have stepped in among us to ferment the destructive leaven prepared by the hands of liberticides. But they will not succeed. I swear it by all that liberty holds most sacred. My attachment to France, my knowledge of the blacks, make it my duty not to leave you ignorant either of the crimes which they meditate or the oath that we renew, to bury ourselves under the ruins of a country revived by liberty rather than suffer the return of slavery.

It is for you, Citizens Directors, to turn from over our heads the storm which the eternal enemies of our liberty are preparing in the shades of silence. It is for you to enlighten the legislature, it is for you to prevent the enemies of the present system from spreading themselves on our unfortunate shores to sully it with new crimes. Do not allow our brothers, our friends, to be sacrificed to men who wish to reign over the ruins of the human species. But no, your wisdom will enable you to avoid the dangerous snares which our common enemies hold out for you. . . .

I send you with this letter a declaration which will acquaint you with the unity that exists between the proprietors of San Domingo who are in France, those in the United States, and those who serve under the English banner. You will see there a resolution, unequivocal and carefully constructed, for the restoration of slavery; you will see there that their determination to succeed has led them to envelop themselves in the mantle of liberty in order to strike it more deadly blows. You will see that they are counting heavily on my complacency in lending myself to their perfidious views by my fear for my children. It is not astonishing that these men who sacrifice their country to their interests are unable to conceive how many sacrifices a true love of country can support in a better father than they, since I unhesitatingly base the happiness of my children on that of my country, which they and they alone wish to destroy.

I shall never hesitate between the safety of San Domingo and my personal happiness; but I have nothing to fear. It is to the solicitude of the French Government that I have confided my children. . . . I would tremble with horror if it was into the hands of the colonists that I had sent them as hostages; but even if it were so, let them know that in punishing them for the fidelity of their father, they would only add one degree more to their barbarism, without any hope of ever making me fail in my duty. . . . Blind as they are! They cannot see how this odious conduct on their part can become the signal of new disasters and irreparable misfortunes, and that far from making them regain what in their eyes liberty for all has made them lose, they expose themselves to a total ruin and the colony to its inevitable destruction. Do they think that men who have been able to enjoy the blessing of liberty will calmly see it snatched away? They supported their chains only so long as they did not know any condition of life more happy than that of slavery. But to-day when they have left it, if they had a thousand lives they would sacrifice them all rather than be forced into slavery again. But no, the same hand which has broken our chains will not enslave us anew. France will not revoke her principles, she will not withdraw from us the greatest of her benefits. She will protect us against all our enemies; she will not permit her sublime morality to be perverted, those principles which do her most honour to be destroyed, her most beautiful achievement to be degraded, and her Decree of 16 Pluviôse which so honours humanity to be revoked. *But if, to re-establish slavery in San Domingo, this was done, then I declare to you it would be to attempt the impossible: we have known how to face dangers to obtain our liberty, we shall know how to brave death to maintain it.*

This, Citizens Directors, is the morale of the people of San Domingo, those are the principles that they transmit to you by me.

My own you know. It is sufficient to renew, my hand in yours, the oath that I have made, to cease to live before gratitude dies in my heart, before I cease to be faithful to France and to my duty, before the god of liberty is profaned and sullied by the liberticides, before they can snatch from my hands that sword, those arms, which France confided to me for the defence of its rights and those of humanity, for the triumph of liberty and equality.

40

SIMÓN BOLÍVAR

A Constitution for Venezuela

As we have seen, the Enlightenment principles of reason, human rights, and equality ignited revolutions on both sides of the Atlantic. In Europe, these revolutions overturned kings and tyrannies, marshaling national citizen armies and creating parliamentary democracies. In the American colonies, the revolutions took shape as anticolonial struggles for independence. Sometimes the effort to create both an independent nation *and* a democracy proved overwhelming.

Simón Bolívar* (1783–1830), called "the Liberator," successfully led the Latin American revolution for independence from Spain between 1810 and 1824. (See Map 6.1.) In 1819, he became president of Venezuela and of what is today Colombia, Ecuador, and Panama, and he gave the speech on the Constitution of Venezuela that follows.

What does Bolívar see as the difference between the independence of Spanish-American colonies and that of the American colonies? What does he mean when he says that Latin Americans have been denied "domestic tyranny"? Would you call Bolívar a "democrat"? Is he more or less democratic than the French or North American revolutionaries? What kind of society do you think would result from the constitution he envisions?

Thinking Historically

How does Bolívar characterize the revolutionary population of South America? How does he think this population differs from the North American revolutionaries? What do you think accounts for this difference?

In what ways did the revolutionaries of South America, North America, and France see their problems and needs differently? How did Bolívar propose to solve what he perceived to be the unique problems of South America? What do you think of his solution?

*see MOHN   boh LEE vahr

Selected Writings of Bolívar, comp. Vincent Lecuna, ed. Harold A. Bierck Jr., 2 vols. (New York: Colonial Press, 1951), 175–91.

Map 6.1 Latin American Independence, 1804–1830

Let us review the past to discover the base upon which the Republic of Venezuela is founded.

America, in separating from the Spanish monarchy, found herself in a situation similar to that of the Roman Empire when its enormous framework fell to pieces in the midst of the ancient world. Each Roman division then formed an independent nation in keeping with its location or interests; but this situation differed from America's in that those members proceeded to reestablish their former associations. We, on the contrary, do not even retain the vestiges of our original being. We are not Europeans; we are not Indians; we are but a mixed species of aborigines and Spaniards. Americans by birth and Europeans by law, we find ourselves engaged in a dual conflict: We are disputing with the natives for titles of ownership, and at the same time we are struggling to maintain ourselves in the country that gave us birth against the opposition of the invaders. Thus our position is most extraordinary and complicated. But there is more. As our role has always been strictly passive and political existence nil, we find that our quest for liberty is now even more difficult of accomplishment; for we, having been placed in a state lower than slavery, had been robbed not only of our freedom but also of the right to exercise an active domestic tyranny. Permit me to explain this paradox.

In absolute systems, the central power is unlimited. The will of the despot is the supreme law, arbitrarily enforced by subordinates who take part in the organized oppression in proportion to the authority that they wield. They are charged with civil, political, military, and religious functions; but, in the final analysis, the satraps of Persia are Persian, the pashas of the Grand Turk are Turks, and the sultans of Tartary are Tartars. China does not seek her mandarins in the homeland of Genghis Khan, her conqueror. America, on the contrary, received everything from Spain, who, in effect, deprived her of the experience that she would have gained from the exercise of an active tyranny by not allowing her to take part in her own domestic affairs and administration. This exclusion made it impossible for us to acquaint ourselves with the management of public affairs; nor did we enjoy that personal consideration, of such great value in major revolutions, that the brilliance of power inspires in the eyes of the multitude. In brief, Gentlemen, we were deliberately kept in ignorance and cut off from the world in all matters relating to the science of government.

Subject to the three-fold yoke of ignorance, tyranny, and vice, the American people have been unable to acquire knowledge, power, or [civic] virtue. The lessons we received and the models we studied, as pupils of such pernicious teachers, were most destructive. We have been ruled more by deceit than by force, and we have been degraded more by vice than by superstition. Slavery is the daughter of darkness: An ignorant people is a blind instrument of its own destruction. Ambition and intrigue abuse the credulity and experience of men lacking all political, economic, and civic knowledge; they adopt pure illusion as reality; they take license for liberty, treachery for patriotism, and vengeance for justice. This situation is similar to that of the robust blind man who, beguiled by his strength, strides forward with all the assurance of one who can see, but, upon hitting every variety of obstacle, finds himself unable to retrace his steps.

If a people, perverted by their training, succeed in achieving their liberty, they will soon lose it, for it would be of no avail to endeavor to explain to them that happiness consists in the practice of virtue; that the rule of law is more powerful than the rule of tyrants, because, as the laws are more inflexible, every one should submit to their beneficent austerity; that proper morals, and not force, are the bases of law; and that to practice justice is to practice liberty. Therefore, Legislators, your work is so much the more arduous, inasmuch as you have to reeducate men who have been corrupted by erroneous illusions and false incentives. Liberty, says Rousseau, is a succulent morsel, but one difficult to digest. Our weak fellow-citizens will have to strengthen their spirit greatly before they can digest the wholesome nutriment of freedom. Their limbs benumbed by chains, their sight dimmed by the darkness of dungeons, and their strength sapped by the pestilence of servitude, are they capable of marching toward the august temple of Liberty without faltering? Can they come near enough to bask in its brilliant rays and to breathe freely the pure air which reigns therein? . . .

The more I admire the excellence of the federal Constitution of Venezuela, the more I am convinced of the impossibility of its application to our state. And to my way of thinking, it is a marvel that its prototype in North America endures so successfully and has not been overthrown at the first sign of adversity or danger. Although the people of North America are a singular model of political virtue and moral rectitude; although the nation was cradled in liberty, reared on freedom, and maintained by liberty alone; and — I must reveal everything — although those people, so lacking in many respects, are unique in the history of mankind, it is a marvel, I repeat, that so weak and complicated a government as the federal system has managed to govern them in the difficult and trying circumstances of their past. But, regardless of the effectiveness of this form of government with respect to North America, I must say that it has never for a moment entered my mind to compare the position and character of two states as dissimilar as the English-American and the Spanish-American. Would it not be most difficult to apply to Spain the English system of political, civil, and religious liberty? Hence, it would be even more difficult to adapt to Venezuela the laws of North America. Does not *L'Esprit des Lois* state that laws should be suited to the people for whom they are made; that it would be a major coincidence if those of one nation could be adapted to another; that laws must take into account the physical conditions of the country, climate, character of the land, location, size, and mode of living of the people; that they should be in keeping with the degree of liberty that the Constitution can sanction respecting the religion of the inhabitants, their inclinations, resources, number, commerce, habits, and customs? This is the code we must consult, not the code of Washington! . . .

Venezuela had, has, and should have a republican government. Its principles should be the sovereignty of the people, division of powers, civil liberty, proscription of slavery, and the abolition of monarchy and privileges. We need equality to recast, so to speak, into a unified nation, the classes of men, political opinions, and public customs.

Among the ancient and modern nations, Rome and Great Britain are the most outstanding. Both were born to govern and to be free and both were built not on ostentatious forms of freedom, but upon solid institutions. Thus I recommend to you, Representatives, the study of the British Constitution, for that body of laws appears destined to bring about the greatest possible good for the peoples that adopt it; but, however perfect it may be, I am by no means proposing that you imitate it slavishly. When I speak of the British government, I only refer to its republican features; and, indeed, can a political system be labelled a monarchy when it recognizes popular sovereignty, division and balance of powers, civil liberty, freedom of conscience and of press, and all that is politically sublime? Can there be more liberty in any other type of republic? Can more be asked of any society? I commend this Constitution to you as that most worthy of serving as model for those who aspire to the enjoyment of the rights of man and who seek all the political happiness which is compatible with the frailty of human nature.

Nothing in our fundamental laws would have to be altered were we to adopt a legislative power similar to that held by the British Parliament. Like the North Americans, we have divided national representation into two chambers; that of Representatives and the Senate. The first is very wisely constituted. It enjoys all its proper functions, and it requires no essential revision, because the Constitution, in creating it, gave it the form and powers which the people deemed necessary in order that they might be legally and properly represented. If the Senate were hereditary rather than elective, it would, in my opinion, be the basis, the tie, the very soul of our republic. In political storms this body would arrest the thunderbolts of the government and would repel any violent popular reaction. Devoted to the government because of a natural interest in its own preservation, a hereditary senate would always oppose any attempt on the part of the people to infringe upon the jurisdiction and authority of their magistrates. It must be confessed that most men are unaware of their best interests, and that they constantly endeavor to assail them in the hands of their custodians — the individual clashes with the mass, and the mass with authority. It is necessary, therefore, that in all governments there be a neutral body to protect the injured and disarm the offender. To be neutral, this body must not owe its origin to appointment by the government or to election by the people, if it is to enjoy a full measure of independence which neither fears nor expects anything from these two sources of authority. The hereditary senate, as a part of the people, shares its interests, its sentiments, and its spirit. For this reason it should not be presumed that a hereditary senate would ignore the interests of the people or forget its legislative duties. The senators in Rome and in the House of Lords in London have been the strongest pillars upon which the edifice of political and civil liberty has rested.

At the outset, these senators should be elected by Congress. The successors to this Senate must command the initial attention of the government, which should educate them in a *colegio* designed especially to train these guardians and future legislators of the nation. They ought to learn the arts, sciences, and letters that enrich the mind of a public figure. From childhood they should understand the career for which they have been destined by Providence, and from earliest youth they should prepare their minds for the dignity that awaits them.

The creation of a hereditary senate would in no way be a violation of political equality. I do not solicit the establishment of a nobility, for as a celebrated republican has said, that would simultaneously destroy equality and liberty. What I propose is an office for which the candidates must prepare themselves, an office that demands great knowledge and the ability to acquire such knowledge. All should not be left to chance and the outcome of elections. The people are more easily deceived than is Nature perfected by art; and, although these senators, it is true, would not be bred in an environment that is all virtue, it is equally true that they would be raised in an atmosphere of enlightened education. Furthermore, the liberators of Venezuela are entitled to occupy forever a high rank in the Republic that they have brought into existence. I believe that posterity would view with regret the effacement of the illustrious names of its first benefactors. I say, moreover, that it is a matter of public interest and national honor, of gratitude on Venezuela's part, to honor gloriously, until the end of time, a race of virtuous, prudent, and persevering men who, overcoming every obstacle, have founded the Republic at the price of the most heroic sacrifices. And if the people of Venezuela do not applaud the elevation of their benefactors, then they are unworthy to be free, and they will never be free.

A hereditary senate, I repeat, will be the fundamental basis of the legislative power, and therefore the foundation of the entire government. It will also serve as a counterweight to both government and people; and as a neutral power it will weaken the mutual attacks of these two eternally rival powers. In all conflicts the calm reasoning of a third party will serve as the means of reconciliation. Thus the Venezuelan senate will give strength to this delicate political structure, so sensitive to violent repercussions; it will be the mediator that will lull the storms and it will maintain harmony between the head and the other parts of the political body.

REFLECTIONS

The Enlightenment and its political legacies — secular order and revolutionary republicanism — were European in origin but global in impact. In this chapter, we have touched on just a few of the crosscurrents of what some historians call an "Atlantic Revolution." A tide of revolutionary fervor swept through France, the United States, and Latin

America, found sympathy in Russia in 1825, and echoed in the Muslim heartland, resulting in secular, modernizing regimes in Turkey and Egypt in the next century.

The appeal of the Enlightenment, of rationally ordered society, and of democratic government continues. Elements of this eighteenth-century revolution — the rule of law; regular, popular elections of representatives; the separation of church and state, of government and politics, and of civil and military authority — are widely recognized ideals and emerging global realities. Like science, the principles of the Enlightenment are universal in their claims and often seem universal in their appeal. Nothing is simpler, more rational, or easier to follow than a call to reason, law, liberty, justice, or equality. And yet every society has evolved its own guidelines under different circumstances, often with lasting results. France had its king and still has a relatively centralized state. The United States began with slavery and still suffers from racism. South American states became free of Europe only to dominate Native Americans, and they continue to do so. One democratic society has a king, another a House of Lords, another a national church. Are these different adaptations of the Enlightenment ideal? Or are these examples of incomplete revolution, cases of special interests allowing their governments to fall short of principle?

The debate continues today as more societies seek to realize responsive, representative government and the rule of law while oftentimes respecting conflicting traditions. Muslim countries and Israel struggle with the competing demands of secular law and religion, citizenship and communalism. Former communist countries adopt market economies and struggle with traditions of collective support and the appeal of individual liberty.

Perhaps these are conflicts within the Enlightenment tradition itself. How is it possible to have both liberty and equality? How can we claim inalienable rights on the basis of a secular, scientific creed? How does a faith in human reason lead to revolution? And how can ideas of order or justice avoid the consequences of history and human nature?

The great revolutionary declarations of the Enlightenment embarrass the modern skeptic with their naïve faith in natural laws, their universal prescriptions to cure all ills, and their hypocritical avoidance of slaves, women, and the colonized. The selections by Diderot, Toussaint, and Wollstonecraft, however, remind us that Enlightenment universalism was based not only on cool reason and calculation and the blind arrogance of the powerful. At least some of the great Enlightenment thinkers based their global prescription on the *felt* needs, even the sufferings, of others. For Diderot, Toussaint, and perhaps especially, Wollstonecraft, the recognition of human commonality began with a capacity for empathy that the Enlightenment may have bequeathed to the modern world.

Capitalism and the Industrial Revolution

Europe and the World, 1750–1900

HISTORICAL CONTEXT

Two principal forces have shaped the modern world: capitalism and the industrial revolution. As influential as the transformations discussed in Chapters 5 and 6 (the rise of science and the democratic revolution), these two forces are sometimes considered to be one and the same, because the industrial revolution occurred first in capitalist countries such as England, Belgium, and the United States. In fact, the rise of capitalism preceded the industrial revolution by centuries.

Capitalism denotes a particular economic organization of a society, whereas *industrial revolution* refers to a particular transformation of technology. Specifically, in capitalism market forces (supply and demand) set money prices that determine how goods are distributed. Before 1500, most economic behavior was regulated by family, religion, tradition, and political authority rather than by markets. Increasingly after 1500 in Europe, feudal dues were converted into money rents, periodic fairs became institutionalized, banks were established, modern bookkeeping procedures were developed, and older systems of inherited economic status were loosened. After 1800, new populations of urban workers had to work for money to buy food and shelter; after 1850 even clothing had to be purchased in the new "department stores." By 1900, the market had become the operating metaphor of society: One sold oneself; everything had its price. Viewed positively, a capitalist society is one in which buyers and sellers, who together compose the market, make most decisions about the production and distribution of resources. Viewed less favorably, it is the capitalists — those who own the resources of the society — who make the decisions about

227

production and distribution. The democratic process of one person, one vote is supplanted by one dollar, one vote.

The industrial revolution made mass production possible with the use of power-driven machines. Mills driven by waterwheels existed in ancient times, but the construction of identical, replaceable machinery — the machine production of machines — revolutionized industry and enabled the coordination of production on a vast scale, occurring first in England's cotton textile mills at the end of the eighteenth century. The market for such textiles was capitalist, though the demand for many early mass-produced goods, such as muskets and uniforms, was government-driven.

The origins of capitalism are hotly debated among historians. Because the world's first cities, five thousand years ago, created markets, merchants, money, and private ownership of capital, some historians refer to an ancient capitalism. In this text, *capitalism* refers to those societies whose markets, merchants, money, and private ownership became central to the way society operated. As such, ancient Mesopotamia, Rome, and Sung dynasty China, which had extensive markets and paper money a thousand years ago, were not among the first capitalist societies. Smaller societies in which commercial interests and merchant classes took hold to direct political and economic matters were the capitalist forerunners. Venice, Florence, Holland, and England, the mercantile states of the fifteenth to seventeenth centuries, exemplify *commercial capitalism* or mercantile capitalism. Thus, the shift to industrial capitalism was more than a change in scale; it was also a transition from a trade-based economy to a manufacturing-based economy, a difference that meant an enormous increase in productivity, profits, and prosperity.

THINKING HISTORICALLY
Distinguishing Causes of Change

Because industry and capitalism are so closely associated, it is difficult to distinguish the effects of one from the other. Still, such a distinction is necessary if we are to understand historical change.

Try to make an analytical distinction between capitalism and industrialization, even when the sources in this chapter do not. By determining what changes can be attributed to each, you will come to understand the changes that capitalism and industrialization might bring to other societies and the impact they may have had in other time periods.

41

ARNOLD PACEY

Asia and the Industrial Revolution

Here a modern historian of technology demonstrates how Indian and East Asian manufacturing techniques were assimilated by Europeans, particularly by the English successors of the Mughal Empire, providing a boost to the industrial revolution in Britain. In what ways was Indian technology considered superior prior to the industrial revolution? How did European products gain greater markets than those of India?

Thinking Historically

Notice how the author distinguishes between capitalism and the industrial revolution. Was India more industrially advanced than capitalistic? Did the British conquest of India benefit more from capitalism, industry, or something else?

Deindustrialization

During the eighteenth century, India participated in the European industrial revolution through the influence of its textile trade, and through the investments in shipping made by Indian bankers and merchants. Developments in textiles and shipbuilding constituted a significant industrial movement, but it would be wrong to suggest that India was on the verge of its own industrial revolution. There was no steam engine in India, no coal mines, and few machines. . . . [E]xpanding industries were mostly in coastal areas. Much of the interior was in economic decline, with irrigation works damaged and neglected as a result of the breakup of the Mughal Empire and the disruption of war. Though political weakness in the empire had been evident since 1707, and a Persian army heavily defeated Mughal forces at Delhi in 1739, it was the British who most fully took advantage of the collapse of the empire. Between 1757 and 1803, they took control of most of India except the Northwest. The result was that the East India Company now administered major sectors of the economy, and quickly reduced the role of the big Indian bankers by changes in taxes and methods of collecting them.

Arnold Pacey, *Technology in World Civilization* (Cambridge: MIT Press, 1990), 128–35.

Meanwhile, India's markets in Europe were being eroded by competition from machine-spun yarns and printed calicoes made in Lancashire, and high customs duties were directed against Indian imports into Britain. Restrictions were also placed on the use of Indian-built ships for voyages to England. From 1812, there were extra duties on any imports they delivered, and that must be one factor in the decline in shipbuilding. A few Indian ships continued to make the voyage to Britain, however, and there was one in Liverpool Docks in 1839 when Herman Melville arrived from America. It was the *Irrawaddy* from Bombay and Melville commented: "Forty years ago, these merchantmen were nearly the largest in the world; and they still exceed the generality." They were "wholly built by the native shipwrights of India, who . . . surpassed the European artisans." Melville further commented on a point which an Indian historian confirms, that the coconut fibre rope used for rigging on most Indian ships was too elastic and needed constant attention. Thus the rigging on the *Irrawaddy* was being changed for hemp rope while it was in Liverpool. Sisal rope was an alternative in India, used with advantage on some ships based at Calcutta.

Attitudes to India changed markedly after the subcontinent had fallen into British hands. Before this, travellers found much to admire in technologies ranging from agriculture to metallurgy. After 1803, however, the arrogance of conquest was reinforced by the rapid development of British industry. This meant that Indian techniques which a few years earlier seemed remarkable could now be equalled at much lower cost by British factories. India was then made to appear rather primitive, and the idea grew that its proper role was to provide raw materials for western industry, including raw cotton and indigo dye, and to function as a market for British goods. This policy was reflected in 1813 by a relaxation of the East India Company's monopoly of trade so that other British companies could now bring in manufactured goods freely for sale in India. Thus the textile industry, iron production, and shipbuilding were all eroded by cheap imports from Britain, and by handicaps placed on Indian merchants.

By 1830, the situation had become so bad that even some of the British in India began to protest. One exclaimed, "We have destroyed the manufactures of India," pleading that there should be some protection for silk weaving, "the last of the expiring manufactures of India." Another observer was alarmed by a "commercial revolution" which produced "so much present suffering to numerous classes in India."

The question that remains is the speculative one of what might have happened if a strong Mughal government had survived. Fernand Braudel argues that although there was no lack of "capitalism" in India, the economy was not moving in the direction of home-grown industrialization. The historian of technology inevitably notes the lack of development of machines, even though there had been some increase in the use of water-wheels during the eighteenth century both in the iron industry and at gunpowder mills. However, it is impossible not to be struck by the achievements of the shipbuilding industry, which produced skilled carpenters and a model of large-scale organizations. It also trained up draughtsmen and people with mechanical interests. It is striking that one of the Wadia shipbuilders installed gas lighting in his home in 1834 and built a small foundry in which he made parts for steam engines. Given an independent and more prosperous India, it is difficult not to believe that a response to British industrialization might well have taken the form of a spread of skill and innovation from the shipyards into other industries.

As it was, such developments were delayed until the 1850s and later, when the first mechanized cotton mill opened. It is significant that some of the entrepreneurs who backed the development of this industry were from the same Parsi families as had built ships in Bombay and invested in overseas trade in the eighteenth century.

Guns and Rails: Asia, Britain, and America

Asian Stimulus

Britain's "conquest" of India cannot be attributed to superior armaments. Indian armies were also well equipped. More significant was the prior breakdown of Mughal government and the collaboration of many Indians. Some victories were also the result of good discipline and bold strategy, especially when Arthur Wellesley, the future Duke of Wellington, was in command. Wellesley's contribution also illustrates the distinctive western approach to the organizational aspect of technology. Indian armies might have had good armament, but because their guns were made in a great variety of different sizes, precise weapons drill was impossible and the supply of shot to the battlefield was unnecessarily complicated. By contrast, Wellesley's forces standardized on just three sizes of field gun, and the commander himself paid close attention to the design of gun carriages and to the bullocks which hauled them, so that his artillery could move as fast as his infantry, and without delays due to wheel breakages.

Significantly, the one major criticism regularly made of Indian artillery concerned the poor design of gun carriages. Many, particularly before 1760, were little better than four-wheeled trolleys. But the guns themselves were often of excellent design and workmanship. Whilst some were imported and others were made with the assistance of foreign craftworkers, there was many a brass cannon and mortar of Indian design, as well as heavy muskets for camel-mounted troops. Captured field guns were often taken over for use by the British, and after capturing ninety guns in one crucial battle, Wellesley wrote that seventy were "the finest brass ordnance I have ever seen." They were probably made in northern India, perhaps at the great Mughal arsenal at Agra.

Whilst Indians had been making guns from brass since the sixteenth century, Europeans could at first only produce this alloy in relatively small quantities because they had no technique for smelting zinc. By the eighteenth century, however, brass was being produced in large quantities in Europe, and brass cannon were being cast at Woolwich Arsenal near London. Several European countries were importing metallic zinc from China for this purpose. However, from 1743 there was a smelter near Bristol in England producing zinc, using coke[1] as fuel, and zinc smelters were also developed in Germany. At the end of the century, Britain's imports of zinc from the Far East were only about forty tons per year. Nevertheless, a British party which visited China in 1797 took particular note of zinc smelting methods. These were similar to the process used in India, which involved vaporizing the metal and then condensing it. There is a suspicion that the Bristol smelting works of 1743 was based on Indian practice, although the possibility of independent invention cannot be excluded.

A much clearer example of the transfer of technology from India occurred when British armies on the subcontinent encountered rockets, a type of weapon of which they had no previous experience. The basic technology had come from the Ottoman Turks or from Syria before 1500, although the Chinese had invented rockets even earlier. In the 1790s, some Indian armies included very large infantry units equipped with rockets. French mercenaries in Mysore had learned to make them, and the British Ordnance Office was enquiring for somebody with expertise on the subject. In response, William Congreve, whose father was head of the laboratory at Woolwich Arsenal, undertook to design a rocket on Indian lines. After a successful demonstration, about two hundred of his rockets were used by the British in an attack on Boulogne in 1806. Fired from over a kilometre away, they set fire to the town. After this success, rockets were adopted quite widely by European armies, though some commanders, notably the Duke of Wellington, frowned on such imprecise weapons, and they tended to drop out of use later in the century. What happened next, however, was typical of the whole British relationship with India. William Congreve set up a factory to manufacture the weapons in 1817, and part of its output was exported to India to equip rocket troops operating there under British command.

Yet another aspect of Asian technology in which eighteenth-century Europeans were interested was the design of farm implements. Reports on seed drills and ploughs were sent to the British Board of Agriculture from India in 1795. A century earlier the Dutch had found much of

---

[1]Fuel from soft coal. [Ed.]

interest in ploughs and winnowing machines of a Chinese type which they saw in Java. Then a Swedish party visiting Guangzhou (Canton) took a winnowing machine back home with them. Indeed, several of these machines were imported into different parts of Europe, and similar devices for cleaning threshed grain were soon being made there. The inventor of one of them, Jonas Norberg, admitted that he got "the initial idea" from three machines "brought here from China," but had to create a new type because the Chinese machines "do not suit our kinds of grain." Similarly, the Dutch saw that the Chinese plough did not suit their type of soil, but it stimulated them to produce new designs with curved metal mould-boards in contrast to the less efficient flat wooden boards used in Europe hitherto.

In most of these cases, and especially with zinc smelting, rockets, and winnowing machines, we have clear evidence of Europeans studying Asian technology in detail. With rockets and winnowers, though perhaps not with zinc, there was an element of imitation in the European inventions which followed. In other instances, however, the more usual course of technological dialogue between Europe and Asia was that European innovation was challenged by the quality or scale of Asian output, but took a different direction, as we have seen in many aspects of the textile industry. Sometimes, the dialogue was even more limited, and served mainly to give confidence in a technique that was already known. Such was the case with occasional references to China in the writings of engineers designing suspension bridges in Britain. The Chinese had a reputation for bridge construction, and before 1700 Peter the Great had asked for bridge-builders to be sent from China to work in Russia. Later, several books published in Europe described a variety of Chinese bridges, notably a long-span suspension bridge made with iron chains.

Among those who developed the suspension bridge in the West were James Finley in America, beginning in 1801, and Samuel Brown and Thomas Telford in Britain. About 1814, Brown devised a flat, wrought-iron chain link which Telford later used to form the main structural chains in his suspension bridges. But beyond borrowing this specific technique, what Telford needed was evidence that the suspension principle was applicable to the problem he was then tackling. Finley's two longest bridges had spanned seventy-four and ninety-three metres, over the Merrimac and Schuylkill Rivers in the eastern United States. Telford was aiming to span almost twice the larger distance with his 176-metre Menai Bridge. Experiments at a Shropshire ironworks gave confidence in the strength of the chains. But Telford may have looked for reassurance even further afield. One of his notebooks contains the reminder, "Examine Chinese bridges." It is clear from the wording which follows that he had seen a recent booklet advocating a "bridge of chains," partly based on a Chinese example, to cross the Firth of Forth in Scotland.

42

ADAM SMITH
From The Wealth of Nations

An Inquiry into the Nature and Causes of the Wealth of Nations might justly be called the bible of free-market capitalism. Written in 1776 in the context of the British (and European) debate over the proper role of government in the economy, Smith's work takes aim at *mercantilism*, or government supervision of the economy. Mercantilists believed that national economies required government assistance and direction to prosper.

Smith argues that free trade will produce greater wealth than mercantilist trade and that free markets allocate resources more efficiently than the government. His notion of *laissez-faire* (literally "let do") capitalism assumes neither that capitalists are virtuous nor that governments should absent themselves entirely from the economy. However, Smith does believe that the greed of capitalists generally negates itself and produces results that are advantageous to, but unimagined by, the individual. "It is not from the benevolence of the butcher, the brewer, or the baker, that we expect our dinner," Smith wrote, "but from their regard of their own interest. We address ourselves not to their humanity, but to their self-love, and never talk to them of our own necessities, but of their advantage."[1] Each person seeks to maximize his or her own gain, thereby creating an efficient market in which the cost of goods is instantly adjusted to exploit changes in supply and demand, while the market provides what is needed at the price people are willing to pay "as if by an invisible hand."

What would Smith say to a farmer or manufacturer who wanted to institute tariffs or quotas to limit the number of cheaper imports entering the country and to minimize competition? What would he say to a government official who wanted to protect an important domestic industry? What would he say to a worker who complained about low wages or boring work?

---

[1]Book I, chapter 2.

Adam Smith, *The Wealth of Nations* (London: Everyman's Library, M. Dent & Sons, Ltd., 1910).

Thinking Historically

The Wealth of Nations was written in defense of free capitalism at a moment when the industrial revolution was just beginning. Some elements of Smith's writing suggest a preindustrial world, as in the quotation about the butcher, brewer, and baker mentioned earlier. Still, Smith was aware how new industrial methods were transforming age-old labor relations and manufacturing processes. In some respects, Smith recognized that capitalism could create wealth, not just redistribute it, because he appreciated the potential of industrial technology.

As you read this selection, note when Smith is discussing capitalism, the economic system, and the power of the new industrial technology. In his discussion of the division of labor, what relationship does Smith see between the development of a capitalistic market and the rise of industrial technology? According to Smith, what is the relationship between money and industry, and which is more important? What would Smith think about a "postindustrial" or "service" economy in which few workers actually make products? What would he think of a prosperous country that imported more than it exported?

Book I: Of the Causes of Improvement in the Productive Powers of Labour, and of the Order According to Which Its Produce Is Naturally Distributed among the Different Ranks of the People

Chapter 1: Of the Division of Labour

The greatest improvement in the productive powers of labour, and the greater part of the skill, dexterity, and judgment with which it is anywhere directed, or applied, seem to have been the effects of the division of labour.

The effects of the division of labour, in the general business of society, will be more easily understood by considering in what manner it operates in some particular manufactures. . . .

To take an example, therefore, from a very trifling manufacture; but one in which the division of labour has been very often taken notice of, the trade of the pin-maker; a workman not educated to this business (which the division of labour has rendered a distinct trade), nor acquainted with the use of the machinery employed in it (to the invention of which the same division of labour has probably given occasion), could scarce, perhaps, with his utmost industry, make one pin in a day, and certainly could not make twenty. But in the way in which this business is now carried on, not only the whole work is a peculiar trade, but it is divided into a number of branches, of which the greater part are likewise peculiar trades. One man draws out the wire, another straights it, a third cuts it, a fourth points it, a fifth grinds it at the top for receiving the head; to make the head requires two or three distinct operations; to put it on is a peculiar business, to whiten the pins is another; it is even a trade by itself to put them into the paper; and the important business of making a pin is, in this manner, divided into about eighteen distinct operations, which, in some manufactories, are all performed by distinct hands, though in others the same man will sometimes perform two or three of them. I have seen a small manufactory of this kind where ten men only were employed, and where some of them consequently performed two or three distinct operations. But though they were very poor, and therefore but indifferently accommodated with the necessary machinery, they could, when they exerted themselves, make among them about twelve pounds of pins in a day. There are in a pound upwards of four thousand pins of a middling size. Those ten persons, therefore, could make among them upwards of forty-eight thousand pins in a day. Each person, therefore, making a tenth part of forty-eight thousand pins, might be considered as making four thousand eight hundred pins in a day. But if they had all wrought separately and independently, and without any of them having been educated to this peculiar business, they certainly could not each of them have made twenty, perhaps not one pin in a day; that is, certainly, not the two hundred and fortieth, perhaps not the four thousand eight hundredth part of what they are at present capable of performing, in consequence of a proper division and combination of their different operations.

In every other art and manufacture, the effects of the division of labour are similar to what they are in this very trifling one; though, in many of them, the labour can neither be so much subdivided, nor reduced to so great a simplicity of operation. . . .

Chapter 3: That the Division of Labour Is Limited by the Extent of the Market

As it is the power of exchanging that gives occasion to the division of labour, so the extent of this division must always be limited by the extent of that power, or, in other words, by the extent of the market. When the market is very small, no person can have any encouragement to dedicate himself entirely to one employment, for want of the power to exchange all that surplus part of the produce of his own labour, which is over and above his own consumption, for such parts of the produce of other men's labour as he has occasion for.

There are some sorts of industry, even of the lowest kind, which can be carried on nowhere but in a great town. A porter, for example, can find employment and subsistence in no other place. A village is by much too narrow a sphere for him. . . .

Chapter 5: Of the Real and Nominal Price of Commodities, or Their Price in Labour, and Their Price in Money

Every man is rich or poor according to the degree in which he can afford to enjoy the necessaries, conveniences, and amusements of human life. But after the division of labour has once thoroughly taken place, it is but a very small part of these with which a man's own labour can supply him. The far greater part of them he must derive from the labour of other people, and he must be rich or poor according to the quantity of that labour which he can command, or which he can afford to purchase. The value of any commodity, therefore, to the person who possesses it, and who means not to use or consume it himself, but to exchange it for other commodities, is equal to the quantity of labour which it enables him to purchase or command. Labour, therefore, is the real measure of the exchangeable value of all commodities. . . .

Chapter 7: Of the Natural and Market Price of Commodities

. . . When the quantity of any commodity which is brought to market falls short of the effectual demand, all those who are willing to pay the whole value of the rent, wages, and profit, which must be paid in order to bring it thither, cannot be supplied with the quantity which they want. Rather than want[1] it altogether, some of them will be willing to give more. A competition will immediately begin among them, and the market price will rise more or less above the natural price, according as either the greatness of the deficiency, or the wealth and wanton luxury of the competitors, happen to animate more or less the eagerness of the competition. Among competitors of equal wealth and luxury the same deficiency will generally occasion a more or less eager competition, according as the acquisition of the commodity happens to be of more or less importance to them. Hence the exorbitant price of the necessaries of life during the blockade of a town or in a famine.

When the quantity brought to market exceeds the effectual demand, it cannot be all sold to those who are willing to pay the whole value of the rent, wages, and profit, which must be paid in order to bring it thither. Some part must be sold to those who are willing to pay less, and the low price which they give for it must reduce the price of the whole. The market price will sink more or less below the natural price, according as the greatness of the excess increases more or less the competition of the sellers, or according as it happens to be more or less important to them to get immediately rid of the commodity. The same excess in the importation of perishables will occasion a much greater

---

[1] Be without it. [Ed.]

competition than in that of durable commodities; in the importation of oranges, for example, than in that of old iron.

When the quantity brought to market is just sufficient to supply the effectual demand, and no more, the market price naturally comes to be either exactly, or as nearly as can be judged of, the same with the natural price. The whole quantity upon hand can be disposed of for this price, and cannot be disposed of for more. The competition of the different dealers obliges them all to accept of this price, but does not oblige them to accept of less.

The quantity of every commodity brought to market naturally suits itself to the effectual demand. It is the interest of all those who employ their land, labour, or stock, in bringing any commodity to market, that the quantity never should exceed the effectual demand; and it is the interest of all other people that it never should fall short of that demand.

Book IV: Of Systems of Political Economy

Chapter 1: Of the Principle of the Commercial or Mercantile System

I thought it necessary, though at the hazard of being tedious, to examine at full length this popular notion that wealth consists in money, or in gold and silver. Money in common language, as I have already observed, frequently signifies wealth, and this ambiguity of expression has rendered this popular notion so familiar to us that even they who are convinced of its absurdity are very apt to forget their own principles, and in the course of their reasonings to take it for granted as a certain and undeniable truth. Some of the best English writers upon commerce set out with observing that the wealth of a country consists, not in its gold and silver only, but in its lands, houses, and consumable goods of all different kinds. In the course of their reasonings, however, the lands, houses, and consumable goods seem to slip out of their memory, and the strain of their argument frequently supposes that all wealth consists in gold and silver, and that to multiply those metals is the great object of national industry and commerce. . . .

Chapter 2: Of Restraints upon the Importation from Foreign Countries of Such Goods as Can Be Produced at Home

. . . The produce of industry is what it adds to the subject or materials upon which it is employed. In proportion as the value of this produce is great or small, so will likewise be the profits of the employer. But it is only for the sake of profit that any man employs a capital in the support of industry; and he will always, therefore, endeavour to employ it in the support of that industry of which the produce is likely to be of the greatest value, or to exchange for the greatest quantity either of money or of other goods.

But the annual revenue of every society is always precisely equal to the exchangeable value of the whole annual produce of its industry, or rather is precisely the same thing with that exchangeable value. As every individual, therefore, endeavours as much as he can both to employ his capital in the support of domestic industry, and so to direct that industry that its produce may be of the greatest value; every individual necessarily labours to render the annual revenue of the society as great as he can. He generally, indeed, neither intends to promote the public interest, nor knows how much he is promoting it. By preferring the support of domestic to that of foreign industry, he intends only his own security; and by directing that industry in such a manner as its produce may be of the greatest value, he intends only his own gain, and he is in this, as in many other cases, led by an invisible hand to promote an end which was no part of his intention. Nor is it always the worse for the society that it was no part of it. By pursuing his own interest he frequently promotes that of the society more effectually than when he really intends to promote it. I have never known much good done by those who affected to trade for the public good. It is an affectation, indeed, not very common among merchants, and very few words need be employed in dissuading them from it.

What is the species of domestic industry which his capital can employ, and of which the produce is likely to be of the greatest value, every individual, it is evident, can, in his local situation, judge much better than any statesman or lawgiver can do for him. The statesman who should attempt to direct private people in what manner they ought to employ their capitals would not only load himself with a most unnecessary attention, but assume an authority which could safely be trusted, not only to no single person, but to no council or senate whatever, and which would nowhere be so dangerous as in the hands of a man who had folly and presumption enough to fancy himself fit to exercise it.

To give the monopoly of the home market to the produce of domestic industry, in any particular art or manufacture, is in some measure to direct private people in what manner they ought to employ their capitals, and must, in almost all cases, be either a useless or a hurtful regulation. If the produce of domestic can be brought there as cheap as that of foreign industry, the regulation is evidently useless. If it cannot, it must generally be hurtful. It is the maxim of every prudent master of a family never to attempt to make at home what it will cost him more to make than to buy. The tailor does not attempt to make his own shoes, but buys them of the shoemaker. The shoemaker does not attempt to make his own clothes, but employs a tailor. The farmer attempts to make neither the one nor the other, but employs those different artificers. All of them find it for their interest to employ their whole industry in a way in which they have some advantage over their neighbours, and to purchase with a part of its produce, or what is the same thing, with the price of a part of it, whatever else they have occasion for.

What is prudence in the conduct of every private family can scarce be folly in that of a great kingdom. If a foreign country can supply us with a commodity cheaper than we ourselves can make it, better buy it of them with some part of the produce of our own industry employed in a way in which we have some advantage. The general industry of the country, being always in proportion to the capital which employs it, will not thereby be diminished, no more than that of the above-mentioned artificers; but only left to find out the way in which it can be employed with the greatest advantage. It is certainly not employed to the greatest advantage when it is thus directed towards an object which it can buy cheaper than it can make. . . .

From The Sadler Report of the House of Commons

Although children were among the ideal workers in the factories of the industrial revolution, according to many factory owners, increasingly their exploitation became a concern of the British Parliament. One important parliamentary investigation, chaired by Michael Sadler, took volumes of testimony from child workers and older people who had worked as children in the mines and factories. The following is a sample of the testimony gathered in the Sadler Report. The report led to child-labor reform in the Factory Act of 1833.

What seem to be the causes of Crabtree's distress? How could they have been alleviated?

From *The Sadler Report: Report from the Committee on the Bill to Regulate the Labour of Children in the Mills and Factories of the United Kingdom* (London: The House of Commons, 1832).

Thinking Historically

To what extent are the problems faced by Matthew Crabtree the inevitable results of machine production? To what extent are his problems caused by capitalism? How might the owner of this factory have addressed these issues?

If you asked the owner why he didn't pay more, shorten the workday, provide more time for meals, or provide medical assistance when it was needed, how do you think he would have responded? Do you think Crabtree would have been in favor of reduced hours if it meant reduced wages?

Friday, 18 May 1832 — Michael Thomas Sadler, Esquire, in the Chair

Mr. Matthew Crabtree, *called in; and Examined.*

What age are you? — Twenty-two.

What is your occupation? — A blanket manufacturer.

Have you ever been employed in a factory? — Yes.

At what age did you first go to work in one? — Eight.

How long did you continue in that occupation? — Four years.

Will you state the hours of labour at the period when you first went to the factory, in ordinary times? — From 6 in the morning to 8 at night.

Fourteen hours? — Yes.

With what intervals for refreshment and rest? — An hour at noon.

Then you had no resting time allowed in which to take your breakfast, or what is in Yorkshire called your "drinking"? — No.

When trade was brisk what were your hours? — From 5 in the morning to 9 in the evening.

Sixteen hours? — Yes.

With what intervals at dinner? — An hour.

How far did you live from the mill? — About two miles.

Was there any time allowed for you to get your breakfast in the mill? — No.

Did you take it before you left your home? — Generally.

During those long hours of labour could you be punctual; how did you awake? — I seldom did awake spontaneously; I was most generally awoke or lifted out of bed, sometimes asleep, by my parents.

Were you always in time? — No.

What was the consequence if you had been too late? — I was most commonly beaten.

Severely? — Very severely, I thought.

In whose factory was this? — Messrs. Hague & Cook's, of Dewsbury.

Will you state the effect that those long hours had upon the state of your health and feelings? — I was, when working those long hours, commonly very much fatigued at night, when I left my work; so much so that I sometimes should have slept as I walked if I had not stumbled and started awake again; and so sick often that I could not eat, and what I did eat I vomited.

Did this labour destroy your appetite? — It did.

In what situation were you in that mill? — I was a piecener.

Will you state to this Committee whether piecening is a very laborious employment for children, or not? — It is a very laborious employment. Pieceners are continually running to and fro, and on their feet the whole day.

The duty of the piecener is to take the cardings from one part of the machinery, and to place them on another? — Yes.

So that the labour is not only continual, but it is unabated to the last? — It is unabated to the last.

Do you not think, from your own experience, that the speed of the machinery is so calculated as to demand the utmost exertions of a child supposing the hours were moderate? — It is as much as they could do at the best; they are always upon the stretch, and it is commonly very difficult to keep up with their work.

State the condition of the children toward the latter part of the day, who have thus to keep up with the machinery. — It is as much as they can do when they are not very much fatigued to keep up with their work, and toward the close of the day, when they come to be more fatigued, they cannot keep up with it very well, and the consequence is that they are beaten to spur them on.

Were you beaten under those circumstances? — Yes.

Frequently? — Very frequently.

And principally at the latter end of the day? — Yes.

And is it your belief that if you had not been so beaten, you should not have got through the work? — I should not if I had not been kept up to it by some means.

Does beating then principally occur at the latter end of the day, when the children are exceedingly fatigued? — It does at the latter end of the day, and in the morning sometimes, when they are very drowsy, and have not got rid of the fatigue of the day before.

What were you beaten with principally? — A strap.

Anything else? — Yes, a stick sometimes; and there is a kind of roller which runs on the top of the machine called a billy, perhaps two or three yards in length, and perhaps an inch and a half, or more in diameter; the circumference would be four or five inches; I cannot speak exactly.

Were you beaten with that instrument? — Yes.

Have you yourself been beaten, and have you seen other children struck severely with that roller? — I have been struck very severely with it myself, so much so as to knock me down, and I have seen other children have their heads broken with it.

You think that it is a general practice to beat the children with the roller? — It is.

You do not think then that you were worse treated than other children in the mill? — No, I was not, perhaps not so bad as some were.

In those mills is chastisement towards the latter part of the day going on perpetually? — Perpetually.

So that you can hardly be in a mill without hearing constant crying? — Never an hour, I believe.

Do you think that if the overlooker were naturally a humane person it would be still found necessary for him to beat the children, in order to keep up their attention and vigilance at the termination of those extraordinary days of labour? — Yes, the machine turns off a regular quantity of cardings, and of course they must keep as regularly to their work the whole of the day; they must keep with the machine, and therefore however humane the slubber may be, as he must keep up with the machine or be found fault with, he spurs the children to keep up also by various means but that which he commonly resorts to is to strap them when they become drowsy.

At the time when you were beaten for not keeping up with your work, were you anxious to have done it if you possibly could? — Yes; the dread of being beaten if we could not keep up with our work was a sufficient impulse to keep us to it if we could.

When you got home at night after this labour, did you feel much fatigued? — Very much so.

Had you any time to be with your parents, and to receive instruction from them? — No.

What did you do? — All that we did when we got home was to get the little bit of supper that was provided for us and go to bed immediately. If the supper had not been ready directly, we should have gone to sleep while it was preparing.

Did you not, as a child, feel it a very grievous hardship to be roused so soon in the morning? — I did.

Were the rest of the children similarly circumstanced? — Yes, all of them; but they were not all of them so far from their work as I was.

And if you had been too late you were under the apprehension of being cruelly beaten? — I generally was beaten when I happened to be too late; and when I got up in the morning the apprehension of that was so great, that I used to run, and cry all the way as I went to the mill.

That was the way by which your punctual attendance was secured? — Yes.

And you do not think it could have been secured by any other means? — No.

Then it is your impression from what you have seen, and from your own experience, that those long hours of labour have the effect of rendering young persons who are subject to them exceedingly unhappy? — Yes.

You have already said it had a considerable effect upon your health? — Yes.

Do you conceive that it diminished your growth? — I did not pay much attention to that; but I have been examined by some persons who said they thought I was rather stunted, and that I should have been taller if I had not worked at the mill.

What were your wages at that time? — Three shillings (per week).

And how much a day had you for overwork when you were worked so exceedingly long? — A halfpenny a day.

Did you frequently forfeit that if you were not always there to a moment? — Yes; I most frequently forfeited what was allowed for those long hours.

You took your food to the mill; was it in your mill, as is the case in cotton mills, much spoiled by being laid aside? — It was very frequently covered by flues from the wool; and in that case they had to be blown off with the mouth, and picked off with the fingers before it could be eaten.

So that not giving you a little leisure for eating your food, but obliging you to take it at the mill, spoiled your food when you did get it? — Yes, very commonly.

And that at the same time that this over-labour injured your appetite? — Yes.

Could you eat when you got home? — Not always.

What is the effect of this piecening upon the hands? — It makes them bleed; the skin is completely rubbed off, and in that case they bleed in perhaps a dozen parts.

The prominent parts of the hand? — Yes, all the prominent parts of the hand are rubbed down till they bleed; every day they are rubbed in that way.

All the time you continue at work? — All the time we are working. The hands never can be hardened in that work, for the grease keeps them soft in the first instance, and long and continual rubbing is always wearing them down, so that if they were hard they would be sure to bleed.

It is attended with much pain? — Very much.

Do they allow you to make use of the back of the hand? — No; the work cannot be so well done with the back of the hand, or I should have made use of that.

44

KARL MARX AND FRIEDRICH ENGELS

From The Communist Manifesto

The Communist Manifesto was written in 1848 in the midst of European upheaval, a time when capitalist industrialization had spread from England to France and Germany. Marx and Engels were Germans who studied and worked in France and England. In the *Manifesto*, they imagine a revolution that will transform all of Europe. What do they see as the inevitable causes of this revolution? How, according to their analysis, is the crisis of "modern" society different from previous crises? Were Marx and Engels correct?

Thinking Historically

Notice how Marx and Engels describe the notions of capitalism and industrialization without using those words. The term *capitalism* developed later from Marx's classic *Das Kapital* (1859), but the term *bourgeoisie*,* as Engels notes in this selection, stands for the capitalist class. For Marx and Engels, the industrial revolution (another later phrase) is the product of a particular stage of capitalist development. Thus, if Marx and Engels were asked whether capitalism or industry was the principal force that created the modern world, what would their answer be?

The Communist Manifesto is widely known as the classic critique of capitalism, but a careful reading reveals a list of achievements of capitalist or "bourgeois civilization." What are these achievements? Did Marx and Engels consider them to be achievements? How could Marx and Engels both praise and criticize capitalism?

Bourgeois and Proletarians[1]

The history of all hitherto existing society is the history of class struggles.

*bohr zhwah ZEE

[1]In French *bourgeois* means a town-dweller. *Proletarian* comes from the Latin, *proletarius*, which meant a person whose sole wealth was his offspring (*proles*). [Ed.]

[Note by Engels] By "bourgeoisie" is meant the class of modern capitalists, owners of the means of social production and employers of wage-labor; by "proletariat," the class of modern wage-laborers who, having no means of production of their own, are reduced to selling their labor power in order to live.

Karl Marx and Friedrich Engels, *Manifesto of the Communist Party* (Arlington Heights, Ill.: Harlan Davidson, 1955). Reprinted in the Crofts Classics Series.

Freeman and slave, patrician and plebeian, lord and serf, guildmaster and journeyman, in a word, oppressor and oppressed, stood in constant opposition to one another, carried on an uninterrupted, now hidden, now open fight, a fight that each time ended, either in a revolutionary reconstitution of society at large, or in the common ruin of the contending classes.

In the earlier epochs of history, we find almost everywhere a complicated arrangement of society into various orders, a manifold gradation of social rank. In ancient Rome we have patricians, knights, plebeians, slaves; in the Middle Ages, feudal lords, vassals, guildmasters, journeymen, apprentices, serfs; in almost all of these classes, again, subordinate gradations.

The modern bourgeois society that has sprouted from the ruins of feudal society, has not done away with class antagonisms. It has but established new classes, new conditions of oppression, new forms of struggle in place of the old ones.

Our epoch, the epoch of the bourgeoisie, possesses, however, this distinctive feature: It has simplified the class antagonisms. Society as a whole is more and more splitting up into the two great hostile camps, into two great classes directly facing each other — bourgeoisie and proletariat.

From the serfs of the Middle Ages sprang the chartered burghers of the earliest towns. From these burgesses the first elements of the bourgeoisie were developed.

The discovery of America, the rounding of the Cape, opened up fresh ground for the rising bourgeoisie. The East-Indian and Chinese markets, the colonization of America, trade with the colonies, the increase in the means of exchange and in commodities generally, gave to commerce, to navigation, to industry, an impulse never before known, and thereby, to the revolutionary element in the tottering feudal society, a rapid development.

The feudal system of industry, in which industrial production was monopolized by closed guilds, now no longer sufficed for the growing wants of the new markets. The manufacturing system took its place. The guildmasters were pushed aside by the manufacturing middle class; division of labor between the different corporate guilds vanished in the face of division of labor in each single workshop.

Meantime the markets kept ever growing, the demand ever rising. Even manufacture[2] no longer sufficed. Thereupon, steam and machin-

---

[2]By *manufacture* Marx meant the system of production which succeeded the guild system but which still relied mainly upon direct human labor for power. He distinguished it from modern industry which arose when machinery driven by water and steam was introduced. [Ed.]

ery revolutionized industrial production. The place of manufacture was taken by the giant, modern industry, the place of the industrial middle class, by industrial millionaires — the leaders of whole industrial armies, the modern bourgeois.

Modern industry has established the world market, for which the discovery of America paved the way. This market has given an immense development to commerce, to navigation, to communication by land. This development has, in its turn, reacted on the extension of industry; and in proportion as industry, commerce, navigation, railways extended, in the same proportion the bourgeoisie developed, increased its capital, and pushed into the background every class handed down from the Middle Ages.

We see, therefore, how the modern bourgeoisie is itself the product of a long course of development, of a series of revolutions in the modes of production and of exchange.

Each step in the development of the bourgeoisie was accompanied by a corresponding political advance of that class. An oppressed class under the sway of the feudal nobility, it became an armed and self-governing association in the medieval commune; here independent urban republic (as in Italy and Germany), there taxable "third estate" of the monarchy (as in France); afterwards, in the period of manufacture proper, serving either the semifeudal or the absolute monarchy as a counterpoise against the nobility, and, in fact, cornerstone of the great monarchies in general — the bourgeoisie has at last, since the establishment of modern industry and of the world market, conquered for itself, in the modern representative state, exclusive political sway. The executive of the modern state is but a committee for managing the common affairs of the whole bourgeoisie.

The bourgeoisie has played a most revolutionary role in history.

The bourgeoisie, wherever it has got the upper hand, has put an end to all feudal, patriarchal, idyllic relations. It has pitilessly torn asunder the motley feudal ties that bound man to his "natural superiors," and has left no other bond between man and man than naked self-interest, than callous "cash payment." It has drowned the most heavenly ecstasies of religious fervor, of chivalrous enthusiasm, of philistine sentimentalism, in the icy water of egotistical calculation. It has resolved personal worth into exchange value, and in place of the numberless indefensible chartered freedoms, has set up that single, unconscionable freedom — Free Trade. In one word, for exploitation, veiled by religious and political illusions, it has substituted naked, shameless, direct, brutal exploitation.

The bourgeoisie has stripped of its halo every occupation hitherto honored and looked up to with reverent awe. It has converted the physician, the lawyer, the priest, the poet, the man of science, into its paid wage-laborers.

The bourgeoisie has torn away from the family its sentimental veil, and has reduced the family relation to a mere money relation.

The bourgeoisie has disclosed how it came to pass that the brutal display of vigor in the Middle Ages, which reactionaries so much admire, found its fitting complement in the most slothful indolence. It has been the first to show what man's activity can bring about. It has accomplished wonders far surpassing Egyptian pyramids, Roman aqueducts, and Gothic cathedrals; it has conducted expeditions that put in the shade all former migrations of nations and crusades.

The bourgeoisie cannot exist without constantly revolutionizing the instruments of production, and thereby the relations of production, and with them the whole relations of society. Conservation of the old modes of production in unaltered form, was, on the contrary, the first condition of existence for all earlier industrial classes. Constant revolutionizing of production, uninterrupted disturbance of all social conditions, everlasting uncertainty and agitation distinguished the bourgeois epoch from all earlier ones. All fixed, fast-frozen relations, with their train of ancient and venerable prejudices and opinions, are swept away, all new-formed ones become antiquated before they can ossify. All that is solid melts into air, all that is holy is profaned, and man is at last compelled to face with sober senses his real conditions of life and his relations with his kind.

The need of a constantly expanding market for its products chases the bourgeoisie over the whole surface of the globe. It must nestle everywhere, settle everywhere, establish connections everywhere.

The bourgeoisie has through its exploitation of the world market given a cosmopolitan character to production and consumption in every country. To the great chagrin of reactionaries, it has drawn from under the feet of industry the national ground on which it stood. All old-established national industries have been destroyed or are daily being destroyed. They are dislodged by new industries, whose introduction becomes a life and death question for all civilized nations, by industries that no longer work up indigenous raw material, but raw material drawn from the remotest zones; industries whose products are consumed, not only at home, but in every quarter of the globe. In place of the old wants, satisfied by the production of the country, we find new wants, requiring for their satisfaction the products of distant lands and climes. In place of the old local and national seclusion and self-sufficiency, we have intercourse in every direction, universal interdependence of nations. And as in material, so also in intellectual production. The intellectual creations of individual nations become common property. National one-sidedness and narrow-mindedness become more and more impossible, and from the numerous national and local literatures there arises a world literature.

The bourgeoisie, by the rapid improvement of all instruments of production, by the immensely facilitated means of communication, draws all nations, even the most barbarian, into civilization. The cheap prices of its commodities are the heavy artillery with which it batters down all Chinese walls, with which it forces the barbarians' intensely obstinate hatred for foreigners to capitulate. It compels all nations, on pain of extinction, to adopt the bourgeois mode of production; it compels them to introduce what it calls civilization into their midst, i.e., to become bourgeois themselves. In a word, it creates a world after its own image.

The bourgeoisie has subjected the country to the rule of the towns. It has created enormous cities, has greatly increased the urban population as compared with the rural, and has thus rescued a considerable part of the population from the idiocy of rural life. Just as it has made the country dependent on the towns, so it has made barbarian and semi-barbarian countries dependent on the civilized ones, nations of peasants on nations of bourgeois, the East on the West.

More and more the bourgeoisie keeps doing away with the scattered state of the population, of the means of production, and of property. It has agglomerated population, centralized means of production, and has concentrated property in a few hands. The necessary consequence of this was political centralization. Independent, or but loosely connected provinces, with separate interests, laws, governments and systems of taxation, became lumped together into one nation, with one government, one code of laws, one national class interest, one frontier and one customs tariff.

The bourgeoisie, during its rule of scarce one hundred years, has created more massive and more colossal productive forces than have all preceding generations together. Subjection of nature's forces to man, machinery, application of chemistry to industry and agriculture, steam-navigation, railways, electric telegraphs, clearing of whole continents for cultivation, canalization of rivers, whole populations conjured out of the ground — what earlier century had even a presentiment that such productive forces slumbered in the lap of social labor?

We see then that the means of production and of exchange, which served as the foundation for the growth of the bourgeoisie, were generated in feudal society. At a certain stage in the development of these means of production and of exchange, the conditions under which feudal society produced and exchanged, the feudal organization of agriculture and manufacturing industry, in a word, the feudal relations of property became no longer compatible with the already developed productive forces; they became so many fetters. They had to be burst asunder; they were burst asunder.

Into their place stepped free competition, accompanied by a social and political constitution adapted to it, and by the economic and political sway of the bourgeois class.

A similar movement is going on before our own eyes. Modern bourgeois society with its relations of production, of exchange and of property, a society that has conjured up such gigantic means of production and exchange, is like the sorcerer who is no longer able to control the powers of the nether world whom he has called up by his spells. For many a decade past the history of industry and commerce is but the history of the revolt of modern productive forces against modern conditions of production, against the property relations that are the conditions for the existence of the bourgeoisie and of its rule. It is enough to mention the commercial crises that by their periodical return put the existence of the entire bourgeoisie society on trial, each time more threateningly. In these crises a great part not only of the existing products, but also of the previously created productive forces, are periodically destroyed. In these crises there breaks out an epidemic that, in all earlier epochs, would have seemed an absurdity — the epidemic of overproduction. Society suddenly finds itself put back into a state of momentary barbarism; it appears as if a famine, a universal war of devastation had cut off the supply of every means of subsistence; industry and commerce seem to be destroyed. And why? Because there is too much civilization, too much means of subsistence, too much industry, too much commerce. The productive forces at the disposal of society no longer tend to further the development of the conditions of bourgeois property; on the contrary, they have become too powerful for these conditions, by which they are fettered, and no sooner do they overcome these fetters than they bring disorder into the whole of bourgeois society, endanger the existence of bourgeois property. The conditions of bourgeois society are too narrow to comprise the wealth created by them. And how does the bourgeoisie get over these crises? On the one hand by enforced destruction of a mass of productive forces; on the other, by the conquest of new markets, and by the more thorough exploitation of the old ones. That is to say, by paving the way for more extensive and more destructive crises, and by diminishing the means whereby crises are prevented.

The weapons with which the bourgeoisie felled feudalism to the ground are now turned against the bourgeoisie itself.

But not only has the bourgeoisie forged the weapons that bring death to itself; it has also called into existence the men who are to wield those weapons — the modern working class — the proletarians.

In proportion as the bourgeoisie, i.e., capital, is developed, in the same proportion is the proletariat, the modern working class, developed — a class of labourers, who live only so long as they find work, and who find work only so long as their labour increases capital. These labourers, who must sell themselves piece-meal, are a commodity, like every other article of commerce, and are consequently exposed to all the vicissitudes of competition, to all the fluctuations of the market.

Owing to the extensive use of machinery and to division of labour, the work of the proletarians has lost all individual character, and consequently, all charm for the workman. He becomes an appendage of the machine, and it is only the most simple, most monotonous, and most easily acquired knack, that is required of him. Hence, the cost of production of a workman is restricted, almost entirely, to the means of subsistence that he requires for his maintenance, and for the propagation of his race. But the price of a commodity, and therefore also of labour, is equal to its cost of production. In proportion therefore, as the repulsiveness of the work increases, the wage decreases. Nay more, in proportion as the use of machinery and division of labour increases, in the same proportion the burden of toil also increases, whether by prolongation of the working hours, by increase of the work exacted in a given time or by increased speed of the machinery, etc.

Modern industry has converted the little workshop of the patriarchal master into the great factory of the industrial capitalist. Masses of labourers, crowded into the factory, are organised like soldiers. As privates of the industrial army they are placed under the command of a perfect hierarchy of officers and sergeants. Not only are they slaves of the bourgeois class, and of the bourgeois State; they are daily and hourly enslaved by the machine, by the over-looker, and, above all, by the individual bourgeois manufacturer himself. The more openly this despotism proclaims gain to be its end and aim, the more petty, the more hateful and the more embittering it is.

The less the skill and exertion of strength implied in manual labour, in other words, the more modern industry becomes developed, the more is the labour of men superseded by that of women. Differences of age and sex have no longer any distinctive social validity for the working class. All are instruments of labour, more or less expensive to use, according to their age and sex.

No sooner is the exploitation of the labourer by the manufacturer, so far, at an end, that he receives his wages in cash, than he is set upon by the other portions of the bourgeoisie, the landlord, the shopkeeper, the pawnbroker, etc.

The lower strata of the middle class — the small tradespeople, shopkeepers, retired tradesmen generally, the handicraftsmen and peasants — all these sink gradually into the proletariat, partly because their diminutive capital does not suffice for the scale on which Modern Industry is carried on, and is swamped in the competition with the large capitalists, partly because their specialized skill is rendered worthless by the new methods of production. Thus the proletariat is recruited from all classes of the population.

$$45$$

PETER N. STEARNS

The Industrial Revolution Outside the West

Stearns, a modern historian, discusses the export of industrial machinery and techniques outside the West (Europe and North America) in the nineteenth century. Again and again, he finds that initial attempts at industrialization — in Russia, India, Egypt, and South America — led to increased production of export crops and resources but failed to stimulate true industrial revolutions. Consequently, as producers of raw materials, these countries became more deeply dependent on Western markets for their products, while at the same time importing from the West more valuable manufactured products like machinery. What common reasons can you find for these failures?

Thinking Historically

Did nineteenth-century efforts to ignite industrial revolutions outside the West fail because these societies neglected to develop capitalism, or did they fail because their local needs were subordinated to those of Western capitalists? Explain.

Before the 1870s no industrial revolution occurred outside Western society. The spread of industrialization within western Europe, while by no means automatic, followed from a host of shared economic, cultural, and political features. The quick ascension of the United States was somewhat more surprising — the area was not European and had been far less developed economically during the eighteenth century. Nevertheless, extensive commercial experience in the northern states and the close mercantile and cultural ties with Britain gave the new nation advantages for its rapid imitation of the British lead. Abundant natural resources and extensive investments from Europe kept the process going, joining the United States to the wider dynamic of industrialization in the nineteenth-century West.

Elsewhere, conditions did not permit an industrial revolution, an issue that must be explored in dealing with the international context for this first phase of the world's industrial experience. Yet the West's in-

Peter N. Stearns, *The Industrial Revolution in World History* (Boulder, Colo.: Westview Press, 1993), 71–79.

dustrial revolution did have substantial impact. It led to a number of pilot projects whereby initial machinery and factories were established under Western guidance. More important, it led to new Western demands on the world's economies that instigated significant change without industrialization; indeed, these demands in several cases made industrialization more difficult.

Pilot Projects

Russia's contact with the West's industrial revolution before the 1870s offers an important case study that explains why many societies could not follow the lead of nations like France or the United States in imitating Britain. Yet Russia did introduce some new equipment for economic and military-political reasons, and these initiatives did generate change — they were not mere window dressing.

More than most societies not directly part of Western civilization, Russia had special advantages in reacting to the West's industrial lead and special motivation for paying attention to this lead. Russia had been part of Europe's diplomatic network since about 1700. It saw itself as one of Europe's great powers, a participant in international conferences and military alliances. The country also had close cultural ties with western Europe, sharing in artistic styles and scientific developments — though Russian leadership had stepped back from cultural alignment because of the shock of the French Revolution in 1789 and subsequent political disorders in the West. Russian aristocrats and intellectuals routinely visited western Europe. Finally, Russia had prior experience in imitating Western technology and manufacturing: importation of Western metallurgy and shipbuilding had formed a major part of Peter the Great's reform program in the early eighteenth century.

Contacts of this sort explain why Russia began to receive an industrial outreach from the West within a few decades of the advent of the industrial revolution. British textile machinery was imported beginning in 1843. Ernst Knoop, a German immigrant to Britain who had clerked in a Manchester cotton factory, set himself up as export agent to the Russians. He also sponsored British workers who installed the machinery in Russia and told any Russian entrepreneur brash enough to ask not simply for British models but for alterations or adaptations: "That is not your affair; in England they know better than you." Despite the snobbism, a number of Russian entrepreneurs set up small factories to produce cotton, aware that even in Russia's small urban market they could make a substantial profit by underselling traditional manufactured cloth. Other factories were established directly by Britons.

Europeans and Americans were particularly active in responding to calls by the tsar's government for assistance in establishing railway and steamship lines. The ~~first steamship appeared in Russia in 1815~~, and by 1820 a regular service ran on the Volga River. The ~~first public railroad,~~ ~~joining St. Petersburg~~ to the ~~imperial residence in the suburbs~~, opened in ~~1837~~. In 1851 the first major line connected St. Petersburg and Moscow, along a remarkably straight route desired by Tsar Nicholas I himself. ~~American engineers were brought in~~, again by the government, to set up a railroad industry so that Russians could build their own locomotives and cars. George Whistler, the father of the painter James McNeill Whistler (and thus husband of Whistler's mother), played an important role in the effort. He and some American workers helped train Russians in the needed crafts, frequently complaining about their slovenly habits but appreciating their willingness to learn.

Russian imports of machinery increased rapidly; they were over thirty times as great in 1860 as they had been in 1825. While in 1851 the nation manufactured only about half as many machines as it imported, by 1860 the equation was reversed, and the number of machine-building factories had quintupled (from nineteen to ninety-nine). The new cotton industry surged forward with most production organized in factories using wage labor.

These were important changes. They revealed that some ~~Russians~~ ~~were alert to the business advantages of Western methods and that~~ ~~some Westerners saw the great profits to be made by setting up shop in~~ ~~a huge but largely agricultural country.~~ The role of the government was vital: The ~~tsars used tax money to offer substantial premiums to West-~~ ~~ern entrepreneurs~~, who liked the adventure of dealing with the Russians but liked their superior profit margins even more.

But Russia did not then industrialize. Modern industrial operations did not sufficiently dent established economic practices. The nation remained overwhelmingly agricultural. High percentage increases in manufacturing proceeded from such a low base that they had little general impact. Several structural barriers impeded a genuine industrial revolution. Russia's cities had never boasted a manufacturing tradition; there were few artisans skilled even in preindustrial methods. Only by the 1860s and 1870s had cities grown enough for an artisan core to take shape — in printing, for example — and even then large numbers of foreigners (particularly Germans) had to be imported. Even more serious was the system of serfdom that kept most Russians bound to agricultural estates. While some free laborers could be found, most rural ~~Russians could not legally leave their land~~, and their ~~obligation to de-~~ ~~vote extensive work service to their lords' estates reduced their incen-~~ ~~tive even for agricultural production~~. Peter the Great had managed to adapt serfdom to a preindustrial metallurgical industry by allowing landlords to sell villages and the labor therein for expansion of iron-works. But this ~~mongrel system~~ was ~~not suitable for change on~~ a ~~grander scale~~, which is precisely ~~what the industrial revolution entailed~~.

Furthermore, the West's industrial revolution, while it provided tangible examples for Russia to imitate, also produced pressures to develop more traditional sectors in lieu of structural change. The West's growing cities and rising prosperity claimed rising levels of Russian timber, hemp, tallow, and, increasingly, grain. These were export goods that could be produced without new technology and without altering the existing labor system. Indeed, many landlords boosted the work-service obligations of the serfs in order to generate more grain production for sale to the West. The obvious temptation was to lock in an older economy — to respond to new opportunity by incremental changes within the traditional system and to maintain serfdom and the rural preponderance rather than to risk fundamental internal transformation.

The proof of Russia's lag showed in foreign trade. It rose but rather modestly, posting a threefold increase between 1800 and 1860. Exports of raw materials approximately paid for the imports of some machinery, factory-made goods from abroad, and a substantial volume of luxury products for the aristocracy. And the regions that participated most in the growing trade were not the tiny industrial enclaves (in St. Petersburg, Moscow, and the iron-rich Urals) but the wheat-growing areas of southern Russia where even industrial pilot projects had yet to surface. Russian manufacturing exported nothing at all to the West, though it did find a few customers in Turkey, central Asia, and China.

The proof of Russia's lag showed even more dramatically in Russia's new military disadvantage. Peter the Great's main goal had been to keep Russian military production near enough to Western levels to remain competitive, with the huge Russian population added into the equation. This strategy now failed, for the West's industrial revolution changed the rules of the game. A war in 1854 pitting Russia against Britain and France led to Russia's defeat in its own backyard. The British and French objected to new Russian territorial gains (won at the expense of Turkey's Ottoman Empire) that brought Russia greater access to the Black Sea. The battleground was the Crimea. Yet British and French steamships connected their armies more reliably with supplies and reinforcements from home than did Russia's ground transportation system with its few railroads and mere three thousand miles of first-class roads. And British and French industry could pour out more and higher-quality uniforms, guns, and munitions than traditional Russian manufacturing could hope to match. The Russians lost the Crimean War, surrendering their gains and swallowing their pride in 1856. Patchwork change had clearly proved insufficient to match the military, much less the economic, power the industrial revolution had generated in the West.

After a brief interlude, the Russians digested the implications of their defeat and launched a period of basic structural reforms. The linchpin was the abolition of serfdom in 1861. Peasants were not entirely freed, and rural discontent persisted, but many workers could now leave the land; the basis for a wage labor force was established. Other reforms focused on improving basic education and health, and while change in these areas was slow, it too set the basis for a genuine commitment to industrialization. A real industrial revolution lay in the future, however. By the 1870s Russia's contact with industrialization had deepened its economic gap vis-à-vis the West but had yielded a few interesting experiments with new methods and a growing realization of the need for further change.

Societies elsewhere in the world — those more removed from traditional ties to the West or more severely disadvantaged in the ties that did exist — saw even more tentative industrial pilot projects during the West's industrialization period. The Middle East and India tried some industrial imitation early on but largely failed — though not without generating some important economic change. Latin America also launched some revealingly limited technological change. Only eastern Asia and sub-Saharan Africa were largely untouched by any explicit industrial imitations until the late 1860s or beyond; they were too distant from European culture to venture a response so quickly.

Prior links with the West formed the key variable, as Russia's experience abundantly demonstrated. Societies that had some familiarity with Western merchants and some preindustrial awareness of the West's steady commercial gains mounted some early experiments in industrialization. Whether they benefited as a result compared with areas that did nothing before the late nineteenth century might be debated.

One industrial initiative in India developed around Calcutta, where British colonial rule had centered since the East India Company founded the city in 1690. A Hindu Brahman family, the Tagores, established close ties with many British administrators. Without becoming British, they sponsored a number of efforts to revivify India, including new colleges and research centers. Dwarkanath Tagore controlled tax collection in part of Bengal, and early in the nineteenth century he used part of his profit to found a bank. He also bought up a variety of commercial landholdings and traditional manufacturing operations. In 1834 he joined with British capitalists to establish a diversified company that boasted holdings in mines (including the first Indian coal mine), sugar refineries, and some new textile factories; the equipment was imported from Britain. Tagore's dominant idea was a British-Indian economic and cultural collaboration that would revitalize his country. He enjoyed a high reputation in Europe and for a short time made a success of his economic initiatives. Tagore died on a trip abroad, and his financial empire declined soon after.

This first taste of Indian industrialization was significant, but it brought few immediate results. The big news in India, even as Tagore launched his companies, was the rapid decline of traditional textiles under the bombardment of British factory competition; millions of Indian villagers were thrown out of work. Furthermore, relations between Britain and the Indian elite worsened after the mid-1830s as British officials sought a more active economic role and became more intolerant of Indian culture. One British official, admitting no knowledge of Indian scholarship, wrote that "all the historical information" and science available in Sanskrit was "less valuable than what may be found in the most paltry abridgements used at preparatory schools in England." With these attitudes, the kind of collaboration that might have aided Indian appropriation of British industry became impossible.

The next step in India's contact with the industrial revolution did not occur until the 1850s when the colonial government began to build a significant railroad network. The first passenger line opened in 1853. Some officials feared that Hindus might object to traveling on such smoke-filled monsters, but trains proved very popular and there ensued a period of rapid economic and social change. The principal result, however, was not industrial development but further extension of commercial agriculture (production of cotton and other goods for export) and intensification of British sales to India's interior. Coal mining did expand, but manufacturing continued to shrink. There was no hint of an industrial revolution in India.

Imitation in the Middle East was somewhat more elaborate, in part because most of this region, including parts of North Africa, retained independence from European colonialism. Muslims had long disdained Western culture and Christianity, and Muslim leaders, including the rulers of the great Ottoman Empire, had been very slow to recognize the West's growing dynamism after the fifteenth century. Some Western medicine was imported, but technology was ignored. Only in the eighteenth century did this attitude begin, haltingly, to change. The Ottoman government imported a printing press from Europe and began discussing Western-style technical training, primarily in relationship to the military.

In 1798 a French force briefly seized Egypt, providing a vivid symbol of Europe's growing technical superiority. Later an Ottoman governor, Muhammed Ali, seized Egypt from the imperial government and pursued an ambitious agenda of expansionism and modernization. Muhammed Ali sponsored many changes in Egyptian society in imitation of Western patterns, including a new tax system and new kinds of schooling. He also destroyed the traditional Egyptian elite. The government encouraged agricultural production by sponsoring major irrigation projects and began to import elements of the industrial revolution from the West in the 1830s. English machinery and technicians were brought in to build textile factories, sugar refineries, paper mills, and weapons shops. Muhammed Ali clearly contemplated a sweeping reform program in which industrialization would play a central role in making Egypt a powerhouse in the Middle East and an equal to the European powers. Many of his plans worked well, but the industrialization effort failed. Egyptian factories could not in the main compete with European imports, and the initial experiments either failed or stagnated. More durable changes involved the encouragement to the production of cash crops like sugar and cotton, which the government required in order to earn tax revenues to support its armies and its industrial imports. Growing concentration on cash crops also enriched a new group of Egyptian landlords and merchants. But the shift actually formalized Egypt's dependent position in the world economy, as European businesses and governments increasingly interfered with the internal economy. The Egyptian reaction to the West's industrial revolution, even more than the Russian response, was to generate massive economic redefinition without industrialization, a strategy that locked peasants into landlord control and made a manufacturing transformation at best a remote prospect.

Spurred by the West's example and by Muhammed Ali, the Ottoman government itself set up some factories after 1839, importing equipment from Europe to manufacture textiles, paper, and guns. Coal and iron mining were encouraged. The government established a postal system in 1834, a telegraph system in 1855, and steamships and the beginning of railway construction from 1866 onward. These changes increased the role of European traders and investors in the Ottoman economy and produced no overall industrial revolution. Again, the clearest result of improved transport and communication was a growing emphasis on the export of cash crops and minerals to pay for necessary manufactured imports from Europe. An industrial example had been set, and, as in Egypt, a growing though still tiny minority of Middle Easterners gained some factory experience, but no fundamental transformation occurred. . . .

Developments of preliminary industrial trappings — a few factories, a few railroads — nowhere outside Europe converted whole economies to an industrialization process until late in the nineteenth century, though they provided some relevant experience on which later (mainly after 1870) and more intensive efforts could build. A few workers became factory hands and experienced some of the same upheaval as their Western counterparts in terms of new routines and pressures on work pace. Many sought to limit their factory experience, leaving for other work or for the countryside after a short time; transience was a problem for much the same reasons as in the West: the clash with traditional work and leisure values. Some technical and business expertise also developed. Governments took the lead in most attempts to imitate the West, which was another portent for the future; with some exceptions, local merchant groups had neither the capital nor the motivation to undertake such ambitious and uncertain projects. By the 1850s a number of governments were clearly beginning to realize that some policy response to the industrial revolution was absolutely essential, lest Western influence become still more overwhelming. On balance, however, the principal results of very limited imitation tended to heighten the economic imbalance with western Europe, a disparity that made it easier to focus on nonindustrial exports. This too was a heritage for the future. . . .

$$46$$

JOHN H. COATSWORTH
Economic Trajectories in Latin America

In this selection, John Coatsworth, a modern economic historian of Latin America, looks at the long-term economic histories of a number of Latin American countries and compares them to those of the United States. What are the main differences between the economic histories of Latin America and the United States? How were Latin American economic histories different, one from the other? What is the significance of those differences?

Thinking Historically

The author is a proponent of two recent trends in economic history. One is called neoclassical and the other is statistical. You can see the importance of statistics in this selection. Coatsworth maintained that an earlier generation of Latin American economic historians made some mistaken assumptions because they lacked the basic data that was necessary to understand the broad changes or trajectories (pathways) of Latin American economic history. How do the statistics presented here change or reinforce any of your assumptions about Latin American history? The neoclassical economic historians used data to measure the kinds of forces that Adam Smith and classical economists had emphasized. How does this essay support Smith's argument about

John H. Coatsworth, "Economic and Institutional Trajectories in Nineteenth-Century Latin America," in *Latin America and the World Economy Since 1800*, ed. John H. Coatsworth and Alan M. Taylor (Cambridge: Harvard University Press, 1998), 23–31.

the "wealth of nations"? Notice that Coatsworth says nothing about the industrial revolution and very little about technology. How can an economic history of Latin America ignore the industrial revolution?

Latin America fell into relative backwardness between roughly 1700 and 1900. At the beginning of this period, the economies of the Iberian colonies in the New World were roughly as productive as those of the British. For most of the ensuing 200 years, the Latin American economies stagnated while those of the North Atlantic achieved sustained increases in productivity. As early as 1800, most of the Latin American economies had already fallen well behind the United States. A century later, most had fallen far enough behind to qualify as "less" (or "under-") developed by contemporary standards.

In the twentieth century, the Latin American economies have achieved respectable rates of economic growth, equal on average to that of the United States. Thus, the relative gap between Latin America and the United States has not changed at all in the past 100 years, though the relative positions of individual countries have shifted. To understand how the Latin American economies fell into relative backwardness, therefore, it is crucial to look at the region's pre-1900 economic history.

Latin America stagnated for most of two crucial centuries because economic institutions distorted incentives and high transport costs left most of the region's abundant natural resources beyond the frontier of profitable exploitation. Early in the colonial era, comparatively high *levels* of productivity were achieved in economies that managed, despite these constraints, to specialize in export production. The successful cases were those that combined relatively scarce supplies of free or slave labor with accessible natural resources and a favorable policy environment. In contrast, colonial economies that relied on relatively cheap indigenous or slave labor to produce exportables in less accessible regions with high tax and regulatory burdens tended to have smaller export sectors and to be less productive. Cycles of export growth and decline, linked to market fluctuations or to freshly discovered and subsequently depleted natural resources, produced variations on these patterns well into the twentieth century in some areas.

Once the opportunities created by more (or less) favorable initial conditions were seized and exploited in a given colony, further economic *growth* usually depended on some combination of institutional modernization and transport innovation. Not until the late nineteenth century did liberalism (or, in some cases, modernizing conservative regimes) and railroads remove the two fundamental obstacles to growth in Latin America and push most of the region's economies onto new trajectories. . . .

Colonial and Nineteenth-Century Trends

As the first permanent English settlers in North America set about chopping down trees to make crude cabins in December of 1620, the Spanish and Portuguese empires in the New World had already passed their first century. It would take the English more than 200 years to catch up to the most prosperous of Spain's possessions. In 1650, Cuba had a gross domestic product (GDP) per capita of roughly $60; the British North American colonies did not reach that level until more than a century later. By 1800, Cuba's GDP per capita was near $90, whereas that of the United States had barely reached $80. The United States did not close the gap with Cuba until the 1830s.

The U.S. performance looks much better in comparison with Spain's mainland colonies. The 13 British colonies probably caught up to Mexico before 1700. Over the eighteenth century, Mexico stagnated as the U.S. economy grew at perhaps a half a percent a year. In 1800, Mexico's per capita GDP of $40 stood at half that of the United States. Brazil, recovering finally from the collapse of its short-lived gold boom (1750–1780), had fallen well behind.

The race ended long before the nineteenth century was over. By 1900, the United States had become a formidable economic power with a GDP per capita, adjusted for purchasing power parity (PPP), nearly four times higher than the mean of Latin America's eight largest economies. Even Argentina, slightly ahead of the United States in 1800 and growing rapidly by the 1870s, had fallen far behind, with a GDP per capita not much more than half that of the United States. . . .

The estimates in Table 7.1 show a consistent pattern of failure from as early as 1700 until at least the end of the nineteenth century. Every Latin American country for which we have estimates grew more slowly on average than the United States for the two centuries up to 1900. Most simply stagnated; some, like Mexico, experienced prolonged periods of economic decline. There is no reason to believe that this record would look any less dismal with more data. The twentieth-century pattern, however, is more mixed. While Argentina declined toward the regional mean of about 27 percent of U.S. GDP per capita in 1994, Brazil and Venezuela rose to meet or surpass it. . . .

In summary, the available quantitative evidence shows that Latin America became an underdeveloped region between the early eighteenth and the late nineteenth centuries. Although all of the Latin American economies fell further behind in this period, the Argentine performance was consistently better than the rest until the twentieth century, that of Brazil almost as consistently the worst. In the twentieth century, these two economies reversed positions, with Brazil consistently outperforming the rest of the region and Argentina far behind. Cuba, with the highest GDP per capita in relation to the United States

Table 7.1 GDP per Capita as Percentage of the U.S. Level, 1700–1994

Country	1700	1800	1850	1900	1913	1950	1994
Argentina		102		52	55	41	37
Brazil		36	39	10	11	15	22
Chile		46		38	40	33	34
Colombia				18	18	19	24
Cuba	167	112	78		39		
Mexico	89	50	37	35	35	27	23
Peru		41		20	20	24	14
Venezuela				10	10	38	37
Mean	128	66	51	27	28	29	27

Note: The last row reports the arithmetic mean of the countries for which there are data for each year. If each country were assigned a weight equal to its share of population, the mean for each year would be lower, since the high-income cases (Argentina and Cuba, for example) had smaller populations. In 1800, the unweighted mean in the table is 66 but the population-weighted mean of the six reported cases would be 51.

in 1700, fell furthest in relative terms over this period, though the lack of GDP estimates for the rest of Latin America (except Mexico) for 1700 makes this conclusion more tentative.

Factor Endowments

The New World factor endowments encountered by the first European entrepreneurs did not matter much. Most of Latin America's potentially exploitable natural resources lay dormant and remained inaccessible throughout the colonial era. Most of the New World's indigenous population died.

Europeans transformed the natural and human resource base of the entire New World, including vast areas they never conquered or even visited. They did so by bringing in pathogens, people, plants, animals, technologies, and institutions hitherto unknown to the Western Hemisphere. The pathogens destroyed most of the New World's inhabitants by the end of the sixteenth century, so the Europeans repopulated the hemisphere with African slaves. Old World plants and animals displaced indigenous species in many areas and in doing so transformed entire landscapes. European technologies and organizational forms, from transoceanic navigation and deep-shaft mining to metal coinage and commercial credit, transformed production and commerce. The Europeans adopted and adapted Amerindian organization, products, and technologies as well, pushing them toward patterns that facilitated money-making in all its forms.

The Europeans did not distribute themselves evenly over the landscape. "Spanish society in the Indies," James Lockhart reminds us, "was import-export oriented at the very base and in every aspect." So, too, was the great Portuguese adventure in Brazil. Publicly licensed but privately financed, the Iberian entrepreneurs who set out to conquer the New World mainly wanted to get rich. Officials and priests in both empires followed them about, careful not to miss any reasonable opportunity to collect a tax, impose a fee, or save a soul. Any exploitable resource, natural or human, that could profitably be turned into silver or gold attracted both private greed and official attention. But vast areas of these New World empires remained unexploited and ungoverned by Europeans or their descendants until long after independence. The "empty spaces" (that is, empty of Europeans) where little or no money could be made added up to more territory than Spain and Portugal actually managed to control or govern in the three centuries after the conquest.

Location determined which of the New World's people and resources the invaders rushed to exploit. The cost of overland transportation proved to be prohibitive for most commodities, even in the relatively easy terrain of plateaus and pampas. Thus, the Europeans and the slaves they brought in from Africa hardly ever settled far from navigable rivers or the seacoast. Since navigable rivers were few (and the few there were, like the Amazon, did not run past much tradable wealth), they eventually settled mainly on islands in the Caribbean and along coastlines. There they produced a variety of plantation products for European markets, including sugar, cacao, tobacco, rice, cotton, and, later in the nineteenth century, coffee, henequen, and bananas. Not until the advent of the railroad did agricultural production for export shift from seacoasts to the interior of the continent.

When Europeans settled further inland during the colonial era, as in central Mexico and parts of the Andes, it was generally to exploit opportunities to profit from the production of commodities with high value-to-bulk ratios or to supply the producers of these commodities with inputs and consumption goods. High transport costs limited the interior regions of the continent to exporting precious metals, gems (like emeralds and diamonds), and dyestuffs such as cochineal and indigo. Local markets took nearly everything else. Where export production generated market demand for food and other inputs and yielded taxes to support the royal bureaucracy, Europeans specialized in these ancillary activities. In the rest of the Americas, they had to make do with whatever they could extort from indigenous populations whose productivity was too low to generate much surplus.

At the time of the Columbus voyages, as many as 50 million Amerindians lived in the vast territories that became Latin America. By the end of the colonial era, more than half of Latin America's population of perhaps 15 million people consisted of Europeans, Africans, and the descendants of Europeans and Africans. Amerindians and mestizos, most of whom lived in Mexico, constituted less than half of the Latin American population in 1820.

The demographic and economic reorganization of New World spaces caused by Latin America's integration into the two Iberian empires with their links to the developing world market can be glimpsed from the data in Table 7.2 on population densities and productivity in 1800. Argentina, a settlement colony with a huge territory and tiny population, was the most thinly populated. Mexico and Cuba were the most densely populated. In Mexico, as in the Andes, the population figures reflect the partial recovery of the indigenous populations, though at comparatively low levels of per capita GDP. In Cuba, the high population density reflects the importation of large numbers of slaves toward the end of the eighteenth century, spurred by the island's high export-based GDP per capita.

As the table suggests, African slaves did not always end up where the marginal product of their labor was highest. Backward Brazil, with a low per capita GDP, imported nearly a third of all slaves that came to the New World, whereas the more productive Spanish islands like Cuba imported far fewer until the end of the eighteenth century. This difference was due in part to Portuguese commercial access to slave-exporting regions of Africa and Spanish restrictions on imports (including slaves) from outside the empire. Slaves were far more costly in the Spanish colonies than anywhere else until the crown relaxed restrictions on slave imports beginning in the late 1760s. In the seventeenth century, the Portuguese brought slaves to Brazil and set them to work in activities where their productivity was low, because slaves cost so little. When slave prices rose in response to Caribbean demand in the eighteenth century, Brazilian production declined. In Cuba, where slaves cost two to three times as much as in Jamaica, Europeans purchased them only when certain that they would be productive enough to compensate for their high price.

Europeans migrated to the New World in much smaller numbers than the Africans they forced to come. Migration to the Spanish colonies from Spain reached a peak at the end of the sixteenth century, but revived somewhat in the eighteenth. Throughout the colonial era, Spain tried to control and limit immigration to the New World and re-

Table 7.2 Population Densities and GDP, 1800

Colony	Area (1000s sq km)	Population (1000s)	Density (Pop. per 1000 sq km)	Total GDP (1000s) (1998 dollars)	GDP per Capita
Argentina	2,777	329	118	26,978	82
Brazil	8,457	3,250	384	94,250	29
Chile	757	535	707	19,795	37
Cuba	115	272	2,365	24,480	90
Mexico	1,967	6,000	3,050	240,340	40
Peru	1,280	1,300	1,016	2,900	33

fused permission for the citizens of other countries (except for naturalized Irish Catholics) to settle in its possessions. By the eighteenth century, low wages on the Spanish American mainland and rising slave imports to the islands kept the flow of Europeans low and made Spain's efforts at controlling immigration fairly easy. Portuguese emigration to Brazil followed a somewhat different trajectory. Like Spanish emigration, that of the Portuguese fell during the seventeenth-century depression, but revived more strongly in the eighteenth century due to the pull of high earnings in the gold and diamond booms in the interior.

In the nineteenth century, slaves continued to arrive in large numbers only in Brazil and Cuba. British pressure finally helped to end the slave trade in the 1850s. Meanwhile, European immigration to Latin America slowed after 1800, reversed during the independence wars from 1810 to the 1820s, and in some cases virtually ceased for up to half a century after independence despite the end of Spanish and Portuguese restrictions. The persistence of slavery tended to discourage European migration to Brazil and Cuba. Low wages compounded by political instability and international war kept numbers down everywhere else. When the slave trade ended, Cuba (for sugar) and Peru (for guano mining as well as sugar) imported large numbers of indentured Chinese laborers. Mass European migration did not begin until the 1870s and 1880s and when it did, most of the immigrants went to Argentina and the southern half of Brazil.

Paradoxically, the most productive economies in Latin America at the beginning of the nineteenth century were the two, Cuba and Argentina, where labor was most costly. No free person would go to Argentina without some assurance of gain; the few that went were not disappointed (especially in high-wage Buenos Aires). In Cuba, no one bought slaves at the high prices prevailing for most of the colonial era without some highly productive use to make of them. The high cost of labor in these two colonies resembled the pattern established in British North America. Most of Latin America, however, consisted of far less productive, low-wage territories with limited access to the sea. None of the Iberian colonies or the nation states that succeeded them, not even the most prosperous in 1800 like Cuba and Argentina, managed to achieve rates of growth comparable to the United States until the nineteenth century had nearly ended.

Access to Trade

Great debates once raged over the impact of trade on the colonial economies. Recent scholarship has tended to reverse the once widely held notion that external trade is necessarily (or even often) harmful to backward economies. Of course, colonial restrictions on trade, such as the commercial monopolies that prohibited direct trade with foreign countries, did impose costs on colonies throughout the New World, but did so precisely because they reduced the gains such regions would otherwise have enjoyed from external trade.

The Latin American case suggests that the static gains from trade can be large, even in economies that experience little or no sustained economic growth. The cross-section data in Table 7.3 compare the export performance of the six major colonial economies in 1800. Note that the colonies are listed in the table in rank order of GDP per capita. The data demonstrate that the Latin American colonial economies with the largest export sectors tended to have the highest GDP per capita. This is because productivity was higher in export industries than in other sectors of the colonial economies, though the gap between export and domestic-use agriculture and industry must have varied considerably. The colonial economies that managed to specialize more did better. . . .

Cuba and Argentina were the most successful exporters in per capita terms by 1800. Argentina also had the largest export sector in relation to GDP, followed by Brazil and Cuba. The mainland economies that produced mainly silver for export (or, in the case of Chile, foodstuffs for export to mining colonies) had much smaller export sectors both in per capita terms and in relation to total output.

Mexico's relative failure as an exporter is perhaps the most surprising. For most of the eighteenth century, Mexico served as the cash cow of the Spanish American empire, regularly exporting huge quantities of silver along with substantial amounts of cochineal and other products. In per capita terms, however, only Chile had a smaller export sector. Although the income generated by the mining industries in Mexico and Peru was substantial, the productivity effect was limited by the relatively small proportion of the labor force employed in mining and the relatively slow growth of silver production even during boom periods.

Throughout the Caribbean, by contrast, exports accounted for a relatively high proportion of GDP. Brazil's export sector was also quite

Table 7.3   Export Performance, circa 1800

Colony	Total Exports (current dollars)	Exports per Capita (current dollars)	Exports as % of GDP	GDP per Capita (current dollars)
Cuba	5,000,000	18.35	20.4	90
Argentina	3,300,000	10.03	12.2	82
Mexico	12,640,800	2.11	5.2	40
Chile	874,072	1.63	4.4	37
Peru	2,998,000	2.31	7.0	33
Brazil	15,526,750	4.78	16.4	29

large, despite its regional concentration in the northeast (except during the gold and diamond export booms further south). The most striking aspect of Brazil's performance, however, is the low level of per capita exports and GDP per capita in comparison with Cuba. This may be explained in part, as mentioned above, by lower slave prices that may have encouraged more marginal producers to enter the market. By the early nineteenth century, Brazil's sugar plantations were notoriously inefficient producers in comparison with those in the Caribbean. In addition, Brazilian sugar was excluded from the markets of the European countries with sugar islands of their own.

Perhaps most surprising is the relative success of Argentina. Table 7.3 includes exports from Buenos Aires that were produced within what became the national territory. They consisted chiefly of cattle hides and salted beef, derived mainly from exploiting the wild herds of the pampas. . . .

In sum, Argentina and Cuba managed to prosper in the colonial era, despite high labor costs, in part because their well-located natural resources allowed them to specialize in export production. The less successful agricultural economies like Brazil managed to substitute cheaper labor for location, pushing export production further from the sea by using low-cost labor to compensate for higher transport costs. The remaining colonies produced small quantities (in relation to GDP) of high-value metals in primitive surroundings, especially in the Andes. Even in ostensibly opulent Mexico, at least 80 percent of the population in 1800 worked in domestic-use agriculture at low levels of productivity.

IWASAKI YATARO

Mitsubishi Letter to Employees

Japan was the first country outside the West to undergo an industrial revolution. After 1854 when American Commodore Perry forced Japan to open its ports to the West, Japanese society underwent a wide range of changes. In 1868, the Meiji (Enlightened) Restoration government proceeded to mobilize the population to learn Western methods of industrial production and many other facets of Western culture and society. Many Japanese were educated in the United States and Europe, especially in Germany. Japanese industry was organized along the German model, with considerable government direction and power vested in leading families. Politics was not democratic, and the economy was not capitalist. In 1870, for example, the Meiji government launched a major railroad construction plan. It hoped to raise capital from private sources, but when none was offered, the government went ahead on its own. Gradually, with the help of foreign loans and Japanese capitalists, a mixed public and private economy developed.

One of the entrepreneurs who directed Japanese industrialization was Iwasaki Yataro* (1835–1885), a clerk for a feudal lord, who used his ability and connections to create a steamship company that in 1873 took the name Mitsubishi. In 1876, the British Peninsular and Oriental Steam Navigation Company challenged Mitsubishi's growing dominance in Japanese coastal trade. Mitsubishi responded by halving its coastal fares and cutting employee wages by one-third. In this letter to his employees, Iwasaki asks for their support.

Notice Iwasaki's appeal to national security and pride. Does the appeal strike you as genuine or contrived? What would Adam Smith or Karl Marx have said about this appeal?

Thinking Historically

Iwasaki Yataro was both a capitalist and an industrialist. While Japanese industrialization enjoyed greater state sponsorship than did British or American industrialization, entrepreneurs like Iwasaki played a crucial role. In this letter, does Iwasaki speak more as a capi-

*ee wah SAH kee   yah TAH roh

David John Lu, *Sources of Japanese History*, vol. 2 (New York: McGraw-Hill, 1974), 80–82.

talist or industrialist? Is there any disparity between these two roles, or are they woven together inextricably?

Many people have expressed differing opinions concerning the principles to be followed and advantages to be obtained in engaging foreigners or Japanese in the task of coastal trade. Granted, we may permit a dissenting voice, which suggests that in principle both foreigners and Japanese must be permitted to engage in coastal trade, but once we look into the question of advantages, we know that coastal trade is too important a matter to be given over to the control of foreigners. If we allow the right of coastal navigation to fall into the hands of foreigners in peacetime, it means a loss of business and employment opportunities for our own people, and in wartime it means yielding the vital right of gathering information to foreigners. In fact, this is not too different from abandoning the rights of our country as an independent nation.

Looking back into the past, at the time when we abandoned the policy of seclusion and entered into an era of friendly intercourse and commerce with foreign nations, we should have been prepared for this very task. However, due to the fact that our people lack knowledge and wealth, we have yet to assemble a fleet sufficient to engage in coastal navigation. Furthermore, we have neither the necessary skills for navigation nor a plan for developing a maritime transportation industry. This condition has attracted foreign shipping companies to occupy our maritime transport lines. Yet our people show not a sense of surprise at it. Some people say that our treaties with foreign powers contain an express provision allowing foreign ships to proceed from Harbor A to Harbor B, and others claim that such a provision must not be regarded as granting foreign ships the right to coastal navigation inasmuch as it is intended not to impose unduly heavy taxes on them. I am not qualified to discuss its legal merit, but the issue remains an important one.

I now propose to do my utmost, and along with my 35 million compatriots, perform my duty as a citizen of this country. That is to recover the right of coastal trade in our hands and not to delegate that task to foreigners. Unless we propose to do so, it is useless for our government to revise the unequal treaties[1] or to change our entrenched customs. We need people who can respond, otherwise all the endeavors of the government will come to naught. This is the reason why the

---

[1] *Unequal treaties* was a term the Chinese used to designate the treaties that were forced upon them by the opium wars; they were "unequal" in the sense that the superior power of the British forced the defeated Chinese to comply with British demands. Here the term refers to the commercial agreements that Japan was made to sign after Admiral Perry's arrival. [Ed.]

government protects our company, and I know that our responsibilities are even greater than the full weight of Mt. Fuji thrust upon our shoulders. There have been many who wish to hinder our progress in fulfilling our obligations. However, we have been able to eliminate one of our worst enemies, the Pacific Mail Company of the United States, from contention by applying appropriate means available to us. Now another rival has emerged. It is the Peninsular & Oriental Steam Navigation Company of Great Britain, which is setting up a new line between Yokohama and Shanghai and is attempting to claim its rights over the ports of Nagasaki, Kobe, and Yokohama. The P & O Company is backed by its massive capital, its large fleet of ships, and by its experiences of operating in Oriental countries. In competing against this giant, what methods can we employ?

I have thought about this problem very carefully and have come to one conclusion. There is no other alternative but to eliminate unnecessary positions and unnecessary expenditures. This is a time-worn solution and no new wisdom is involved. Even though it is a familiar saying, it is much easier said than done, and this indeed has been the root cause of difficulties in the past and present times. Therefore, starting immediately, I propose that we engage in this task. By eliminating unnecessary personnel from the payroll, eliminating unnecessary expenditures, and engaging in hard and arduous tasks, we shall be able to solidify the foundation of our company. If there is a will, there is a way. Through our own efforts, we shall be able to repay the government for its protection and answer our nation for its confidence shown in us. Let us work together in discharging our obligations and let us not be ashamed of ourselves. Whether we succeed or fail, whether we can gain profit or sustain loss, we cannot anticipate at this time. Hopefully, all of you will join me in a singleness of heart to attain this cherished goal, forbearing and undaunted by setbacks, to restore to our own hands the right to our own coastal trade. If we succeed it will not only be an accomplishment for our company but also a glorious event for our Japanese Empire, which shall let its light shine to all four corners of the earth. We may succeed and we may fail, and it depends on your effort or lack of it. Do your utmost in this endeavor!

REFLECTIONS

It was because of certain traits in private capitalism that the machine — which was a neutral agent — has often seemed, and in fact has sometimes been, a malicious element in society, careless of human life, indifferent to human interests. The machine has suffered for the sins of capitalism; contrariwise, capitalism has often taken credit for the virtues of the machine.[1]

Our chapter turns writer Lewis Mumford's proposition into a series of questions: What has been the impact of capitalism? Is the machine only neutral, or does it have its own effects? How can we distinguish between the economic and the technological chains of cause and effect?

Capitalism and industrialization are difficult concepts to distinguish. Adam Smith illustrated the power of the market and the division of labor by imagining their impact not on a shop or trading firm, but on a pin factory, an early industrial enterprise. Karl Marx summarized the achievements of the capitalist age by enumerating "wonders far surpassing Egyptian pyramids," which included chemical industries, steam navigation, railroads, and electric telegraphs. Neither Smith nor Marx used the terms *capitalism* or *industrial revolution*, although such variants as *capitalist* and *industrial* were already in circulation. Modern historians fought over their meaning and relevance as explanations of change through most of the last century. To understand the great transformation into modernity, some emphasized the expansion of market capitalism; others emphasized the power of the machine. The rise of state-capitalist and communist industrial societies politicized the debate, but even after the fall of communism, the historical questions remained. Peter Stearns looks for the forces that spread or retarded industrialization. John Coatsworth sees the root cause of change in trade and markets.

After 1900 the industrial revolution spread throughout the world, but its pace was not always revolutionary. Even today some societies are still largely rural with a majority of workers engaged in subsistence farming or small-scale manufacturing by hand. But over the long course of history people have always tried to replace human labor with machines and increase the production of machine-made goods. In some cases, the transformation has been dramatic. Malaysia, once a languid land of tropical tea and rubber plantations, sprouted enough microchip and electronics factories after 1950 to account for 60 percent of its exports by the year 2000. By the 1990s an already highly industrialized country like Japan could produce luxury cars in factories that needed

---

[1]Lewis Mumford, *Technics and Civilization* (New York: Harcourt Brace, 1963), 27.

only a handful of humans to monitor the work of computer-driven robots. Despite occasional announcements of the arrival of a "postindustrial" society, the pressure to mechanize continues unabated in the twenty-first century.

The fate of capitalism in the twentieth century was more varied. The second wave of industrial revolutions — beginning with Germany after 1850 and Japan after 1880 — was directed by governments as much as capitalists. Socialist parties won large support in industrial countries in the first half of the twentieth century, creating welfare states in some after World War II. In Russia after 1917, the Communist party pioneered a model of state-controlled industrialization that attracted imitators from China to Chile and funded anticapitalist movements throughout the world.

The Cold War (1947–1991) between the United States and the Soviet Union, though largely a power struggle between two superpowers, was widely seen as an ideological contest between capitalism and socialism. Thus, the demise of the Soviet Union and its Communist party in 1991 was heralded as the victory of capitalism over socialism. As Russia, China, and other previously communist states embraced market economies, socialism was declared dead.

But could proclaiming the death of socialism be as premature as heralding the end of industrial society? *The Communist Manifesto* of 1848 long predates the Russian revolution of 1917. Karl Marx died in 1883. Socialists like Rosa Luxembourg criticized Lenin and the Russian communists for misinterpreting Marxism in their impatience to transform Russian society. Socialists, even Marxists, continue to write, advise, and govern today, often urging restraints on the spread of global capital markets and the threat of unregulated capitalism on the global environment. Rarely are they willing to relinquish the advantages of industrial technology. Rather they seek to release the "virtues of the machine."

8

Colonized and Colonizers

Europeans in Africa and Asia, 1850–1930

HISTORICAL CONTEXT

The first stage of European colonialism, beginning with Columbus, was a period in which Europeans — led by the Spanish and Portuguese — settled in the Western Hemisphere and created plantations with African labor. From 1492 to 1776, European settlement in Asia was limited to a few coastal port cities where merchants and missionaries operated. The second stage — the years between 1776, when Britain lost most of its American colonies, and 1880, when the European scramble for African territory began — has sometimes been called a period of *free-trade imperialism*. This term refers to the desire by European countries in general and by Britain in particular to expand their zones of free trade. It also refers to a widespread opposition to the expense of colonization, a conviction held especially among the British, who garnered all of the advantages of political empire without the costs of occupation and outright ownership.

The British used to quip that their second global empire was created in the nineteenth century "in a fit of absentmindedness." But colonial policy in Britain and the rest of Europe was more planned and continuous than that comment might suggest. British control of India (including Burma) increased throughout the nineteenth century, as did British control of South Africa, Australia, the Pacific, and parts of the Americas. At the same time, France, having lost most of India to the British, began building an empire that included parts of North Africa, Southeast Asia, and the Pacific.

Thus, a third stage of colonialism, beginning in the mid-nineteenth century, reached a fever pitch with the partition of Africa after 1880. The period between 1888 and 1914 spawned renewed settlement and massive population transfers, with most European migrants settling in

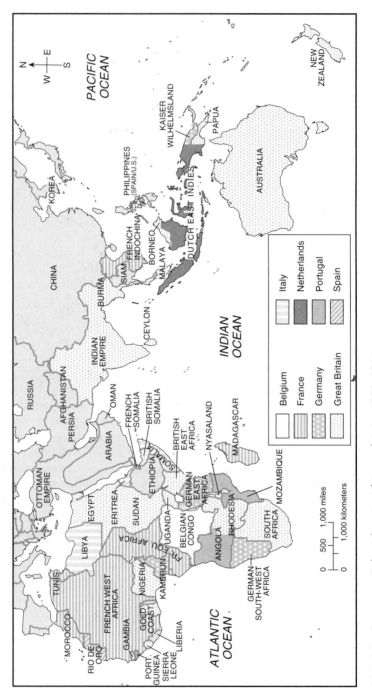

Map 8.1   European Colonialism in Africa and Asia, 1880–1914.

the older colonies of the Americas (as well as in South Africa and Australia), where indigenous populations had been reduced. Even where settlement remained light, however, Europeans took political control of large areas of the Earth's surface (see Map 8.1).

In the first reading in this chapter, a historian offers a brief history of this second stage of European colonialism and describes what the renewed era of colonization meant, both for the colonizers and the colonized. Subsequent readings examine aspects of colonial society across the globe.

THINKING HISTORICALLY
Using Literature in History

This chapter also explores whether literature can and should be used in the quest to better understand history. Beginning with some basic questions about the differences between literary and historical approaches, we examine a number of fictional accounts of colonialism, some written by the colonizers, others by the colonized or their descendants. How do these literary accounts add to, or detract from, a historical understanding of colonialism? The rich, evocative literature of the colonial period aids us in determining how we separate fact from fiction, construct historical knowledge, and appreciate the past in all its dimensions.

$$48$$

JURGEN OSTERHAMMEL
From Colonialism

In this selection, modern historian Jurgen Osterhammel provides us with an overview of European colonialism. In the first part, "Colonial Epochs," the author discusses ways in which European colonialism changed from the late eighteenth to the early twentieth century. In the second section, "Colonial Societies," he discusses the special character of the colonial social order throughout this period.

Jurgen Osterhammel, *Colonialism*, trans. Shelly Frisch (Princeton: Markus Wiener, 1997), 32–34, 86–89.

How, according to Osterhammel, did colonialism change between 1760 and 1930? How were these changes reflected in the evolution of "colonial society"?

Thinking Historically

Unlike philosophy, which tends to deal with general principles, history studies specific details. Yet as this general overview of colonialism shows, history can include summaries of long-term change and generalizations about different parts of the world over entire centuries as well as specific names and dates. What sorts of generalizations are made in this excerpt?

History, like fiction, is a form of storytelling. Fictional storytelling tends to be far more specific than history, usually documenting minutes or hours in the amount of space that it takes many historians to cover years and Osterhammel to cover centuries. Does this selection tell you a story in any sense, or is it too general to do that?

Colonial Epochs

The most important colonial advance of the period [1760–1830] was the extension of the British position in *India*. The British East India Company (EIC) originally conducted trade from port cities. Later on, it becomes increasingly involved in Indian domestic politics, which were determined by the antagonisms of regional powers in the declining phase of the Mughal empire. Unlike the Spanish in Central America, the British in India at first pursued no plans to conquer and certainly no plans to proselytize. They were far from possessing military advantages over the Indian states until about the middle of the century. In Bengal, where British trade interests were increasingly concentrated, a mutually advantageous agreement was reached with the regional prince, the Nabob. Only when a collapse of this "collaboration" was brought about by a concatenation of causes did the idea of territorial rule originate. In 1755, Robert Clive, the future conqueror of Bengal, expressed a hitherto unthinkable idea: "We must indeed become the Nabobs ourselves." From then on the British pursued a strategy of subjugation within a polycentric Indian state system, interrupted repeatedly by phases of deadlock and consolidation. Until the end of the colonial period in 1947, hundreds of seemingly autonomous principalities continued to exist, but after 1818 the British could consider themselves the "paramount power" on the subcontinent.

The East India Company continued to play its double role as business enterprise and state organization. Under constant supervision of the government in London it accompanied the military expansion of its sphere of power with the gradual establishment of colonial structures, which, in rough schematic terms, passed through a characteristic sequence of steps: (1) securing an effective trade monopoly, (2) securing military dominance and disarmament of any subjugated indigenous powers, (3) achieving a tax collection system, (4) stabilizing government by comprehensive legal regulations and the establishment of a bureaucratic administration, and (5) intervening in the indigenous society for purposes of social and humanitarian reform. This fifth stage was reached in the early 1830s. Not only did the age of European rule over highly civilized Asian societies begin in India, but India also became the prototype of an exploitation colony without settlers, a model for British expansion in other parts of Asia and Africa.

The period between 1830 and 1880 was certainly not a calm interlude in the history of European expansion. Only the Caribbean, once so rich, became a "forgotten derelict corner of the world." In an age of "free trade imperialism," China, Japan, Siam (Thailand) and, to a greater extent than was previously the case, the Ottoman Empire as well as Egypt, now de facto independent from it, were forced to open their economies. Sovereignty limitations characteristic of "informal empires" were imposed on them. Latin America, which was *no longer* colonial, and West Africa, which was rid of the slave trade but *not yet* colonized, were integrated into the world economy more closely than ever. On Java, the major island of the Netherlands East Indies, direct colonial intervention in the utilization of land began after 1830; the outer Indonesian islands were gradually subjugated in the period to follow. Foreign encroachment on continental Southeast Asia began after about 1820. First the lowlands near the coast fell into foreign hands: in 1852–1853 Lower Burma, and in 1857 Cochin China. By 1870, the later colonial borders could be distinguished clearly. During the entire period, the Tsarist Empire advanced in the Caucasus and Central Asia with military force, and shortly thereafter in the Far East with somewhat more diplomatic means, thereby intensifying the so-called "Great Game," a sustained cold war between the two Asiatic Great Powers Russia and Great Britain.

Despite these continuities of European world conquest and of ties between classic European diplomacy and "high imperialism," there is something to be said for marking a new epoch around 1870–1880. Most of the reasons can be found in the broader imperialist environment of colonialism, that is, in the structural changes of the world economy and international system. In terms of *colonial* history, the chief development over the last two decades of the nineteenth century was the European occupation of Africa, a singularly condensed expropriation of an entire continent termed the "partition of Africa." On the eve of this process, only South Africa and Algeria had been regions of European colonization, South Africa since 1652 and Algeria since

1830. Elsewhere the Portuguese (Angola, Mozambique), French (Senegal), and British (Sierra Leone, Lagos) made their presence felt in a more limited way. After all, by 1870 over 270,000 white people were already living in Algeria and about 245,000 in South Africa (including the two Boer Republics). The further expansion of these early cores of colonization was also an impetus for the occupation of Africa in the last quarter of the century. The discovery of diamond deposits in 1867 and of gold in 1886 unleashed a development that changed South Africa into a capitalist center of growth and a magnet for international capital. At the same time, it strengthened white supremacy. In Algeria the same result was achieved simultaneously under almost purely agrarian conditions by extensive land transfers from the Arabs to a rapidly growing settlement population.

The actual "partition" of Africa in the years between the occupation of Tunis by the French in 1881 and of Egypt by the British in 1882 on the one hand and the Boer War of the years 1899–1902 on the other was initially a somewhat symbolic process. With treaties *amongst themselves,* the European Great Powers committed themselves to mutual recognition of colonies, protectorates, and spheres of influence. "Paper partition" was only slowly and incompletely transformed into effective occupation, "partition on the ground." However, the borders that were drawn endured with the later establishment of independent African national states. For Africans, the so-called partition of their continent often meant the brutal disruption of bonds and established ways of life. However, partition could also result in the exact opposite: "a ruthless act of political amalgamation, whereby something of the order of ten thousand units was reduced to a mere forty." Particularly in Islamic North Africa (Egypt, Morocco, Tunisia, and Algeria) as well as in parts of Asia (Vietnam, Korea, and Burma), colonialism encountered fairly complex proto-nation-states. Colonial rule in these countries was considered even less legitimate than elsewhere.

Colonial Societies

. . . Characteristic of the social and cultural history of modern colonialism, especially in Asia, was the increasing alienation between two societies that had shared the bond of a colonial relationship since the late eighteenth century. While the status scale in Iberian America was rapidly refined, thereby placing renewed emphasis on racial criteria, the dualization of the colonial social landscape intensified in Asia and Africa. Only in Portuguese Asia was there significant progress in societal interaction, especially where native clergy were concerned, owing to the enlightened politics of the crown under the Marquis de Pombal in the 1760s and 1770s. The sealing off of the European communities from the indigenous environment had many causes, which were manifested in varying combinations: (1) Although Portugal and the Netherlands in particular had officially encouraged marriage between European men and Asian women at first, and the other colonial powers had tolerated it tacitly, immigration of European women raised the sexual autarky of the colonial societies. (2) The transition from trade to rule and often to direct production with dependent workers transformed the "age of partnership" into an age of subordination. (3) Violent resistance by the natives, such as the Native American massacre of colonists in Virginia in 1622 and the Indian rebellion of 1857–1858, strengthened the resolve of white minorities to shield themselves for self-protection. (4) A European attitude of superiority over the rest of the world, stemming from the Christian Eurocentricism of early encounters, made it appear increasingly "unreasonable" to Europeans to maintain close egalitarian relationships with non-Europeans and to make cultural accommodations to them. (5) After the gradual abolition of slave trade and slavery, racist thought lived in the less blatant, but now "scientifically" legitimated forms. It bears pointing out, however, that racism is often not the *cause* of segregation, but the *effect*. Racism has often been used to justify segregation after the fact.

Ethnosocial distancing was an outgrowth of societal interaction and was not always based on discriminatory laws. A telling example was Batavia, the most populous and resplendent city in Asia that was governed by Europe. In the first half of the seventeenth century, a mixed society was formed based on house slavery and the expansion of "Creole" family and patronage networks with relatively high tolerance for interracial family relationships. This society resembled its counterpart in Mexico and was even more akin to Portuguese colonization in Asia (Goa). In the manner of living of its upper class, the mixed society of Batavia conformed almost as closely to its Javanese surroundings as it did to Holland. A distinct demarcation between the European and Asian spheres commenced with the British interregnum of 1811–1816. In the eyes of the British, the Batavian Dutch were appallingly infected by their contact with Asians. Cultural decontamination was decreed. The whites in the city and their mestizo relatives were told to develop an identity as civilized Europeans and clearly display it in their appearances before the Javanese public.

The English in India had always been somewhat more detached from the indigenous environment than the Dutch in Indonesia. After the 1780s, their isolation gradually intensified and became obvious with the decline in status of Eurasian Anglo-Indians, even though some influential Indian politicians in 1830 were still dreaming of a racially mixed India modelled on Mexico. The club became the center of British social life in India and the other Asian colonies during the Victorian era. In clubs, one could feel like a gentleman among other gentlemen while being served by a native staff. In Kuala Lumpur, very few non-Europeans were admitted before 1940; in Singapore no non-Europeans were allowed in at all. The large clubs of Calcutta remained closed to Indians until 1946. This type of color bar was especially disturbing because it excluded from social recognition the very people who had carried their self-Anglicizing the furthest and loyally supported British rule. Even Indian members of the Indian Civil Service were excluded.

In most regions of Africa, the colonial period began at a time when exclusionist thought and action were most pronounced. In Africa there was virtually no history of intercultural proximity and therefore no need for policies enforcing detachment. The Europeans saw themselves as foreign rulers separated from the African cultures by an abyss. This absolute aloofness extended even to Islam, which they certainly did not consider "primitive," but rather historically obsolete. Color bars in Africa varied in height; they were lowest in West Africa and highest in the settlement colonies of the far north and the deep south. A process of great symptomatic significance was the rejection of the highly educated West Africans who had worked with the early mission. They had envisioned the colonial takeover as an opportunity for a joint European-African effort to modernize and civilize Africa. Instead, they were now, as "white Negroes," despised by all.

$$49$$

GEORGE ORWELL

From Burmese Days

This selection, from one of the great novels on colonialism, captures the life of the British colonial class in a remote "upcountry" town in Burma in the 1920s. The chapter is set in the European club. Flory, the principal character, is the only Englishman at all sympathetic to the Burmese. Though he has befriended the Indian physician, Dr. Veraswami, Flory is too weak to propose him as the first "native" member of the club. The other main characters are Westfield, District Superintendent of Police; Ellis, local company manager and the most racist of the group; Lackersteen, local manager of a timber company

George Orwell, *Burmese Days* (1934; reprint, San Diego: Harcourt Brace, 1962), 17–27.

who is usually drunk; Maxwell, a forest officer; and Macgregor, Deputy Commissioner and secretary of the club.

Why does the club loom so large in the lives of these Englishmen? If they complain so much, why are they in Burma? How do you account for the virulent racism of these men? Why does Ellis "correct" the butler's English? What does this story suggest about women in the colonial world?

Thinking Historically

As different as this selection is from Osterhammel's historical overview, both touch on the subjects of dual society, the European club, and colonial racism. How does this selection from Orwell support some of Osterhammel's generalizations? How does it deepen your understanding of these subjects?

The structure of a novel like this one bears certain similarities to history — a description of a place, proper names and biographies, descriptions of human interactions, an accounting of change, and a story. There are also structural differences in a novel — a lot of dialogue, greater attention to physical appearance and character, and a more prominent narrative. Do the fictional constructs in this selection detract from our historical understanding? Can such elements add to our understanding of what actually happened?

Of course, the problem with structural elements such as dialogue and story is that they are fiction. The author of a novel makes no pretense of telling the truth. Nevertheless, an author draws on what he or she knows to create a plausible scenario that is recognizable and consistent. Interestingly, Orwell knew Burma quite well. He was born in India in 1903. His father worked in the Opium Department of the Indian Civil Service. After attending school at Eton in England, Orwell returned to Burma, where he spent five years as a member of the Indian Imperial Police. Orwell, therefore, had a broad knowledge of Burma on which to base his story. Is there any way to determine what Orwell invented and what he merely described in this account?

Orwell was politically engaged throughout his life. Would political ideas make him better or worse as a historian or novelist? How so?

Flory's house was at the top of the maidan,[1] close to the edge of the jungle. From the gate the maidan sloped sharply down, scorched and khaki-coloured, with half a dozen dazzling white bungalows scattered round it. All quaked, shivered in the hot air. There was an English

[1]Parade-ground. [Ed.]

cemetery within a white wall half-way down the hill, and nearby a tiny tin-roofed church. Beyond that was the European Club, and when one looked at the Club — a dumpy one-storey wooden building — one looked at the real centre of the town. In any town in India the European Club is the spiritual citadel, the real seat of the British power, the Nirvana for which native officials and millionaires pine in vain. It was doubly so in this case, for it was the proud boast of Kyauktada Club that, almost alone of Clubs in Burma, it had never admitted an Oriental to membership. Beyond the Club, the Irrawaddy flowed huge and ochreous, glittering like diamonds in the patches that caught the sun; and beyond the river stretched great wastes of paddy fields, ending at the horizon in a range of blackish hills.

The native town, and the courts and the jail, were over to the right, mostly hidden in green groves of peepul trees. The spire of the pagoda rose from the trees like a slender spear tipped with gold. Kyauktada was a fairly typical Upper Burma town, that had not changed greatly between the days of Marco Polo and 1910, and might have slept in the Middle Ages for a century more if it had not proved a convenient spot for a railway terminus. In 1910 the Government made it the headquarters of a district and a seat of Progress — interpretable as a block of law courts, with their army of fat but ravenous pleaders, a hospital, a school, and one of those huge, durable jails which the English have built everywhere between Gibraltar and Hong Kong. The population was about four thousand, including a couple of hundred Indians, a few score Chinese and seven Europeans. There were also two Eurasians named Mr. Francis and Mr. Samuel, the sons of an American Baptist missionary and a Roman Catholic missionary respectively. The town contained no curiosities of any kind, except an Indian fakir who had lived for twenty years in a tree near the bazaar, drawing his food up in a basket every morning.

Flory yawned as he came out of the gate. He had been half drunk the night before, and the glare made him feel liverish. "Bloody, bloody hole!" he thought, looking down the hill. And, no one except the dog being near, he began to sing aloud, "Bloody, bloody, bloody, oh, how thou art bloody" to the tune of "Holy, holy, holy, oh how Thou art holy," as he walked down the hot red road, switching at the dried-up grasses with his stick. It was nearly nine o'clock and the sun was fiercer every minute. The heat throbbed down on one's head with a steady, rhythmic thumping, like blows from an enormous bolster. Flory stopped at the Club gate, wondering whether to go in or to go farther down the road and see Dr. Veraswami. Then he remembered that it was "English mail day" and the newspapers would have arrived. He went in, past the big tennis screen, which was overgrown by a creeper with starlike mauve flowers.

In the borders beside the path swathes of English flowers, phlox and larkspur, hollyhock and petunia, not yet slain by the sun, rioted in vast size and richness. The petunias were huge, like trees almost. There was no lawn, but instead a shrubbery of native trees and bushes — gold mohur trees like vast umbrellas of blood-red bloom, frangipanis with creamy, stalkless flowers, purple bougainvillea, scarlet hibiscus, and the pink, Chinese rose, bilious-green crotons, feathery fronds of tamarind. The clash of colours hurt one's eyes in the glare. A nearly naked *mali*,[2] watering-can in hand, was moving in the jungle of flowers like some large nectar-sucking bird.

On the Club steps a sandy-haired Englishman, with a prickly moustache, pale grey eyes too far apart, and abnormally thin calves to his legs, was standing with his hands in the pockets of his shorts. This was Mr. Westfield, the District Superintendent of Police. With a very bored air he was rocking himself backwards and forwards on his heels and pouting his upper lip so that his moustache tickled his nose. He greeted Flory with a slight sideways movement of his head. His way of speaking was clipped and soldierly, missing out every word that well could be missed out. Nearly everything he said was intended for a joke, but the tone of his voice was hollow and melancholy.

"Hullo, Flory me lad. Bloody awful morning, what?"

"We must expect it at this time of year, I suppose," Flory said. He had turned himself a little sideways, so that his birthmarked cheek was away from Westfield.

"Yes, dammit. Couple of months of this coming. Last year we didn't have a spot of rain till June. Look at that bloody sky, not a cloud in it. Like one of those damned great blue enamel saucepans. God! What'd you give to be in Piccadilly now, eh?"

"Have the English papers come?"

"Yes. Dear old *Punch, Pink'un,* and *Vie Parisienne.* Makes you homesick to read 'em, what? Let's come in and have a drink before the ice all goes. Old Lackersteen's been fairly bathing in it. Half pickled already."

They went in, Westfield remarking in his gloomy voice, "Lead on, Macduff." Inside, the Club was a teak-walled place smelling of earth-oil, and consisting of only four rooms, one of which contained a forlorn "library" of five hundred mildewed novels, and another an old and mangy billiard-table — this, however, seldom used, for during most of the year hordes of flying beetles came buzzing round the lamps and littered themselves over the cloth. There were also a card-room and a "lounge" which looked towards the river, over a wide veranda; but at

---

[2]Gardener. [Ed.]

this time of day all the verandas were curtained with green bamboo chicks. The lounge was an unhomelike room, with coco-nut matting on the floor, and wicker chairs and tables which were littered with shiny illustrated papers. For ornament there were a number of "Bonzo" pictures, and the dusty skulls of sambhur. A punkah,[3] lazily flapping, shook dust into the tepid air.

There were three men in the room. Under the punkah a florid, fine-looking, slightly bloated man of forty was sprawling across the table with his head in his hands, groaning in pain. This was Mr. Lackersteen, the local manager of a timber firm. He had been badly drunk the night before, and he was suffering for it. Ellis, local manager of yet another company, was standing before the notice board studying some notice with a look of bitter concentration. He was a tiny wiry-haired fellow with a pale, sharp-featured face and restless movements. Maxwell, the acting Divisional Forest Officer, was lying in one of the long chairs reading the *Field,* and invisible except for two large-boned legs and thick downy forearms.

"Look at this naughty old man," said Westfield, taking Mr. Lackersteen half affectionately by the shoulders and shaking him. "Example to the young, what? There, but for the grace of God and all that. Gives you an idea what you'll be like at forty."

Mr. Lackersteen gave a groan which sounded like "brandy."

"Poor old chap," said Westfield; "regular martyr to booze, eh? Look at it oozing out of his pores. Reminds me of the old colonel who used to sleep without a mosquito net. They asked his servant why and the servant said: 'At night, master too drunk to notice mosquitoes; in the morning, mosquitoes too drunk to notice master.' Look at him — boozed last night and then asking for more. Got a little niece coming to stay with him, too. Due tonight, isn't she, Lackersteen?"

"Oh, leave that drunken sot alone," said Ellis without turning round. He had a spiteful cockney voice. Mr. Lackersteen groaned again, "— the niece! Get me some brandy, for Christ's sake."

"Good education for the niece, eh? Seeing uncle under the table seven times a week. — Hey, butler! Bringing brandy for Lackersteen master!"

The butler, a dark, stout Dravidian[4] with liquid, yellow-irised eyes like those of a dog, brought the brandy on a brass tray. Flory and Westfield ordered gin. Mr. Lackersteen swallowed a few spoonfuls of brandy and sat back in his chair, groaning in a more resigned way. He had a beefy, ingenuous face, with a toothbrush moustache. He was re-

---

[3]Large cloth panel fan hanging from the ceiling, usually pulled by a rope to move the air. [Ed.]

[4]Dated racial term used to refer to darker skinned inhabitants of southern India. [Ed.]

ally a very simple-minded man, with no ambitions beyond having what he called "a good time." His wife governed him by the only possible method, namely, by never letting him out of her sight for more than an hour or two. Only once, a year after they were married, she had left him for a fortnight, and had returned unexpectedly a day before her time, to find Mr. Lackersteen, drunk, supported on either side by a naked Burmese girl, while a third up-ended a whisky bottle into his mouth. Since then she had watched him, as he used to complain, "like a cat over a bloody mousehole." However, he managed to enjoy quite a number of "good times," though they were usually rather hurried ones.

"My Christ, what a head I've got on me this morning," he said. "Call that butler again, Westfield. I've got to have another brandy before my missus gets here. She says she's going to cut my booze down to four pegs a day when our niece gets here. God rot them both!" he added gloomily.

"Stop playing the fool, all of you, and listen to this," said Ellis sourly. He had a queer wounding way of speaking, hardly ever opening his mouth without insulting somebody. He deliberately exaggerated his cockney accent, because of the sardonic tone it gave to his words. "Have you seen this notice of old Macgregor's? A little nosegay for everyone. Maxwell, wake up and listen!"

Maxwell lowered the *Field*. He was a fresh-coloured blond youth of not more than twenty-five or six — very young for the post he held. With his heavy limbs and thick white eyelashes he reminded one of a carthorse colt. Ellis nipped the notice from the board with a neat, spiteful little movement and began reading it aloud. It had been posted by Mr. Macgregor, who, besides being Deputy Commissioner, was secretary of the Club.

"Just listen to this. 'It has been suggested that as there are as yet no Oriental members of this club, and as it is now usual to admit officials of gazetted rank, whether native or European, to membership of most European Clubs, we should consider the question of following this practice in Kyauktada. The matter will be open for discussion at the next general meeting. On the one hand it may be pointed out' — oh, well, no need to wade through the rest of it. He can't even write out a notice without an attack of literary diarrhœa. Anyway, the point's this. He's asking us to break all our rules and take a dear little nigger-boy into this Club. *Dear* Dr. Veraswami, for instance. Dr. Very-slimy, I call him. That *would* be a treat, wouldn't it? Little pot-bellied niggers breathing garlic in your face over the bridge-table. Christ, to think of it! We've got to hang together and put our foot down on this at once. What do you say, Westfield? Flory?"

Westfield shrugged his thin shoulders philosophically. He had sat down at the table and lighted a black, stinking Burma cheroot.

"Got to put up with it, I suppose," he said. "B_____s of natives are getting into all the Clubs nowadays. Even the Pegu Club, I'm told. Way this country's going, you know. We're about the last Club in Burma to hold out against 'em."

"We are; and what's more, we're damn well going to go on holding out. I'll die in the ditch before I'll see a nigger in here." Ellis had produced a stump of pencil. With the curious air of spite that some men can put into their tiniest action, he re-pinned the notice on the board and pencilled a tiny, neat "B. F." against Mr. Macgregor's signature — "There, that's what I think of his idea. I'll tell him so when he comes down. What do *you* say, Flory?"

Flory had not spoken all this time. Though by nature anything but a silent man, he seldom found much to say in Club conversations. He had sat down at the table and was reading G. K. Chesterton's article in the *London News*, at the same time caressing Flo's [his dog] head with his left hand. Ellis, however, was one of those people who constantly nag others to echo their own opinions. He repeated his question, and Flory looked up, and their eyes met. The skin round Ellis's nose suddenly turned so pale that it was almost grey. In him it was a sign of anger. Without any prelude he burst into a stream of abuse that would have been startling, if the others had not been used to hearing something like it every morning.

"My God, I should have thought in a case like this, when it's a question of keeping those black, stinking swine out of the only place where we can enjoy ourselves, you'd have the decency to back me up. Even if that pot-bellied, greasy little sod of a nigger doctor *is* your best pal. *I* don't care if you choose to pal up with the scum of the bazaar. If it pleases you to go to Veraswami's house and drink whisky with all his nigger pals, that's your look-out. Do what you like outside the Club. But, by God, it's a different matter when you talk of bringing niggers in here. I suppose you'd like little Veraswami for a Club member, eh? Chipping into our conversation and pawing everyone with his sweaty hands and breathing his filthy garlic breath in our faces. By God, he'd go out with my boot behind him if ever I saw his black snout inside that door. Greasy, pot-bellied little ———— !" etc.

This went on for several minutes. It was curiously impressive, because it was so completely sincere. Ellis really did hate Orientals — hated them with a bitter, restless loathing as of something evil or unclean. Living and working, as the assistant of a timber firm must, in perpetual contact with the Burmese, he had never grown used to the sight of a black face. Any hint of friendly feeling towards an Oriental seemed to him a horrible perversity. He was an intelligent man and an able servant of his firm, but he was one of those Englishmen — common, unfortunately — who should never be allowed to set foot in the East.

Flory sat nursing Flo's head in his lap, unable to meet Ellis's eyes. At the best of times his birthmark made it difficult for him to look people straight in the face. And when he made ready to speak, he could feel his voice trembling — for it had a way of trembling when it should have been firm; his features, too, sometimes twitched uncontrollably.

"Steady on," he said at last, sullenly and rather feebly. "Steady on. There's no need to get so excited. *I* never suggested having any native members in here."

"Oh, didn't you? We all know bloody well you'd like to, though. Why else do you go to that oily little babu's house every morning, then? Sitting down at table with him as though he was a white man, and drinking out of glasses his filthy black lips have slobbered over — it makes me spew to think of it."

"Sit down, old chap, sit down," Westfield said. "Forget it. Have a drink on it. Not worth while quarrelling. Too hot."

"My God," said Ellis a little more calmly, taking a pace or two up and down, "my God, I don't understand you chaps. I simply don't. Here's that old fool Macgregor wanting to bring a nigger into this Club for no reason whatever, and you all sit down under it without a word. Good God, what are we supposed to be doing in this country? If we aren't going to rule, why the devil don't we clear out? Here we are, supposed to be governing a set of damn black swine who've been slaves since the beginning of history, and instead of ruling them in the only way they understand, we go and treat them as equals. And all you silly b———s take it for granted. There's Flory, makes his best pal of a black babu who calls himself a doctor because he's done two years at an Indian so-called university. And you, Westfield, proud as Punch of your knock-kneed, bribe-taking cowards of policemen. And there's Maxwell, spends his time running after Eurasian tarts. Yes, you do, Maxwell; I heard about your goings-on in Mandalay with some smelly little bitch called Molly Pereira. I supposed you'd have gone and married her if they hadn't transferred you up here? You all seem to *like* the dirty black brutes. Christ, I don't know what's come over us all. I really don't."

"Come on, have another drink," said Westfield. "Hey, butler! Spot of beer before the ice goes, eh? Beer, butler!"

The butler brought some bottles of Munich beer. Ellis presently sat down at the table with the others, and he nursed one of the cool bottles between his small hands. His forehead was sweating. He was sulky, but not in a rage any longer. At all times he was spiteful and perverse, but his violent fits of rage were soon over, and were never apologised for. Quarrels were a regular part of the routine of Club life. Mr. Lackersteen was feeling better and was studying the illustrations in *La Vie Parisienne*. It was after nine now, and the room, scented with the acrid smoke of Westfield's cheroot, was stifling hot. Everyone's shirt stuck to his back with the first sweat of the day. The invisible *chokra*[5] who pulled the punkah rope outside was falling asleep in the glare.

"Butler!" yelled Ellis, and as the butler appeared, "go and wake that bloody *chokra* up!"

"Yes, master."

"And butler!"

"Yes, master?"

"How much ice have we got left?"

"'Bout twenty pounds, master. Will only last to-day, I think. I find it very difficult to keep ice cool now."

"Don't talk like that, damn you — 'I find it very difficult!' Have you swallowed a dictionary? 'Please, master, can't keeping ice cool' — that's how you ought to talk. We shall have to sack this fellow if he gets to talk English too well. I can't stick servants who talk English. D'you hear, butler?"

"Yes, master," said the butler, and retired.

"God! No ice till Monday," Westfield said. "You going back to the jungle, Flory?"

"Yes. I ought to be there now. I only came in because of the English mail."

"Go on tour myself, I think. Knock up a spot of Travelling Allowance. I can't stick my bloody office at this time of year. Sitting there under the damned punkah, signing one chit after another. Paper-chewing. God, how I wish the war was on again!"

"I'm going out the day after to-morrow," Ellis said. "Isn't that damned padre coming to hold his service this Sunday? I'll take care not to be in for that, anyway. Bloody knee-drill."

"Next Sunday," said Westfield. "Promised to be in for it myself. So's Macgregor. Bit hard on the poor devil of a padre, I must say. Only gets here once in six weeks. Might as well get up a congregation when he does come."

"Oh, hell! I'd snivel psalms to oblige the padre, but I can't stick the way these damned native Christians come shoving into our church. A pack of Madrassi servants and Karen school-teachers. And then those two yellow-bellies, Francis and Samuel — they call themselves Christians too. Last time the padre was here they had the nerve to come up and sit on the front pews with the white men. Someone ought to speak to the padre about that. What bloody fools we were ever to let those missionaries loose in this country! Teaching bazaar sweepers they're as good as we are. 'Please, sir, me Christian same like master.' Damned cheek."

---

[5]Person who pulls the punkah rope that moves a large panel to let in a breeze. [Ed.]

50

DAVID CANNADINE
From Ornamentalism

In the following selection from his work *Ornamentalism,* David Cannadine, a modern historian, challenges a traditional interpretation of the British Empire. What is that traditional interpretation? What view does the author propose instead? Do you find his new interpretation convincing?

Thinking Historically

Does your reading of *Burmese Days* support or contradict Cannadine's interpretation of British imperialism? What evidence do you see in *Burmese Days* that social distinctions were more important than racial ones? What literary evidence does Cannadine present to support his thesis?

Nations, it has recently become commonplace to observe, are in part imagined communities, depending for their credibility and identity both on the legitimacy of government and the apparatus of the state, and on invented traditions, manufactured myths, and shared perceptions of the social order that are never more than crude categories and oversimplified stereotypes. If this has been true (as indeed it has) of a relatively compact and contained country like Britain, then how much more true must this have been of the empire that the British conquered and peopled, administered, and ruled? At its territorial zenith, shortly after the end of the First World War, it consisted of naval stations and military bases extending from Gibraltar to Hong Kong, the four great dominions of settlement, the Indian Empire that occupied an entire subcontinent, the crown colonies in Asia, Africa, and the Caribbean, and the League of Nations Mandates, especially in the Middle East. But, as with all such transoceanic realms, the British Empire was not only a geopolitical entity: it was also a culturally created and imaginatively constructed artifact. How, then, in the heyday of its existence, did Britons imagine and envisage their unprecedentedly vast and varied imperium, not so much geographically as sociologically? How did they try

David Cannadine, *Ornamentalism: How the British Saw Their Empire* (Oxford: Oxford University Press, 2001), 3–10.

to organize and to arrange their heterogeneous imperial society, as they settled and conquered, governed and ruled it, and what did they think the resulting social order looked like?

To the extent that they tried to conceive of these diverse colonies and varied populations beyond the seas as "an entire interactive system, one vast interconnected world," most Britons followed the standard pattern of human behaviour when contemplating and comprehending the unfamiliar. Their "inner predisposition" was to begin with what they knew — or what they thought they knew — namely, the social structure of their own home country. But what sort of a starting point was this, and what were the implications and consequences of British perceptions of their domestic social order for British perceptions of their imperial social order? From Hegel to Marx, and from Engels to Said, it has been commonplace to suggest that Britons saw their own society (and, by extension, that of what became their settler dominions) as dynamic, individualistic, egalitarian, modernizing — and thus superior. By comparison with such a positive and progressive metropolitan perception, this argument continues, Britons saw society in their "tropical" and "oriental" colonies as enervated, hierarchical, corporatist, backward — and thus inferior. But among its many flaws, this appealingly simplistic (and highly influential) contrast is based on a mistaken premise, in that it fundamentally misunderstands most Britons' perceptions of their domestic social world when their nation was at its zenith as an imperial power.

Far from seeing themselves as atomized individuals with no rooted sense of identity, or as collective classes coming into being and struggling with each other, or as equal citizens whose modernity engendered an unrivalled sense of progressive superiority, Britons generally conceived of themselves as belonging to an unequal society characterized by a seamless web of layered gradations, which were hallowed by time and precedent, which were sanctioned by tradition and religion, and which extended in a great chain of being from the monarch at the top to the humblest subject at the bottom. That was how they saw themselves, and it was from that starting point that they contemplated and tried to comprehend the distant realms and diverse society of their empire. This in turn meant that for the British, their overseas realms were at least as much about sameness as they were about difference. For insofar as they regarded their empire as "one vast interconnected world," they did not necessarily do so in disadvantaged or critical contrast to the way they perceived their own metropolitan society. Rather, they were at least as likely to envisage the social structure of their empire — as their predecessors had done before them — by analogy to what they knew of "home," or in replication of it, or in parallel to it, or in extension of it, or (sometimes) in idealization of it, or (even, and increasingly) in nostalgia for it.

This means that we need to be much more attentive to the varied — sometimes, even, contradictory — ways in which the British understood, visualized, and imagined their empire hierarchically. To be sure, *one* of the ways in which they did so was in racial terms of superiority and inferiority. Like all post-Enlightenment imperial powers, only more so, Britons saw themselves as the lords of all the world and thus of humankind. They placed themselves at the top of the scale of civilization and achievement, they ranked all other races in descending order beneath them, according to their relative merits (and de-merits), and during the period 1780 to 1830 they increasingly embodied these views in imperial institutions and codes. And when it came to the systematic settlement of Canada, Australia, New Zealand, and South Africa, they did not hesitate to banish the indigenous peoples to the margins of the new, imperial society. By the end of the nineteenth century these notions of racial hierarchy, supremacy, and stereotyping had become more fully developed, and stridently hardened, as exemplified in Cecil Rhodes's remark that "the British are the finest race in the world, and the more of the world they inhabit, the better it will be for mankind," or in Lord Cromer's belief that the world was divided between those who were British and those who were merely "subject races."

In short, and as Peter Marshall has observed, "Empire reinforced a hierarchical view of the world, in which the British occupied a preeminent place among the colonial powers, while those subjected to colonial rule were ranged below them, in varying degrees of supposed inferiority." These facts are familiar and incontrovertible. But this mode of imperial ranking and imaging was not just based on the Enlightenment view of the intrinsic inferiority of dark-skinned peoples: it was also based on notions of metropolitan–peripheral analogy and sameness. For as the British contemplated the unprecedented numbers massed together in their new industrial cities, they tended to compare these great towns at home with the "dark continents" overseas, and thus equate the workers in factories with coloured peoples abroad. The "shock cities" of the 1830s and 1840s were seen as resembling "darkest Africa" in their distant, unknown, and unfathomable menaces; and during the third quarter of the nineteenth century London's newly discovered "residuum" and "dangerous classes" were likened — in their character and their conduct — to the "negroes" of empire. And these domestic–imperial analogies were worked and extended in the opposite direction as well: one additional reason why "natives" in the empire were regarded as collectively inferior was that they were seen as the overseas equivalent of the "undeserving poor" in Britain.

To some degree, then, these analogies and comparisons that Britons drew and made between domestic and overseas societies, from the eighteenth to the twentieth centuries, served to reinforce the prevailing

Enlightenment notions of racial superiority and inferiority. And it is from this premise that the British Empire has been viewed by contemporaries and by historians as an enterprise that was built and maintained on the basis of the collective, institutionalized, and politicized ranking of races. But, as these analogies and comparisons also suggest, this was not the only way in which Britons envisioned their empire, and its imperial society, as an essentially hierarchical organism. For there was another vantage-point from which they regarded the inhabitants of their far-flung realms, which was also built around notions of superiority and inferiority, but which frequently cut across, and sometimes overturned and undermined, the notion that the British Empire was based solely and completely on a hierarchy of race. This alternative approach was, indeed, the conventional way in which the English (and latterly the British) had regarded the inhabitants of other, alien worlds, for it was a perspective that long antedated the Enlightenment.

It has certainly been traced back to the sixteenth and seventeenth centuries, for when the English first encountered the native peoples of North America, they did not see them collectively as a race of inferior savages; on the contrary, they viewed them individually as fellow human beings. It was from this pre-Enlightenment perspective that the English concluded that North American society closely resembled their own: a carefully graded hierarchy of status, extending in a seamless web from chiefs and princes at the top to less worthy figures at the bottom. Moreover, these two essentially hierarchical societies were seen as coexisting, not in a relationship of (English) superiority and (North American) inferiority, but in a relationship of equivalence and similarity: princes in one society were the analogues to princes in another, and so on and so on, all the way down these two parallel social ladders. In short, when the English initially contemplated native Americans, they saw them as social equals rather than as social inferiors, and when they came to apply their conventionally hierarchical tools of observation, their prime grid of analysis was individual status rather than collective race.

It is the argument of this book that these attitudes, whereby social ranking was as important as (perhaps more important than?) colour of skin in contemplating the extra-metropolitan world, remained important for the English and, latterly, for the British long after it has been generally supposed they ceased to matter. To be sure, the Enlightenment brought about a new, collective way of looking at peoples, races, and colours, based on distance and separation and otherness. But it did not subvert the earlier, individualistic, analogical way of thinking, based on the observation of status similarities and the cultivation of affinities, that projected domestically originated perceptions of the social order overseas. On the contrary, this essentially pre-racial way of seeing things lasted for as long as the British Empire lasted. Here is one example. In the summer of 1881 King Kalakaua of Hawaii was visiting England and, in the course of an extensive round of social engagements, he found himself the guest at a party given by Lady Spencer. Also attending were the prince of Wales, who would eventually become King Edward VII, and the German crown prince, who was his brother-in-law and the future kaiser. The prince of Wales insisted that the king should take precedence over the crown prince, and when his brother-in-law objected, he offered the following pithy and trenchant justification: "Either the brute is a king, or he's a common or garden nigger; and if the latter, what's he doing here?"

Read one way, this is, to our modern sensibilities, a deeply insensitive and offensively racist observation; read from another viewpoint, this was, by the conventions of its own time, a very *un*racist remark. The traditional, pre-Enlightenment freemasonry based on the shared recognition of high social rank — a freemasonry to which Martin Malia has suggestively given the name "aristocratic internationalism" — both trumped and transcended the alternative and more recent freemasonry based on the unifying characteristic of shared skin colour. From *this* perspective, the hierarchical principle that underlay Britons' perceptions of their empire was not exclusively based on the collective, colour-coded ranking of social groups, but depended as much on the more venerable colour-blind ranking of individual social prestige. This means there were at least two visions of empire that were essentially (and elaborately) hierarchical: one centred on colour, the other on class. So, in the *Raj Quartet*, Major Ronald Merrick, whose social background was relatively lowly, believed that "the English were superior to all other races, especially black." But the Cambridge-educated Guy Perron feels a greater affinity with the Indian Hari Kumar, who went to the same public school as he did, than he does with Merrick, who is very much his social inferior.

The British Empire has been extensively studied as a complex *racial* hierarchy (and also as a less complex *gender* hierarchy); but it has received far less attention as an equally complex *social* hierarchy or, indeed, as a social organism, or construct, of any kind. This constant (and largely unquestioned) privileging of colour over class, of race over rank, of collectivities over individualities, in the scholarly literature has opened up many important new lines of inquiry. But it has also meant that scarcely any attention has been paid to empire as a functioning social structure and as an imagined social entity, in which, as Karen Ordahl Kupperman puts it, "status is fundamental to all other categories." Yet throughout its history, the views expressed by the prince of Wales reflected generally held opinions about the social arrangements existing in the empire. These attitudes and perceptions were certainly still in existence in the late eighteenth and early nineteenth centuries. But they were no less important between the 1850s and the 1950s, when the ideal of social hierarchy was seen as the model towards which the great dominions should approximate, when it formed the basis of the fully elaborated Raj in India, when it provided the key to the doctrine of "indirect rule" in Africa, when it formed the template for the new nations created in the British Middle East, when it was codified and rationalized by the imperial honours system, and when it was legitimated and unified by the imperial monarchy. In all these ways, the theory and the practice of social hierarchy served to eradicate the differences, and to homogenize the heterogeneities, of empire. . . .

We should never forget that the British Empire was first and foremost a class act, where individual social ordering often took precedence over collective racial othering.

51

JOSEPH CONRAD
From Heart of Darkness

Although his native tongue was Polish (and French his second language), Joseph Conrad (1857–1924) became one of the leading English novelists of the era of British imperialism. Drawing on his experience as a mariner and ship captain, he secured a post as an officer on river steamboats on the Congo River in 1890. Nine years later he published *Heart of Darkness*, a novel which has introduced generations since to Africa, the Congo, the era of colonialism, and European ideas of "the other."

In this selection from the novel, Conrad's narrator, Marlow, tells of his voyage up the Congo to meet the enigmatic European Kurtz who has secured prodigious amounts of ivory for his Belgian employer but (we learn at the end of the novel) lost his mind in the process.

What impression does *Heart of Darkness* give of Africa and of European exploration of Africa?

Joseph Conrad, *Heart of Darkness*, A Norton Critical Edition (New York: Norton, 1988), 35–39. Originally published by *Blackwood's Magazine* (London, 1899, 1902).

Thinking Historically

Like many novels, *Heart of Darkness* is based on the actual experiences of the author. Despite the basis in fact, however, it is very different from historical writing. Imagine Conrad writing a history of the events described in this selection. How would it be different? Would one account be truer, or merely reveal different truths?

Going up that river was like travelling back to the earliest beginnings of the world, when vegetation rioted on the earth and the big trees were kings. An empty stream, a great silence, an impenetrable forest. The air was warm, thick, heavy, sluggish. There was no joy in the brilliance of sunshine. The long stretches of the waterway ran on, deserted, into the gloom of overshadowed distances. On silvery sandbanks hippos and alligators sunned themselves side by side. The broadening waters flowed through a mob of wooded islands. You lost your way on that river as you would in a desert and butted all day long against shoals trying to find the channel till you thought yourself bewitched and cut off for ever from everything you had known once — somewhere — far away — in another existence perhaps. There were moments when one's past came back to one, as it will sometimes when you have not a moment to spare to yourself; but it came in the shape of an unrestful and noisy dream remembered with wonder amongst the overwhelming realities of this strange world of plants and water and silence. And this stillness of life did not in the least resemble a peace. It was the stillness of an implacable force brooding over an inscrutable intention. It looked at you with a vengeful aspect. I got used to it afterwards. I did not see it any more. I had no time. I had to keep guessing at the channel; I had to discern, mostly by inspiration, the signs of hidden banks; I watched for sunken stones; I was learning to clap my teeth smartly before my heart flew out when I shaved by a fluke some infernal sly old snag that would have ripped the life out of the tin-pot steamboat and drowned all the pilgrims; I had to keep a look-out for the signs of dead wood we could cut up in the night for next day's steaming. When you have to attend to things of that sort, to the mere incidents of the surface, the reality — the reality I tell you — fades. The inner truth is hidden — luckily, luckily. But I felt it all the same; I felt often its mysterious stillness watching me at my monkey tricks. . . .

"I managed not to sink that steamboat on my first trip. It's a wonder to me yet. Imagine a blindfolded man set to drive a van over a bad road. I sweated and shivered over that business considerably, I can tell you. After all, for a seaman, to scrape the bottom of the thing that's supposed to float all the time under his care is the unpardonable sin.

No one may know of it, but you never forget the thump — eh? A blow on the very heart. You remember it, you dream of it, you wake up at night and think of it — years after — and go hot and cold all over. I don't pretend to say that steamboat floated all the time. More than once she had to wade for a bit, with twenty cannibals splashing around and pushing. We had enlisted some of these chaps on the way for a crew. Fine fellows — cannibals — in their place. They were men one could work with, and I am grateful to them. And, after all, they did not eat each other before my face: they had brought along a provision of hippo-meat which went rotten and made the mystery of the wilderness stink in my nostrils. Phoo! I can sniff it now. I had the Manager on board and three or four pilgrims with their staves — all complete. Sometimes we came upon a station close by the bank clinging to the skirts of the unknown, and the white men rushing out of a tumble-down hovel with great gestures of joy and surprise and welcome seemed very strange, had the appearance of being held there captive by a spell. The word 'ivory' would ring in the air for a while — and on we went again into the silence, along empty reaches, round the still bends, between the high walls of our winding way, reverberating in hollow claps the ponderous beat of the stern-wheel. Trees, trees, millions of trees, massive, immense, running up high, and at their foot, hugging the bank against the stream, crept the little begrimed steamboat like a sluggish beetle crawling on the floor of a lofty portico. It made you feel very small, very lost, and yet it was not altogether depressing, that feeling. After all, if you were small, the grimy beetle crawled on — which was just what you wanted it to do. Where the pilgrims imagined it crawled to I don't know. To some place where they expected to get something, I bet! For me it crawled towards Kurtz — exclusively; but when the steam-pipes started leaking we crawled very slow. The reaches opened before us and closed behind, as if the forest had stepped leisurely across the water to bar the way for our return. We penetrated deeper and deeper into the heart of darkness. It was very quiet there. At night sometimes the roll of drums behind the curtain of trees would run up the river and remain sustained faintly, as if hovering in the air high over our heads till the first break of day. Whether it meant war, peace, or prayer we could not tell. The dawns were heralded by the descent of a chill stillness. The woodcutters slept, their fires burned low, the snapping of a twig would make you start. We were wanderers on a prehistoric earth, on an earth that wore the aspect of an unknown planet. We could have fancied ourselves the first of men taking possession of an accursed inheritance, to be subdued at the cost of profound anguish and of excessive toil. But suddenly as we struggled round a bend there would be a glimpse of rush walls, of peaked grass-roofs, a burst of yells, a whirl of black limbs, a mass of hands clapping, of feet stamping, of bodies swaying, of eyes rolling under the droop of heavy and motionless foliage. The steamer toiled along slowly on the edge of a black and incomprehensible frenzy. The prehistoric man was cursing us, praying to us, welcoming us — who could tell? We were cut off from the comprehension of our surroundings; we glided past like phantoms, wondering and secretly appalled, as sane men would be before an enthusiastic outbreak in a madhouse. We could not understand because we were too far and could not remember because we were travelling in the night of first ages, of those ages that are gone, leaving hardly a sign — and no memories.

"The earth seemed unearthly. We are accustomed to look upon the shackled form of a conquered monster, but there — there you could look at a thing monstrous and free. It was unearthly and the men were. . . . No they were not inhuman. Well, you know that was the worst of it — this suspicion of their not being inhuman. It would come slowly to one. They howled and leaped and spun and made horrid faces, but what thrilled you was just the thought of their humanity — like yours — the thought of your remote kinship with this wild and passionate uproar. Ugly. Yes, it was ugly enough, but if you were man enough you would admit to yourself that there was in you just the faintest trace of a response to the terrible frankness of that noise, a dim suspicion of there being a meaning in it which you — you so remote from the night of first ages — could comprehend. And why not? The mind of man is capable of anything — because everything is in it, all the past as well as all the future. What was there after all? Joy, fear, sorrow, devotion, valour, rage — who can tell? — but truth — truth stripped of its cloak of time. Let the fool gape and shudder — the man knows and can look on without a wink. But he must at least be as much of a man as these on the shore. He must meet that truth with his own true stuff — with his own inborn strength. Principles? Principles won't do. Acquisitions, clothes, pretty rags — rags that would fly off at the first good shake. No. You want a deliberate belief. An appeal to me in this fiendish row — is there? Very well. I hear, I admit, but I have a voice too, and for good or evil mine is the speech that cannot be silenced. Of course, a fool, what with sheer fright and fine sentiments, is always safe. Who's that grunting? You wonder I didn't go ashore for a howl and a dance? Well, no — I didn't. Fine sentiments, you say? Fine sentiments be hanged! I had no time. I had to mess about with white-lead and strips of woollen blanket helping to put bandages on those leaky steam-pipes — tell you. I had to watch the steering and circumvent those snags and get the tin-pot along by hook or by crook. There was surface-truth enough in these things to save a wiser man. And between whiles I had to look after the savage who was fireman. He was an improved specimen; he could fire up a vertical boiler. He was there below me and, upon my word, to look at him was as edifying as seeing a dog in a parody of breeches and a feather hat walking on his hind legs. A few months of training had done for that really fine chap. He squinted at the steam-gauge and at the water-gauge with an evident effort of intrepidity — and he had filed teeth too, the poor devil, and the wool of his pate shaved into queer patterns, and three ornamental scars on each of his cheeks. He ought to have been clapping his hands and stamping his feet on the bank, instead of which he was hard at work, a thrall to strange witchcraft, full of improving knowledge. He was useful because he had been instructed; and what he knew was this — that should the water in that transparent thing disappear the evil spirit inside the boiler would get angry through the greatness of his thirst and take a terrible vengeance. So he sweated and fired up and watched the glass fearfully (with an impromptu charm, made of rags, tied to his arm and a piece of polished bone as big as a watch stuck flatways through his lower lip) while the wooded banks slipped past us slowly, the shore noise was left behind, the interminable miles of silence — and we crept on, towards Kurtz.

$$\boxed{52}$$

CHINUA ACHEBE

An Image of Africa: Racism in Conrad's *Heart of Darkness*

Chinua Achebe* is modern Africa's most read novelist. His *Things Fall Apart*, about the impact of European missionaries in his native Nigeria at the end of the nineteenth century, is a classic that is as widely read as *Heart of Darkness*. In this selection, which first took form as an address to an American college audience in 1975, Achebe tackles *Heart of Darkness*. What is his argument? Are you persuaded? How, if at all, does this reading change your evaluation of the selection from David Cannadine's *Ornamentalism*?

*chih NOO ah   ah CHEH bay

Chinua Achebe, "An Image of Africa: Racism in Conrad's *Heart of Darkness*," an emended version (1987) of the second Chancellor's Lecture at the University of Massachusetts, Amherst, February 18, 1975; later published in the *Massachusetts Review*, 18 (1977). Reprinted in *Heart of Darkness*, A Norton Critical Edition (New York: Norton, 1988), 252–54, 257–60.

Thinking Historically

Achebe is a novelist criticizing another novelist for distorting history. What are the responsibilities of a novelist to historical accuracy?

Heart of Darkness projects the image of Africa as "the other world," the antithesis of Europe and therefore of civilization, a place where man's vaunted intelligence and refinement are finally mocked by triumphant bestiality. The book opens on the River Thames, tranquil, resting, peacefully "at the decline of day after ages of good service done to the race that peopled its banks." But the actual story will take place on the River Congo, the very antithesis of the Thames. The River Congo is quite decidedly not a River Emeritus. It has rendered no service and enjoys no old-age pension. We are told that "Going up that river was like travelling back to the earliest beginnings of the world."

Is Conrad saying then that these two rivers are very different, one good, the other bad? Yes, but that is not the real point. It is not the differentness that worries Conrad but the lurking hint of kinship, of common ancestry. For the Thames too "has been one of the dark places of the earth." It conquered its darkness, of course, and is now in daylight and at peace. But if it were to visit its primordial relative, the Congo, it would run the terrible risk of hearing grotesque echoes of its own forgotten darkness, and falling victim to an avenging recrudescence of the mindless frenzy of the first beginnings.

These suggestive echoes comprise Conrad's famed evocation of the African atmosphere in *Heart of Darkness*. In the final consideration his method amounts to no more than a steady, ponderous, fake-ritualistic repetition of two antithetical sentences, one about silence and the other about frenzy. We can inspect samples of this on pages 36 and 37 of the present edition: a) *It was the stillness of an implacable force brooding over an inscrutable intention* and b) *The steamer toiled along slowly on the edge of a black and incomprehensible frenzy.* Of course there is a judicious change of adjective from time to time, so that instead of *inscrutable*, for example, you might have *unspeakable*, even plain *mysterious*, etc., etc.

The eagle-eyed English critic F. R. Leavis drew attention long ago to Conrad's "adjectival insistence upon inexpressible and incomprehensible mystery." That insistence must not be dismissed lightly, as many Conrad critics have tended to do, as a mere stylistic flaw; for it raises serious questions of artistic good faith. When a writer while pretending to record scenes, incidents, and their impact is in reality engaged in inducing hypnotic stupor in his readers through a bombardment of emotive words and other forms of trickery much more has to be at stake than stylistic felicity. Generally normal readers are well armed to detect and resist such underhand activity. But Conrad chose his subject well — one which was guaranteed not to put him in conflict with the psychological pre-disposition of his readers or raise the need for him to contend with their resistance. He chose the role of purveyor of comforting myths.

The most interesting and revealing passages in *Heart of Darkness* are, however, about people. I must crave the indulgence of my reader to quote almost a whole page from about the middle of the story when representatives of Europe in a steamer going down the Congo encounter the denizens of Africa.

> We were wanderers on a prehistoric earth, on an earth that wore the aspect of an unknown planet. We could have fancied ourselves the first of men taking possession of an accursed inheritance, to be subdued at the cost of profound anguish and of excessive toil. But suddenly as we struggled round a bend there would be a glimpse of rush walls, of peaked grass-roofs, a burst of yells, a whirl of black limbs, a mass of hands clapping, of feet stamping, of bodies swaying, of eyes rolling under the droop of heavy and motionless foliage. The steamer toiled along slowly on the edge of a black and incomprehensible frenzy. The prehistoric man was cursing us, praying to us, welcoming us — who could tell? We were cut off from the comprehension of our surroundings; we glided past like phantoms, wondering and secretly appalled, as sane men would be before an enthusiastic outbreak in a madhouse. We could not understand because we were too far and could not remember, because we were travelling in the night of first ages, of those ages that are gone, leaving hardly a sign — and no memories.
>
> The earth seemed unearthly. We are accustomed to look upon the shackled form of a conquered monster, but there — there you could look at a thing monstrous and free. It was unearthly and the men were. . . . No they were not inhuman. Well, you know that was the worst of it — this suspicion of their not being inhuman. It would come slowly to one. They howled and leaped and spun and made horrid faces, but what thrilled you was just the thought of their humanity — like yours — the thought of your remote kinship with this wild and passionate uproar. Ugly. Yes, it was ugly enough, but if you were man enough you would admit to yourself that there was in you just the faintest trace of a response to the terrible frankness of that noise, a dim suspicion of there being a meaning in it which you — you so remote from the night of first ages — could comprehend.

Herein lies the meaning of *Heart of Darkness* and the fascination it holds over the Western mind: "What thrilled you was just the thought of their humanity — like yours. . . . Ugly."

Having shown us Africa in the mass, Conrad then zeros in, half a page later, on a specific example, giving us one of his rare descriptions of an African who is not just limbs or rolling eyes:

And between whiles I had to look after the savage who was fireman. He was an improved specimen; he could fire up a vertical boiler. He was there below me and, upon my word, to look at him was as edifying as seeing a dog in a parody of breeches and a feather hat walking on his hind legs. A few months of training had done for that really fine chap. He squinted at the steam-gauge and at the water-gauge with an evident effort of intrepidity — and he had filed his teeth too, the poor devil, and the wool of his pate shaved into queer patterns, and three ornamental scars on each of his cheeks. He ought to have been clapping his hands and stamping his feet on the bank, instead of which he was hard at work, a thrall to strange witchcraft, full of improving knowledge.

As everybody knows, Conrad is a romantic on the side. He might not exactly admire savages clapping their hands and stamping their feet but they have at least the merit of being in their place, unlike this dog in a parody of breeches. For Conrad things being in their place is of the utmost importance.

"Fine fellows — cannibals — in their place," he tells us pointedly. Tragedy begins when things leave their accustomed place, like Europe leaving its safe stronghold between the policeman and the baker to take a peep into the heart of darkness. . . .

The point of my observations should be quite clear by now, namely that Joseph Conrad was a thoroughgoing racist. That this simple truth is glossed over in criticisms of his work is due to the fact that white racism against Africa is such a normal way of thinking that its manifestations go completely unremarked. Students of *Heart of Darkness* will often tell you that Conrad is concerned not so much with Africa as with the deterioration of one European mind caused by solitude and sickness. They will point out to you that Conrad is, if anything, less charitable to the Europeans in the story than he is to the natives, that the point of the story is to ridicule Europe's civilizing mission in Africa. A Conrad student informed me in Scotland that Africa is merely a setting for the disintegration of the mind of Mr. Kurtz.

Which is partly the point. Africa as setting and backdrop which eliminates the African as human factor. Africa as a metaphysical battlefield devoid of all recognizable humanity, into which the wandering European enters at his peril. Can nobody see the preposterous and perverse arrogance in thus reducing Africa to the role of props for the break-up of one petty European mind? But that is not even the point. The real question is the dehumanization of Africa and Africans which this age-long attitude has fostered and continues to foster in the world. And the question is whether a novel which celebrates this dehumanization, which depersonalizes a portion of the human race, can be called a great work of art. My answer is: No, it cannot. I do not doubt Conrad's great talents. Even *Heart of Darkness* has its memorably good passages and moments:

> The reaches opened before us and closed behind, as if the forest had stepped leisurely across the water to bar the way for our return.

Its exploration of the minds of the European characters is often penetrating and full of insight. But all that has been more than fully discussed in the last fifty years. His obvious racism has, however, not been addressed. And it is high time it was!

Conrad was born in 1857, the very year in which the first Anglican missionaries were arriving among my own people in Nigeria. It was certainly not his fault that he lived his life at a time when the reputation of the black man was at a particularly low level. But even after due allowances have been made for all the influences of contemporary prejudice on his sensibility there remains still in Conrad's attitude a residue of antipathy to black people which his peculiar psychology alone can explain. His own account of his first encounter with a black man is very revealing:

> A certain enormous buck nigger encountered in Haiti fixed my conception of blind, furious, unreasoning rage, as manifested in the human animal to the end of my days. Of the nigger I used to dream for years afterwards.

Certainly Conrad had a problem with niggers. His inordinate love of that word itself should be of interest to psychoanalysts. Sometimes his fixation on blackness is equally interesting as when he gives us this brief description:

> A black figure stood up, strode on long black legs, waving long black arms. . . .

as though we might expect a black figure striding along on black legs to wave white arms! But so unrelenting is Conrad's obsession. . . .

Whatever Conrad's problems were, you might say he is now safely dead. Quite true. Unfortunately his heart of darkness plagues us still. Which is why an offensive and deplorable book can be described by a serious scholar as "among the half dozen greatest short novels in the English language." And why it is today perhaps the most commonly prescribed novel in twentieth-century literature courses in English Departments of American universities.

There are two probable grounds on which what I have said so far may be contested. The first is that it is no concern of fiction to please people about whom it is written. I will go along with that. But I am not talking about pleasing people. I am talking about a book which parades in the most vulgar fashion prejudices and insults from which a section of mankind has suffered untold agonies and atrocities in the past and continues to do so in many ways and many places today. I am talking about a story in which the very humanity of black people is called in question.

Secondly, I may be challenged on the grounds of actuality. Conrad, after all, did sail down the Congo in 1890 when my own father was still a babe in arms. How could I stand up more than fifty years after his death and purport to contradict him? My answer is that as a sensible man I will not accept just any traveller's tales solely on the grounds that I have not made the journey myself. I will not trust the evidence even of a man's very eyes when I suspect them to be as jaundiced as Conrad's. And we also happen to know that Conrad was, in the words of his biographer, Bernard C. Meyer, "notoriously inaccurate in the rendering of his own history."

But more important by far is the abundant testimony about Conrad's savages which we could gather if we were so inclined from other sources and which might lead us to think that these people must have had other occupations besides merging into the evil forest or materializing out of it simply to plague Marlow and his dispirited band. For as it happened, soon after Conrad had written his book an event of far greater consequence was taking place in the art world of Europe. This is how Frank Willett, a British art historian, describes it:

> Gaugin had gone to Tahiti, the most extravagant individual act of turning to a non-European culture in the decades immediately before and after 1900, when European artists were avid for new artistic experiences, but it was only about 1904–5 that African art began to make its distinctive impact. One piece is still identifiable; it is a mask that had been given to Maurice Vlaminck in 1905. He records that Derain was "speechless" and "stunned" when he saw it, bought it from Vlaminck and in turn showed it to Picasso and Matisse, who were also greatly affected by it. Ambroise Vollard then borrowed it and had it cast in bronze. . . . The revolution of twentieth century art was under way!

The mask in question was made by other savages living just north of Conrad's River Congo. They have a name too: the Fang people, and are without a doubt among the world's greatest masters of the sculptured form. The event Frank Willett is referring to marked the beginning of cubism and the infusion of new life into European art, which had run completely out of strength.

The point of all this is to suggest that Conrad's picture of the peoples of the Congo seems grossly inadequate even at the height of their subjection to the ravages of King Leopold's International Association for the Civilization of Central Africa.

RUDYARD KIPLING

The White Man's Burden

This poem, written by Rudyard Kipling (1865–1936), is often presented as the epitome of colonialist sentiment, though some readers see in it a critical, satirical attitude toward colonialism. Do you find the poem to be for or against colonialism? Can it be both?

Thinking Historically

"The White Man's Burden" is a phrase normally associated with European colonialism in Africa. In fact, however, Kipling wrote the poem in response to the annexation of the Philippines by the United States. How does this historical context change the meaning of the poem for you? Does the meaning of a literary work depend on the motives of the writer, the historical context in which it is written, or both?

Take up the White Man's burden —
Send forth the best ye breed —
Go, bind your sons to exile
To serve your captives' need;
To wait, in heavy harness,
On fluttered folk and wild —
Your new-caught sullen peoples,
Half devil and half child.

Take up the White Man's burden —
In patience to abide,
To veil the threat of terror
And check the show of pride;
By open speech and simple,
An hundred times made plain,
To seek another's profit
And work another's gain.

Rudyard Kipling, "The White Man's Burden," *McClure's Magazine* 12, no. 4 (February 1899): 290–91.

Take up the White Man's burden —
The savage wars of peace —
Fill full the mouth of Famine,
And bid the sickness cease;
And when your goal is nearest
(The end for others sought)
Watch sloth and heathen folly
Bring all your hope to nought.

Take up the White Man's burden —
No iron rule of kings,
But toil of serf and sweeper —
The tale of common things.
The ports ye shall not enter,
The roads ye shall not tread,
Go, make them with your living
And mark them with your dead.

Take up the White Man's burden,
And reap his own reward —
The blame of those ye better
The hate of those ye guard —
The cry of hosts ye humour
(Ah, slowly!) toward the light: —
"Why brought ye us from bondage,
Our loved Egyptian night?"

Take up the White Man's burden —
Ye dare not stoop to less —
Nor call too loud on Freedom
To cloke your weariness.
By all ye will or whisper,
By all ye leave or do,
The silent sullen peoples
Shall weigh your God and you.

Take up the White Man's burden!
Have done with childish days —
The lightly-proffered laurel,
The easy ungrudged praise:
Comes now, to search your manhood
Through all the thankless years,
Cold, edged with dear-bought wisdom,
The judgment of your peers.

REFLECTIONS

Many of the selections within this chapter as well as its title point to the dual character of colonial society. There are the colonized and the colonizers, the "natives" and the Europeans, and as racial categories hardened in the second half of the nineteenth century, the blacks and the whites. Colonialism centered on the construction of an accepted inequality. The dominant Europeans invested enormous energy in keeping the double standards, dual pay schedules, separate rules and residential areas — the two castes.

One problem with maintaining a neat division between the colonized and the colonizers is that the Europeans were massively outnumbered by the indigenous people. Thus, the colonizers needed a vast class of middle-status people to staff the army, police, and bureaucracy. These people who Osterhammel reminds us were often unkindly seen as "white negroes," might be educated in Paris or London, raised in European culture, and encouraged to develop a sense of pride in their similarity to the Europeans ("me Christian, same like master") and their differences from the other "natives." Often, like the Indian Dr. Veraswami, they were chosen for their ethnic or religious differences from the rest of the colonized population.

In short, colonialism created a whole class of people who were neither fully colonized nor colonizers. They were in between. To the extent that the colonial enterprise was an extension of European conceits of social class, as Cannadine argues, these in-between people could be British as well as Indian. Orwell's Flory is only one of the characters in *Burmese Days* caught between two inhospitable worlds. One of the most notorious of this class of Europeans "gone native" is the Mr. Kurtz that Conrad's crew will meet upriver. Achebe's point that Africa becomes a setting for the breakup of a European mind might be generalized to apply to the European perception of the colonial experience. It is certainly one of the dominant themes of the European colonial novel. Even the great ones often center on the real or imagined rape, ravishing, or corruption of the European by the seething foreign unknown. This attitude also helps us understand how Kipling could be both anti-imperialist and racist. Imperialism could seem like a thankless act to those who tried to carry civilization to "sullen peoples, half devil and half child."

All the novels and poetry excerpted in this chapter are well worth reading in their entirety, and many other excellent colonial novels can be chosen from this period as well as from the 1930s and 1940s. E. M. Forster's *A Passage to India* and Paul Scott's *The Raj Quartet* stand out as fictional introductions to British colonialism in India. (Both have also received excellent adaptations to film, the latter as the series for television called *The Jewel in the Crown.*) In addition to Chinua Achebe, Amos Tutuola and Wole Soyinka have written extensively on Nigeria; as well, Francis Bebey, Ferdinand Oyono, and Mongo Beti address French colonialism in Africa. On South Africa, the work of Alan Payton, Andre Brink, J. M. Coetzee, Peter Abrams, and James McClure, among many others, stands out.

The advantage of becoming engrossed in a novel is that we feel part of the story and have a sense that we are learning something firsthand. Of course, we are reading a work of fiction, not gaining firsthand experience or reading an accurate historical account of events. A well-made film poses an even greater problem. Its visual and aural impact imparts a psychological reality that becomes part of our experience. If it is about a subject of which we know little, the film quickly becomes our "knowledge" of the subject, and this knowledge may be incomplete or inaccurate.

On the other hand, a well-written novel or film can whet our appetite and inspire us to learn more. Choose and read a novel about colonialism or some other historical subject. Then read a biography of the author or research his or her background to determine how much the author knew about the subject. Next, read a historical account of the subject. How much attention does the historian give to the novelist's subject? How does the novel add depth to the historical account? How does the historical account place the novel in perspective? Finally how does the author's background place the novel in historical context?

Nationalism and Westernization

Japan, India, and the Americas, 1880–1930

HISTORICAL CONTEXT

As peoples of Asia, Africa, and the Americas adapted to Western colonialism or struggled to free themselves from it, they inevitably faced the issue of Westernization. To become Westernized was to accept and adopt the ways of the powerful colonial powers of the West: Western Europe and its more distant western offshoot, the United States. All colonized peoples were exposed to some degree of Western education, indoctrination, or control. As they sought their independence and worked to create their own national identities, they frequently revived older indigenous traditions, languages, and religions — ideas that had fallen into disuse or had been replaced by Western culture. This rebirth of traditional culture often meant a specific and determined rejection of Western ways.

This chapter explores a number of responses to Westernization at the end of the nineteenth and the beginning of the twentieth century. The first selection gives an overall picture of how these societies came to grips with the West, culturally as well as politically. In every case, a people who sought its own national identity had to determine the degree of Westernization, if any, it desired to retain.

We examine Westernization in Japan, a country that was never colonized but that experienced cultural discord as it strove to "catch up" with the West. Japan's economic and industrial Westernization was so successful that many other countries were inspired by its example. What was the range of attitudes toward the West in Japan, and how strong was the impact of Westernization on its people?

We then turn to India for comparison. While Japan adopted Western ways in its successful effort to escape Western colonization, India's colonization by the British led to various forms of Westernization. However, the Westernization of India was not a monolithic process. There were both English colonials who opposed it and Indians who favored it. India was more fully Westernized than Japan, but its opposition to Westernization was more intense and eventually provided a foundation for rejecting British rule.

The North America of European immigrants joined the club of rich and powerful Western nations in the nineteenth century. Others in the Western hemisphere — Native Americans, African Americans, and many Latin Americans — struggled with the same issues of nationalist versus Western identity as did the colonized and former colonized peoples of Asia. Native Americans, in North and South America, experienced a European colonial expansion very much like that of colonized peoples in Asia. In South America, many states gained their political independence early in the nineteenth century, but often the political and military power of Spain was replaced by the dominance of the United States. In Cuba and New York, political activist José Martí looked to a free Cuba and a more global American identity.

What accounted for the appeal of the West in these different settings? Did the intellectuals of Japan and India mean the same thing by "the West"? Did the Westernizers seek to imitate different aspects of the West? And what motivated those who rejected the West? Did they have similar or different agendas?

THINKING HISTORICALLY
Appreciating Contradictions

The process of Westernization, like the experience of conquest and colonization that often preceded it, was fraught with conflict and led to frequent contradictions. Often, the struggle for national independence meant the borrowing of Western practices and ideologies: both Marxist and liberal. Indeed, the idea of national self-determination was a product of the French and American revolutions, as we have seen. Even the words and languages employed in the debate reflected Western origins as English or French was often the only common language of educated colonized peoples. Therefore, it is not surprising that contradictory behavior and ambivalent relationships were endemic in the postcolonial world, just as they had been under colonialism. These contradictions usually manifested themselves in an individual's cultural identity. How do colonized persons adopt Western ways, embrace traditional culture, and not feel as though their identity has been divided between the two? Such individuals may not fit entirely into either world and so may be torn between who they were and who they have become. The somewhat anguished experiences of these colonized people are difficult to understand. We typically want to accept one view or another, to praise or to blame. But as we have learned, the history of peoples and nations is rarely that clear. In examining some of the fundamental contradictions in the history of Westernization, we might better understand how people were variously affected.

The historical thinking skill one learns in reading documents from people torn between different ideals is the appreciation of contradictions. This operates on a number of levels. We learn that people can hold two contradictory ideas in their minds at the same time; and, in consequence, we learn to do it ourselves. This prevents us from jumping to conclusions or oversimplifying the historical process. In addition, we learn how the struggle over contradictory goals, whether internalized or expressed in group conflict, moves history forward.

$$54$$

THEODORE VON LAUE

From The World Revolution of Westernization

Western colonialism, according to von Laue, a modern historian, brought about a "world revolution of Westernization," the victory of Western culture that accompanied Western political domination. What, according to von Laue, are these Western ideas that spread throughout the world during the nineteenth century? Did these ideas spread peacefully or were they forced on non-Western peoples? What groups of people were most attracted to Western ideas? Why did some non-Western people prefer Western culture to their own?

Does von Laue believe that this "world revolution" was a good thing? Does he believe it is over? What, according to von Laue, must still be done?

Theodore von Laue, *The World Revolution of Westernization* (New York: Oxford University Press, 1987), 27–34.

Thinking Historically

Von Laue is particularly interested in the plight of what he calls the "Westernized non-Western intelligentsia." Who are these people? What is their problem? What does von Laue mean when he says that "as a result of their Westernization they became anti-Western nationalists"? How could Westernization make people anti-Western?

Throughout this selection, von Laue discusses paradoxical or ironic behavior. He writes of people learning lessons that were not formally taught and of psychological conflicts or love-hate attitudes. At one point he generalizes this phenomenon of seemingly contradictory behavior by quoting an eighteenth-century maxim that states, "To do just the opposite is also a form of imitation." Is von Laue describing some paradoxical aspect of human nature, or are these conflicts a particular product of colonialism?

While the world revolution of Westernization created a political world order radically above the horizons of all past human experience, it also unhinged, in the revolutionary manner sensed by Lord Lytton,[1] the depths of non-Western societies constituting the bulk of humanity. As he had said, "The application of the most refined principles of European government and some of the most artificial institutions of European society to a . . . vast population in whose history, habits, and traditions they have had no previous existence" was a risky enterprise, perhaps more than he had anticipated.

Examining the history of colonial expansion, one can discern a rough but generally applicable pattern for the revolutionary subversion of non-Western societies. Subversion began at the apex, with the defeat, humiliation, or even overthrow of traditional rulers. The key guarantee of law, order, and security from external interference was thus removed. With it went the continuity of tradition, whether of governance or of all other social institutions down to the subtle customs regulating the individual psyche. Thus ended not only political but also cultural self-determination. Henceforth, the initiatives shaping collective existence came from without, "mysterious formulas of a foreign and more or less uncongenial system" not only of administration but also of every aspect of life.

Once the authority of the ruler (who often was the semi-divine intermediary between Heaven and Earth) was subverted, the Western attack on the other props of society intensified. Missionaries, their

---

[1] British viceroy of India from 1876 to 1880.

security guaranteed by Western arms, discredited the local gods and their guardians, weakening the spiritual foundations of society. At the same time, colonial administrators interfered directly in indigenous affairs by suppressing hallowed practices repulsive to them, including human sacrifice, slavery, and physical cruelty in its many forms. Meanwhile, Western businessmen and their local agents redirected the channels of trade and economic life, making local producers and consumers dependent on a world market beyond their comprehension and control. In a thousand ways the colonial administration and its allies, though not necessarily in agreement with each other, introduced a new set of rewards and punishments, of prestige and authority. The changeover was obvious even in the externals of dress. Africans became ashamed of their nudity, women covered their breasts; Chinese men cut off their queues and adopted Western clothes. The boldest even tried to become like Westerners "in taste, in opinion, in morals, and intellect."

The pathways of subversion here outlined indicate the general pattern and the directions which it followed over time. Its speed depended on Western policy and the resilience of local society. Things seemingly fell apart quickly in the case of the most vulnerable small-scale societies of Africa and much more slowly in India or China, if at all in Japan. Often the colonial administration itself, under the policy of "indirect rule," slowed the Western impact for fear of causing cultural chaos and making trouble for itself. In all cases, tradition (however subverted) persisted in a thousand forms, merely retreating from the external world into the subliminally conditioned responses of the human psyche, its last refuge. It is still lurking in the promptings of "soul" today.

And did things really fall apart? The world revolution of Westernization prevailed by the arts of both war and peace. Certain aspects of Western power possessed an intrinsic appeal which, even by indigenous judgment, enhanced life. New crops often brought ampler food; European rule often secured peace. Through their command of the seas and of worldwide trade Europeans and Americans opened access to survival and opportunity in foreign lands to countless millions of people in China and India. Or take even the persuasion of raw power: Once convinced of the superiority of European weapons, who would not crave possession of them too? And more generally, being associated with European power also carried weight; it patently held the keys to the future. More directly perhaps, doing business with Westerners promised profit. If they played it right, compradors would get rich.

More subtly, certain categories of the local population eagerly took to foreign ways. Missionaries sheltered outcasts: slaves held for sacrifice, girls to be sold into prostitution or abandoned, or married women feeling abused and oppressed. The struggle for sexual equality is still raging in our midst, yet by comparison even Victorian England offered hope to women in Africa or East Asia. Regarding Japan, Fukuzawa[2] related the story of a highborn dowager lady who "had had some unhappy trials in earlier days." She was told of "the most remarkable of all the Western customs . . . the relations between men and women," where "men and women had equal rights, and monogamy was the strict rule in any class of people. . . ." It was, Fukuzawa reported, "as if her eyes were suddenly opened to something new. . . ." As a messenger of women's rights he certainly had Japanese women, "especially the ladies of the higher society," on his side. In China liberated women rushed to unbind their feet.

In addition, the Westerners introduced hospitals and medicines that relieved pain and saved lives, a fact not unappreciated. Besides, whose greed was not aroused by the plethora of Western goods, all fancier than local products: stronger liquor, gaudier textiles, faster transport? Simple minds soon preferred Western goods merely because they were Western. Given the comparative helplessness of local society, was it surprising that everything Western tended to be judged superior?

The Westerners with their sense of mission also introduced their education. It was perhaps not enough, according to anti-Western nationalists suspicious of European desires, to keep the natives down, yet it offered access to Western skills at some sacrifice on the part of teachers willing to forgo the easier life in their own culture. Privileged non-Westerners even attended schools and universities in the West. Thus, as part of the general pattern of Westernization, a new category of cultural half-breeds was created, the Westernized non-Western intelligentsia. It differed somewhat according to cultural origins, but shared a common predicament. Product of one culture, educated in another, it was caught in invidious comparison. As [philosopher] Thomas Hobbes observed "Man, whose Joy consisteth in comparing himselfe with other men, can relish nothing but what is eminent." Riveted to Western preeminence, this intelligentsia struggled for purpose, identity, and recognition in the treacherous no-man's-land in between — and most furiously in lands where skin color added to its disabilities. Talented and industrious, these intellectuals threw themselves heroically into the study of Western society and thought so alien to their own.

Along the way they soon acquired a taste for the dominant ideals of the West, foremost the liberal plea for equality, freedom, and self-determination and the socialists' cry of social justice for all exploited and oppressed peoples and classes. They were delighted by the bitter self-criticism they discovered among Westerners — Western society produced many doubters, especially among its fringes in central and eastern Europe. At the same time, non-Western intellectuals quickly perceived

[2]See selection 55. [Ed.]

the pride that lurked behind Western humanitarianism. They might be treated as equals in London or Paris, but "east of Aden" on the Indian circuit or anywhere in the colonies, they were "natives" — natives hypersensitive to the hypocrisy behind the Western mission of exporting high ideals without the congenital ingredient of equality. Thus they learned the lessons of power not formally taught by their masters. They needed power — state power — not only to carry the Western vision into practice on their own but also to make equality real.

Inevitably, the non-Western intellectuals turned their lessons to their own use. The ideals of freedom and self-determination justified giving free rein not only to the promptings of their own minds and souls, but also to protests over the humiliation of their countries and cultures. As a result of their Westernization they became anti-Western nationalists, outwardly curtailing, in themselves and their compatriots, the abject imitation of the West. Yet, as an 18th-century German wag had said, "To do just the opposite is also a form of imitation." Anti-Western self-assertion was a form of Westernization copying the cultural self-assertion of the West. Moreover, limiting Western influence in fact undercut any chance of matching Western power (and the issue of power was never far from their minds). Thus anti-Western intellectuals were caught in a love-hate attitude toward the West, anti-Western purveyors of further Westernization.

Take Mohandas Gandhi,[3] perhaps the greatest among the Westernized non-Western intellectuals. Born into a prominent tradition-oriented Hindu family and of a lively, ambitious mind, he broke with Hindu taboo and studied English law in London, fashionably dressed and accepted in the best society, though by preference consorting with vegetarians and students of Eastern religion. After his return he confessed that "next to India, [he] would rather live in London than in any other place in the world." From 1892 to 1914, however, he lived in South Africa, using his legal training for defending the local Indian community against white discrimination. There he put together from Indian and Western sources a philosophy as well as a practice of non-violent resistance, strengthening the self-confidence and civil status of his clients. . . .

One of Gandhi's precursors, Narendranath Datta, better known as Swami Vivekananda, had gone even further. At a lecture in Madras he exhorted his audience: "This is the great ideal before us, and everyone must be ready for it — the conquest of the whole world by India — nothing less than that. . . . Up India and conquer the world with your spirituality." Western globalized nationalism, obviously, was working its way around the world, escalating political ambition and cultural messianism to novel intensity. . . .

---

[3]See selection 57. [Ed.]

. . . [T]he run of Westernized non-Western intellectuals led awkward lives — "in a free state," as [Indian novelist] V. S. Naipaul has put it — forever in search of roots, and certitude; inwardly split, part backward, part Western, camouflaging their imitation of the West by gestures of rejection; forever aspiring to build lofty halfway houses that bridged the disparate cultural universes, often in all-embracing designs, never admitting the fissures and cracks in their lives and opinions; and always covering up their unease with a compensating presumption of moral superiority based on the recognition that the promptings of heart and soul are superior to the dictates of reason. Knowing their own traditions and at least some of the essentials of the West, they sensed that they had a more elevated grasp of human reality; the future belonged to them rather than to the "decadent" West. Out of that existential misery of "heightened consciousness" (as [Russian novelist] Dostoyevsky called it) have come some of the most seminal contributions to the intellectual and political developments of the 20th century, including the anti-Western counterrevolutions.

. . . Let it be said first that the relations between the colonized and the colonizer are exceedingly subtle and complex, subject to keen controversy among all observers, all of them partisans, all of them now judging not by indigenous but by Westernized standards. Western ideals and practices have shaped and intensified the protests of Westernized non-Western intellectuals taking full advantage of the opportunities offered by Western society. Their protests, incidentally, were hardly ever turned against past inhumanities committed by their own kind (because traditionally they were not considered as such).

Next, having already surveyed the not inconsiderable side benefits of Western domination, let us ask: Did the Westerners in their expansion behave toward the non-Westerners worse than they behaved toward themselves? While they never treated their colonial subjects as equals, they never killed as many people in all their colonial campaigns as they did in their own wars at home (the brutality of Europe's cultural evolution has been carefully rinsed out of all current historical accounts). And in their peaceful intercourse with non-Westerners we find the whole range of emotions common in Western society. It was darkness at heart on one extreme and saintliness on the other, and every mix in between, with the balance perhaps tending toward darkness. As one colonial officer in East Africa confided to his diary: "It is but a small percentage of white men whose characters do not in one way or another undergo a subtle process of deteriorization when they are compelled to live for any length of time among savage races and under conditions as exist in tropical climates." The colonial district commissioner, isolated among people whose ways sharply contradicted his own upbringing, often suffering from tropical sickness, and scared at heart, found himself perhaps in a worse dilemma than the Westernized non-Western intellectuals. Some of them, no doubt, were unscrupulous opportunists seeking escape from the trammels of civic conformity at home; they turned domineering sadists in the colonies. On the other hand, missionaries often sacrificed their lives, generally among uncomprehending local folk. It was perhaps a credit to the Westerners that the victims of imperialism found considerable sympathy in their own midst. The evils stood out while the good intentions were taken for granted.

Yet — to take a longer view — even compassionate Western observers generally overlook the fact that among all the gifts of the West the two most crucial boons were missing: cultural equality as the basis for political equality and reasonable harmony in the body politic. The world revolution of Westernization perpetuated inequality and ruinous cultural subversion while at the same time improving the material conditions of life. More people survived, forever subject to the agonies of inequality and disorientation resulting from enforced change originating beyond their ken. Collectively and individually, they straddled the border between West and non-West, on the one side enjoying the benefits of Western culture, on the other feeling exploited as victims of imperialism. Indigenous populations always remained backward and dependent, unable to match the resources and skills of a fast-advancing West.

What we should weigh, then, in any assessment of Western colonial expansion before World War I is perhaps not only the actions, good or evil, of the colonial powers, but also the long-run consequences thereafter. The victims of Western colonialism do not include only the casualties of colonial wars but also the far greater multitudes killed or brutalized in the civil commotions in the emerging modern nation-states. Whatever the mitigating circumstances, the anti-Western fury has its justifications indeed.

And yet, in the all-inclusive global perspective, is it morally justified? Was the outreach with all its outrages planned by the Westerners? Was it based on a deliberate design of conquest? Or was it the accidental result of stark imbalances in the resources of power for both war and peace which had come about through circumstances beyond human control? Why were the Westerners so powerful? Their stock answer has been: because of their ideals embedded in their religion, culture, and political institutions, adding up to their overwhelming material superiority. That answer, however, will not suffice for the overview appropriate to this age. In the enlarged contexts of global interaction human beings appear far more helpless than in their smaller settings, where they may claim a measure of control. As argued above, it was merely by historical and geographic accident that the Europeans were enabled to create the cultural hothouse that made them uniquely powerful in the world.

. . . As we now see the grand connections more clearly, we also understand that the burden of responsibility for bringing about cultural equality falls more heavily on those who have been so privileged, so spoiled, by circumstances beyond their control. They have furnished the energies behind the world revolution of Westernization; they carry the obligation to complete it according to their ideals of freedom, equality, and human dignity and in a manner beneficial to all humanity.

$$\boxed{55}$$

FUKUZAWA YUKICHI
Good-bye Asia

Fukuzawa* Yukichi (1835–1901) was one of the most important Japanese Westernizers during Japan's late-nineteenth-century rush to catch up with the West. The son of a lower samurai (military) family, Fukuzawa's pursuit of Western knowledge took him to a Dutch school in Osaka, where he studied everything from the Dutch language to chemistry, physics, and anatomy, and to Yedo where he studied English. Due to his privileged background and Western schooling, he was naturally included in the first Japanese mission to the United States in 1860 as well as in the first diplomatic mission to Europe in 1862. After Fukuzawa returned to Japan, he spent many years teaching and writing the books that would make him famous. The best known of these was *Seiyo Jijo* (*Things Western*), which in 1866 introduced Japanese readers to the daily life and typical institutions of Western society. According to Fukuzawa, the main obstacle that prevented Japanese society from catching up with the West was a long heritage of Chinese Confucianism, which stifled educational independence.

In the years after the Meiji Restoration of 1868, in which feudalism was abolished and power was restored to the emperor, Fukuzawa

*foo koo ZAH wah

Fukuzawa Yukichi, "Datsu-a Ron" ("On Saying Good-bye to Asia"), in *Japan: A Documentary History*, vol. II, ed. David J. Lu (Armonk, NY: M. E. Sharpe, 1997), 351–53. From Takeuchi Yoshimi, ed., *Azia Shugi* (*Asianism*) *Gendai Nihon Shisō Taikei* (*Great Compilation of Modern Japanese Thought*), vol. 8 (Tokyo: Chikuma Shobō, 1963), 38–40.

became the most popular spokesman for the Westernizing policies of the new government. In this essay, "Good-bye Asia," written in 1885, Fukuzawa describes the spread of Western civilization in Japan. Does he believe that it is both inevitable and desirable? Why? What do you make of Fukuzawa's attitude toward Chinese and Korean civilizations?

Thinking Historically

Does this selection from Fukuzawa display any of the contradictions, ambivalence, or love-hate feelings that von Laue describes as common among Westernized non-Western intellectuals? Were such conflicts inevitable? How might someone like Fukuzawa avoid this conflict, ambivalence, or uncertainty?

Transportation has become so convenient these days that once the wind of Western civilization blows to the East, every blade of grass and every tree in the East follow what the Western wind brings. Ancient Westerners and present-day Westerners are from the same stock and are not much different from one another. The ancient ones moved slowly, but their contemporary counterparts move vivaciously at a fast pace. This is possible because present-day Westerners take advantage of the means of transportation available to them. For those of us who live in the Orient, unless we want to prevent the coming of Western civilization with a firm resolve, it is best that we cast our lot with them. If one observes carefully what is going on in today's world, one knows the futility of trying to prevent the onslaught of Western civilization. Why not float with them in the same ocean of civilization, sail the same waves, and enjoy the fruits and endeavors of civilization?

The movement of a civilization is like the spread of measles. Measles in Tokyo start in Nagasaki and come eastward with the spring thaw. We may hate the spread of this communicable disease, but is there any effective way of preventing it? I can prove that it is not possible. In a communicable disease, people receive only damages. In a civilization, damages may accompany benefits, but benefits always far outweigh them, and their force cannot be stopped. This being the case, there is no point in trying to prevent their spread. A wise man encourages the spread and allows our people to get used to its ways.

The opening to the modern civilization of the West began in the reign of Kaei (1848–58). Our people began to discover its utility and gradually and yet actively moved toward its acceptance. However, there was an old-fashioned and bloated government that stood in the way of progress. It was a problem impossible to solve. If the government were allowed to continue, the new civilization could not enter. The modern civilization and Japan's old conventions were mutually exclusive. If we were to discard our old conventions, that government also had to be abolished. We could have prevented the entry of this civilization, but it would have meant loss of our national independence. The struggles taking place in the world civilization were such that they would not allow an Eastern island nation to slumber in isolation. At that point, dedicated men (*shijin*) recognized the principle of "the country is more important than the government," relied on the dignity of the Imperial Household, and toppled the old government to establish a new one. With this, public and the private sectors alike, everyone in our country accepted the modern Western civilization. Not only were we able to cast aside Japan's old conventions, but we also succeeded in creating a new axle toward progress in Asia. Our basic assumptions could be summarized in two words: "Good-bye Asia (*Datsu-a*)."

Japan is located in the eastern extremities of Asia, but the spirit of her people have already moved away from the old conventions of Asia to the Western civilization. Unfortunately for Japan, there are two neighboring countries. One is called China and another Korea. These two peoples, like the Japanese people, have been nurtured by Asiatic political thoughts and mores. It may be that we are different races of people, or it may be due to the differences in our heredity or education; significant differences mark the three peoples. The Chinese and Koreans are more like each other and together they do not show as much similarity to the Japanese. These two peoples do not know how to progress either personally or as a nation. In this day and age with transportation becoming so convenient, they cannot be blind to the manifestations of Western civilization. But they say that what is seen or heard cannot influence the disposition of their minds. Their love affairs with ancient ways and old customs remain as strong as they were centuries ago. In this new and vibrant theater of civilization when we speak of education, they only refer back to Confucianism. As for school education, they can only cite [Chinese philosopher Mencius's] precepts of humanity, righteousness, decorum, and knowledge. While professing their abhorrence to ostentation, in reality they show their ignorance of truth and principles. As for their morality, one only has to observe their unspeakable acts of cruelty and shamelessness. Yet they remain arrogant and show no sign of self-examination.

In my view, these two countries cannot survive as independent nations with the onslaught of Western civilization to the East. Their concerned citizens might yet find a way to engage in a massive reform, on the scale of our Meiji Restoration, and they could change their governments and bring about a renewal of spirit among their peoples. If that could happen they would indeed be fortunate. However, it is more likely that would never happen, and within a few short years they will be wiped out from the world with their lands divided among the civilized nations. Why is this so? Simply at a time when the spread of civilization and enlightenment (*bummei kaika*) has a force akin to that of measles, China and Korea violate the natural law of its spread. They forcibly try to avoid it by shutting off air from their rooms. Without air, they suffocate to death. It is said that neighbors must extend helping hands to one another because their relations are inseparable. Today's China and Korea have not done a thing for Japan. From the perspectives of civilized Westerners, they may see what is happening in China and Korea and judge Japan accordingly, because of the three countries' geographical proximity. The governments of China and Korea still retain their autocratic manners and do not abide by the rule of law. Westerners may consider Japan likewise a lawless society. Natives of China and Korea are deep in their hocus pocus of nonscientific behavior. Western scholars may think that Japan still remains a country dedicated to the *yin* and *yang* and five elements.[1] Chinese are mean-spirited and shameless, and the chivalry of the Japanese people is lost to the Westerners. Koreans punish their convicts in an atrocious manner, and that is imputed to the Japanese as heartless people. There are many more examples I can cite. It is not different from the case of a righteous man living in a neighborhood of a town known for foolishness, lawlessness, atrocity, and heartlessness. His action is so rare that it is always buried under the ugliness of his neighbors' activities. When these incidents are multiplied, that can affect our normal conduct of diplomatic affairs. How unfortunate it is for Japan.

What must we do today? We do not have time to wait for the enlightenment of our neighbors so that we can work together toward the development of Asia. It is better for us to leave the ranks of Asian nations and cast our lot with civilized nations of the West. As for the way of dealing with China and Korea, no special treatment is necessary just because they happen to be our neighbors. We simply follow the manner of the Westerners in knowing how to treat them. Any person who cherishes a bad friend cannot escape his bad notoriety. We simply erase from our minds our bad friends in Asia.

---

[1] *Yin* and *yang* is a traditional Chinese duality (hot/cold, active/passive, male/female) illustrated by a circle divided by an "s" to show unity within duality. The five elements suggest another traditional, prescientific idea that everything is made of five basic ingredients.

56

Images from Japan: Views of Westernization

This selection consists of three prints by Japanese artists. The first print, Figure 9.1, called *Beef Eater*, illustrates a character in Kanagaki Robun's *Aguranabe* (1871). The author, a popular newspaper humorist, parodies a new class of urban Westernized Japanese who carry watches and umbrellas and eat beef (banned by Buddhist law for centuries but added to the Japanese diet by Westerners). What response in the viewer does the artist seek to evoke?

The second piece, Figure 9.2, is called *Monkey Show Dressing Room* (1879), by Honda Kinkachiro. What is this print's message? What is the artist's attitude toward Westernization?

The third piece, Figure 9.3, *The Exotic White Man*, shows a child born to a Western man and a Japanese woman. What is the artist's message? Does the artist favor such unions? What does the artist think of Westerners?

Thinking Historically

Prints, like cartoons, are a shorthand that must capture an easily recognizable trait. What, evidently, were the widely understood Japanese images of the West? Where do you think these stereotypes of the West came from? Do you see any signs in these prints of ambivalence on the part of the artist?

Figure 9.1 Beef Eater.

Source: *Beef Eater*, from Kanagaki Robun, *Aguranabe* (1871) in G. B. Sansom, *The Western World and Japan* (Tokyo: Charles E. Tuttle Co., 1977).

322

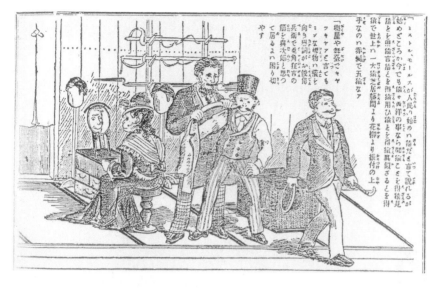

Figure 9.2   Monkey Show Dressing Room.
Source: Honda Kinkachiro, *Monkey Show Dressing Room*, in Julia Meech-Pekarik, *The World of the Meiji Print* (New York: John Weatherhill, 1986).

Figure 9.3 The Exotic White Man.

    Source: Japanese color print, late 19th c., Dutch private collection, in C. A. Burland, *The Exotic White Man* (New York: McGraw-Hill, 1969), fig. 38.

57

MOHANDAS K. GANDHI
From Hind Swaraj

Mohandas K. Gandhi (1869–1948), the father of Indian independence, combined the education of an English lawyer with the tempera-
ment of an Indian ascetic to lead a national resistance movement
against the British. In the century that followed British-supported reforms to the Indian education system (in the early nineteenth century),
British rule had become far more pervasive and increasingly hostile toward Indian culture. Unlike Indian educational reformers, who had
embraced Western culture as a means to uplift Indians, Gandhi was
extremely critical of Western culture as he witnessed the havoc British
rule wreaked on his country.

Gandhi began to develop his ideas of *Hind Swaraj,** or Indian
Home Rule, while he sailed from England to South Africa in 1909
where he served as a lawyer for fellow Indians. An early version of
this essay, published then, was reissued in its present form in 1921,
two years after he returned to his birthplace, India, and again in 1938,
in the last years of struggle against British rule.

After Gandhi's introduction, the essay takes the form of questions
and answers. The questions are posed by a presumed "reader" of
Gandhi's pamphlet. As "editor," Gandhi explains what he means.
How does Gandhi compare life in Europe and India? What does he
think of the possibility of Hindus and Muslims living together? What
does he mean by passive resistance or soul-force (Satyagraha)? Why
does he think it is preferable to violence, or body-force? Gandhi was
assassinated by a Hindu extremist in 1948 before he had a chance to
shape the new nation. What kind of India would Gandhi have tried to
create had he lived?

Thinking Historically

Some historians have argued that Gandhi's contradictory roles —
Hindu philosopher espousing secular nationalism and anti-modernist
revolutionary — were ultimately unbridgeable. Notice how Gandhi
makes a lawyer's case for traditional Indian values. How does he combine both religious and secular goals for India? How does he combine
Hindu religious ideas with respect for Muslims? Were Gandhi's contradictions a fatal flaw, or could they have been his strength?

*hihnd swah RAHJ

M. K. Gandhi, *Hind Swaraj* (Ahmedabad, India: Navajivan, 1938), 15–16, 26–27, 28, 30–31,
32–33, 58–60, 69–71, 82–85.

Civilization

READER: Now you will have to explain what you mean by civilization.

EDITOR: Let us first consider what state of things is described by the word "civilization." Its true test lies in the fact that people living in it make bodily welfare the object of life. We will take some examples. The people of Europe today live in better-built houses than they did a hundred years ago. This is considered an emblem of civilization, and this is also a matter to promote bodily happiness. Formerly, they wore skins, and used spears as their weapons. Now, they wear long trousers, and, for embellishing their bodies, they wear a variety of clothing, and, instead of spears, they carry with them revolvers containing five or more chambers. If people of a certain country, who have hitherto not been in the habit of wearing much clothing, boots, etc., adopt European clothing, they are supposed to have become civilized out of savagery. Formerly, in Europe, people ploughed their lands mainly by manual labour. Now, one man can plough a vast tract by means of steam engines and can thus amass great wealth. This is called a sign of civilization. Formerly, only a few men wrote valuable books. Now, anybody writes and prints anything he likes and poisons people's minds. Formerly, men travelled in waggons. Now, they fly through the air in trains at the rate of four hundred and more miles per day. This is considered the height of civilization. It has been stated that, as men progress, they shall be able to travel in airship and reach any part of the world in a few hours. Men will not need the use of their hands and feet. They will press a button, and they will have their clothing at their side. They will press another button, and they will have their newspaper. A third, and motor-car will be in waiting for them. They will have a variety of delicately dished up food. Everything will be done by machinery. Formerly, when people wanted to fight with one another, they measured between them their bodily strength; now it is possible to take away thousands of lives by one man working behind a gun from a hill. This is civilization. Formerly, men worked in the open air only as much as they liked. Now thousands of workmen meet together and for the sake of maintenance work in factories or mines. Their condition is worse than that of beasts. They are obliged to work, at the risk of their lives, at most dangerous occupations, for the sake of millionaires. Formerly, men were made slaves under physical compulsion. Now they are enslaved by temptation of money and of the luxuries that money can buy. There are now diseases of which people never dreamt before, and an army of doctors is engaged in finding out their cures, and so hospitals have increased. This is a test of civilization. Formerly, special messengers were required and much expense was incurred in order to send letters; today, anyone can abuse his fellow by means of a letter for one penny. True, at the same cost, one can send one's thanks also. Formerly, people had two or three meals consisting of home-made bread and vegetables; now, they require something to eat every two hours so that they have hardly leisure for anything else. What more need I say? . . . Even a child can understand that in all I have described above there can be no inducement to morality.

The Hindus and the Mahomedans

READER: Has the introduction to Mahomedanism [Islam] not un-made the nation?

EDITOR: India cannot cease to be one nation because people belonging to different religions live in it. The introduction of foreigners does not necessarily destroy the nation; they merge in it. A country is one nation only when such a condition obtains in it. That country must have a faculty for assimilation. India has ever been such a country. In reality there are as many religions as there are individuals; but those who are conscious of the spirit of nationality do not interfere with one another's religion. If they do, they are not fit to be considered a nation. If the Hindus believe that India should be peopled only by Hindus, they are living in dreamland. The Hindus, the Mahomedans, the Parsis and the Christians who have made India their country are fellow-country-men, and they will have to live in unity, if only for their own interest. In no part of the world are one nationality and one religion synonymous terms; nor has it ever been so in India.

READER: But what about the inborn enmity between Hindus and Mahomedans?

EDITOR: That phrase has been invented by our mutual enemy. When the Hindus and Mahomedans fought against one another, they certainly spoke in that strain. They have long since ceased to fight. How, then, can there be any inborn enmity? Pray remember this too, that we did not cease to fight only after British occupation. The Hindus flourished under Moslem sovereigns and Moslems under the Hindu. Each party recognized that mutual fighting was suicidal, and that neither party would abandon its religion by force of arms. Both parties, therefore, decided to live in peace. With the English advent quarrels recommenced. . . .

How Can India Become Free?

READER: If Indian civilization is, as you say, the best of all, how do you account for India's slavery?

EDITOR: This civilization is unquestionably the best, but it is to be observed that all civilizations have been on their trial. That civilization which is permanent outlives it. Because the sons of India were found wanting, its civilization has been placed in jeopardy. But its strength is to be seen in its ability to survive the shock. Moreover, the whole of India is not touched. Those alone who have been affected by Western civilization have become enslaved. We measure the universe by our own miserable foot-rule. When we are slaves, we think that the whole universe is enslaved. Because we are in an abject condition, we think that the whole of India is in that condition. As a matter of fact, it is not so, yet it is as well to impute our slavery to the whole of India. But if we bear in mind the above fact, we can see that if we become free, India is free. And in this thought you have a definition of Swaraj. It is Swaraj when we learn to rule ourselves. It is, therefore, in the palm of our hands. Do not consider this Swaraj to be like a dream. There is no idea of sitting still. The Swaraj that I wish to picture is such that, after we have once realized it, we shall endeavour to the end of our life-time to persuade others to do likewise. But such Swaraj has to be experienced, by each one for himself. One drowning man will never save another. Slaves ourselves, it would be a mere pretension to think of freeing others. Now you will have seen that it is not necessary for us to have as our goal the expulsion of the English. If the English become Indianized, we can accommodate them. If they wish to remain in India along with their civilization, there is no room for them. It lies with us to bring about such a state of things. . . .

Passive Resistance

READER: Is there any historical evidence as to the success of what you have called soul-force or truth-force? No instance seems to have happened of any nation having risen through soul-force. I still think that the evil-doers will not cease doing evil without physical punishment.

EDITOR: The [Hindu] poet Tulsidas [1532–1623] has said: "Of religion, pity, or love, is the root, as egotism of the body. Therefore, we should not abandon pity so long as we are alive." This appears to me to be a scientific truth. We have evidence of its working at every step. The universe would disappear without the existence of that force. . . .

The fact that there are so many men still alive in the world shows that it is based not on the force of arms but on the force of truth or love. Therefore, the greatest and most unimpeachable evidence of the success of this force is to be found in the fact that, in spite of the wars of the world, it still lives on.

Thousands, indeed tens of thousands, depend for their existence on a very active working of this force. Little quarrels of millions of families in their daily lives disappear before the exercise of this force. Hundreds of nations live in peace. History does not and cannot take note of this fact. History is really a record of every interruption of the even working of the force of love or of the soul. Two brothers quarrel; one of them repents and re-awakens the love that was lying dormant in him; the two again begin to live in peace; nobody takes note of this. But if the two brothers, through the intervention of solicitors or some other reason take up arms or go to law — which is another form of the exhibition of brute force, — their doings would be immediately noticed in the press, they would be the talk of their neighbours and would probably go down to history. And what is true of families and communities is true of nations. There is no reason to believe that there is one law for families and another for nations. History, then, is a record of an interruption of the course of nature. Soul-force, being natural, is not noted in history.

READER: According to what you say, it is plain that instances of this kind of passive resistance are not to be found in history. It is necessary to understand this passive resistance more fully. It will be better, therefore, if you enlarge upon it.

EDITOR: Passive resistance is a method of securing rights by personal suffering; it is the reverse of resistance by arms. When I refuse to do a thing that is repugnant to my conscience, I use soul-force. For instance, the Government of the day has passed a law which is applicable to me. I do not like it. If by using violence I force the Government to repeal the law, I am employing what may be termed body-force. If I do not obey the law and accept the penalty for its breach, I use soul-force. It involves sacrifice of self.

$$\boxed{58}$$

JAWAHARLAL NEHRU

Gandhi

Mohandas K. Gandhi and Jawaharlal Nehru* were the two most important leaders of India's national independence movement. In 1942, Nehru published his autobiography, excerpted here, in which he had much to say about the importance of Gandhi in his life. Though they worked together and Nehru was Gandhi's choice as the first Indian prime minister, they expressed in their personalities and ideas two

*jah wah HAHR lahl   NAY roo

J. Nehru, *Toward Freedom: The Autobiography of Jawaharlal Nehru* (New York: John Day Company, 1942).

very different Indias. How would you describe these two Indias? Was
it Gandhi's or Nehru's vision of the future that was realized? Who do
you think was a better guide for India?

Thinking Historically

Think of Gandhi and Nehru as the two sides of the Indian struggle for
independence. Did India benefit from having both of these sides represented? What would have happened if there had been only Gandhi's
view or only Nehru's?

How was the debate in India about the influence of the West different from the debate in Japan?

I imagine that Gandhiji[1] is not so vague about the objective as he sometimes appears to be. He is passionately desirous of going in a certain direction, but this is wholly at variance with modern ideas and conditions, and he has so far been unable to fit the two, or to chalk out all
the intermediate steps leading to his goal. Hence the appearance of
vagueness and avoidance of clarity. But his general inclination has been
clear enough for a quarter of a century, ever since he started formulating his philosophy in South Africa. I do not know if those early writings still represent his views. I doubt if they do so in their entirety, but
they do help us to understand the background of his thought.

"India's salvation consists," he wrote in 1909, "in unlearning what
she has learned during the last fifty years. The railways, telegraphs,
hospitals, lawyers, doctors, and suchlike have all to go; and the
so-called upper classes have to learn consciously, religiously, and deliberately the simple peasant life, knowing it to be a life giving true happiness." And again: "Every time I get into a railway car or use a motor
bus I know that I am doing violence to my sense of what is right"; "to
attempt to reform the world by means of highly artificial and speedy lo-
comotion is to attempt the impossible."

All this seems to me utterly wrong and harmful doctrine, and impossible of achievement. Behind it lies Gandhiji's love and praise of poverty
and suffering and the ascetic life. For him progress and civilization consist not in the multiplication of wants, of higher standards of living,
"but in the deliberate and voluntary restriction of wants, which promotes real happiness and contentment, and increases the capacity for
service." If these premises are once accepted, it becomes easy to follow
the rest of Gandhiji's thought and to have a better understanding of his
activities. But most of us do not accept those premises, and yet we complain later on when we find that his activities are not to our liking.

[1]Term of endearment. [Ed.]

Personally I dislike the praise of poverty and suffering. I do not think they are at all desirable, and they ought to be abolished. Nor do I appreciate the ascetic life as a social ideal, though it may suit individuals. I understand and appreciate simplicity, equality, self-control; but not the mortification of the flesh. Just as an athlete requires to train his body, I believe that the mind and habits have also to be trained and brought under control. It would be absurd to expect that a person who is given to too much self-indulgence can endure much suffering or show unusual self-control or behave like a hero when the crisis comes. To be in good moral condition requires at least as much training as to be in good physical condition. But that certainly does not mean asceticism or self-mortification.

Nor do I appreciate in the least the idealization of the "simple peasant life." I have almost a horror of it, and instead of submitting to it myself I want to drag out even the peasantry from it, not to urbanization, but to the spread of urban cultural facilities to rural areas. Far from his life's giving me true happiness, it would be almost as bad as imprisonment for me. What is there in "The Man with the Hoe" to idealize over? Crushed and exploited for innumerable generations, he is only little removed from the animals who keep him company.

> Who made him dead to rapture and despair,
> A thing that grieves not and that never hopes,
> Stolid and stunned, a brother to the ox?

This desire to get away from the mind of man to primitive conditions where mind does not count, seems to me quite incomprehensible. The very thing that is the glory and triumph of man is decried and discouraged, and a physical environment which will oppress the mind and prevent its growth is considered desirable. Present-day civilization is full of evils, but it is also full of good; and it has the capacity in it to rid itself of those evils. To destroy it root and branch is to remove that capacity from it and revert to a dull, sunless, and miserable existence. But even if that were desirable it is an impossible undertaking. We cannot stop the river of change or cut ourselves adrift from it, and psychologically we who have eaten of the apple of Eden cannot forget that taste and go back to primitiveness.

59

LUTHER STANDING BEAR

From Land of the Spotted Eagle

Most European-Americans accepted the idea of the magazine editor John O'Sullivan, writing in 1845, that "Our manifest destiny [is] to overspread the continent allotted by Providence for the free development of our yearly multiplying millions." Most Americans of European ancestry were not used to thinking of White settlement of Indian lands as colonialism. But manifest destiny, or not, Whites won the west by force, and the Indians who survived were herded into reservations where they lived like colonial subjects.

The American Indian confrontation with the ways of the West was not that different from that of the people of India or other European colonies. Each struggled with the conflict between Western advantage and traditional cultural identity, and each shaped a personal identity from that conflict.

Luther Standing Bear (1868–1939), born Plenty Kill, son of Standing Bear, describes his own struggle for identity in his years at boarding school in Carlisle, Pennsylvania, after he had been separated from his Lakota people. What did he see as the advantages and disadvantages of his education at Carlisle?

Thinking Historically

Would you describe the author's attitude toward Westernization as conflicted, ambiguous, compromising, practical, or something else? How does the author show us that assimilation to Western values or "civilizing" was not just an intellectual process? Change, whether or not we choose it, can have physical manifestations. Can you recall an experience where you struggled over two competing or contradictory pulls to your identity? Do you remember any physical manifestation of the conflict?

I grew up leading the traditional life of my people, learning the crafts of hunter, scout, and warrior from father, kindness to the old and feeble from mother, respect for wisdom and council from our wise men, and was trained by grandfather and older boys in the devotional rites to the Great Mystery. This was the scheme of existence as followed by my

---

Luther Standing Bear, *Land of the Spotted Eagle* (Lincoln: University of Nebraska Press, 1933), 229–37.

forefathers for many centuries, and more centuries might have come and gone in much the same way had it not been for a strange people who came from a far land to change and reshape our world.

At the age of eleven years, ancestral life for me and my people was most abruptly ended without regard for our wishes, comforts, or rights in the matter. At once I was thrust into an alien world, into an environment as different from the one into which I had been born as it is possible to imagine, to remake myself, if I could, into the likeness of the invader.

By 1879, my people were no longer free, but were subjects confined on reservations under the rule of agents. One day there came to the agency a party of white people from the East. Their presence aroused considerable excitement when it became known that these people were school teachers who wanted some Indian boys and girls to take away with them to train as were white boys and girls.

Now, father was a "blanket Indian,"[1] but he was wise. He listened to the white strangers, their offers and promises that if they took his son they would care well for him, teach him how to read and write, and how to wear white man's clothes. But to father all this was just "sweet talk," and I know that it was with great misgivings that he left the decision to me and asked if I cared to go with these people. I, of course, shared with the rest of my tribe a distrust of the white people, so I know that for all my dear father's anxiety he was proud to hear me say "Yes." That meant that I was brave.

I could think of no reason why white people wanted Indian boys and girls except to kill them, and not having the remotest idea of what a school was, I thought we were going East to die. But so well had courage and bravery been trained into us that it became a part of our unconscious thinking and acting, and personal life was nothing when it came time to do something for the tribe. . . . Thus, in giving myself up to go East I was proving to my father that he was honored with a brave son. In my decision to go, I gave up many things dear to the heart of a little Indian boy, and one of the things over which my child mind grieved was the thought of saying good-bye to my pony. I rode him as far as I could on the journey, which was to the Missouri River, where we took the boat. There we parted from our parents, and it was a heart-breaking scene, women and children weeping. Some of the children changed their minds and were unable to go on the boat, but for many who did go it was a final parting.

On our way to school we saw many white people, more than we ever dreamed existed, and the manner in which they acted when they saw us quite indicated their opinion of us. It was only about three years

---

[1]An Indian who prefers traditional ideas, dress, ways. [Ed.]

after the Custer battle, and the general opinion was that the Plains people merely infested the earth as nuisances. . . . At one place we were taken off the train and marched a distance down the street to a restaurant. We walked down the street between two rows of uniformed men whom we called soldiers, though I suppose they were policemen. This must have been done to protect us, for it was surely known that we boys and girls could do no harm. Back of the rows of uniformed men stood the white people craning their necks, talking, laughing, and making a great noise. They yelled and tried to mimic us by giving what they thought were war-whoops. We did not like this, and some of the children were naturally very much frightened. . . . In my mind I often recall that scene — eighty-odd blanketed boys and girls marching down the street surrounded by a jeering, unsympathetic people whose only emotions were those of hate and fear; the conquerors looking upon the conquered. And no more understanding us than if we had suddenly been dropped from the moon.

At last at Carlisle the transforming, the "civilizing" process began. It began with clothes. Never, no matter what our philosophy or spiritual quality, could we be civilized while wearing the moccasin and blanket. The task before us was not only that of accepting new ideas and adopting new manners, but actual physical changes and discomfort has to be borne uncomplainingly until the body adjusted itself to new tastes and habits. Our accustomed dress was taken and replaced with clothing that felt cumbersome and awkward. Against trousers and handkerchiefs we had a distinct feeling — they were unsanitary and the trousers kept us from breathing well. High collars, stiff-bosomed shirts, and suspenders fully three inches in width were uncomfortable, while leather boots caused actual suffering. We longed to go barefoot, but were told that the dew on the grass would give us colds. . . . red flannel undergarments were given us for winter wear, and for me, at least, discomfort grew into actual torture. I used to endure it as long as possible, then run upstairs and quickly take off the flannel garments and hide them. . . . I still remember those horrid, sticky garments which we had to wear next to the skin, and I still squirm and itch when I think of them. Of course, our hair was cut, and then there was much disapproval. But that was part of the transformation process and in some mysterious way long hair stood in the path of our development. For all the grumbling among the bigger boys, we soon had our heads shaven. How strange I felt! Involuntarily, time and time again, my hands went to my head, and that night it was a long time before I went to sleep. If we did not learn much at first, it will not be wondered at, I think. Everything was queer, and it took a few months to get adjusted to the new surroundings.

Almost immediately our names were changed to those in common use in the English language. Instead of translating our names into English and calling Zinkcaziwin, Yellow Bird, and Wanbli K'leska, Spotted Eagle, which in itself would have been educational, we were just John, Henry, or Maggie, as the case might be. I was told to take a pointer and select a name for myself from the list written on the blackboard. I did, and since one was just as good as another, and as I could not distinguish any difference in them, I placed the pointer on the name Luther. I then learned to call myself by that name and got used to hearing others call me by it, too. By that time we had been forbidden to speak our mother tongue, which is the rule in all boarding-schools. This rule is uncalled for, and today is not only robbing the Indian, but America of a rich heritage. The language of a people is part of their history. Today we should be perpetuating history instead of destroying it, and this can only be effectively done by allowing and encouraging the young to keep it alive. . . .

Of all the changes we were forced to make, that of diet was doubtless the most injurious, for it was immediate and drastic. White bread we had for the first meal and thereafter, as well as coffee and sugar. Had we been allowed our own simple diet of meat, either boiled with soup or dried, and fruit, with perhaps a few vegetables, we should have thrived. But the change in clothing, housing, food, and confinement combined with lonesomeness was too much, and in three years nearly one half of the children from the Plains were dead and through with all earthly schools. In the graveyard at Carlisle most of the graves are those of little ones.

I am now going to confess that I had been at Carlisle a full year before I decided to learn all I could of the white man's ways, and then the inspiration was furnished by my father, the man who has been the greatest influence in all my life. When I had been in school a year, father made his first trip to see me. After I had received permission to speak to him, he told me that on his journey he had seen that the land was full of "Long Knives." "They greatly outnumber us and are here to stay," he said, and advised me, "Son, learn all you can of the white man's ways and try to be like him." From that day on I tried. Those few words of my father I remember as if we talked but yesterday, and in the maturity of my mind I have thought of what he said. He did not say that he thought the white man's ways better than our own; neither did he say that I could be like a white man. He said, "Son, try to be like a white man." So, in two more years I had been "made over." I was Luther Standing Bear wearing the blue uniform of the school, shorn of my hair, and trying hard to walk naturally and easily in stiff-soled cowhide boots. I was now "civilized" enough to go to work in John Wanamaker's fine store in Philadelphia.

I returned from the East at about the age of sixteen, after five years' contact with the white people, to resume life upon the reservation. But I returned, to spend some thirty years before again leaving, just as I had gone — a Lakota.

Outwardly I lived the life of the white man, yet all the while I kept in direct contact with tribal life. While I had learned all that I could of the white man's culture, I never forgot that of my people. I kept the language, tribal manners and usages, sang the songs and danced the dances. I still listened to and respected the advice of the older people of the tribe. I did not come home so "progressive" that I could not speak the language of my father and mother. I did not learn the vices of chewing tobacco, smoking, drinking, and swearing, and for all this I am grateful. I have never, in fact, "progressed" that far.

But I soon began to see the sad sight, so common today, of returned students who could not speak their native tongue, or, worse yet, some who pretended they could no longer converse in the mother tongue. They had become ashamed and this led them into deception and trickery. The boys came home wearing stiff paper collars, tight patent-leather boots, and derby hats on heads that were meant to be clothed in the long hair of the Lakota brave. The girls came home wearing muslin dresses and long ribbon sashes in bright hues which were very pretty. But they were trying to squeeze their feet into heeled shoes of factory make and their waists into binding apparatuses that were not garments — at least they served no purpose of a garment, but bordered on some mechanical device. However, the wearing of them was part of the "civilization" received from those who were doing the same thing. So we went to school to copy, to imitate; not to exchange languages and ideas, and not to develop the best traits that had come out of uncountable experiences of hundreds and thousands of years living upon this continent. Our annals, all happenings of human import, were stored in our song and dance rituals, our history differing in that it was not stored in books, but in the living memory. So, while the white people had much to teach us, we had much to teach them, and what a school could have been established upon that idea! However, this was not the attitude of the day, though the teachers were sympathetic and kind, and some came to be my lifelong friends. But in the main, Indian qualities were undivined and Indian virtues not conceded. And I can well remember when Indians in those days were stoned upon the streets as were the dogs that roamed them. We were "savages," and all who had not come under the influence of the missionary were "heathen," and Wakan Tanka [the Great Mystery], who had since the beginning watched over the Lakota and his land, was denied by these men of God. Should we not have been justified in thinking them heathen? And so the "civilizing" process went on, killing us as it went.

60

JOSÉ MARTÍ
Letters from New York

José Martí* (1853–1895) is the national hero of Cuba. As poet, journalist, and organizer, he devoted his life to Cuban independence. He fought Spain during the Ten Year War, 1868–1878, and directed the independence movement to the successful war of 1895–1898 but was killed in one of the first battles. Because of his revolutionary activities, Martí spent much of his life in exile in Spain, Mexico, Guatemala, and the United States. In the last fifteen years of his life he lived in New York, where he represented various Latin American governments and wrote widely for Latin American publications. This selection includes excerpts from two of his "Letters from New York." The first, an early one published in Colombia, describes the new Coney Island amusement park to Latin American readers. The second, published in the Spanish *Illustrated Review of New York*, lays out his larger nationalist vision for Cuba and the other countries of Latin America. What in New York appeals to Martí? What bothers him about North American life? What does Martí mean by "our America"? What most concerns him about Latin America in 1891? What does he think needs to be done?

Thinking Historically

Martí's life embodied the contradictions of the nationalist in exile. Living in New York from 1880 to the end of his life, he continually interpreted each America to the other. But his stance was hardly neutral. How did he balance the ways of North America and Latin America? How was Martí both pro–United States and pro–Latin American? In what ways was he both a nationalist and a globalist?

*hoh SAY   mahr TEE

José Martí, "Coney Island," trans. Esther Allen, in *Selected Writings* (New York: Penguin Books, 2002), 89–94. Originally published in *La Pluma* (Bogota, Colombia), December 3, 1881. José Martí, "Our America," is edited from the Web site of the Cuban ministry of foreign affairs, http://www.cubaminrex.cu/English/index.asp. Originally published as "Nuestra América" in *La Revista Ilustrada de Nueva York*, January 1, 1891.

Coney Island (1881)

Nothing in the annals of humanity can compare to the marvelous prosperity of the United States of the North. Does the country lack deep roots? Are ties of sacrifice and shared suffering more lasting within countries than those of common interest? Does this colossal nation contain ferocious and terrible elements? Does the absence of the feminine spirit, source of artistic sensibility and complement to national identity, harden and corrupt the heart of this astonishing people? Only time will tell.

For now it is certain that never has a happier, more joyous, better equipped, more densely packed, more jovial, or more frenetic multitude lived in such useful labor in any land on earth, or generated and enjoyed greater wealth, or covered rivers and seas with more gaily bedecked steamers, or spread out with more bustling order and naive merriment across gentle coastlines, gigantic piers, and fantastical, glittering promenades.

The North American newspapers are full of hyperbolic descriptions of the original beauties and unique attractions of one of those summer resorts, overflowing with people, dotted with sumptuous hotels, crosshatched by an aerial tramway, and colored in with gardens, kiosks, small theaters, saloons, circuses, tents, droves of carriages, picturesque assemblies, bathing machines, auctioneers, fountains.

Echoes of its fame have reached the French newspapers.

From the farthest reaches of the American Union, legions of intrepid ladies and gallant rustics arrive to admire the splendid landscapes, the unrivaled wealth, the bedazzling variety, the Herculean effort, the astonishing sight of the now world-famous Coney Island. Four years ago it was a barren heap of dirt, but today it is a spacious place of relaxation, shelter, and amusement for the hundred thousand or so New Yorkers who repair to its glad beaches each day.

[Martí goes on to describe the town and beach of Gable where Coney Island was located.] But the main attraction of the island is not far-off Rockaway or monotonous Brighton or grave and aristocratic Manhattan Beach: it is Gable, laughing Gable, with its elevator that goes higher than the spire of Trinity Church in New York — twice as high as the spire of our cathedral — and allows travelers to rise to the dizzying heights of its summit, suspended in a tiny, fragile cage. Gable, with its two iron piers that advance on elegant pillars for three blocks out over the sea, and its Sea Beach Palace, which is only a hotel now but was the famous Agricultural Building at the Philadelphia Centennial Exposition, transported to New York as if by magic and rebuilt in its original form down to the last shingle on the coast of Coney Island. Gable, with its fifty-cent museums exhibiting human freaks, preposterous fish, bearded ladies, melancholy dwarves, and stunted elephants grandiloquently advertised as the largest on earth; Gable, with its hundred orchestras, its mirthful dances, its battalions of baby carriages, its gigantic cow, perpetually milked and perpetually giving milk, its twenty-five-cent glasses of fresh cider, its innumerable pairs of amorous wanderers. . . .

Gable, where families gather to seek respite from the rank, unwholesome New York air in the healthy and invigorating seaside breeze; where impoverished mothers — as they empty the enormous box containing the family's lunch onto one of the tables provided without cost in vast pavilions. . . .

Ferries come and go; trains blow their whistles, belch smoke, depart, and arrive, their serpentine bosoms swollen with families they disgorge onto the beach. The women rent blue flannel bathing costumes and rough straw hats that they tie under their chins; the men, in less complicated garments, hold the women's hands and go into the sea, while barefoot children wait along the shore for the roaring wave to drench them, and flee as it reaches them, hiding their terror behind gales of laughter, then return in bands — the better to defy the enemy — to this game of which these innocents, prostrate an hour earlier from the terrible heat, never tire. . . . The amazing thing here is the size, the quantity, this sudden result of human activity, this immense valve of pleasure opened to an immense people, these dining rooms that, seen from afar, look like the encampments of armies, these roads that from two miles away are not roads at all but long carpets of heads, the daily surge of a prodigious people onto a prodigious beach, this mobility, this faculty for progress, this enterprise, this altered form, this fevered rivalry in wealth, the monumentality of the whole, which makes this seaside resort comparable in majesty to the earth that bears it, the sea that caresses it, and the sky that crowns it, this rising tide, this overwhelming and invincible, constant and frenetic drive to expand, and the taking for granted of these very wonders — that is the amazing thing here.

Other peoples — ourselves among them — live in prey to a sublime inner demon that drives us to relentless pursuit of an ideal of love or glory. And when, with the joy of grasping an eagle, we seize the degree of ideal we were pursuing, a new zeal inflames us, a new ambition spurs us on, a new aspiration catapults us into a new and vehement longing, and from the captured eagle goes a free, rebellious butterfly, as if defying us to follow it and chaining us to its restless flight.

Not so these tranquil spirits, disturbed only by their eagerness to possess wealth. The eyes travel across these reverberating beaches; the traveler goes in and out of these dining rooms, vast as the pampas, and climbs to the tops of these colossal buildings, high as mountains; seated in a comfortable chair by the sea, the passerby fills his lungs with that powerful and salubrious air, and yet it is well known that a sad melancholy steals over the men of our Hispanoamerican peoples who live here. They seek each other in vain, and however much the first impressions may have gratified their senses, enamored their eyes, and dazzled and befuddled their minds, the anguish of solitude possesses them in the end. Nostalgia for a superior spiritual world invades and afflicts them; they feel like lambs with no mother or shepherd, lost from the flock, and though their eyes may be dry, the frightened spirit breaks into a torrent of the bitterest tears because this great land is devoid of spirit.

But what comings and goings! What spendings of money! What opportunities for every pleasure! What absolute absence of any visible sadness or poverty! Everything is out in the open: the noisy groups, the vast dining rooms, the peculiar courtship of the North Americans — almost wholly devoid of the elements that comprise the bashful, tender, and elevated courtship of our lands — the theater, the photographer, the bathhouse — all of it out in the open. Some weigh themselves, because for the North Americans it is a matter of positive joy or real grief to weigh a pound more or less; others, for fifty cents, receive from the hands of a robust German girl an envelope containing their fortune; others, with incomprehensible delight, drink unpalatable mineral waters from glasses as long and narrow as artillery shells.

Our America (1891)

The conceited villager believes the entire world to be his village. Provided that he can be mayor, humiliate the rival who stole his sweetheart, or add to the savings in his strongbox, he considers the universal order good, unaware of those giants with seven-league boots who can crush him underfoot, or of the strife in the heavens between comets that go through the air asleep, gulping down worlds. What remains of the village in America must rouse itself. These are not the times for sleeping in a nightcap, but with weapons for a pillow, like the warriors of Juan de Castellanos[1]: weapons of the mind, which conquer all others. Barricades of ideas are worth more than barricades of stones.

There is no prow that can cut through a cloudbank of ideas. A powerful idea, waved before the world at the proper time, can stop a squadron of iron-clad ships, like the mystical flag of the last judgment. Nations that do not know one another should quickly become acquainted, as men who are to fight a common enemy. Those who shake their fists, like jealous brothers coveting the same tract of land, or like the modest cottager who envies the esquire his mansion, should clasp hands and become one. . . . We can no longer be a people of leaves, liv-

---

[1](1522–1607), chronicler and participant in Spanish conquest of Colombia. [Ed.]

ing in the air, our foliage heavy with blooms and crackling or humming at the whim of the sun's caress, or buffeted and tossed by the storms. The trees must form ranks to keep the giant with seven-league boots from passing! It is the time of mobilization, of marching together, and we must go forward in close ranks, like silver in the veins of the Andes.

. . . Those born in America who are ashamed of the mother that reared them, because she wears an Indian apron, and, who disown their sick mothers, the scoundrels, abandoning her on her sickbed! Then who is a real man? He who stays with his mother and nurses her in her illness, or he who puts her to work out of sight, and lives at her expense on decadent lands, sporting fancy neckties, cursing the womb that carried him, displaying the sign of the traitor on the back of his paper frockcoat? These sons of our America, which will be saved by its Indians in blood and is growing better; these deserters who take up arms in the army of a North America that drowns its Indians in blood and is growing worse! . . .

For in what lands can men take more pride than in our long-suffering American republics, raised up among the silent Indian masses by the bleeding arms of a hundred apostles, to the sound of battle between the book and processional candle? Never in history have such advanced and united nations been forged in so short a time from such disorganized elements. The presumptuous man feels that the earth was made to serve as his pedestal, because he happens to have a facile pen or colorful speech, and he accuses his native land of being worthless and beyond redemption because its virgin jungles fail to provide him with a constant means of traveling over the world, driving Persian ponies and lavishing champagne like a tycoon. The incapacity does not lie with the emerging country in quest of suitable forms and utilitarian greatness; it lies rather with those who attempt to rule nations of a unique and violent character by means of laws inherited from four centuries of freedom in the United States and nineteen centuries of monarchy in France. A decree by Hamilton does not halt the charge of a gaucho's horse. A phrase by Sieyes[2] does nothing to quicken the stagnant blood of the Indian race. To govern well, one must see things as they are. And the able governor in America is not the one who knows how to govern the Germans or the French; he must know the elements that make up his own country, and how to bring them together, using methods and institutions originating within the country, to reach that desirable state where each man can attain self-realization and all may enjoy the abundance that Nature has bestowed on everyone in the nation to enrich with their toil and defend with their lives. Government must

---

[2]French priest whose question "What is the third estate, if not the entire nation?" was said to spark the French Revolution of 1789. [Ed.]

originate in the country. The spirit of government must be that of the country. Its structure must conform to rules appropriate to the country. Good government is nothing more than the balance of the country's natural elements.

That is why in America the imported book has been conquered by the natural man. Natural men have conquered learned and artificial men. The native half-breed has conquered the exotic Creole. The struggle is not between civilization and barbarity, but between false erudition and Nature. The natural man is good, and he respects and rewards superior intelligence as long as his humility is not turned against him. . . . Republics have paid with oppression for their inability to recognize the true elements of their countries, to derive from them the right kind of government, and to govern accordingly. In a new nation a government means a creator.

In nations composed of both cultured and uncultured elements, the uncultured will govern because it is their habit to attack and resolve doubts with their fists in cases where the cultured have failed in the art of governing. The uncultured masses are lazy and timid in the realm of intelligence, and they want to be governed well. But if the government hurts them, they shake it off and govern themselves. How can the universities produce governors if not a single university in America teaches the rudiments of the art of government, the analysis of elements peculiar to the peoples of America? The young go out into the world wearing Yankee or French spectacles, hoping to govern a people they do not know. . . . To know one's country and govern it with that knowledge is the only way to free it from tyranny. The European university must bow to the American university. The history of America, from the Incas to the present, must be taught in clear detail and to the letter, even if the archons of Greece are overlooked. Our Greece must take priority over the Greece which is not ours. We need it more. Nationalist statement must replace foreign statement. Let the world be grafted onto our republics, but the trunk must be our own. And let the vanquished pedant hold his tongue, for there are no lands in which a man may take greater pride than in our long-suffering American republics. . . .

We were a phenomenon with the chest of an athlete, the hands of a dandy, and the brain of a child. We were a masquerader in English breeches, Parisian vest, North American jacket, and Spanish cap. The Indian hovered near us in silence, and went off to hills to baptize his children. The Negro, pursued from afar, poured out the songs of his heart at night, alone and unrecognized between the waves and wild beasts. The peasant, the creator, turned in blind indignation against the disdainful city, against his own child. We wore epaulets and judges' robes in countries that came into the world wearing hemp sandals and headbands. . . . Neither the Europeans nor the Yankee could provide the key to the Spanish American riddle. So the people tried hatred instead, and every year the countries amounted to less. Exhausted by useless hatred, by the senseless struggle between the book and the lance, between reason and the processional candle, between the city and the country, weary of the impossible rule by rival urban cliques over the natural nation tempestuous or inert by turns, we are beginning almost unconsciously to try love. Nations stand up and greet one another. "What are we?" is the mutual question, and little by little they furnish answers. When a problem arises in Cojímar,[3] they do not seek its solution in Danzig. The frockcoats are still French, but thought begins to be American. The youth of America are rolling up their sleeves, digging their hands in the dough, and making it rise with the sweat of their brows. They realize that there is too much imitation, and that creation holds the key to salvation. "Create" is the password of this generation. Make wine from plantains; it may be sour, but it is our own wine! . . . Thaw out frozen America with the fire of your hearts! Make the natural blood of the nations course vigorously through their veins! The new Americans are on their feet, saluting each other from nation to nation, the eyes of the laborers shining with joy. The natural statesman arises, schooled in the direct study of Nature. He reads to apply his knowledge, not to imitate. Economists study the problems at their point of origin. Speakers begin a policy of moderation. Playwrights bring native characters to the stage. Academies discuss practical subjects. Poetry shears off its . . . locks and hangs its red vest on the glorious tree. Selective and sparkling prose is filled with ideas. In the Indian republics, the governors are learning Indian languages. . . .

There can be no racial animosity, because there are no races. The theorist and feeble thinkers string together and warm over the bookshelf races which the well-disposed observer and the fair-minded traveler vainly seek in the justice of Nature where man's universal identity springs forth from triumphant love and the turbulent hunger for life. The soul, equal and eternal, emanates from bodies of different shapes and colors. Whoever foments and spreads antagonism and hate between the races, sins against humanity. With a single voice the hymn is already being sung; the present generation is carrying industrious America along the road enriched by their sublime fathers; from Rio Grande to the strains of Magellan, the Great Cemí,[4] astride its condor, has scattered the seeds of the new America over the romantic nations of the continent and the sorrowful islands of the sea!

[3]Near Havana, Cuba. [Ed.]
[4]Spirit worshipped by the Taino people of the Caribbean. [Ed.]

REFLECTIONS

We have looked at the conflict between Westernization and nationalism through windows on three different societies: Japan, India, and the Americas. For the Japanese, the borrowing of Western institutions and ideas provided an escape from colonization. By the time India gained political independence in 1947, it had become partially Westernized by three hundred years of colonialism. Yet in both countries, as in the countries of the Americas, there were those who resisted Western ways, those who embraced them, and others still who developed what von Laue called (after Dostoyevski) "heightened consciousness" from the contrary experiences or "love-hate" feelings within their own hearts.

This last response — accepting the contradictions: treasuring the traditional while trying the new — may have been the most difficult, but ultimately the most useful. It must have been far easier to cast off everything Asian, as Fukuzawa urged, or make fun of any contact with the West as buffoonery, monkeying around, or frightful miscegenation, as the Japanese cartoons suggested. Japan may have made the most successful non-Western transition to industrial modernity because it steered a path between Fukuzawa's prescription for wholesale cultural capitulation and the cartoonists' blanket rejection of anything new and foreign.

India, with older indigenous traditions than Japan, but also a longer period confronting the influence of Western culture, approached independence in 1947 with a political elite trained in English law, liberal and Marxist political parties, a literate English-speaking middle class, and a long-suppressed hunger for economic freedom and material well-being. Gandhi feared violence, anticolonial in 1909 and anti-Muslim in 1947, more than the repressions of the old society. While he sought a new social cohesion in traditional religious spiritualism, Nehru hoped to forge a new solidarity along the Western industrial socialist model.

In America, when the ideal of assimilation was not just a sham (as it was for many Africans and Native Americans), it required a cultural whitewashing in exchange for material success. Few could condemn themselves or their countrymen to economic dependence, but Martí, and others among the best and brightest, could insist on the need to find their own way.

Our brief summary of Westernization raises many questions. Why do so many nationalist leaders emerge from outside their native countries? Did Gandhi become more Indian in England or South Africa? Were Indians who lived overseas more free to express themselves, better able to contribute financially, or more optimistic about changing societies? Did Martí become a Cuban and first citizen of all the Americas through his travels, or his life in Nueva York? We cannot overlook the international aspects of nationalist movements in the twentieth century; Westernizers and anti-Westernizers seem to have been profoundly influenced by their foreign travel experiences. Is the history of Westernization, and of the opposition to Westernization, ultimately a global story? And are the global processes such that the story eventually becomes irrelevant?

In his book *The Birth of the Modern World, 1780–1914*, historian C. A. Bayly observes that at the beginning of the twenty-first century, it is difficult to distinguish Westernization from globalization, as the forces that threaten the national economies or cultures of Asia, Africa, and Latin America tend to come from every direction. Perhaps future generations will see Westernization as only the initial stage of a larger process of economic and cultural integration, which we now call globalization.

10

World War I and
Its Consequences

Europe and the Soviet Union, 1914–1920

HISTORICAL CONTEXT

The Europe that so many non-European intellectuals sought to imitate or reject between 1880 and 1920 came very close to self-destructing between 1914 and 1918, and bringing many of the world's peoples from Asia, Africa, and the Americas down with it. The orgy of bloodletting, then known as the "Great War," put seventy million men in uniform, of whom ten million were killed and twenty million were wounded. Most of the soldiers were Western European, though Russia contributed more soldiers than France or Germany, while Japan enlisted as many as the Austro-Hungarian empire that began the war. Enlisted men also came from the United States, Canada, Australia, New Zealand, South Africa, and the colonies: India, French West Africa, German East Africa, among others. The majority of soldiers were killed in Europe, especially along the German Western front — four hundred miles of trenches that spanned from Switzerland to the English Channel, across northeastern France. But battles were also fought along the borders of German, French, and English colonies in Africa, and there were high Australian casualties on the coast of Gallipoli in Ottoman Turkey.

The readings in this chapter focus on the lives and deaths of the soldiers, as well as the efforts of some of their political leaders to redefine the world around them. We examine the experiences of soldiers and how the war changed the lives of those who survived its devastating toll. We compare the accounts of those who fought on both sides of the great divide. Germany and the Austro-Hungarian empire, joined by the Ottoman Empire, formed an alliance called the Central Powers (see Map 10.1). In opposition, England, France, and Russia, the Allied Powers, were later joined by Italy, Greece, Japan, and the United

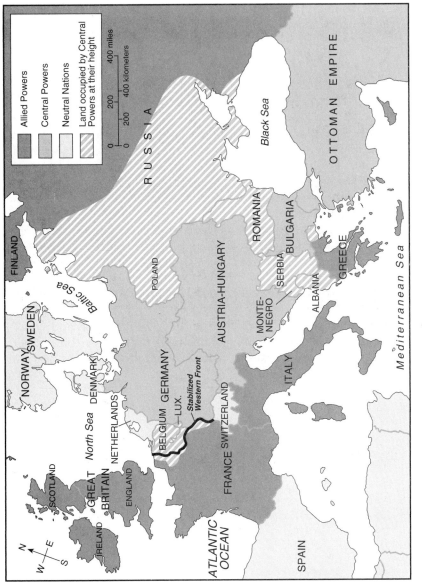

Map 10.1   Allied Powers and Central Powers in World War I.

States. We compare views across the generational divide as well as from the trenches and government offices.

THINKING HISTORICALLY
Understanding Causes and Consequences

From 1914 to 1920, the greatest divide was the war itself. It marked the end of one era and the beginning of another. Few events have left the participants with such a profound sense of fundamental change. And so our study of the war is an appropriate place to ask two of the universal questions of major historical change: What caused it? What were the consequences?

The *causes* are those events or forces that came before; the *consequences* are the results, what the war itself prompted to occur. Thus, causes and consequences are part of the same continuum. Still, we must remember that not everything that happened before the war was a cause of the war. Similarly, not everything that happened afterward was a result of the war.

In this chapter we explore specific ideas about cause and consequence. Our goal is not to compile a definitive list of either but, rather, to explore some of the ways that historians and thoughtful readers can make sense of the past.

61

SALLY MARKS

The Coming of the First World War

Sally Marks, a modern scholar, begins the following selection by declaring that, after much debate, historians have recently come to agree that Germany was the country primarily responsible for causing the First World War. Other countries were not blameless, however, and waging war in the twentieth century required willing recruits and popular support on all sides. Further, as Marks notes, there were secondary or background causes that precipitated the outbreak of war. What were these secondary causes? How important were they?

Thinking Historically

In studying the causes of major historical events, historians distinguish between structural or long-term causes, direct or immediate causes, and contingent events or accidents. Which events and circumstances leading up to the First World War would you place in each of these categories? Marks writes mainly of political decisions made by governments, which are often the most immediate causes of war. She also writes of long-term historic developments, however, such as competition for colonies, the difference between "young" and "old" states, the balance of power in international politics, the development of nationalism, as well as more personal factors such as leaders' fears and miscalculations. Were any of these long-term developments "causes" of war? How important does Marks think they were? Why does she think German political decisions were more important?

There is little that historians debate more endlessly than causation, and certainly much ink has been expended in arguing the origins of World War I. In recent years, however, a degree of consensus has emerged, even among German scholars, that primary responsibility should be assigned to the Second Reich, though debate continues about German motives and intentions. It now seems clear that Germany's

Sally Marks, *The Ebbing of European Ascendancy: An International History of the World, 1914–1945* (New York: Oxford University Press, 2002), 19–22, 25, 26, 31–36.

power, policies, actions, and diplomatic style provided a continual factor between its creation in 1870–1871 and the great collision of 1914.

Germany's unification, coupled with its industrial and demographic growth, brought a young but very strong power to the center of the European stage, hitherto a comparatively weak area. The power balance was at once implicitly altered. But Prince Otto von Bismarck, Chancellor of the new Germany until 1890, chose not to make this explicit in Europe or elsewhere. Preferring to build the Reich's institutions and industry, he restored the Concert of Europe, used it to settle quarrels threatening the peace and his new empire, and eschewed colonies. Between 1894 and 1914, however, a series of political, economic, and diplomatic events contributed to a gradual coalescing of the great power alliances — Russia, France, Great Britain (and later Italy) on the one side, and Germany, Austria-Hungary, and Turkey on the other — that would confront each other in World War I. Other key developments in this period and leading up to 1914 included Germany's growing policy of expansion, hunger for colonies, and military buildup, this last evolving into a fast-escalating naval race with Great Britain.

Although the old Concert was not quite moribund, all European powers of consequence were thus aligned in the two blocs, the Triple Alliance down the center of Europe, and the Triple Entente on the edges. Germany saw the Entente policy of containment as encirclement, and its fears in this respect only increased "the amalgam of insecurity and self-assertion in her make-up. . .". Thus its diplomacy became more bullying, which had the effect of driving Britain and France together, causing the Triple Entente to solidify. Both Germany's insistent claims and Russia's return from East Asia to compete with Austria in the Balkans contributed to growing conflict and tension between the two alignments.

Most of the conflicts concerned imperial matters although a European power struggle underlay them all. Part of the trouble was that the days when there were plenty of colonies available for everybody had passed, and as the powers bumped into each other, the latecomers were dissatisfied. Timing proved crucial to the imperial race; those who did not seize the moment encountered difficulties in doing later what other powers had done earlier. The latecomers were Germany, Japan, and Italy, impatient youngsters who remained dissatisfied, always seeking more until they went down to decisive defeat in World War II. But in the decade before the First World War, the collisions were not only in Africa and Asia, but also in the Balkans, as Russia turned to Austria's sole remaining sphere. Wherever confrontations occurred they brought with them the risk of a major conflagration, not merely a local conflict between two states, but a global struggle between two alignments of powers.

War among the major powers was avoided for a decade despite a series of crises, but only at the price of exhausting options and reducing flexibility, thus rendering resolution more difficult for the future. Great powers, especially the more precarious ones, could not repeatedly accept defeat and humiliation and still remain great powers. Another option which several states exhausted was that of not supporting an ally. With Europe divided into two camps, both of which were arming briskly, retaining one's allies was vital. However, one can desert an ally only so often and still keep it as an ally. Equally, the need for allies meant that both crises and atonements for desertion tended to solidify the two rival alignments, further reducing flexibility.

During the decade before 1914 the Anglo-German naval competition continued, despite British efforts to come to terms, and crises, often entailing lack of support from allies or diplomatic defeat, were too numerous to recount briefly. Though all depleted the reservoirs of good will and elasticity, only a few were so serious that they brought the risk of a pan-European war. Nonetheless, the fact that Europe came to the brink of a great war five or six times in ten short years is indicative of the instability and tension which were mounting.

Part of the problem was that Europe's power system was increasingly out of balance. The Habsburg Empire was no longer really a great power, while France was fading in comparative terms. Russia's vast size did not fully compensate for technological and organizational weakness, especially after the regime was shaken by defeat and revolution in 1905, while at the other end of the continent, Britain's economic lead was less commanding than before. In the middle of Europe Germany was becoming comparatively something of a superpower, already dominant economically, especially in relation to its neighbours, and aspiring to a comparable political and world position. And this young, thrustingly ambitious Reich pursued a high-risk policy of confrontation which created or aggravated crises, contributing to ten years of international tension. . . .

In the chanceries of Europe, a major war was anticipated before long. Some leaders thought that sooner rather than later would be more advantageous for their countries. All assumed that a pan-European war would be short — for economic and technological reasons. But despite the decade of crises and mounting tension, the situation seemed more serene in 1914. In particular, Anglo-German relations appeared improved. The two countries had worked together at the conference of ambassadors in London in 1913 to prevent an Austro-Serbian war, though the German calculations and hope was that if war came, Russia would be blamed and Britain would remain neutral. But that was not public knowledge. However, the citizenry did know that there had not been a major European war for a hundred years; collisions between the great powers had been short and snappy, especially since mid-century, and the last one had occurred nearly 45 years before. A widespread assumption had developed that wars were something which occurred only overseas or in the backward Balkans among quarrelsome infant states. Even Anglo-German naval relations were now less tense, and in July of 1914 the two countries reached an agreement about the Berlin to Baghdad railway. For these and other reasons, the prospects for peace looked better than in the recent past as the spectacularly beautiful summer of 1914 opened.

The sunny calm was shattered on 28 June 1914 by the assassination of the heir to the Austrian throne and his wife in Sarajevo, the capital of Bosnia, by young Bosnian nationalists backed by Unification or Death,[1] a secret Serbian society in which key Serbian army officers were dominant. Their complicity is clear; members of the Serbian cabinet may have had partial foreknowledge as well. The chanceries of Europe anticipated an Austrian reaction directed against Serbia, whose involvement was widely assumed, but not a major war. However, the assassination led to the July crisis of 1914, culminating in World War I. . . .

Austria's actions played a substantial contributory role, and the Habsburg monarchy is usually assigned secondary responsibility for causing World War I, but only secondary, because Austria's actions were obviously contingent. It is beyond serious doubt that it would not have acted against Serbia or risked war with Russia without solid German support. Berlin not only gave that support and repeatedly urged Austria on but also decided upon war now and declared it against Russia and France without any direct provocation from either. A leading German scholar of the July crisis has concluded that "the German Government opened Pandora's box in an act of sheer political and ideological despair."

One must ask what brought the European continent's strongest power to such despair and created a situation where it almost desperately opted to set off a continental war with the risk of world war. Some of the answers lie within German domestic politics and the psychological frame of reference of its leaders. Additional answers lie, as do the contributory errors from other powers, in broader aspects of the European scene in 1914.

For example, there were both men and nations which could ill afford to back down. Too often in the past, the Russian foreign minister, his Austrian counterpart, and the German Kaiser had all displayed timidity, hesitation, and reluctance to commit themselves to firm action. Kaiser Wilhelm in particular was determined to prove that he was not a coward, and, like the Russian foreign minister, he was rather unstable. Similarly, it was doubtful whether the Austrian and Russian regimes could survive major diplomatic defeats. Austria was internally

---

[1] Popularly known as the Black Hand.

so precarious and Russia had sustained so many recent humiliations that disintegration of the one and revolution in the other were real possibilities. This factor loomed large in the calculations of leaders in Vienna, St. Petersburg, and Berlin. Paris concentrated more on retaining its Russian ally. Moreover, the intensity of public opinion in most countries made backing down almost impossible for weak regimes and politicians who wished to retain office. Under the circumstances, it was easy to hope that a strong stand would deter others and solve the problem.

The stronger great powers feared that their allies would cease to be great powers and, to varying degrees, felt a need to bolster them. There was also a widespread fear of losing an ally altogether. Both Britain and France had worried in past crises about losing Russia: France because she compensated for her own deficiencies with the Russian tie, Britain from fear of adding Russia to its enemies. Austria and Germany feared losing each other: Austria because its need was great, Germany from a sense of isolation. Both France and Germany worried that Russia and Austria would fight only if their own interests were involved. Each concluded that it was better for war to come on an issue where the ally's concerns were directly engaged.

Most states feared losing prestige and great power status. This was of intense concern to Austria and Russia, and in both instances was focused primarily on the Balkans, which impacted on domestic concerns and where the situation had changed so rapidly with the removal of Turkey. Yet dread of the results of backing down was widespread and extended even to Britain, master of the seas and of the world's greatest empire. On 31 July 1914, a senior British official argued for action by saying, "The theory that England cannot engage in a big war means her abdication as an independent state. . . . A balance of power cannot be maintained by a State that is incapable of fighting and consequently carries no weight."

Threats to prestige, authority, and vital interests were almost universally perceived. Britain had long recognized a German challenge on and beyond the seas; the invasion of Belgium seemed to be striking at the British heartland. France, aside from other considerations, could hardly hand over her border forts without becoming a defenceless laughing stock. Russia felt its future in the Balkans and among the Slavs was at stake. Austria saw Serbia as a danger to its very existence, whereas Germany perceived a Russian threat and perhaps was as obsessed by Russia as Britain had been in the mid-nineteenth century and the United States would be in the mid-twentieth century. Clearly, some threats were more real and immediate than others, but leaders acted upon their perceptions, even if erroneous.

Nationalism, whether unifying or divisive, and imperialism contributed to the crises and tensions of the pre-war years, if they did not themselves directly cause the war. And certainly Austria-Hungary's ageing, archaic multinational empire, trying to maintain itself against mounting nationalist pressures, was a major contributing factor, as was the Austro-Russian rivalry among the infant national states of the Balkans. The pre-war arms race contributed to the international tension of the era but of itself was not a direct causal factor, despite the beliefs of a later generation, particularly of Americans.

More important, probably, was a widespread pseudo-Darwinian view of international politics, an assumption that it was a question of dog eat dog with the strongest and speediest dog surviving. Furthermore, crises had become the norm, so much so that some leaders expected war before long. Especially in Germany, there was a belief that war and Darwinian struggle were unavoidable, which perhaps explains the preoccupation with an assumed Russian threat and a fatalistic view that a Russo-German war was inevitable soon. Nowhere was there any awareness of what a war would be like; as a result there was scant caution about the dangers war would bring. The short war illusion was widespread and had contributed to the arms race on the assumption that the war would be fought with what equipment one had at the outset. The businessmen would see to it that the war was brief (if they did not prevent it altogether, as some believed, but not those determining national policies). Few in power had much appreciation of what the industrialization, nationalization, and democratization of war signified. Indeed, it was widely held that war was good and glorious and cleansing.

In some countries, military men and military plans played a considerable role. The military plans were rigid, too few in number, and had tight timetables; the military men were wedded to them. The generals tended to be more eager for war than the civilian leaders; even where they were not, there was a fear that any delay in mobilization would be catastrophic. Initially there was often lack of co-ordination between civilian and military leaders, thanks to administrative inadequacy at the top, especially in Germany and Russia, and then tugs-of-war ensued, particularly to sway the autocrat. At a more fundamental level, appreciations in various countries of the military balance of power, then and as it would be in the future, clearly contributed to the pressures toward war.

The alliance system did not of itself cause any war, local, continental, or world. But it constituted a substantial reason why a local crisis became a world war, and partially explains why a murder in Bosnia caused Germany to invade Belgium and why that event in turn led to a world war, with Japan occupying Germany's Asian colonies. This is particularly true in view of the suddenness and speed of the crisis. Peace movements collapsed, and little time was left for diplomacy. Furthermore, previous crises had made the alliances more rigid. Europe had managed to edge past the abyss repeatedly in recent years, but only at the price of expending options and losing flexibility. Now governments felt they had few choices left. . . .

In the end, the debate always comes back to Germany. Clearly, Austria intended to start nothing without Germany at its side, and none of the Entente powers actively wanted a war in 1914. There was no Entente equivalent to Wilhelm's "Now or never." Thus, one must ask whether Germany wanted war in 1914, if so why, and what its reasons and motives were. Why did it encourage local war, accept continental war, and risk world war? The answers are contradictory, thanks to illogic, conflicts, and differing perceptions within Berlin's upper echelons, where policy-making was disorganized. . . .

War came when it did primarily because Germany opted for a war, if not necessarily for the war which eventuated. There has been a good deal of debate about why Germany did so and to what end. Was it largely a matter of miscalculation? Had there been a systematic two-year German plan for world conquest? Was Germany running a calculated risk, hoping to get its way without intent of war? Was the goal a preventive war, to deter future Russian aggression, or was Germany itself engaging in an opportunistic war of aggression?

The answers to these questions are a matter of opinion and the object of heated historical debate. Certainly there was miscalculation aplenty, and repeated gambles constituted calculated or miscalculated risks. It is perhaps begging the question to say that little German policy formulation was systematic, but, despite conferences debating war in December 1912 and thereafter, evidence for a conscious systematic two-year drive toward a world war depends heavily on interpretation and is hotly disputed. Clearly, Germany seized the opportunity for a war of aggression, but the question is why it thought it should.

Perhaps it is best to let German leaders speak for themselves. In February 1918 Bethmann Hollweg, who had been Chancellor in 1914, explained privately, "Yes, my god, in a certain sense it was a preventive war. But when war was hanging above us, when it had to come in two years even more dangerously and more inescapably, and when the generals said, now it is still possible, without defeat, but not in two years time." And in August 1916, Bethmann's close aide and confidante, who himself propounded the theory of the calculated risk, explained that the purpose of the war was "defence against present-day France, preventive war against the Russia of the future, struggle with Britain for world domination."

62

ERICH MARIA REMARQUE

From All Quiet on the Western Front

In this selection, the beginning of one of the most famous war novels ever written, we are introduced to the main characters and to the daily routines of the German army on "the Western Front," the long line of trenches that stretched across northern France from Switzerland to the English Channel for most of the war between 1914 and 1918. What does this selection suggest about the types of people recruited to serve in the army? How does Remarque view friendship, authority, and discipline in the army? Do you imagine these German soldiers behaved very differently from French or English soldiers?

Thinking Historically

Remarque's novel is not intended as an explanation of the causes of war, but this excerpt offers an explanation of how young men were recruited to fight and gives us some idea of their mental state. How might you use material from this novel, assuming that it is factual, to propose at least one cause of World War I?

In this brief selection, the author also suggests something about the consequences of the war. What, according to Remarque, are the war's likely outcomes? The consequences described here are arrived at very early in the war. Is it likely that they will change significantly as the war continues?

Kantorek had been our schoolmaster, a stern little man in a grey tail-coat, with a face like a shrew mouse. He was about the same size as Corporal Himmelstoss, the "terror of Klosterberg." It is very queer that the unhappiness of the world is so often brought on by small men. They are so much more energetic and uncompromising than the big fellows. I have always taken good care to keep out of sections with small company commanders. They are mostly confounded little martinets.

During drill-time Kantorek gave us long lectures until the whole of our class went, under his shepherding, to the District Commandant and

Erich Maria Remarque, *All Quiet on the Western Front,* trans. A. W. Wheen (New York: Fawcett Books, 1929), 1–18.

volunteered. I can see him now, as he used to glare at us through his spectacles and say in a moving voice: "Won't you join up, Comrades?"

These teachers always carry their feelings ready in their waistcoat pockets, and trot them out by the hour. But we didn't think of that then.

There was, indeed, one of us who hesitated and did not want to fall into line. That was Joseph Behm, a plump, homely fellow. But he did allow himself to be persuaded, otherwise he would have been ostracized. And perhaps more of us thought as he did, but no one could very well stand out, because at that time even one's parents were ready with the word "coward"; no one had the vaguest idea what we were in for. The wisest were just the poor and simple people. They knew the war to be a misfortune, whereas those who were better off, and should have been able to see more clearly what the consequences would be, were beside themselves with joy.

Katczinsky said that was a result of their upbringing. It made them stupid. And what Kat said, he had thought about.

Strange to say, Behm was one of the first to fall. He got hit in the eye during an attack, and we left him lying for dead. We couldn't bring him with us, because we had to come back helter-skelter. In the afternoon suddenly we heard him call, and saw him crawling about in No Man's Land. He had only been knocked unconscious. Because he could not see, and was mad with pain, he failed to keep under cover, and so was shot down before anyone could go and fetch him in.

Naturally we couldn't blame Kantorek for this. Where would the world be if one brought every man to book? There were thousands of Kantoreks, all of whom were convinced that they were acting for the best — in a way that cost them nothing.

And that is why they let us down so badly.

For us lads of eighteen they ought to have been mediators and guides to the world of maturity, the world of work, of duty, of culture, of progress — to the future. We often made fun of them and played jokes on them, but in our hearts we trusted them. The idea of authority, which they represented, was associated in our minds with a greater insight and a more humane wisdom. But the first death we saw shattered this belief. We had to recognize that our generation was more to be trusted than theirs. They surpassed us only in phrases and in cleverness. The first bombardment showed us our mistake, and under it the world as they had taught it to us broke in pieces.

While they continued to write and talk, we saw the wounded and dying. While they taught that duty to one's country is the greatest thing, we already knew that death-throes are stronger. But for all that we were no mutineers, no deserters, no cowards — they were very free with all these expressions. We loved our country as much as they; we went courageously into every action; but also we distinguished the false from true, we had suddenly learned to see. And we saw that there was nothing of their world left. We were all at once terribly alone; and alone we must see it through.

Before going over to see Kemmerich we pack up his things: He will need them on the way back.

In the dressing station there is great activity: It reeks as ever of carbolic, pus, and sweat. We are accustomed to a good deal in the billets, but this makes us feel faint. We ask for Kemmerich. He lies in a large room and receives us with feeble expressions of joy and helpless agitation. While he was unconscious someone had stolen his watch.

Müller shakes his head: "I always told you that nobody should carry as good a watch as that."

Müller is rather crude and tactless, otherwise he would hold his tongue, for anybody can see that Kemmerich will never come out of this place again. Whether he finds his watch or not will make no difference, at the most one will only be able to send it to his people.

"How goes it, Franz?" asks Kropp.

Kemmerich's head sinks.

"Not so bad . . . but I have such a damned pain in my foot."

We look at his bed covering. His leg lies under a wire basket. The bed covering arches over it. I kick Müller on the shin, for he is just about to tell Kemmerich what the orderlies told us outside: that Kemmerich has lost his foot. The leg is amputated. He looks ghastly, yellow and wan. In his face there are already the strained lines that we know so well, we have seen them now hundreds of times. They are not so much lines as marks. Under the skin the life no longer pulses, it has already pressed out the boundaries of the body. Death is working through from within. It already has command in the eyes. Here lies our comrade, Kemmerich, who a little while ago was roasting horse flesh with us and squatting in the shellholes. He it is still and yet it is not he any longer. His features have become uncertain and faint, like a photographic plate from which two pictures have been taken. Even his voice sounds like ashes.

I think of the time when we went away. His mother, a good plump matron, brought him to the station. She wept continually, her face was bloated and swollen. Kemmerich felt embarrassed, for she was the least composed of all; she simply dissolved into fat and water. Then she caught sight of me and took hold of my arm again and again, and implored me to look after Franz out there. Indeed he did have a face like a child, and such frail bones that after four weeks' pack-carrying he already had flat feet. But how can a man look after anyone in the field!

"Now you will soon be going home," says Kropp. "You would have had to wait at least three or four months for your leave."

Kemmerich nods. I cannot bear to look at his hands, they are like wax. Under the nails is the dirt of the trenches, it shows through blue-black like poison. It strikes me that these nails will continue to grow like lean fantastic cellar-plants long after Kemmerich breathes no more. I see the picture before me. They twist themselves into corkscrews and grow and grow, and with them the hair on the decaying skull, just like grass in a good soil, just like grass, how can it be possible ———

Müller leans over. "We have brought your things, Franz."

Kemmerich signs with his hands. "Put them under the bed."

Müller does so. Kemmerich starts on again about the watch. How can one calm him without making him suspicious?

Müller reappears with a pair of airman's boots. They are fine English boots of soft, yellow leather which reach to the knees and lace up all the way — they are things to be coveted.

Müller is delighted at the sight of them. He matches their soles against his own clumsy boots and says: "Will you be taking them with you then, Franz?"

We all three have the same thought; even if he should get better, he would be able to use only one — they are no use to him. But as things are now it is a pity that they should stay here; the orderlies will of course grab them as soon as he is dead.

"Won't you leave them with us?" Müller repeats.

Kemmerich doesn't want to. They are his most prized possessions.

"Well, we could exchange," suggests Müller again. "Out here one can make some use of them." Still Kemmerich is not to be moved.

I tread on Müller's foot; reluctantly he puts the fine boots back again under the bed.

We talk a little more and then take our leave.

"Cheerio, Franz."

I promise him to come back in the morning. Müller talks of doing so, too. He is thinking of the lace-up boots and means to be on the spot.

Kemmerich groans. He is feverish. We get hold of an orderly outside and ask him to give Kemmerich a dose of morphia.

He refuses. "If we were to give morphia to everyone we would have to have tubs full ———"

"You only attend to officers properly," says Kropp viciously.

I hastily intervene and give him a cigarette. He takes it.

"Are you usually allowed to give it, then?" I ask him.

He is annoyed. "If you don't think so, then why do you ask?"

I press a few more cigarettes into his hand. "Do us the favour ———"

"Well, all right," he says.

Kropp goes in with him. He doesn't trust him and wants to see. We wait outside.

Müller returns to the subject of the boots. "They would fit me perfectly. In these boots I get blister after blister. Do you think he will last till tomorrow after drill?" If he passes out in the night, we know where the boots ———"

Kropp returns. "Do you think ———?" he asks.

"Done for," said Müller emphatically.

We go back to the huts. I think of the letter that I must write tomorrow to Kemmerich's mother. I am freezing. I could do with a tot of rum. Müller pulls up some grass and chews it. Suddenly little Kropp throws his cigarette away, stamps on it savagely, and looking around him with a broken and distracted face, stammers "Damned shit, the damned shit!"

We walk on for a long time. Kropp has calmed himself; we understand, he saw red; out there every man gets like that sometime.

"What has Kantorek written to you?" Müller asks him.

He laughs. "We are the Iron Youth."

We all three smile bitterly, Kropp rails: He is glad that he can speak.

Yes, that's the way they think, these hundred thousand Kantoreks! Iron Youth! Youth! We are none of us more than twenty years old. But young? Youth? That is long ago. We are old folk.

63

World War I Propaganda Posters

Posters were the communication medium of the First World War. In an age when governments had still not taught most people how to read but increasingly needed their consent or compliance, images often spoke louder than words, but those images had to be *persuasive.*

The American poster from 1917 and the German poster from 1915–1916 (Figures 10.1 and 10.3) implore men to enlist in the army; the Italian poster from 1917 (Figure 10.2) encourages people to buy war bonds. What do you think accounts for the similar graphic style used in these three posters? How effective do you think they were and why?

Another strategy for promoting loyalty, patriotism, and support for a war that was lasting far longer than anyone had anticipated was to demonize or ridicule the enemy. What feelings does the U.S. anti-German poster from 1916 (Figure 10.4) attempt to provoke in viewers and how does the scene shown achieve this? Compare this portrayal of German brutishness to the narrator of *All Quiet on the Western Front* and his soldier companions. Why is it often essential to dehumanize the enemy in wartime? Figure 10.5, a German propaganda

Figure 10.1   Recruiting Poster for U.S. Army.

poster, takes a different tack, depicting the Allied Powers as a series of ineffectual toy soldiers. The caption in German mockingly confirms this notion: "You six aren't worth the waste of shot and powder." Although it may be difficult to discern, each soldier bears a letter above or next to his head indicating his country of origin. Viewing them left to right the soldiers are Montenegrin, Serbian, Russian, English, French, and Belgian. What cultural and ethnic stereotypes do these figures reveal?

The signing of the armistice in 1918 did not mean the end of propaganda, as Figure 10.6, a lithograph from 1920 exhorting French citizens to help repay the war debt, shows. The female figure striding optimistically forward is the goddess Victory holding aloft an olive branch, a symbol of peace. What do you make of the other elements in this print? What sentiments does this picture appeal to?

Figure 10.2 Italian Poster for National War Loan, 1917.
Source: Snark/Art Resource, N.Y.

Figure 10.3 Recruiting Poster for German Army, 1915–1916.

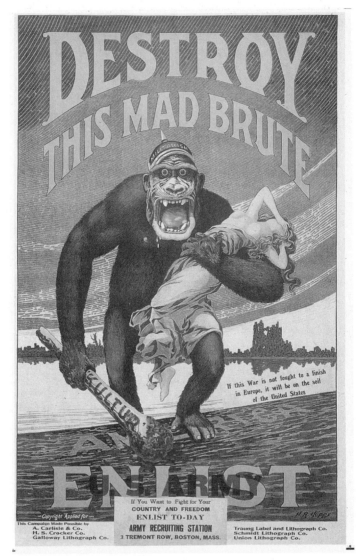

Figure 10.4 Propaganda Poster, United States, 1916.

Figure 10.5 German Propaganda Poster, 1916.
Source: Roger Viollet/Getty Images.

Figure 10.6 French War Loan Poster, 1920.
Source: The Image Works.

Thinking Historically

When war broke out overseas, President Woodrow Wilson declared it a European matter that had nothing to do with the United States and most Americans agreed. Indeed, the United States did not join the war and throw its crucial weight behind the Allied Powers until April 1917. What role do you think propaganda such as Figure 10.4 played in swaying public opinion? This and the other posters illustrate both sides' efforts to promote and sustain the cause of war. But do they reveal anything about the changes wrought by the war?

SIEGFRIED SASSOON
Base Details

An English gentleman and pastoral poet before the war, Siegfried Sassoon (1886–1967) enlisted with a noble innocence soon challenged on the battlefield. In addition to his own sobering experiences, his brother and a fellow officer were among the many slaughtered in the failed Allied effort of 1915 to conquer Turkish defenses at Gallipoli. What is the message of this poem?

Thinking Historically

Poems are not, of course, exercises in historical explanation. Nevertheless, there is here a partial explanation of the continuation, if not the cause, of the war. What is that explanation? How is it similar to, or different from, others you have read in this chapter?

Siegfried Sassoon, *Counter-Attack and Other Poems* (London: W. Heinemann, 1918).

If I were fierce, and bald, and short of breath,
   I'd live with scarlet Majors at the Base,
And speed glum heroes up the line to death.
   You'd see me with my puffy petulant face,
Guzzling and gulping in the best hotel,
   Reading the Roll of Honour. "Poor young chap,"
I'd say — "I used to know his father well;
   Yes, we've lost heavily in this last scrap."
And when the war is done and youth stone dead,
   I'd toddle safely home and die — in bed.

65

WILFRED OWEN

Dulce et Decorum Est

Wilfred Owen (1893–1918) enlisted in the British Army in 1915, was wounded in 1917, and was hospitalized, released, and sent back to the front, where he died on November 4, 1918, one week before the end of the war. In this poem, he describes a poison gas attack. Like the machine gun and the airplane, gas was a common element of the new mechanized mass warfare. Owen describes how physically debilitating the effects of gas were. Why was gas such an effective and deadly weapon? How, according to Owen, had the nature of war changed?

Thinking Historically

The concluding phrase, which means "Sweet and proper it is to die for one's country," was a Latin declaration of patriotic duty that English students repeated as a lesson, not only in Latin classes but, more important, in their political education as subjects of the British empire. How does Owen portray this lesson as a cause of the war? What does he imagine to be the consequences of fighting a war with such patriotic slogans in mind?

Wilfred Owen, *Poems*, ed. Siegfried Sassoon (London: Chatto and Windus, 1920).

Dulce et Decorum Est

Bent double, like old beggars under sacks,
Knock-kneed, coughing like hags, we cursed
   through sludge,
Till on the haunting flares we turned our backs
And towards our distant rest began the trudge.
Men marched asleep. Many had lost their boots
But limped on, blood-shod. All went lame; all
   blind;
Drunk with fatigue; deaf even to the hoots
Of tired, outstripped Five-Nines[1] that dropped
   behind.

Gas! GAS! Quick, boys! — An ecstasy of
   fumbling,
Fitting the clumsy helmets just in time;
But someone still was yelling out and stumbling,
And flound'ring like a man in fire or lime. . . .
Dim, through the misty panes and thick green
   light,
As under a green sea, I saw him drowning.

In all my dreams, before my helpless sight,
He plunges at me, guttering, choking,
   drowning.

If in some smothering dreams you too could
   pace
Behind the wagon that we flung him in,
And watch the white eyes writhing in his face,
His hanging face, like a devil's sick of sin;
If you could hear, at every jolt, the blood
Come gargling from the froth-corrupted lungs,
Obscene as cancer, bitter as the cud
Of vile, incurable sores on innocent tongues,
My friend, you would not tell with such high
   zest,
To children ardent for some desperate glory.
The old Lie: Dulce et decorum est
Pro patria mori.

[1]German artillery shells. [Ed.]

66

ROSA LUXEMBURG
The Junius[1] Pamphlet

Many Europeans greeted the onset of war with enthusiasm, expecting a quick victory. Before 1914 the socialist parties of Europe were among the few voices for peace and international cooperation. But when war came, the socialist parties of Germany, England, and France were swept up in the nationalist furor for war, like everyone else. Rosa Luxemburg (1871–1919), a Polish refugee who had earned a doctorate in Switzerland and became a leader of German socialism, feared their capitulation. When it happened she broke with the German Social Democratic party and founded the more radical Spartacus League. Because of her activities, she spent most of the war in jail. There she wrote the Junius Pamphlet in 1915. What reasons did she give for opposing the war?

Thinking Historically

Rosa Luxemburg's opposition to the war was based on a Marxist interpretation of history according to which the wars of capitalist societies were products of particular causes. What were these causes? What, according to this view, would be the consequences of capitalist wars?

The scene has changed fundamentally. The six weeks' march to Paris has grown into a world drama.[2] Mass slaughter has become the tiresome and monotonous business of the day and the end is no closer. Bourgeois statecraft is held fast in its own vise. The spirits summoned up can no longer be exorcised.

Gone is the euphoria. Gone the patriotic noise in the streets, the chase after the gold-colored automobile, one false telegram after another, the wells poisoned by cholera, the Russian students heaving

---

[1]Perhaps a reference to Lucius Junius Brutus, a republican hero of ancient Rome, legendary founder of the Roman Republic, c. 509 B.C.E. [Ed.]

[2]Six weeks was the time allotted for victory on the Western Front by the Schlieffen Plan. The general staff was forced to scrap the plan in October 1914, as the war of movement swiftly devolved into grinding trench warfare. [Ed.]

"Die Krise der Sozialdemokratie (Junius-Broschüre)," trans. Richard S. Levy, in Rosa Luxemburg, *Politische Schriften*, Günter Radczun, ed. (Leipzig, 1970), 229–43, 357–72. Also available on-line at http://h-net.org/~german/gtext/kaiserreich/lux.html.

bombs over every railway bridge in Berlin, the French airplanes over Nuremberg, the spy hunting public running amok in the streets, the swaying crowds in the coffee shops with ear-deafening patriotic songs surging ever higher, whole city neighborhoods transformed into mobs ready to denounce, to mistreat women, to shout hurrah and to induce delirium in themselves by means of wild rumors. . . .

The spectacle is over. German scholars, those "stumbling lemurs," have been whistled off the stage long ago. The trains full of reservists are no longer accompanied by virgins fainting from pure jubilation. They no longer greet the people from the windows of the train with joyous smiles. Carrying their packs, they quietly trot along the streets where the public goes about its daily business with aggrieved visages.

In the prosaic atmosphere of pale day there sounds a different chorus — the hoarse cries of the vulture and the hyenas of the battlefield. Ten thousand tarpaulins guaranteed up to regulations! A hundred thousand kilos of bacon, cocoa powder, coffee-substitute — c.o.d., immediate delivery! Hand grenades, lathes, cartridge pouches, marriage bureaus for widows of the fallen, leather belts, jobbers for war orders — serious offers only! The cannon fodder loaded onto trains in August and September is moldering in the killing fields of Belgium, the Vosges, and Masurian Lakes where the profits are springing up like weeds. It's a question of getting the harvest into the barn quickly. Across the ocean stretch thousands of greedy hands to snatch it up.

Business thrives in the ruins. Cities become piles of ruins; villages become cemeteries; countries, deserts; populations are beggared; churches, horse stalls. International law, treaties and alliances, the most sacred words and the highest authority have been torn in shreds. Every sovereign "by the grace of God" is called a rogue and lying scoundrel by his cousin on the other side. Every diplomat is a cunning rascal to his colleagues in the other party. Every government sees every other as dooming its own people and worthy only of universal contempt. There are food riots in Venice, in Lisbon, Moscow, Singapore. There is plague in Russia, and misery and despair everywhere.

Violated, dishonored, wading in blood, dripping filth — there stands bourgeois society. This is it [in reality]. Not all spic and span and moral, with pretense to culture, philosophy, ethics, order, peace, and the rule of law — but the ravening beast, the witches' sabbath of anarchy, a plague to culture and humanity. Thus it reveals itself in its true, its naked form.

In the midst of this witches' sabbath a catastrophe of world-historical proportions has happened: International Social Democracy has capitulated. To deceive ourselves about it, to cover it up, would be the most foolish, the most fatal thing the proletariat could do. . . .

Friedrich Engels once said: "Bourgeois society stands at the cross-roads, either transition to socialism or regression into barbarism.". . .

This world war is a regression into barbarism. The triumph of imperialism leads to the annihilation of civilization. . . .

The war means ruin for all the belligerents, although more so for the defeated. On the day after the concluding of peace, preparations for a new world war will be begun under the leadership of England in order to throw off the yoke of Prusso-German militarism burdening Europe and the Near East. A German victory would be only a prelude to a soon-to-follow second world war; and this would be the signal for a new, feverish arms race as well as the unleashing of the blackest reaction in all countries, but first and foremost in Germany itself. . . . from this side, too, [an Anglo-French] victory would lead to a new feverish armaments race among all the states — with defeated Germany obviously in the forefront. An era of unalloyed militarism and reaction would dominate all Europe with a new world war as its ultimate goal. . . .

The world war today is demonstrably not only murder on a grand scale; it is also suicide of the working classes of Europe. The soldiers of socialism, the proletarians of England, France, Germany, Russia, and Belgium have for months been killing one another at the behest of capital. They are driving the cold steel of murder into each other's hearts. Locked in the embrace of death, they tumble into a common grave.

"*Deutschland, Deutschland über Alles!* Long live democracy! Long live the Tsar and Slav-dom! Ten thousand tarpaulins guaranteed up to regulations! A hundred thousand kilos of bacon, coffee-substitute for immediate delivery!" . . . Dividends are rising, and the proletarians are falling. And with every one there sinks into the grave a fighter of the future, a soldier of the revolution, mankind's savior from the yoke of capitalism.

The madness will cease and the bloody demons of hell will vanish only when workers in Germany and France, England and Russia finally awake from their stupor, extend to each other a brotherly hand, and drown out the bestial chorus of imperialist war-mongers and the shrill cry of capitalist hyenas with labor's old and mighty battle cry: Proletarians of all lands, unite!

67

V. I. LENIN

From War and Revolution

One of the great casualties of the First World War was the Russian empire, including the czar, his family, many of the members of their class, and its centuries-old autocratic system. The burden of war was simply too much for Russian society to bear. The disillusionment in the army and civilian society, along with the overwhelming costs of war, fueled uprisings among civilians and the army and Czar Nicholas II was forced to abdicate in February of 1917. The government that emerged, under Alexander Kerensky, proved unable to satisfy the growing demands of peasants, veterans, and urban workers for "land, peace, and bread," a slogan that V. I. Lenin (1870–1924) and the communists exploited, successfully seizing power from the moderate parliamentarians in October of that year.

As a Marxist, Lenin believed that he could establish a socialist society in Russia, but he argued that Russian conditions (e.g., economic underdevelopment; the devastation of war; the opposition of Europe, the United States, and Russian nobles to the revolution) made a democratic transition impossible. According to Lenin, a self-appointed government acting in the interests of the working class was the only way to a socialist Soviet Union. Lenin called this government "the dictatorship of the proletariat." Rosa Luxemburg was one of Lenin's fiercest critics on this point, arguing that capitalism in Russia was not sufficiently developed to allow for a democratic socialist revolution, and that dictatorial means would result in dictatorial ends.

Lenin delivered his "War and Revolution" address in May of 1917, during the fateful summer that followed the liberal February revolution and preceded the Bolshevik revolution in October. How did Lenin view the First World War and Russia's continued participation in it? What did he hope to accomplish in the summer of 1917? How did he hope to accomplish it? The most important news for Russia's allies, England and France, in the summer of 1917 was the United States' entry into the war on their behalf. What was Lenin's reaction to this development?

V. I. Lenin, *Collected Works*, vol. 24, 4th English ed. (Moscow: Progress Publishers, 1964), 398–421.

Thinking Historically

According to Lenin, what were the causes of the First World War? What did he believe to be the main cause of the Russian revolution that occurred in February? What were the consequences of that revolution? What did he think would be the causes of a new revolution in Russia?

What we have at present is primarily two leagues, two groups of capitalist powers. We have before us all the world's greatest capitalist powers — Britain, France, America, and Germany — who for decades have doggedly pursued a policy of incessant economic rivalry aimed at achieving world supremacy, subjugating the small nations, and making threefold and tenfold profits on banking capital, which has caught the whole world in the net of its influence. That is what Britain's and Germany's policies really amount to. . . .

These policies show us just one thing — continuous economic rivalry between the world's two greatest giants, capitalist economies. On the one hand we have Britain, a country which owns the greater part of the globe, a country which ranks first in wealth, which has created this wealth not so much by the labour of its workers as by the exploitation of innumerable colonies, by the vast power of its banks which have developed at the head of all the others into an insignificantly small group of some four or five super-banks handling billions of rubles, and handling them in such a way that it can be said without exaggeration that there is not a patch of land in the world today on which this capital has not laid its heavy hand, not a patch of land which British capital has not enmeshed by a thousand threads. . . .

On the other hand, opposed to this, mainly Anglo-French group, we have another group of capitalists, an even more rapacious, even more predatory one, a group who came to the capitalist banqueting table when all the seats were occupied, but who introduced into the struggle new methods for developing capitalist production, improved techniques, and superior organization, which turned the old capitalism, the capitalism of the free-competition age, into the capitalism of giant trusts, syndicates, and cartels. This group introduced the beginnings of state-controlled capitalist production, combining the colossal power of capitalism with the colossal power of the state into a single mechanism and bringing tens of millions of people within the single organization of state capitalism. Here is economic history, here is diplomatic history, covering several decades, from which no one can get away. It is the one and only guide-post to a proper solution of the problem of war; it leads you to the conclusion that the present war, too, is the outcome of the policies of the classes who have come to grips in it, of the two supreme giants, who, long before the war, had caught the whole world, all countries, in the net of financial exploitation and economically divided the globe up among themselves. They were bound to clash, because a redivision of this supremacy, from the point of view of capitalism, had become inevitable. . . .

The present war is a continuation of the policy of conquest, of the shooting down of whole nationalities, of unbelievable atrocities committed by the Germans and the British in Africa, and by the British and the Russians in Persia — which of them committed most it is difficult to say. It was for this reason that the German capitalists looked upon them as their enemies. Ah, they said, you are strong because you are rich? But we are stronger, therefore we have the same "sacred" right to plunder. That is what the real history of British and German finance capital in the course of several decades preceding the war amounts to. That is what the history of Russo-German, Russo-British, and German-British relations amounts to. There you have the clue to an understanding of what the war is about. That is why the story that is current about the cause of the war is sheer duplicity and humbug. Forgetting the history of finance capital, the history of how this war had been brewing over the issue of redivision, they present the matter like this: Two nations were living at peace, then one attacked the other, and the other fought back. All science, all banks are forgotten, and the peoples are told to take up arms, and so are the peasants, who know nothing about politics. . . .

. . . What revolution did we make? We overthrew Nicholas. The revolution was not so very difficult compared with one that would have overthrown the whole class of landowners and capitalists. Who did the revolution put in power? The landowners and capitalists — the very same classes who have long been in power in Europe. . . . The [February] Russian revolution has not altered the war, but it has created organizations which exist in no other country and were seldom found in revolutions in the West. . . . We have all over Russia a network of Soviets of Workers', Soldiers', and Peasants' Deputies. Here is a revolution which has not said its last word yet. . . .

. . . In the two months following the revolution the industrialists have robbed the whole of Russia. Capitalists have made staggering profits; every financial report tells you that. And when the workers, two months after the revolution, had the "audacity" to say they wanted to live like human beings, the whole capitalist press throughout the country set up a howl.

On the question of America entering the war I shall say this. People argue that America is a democracy, America has the White House. I say: Slavery was abolished there half a century ago. The anti-slave war ended in 1865. Since then multimillionaires have mushroomed. They have the whole of America in their financial grip. They are making ready to subdue Mexico and will inevitably come to war with Japan over a carve-up of the Pacific. This war has been brewing for several decades. All literature speaks about it. America's real aim in entering the war is to prepare for this future war with Japan. The American people do enjoy considerable freedom and it is difficult to conceive them standing for compulsory military service, for the setting up of an army pursuing any aims of conquest — a struggle with Japan, for instance. The Americans have the example of Europe to show them what this leads to. The American capitalists have stepped into this war in order to have an excuse, behind a smoke-screen of lofty ideals championing the rights of small nations, for building up a strong standing army. . . .

. . . Tens of millions of people are facing disaster and death; safeguarding the interests of the capitalists is the last thing that should bother us. The only way out is for all power to be transferred to the Soviets, which represent the majority of the population. Possibly mistakes may be made in the process. No one claims that such a difficult task can be disposed of offhand. We do not say anything of the sort. We are told that we want the power to be in the hands of the Soviets, but they don't want it. We say that life's experience will suggest this solution to them, and the whole nation will see that there is no other way out. We do not want a "seizure" of power, because the entire experience of past revolutions teaches us that the only stable power is the one that has the backing of the majority of the population. "Seizure" of power, therefore, would be adventurism, and our Party will not have it. . . .

Nothing but a workers' revolution in several countries can defeat this war. The war is not a game, it is an appalling thing taking a toll of millions of lives, and it is not to be ended easily.

. . . The war has been brought about by the ruling classes and only a revolution of the working class can end it. Whether you will get a speedy peace or not depends on how the revolution will develop.

Whatever sentimental things may be said, however much we may be told: Let us end the war immediately — this cannot be done without the development of the revolution. When power passes to the Soviets the capitalists will come out against us. Japan, France, Britain — the governments of all countries will be against us. The capitalists will be against, but the workers will be for us. That will be the end of the war which the capitalists started. There you have the answer to the question of how to end the war.

68

WOODROW WILSON

Fourteen Points

Woodrow Wilson (1856–1924) was president of the United States during the First World War. He presented these "Fourteen Points" to Congress in January 1918 as a basis for a just peace treaty to end the war.

You may wish to compare these proposals with the actual peace settlement. Only points VII, VIII, X, and XIV were realized. Point IV was applied only to the defeated nations. The Versailles Treaty, which the defeated Germans were forced to sign on June 28, 1919, contained much harsher terms, including the famous "war guilt" clause (Article 231):

> The Allied and Associated Governments affirm and Germany accepts the responsibility of Germany and her allies for causing all the loss and damage to which the Allied and Associated Governments and their nationals have been subjected as a consequence of the war imposed upon them by the aggression of Germany and her allies.

Why do you think there was such a gap between Wilson's ideals and the actual treaty? How might Wilson have improved on these Fourteen Points? Could he reasonably expect all of them to be accepted?

Thinking Historically

What does the first paragraph suggest Wilson thought was one cause of the war? What does the beginning of the second paragraph suggest about the cause for U.S. entry into the war? What would have been the consequences of a peace fashioned along the lines Wilson envisioned in his Fourteen Points?

It will be our wish and purpose that the processes of peace, when they are begun, shall be absolutely open, and that they shall involve and permit henceforth no secret understandings of any kind. The day of

Woodrow Wilson, *War and Peace: Presidential Messages, Addresses, and Public Papers (1917–1924)*, vol. 1, ed. Ray Stannard Baker and William E. Dodd (New York: Harper Brothers, 1927).

conquest and aggrandizement is gone by; so is also the day of secret covenants entered into in the interest of particular Governments and likely at some unlooked-for moment to upset the peace of the world. It is this happy fact, now clear to the view of every public man whose thoughts do not still linger in an age that is dead and gone, which makes it possible for every nation whose purposes are consistent with justice and the peace of the world to avow now or at any other time the objects it has in view.

We entered this war because violations of right had occurred which touched us to the quick and made the life of our own people impossible unless they were corrected and the world secured once for all against their recurrence. What we demand in this war, therefore, is nothing peculiar to ourselves. It is that the world be made fit and safe to live in; and particularly that it be made safe for every peace-loving nation which, like our own, wishes to live its own life, determine its own institutions, be assured of justice and fair dealing by the other peoples of the world as against force and selfish aggression. All the peoples of the world are in effect partners in this interest, and for our own part we see very clearly that unless justice be done to others it will not be done to us. The program of the world's peace, therefore, is our program; and that program, the only possible program, as we see it, is this:

I. Open covenants of peace, openly arrived at, after which there shall be no private international understandings of any kind but diplomacy shall proceed always frankly and in the public view.

II. Absolute freedom of navigation upon the seas, outside territorial waters, alike in peace and in war, except as the seas may be closed in whole or in part by international action. . . .

III. The removal, so far as possible, of all economic barriers and the establishment of an equality of trade conditions among all the nations consenting to the peace and associating themselves for its maintenance.

IV. Adequate guarantees given and taken that national armaments will be reduced to the lowest point consistent with domestic safety.

V. A free, open-minded, and absolutely impartial adjustment of all colonial claims, based upon a strict observance of the principle that in determining all such questions of sovereignty the interests of the populations concerned must have equal weight with the equitable claims of the government whose title is to be determined.

VI. The Evacuation of all Russian territory and such a settlement of all questions affecting Russia as will secure the best and freest cooperation of the other nations of the world in obtaining for her an unhampered and unembarrassed opportunity for the independent determination of her own political development and national policy and assure her of a sincere welcome into the society of free nations under institutions of her own choosing; and, more than a welcome, assistance also of every kind that she may need and may herself desire. The treatment accorded Russia by her sister nations in the months to come will be the acid test of their good will, of their comprehension of her needs as distinguished from their own interests, and of their intelligent and unselfish sympathy.

VII. Belgium, the whole world will agree, must be evacuated and restored, without any attempt to limit the sovereignty which she enjoys in common with all other free nations. No other single act will serve to restore confidence among the nations in the laws which they have themselves set and determined for the government of their relations with one another. Without this healing act the whole structure and validity of international law is forever impaired.

VIII. All French territory should be freed and the invaded portions restored, and the wrong done to France by Prussia in 1871 in the matter of Alsace-Lorraine, which has unsettled the peace of the world for nearly fifty years, should be righted, in order that peace may once more be made secure in the interest of all.

IX. A readjustment of the frontiers of Italy should be effected along clearly recognizable lines of nationality.

X. The peoples of Austria-Hungary, whose place among the nations we wish to see safeguarded and assured, should be accorded the freest opportunity of autonomous development.

XI. Rumania, Serbia, and Montenegro should be evacuated; occupied territories restored; Serbia accorded free and secure access to the sea; and the relations of the several Balkan states to one another determined by friendly counsel along historically established lines of allegiance and nationality; and international guarantees of the political and economic independence and territorial integrity of the several Balkan states should be entered into.

XII. The Turkish portions of the present Ottoman Empire should be assured a secure sovereignty, but the other nationalities which are now under Turkish rule should be assured an undoubted security of life and an absolutely unmolested opportunity of autonomous development, and the Dardanelles should be permanently opened as a free passage to the ships and commerce of all nations under international guarantees.

XIII. An independent Polish state should be erected which should include the territories inhabited by indisputably Polish populations, which should be assured a free and secure access to the sea, and whose political and economic independence and territorial integrity should be guaranteed by international covenant.

XIV. A general association of nations must be formed under specific covenants for the purpose of affording mutual guarantees of political independence and territorial integrity to great and small states alike.

In regard to these essential rectifications of wrong and assertions of right we feel ourselves to be intimate partners of all the governments and peoples associated together against the Imperialists. We cannot be separated in interest or divided in purpose. We stand together until the end.

For such arrangements and covenants we are willing to fight and to continue to fight until they are achieved; but only because we wish the right to prevail and desire a just and stable peace such as can be secured only by removing the chief provocations to war, which this program does remove. We have no jealousy of German greatness, and there is nothing in this program that impairs it. We grudge her no achievement or distinction of learning or of pacific enterprise such as have made her record very bright and very enviable. We do not wish to injure her or to block in any way her legitimate influence or power. We do not wish to fight her either with arms or with hostile arrangements of trade if she is willing to associate herself with us and the other peace-loving nations of the world in covenants of justice and law and fair dealing. We wish her only to accept a place of equality among the peoples of the world, — the new world in which we now live — instead of a place of mastery.

. . . An evident principle runs through the whole program I have outlined. It is the principle of justice to all peoples and nationalities, and their right to live on equal terms of liberty and safety with one another, whether they be strong or weak. Unless this principle be made its foundation no part of the structure of international justice can stand. The people of the United States could act upon no other principle; and to the vindication of this principle they are ready to devote their lives, their honor, and everything that they possess. The moral climax of this the culminating and final war for human liberty has come, and they are ready to put their own strength, their own highest purpose, their own integrity and devotion to the test.

REFLECTIONS

By studying causes and consequences of world events, we learn how things change but more important we learn how to avoid repeating past mistakes. History is full of lessons that breed humility as well as confidence. In *The Origins of the First World War*,[1] historian James Joll points out how unprepared people were for the war as late as the summer of 1914. Even after the Austrian ultimatum to Serbia was issued on July 23 (almost a month after the assassination of the Archduke Franz Ferdinand on June 28), diplomats across Europe left for their summer holidays. By August, all of Europe was at war, though as Sally Marks noted, the expectation was that it would be over in a month.

---

[1] James Joll, *The Origins of the First World War* (London: Longman, 1992), 200.

We could make a good case for diplomatic blundering as an important cause of the First World War. It is safe to say that few statesmen had any inkling of the consequences of their actions in 1914. And yet, if we concentrate on the daily decisions of diplomats that summer, we may pay attention only to the tossing of lit matches by people sitting on powder kegs rather than on the origins of the powder kegs themselves.

President Wilson blamed secret diplomacy, the international system of alliances, and imperialism as the chief causes of the war. On the importance of imperialism, Wilson's conclusion was the same as that of Lenin and Luxemburg, though he certainly did not share their conviction that capitalism was the root cause of imperialism and, in 1919, neither alliances nor imperialism were regarded as un-American or likely to end any time soon. Still, Wilson's radical moral aversion to reviving Old World empires might have prevented a new stage of imperialism in the League of Nations mandate system. One of the consequences of a Wilsonian peace might have been the creation of independent states in the Middle East and Africa a generation earlier.

The principle of the "self-determination of nations" that Wilson espoused, however, was a double-edged sword. The fact that the war had been "caused" by a Bosnian Serb nationalist assassin in 1914 might have been a warning that national self-determination could become an infinite regress in which smaller and smaller units sought to separate themselves from "foreign" domination. On the issue of nationalism versus internationalism, Wilson might have benefited from listening to Rosa Luxemburg. When asked about anti-Semitism, Luxemburg, a Jew from Russian Poland, answered:

> What do you want with this particular suffering of the Jews? The poor victims of the rubber plantations of Putumayo, the Negroes of Africa with whose bodies the Europeans play a game of catch are just as near to me. . . . I have no special corner of my heart reserved for the ghetto: I am at home wherever in the world there are clouds, birds, and human tears.[2]

Woodrow Wilson was a historian and president of Princeton University before he became president of the United States. Rosa Luxemburg was a professional revolutionary — perhaps the leading socialist theorist in Europe. Both were trained to think historically. Which of the two better understood the causes and consequences of the First World War? Which of the two had a better appreciation of the problems of nationalism that were to continue to haunt the twentieth century?

[2]Jay Winter and Blaine Baggett, *The Great War* (New York: Penguin, 1996), 248, quoting Rosa Luxemburg.

The rise of nationalist movements and international organizations were only two consequences of the First World War. Historians have attributed many other aspects of the twentieth century to the war. In an engaging account of his own search for the evidence of war along the Western Front, Stephen O'Shea writes:

> It is generally accepted that the Great War and its fifty-two months of senseless slaughter encouraged, or amplified, among other things: the loss of a belief in progress, a mistrust of technology, the loss of religious faith, the loss of a belief in Western cultural superiority, the rejection of class distinctions, the rejection of traditional sexual roles, the birth of the Modern [in art], the rejection of the past, the elevation of irony to a standard mode of apprehending the world, the unbuttoning of moral codes, and the conscious embrace of the irrational.[3]

What evidence can you find of any of these consequences in the accounts of this chapter?

---

[3]Stephen O'Shea, *Back to the Front: An Accidental Historian Walks the Trenches of World War I* (New York: Avon Books, 1996), 9.

World War II and Genocide

Europe, Japan, China, Rwanda,
and Guatemala, 1931–1994

HISTORICAL CONTEXT

It is easier to understand the causes of the Second World War than of the First World War. In 1914, we might have pointed to Serbia or Austria, Germany or England, even the bellicosity of Russia and France. But in 1939, it was Hitler's invasion of Poland that led to war with France (which was occupied by the Germans along with most of Europe in 1940), England, and the nations of the British Commonwealth, followed by the Soviet Union after 1940 and the United States after 1941. As in 1914, Germany was allied with Austria (a remnant of the former empire annexed by Germany after 1937) and the new Axis alliance of Japan and Italy.

World War II was even more of a global conflict than World War I. That conflict began with the Japanese invasion of Manchuria in 1931, continuing with Japan's conquest of most of China in 1937 and of Southeast Asia and the Pacific in 1941. For Africans, the war began with the Italian invasion of Ethiopia in 1935. After 1940, North Africa became an increasingly important battleground. As in World War I, soldiers were drawn from all over the world, from Africa and India, the Caribbean and Middle East, but especially in the end, from the United States, Canada, Australia, and New Zealand.

The death toll from World War II may have approached one hundred million, soldiers and civilians combined. Civilian casualties in an age of lightning tank attacks, military occupation of cities, and aerial bombing were enormous. World War I blurred the distinction between soldiers and civilians; World War II ended it. Millions of civilians died in Eastern Europe — along the paths of invading armies — in the great cities of China, and in the bombed-out cities of Germany and Japan. The numbers of wounded, mentally or physically, cannot be counted and the hunger, disease, and deprivation continued long after the end of the war in 1945.

Death tolls offer a crude glimpse of war, and clearly World War II was one of the worst. This chapter focuses on a terrifying aspect of this and more recent conflicts: genocide. Hitler's attempt to rid the world of Jews was genocide. The systematic roundup and murder of the Roma and Sinti peoples,[1] homosexuals, and psychiatric patients, among others, was part of his larger attempt at racial "cleansing" and "Aryan" domination for which the war was little more than a pretext. In addition, Hitler undertook the mass slaughter of all leaders and educated civilians in occupied Poland and Russia for the express purpose of turning those nations into docile armies of brute labor for German industry.

The Nazis' gross indifference to human life, their sadistic killing of defenseless civilians — among them women and children, the helpless, infirm, and aged — reached unimagined heights. Whether or not this was due to factors that distinguish the twentieth century from earlier eras (e.g., the anonymity of mass society, the rise of racist ideas, economic depression, the rise of fascism, the militarization of political life) we do not know. We do know that the Nazi experience was not singular. Imperial Japan, run by a militaristic fascist government in the 1930s, encouraged similar racist and inhumane behavior in its troops in Manchuria, China, and Southeast Asia. Were such barbarities limited to these two countries and this particular era? Certainly not, for aspects of earlier twentieth-century conflicts prepared the ground for mid-century genocide. During the Boer War (1899–1902) British troops in South Africa burned the homes of Dutch "Boer" settlers, forcing women and children into refugee or concentration camps where many died. Shortly thereafter in neighboring German South-West Africa, as recounted in selection 73, German colonial officials put the indigenous Herero people in work camps and concentration camps as part of a policy of extermination and control. During World War I, hundreds of thousands of Armenians in Eastern Turkey were evacuated and massacred. Hitler famously commented: "Who, after all, remembers the Armenians?"

Nor, unfortunately, did genocide end with the Second World War. We will look at two recent examples from the early 1990s — Rwanda and Guatemala — where genocide was committed. We might just as readily explore the cases of ethnic cleansing in the breakup of Yugoslavia in the same period, the annihilation of urban Cambodians in the 1970s, or more recent ethnic conflicts in Darfur, Sudan. One might have thought that the horrendous revelation of the Nazi holocaust

---

[1]The West commonly refers to the Roma and Sinti as "Gypsies" — a misnomer based on the mistaken belief that they were from Egypt. These peoples consider this a pejorative term.

would have ensured a global "Amen" to the declaration: "Never Again." We will do our best to understand why it did not.

THINKING HISTORICALLY
Understanding and Explaining the Unforgivable

Occasionally when we learn of something horrendous, we simply say, "I don't believe it." Our disbelief harbors two feelings: first, our sense of outrage and anger, a rejection of what was done; second, our unwillingness to believe that such a thing could happen or did happen. Our choice of words expresses the difficulty we have making sense of the senseless.

We must try, however, to understand such catastrophes so that we can help to prevent similar horrors in the future. Understanding requires a level of empathy that is often difficult to arouse when we find someone's actions reprehensible. As you read these selections, you will be encouraged to understand and explain, not to forgive.

JOACHIM C. FEST
The Rise of Hitler

World War II had its origins in World War I. The peace terms imposed by the victors demanded the removal of the kaiser, the demilitarization of Germany, the transfer of Germany's industrial heartland to France, and the payment of enormous sums in reparation for the war. In addition, the revolutionary establishment of a republic by the German socialist party was followed by the unsuccessful uprising by the far more radical Spartacus League, which had raised the specter of a Bolshevik coup that would later turn Germany into a communist state.

In this essay, historian Joachim Fest explores the response of German conservative, nationalist, and middle-class groups to these developments. The National Socialists (the Nazi party) was just one of many fascist groups in Germany. Initiated by Mussolini in Italy in

Joachim C. Fest, *Hitler*, trans. Clara and Richard Winston (New York: Harcourt Brace and Co., 1974), 89–91, 92–93, 99–102, 104–5.

1922, fascism was a movement that spread throughout Europe. As defined by Mussolini, in fascism the state dominates everything else:

> For the Fascist the state is all-embracing; outside it no human or spiritual values exist, much less have worth. In this sense Fascism is totalitarian, and the Fascist State — a synthesis and a unity of all values — interprets, develops, and gives power to the whole life of the people.[1]

Why did fascism appeal more to the middle class than to the working class? Was Hitler typical of those who were attracted to fascism? Was Hitler out of touch with reality, or was he tuned in to the feelings of many?

Thinking Historically

Fest helps us understand some of the appeal of fascism by putting it into the context of Germany's defeat in World War I and the real or imagined threat of a Bolshevik revolution. Can you imagine empathizing with antirevolutionary fears if you lived then? Imagine how you might have responded to some of the other fascist appeals: fewer politicians, more police? The nobility of sacrificing for higher purposes; challenging the gray ordinariness of modern life; following instinct rather than reason; and war as authentic experience?

At the end of the First World War the victory of the democratic idea seemed beyond question. Whatever its weaknesses might be, it rose above the turmoil of the times, the uprisings, the dislocations, and the continual quarrels among nations as the unifying principle of the new age. For the war had not only decided a claim to power. It had at the same time altered a conception of government. After the collapse of virtually all the governmental structures of Central and Eastern Europe, many new political entities had emerged out of turmoil and revolution. And these for the most part were organized on democratic principles. In 1914 there had been only three republics alongside of seventeen monarchies in Europe. Four years later there were as many republics as monarchies. The spirit of the age seemed to be pointing unequivocally toward various forms of popular rule.

Only Germany seemed to be opposing this mood of the times, after having been temporarily gripped and carried along by it. Those who would not acknowledge the reality created by the war organized into a fantastic swarm of *völkisch* (racist-nationalist) parties, clubs, and free

---

[1]*Enciclopedia Italiana*, vol. xiv, s.v. "fascism," signed by Mussolini but actually written by the philosopher Giovanni Gentile (1932), 847.

corps. To these groups the revolution had been an act of treason; parliamentary democracy was something foreign and imposed from without, merely a synonym for "everything contrary to the German political will," or else an "institution for pillaging created by Allied capitalism."

Germany's former enemies regarded the multifarious symptoms of nationalistic protest as the response of an inveterately authoritarian people to democracy and civic responsibility. To be sure, the Germans were staggering beneath terrible political and psychological burdens: There was the shock of defeat, the moral censure of the Versailles Treaty, the loss of territory and the demand for reparations, the impoverishment and spiritual undermining of much of the population. Nevertheless, the conviction remained that a great moral gap existed between the Germans and most of their neighbours. Full of resentment, refusing to learn a lesson, this incomprehensible country had withdrawn into its reactionary doctrines, made of them a special virtue, abjured Western rationality and humanity, and in general set itself against the universal trend of the age. For decades this picture of Germany dominated the discussion of the reasons for the rise of National Socialism.

But the image of democracy victorious was also deceptive. The moment in which democracy seemed to be achieving historic fulfillment simultaneously marked the beginning of its crisis. Only a few years later the idea of democracy was challenged in principle as it had never been before. Only a few years after it had celebrated its triumph it was overwhelmed or at least direly threatened by a new movement that had sprung to life in almost all European countries.

This movement recorded its most lasting successes in countries in which the war had aroused considerable discontent or made it conscious of existing discontent, and especially in countries in which the war had been followed by leftist revolutionary uprisings. In some places these movements were conservative, harking back to better times when men were more honorable, the valleys more peaceable, and money had more worth; in others these movements were revolutionary and vied with one another in their contempt for the existing order of things. Some attracted chiefly the petty bourgeois elements, others the peasants, others portions of the working class. Whatever their strange compound of classes, interests, and principles, all seemed to be drawing their dynamic force from the less conscious and more vital lower strata of society. National Socialism was merely one variant of this widespread European movement of protest and opposition aimed at overturning the general order of things.

National Socialism rose from provincial beginnings, from philistine clubs, as Hitler scornfully described them, which met in Munich bars over a few rounds of beer to talk over national and family troubles. No one would have dreamed that they could ever challenge, let alone outdo, the powerful, highly organized Marxist parties. But the following years proved that in these clubs of nationalistic beer drinkers, soon swelled by disillusioned homecoming soldiers and proletarianized members of the middle class, a tremendous force was waiting to be awakened, consolidated, and applied.

In Munich alone there existed, in 1919, nearly fifty more or less political associations, whose membership consisted chiefly of confused remnants of the prewar parties that had been broken up by war and revolution. . . . What united them all and drew them together theoretically and in reality was nothing but an overwhelming feeling of anxiety.

First of all, and most immediate, there was the fear of revolution, that *grande peur* which after the French Revolution had haunted the European-bourgeoisie throughout the nineteenth century. The notion that revolutions were like forces of nature, elemental mechanisms operating without reference to the will of the actors in them, following their own logic and leading perforce to reigns of terror, destruction, killing, and chaos — that notion was seared into the public mind. That was the unforgettable experience, not [German philosopher Immanuel] Kant's belief that the French Revolution had also shown the potentiality for betterment inherent in human nature. For generations, particularly in Germany, this fear stood in the way of any practical revolutionary strivings and produced a mania for keeping things quiet, with the result that every revolutionary proclamation up to 1918 was countered by the standard appeal to law and order.

This old fear was revived by the pseudorevolutionary events in Germany and by the menace of the October Revolution in Russia. Diabolical traits were ascribed to the Reds. The refugees pouring into Munich described bloodthirsty barbarians on a rampage of killing. Such imagery had instant appeal to the nationalists. . . .

This threat dominated Hitler's speeches of the early years. In garish colors he depicted the ravages of the "Red squads of butchers," the "murderous communists," the "bloody morass of Bolshevism." In Russia, he told his audiences, more than thirty million persons had been murdered, "partly on the scaffold, partly by machine guns and similar means, partly in veritable slaughterhouses, partly, millions upon millions, by hunger; and we all know that this wave of hunger is creeping on . . . and see that this scourge is approaching, that it is also coming upon Germany." The intelligentsia of the Soviet Union, he declared, had been exterminated by mass murder, the economy utterly smashed. Thousands of German prisoners-of-war had been drowned in the Neva or sold as slaves. Meanwhile, in Germany the enemy was boring away at the foundations of society "in unremitting, ever unchanging undermining work." The fate of Russia, he said again and again, would soon be ours! . . .

National Socialism owed a considerable part of its emotional appeal, its militancy, and its cohesion to this defensive attitude toward the threat of Marxist revolution. The aim of the National Socialist Party, Hitler repeatedly declared, "is very brief: Annihilation and extermination of the Marxist world view." This was to be accomplished by an "incomparable, brilliantly orchestrated propaganda and information organization" side by side with a movement "of the most ruthless force and most brutal resolution, prepared to oppose all terrorism on the part of the Marxists with tenfold greater terrorism." At about the same time, for similar reasons, Mussolini was founding his Fasci di combattimento [battle group]. Henceforth, the new movements were to be identified by the general name of "Fascism."

But the fear of revolution would not have been enough to endow the movement with that fierce energy, which for a time seemed to stem the universal trend toward democracy. After all, for many people revolution meant hope. A stronger and more elemental motivation had to be added. And in fact Marxism was feared as the precursor of a far more comprehensive assault upon all traditional ideas. It was viewed as the contemporary political aspect of a metaphysical upheaval, as a "declaration of war upon the European . . . idea of culture." Marxism itself was only the metaphor for something dreaded that escaped definition. . . .

This first phase of the postwar era was characterized both by fear of revolution and anticivilizational resentments; these together, curiously intertwined and reciprocally stimulating each other, produced a syndrome of extraordinary force. Into the brew went the hate and defense complexes of a society shaken to its foundations. German society had lost its imperial glory, its civil order, its national confidence, its prosperity, and its familiar authorities. The whole system had been turned topsy-turvy, and now many Germans blindly and bitterly wanted back what they thought had been unjustly taken from them. These general feelings of unhappiness were intensified and further radicalized by a variety of unsatisfied group interests. The class of white-collar workers, continuing to grow apace, proved especially susceptible to the grand gesture of total criticism. For the industrial revolution had just begun to affect office workers and was reducing the former "non-commissioned officers of capitalism" to the status of last victims of "modern slavery." It was all the worse for them because unlike the proletarians they had never developed a class pride of their own or imagined that the breakdown of the existing order was going to lead to their own apotheosis. Small businessmen were equally susceptible because of their fear of being crushed by corporations, department stores, and rationalized competition. Another unhappy group consisted of farmers who, slow to change and lacking capital, were fettered to backward modes of production. Another group were the academics and formerly solid bourgeois who felt themselves caught in the tremendous suction of proletarianization. Without outside support you found yourself "at once

despised, declassed; to be unemployed is the same as being a communist," one victim stated in a questionnaire of the period. No statistics,
no figures on rates of inflation, bankruptcies, and suicides can describe
the feelings of those threatened by unemployment or poverty, or can
express the anxieties of those others who still possessed some property
and feared the consequences of so much accumulated discontent. . . .

The vigilante groups and the free corps that were being organized
in great numbers, partly on private initiative, partly with covert government support, chiefly to meet the threat of Communist revolution,
formed centers of bewildered but determined resistance to the *status
quo*. The members of these paramilitary groups were vaguely looking
around for someone to lead them into a new system. At first there was
another reservoir of militant energies alongside the parliamentary
groups: the mass of homecoming soldiers. Many of these stayed in the
barracks dragging out a pointless military life, baffled and unable to
say good-bye to the warrior dreams of their recent youth. In the front-
line trenches they had glimpsed the outlines of a new meaning to life; in
the sluggishly resuming normality of the postwar period they tried in
vain to find that meaning again. They had not fought and suffered for
years for the sake of this weakened regime with its borrowed ideals
which, as they saw it, could be pushed around by the most con-
temptible of their former enemies. And they also feared, after the exalting sense of life the war had given them, the ignobility of the commonplace bourgeois world.

It remained for Hitler to bring together these feelings and to ap-
point himself their spearhead. Indeed, Hitler regarded as a phenomenon seems like the synthetic product of all the anxiety, pessimism, nostalgia, and defensiveness we have discussed. For him, too, the war had
been education and liberation. If there is a "Fascistic" type, it was embodied in him. More than any of his followers he expressed the underlying psychological, social, and ideological motives of the movement.
He was never just its leader; he was also its exponent.

His early years had contributed their share to that experience of
overwhelming anxiety which dominated his intellectual and emotional
constitution. That lurking anxiety can be seen at the root of almost all
his statements and reactions. It had everyday as well as cosmic dimensions. Many who knew him in his youth have described his pallid,
"timorous" nature, which provided the fertile soil for his lush fantasies.
His "constant fear" of contact with strangers was another aspect of
that anxiety, as was his extreme distrust and his compulsion to wash
frequently, which became more and more pronounced in later life. The
same complex is apparent in his oft-expressed fear of venereal disease
and his fear of contagion in general. He knew that "microbes are rushing at me." He was ridden by the Austrian Pan-German's fear of being
overwhelmed by alien races, by fear of the "locust-like immigration of

Russian and Polish Jews," by fear of "the niggerizing of the Germans," by fear of the Germans' "expulsion from Germany," and finally by fear that the Germans would be "exterminated." He had the *Völkische Boebachter* print an alleged French soldier's song whose refrain was: "Germans, we will possess your daughters!" Among his phobias were American technology, the birth rate of the Slavs, big cities, "industrialization as unrestricted as it is harmful," the "economization of the nation," corporations, the "morass of metropolitan amusement culture," and modern art, which sought "to kill the soul of the people" by painting meadows blue and skies green. Wherever he looked he discovered the "signs of decay of a slowly ebbing world." Not an element of pessimistic anticivilizational criticism was missing from his imagination.

What linked Hitler with the leading Fascists of other countries was the resolve to halt this process of degeneration. What set him apart from them, however, was the manic single-mindedness with which he traced all the anxieties he had ever felt back to a single source. For at the heart of the towering structure of anxiety, black and hairy, stood the figure of the Jew: evil-smelling, smacking his lips, lusting after blonde girls, eternal contaminator of the blood, but "racially harder" than the Aryan, as Hitler uneasily declared as late as the summer of 1942. A prey to his psychosis, he saw Germany as the object of a worldwide conspiracy, pressed on all sides by Bolshevists, Freemasons, capitalists, Jesuits, all hand in glove with each other and directed in their nefarious projects by the "bloodthirsty and avaricious Jewish tyrant." *The* Jew had 75 per cent of world capital at his disposal. He dominated the stock exchanges and the Marxist parties, the Gold and Red Internationals. He was the "advocate of birth control and the idea of emigration." He undermined governments, bastardized races, glorified fratricide, fomented civil war, justified baseness, and poisoned nobility: "the wirepuller of the destinies of mankind." The whole world was in danger, Hitler cried imploringly; it had fallen "into the embrace of this octopus." He groped for images in which to make his horror tangible, saw "creeping venom," "belly-worms," and "adders devouring the nation's body." . . .

The appearance of Hitler signaled a union of those forces that in crisis conditions had great political potential. The Fascistic movements all centered on the charismatic appeal of a unique leader. The leader was to be the resolute voice of order controlling chaos. He would have looked further and thought deeper, would know the despairs but also the means of salvation. This looming giant had already been given established form in a prophetic literature that went back to German folklore. Like the mythology of many other nations unfortunate in their history, that of the Germans has its sleeping leaders dreaming away the centuries in the bowels of a mountain, but destined some day to return to rally their people and punish the guilty world. . . .

The success of Fascism in contrast to many of its rivals was in large part due to its perceiving the essence of the crisis, of which it was itself the symptom. All the other parties affirmed the process of industrialization and emancipation, whereas the Fascists, evidently sharing the universal anxiety, tried to deal with it by translating it into violent action and histrionics. . . .

70

HEINRICH HIMMLER

Speech to the SS

Heinrich Himmler (1900–1945) was one of the most powerful leaders of Nazi Germany. He was the head of the SS, or *Schutzstaffel*, an elite army that was responsible for, among other things, running the many concentration camps. Hitler gave Himmler the task of implementing the "final solution of the Jewish question": killing the Jewish population of Germany and the other countries the Nazis occupied. The horror that resulted is today often referred to by the biblical word *holocaust*.

The following reading is an excerpt from a speech Himmler gave to SS leaders on October 4, 1943. What was Himmler's concern in this speech? What kind of general support for the extermination of the Jews does this excerpt suggest existed?

Thinking Historically

Psychiatrists say that people use various strategies to cope when they must do something distasteful. We might summarize these strategies as denial, distancing, compartmentalizing, ennobling, rationalizing, and scapegoating. *Denial* is pretending that something has not happened. *Distancing* removes the idea, memory, or reality from the mind, placing it at a distance. *Compartmentalizing* separates one action, memory, or idea from others, allowing one to "put away" certain feelings. *Ennobling* makes the distasteful act a matter of pride rather than guilt, nobility rather than disgrace. *Rationalizing* creates

---

Heinrich Himmler, "Secret Speech at Posen," *A Holocaust Reader*, ed. Lucy S. Dawidowicz (New York: Behrman House, 1976), 132–33.

"good" reasons for doing something, while *scapegoating* puts blame on someone else.

What evidence do you see of these strategies in Himmler's speech? Judging from the speech, which of these strategies do you think his listeners used to rationalize their actions?

I also want to make reference before you here, in complete frankness, to a really grave matter. Among ourselves, this once, it shall be uttered quite frankly; but in public we will never speak of it. Just as we did not hesitate on June 30, 1934, to do our duty as ordered, to stand up against the wall comrades who had transgressed,[1] and shoot them, so we have never talked about this and never will. It was the tact which I am glad to say is a matter of course to us that made us never discuss it among ourselves, never talk about it. Each of us shuddered, and yet each one knew that he would do it again if it were ordered and if it were necessary.

I am referring to the evacuation of the Jews, the annihilation of the Jewish people. This is one of those things that are easily said. "The Jewish people is going to be annihilated," says every party member. "Sure, it's in our program, elimination of the Jews, annihilation — we'll take care of it." And then they all come trudging, 80 million worthy Germans, and each one has his one decent Jew. Sure, the others are swine, but this one is an A-1 Jew. Of all those who talk this way, not one has seen it happen, not one has been through it. Most of you must know what it means to see a hundred corpses lie side by side, or five hundred, or a thousand. To have stuck this out — excepting cases of human weakness — to have kept our integrity, that is what has made us hard. In our history, this is an unwritten and never-to-be-written page of glory, for we know how difficult we would have made it for ourselves if today — amid the bombing raids, the hardships, and the deprivations of war — we still had the Jews in every city as secret saboteurs, agitators, and demagogues. If the Jews were still ensconced in the body of the German nation, we probably would have reached the 1916–17 stage by now.[2]

The wealth they had we have taken from them. I have issued a strict order, carried out by SS-Obergruppenfuhrer Pohl, that this wealth in its entirety is to be turned over to the Reich as a matter of course.

---

[1] A reference to the "Night of the Long Knives," when Hitler ordered the SS to murder the leaders of the SA, a Nazi group he wished to suppress. [Ed.]

[2] Here Himmler is apparently referring to the stalemate on Germany's western front in World War I. [Ed.]

We have taken none of it for ourselves. Individuals who transgress will be punished in accordance with an order I issued at the beginning, threatening that whoever takes so much as a mark of it for himself is a dead man. A number of SS men — not very many — have transgressed, and they will die, without mercy. We had the moral right, we had the duty toward our people, to kill this people which wanted to kill us. But we do not have the right to enrich ourselves with so much as a fur, a watch, a mark, or a cigarette, or anything else. Having exterminated a germ, we do not want, in the end, to be infected by the germ, and die of it. I will not stand by and let even a small rotten spot develop or take hold. Wherever it may form, we together will cauterize it. All in all, however, we can say that we have carried out this heaviest of our tasks in a spirit of love for our people. And our inward being, our soul, our character has not suffered injury from it.

$$\boxed{71}$$

JEAN-FRANÇOIS STEINER
From Treblinka

Treblinka, in Poland, was one of several Nazi death camps. (Auschwitz was the largest camp.) (See Map 11.1.) In these "death factories," the Nazis murdered millions of Jews as well as many thousands of Roma and Sinti, socialists, Soviet prisoners of war, and other people. In this selection, Steiner, who lost his father at Treblinka, reveals how "rational" and "scientific" mass murder can be. How could this happen? Can it happen again?

Thinking Historically

Try to imagine what went through the mind of Lalka as he designed the extermination process at Treblinka. How did concerns for efficiency and humanity enter into his deliberations? Do you think he found his work distasteful? If so, which of the strategies mentioned in the previous selection did he adopt?

Jean-François Steiner, *Treblinka* (New York: Simon & Schuster, 1967), 153–54, 155–58, 159–60.

Legend:
- □ Extermination camps
- ■ Main concentration, labor, transit camps

Scale:
0 — 125 — 250 miles
0 — 125 — 500 kilometers

N, E, W, S compass

Map 11.1 Major Nazi Concentration Camps in World War II.

What would it have been like to be a sign-painter, guard, or hair-cutter at Treblinka?

Each poorly organized debarkation [of deportees from trains arriving at Treblinka] gave rise to unpleasant scenes — uncertainties and confusion for the deportees, who did not know where they were going and were sometimes seized with panic.

So, the first problem was to restore a minimum of hope. Lalka[1] had many faults, but he did not lack a certain creative imagination. After a few days of reflection he hit upon the idea of transforming the platform where the convoys [trains] arrived into a false station. He had the ground filled in to the level of the doors of the cars in order to give the appearance of a train platform and to make it easier to get off the trains. . . . On [a] wall Lalka had . . . doors and windows painted in gay and pleasing colors. The windows were decorated with cheerful curtains and framed by green blinds which were just as false as the rest. Each door was given a special name, stencilled at eye level: "Stationmaster," "Toilet," "Infirmary" (a red cross was painted on this door). Lalka carried his concern for detail so far as to have his men paint two doors leading to the waiting rooms, first and second class. The ticket window, which was barred with a horizontal sign reading, "Closed," was a little masterpiece with its ledge and false perspective and its grill, painted line for line. Next to the ticket window a large timetable announced the departure times of trains for Warsaw, Bialystok, Wolkowysk, etc. . . . Two doors were cut into the [wall]. The first led to the "hospital," bearing a wooden arrow on which "Wolkowysk" was painted. The second led to the place where the Jews were undressed; that arrow said "Bialystok." Lalka also had some flower beds designed, which gave the whole area a neat and cheery look. . . .

Lalka also decided that better organization could save much time in the operations of undressing and recovery of the [deportees'] baggage. To do this you had only to rationalize the different operations, that is, to organize the undressing like an assembly line. But the rhythm of this assembly line was at the mercy of the sick, the old, and the wounded, who, since they were unable to keep the pace, threatened to bog down the operation and make it proceed even more slowly than before. . . . Individuals of both sexes over the age of ten, and children under ten, at a maximum rate of two children per adult, were judged fit to follow the complete circuit,[2] as long as they did not show

[1]Kurt Franz, whom the prisoners called Lalka, designed the highly efficient system of extermination at Treblinka. [Ed.]

[2]The "complete" circuit was getting off the train, walking along the platform through the door to the men's or women's barracks, undressing, and being led to the gas chamber "showers." [Ed.]

serious wounds or marked disability. Victims who did not correspond to the norms were to be conducted to the "hospital" by members of the blue commando and turned over to the Ukrainians [guards] for special treatment. A bench was built all around the ditch of the "hospital" so that the victims would fall of their own weight after receiving the bullet in the back of the head. This bench was to be used only when Kurland[3] was swamped with work. On the platform, the door which these victims took was surmounted by the Wolkowysk arrow. In the Sibylline language of Treblinka, "Wolkowysk" meant the bullet in the back of the neck or the injection. "Bialystok" meant the gas chamber.

Beside the "Bialystok" door stood a tall Jew whose role was to shout endlessly, "Large bundles here, large bundles here!" He had been nicknamed "Groysse Pack." As soon as the victims had gone through, Groysse Pack and his men from the red commando carried the bundles at a run to the sorting square, where the sorting commandos immediately took possession of them. As soon as they had gone through the door came the order, "Women to the left, men to the right." This moment generally gave rise to painful scenes.

While the women were being led to the left-hand barracks to undress and go to the hairdresser, the men, who were lined up double file, slowly entered the production line. This production line included five stations. At each of these a group of "reds" shouted at the top of their lungs the name of the piece of clothing that it was in charge of receiving. At the first station the victim handed over his coat and hat. At the second, his jacket. (In exchange, he received a piece of string.) At the third he sat down, took off his shoes, and tied them together with the string he had just received. Until then the shoes were not tied together in pairs, and since the yield was at least fifteen thousand pairs of shoes per day, they were all lost, since they could not be matched up again.) At the fourth station the victim left his trousers, and at the fifth his shirt and underwear.

After they had been stripped, the victims were conducted, as they came off the assembly line, to the right-hand barracks and penned in until the women had finished: ladies first. However, a small number, chosen from among the most able-bodied, were singled out at the door to carry the clothing to the sorting square. They did this while running naked between two rows of Ukrainian guards. Without stopping once they threw their bundles onto the pile, turned around, and went back for another.

Meanwhile the women had been conducted to the barracks on the left. This barracks was divided into two parts: a dressing room and a

---

[3]Kurland was a Jew assigned to the "hospital," where he gave injections of poison to those who were too ill or crippled to make the complete circuit. [Ed.]

beauty salon. "Put your clothes in a pile so you will be able to find them after the shower," they were ordered in the first room. The "beauty salon" was a room furnished with six benches, each of which could seat twenty women at a time. Behind each bench twenty prisoners of the red commando, wearing white tunics and armed with scissors, waited at attention until all the women were seated. Between hair-cutting sessions they sat down on the benches and, under the direction of a *kapo* [prisoner guard] who was transformed into a conductor, they had to sing old Yiddish melodies.

Lalka, who had insisted on taking personal responsibility for every detail, had perfected the technique of what he called the "Treblinka cut." With five well-placed slashes the whole head of hair was trans-ferred to a sack placed beside each hairdresser for this purpose. It was simple and efficient. How many dramas did this "beauty salon" see? From the very beautiful young woman who wept when her hair was cut off, because she would be ugly, to the mother who grabbed a pair of scissors from one of the "hairdressers" and literally severed a Ukrain-ian's arm; from the sister who recognized one of the "hairdressers" as her brother to the young girl, Ruth Dorfman, who, suddenly under-standing and fighting back her tears, asked whether it was difficult to die and admitted in a small brave voice that she was a little afraid and wished it were all over.

When they had been shorn the women left the "beauty salon" double file. Outside the door, they had to squat in a particular way also specified by Lalka, in order to be intimately searched. Up to this point, doubt had been carefully maintained. Of course, a discriminating eye might have observed that . . . the smell was the smell of rotting bodies. A thousand details proved that Treblinka was not a transient camp, and some realized this, but the majority had believed in the impossible for too long to begin to doubt at the last moment. The door of the bar-racks, which opened directly onto the "road to heaven," represented the turning point. Up to here the prisoners had been given a minimum of hope, from here on this policy was abandoned.

This was one of Lalka's great innovations. After what point was it no longer necessary to delude the victims? This detail had been the sub-ject of rather heated controversy among the Technicians. At the Nurem-berg trials, Rudolf Höss, Commandant of Auschwitz, criticized Tre-blinka where, according to him, the victims knew that they were going to be killed. Höss was an advocate of the towel distributed at the door to the gas chamber. He claimed that this system not only avoided disor-der, but was more humane, and he was proud of it. But Höss did not invent this "towel technique"; it was in all the manuals, and it was uti-lized at Treblinka until Lalka's great reform.

Lalka's studies had led to what might be called the "principle of the cutoff." His reasoning was simple: Since sooner or later the victims must realize that they were going to be killed, to postpone this moment was only false humanity. The principle "the later the better" did not apply here. Lalka had been led to make an intensive study of this problem upon observing one day completely by chance, that winded victims died much more rapidly than the rest. The discovery had led him to make a clean sweep of accepted principles. Let us follow his industrialist's logic, keeping well in mind that his great preoccupation was the saving of time. A winded victim dies faster. Hence, a saving of time. The best way to wind a man is to make him run — another saving of time. Thus Lalka arrived at the conclusion that you must make the victims run. A new question had then arisen: At what point must you make the victims run and thus create panic (a further aid to breathlessness)? The question had answered itself: As soon as you have nothing more to make them do. Franz located the exact point, the point of no return: the door of the barracks.

The rest was merely a matter of working out the details. Along the "road to heaven" and in front of the gas chambers he stationed a cordon of guards armed with whips, whose function was to make the victims run, to make them rush into the gas chambers of their own accord in search of refuge. One can see that this system is more daring than the classic system, but one can also see the danger it represents. Suddenly abandoned to their despair, realizing that they no longer had anything to lose, the victims might attack the guards. Lalka was aware of this risk, but he maintained that everything depended on the pace. "It's close work," he said, "but if you maintain a very rapid pace and do not allow a single moment of hesitation, the method is absolutely without danger." There were still further elaborations later on, but from the first day, Lalka had only to pride himself on his innovation: It took no more than three quarters of an hour, by the clock, to put the victims through their last voyage, from the moment the doors of the cattle cars were unbolted to the moment the great trap doors of the gas chamber were opened to take out the bodies. . . .

But let us return to the men. The timing was worked out so that by the time the last woman had emerged from the left-hand barracks, all the clothes had been transported to the sorting square. The men were immediately taken out of the right-hand barracks and driven after the women into the "road to heaven," which they reached by way of a special side path. By the time they arrived at the gas chambers the toughest, who had begun to run before the others to carry the bundles, were just as winded as the weakest. Everyone died in perfect unison for the greater satisfaction of that great Technician Kurt Franz, the Stakhanovite [model worker] of extermination.

72

IRIS CHANG

From The Rape of Nanking

Nazi genocide was not the only systematic murder of civilian populations during World War II. The military government of Japan, a German ally during the war, engaged in some of the same tactics of brutal
and indiscriminate mass murder of civilians. In fact, atrocities in
Japan preceded those in Germany.

While for Europeans World War II began with the German invasion of Poland on September 1, 1939, and for Americans with the
Japanese attack at Pearl Harbor, Hawaii, on December 7, 1941, for
the Chinese it began ten years earlier with the Japanese invasion of
Manchuria in 1931. By 1937, Japanese troops occupied Peking and
Shanghai as well as the old imperial capital of Nanking. It is estimated
that more than twenty-five thousand civilians were killed by Japanese
soldiers in the months after the fall of Nanking on December 13,
1937. But it was the appalling brutality of Japanese troops that foreign residents remembered, even those who could recall the brutality
of the Chinese nationalist troops who captured the city in 1927. In the
Introduction to *The Rape of Nanking*, Iris Chang writes:

> The Rape of Nanking should be remembered not only for the
> number of people slaughtered but for the cruel manner in which
> many met their deaths. Chinese men were used for bayonet prac-
> tice and in decapitation contests. An estimated 20,000 to 80,000
> Chinese women were raped. Many soldiers went beyond rape to
> disembowel women, slice off their breasts, nail them alive to
> walls. Fathers were forced to rape their daughters, and sons their
> mothers, as other family members watched. Not only did live
> burials, castration, the carving of organs, and the roasting of
> people become routine, but more diabolical tortures were prac-
> ticed, such as hanging people by their tongues on iron hooks or
> burying people to their waist and watching them get torn apart by
> German shepherds. So sickening was the spectacle that even the
> Nazis in the city were horrified, one declaring the massacre to be
> the work of "bestial machinery." (p. 6)

In the selection that follows, the author asks how Japanese soldiers
were capable of such offenses. What is her answer?

Iris Chang, *The Rape of Nanking* (New York: Basic Books, 1997), 55–59.

Thinking Historically

What would have happened to these recruits if they had refused an order to kill a prisoner or noncombatant? Once they had killed one prisoner, why did they find it easier to kill another? Did they eventually enjoy it, feel pride, or think it insignificant? The last informant, Nagatomi, says he had been a "devil." Had he been possessed? By whom?

How then do we explain the raw brutality carried out day after day after day in the city of Nanking? Unlike their Nazi counterparts, who have mostly perished in prisons and before execution squads or, if alive, are spending their remaining days as fugitives from the law, many of the Japanese war criminals are still alive, living in peace and comfort, protected by the Japanese government. They are therefore some of the few people on this planet who, without concern for retaliation in a court of international law, can give authors and journalists a glimpse of their thoughts and feelings while committing World War II atrocities.

Here is what we learn. The Japanese soldier was not simply hardened for battle in China; he was hardened for the task of murdering Chinese combatants and noncombatants alike. Indeed, various games and exercises were set up by the Japanese military to numb its men to the human instinct against killing people who are not attacking.

For example, on their way to the capital, Japanese soldiers were made to participate in killing competitions, which were avidly covered by the Japanese media like sporting events. The most notorious one appeared in the December 7 issue of the *Japan Advertiser* under the headline "Sub-Lieutenants in Race to Fell 100 Chinese Running Close Contest."

> Sub-Lieutenant Mukai Toshiaki and Sub-Lieutenant Noda Takeshi, both of the Katagiri unit at Kuyung, in a friendly contest to see which of them will first fell 100 Chinese in individual sword combat before the Japanese forces completely occupy Nanking, are well in the final phase of their race, running almost neck to neck. On Sunday [December 5] . . . the "score," according to the Asahi, was: Sub-Lieutenant Mukai, 89, and Sub-Lieutenant Noda, 78.

A week later the paper reported that neither man could decide who had passed the 100 mark first, so they upped the goal to 150. "Mukai's blade was slightly damaged in the competition," the *Japan Advertiser* reported. "He explained that this was the result of cutting a Chinese in half, helmet and all. The contest was 'fun' he declared. " . . .

For new soldiers, horror was a natural impulse. One Japanese wartime memoir describes how a group of green Japanese recruits failed to conceal their shock when they witnessed seasoned soldiers torture a group of civilians to death. Their commander expected this reaction and wrote in his diary: "All new recruits are like this, but soon they will be doing the same things themselves."

But new officers also required desensitization. A veteran officer named Tominaga Shozo recalled vividly his own transformation from innocent youth to killing machine. Tominaga had been a fresh second lieutenant from a military academy when assigned to the 232nd Regiment of the 39th Division from Hiroshima. When he was introduced to the men under his command, Tominaga was stunned. "They had evil eyes," he remembered. "They weren't human eyes, but the eyes of leopards or tigers."

On the front Tominaga and other new candidate officers underwent intensive training to stiffen their endurance for war. In the program an instructor had pointed to a thin, emaciated Chinese in a detention center and told the officers: "These are the raw materials for your trial of courage." Day after day the instructor taught them how to cut off heads and bayonet living prisoners.

> On the final day, we were taken out to the site of our trial. Twenty-four prisoners were squatting there with their hands tied behind their backs. They were blindfolded. A big hole had been dug — ten meters long, two meters wide, and more than three meters deep. The regimental commander, the battalion commanders, and the company commanders all took the seats arranged for them. Second Lieutenant Tanaka bowed to the regimental commander and reported, "We shall now begin." He ordered a soldier on fatigue duty to haul one of the prisoners to the edge of the pit; the prisoner was kicked when he resisted. The soldiers finally dragged him over and forced him to his knees. Tanaka turned toward us and looked into each of our faces in turn. "Heads should be cut off like this," he said, unsheathing his army sword. He scooped water from a bucket with a dipper, then poured it over both sides of the blade. Swishing off the water, he raised his sword in a long arc. Standing behind the prisoner, Tanaka steadied himself, legs spread apart, and cut off the man's head with a shout, "Yo!" The head flew more than a meter away. Blood spurted up in two fountains from the body and sprayed into the hole.
>
> The scene was so appalling that I felt I couldn't breathe.

But gradually, Tominaga Shozo learned to kill. And as he grew more adept at it, he no longer felt that his men's eyes were evil. For him, atrocities became routine, almost banal. Looking back on his experience, he wrote: "We made them like this. Good sons, good daddies, good elder brothers at home were brought to the front to kill each other. Human beings turned into murdering demons. Everyone became a demon within three months."

Some Japanese soldiers admitted it was easy for them to kill because they had been taught that next to the emperor, all individual life — even their own — was valueless. Azuma Shiro, the Japanese soldier who witnessed a series of atrocities in Nanking, made an excellent point about his comrades' behavior in his letter to me. During his two years of military training in the 20th Infantry Regiment of Kyoto-fu Fukuchi-yama, he was taught that "loyalty is heavier than a mountain, and our life is lighter than a feather." He recalled that the highest honor a soldier could achieve during war was to come back dead: To die for the emperor was the greatest glory, to be caught alive by the enemy the greatest shame. "If my life was not important," Azuma wrote to me, "an enemy's life became inevitably much less important. . . . This philosophy led us to look down on the enemy and eventually to the mass murder and ill treatment of the captives."

In interview after interview, Japanese veterans from the Nanking massacre reported honestly that they experienced a complete lack of remorse or sense of wrongdoing, even when torturing helpless civilians. Nagatomi Hakudo spoke candidly about his emotions in the fallen capital:

> I remember being driven in a truck along a path that had been cleared through piles of thousands and thousands of slaughtered bodies. Wild dogs were gnawing at the dead flesh as we stopped and pulled a group of Chinese prisoners out of the back. Then the Japanese officer proposed a test of my courage. He unsheathed his sword, spat on it, and with a sudden mighty swing he brought it down on the neck of a Chinese boy cowering before us. The head was cut clean off and tumbled away on the group as the body slumped forward, blood spurting in two great gushing fountains from the neck. The officer suggested I take the head home as a souvenir. I remember smiling proudly as I took his sword and began killing people.

After almost sixty years of soul-searching, Nagatomi is a changed man. A doctor in Japan, he has built a shrine of remorse in his waiting room. Patients can watch videotapes of his trial in Nanking and a full confession of his crimes. The gentle and hospitable demeanor of the doctor belies the horror of his past, making it almost impossible for one to imagine that he had once been a ruthless murderer.

"Few know that soldiers impaled babies on bayonets and tossed them still alive into pots of boiling water," Nagatomi said. "They gang-raped women from the ages of twelve to eighty and then killed them when they could no longer satisfy sexual requirements. I beheaded people, starved them to death, burned them, and buried them alive, over two hundred in all. It is terrible that I could turn into an animal and do these things. There are really no words to explain what I was doing. I was truly a devil."

73

MAHMOOD MAMDANI
Thinking about Genocide

On December 11, 1946, the General Assembly of the United Nations declared genocide a crime under international law. In 1948 the international body defined genocide as "acts committed with intent to destroy, in whole or in part, a national, ethnical, racial, or religious group." Before the signatures dried on the second document, the world witnessed the bloody partition of British India between Hindus and Muslims and the beginnings of an international balance of terror depending on the threat of mutual nuclear destruction. By and large, the ethnic, national, and religious violence of the immediate post-war was not called genocide. The term was limited to the Nazi attempt to exterminate Jews.

In the early 1990s, the specter of genocide returned in the breakup of Yugoslavia and in the African state of Rwanda. (See Map 11.2.) While Yugoslavia died a slow death, the outburst of killing in Rwanda in 1994 was remarkable for its suddenness. Within a matter of months, the majority Hutu population slaughtered almost a million of the minority Tutsis. Under German and then Belgian colonialism, the Tutsis had been designated a superior race and given special power and privileges. This was a common divide-and-rule tactic of European colonial control. In the period of independence (1959–1962), Hutu resentment against Tutsis came to a boil. Thousands of Tutsis were killed and hundreds of thousands were expelled. Hutus took their place and controlled the government and resources. Over the next decades, Tutsis came back to the densely populated country, formed a political party, and became stronger. By 1994, the Hutu president and many of his supporters feared a return of Tutsi rule. When the president and many of his advisors were killed in a plane crash, the Hutu media and militant groups marshaled a campaign of extermination.

In this selection, Mahmood Mamdani, born in Uganda and currently director of the Institute of African Studies at Columbia University, reflects on the meaning of that genocide committed so soon after the world community had declared "never again." How, according to the author, was the Hutu genocide different from that of the Nazis? What is the significance of that difference? Does it matter?

Mahmood Mamdani, *When Victims Become Killers: Colonialism, Nativism and Genocide in Rwanda* (Princeton, N.J.: Princeton University Press, 2001), 3–14.

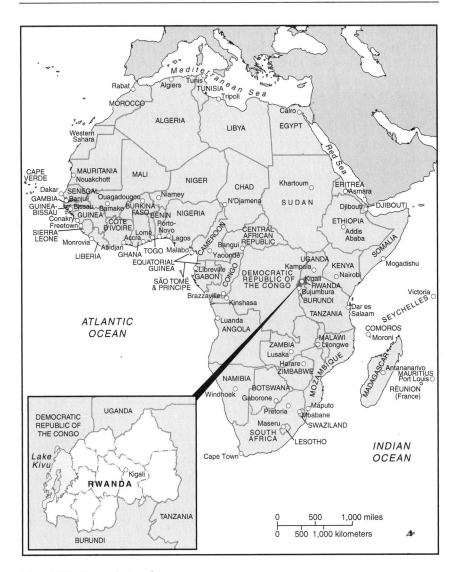

Map 11.2   Rwanda in Africa.

Thinking Historically

The author says that the "violence cannot be understood as rational: yet we need to understand it as thinkable" (p. 409). What does he mean? Do you agree? How does he help you to understand it as thinkable?

I visited Rwanda roughly a year after the genocide. On July 22, 1995, I went to Ntarama, about an hour and a half by car from Kigali, on a dirt road going south toward the Burundi border. We arrived at a village church, made of brick and covered with iron sheets. Outside there was a wood and bamboo rack, bearing skulls. On the ground were assorted bones, collected and pressed together inside sacks, but sticking out of their torn cloth. . . .

The church was about twenty by sixty feet. Inside, wooden planks were placed on stones. I supposed they were meant as benches. I peered inside and saw a pile of belongings — shoulder sacks, tattered clothing, a towel, a wooden box, a *suferia* (cooking pot), plastic mugs and plates, straw mats and hats — the worldly goods of the poor. Then, amidst it all, I saw bones, and then entire skeletons, each caught in the posture in which it had died. Even a year after the genocide, I thought the air smelled of blood, mixed with that of bones, clothing, earth — a human mildew.

I scanned the walls with their gaping holes. The guide explained these were made by the Interahamwe (youth militia of the ruling party) so they could throw grenades into the building. He said that those in the church were lucky. They died, almost instantly. Those outside had a protracted, brutal death, in some cases drawn out over as long as a week, with one part of the body cut daily.

I raised my eyes, away from the skeletons, to look at the church wall. Much of it was still covered with some old posters. They read like exhortations common to radical regimes with a developmental agenda, regimes that I was familiar with and had lived under for decades. One read: "Journée Internationale de la Femme." And below it, was another, this time in bold: "ÉGALITÉ — PAIX — DÉVELOPPEMENT."

I was introduced to a man called Callixte, a survivor of the massacre in Ntarama. "On the 7th of April [1994], in the morning," he explained, "they started burning houses over there and moving towards here. Only a few were killed. The burning pushed us to this place. Our group decided to run to this place. We thought this was God's house, no one would attack us here. On the 7th, 8th, up to the 10th, we were fighting them. We were using stones. They had *pangas* (machetes), spears, hammers, grenades. On the 10th, their numbers were increased. On the 14th, we were being pushed inside the church. The church was attacked on the 14th and the 15th. The actual killing was on the 15th.

"On the 15th, they brought Presidential Guards. They were supporting Interahamwe, brought in from neighboring communes. I was not in the group here. Here, there were women, children, and old men. The men had formed defense units outside. I was outside. Most men died fighting. When our defense was broken through, they came and killed everyone here. After that, they started hunting for those hiding in the hills. I and others ran to the swamp."

I asked about his *secteur,* about how many lived in it, how many Tutsi, how many Hutu, who participated in the killing. "In my *secteur,* Hutu were two-thirds, Tutsi one-third. There were about 5,000 in our *secteur.* Of the 3,500 Hutu, all the men participated. It was like an order, except there were prominent leaders who would command. The rest followed."

I asked whether there were no intermarriages in the *secteur.* "Too many. About one-third of Tutsi daughters would be married to Hutu. But Hutu daughters married to Tutsi men were only 1 per cent: Hutu didn't want to marry their daughters to Tutsi who were poor and it was risky. Because the Tutsi were discriminated against, they didn't want to give their daughters where there was no education, no jobs . . . risky. Prospects were better for Tutsi daughters marrying Hutu men. They would get better opportunities.

"Tutsi women married to Hutu were killed. I know only one who survived. The administration forced Hutu men to kill their Tutsi wives before they go to kill anyone else — to prove they were true Interahamwe. One man tried to refuse. He was told he must choose between the wife and himself. He then chose to save his own life. Another Hutu man rebuked him for having killed his Tutsi wife. That man was also killed. Kallisa — the man who was forced to kill his wife — is in jail. After killing his wife, he became a convert. He began to distribute grenades all around.

"The killing was planned, because some were given guns. During the war with the RPF, many young men were taken in the reserves and trained and given guns. Those coming from training would disassociate themselves from Tutsi. Some of my friends received training. When they returned, they were busy mobilizing others. They never came to see me. I am fifty-seven. Even people in their sixties joined in the killing, though they were not trained. The trained were Senior 6 or Technical School leavers." I asked how such killers could have been his friends. "I was a friend to their fathers. It was a father-son relationship. I think the fathers must have known."

Who were the killers in Ntarama? Units of the Presidential Guard came from Kigali. The Interahamwe were brought in from neighboring communes. Youth who had been trained in self-defense units after the civil war began provided the local trained force. But the truth is that everybody participated, at least all men. And not only men, women, too: cheering their men, participating in auxiliary roles, like the second line in a street-to-street battle.

No one can say with certainty how many Tutsi were killed between March and July of 1994 in Rwanda. In the fateful one hundred days that followed the downing of the presidential plane — and the coup d'état thereafter — a section of the army and civilian leadership organized the Hutu majority to kill all Tutsi, even babies. In the process, they also killed not only the Hutu political opposition, but also many nonpolitical Hutu who showed reluctance to perform what was touted as a "national" duty. The estimates of those killed vary: between ten and fifty thousand Hutu, and between 500,000 and a million Tutsi. Whereas the Hutu were killed as individuals, the Tutsi were killed as a group, recalling German designs to extinguish the country's Jewish population. This explicit goal is why the killings of Tutsi between March and July of 1994 must be termed "genocide." This single fact underlines a crucial similarity between the Rwandan genocide and the Nazi Holocaust.

In the history of genocide, however, the Rwandan genocide raises a difficult political question. Unlike the Nazi Holocaust, the Rwandan genocide was not carried out from a distance, in remote concentration camps beyond national borders, in industrial killing camps operated by agents who often did no more than drop Zyklon B crystals into gas chambers from above. The Rwandan genocide was executed with the slash of machetes rather than the drop of crystals, with all the gruesome detail of a street murder rather than the bureaucratic efficiency of a mass extermination. The difference in technology is indicative of a more significant social difference. The technology of the holocaust allowed a few to kill many, but the machete had to be wielded by a single pair of hands. It required not one but many hacks of a machete to kill even one person. With a machete, killing was hard work; that is why there were often several killers for every single victim. Whereas Nazis made every attempt to separate victims from perpetrators, the Rwandan genocide was very much an intimate affair. It was carried out by hundreds of thousands, perhaps even more, and witnessed by millions. . . .

The Rwandan genocide unfolded in just a hundred days. "It was not just a small group that killed and moved," a political commissar in the police explained to me in Kigali in July 1995. "Because genocide was so extensive, there were killers in every locality — from ministers to peasants — for it to happen in so short a time and on such a large scale." Opening the international conference on Genocide, Impunity and Accountability in Kigali in late 1995, the country's president, Pasteur Bizimungu, spoke of "hundreds of thousands of criminals" evenly spread across the land:

> Each village of this country has been affected by the tragedy, either because the whole population was mobilized to go and kill elsewhere, or

because one section undertook or was pushed to hunt and kill their fellow villagers. The survey conducted in Kigali, Kibungo, Byumba, Gitarama, and Butare Préfectures showed that genocide had been characterized by torture and utmost cruelty. About forty-eight methods of torture were used countrywide. They ranged from burying people alive in graves they had dug up themselves, to cutting and opening wombs of pregnant mothers. People were quartered, impaled or roasted to death.

On many occasions, death was the consequence of ablation of organs, such as the heart, from alive people. In some cases, victims had to pay fabulous amounts of money to the killers for a quick death. The brutality that characterised the genocide has been unprecedented. . . .

The violence of the genocide was the result of both planning and participation. The agenda imposed from above became a gruesome reality to the extent it resonated with perspectives from below. Rather than accent one or the other side of this relationship and thereby arrive at either a state-centered or a society-centered explanation, a complete picture of the genocide needs to take both sides into account. For this was neither just a conspiracy from above that only needed enough time and suitable circumstance to mature, nor was it a popular *jacquerie* gone berserk. If the violence from below could not have spread without cultivation and direction from above, it is equally true that the conspiracy of the tiny fragment of *génocidaires* could not have succeeded had it not found resonance from below. The design from above involved a tiny minority and is easier to understand. The response and initiative from below involved multitudes and presents the true moral dilemma of the Rwandan genocide.

In sum, the Rwandan genocide poses a set of deeply troubling questions. Why did hundreds of thousands, those who had never before killed, take part in mass slaughter? Why did such a disproportionate number of the educated — not just members of the political elite but, as we shall see, civic leaders such as doctors, nurses, judges, human rights activists, and so on — play a leading role in the genocide? Similarly, why did places of shelter where victims expected sanctuary — churches, hospitals, and schools — turn into slaughterhouses where innocents were murdered in the tens and hundreds, and sometimes even thousands? . . .

We may agree that genocidal violence cannot be understood as rational; yet, we need to understand it as thinkable. Rather than run away from it, we need to realize that it is the "popularity" of the genocide that is its uniquely troubling aspect. In its social aspect, Hutu/Tutsi violence in the Rwandan genocide invites comparison with Hindu/Muslim violence at the time of the partition of colonial India. Neither can be explained as simply a state project. One shudders to put the words "popular" and "genocide" together, therefore I put "popularity" in quotation marks. And yet, one needs to explain the large-scale civilian involvement in the genocide. To do so is to contextualize it, to understand the logic of its development. . . .

Colonialism and Genocide

The genocidal impulse to eliminate an enemy may indeed be as old as organized power. Thus, God instructed his Old Testament disciples through Moses, saying:

> Avenge the children of Israel of the Medianites: afterward shalt thou be gathered unto thy people. And Moses spake unto the people saying, Arm ye men from among you for the war, that they may go against Median, to execute the LORD's vengeance on Median. . . . And they warred against Median, as the LORD commanded Moses, and they slew every male. . . . And the children of Israel took captive the women of Median and their little ones; and all their cattle, and all their flocks, and all their goods, they took for a prey. And all their cities in the places wherein they dwelt, and all their encampments, they burnt with fire. And they took all the spoil, and all the prey, both of man and of beast. . . . And Moses said unto them, Have you saved all the women alive? Behold, these caused the children of Israel, through the counsel of Balaam, to commit trespass against the LORD in the matter of Peor, and so the plague was among the congregation of the LORD. Now therefore kill every male among the little ones, and kill every woman that hath known man by lying with him. But all the women children that have not known man by lying with him, keep alive for yourselves.

If the genocidal impulse is as old as the organization of power, one may be tempted to think that all that has changed through history is the technology of genocide. Yet, it is not simply the technology of genocide that has changed through history, but surely also how that impulse is organized and its target defined. Before you can try and eliminate an enemy, you must first define that enemy. The definition of the political self and the political other has varied through history. The history of that variation is the history of political identities, be these religious, national, racial, or otherwise.

I argue that the Rwandan genocide needs to be thought through within the logic of colonialism. The horror of colonialism led to two types of genocidal impulses. The first was the genocide of the native by the settler, to become a reality where the violence of colonial pacification took on extreme proportions. The second was the native impulse to eliminate the settler. Whereas the former was obviously despicable, the latter was not. The very political character of native violence made it difficult to think of it as an impulse to genocide. Because it was derivative of settler violence, the natives' violence appeared less of an outright aggression and more a self defense in the face of continuing aggression. Faced with the violent denial of his humanity by the settler, the native's violence began as a counter to violence. It even seemed more like the affirmation of the native's humanity than the brutal extinction of life that it came to be. When the native killed the settler, it was violence by yesterday's victims. More of a culmination of anticolonial resistance than a direct assault on life and freedom, this violence of victims-turned-perpetrators always provoked a greater moral ambiguity than did the settlers' violence. . . .

Settlers' Genocide

It is more or less a rule of thumb that the more Western settlement a colony experienced, the greater was the violence unleashed against the native population. The reason was simple: settler colonization led to land deprivation. Whereas the prototype of settler violence in the history of modern colonialism is the near-extermination of Amerindians in the New World, the prototype of settler violence in the African colonies was the German annihilation of over 80 percent of the Herero population in the colony of German South West Africa in a single year, 1904. Its context was Herero resistance to land and cattle appropriation by German settlers and their *Schutztruppe* allies. Faced with continuing armed resistance by the Herero, German opinion divided between two points of views, one championed by General Theodor Leutwein, who commanded the army in the colony, and the other by General Lothar von Trotha, who took over the military command when General Leutwein failed to put down native resistance. The difference between them illuminates the range of political choice in a colonial context.

General Trotha explained the difference in a letter:

> Now I have to ask myself how to end the war with the Hereros. The views of the Governor and also a few old Africa hands [*alte Afrikaner*] on the one hand, and my views on the other, differ completely. The first wanted to negotiate for some time already and regard the Herero nation as necessary labour material for the future development of the country. I believe that the nation as such should be annihilated, or, if this was not possible by tactical measures, have to be expelled from the country by operative means and further detailed treatment. This will be possible if the water-holes from Grootfontein to Gobabis are occupied. The constant movement of our troops will enable us to find the small groups of the nation who have moved back westwards and destroy them gradually.

Equally illuminating is General Trotha's rationale for the annihilation policy: "My intimate knowledge of many central African tribes (Bantu and others) has everywhere convinced me of the necessity that the Negro does not respect treaties but only brute force."

The plan Trotha laid out in the letter is more or less the fate he meted to the Herero on the ground. To begin with, the army exterminated as many Herero as possible. For those who fled, all escape routes except the one southeast to the Omeheke, a waterless sandveld in the Kalahari Desert, were blocked. The fleeing Herero were forcibly separated from their cattle and denied access to water holes, leaving them with but one option: to cross the desert into Botswana, in reality a march to death. This, indeed, is how the majority of the Herero perished. It was a fate of which the German general staff was well aware, as is clear from the following gleeful entry in its official publication, *Der Kampf*: "No efforts, no hardships were spared in order to deprive the enemy of his last reserves of resistance; like a half-dead animal he was hunted from water-hole to water-hole until he became a lethargic victim of the nature of his own country. The waterless Omaheke was to complete the work of the German arms: the annihilation of the Herero people."

Lest the reader be tempted to dismiss General Lothar von Trotha as an improbable character come to life from the lunatic fringe of the German officer corps, one given a free hand in a distant and unimportant colony, I hasten to point out that the general had a distinguished record in the annals of colonial conquest, indeed the most likely reason he was chosen to squash a protracted rebellion. Renowned for his brutal involvement in the suppression of the Chinese Boxer Rebellion in 1900, and a veteran of bloody suppression of African resistance to German occupation in Rwanda, Burundi, and Tanzania, General Trotha often enthused about his own methods of colonial warfare: "The exercise of violence with crass terrorism and even with gruesomeness was and is my policy. I destroy the African tribes with streams of blood and streams of money. Only following this cleansing can something new emerge, which will remain."

Opposition to Trotha's annihilation policy had come from two sources: colonial officials who looked at the Herero as potential labor, and church officials who saw them as potential converts. Eventually, the Herero who survived were gathered by the German army with the help of missionary societies and were put in concentration camps, also run by missionaries along with the German army. By 1908, inmates of these concentration camps were estimated at 15,000. Put to slave labor, overworked, hungry, and exposed to diseases such as typhoid and smallpox, more Herero men perished in these camps. Herero women, meanwhile, were turned into sex slaves. At the same time, those who survived were converted en masse to Christianity. When the camps were closed in 1908, the Herero were distributed as laborers among the settlers. Henceforth, all Herero over the age of seven were expected to carry around their necks a metal disk bearing their labor registration number.

The genocide of the Herero was the first genocide of the twentieth century. The links between it and the Holocaust go beyond the building of concentration camps and the execution of an annihilation policy and are worth exploring. It is surely of significance that when General Trotha wrote, as above, of destroying "African tribes with streams of blood," he saw this as some kind of a Social Darwinist "cleansing" after which "something new" would "emerge." It is also relevant that, when the general sought to distribute responsibility for the genocide, he accused the missions of inciting the Herero with images "of the blood-curdling Jewish history of the Old Testament." . . . It seems to me that Hannah Arendt erred when she presumed a relatively uncomplicated relationship between settlers' genocide in the colonies and the Nazi Holocaust at home: When Nazis set out to annihilate Jews, it is far more likely that they thought of themselves as natives, and Jews as settlers. Yet, there is a link that connects the genocide of the Herero and the Nazi Holocaust to the Rwandan genocide. That link is *race branding*, whereby it became possible not only to set a group apart as an enemy, but also to exterminate it with an easy conscience.

Natives' Genocide

In the annals of colonial history, the natives' genocide never became a historical reality. Yet, it always hovered on the horizon as a historical possibility. None sensed it better than Frantz Fanon, whose writings now read like a foreboding. For Fanon, the native's violence was not life denying, but life affirming: "For he knows that he is not an animal; and it is precisely when he realizes his humanity that he begins to sharpen the weapons with which he will secure its victory." What distinguished native violence from the violence of the settler, its saving grace, was that it was the violence of yesterday's victims who have turned around and decided to cast aside their victimhood and become masters of their own lives. "He of whom they have never stopped saying that the only language he understands is that of force, decides to give utterance by force." Indeed, "the argument the native chooses has been furnished by the settler, and by an ironic turning of the tables it is the native who now affirms that the colonialist understands nothing but force." What affirmed the natives' humanity for Fanon was not that they were willing to take the settler's life, but that they were willing to risk their own: "The colonized man finds his freedom in and through violence." If its outcome would be death, of settlers by natives, it would need to be understood as a derivative outcome, a result of a prior logic, the genocidal logic of colonial pacification and occupation infecting anticolonial resistance. "The settler's work is to make even dreams of liberty impossible for the native. The native's work is to imagine all possible methods for destroying the settler. . . . For the native, life can only spring up again out of the rotting corpse of the settler . . . for the colonized people, this violence, because it constitutes their only work, invests their character with positive and creative qualities. The practice of violence binds them together as a whole, since each individual forms a violent link in the great chain, a part of the great organism of violence which has surged upwards in reaction to the settler's violence in the beginning."

The great crime of colonialism went beyond expropriating the native, the name it gave to the indigenous population. *The greater crime was to politicize indigeneity in the first place*: first negatively, as a settler libel of the native; but then positively, as a native response, as a self-assertion. The dialectic of the settler and the native did not end with colonialism and political independence. To understand the logic of genocide, I argue, it is necessary to think through the political world that colonialism set into motion. This was the world of the settler and the native, a world organized around a binary preoccupation that was as compelling as it was confining. It is in this context that Tutsi, a group with a privileged relationship to power before colonialism, got constructed as a privileged *alien settler* presence, first by the great nativist revolution of 1959, and then by Hutu Power propaganda after 1990.

In its motivation and construction, I argue that the Rwandan genocide needs to be understood as a natives' genocide. It was a genocide by those who saw themselves as sons — and daughters — of the soil, and their mission as one of clearing the soil of a threatening *alien* presence. This was not an "ethnic" but a "racial" cleansing, not a violence against one who is seen as a neighbor but against one who is seen as a foreigner; not a violence that targets a transgression across a boundary into home but one that seeks to eliminate a foreign presence from home soil, literally and physically. From this point of view, we need to distinguish between racial and ethnic violence: ethnic violence can result in massacres, but not genocide. Massacres are about transgressions, excess; genocide questions the very legitimacy of a presence as alien. For the Hutu who killed, the Tutsi was a settler, not a neighbor. Rather than take these identities as a given, as a starting point of analysis, I seek to ask: When and how was Hutu made into a native identity and Tutsi into a settler identity? The analytical challenge is to understand the historical dynamic through which Hutu and Tutsi came to be synonyms for native and settler.

74

GLENN GARVIN AND EDWARD HEGSTROM

Report: Maya Indians Suffered Genocide

In 1994, the United Nations–brokered Accord of Oslo brought an end to the civil war that had wracked Guatemala for almost four decades. The Accord created a Guatemalan truth commission, the Commission for Historical Clarification, "in order to clarify with objectivity, equity and impartiality, the human rights violations and acts of violence connected with the armed confrontation that caused suffering among the Guatemalan people."[1] The commission examined 42,275 cases of human rights abuses, including the destruction of over 400 villages and more than 626 massacres. It concluded that 93 percent of the abuses were committed by the U.S.-backed military and paramilitary forces and 3 percent were committed by the rebels. (The cause of 4 percent could not be determined.) The report, issued in 1999, concluded that genocide had occurred.

Major U.S. involvement in Guatemala dates back to the early 1950s in the aftermath of the country's first free election. In 1950, Jacobo Arbenz Guzman, a reformer, won 60 percent of the vote and became president of Guatemala. His efforts to redistribute about 1 percent of the land to the poor raised fears in the Eisenhower administration of the spread of communism in the hemisphere. In 1954, the CIA organized a coup that ousted Arbenz and installed a military junta that plunged the country into thirty-six years of political turbulence. (See Map 11.3.) During that period the U.S. government maintained close relations with the junta and trained and aided its army.

This was the first time a United Nations–sponsored report reached the conclusion that events in a Latin American country constituted genocide. Using the categories of genocide suggested by Mahmood Mamdani in the previous selection, what kind of genocide was committed in Guatemala? One commentator, Andrew Reding, writing in the *Journal of Commerce*[2] declared Guatemala America's Rwanda and urged the creation of a United Nations–sponsored genocide

[1]Guatemala Memory of Silence: Report of the Commission for Historical Clarification, Conclusions and Recommendations; Prologue. See http://shr.aaas.org/guatemala/ceh/report/english/prologue.html.
[2]March 18, 1999.

Glenn Garvin and Edward Hegstrom, "Report: Maya Indians Suffered Genocide," *Miami Herald*, February 25, 1999.

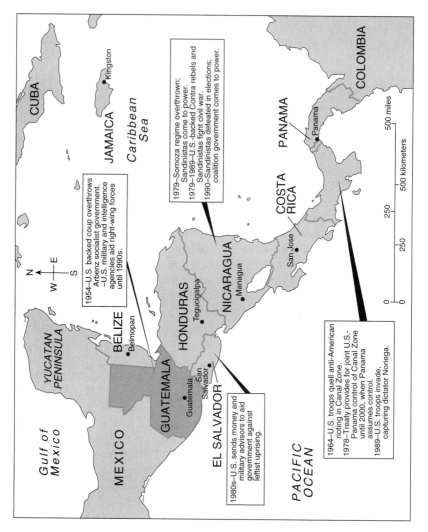

1954—U.S. backed coup overthrows
Arbenz socialist government.
—U.S. military and intelligence
agencies aid right-wing forces
until 1990s.

1979—Somoza regime overthrown;
Sandinistas come to power.
1979–1989—U.S.-backed Contra rebels and
Sandinistas fight civil war.
1990—Sandinistas defeated in elections;
coalition government comes to power.

1980s—U.S. sends money and
military advisors to aid
government against
leftist uprising.

1964—U.S. troops quell anti-American
rioting in Canal Zone.
1978—Treaty provides for joint U.S.-
Panama control of Canal Zone
until 2000, when Panama
assumes control.
1989—U.S. troops invade,
capturing dictator Noriega.

Map 11.3 U.S. Involvement in Central America.

416

tribunal, similar to that for Rwanda. What do you think of this idea? Should government officials of the United States be held to international laws?

Thinking Historically

How should one respond to charges of genocide? When the report was released, President Clinton apologized to the people of Guatemala. He said: "It is important that I state clearly that support for military forces or intelligence units which engaged in violent and widespread repression of the kind described in the report was wrong. And the United States must not repeat that mistake. We must, and we will, instead continue to support the peace and reconciliation process in Guatemala." What do you think of Clinton's characterization of these events as a "mistake"? Compare his response to that of the diplomats described in the news article. How would you describe the attitude of the reporters for the *Miami Herald*? If the actions of the United States do not appear to be rational, how were they "thinkable"? In other words, how did this happen?

GUATEMALA CITY — A Guatemalan truth commission investigating the country's vicious 36-year civil war issued a final report Thursday placing the blame for most of the 200,000 deaths on a "racist" Guatemalan government that received considerable support from the United States. Guatemala's Maya Indian population, which suffered "acts of genocide," bore the brunt of the government's repression, the report said. More than 80 percent of the victims of human rights abuses during the war were Indians, the Commission for Historical Clarification concluded.

"The massacres, scorched-earth operations, forced disappearances, and executions of Maya authorities, leaders, and spiritual guides were not only an attempt to destroy the social base of the guerrillas," the report said, "but above all, to destroy the cultural values that ensured cohesion and collective action in Maya communities."

Although the report was couched in relatively moderate language when it came to assigning blame to non-Guatemalan participants, Commission Chairman Christian Tomuschat accused the United States of being responsible for much of the bloodshed. As seething U.S. diplomats looked on, Tomuschat said the Guatemalan army carried out hundreds of massacres of civilians at a time when "the United States government and U.S. private companies exercised pressure to maintain the country's archaic and unjust socioeconomic structure."

Tomuschat said the CIA and other U.S. agencies "lent direct and indirect support to some illegal state operations." This encouraged a

Guatemalan military government that was committing genocide against the country's Indian population, he added.

Tomuschat spoke at the unveiling of the commission's 3,600-page report on human rights abuses during the civil war that ended in 1996. The report took 18 months to assemble. Hundreds of spectators — many of them former Marxist guerrillas who battled the government — burst into wild applause after Tomuschat, a German law professor, finished his attack on the United States.

A contingent of U.S. diplomats, including Ambassador Donald Planty and Mark Schneider, an assistant administrator of the Agency for International Development (USAID), stared stonily ahead during Tomuschat's speech. Afterward, a clearly furious Planty said the attack was unfair. "Everyone knows the historical context in which the conflict took place," Planty said. "But that doesn't obscure the fact that the violence was committed by Guatemalans against Guatemalans."

The surprise of Planty and other U.S. diplomats was compounded by the fact that USAID financed much of the commission's work with a donation of $1.5 million. One of the three members of the commission, bilingual education expert Otilia Lux de Coti, is a USAID employee who took a leave of absence to work on the report.

Cold War Impact Cited

The report's 100-page executive summary, while noting that Cold War policies in both the United States and Cuba "had a bearing" on the war, said the Guatemalan government used a relatively small Marxist insurgency as an excuse for the "physical annihilation" of all its political opponents in a war that claimed 200,000 lives, the vast majority of them civilians. "The inclusion of all opponents under one banner, democratic or otherwise, pacifist or guerrilla, legal or illegal, communist or noncommunist, served to justify numerous and serious crimes," the report said.

Coup Attempt Sparked War

The Guatemalan civil war began in November 1960, when leftist officers attempted a coup against the country's right-wing military government. When they failed, many of the officers went into the countryside to form guerrilla groups. Many political analysts, however, say the roots of the war lay in the 1950s, when a coup supported by the CIA toppled the Marxist government of President Jacobo Arbenz and put in place the first of a series of military governments.

Tomuschat's searing comments on the United States clearly delighted many Guatemalan human rights activists. "Today, Tomuschat spoke the truth about Guatemala as it has never been spoken before," said Frank La Rue, who runs a human rights legal foundation.

Others, however, said Guatemalans might be trying to let themselves off the hook, pretending they were merely pawns in the Cold War rather than enthusiastic participants. "Blaming the U.S. is a national pastime here," said David Holiday, an American political consultant based in Guatemala. "That unjustly exonerates the Guatemala players."

Offenders Not Named

The report does not include names of individual human rights offenders. It does single out a handful of senior officials for blame — like former military strongman Efrain Rios Montt — who already have been excoriated in numerous other human rights reports.

The last time a highly publicized human rights report was unveiled in Guatemala, it was followed 48 hours later by the murder of its principal author. Bishop Juan Gerardi was beaten to death two days after the Roman Catholic Church's human rights office issued a report similar to the one released Thursday.

Gerardi's killing remains unsolved and it has not been determined that it was related to the bishop's human rights work. Nonetheless, all three members of the Commission for Historical Clarification are reportedly leaving Guatemala for lengthy stays overseas.

REFLECTIONS

Short of war, the world community has adopted three strategies to counter genocide and mass murder. The first is trial of war criminals. At the conclusion of World War II, war-crime trials of Nazis and Japanese were conducted. The terms *war crimes* and *war criminals* are unfortunate misnomers because they suggest a criminalization of military activities. In fact, the crimes recounted in this chapter were not crimes of the battlefield but, rather, massive crimes against civilian populations.

Developing and refining international laws respecting human rights is the second strategy. The "Declaration of Human Rights" passed by the United Nations, itself a shaper and guardian of international law, offers a recognized standard and continuing process for defining and preventing genocide, mass murder, and "crimes against humanity."

The third strategy, one in which all of us can participate, is the dissemination of information and concerted efforts toward understanding.

To promote understanding, archives must be opened, and laws such as the Freedom of Information Act must be used aggressively. We must develop sensitivity to the plight of victims, knowledge of the victimizers' motives, and understanding about the ways that the horrendous can happen.

In recent years "truth and reconciliation" commissions have been formed in South Africa and El Salvador to enable those countries to get beyond years of government-sponsored terrorism. In cases like these, when such governments have relinquished power but their personnel are either too powerful or too numerous to be brought to justice, the new democratic governments and their truth and reconciliation commissions have asked for a complete and remorseful accounting of past crimes. Some say these commissions have been able to accept truth instead of revenge; others find it to be truth instead of justice. The cases of Yugoslavia and Rwanda, which have followed the route of international trials rather than truth and justice commissions, continue in the International Court of Justice at the Hague and the International Criminal Tribunal for Rwanda in Tanzania as this is written. The case of Guatemala has gone no further than the United Nations report issued in 1999. It is the U.S. position that international tribunals are not appropriate for its citizens or officials. Do you think U.S. citizens should be exempt from international law or immune from prosecution in international courts? If so, how would you make that case to citizens of other countries? If international criminal courts are not appropriate, should the United States form a truth and reconciliation commission for events in Guatemala? Truth can be an amazing restorative, especially when it is linked with genuine contrition. The price of amnesty can hardly be less. Forgiveness may be much more. Which, if any, of the crimes recalled in this chapter would you be willing to forgive? What should be necessary for acquittal or amnesty? How do we prevent such things from occurring again and again?

Religion and Politics

*Israel, Palestine, and the West,
1896 to the Present*

HISTORICAL CONTEXT

Many of the political conflicts of the mid- to late twentieth century turned on, or were expressed in, the language of religion: Catholics and Protestants in Northern Ireland; Hindus and Muslims in India, Pakistan, and the disputed areas of Kashmir; Jews and Muslims in Palestine and Israel. None of these conflicts were new to the twentieth century but were continuations of conflicts hundreds or thousands of years old. Yet the post–World War II end of European colonialism unleashed sectarian religious forces that were dormant or suppressed for centuries.

The great colonial empires were not above favoring one religion or ethnic group over another. The British invented their "martial races"[1] to serve as elite enforcers; the Austro-Hungarian Empire favored Austrians and Hungarians over Slavs, Serbs, and almost everyone else. But ethnic or religious sectarianism could be the death of empires. In the case of the Austro-Hungarian Empire, it was. Consequently most great empires attempted to stress more universal identities: the Islamic brotherhood of the Ottomans or the Socialist unity of the Soviets. The demise of the great empires left kindling resentments that could be blown into full flame.

This chapter will explore one of these post–World War II political conflicts fueled by religious nationalism. The conflict between Israel and Palestine may not be representative of other struggles, like those between Catholics and Protestants, or Muslims and Hindus. In some ways the creation of a Jewish homeland in the Arab Middle East was a unique event. But nothing under the sun is entirely new, and no two cases are the same. We will study the role of religion and politics in a particular place

---

[1]Sikhs in India, Nepali Gurkhas, Hausas in West Africa, and the Kamba in East Africa were thought to be naturally warlike and were selected for police or army overrepresentation.

421

at a particular time, but it is a place that has appeared at the very center of world maps for millennia and its conflicts still shake our world.

THINKING HISTORICALLY
Making Use of the Unexpected

The most lasting learning comes from making our own meanings. We do that to a certain extent when we read something and put it in our own words. But most of what we read washes over us. We remember it or not, but generally we do not make our own meaning out of information and ideas that are expected or unexceptional.

Sometimes, however, we come across details, ideas, or statements that surprise us. They stop us in our tracks because they are unexpected: They seem wrong, unbelievable, or senseless. The most common response to the unexpected may be to ignore it and move on, but by doing so we may miss an opportunity to learn something new. The unexpected can provide an entry point into a document, period, culture, or movement that opens up a whole new realm of understanding. In this chapter, you will be encouraged to reflect on the unexpected so that you might use it as an opportunity to create new meaning and deepen your understanding.

$$\boxed{75}$$

THEODOR HERZL
From The Jewish State

Born and raised in an assimilated Hungarian family, Theodor Herzl* (1860–1904) first experienced anti-Semitism as a student at the University of Vienna, but he was most profoundly shaken by the Dreyfus Affair in France. In 1894, Captain Alfred Dreyfus[†], a Jewish officer in the French army, was falsely convicted of treason on a wave of public

*HAYR tzuhl
[†]DRY fuhs

Theodor Herzl, *The Jewish State,* trans. Sylvie D'Avigdor (American Zionist Emergency Council, 1946), selections from Chapters 2 and 5. Originally published in German in 1896. Also available online at http://www.jewishvirtuallibrary.org/jsource/Zionism/herzl2e.html.

hostility toward Jews. Herzl, a reporter in Paris at the time, was shocked to hear French mobs shouting "Death to the Jews." The events, he later wrote, radically transformed him. In 1896 he published *The Jewish State*. What reasons did he give for forming a Jewish state? How and where did he intend to create this Jewish state? How "religious" was this state to be? What did he see as the potential problems of a Jewish state and how did he propose to solve those problems?

Thinking Historically

Different details may surprise different readers. The more we know, perhaps the smaller or less obvious the surprise. Nevertheless, even the least knowledgeable student of modern history will likely be surprised by the appearance in this text of the word "Argentine." Why is that a surprise? What does its presence in the text tell you about Herzl or early Zionism? (Uganda, too, was an early candidate for a Jewish homeland.)

Details like this seem unlikely from the perspective of the present. Our contemporary association of Israel as "the home of the Jews" is so strong, it is difficult to imagine the possibility of a different historical outcome. And perhaps there was not. But clearly, the possibilities of the early twentieth century were more fluid than those of today. What other unexpected details do you see in the document? How might they lead to new ways of thinking about the subject?

Chapter 2

The Jewish Question

No one can deny the gravity of the situation of the Jews. Wherever they live in perceptible numbers, they are more or less persecuted. Their equality before the law, granted by statute, has become practically a dead letter. They are debarred from filling even moderately high positions, either in the army, or in any public or private capacity. And attempts are made to thrust them out of business also: "Don't buy from Jews!"

Attacks in Parliaments, in assemblies, in the press, in the pulpit, in the street, on journeys — for example, their exclusion from certain hotels — even in places of recreation, become daily more numerous. The forms of persecution vary according to the countries and social circles in which they occur. In Russia, imposts are levied on Jewish villages; in Rumania, a few persons are put to death; in Germany, they get a good beating occasionally; in Austria, Anti-Semites exercise terrorism over all public life; in Algeria, there are traveling agitators; in Paris, the Jews are shut out of the so-called best social circles and excluded from clubs. Shades of anti-Jewish feeling are innumerable. But this is not to be an attempt to make out a doleful category of Jewish hardships.

I do not intend to arouse sympathetic emotions on our behalf. That would be a foolish, futile, and undignified proceeding. I shall content myself with putting the following questions to the Jews: Is it not true that, in countries where we live in perceptible numbers, the position of Jewish lawyers, doctors, technicians, teachers, and employees of all descriptions becomes daily more intolerable? Is it not true, that the Jewish middle classes are seriously threatened? Is it not true, that the passions of the mob are incited against our wealthy people? Is it not true, that our poor endure greater sufferings than any other proletariat? I think that this external pressure makes itself felt everywhere. In our economically upper classes it causes discomfort, in our middle classes continual and grave anxieties, in our lower classes absolute despair.

Everything tends, in fact, to one and the same conclusion, which is clearly enunciated in that classic Berlin phrase: "Juden Raus" (Out with the Jews!).

I shall now put the Question in the briefest possible form: Are we to "get out" now and where to? . . .

The Plan

The whole plan is in its essence perfectly simple, as it must necessarily be if it is to come within the comprehension of all.

Let the sovereignty be granted us over a portion of the globe large enough to satisfy the rightful requirements of a nation; the rest we shall manage for ourselves.

The creation of a new State is neither ridiculous nor impossible. We have in our day witnessed the process in connection with nations which were not largely members of the middle class, but poorer, less educated, and consequently weaker than ourselves. The Governments of all countries scourged by Anti-Semitism will be keenly interested in assisting us to obtain the sovereignty we want.

The plan, simple in design, but complicated in execution, will be carried out by two agencies: The Society of Jews and the Jewish Company.

The Society of Jews will do the preparatory work in the domains of science and politics, which the Jewish Company will afterwards apply practically.

The Jewish Company will be the liquidating agent of the business interests of departing Jews, and will organize commerce and trade in the new country.

We must not imagine the departure of the Jews to be a sudden one. It will be gradual, continuous, and will cover many decades. The poorest will go first to cultivate the soil. In accordance with a preconceived plan, they will construct roads, bridges, railways, and telegraph installations; regulate rivers; and build their own dwellings; their labor will create trade, trade will create markets, and markets will attract new settlers, for every man will go voluntarily, at his own expense and his own risk. The labor expended on the land will enhance its value, and the Jews will soon perceive that a new and permanent sphere of operation is opening here for that spirit of enterprise which has heretofore met only with hatred and obloquy. . . .

The emigrants standing lowest in the economic scale will be slowly followed by those of a higher grade. Those who at this moment are living in despair will go first. They will be led by the mediocre intellects which we produce so superabundantly and which are persecuted everywhere.

This pamphlet will open a general discussion on the Jewish Question, but that does not mean that there will be any voting on it. Such a result would ruin the cause from the outset, and dissidents must remember that allegiance or opposition is entirely voluntary. He who will not come with us should remain behind.

Let all who are willing to join us, fall in behind our banner and fight for our cause with voice and pen and deed.

Those Jews who agree with our idea of a State will attach themselves to the Society, which will thereby be authorized to confer and treat with Governments in the name of our people. The Society will thus be acknowledged in its relations with Governments as a State-creating power. This acknowledgment will practically create the State.

Should the Powers declare themselves willing to admit our sovereignty over a neutral piece of land, then the Society will enter into negotiations for the possession of this land. Here two territories come under consideration, Palestine and Argentine. In both countries important experiments in colonization have been made, though on the mistaken principle of a gradual infiltration of Jews. An infiltration is bound to end badly. It continues till the inevitable moment when the native population feels itself threatened, and forces the Government to stop a further influx of Jews. Immigration is consequently futile unless we have the sovereign right to continue such immigration.

The Society of Jews will treat with the present masters of the land, putting itself under the protectorate of the European Powers, if they prove friendly to the plan. We could offer the present possessors of the land enormous advantages, assume part of the public debt, build new roads for traffic, which our presence in the country would render necessary, and do many other things. The creation of our State would be beneficial to adjacent countries, because the cultivation of a strip of land increases the value of its surrounding districts in innumerable ways.

Palestine or Argentine?

Shall we choose Palestine or Argentine? We shall take what is given us, and what is selected by Jewish public opinion. The Society will determine both these points.

Argentine is one of the most fertile countries in the world, extends over a vast area, has a sparse population and a mild climate. The Argentine Republic would derive considerable profit from the cession of a portion of its territory to us. The present infiltration of Jews has certainly produced some discontent, and it would be necessary to enlighten the Republic on the intrinsic difference of our new movement.

Palestine is our ever-memorable historic home. The very name of Palestine would attract our people with a force of marvelous potency. If His Majesty the Sultan were to give us Palestine, we could in return undertake to regulate the whole finances of Turkey. We should there form a portion of a rampart of Europe against Asia, an outpost of civilization as opposed to barbarism. We should as a neutral State remain in contact with all Europe, which would have to guarantee our existence. The sanctuaries of Christendom would be safeguarded by assigning to them an extra-territorial status such as is well-known to the law of nations. We should form a guard of honor about these sanctuaries, answering for the fulfillment of this duty with our existence. This guard of honor would be the great symbol of the solution of the Jewish question after eighteen centuries of Jewish suffering.

Chapter 5

Language

It might be suggested that our want of a common current language would present difficulties. We cannot converse with one another in Hebrew. Who amongst us has a sufficient acquaintance with Hebrew to ask for a railway ticket in that language! Such a thing cannot be done. Yet the difficulty is very easily circumvented. Every man can preserve the language in which his thoughts are at home. Switzerland affords a conclusive proof of the possibility of a federation of tongues. We shall remain in the new country what we now are here, and we shall never cease to cherish with sadness the memory of the native land out of which we have been driven.

We shall give up using those miserable stunted jargons, those Ghetto languages which we still employ, for these were the stealthy tongues of prisoners. Our national teachers will give due attention to this matter; and the language which proves itself to be of greatest utility for general intercourse will be adopted without compulsion as our national tongue. Our community of race is peculiar and unique, for we are bound together only by the faith of our fathers.

Theocracy

Shall we end by having a theocracy? No, indeed. Faith unites us, knowledge gives us freedom. We shall therefore prevent any theocratic tendencies from coming to the fore on the part of our priesthood. We shall keep our priests within the confines of their temples in the same way as we shall keep our professional army within the confines of their barracks. Army and priesthood shall receive honors high as their valuable functions deserve. But they must not interfere in the administration of the State which confers distinction upon them, else they will conjure up difficulties without and within.

Every man will be as free and undisturbed in his faith or his disbelief as he is in his nationality. And if it should occur that men of other creeds and different nationalities come to live amongst us, we should accord them honorable protection and equality before the law. We have learnt toleration in Europe. This is not sarcastically said; for the Anti-Semitism of today could only in a very few places be taken for old religious intolerance. It is for the most part a movement among civilized nations by which they try to chase away the spectres of their own past. . . .

The Army

The Jewish State is conceived as a neutral one. It will therefore require only a professional army, equipped, of course, with every requisite of modern warfare, to preserve order internally and externally.

The Flag

We have no flag, and we need one. If we desire to lead many men, we must raise a symbol above their heads.

I would suggest a white flag, with seven golden stars. The white field symbolizes our pure new life; the stars are the seven golden hours of our working-day. For we shall march into the Promised Land carrying the badge of honor.

DAVID FROMKIN

On the Balfour Declaration

In a brief note, dated November 2, 1917, British Foreign Secretary Lord Balfour declared that Britain was in favor of the creation of a "national home" for Jews in Palestine. The note, delivered to Lord Rothschild, a leading British Zionist, marked a crucial turning point in British policy. It suddenly turned Zionism from a quixotic dream to a strategic movement. Yet, as the following selection from a history of the Middle East reveals, the Balfour Declaration was issued despite, considerable domestic opposition and numerous British misconceptions about the needs and beliefs of its allies and enemies. Recall that the Great War of 1914–1918 pitted England, France, and Russia against Germany, Austria, and the Ottoman Empire. Palestine was part of the Ottoman Empire until taken from Turkey by British troops and Arab allies shortly after the Declaration was issued. The Arabs expected to govern the land themselves. Neither they nor the French or Russians were consulted or advised of Balfour's plans.

According to Fromkin's history, what were the reasons for the British and American support of a Jewish homeland in Palestine? Who was in favor of a creation of a Jewish homeland in Palestine, and who was opposed? What did the British government expect to gain? Were they successful?

Thinking Historically

Here you have the actual document and a modern historian's account of the political considerations that finally led to passage of the Balfour Declaration. What elements in either the Declaration or Fromkin's history surprise you? What do you make of such surprises? How, if at all, are they related to the surprises in the other selections?

The Prime Minister had always planned to carry through a Zionist program; and while he did not express an interest in declaring Britain's intentions in advance, neither did he place any obstacle in the way of his government's doing so once his colleagues thought it useful.

Yet the proposal that Balfour should issue his pro-Zionist declaration suddenly encountered opposition that brought it to a halt. The op-

David Fromkin, *A Peace to End All Peace* (New York: Avon Books, 1989), 294–330.

position came from leading figures in the British Jewish community. Edwin Montagu, Secretary of State for India, led the opposition group within the Cabinet. He, along with his cousin, Herbert Samuel, and Rufus Isaacs (Lord Reading) had broken new ground for their co-religionists: they had been the first Jews to sit in a British Cabinet.[1] The second son of a successful financier who had been ennobled, Montagu saw Zionism as a threat to the position in British society that he and his family had so recently, and with so much exertion, attained. Judaism, he argued, was a religion, not a nationality, and to say otherwise was to say that he was less than 100 percent British.

Montagu was regarded as by far the most capable of the younger men in the Liberal ranks, and it was deemed a political masterstroke for the Prime Minister to have taken him and Churchill away from Asquith. Yet a typical political comment at the time (from Lord Derby, the War Minister) was, "The appointment of Montagu, a Jew, to the India Office has made, as far as I can judge, an uneasy feeling both in India and here"; though Derby added that "I, personally, have a very high opinion of his capability and I expect he will do well." It bothered Montagu that, despite his lack of religious faith, he could not avoid being categorized as a Jew. He was the millionaire son of an English lord, but was driven to lament that "I have been striving all my life to escape from the Ghetto."

The evidence suggested that in his non-Zionism, Montagu was speaking for a majority of Jews. As of 1913, the last date for which there were figures, only about one percent of the world's Jews had signified their adherence to Zionism. British Intelligence reports indicated a surge of Zionist feeling during the war in the Pale of Russia, but there were no figures either to substantiate or to quantify it. In Britain, the Conjoint Committee, which represented British Jewry in all matters affecting Jews abroad, had been against Zionism from the start and remained so.

Montagu's opposition brought all matters to a halt. In disgust, Graham reported that the proposed declaration was "hung up" by Montagu, "who represents a certain section of the rich Jews and who seems to fear that he and his like will be expelled from England and asked to cultivate farms in Palestine."

The sub-Cabinet officials who were pushing for a pro-Zionist commitment attempted to allay such fears. Amery, who was helping Milner redraft the proposed Declaration, explained the concept behind it to a Cabinet member as not really being addressed to British subjects of the Jewish faith, but to Jews who resided in countries that denied them real citizenship. "Apart from those Jews who have become citizens of this

---

[1] Disraeli, of course, though of Jewish ancestry, was baptized a Christian.

or any other country in the fullest sense, there is also a large body, more particularly of the Jews in Poland and Russia . . . who are still in a very real sense a separate nation. . . ." Denied the right to become Russians, they would be offered a chance to rebuild their own homeland in Palestine.

Montagu, however, took little interest in the position of Jews in other countries. It was the position of Jews in British society that concerned him; feeling threatened, he fought back with a ferocity that brought the Cabinet's deliberations on the matter to a standstill.

Montagu was aided by Lord Curzon, who argued that Palestine was too meagre in resources to accommodate the Zionist dream. More important, he was aided by Andrew Bonar Law — leader of the dominant party in the Coalition government and the Prime Minister's powerful political partner — who urged delay. Bonar Law argued that the time was not yet ripe for a consideration of the Zionist issue.

Montagu was also aided by the United States, which, until mid-October 1917, cautiously counselled delay. President Wilson was sympathetic to Zionism, but suspicious of British motives; he favored a Jewish Palestine but was less enthusiastic about a British Palestine. As the British Cabinet considered issuing the Balfour Declaration, it solicited the advice, and by implication the support, of President Wilson. The proposed Declaration was described by the Cabinet to the American government as an expression of sympathy for Zionist aspirations, as though it were motivated solely by concern for the plight of persecuted Jews. Wilson's foreign policy adviser, Colonel House, translated this as follows: "The English naturally want the road to Egypt and India blocked, and Lloyd George is not above using us to further this plan."

This was a fair interpretation of the views of the Prime Minister and of the Milner circle which advised him. According to Chaim Weizmann, Philip Kerr (the former Milner aide who served as Lloyd George's secretary) "saw in a Jewish Palestine a bridge between Africa, Asia, and Europe on the road to India." It was not, however, a fair interpretation of the views of the Foreign Office, which had been won over by the argument that a pro-Zionist declaration would prove a crucial weapon against Germany in the war and afterward. The Foreign Office believed that the Jewish communities in America and, above all, Russia, wielded great power. The British ambassador in Petrograd, well aware that Jews were a weak and persecuted minority in imperial Russia and of no political consequence, reported that Zionists could not affect the outcome of the struggle for power in Russia. His home government persisted in believing, however, that the Jewish community in Russia could keep the government that ruled them in the Allied camp. As the crisis in Russia deepened, the Foreign Office was seized by a sense of urgency in seeking Jewish support.

IV

Fear begets fear. In Germany the press was aroused by rumors of what the British Foreign Office intended to do. In June 1917 Sir Ronald Graham received from Chaim Weizmann an issue of a Berlin newspaper known for its close relationship to the government, reporting that the British were flirting with the idea of endorsing Zionism in order to acquire the Palestinian land bridge on the road from Egypt to India, and proposing that Germany forestall the maneuver by endorsing Zionism first. (Though the British did not know it, the German government took little interest in adopting a pro-Zionist stance; it was the German press that took an interest in it.)

That summer Graham communicated his fears to Balfour. In his minute, Graham wrote that he had heard there was to be another postponement which he believed would "jeopardise the whole Jewish situation." This endangered the position in Russia where, he asserted, the Jews were all anti-Ally and, to a lesser extent, it would antagonize public opinion in the United States. Warning that Britain must not "throw the Zionists into the arms of the Germans," he argued that "We might at any moment be confronted by a German move on the Zionist question and it must be remembered that Zionism was originally if not a German Jewish at any rate an Austrian Jewish idea."

Graham attached to his minute a list of dates showing how extensive the government's delays had been in dealing with the Zionist matter. In October, Balfour forwarded the minute to the Prime Minister, along with the list of dates which he said showed that the Zionists had reasonable cause to complain, to which he added his own recommendation that the question be taken up by the Cabinet as soon as possible.

On 26 October 1917, *The Times* published a leading article attacking the continuing delay. Stating that it was no secret that British and Allied governments had been considering a statement about Palestine, *The Times* argued that the time had come to make one.

> Do our statesmen fail to see how valuable to the Allied cause would be the hearty sympathy of the Jews throughout the world which an unequivocal declaration of British policy might win? Germany has been quick to perceive the danger to her schemes and to her propaganda that would be involved in the association of the Allies with Jewish national hopes, and she has not been idle in attempting to forestall us.

On 31 October 1917 the Cabinet overrode the opposition of Montagu and Curzon and authorized the Foreign Secretary to issue a much-diluted version of the assurance of support that Weizmann had requested. An ebullient Sykes rushed over with the news, "Dr. Weizmann, it's a boy"; but the Zionist leader was unhappy that the original language had been so watered down.

Addressed to the most illustrious name in British Jewry, the Foreign Secretary's letter of 2 November 1917 stated:

Dear Lord Rothschild,
I have much pleasure in conveying to you, on behalf of His Majesty's Government, the following declaration of sympathy with Jewish Zionist aspirations which has been submitted to, and approved by, the Cabinet: "His Majesty's Government view with favour the establishment in Palestine of a national home for the Jewish people, and will use their best endeavours to facilitate the achievement of this object, it being clearly understood that nothing shall be done which may prejudice the civil and religious rights of existing non-Jewish communities in Palestine, or the rights and political status enjoyed by Jews in any other country." I should be grateful if you would bring this declaration to the knowledge of the Zionist Federation.

Britain's leaders anticipated no adverse reaction from their Arab allies; they had seen France as their only problem in this connection, and that had been resolved. The Prime Minister later wrote of the Arab leaders that "Palestine did not seem to give them much anxiety." He pointed out that his government had informed King Hussein and Prince Feisal of its plans to re-create a Jewish homeland in the Holy Land. He caustically added that "We could not get in touch with the Palestinian Arabs as they were fighting against us."

The public announcement of the Balfour Declaration was delayed until the following Friday, the publication date of the weekly *Jewish Chronicle*. By then the news was overshadowed by reports from Petrograd that Lenin and Trotsky had seized power. The Foreign Office had hoped the Balfour Declaration would help to swing Russian Jewish support to the Allied side and against Bolshevism. This hope remained alive until the Bolsheviks decisively won the Russian Civil War in the early 1920s. In November of 1917 the battle against Bolshevism in Russia had just begun, and those Britons who supported the Balfour Declaration, because they mistakenly believed Russian Jews were powerful and could be valuable allies, were driven to support it all the more by the dramatic news from Petrograd.

It was not until 9 November that *The Times* was able to report the announcement of the Balfour Declaration, and not until 3 December that it published comments approving it. The comments followed upon a celebration at the London Opera House on 2 December organized by the British Zionist Federation. In addition to the Zionist leaders, speakers included Lord Robert Cecil, Sir Mark Sykes, and William Ormsby-Gore, as well as a Syrian Christian, an Arab nationalist, and spokesmen for Armenia. The theme of the meeting, eloquently pursued by many of the speakers, was the need for Jews, Arabs, and Armenians to help one another and to move forward in harmony. The opinion of *The Times* was that "The presence and the words of influential representatives of the Arab and Armenian peoples, and their assurances of agreement and cooperation with the Jews, would alone have sufficed to make the meeting memorable."

Of the meeting, *The Times* wrote that "its outstanding features were the Old Testament spirit which pervaded it and the feeling that, in the somewhat incongruous setting of a London theatre, the approaching fulfillment of ancient prophecy was being celebrated with faith and fervour." It was appropriate that it should be so: Biblical prophecy was the first and most enduring of the many motives that led Britons to want to restore the Jews to Zion.

The Prime Minister planned to foster a Jewish home in Palestine, in any event, and later wrote that the peace treaty would have provided that Palestine should be a homeland for the Jews "even had there been no previous pledge or promise." The importance of the Balfour Declaration, he wrote, was its contribution to the war effort. He claimed that Russian Jews had given invaluable support to the war against Germany because of it. The grateful Zionist leaders had promised to work toward an Allied victory — and had done so. Writing two decades later, as the British government was about to abandon the Balfour Declaration, he said that the Zionists "kept their word in the letter and the spirit, and the only question that remains now is whether we mean to honour ours."

The Prime Minister underestimated the effect of the Balfour Declaration on the eventual peace settlement. Its character as a public document — issued with the approval of the United States and France and after consultation with Italy and the Vatican, and greeted with approval by the public and the press throughout the western world — made it a commitment that was difficult to ignore when the peace settlement was being negotiated. It took on a life and momentum of its own.

V

The Declaration also played a role in the development of the Zionist movement in the American Jewish community. American Zionism had been a tiny movement when the war began. Of the roughly three million Jews who then lived in the United States, only 12,000 belonged to the often ephemeral groups loosely bound together in the amateurishly led Zionist Federation. The movement's treasury contained 15,000 dollars; its annual budget never exceeded 5,200 dollars. The largest single donation the Federation ever received prior to 1914 was 200 dollars. In New York the movement had only 500 members.

Louis D. Brandeis, an outstanding Boston lawyer not previously identified with specifically Jewish causes, had become a Zionist in 1912 and took over leadership of the movement in 1914. As the intellectual giant of the Progressive movement in American politics, he was believed to exert great influence over President Wilson. Brandeis was perhaps the first Jew to play an important part in American politics since the Civil War. Only one Jew had ever been a member of a president's cabinet,[2] and Brandeis himself was to become the first Jewish member of the U.S. Supreme Court.

The great waves of Jewish immigration into the United States were recent, and most immigrants were anxious to learn English, to shed their foreign accents and ways, and to become American. American-born Jews, too, wanted to distance themselves from any foreign taint and feared that attachment to Zionism on their part might make them seem less than wholehearted in their loyalty to the United States.

It was this issue, above all, that Brandeis set out to address. As he saw it, American Jews lacked something important that other Americans possessed: a national past. Others could point to an ancestral homeland and take pride in it and in themselves. Brandeis especially admired Irish-Americans in this respect and for manifesting their opposition to continued British rule in Ireland.

Arguing that this kind of political concern and involvement is entirely consistent with American patriotism, and indeed enhances it, he proclaimed that "Every Irish-American who contributed towards advancing home rule was a better man and a better American for the sacrifice he made. Every American Jew who aids in advancing the Jewish settlement in Palestine . . . will likewise be a better man and a better American for doing so."

The ethical idealism of Brandeis made a powerful impression on Arthur Balfour when the British Foreign Secretary visited the United States in 1917 and discussed the future of Palestine. In turn, the Balfour Declaration vindicated the arguments that Brandeis had used in his appeals to the American Jewish community. It showed that Zionism was in harmony with patriotism in wartime because a Jewish Palestine was an Allied war goal. Soon afterward it also became an officially supported American goal. On the occasion of the Jewish New Year in September 1918, President Wilson endorsed the principles of the Balfour Declaration in a letter of holiday greetings to the American Jewish community.

Whether because of the Balfour Declaration or because of Brandeis's effective and professional leadership, support for Zionism within the Jewish community grew dramatically. In 1919 membership of the Zionist Federation grew to more than 175,000, though Zionist supporters remained a minority group within American Jewry and still en-

---

[2]Oscar Straus, Secretary of Commerce and Labor from 1906 to 1909.

countered fierce opposition from the richer and more established Jews — opposition that was not really overcome until the 1940s. But Brandeis had made American Zionism into a substantial organization along the lines pioneered by Irish-Americans who supported independence for Ireland; and the Balfour Declaration had helped him to do so — even though the Foreign Office had issued the declaration in part because they supposed such a force was already in existence and needed to be appeased.

The Zionist and Arab Cases to the Anglo-American Committee of Inquiry

After World War I, the victorious allies transferred control of Palestine from defeated Turkey to Britain. The new League of Nations sanctioned the mandate system as a preparatory stage to eventual independence. Jewish immigration to Palestine continued, but in response to Arab rebellions from 1936 to 1939, Britain effectively rescinded the Balfour Declaration and ended Jewish immigration in 1939. In 1942, in the midst of World War II, leading figures in the Zionist movement gathered at the Biltmore Hotel in New York City. Their "Biltmore Program" demanded renewed immigration, a British return to the policy of the Balfour Declaration, and the establishment of Palestine not only as "a home" for Jews, but as a Jewish state.

In the immediate aftermath of the Second World War, in November 1945, the new United Nations established the Anglo-American Committee of Inquiry to find a solution. The committee took testimony from Jews and Arabs, in Europe, America, Palestine, and the Middle East. In the following selections the committee's report, published in May 1946, summarized what it called "The Jewish Attitude" and "The Arab Attitude" towards the British Mandate of Palestine. What were the arguments of both sides in 1946? Were these two sides reconcilable?

Reports of the Anglo-American Committee of Inquiry, Confidential Files, Re, Palestine, 1944–1946, Chapter 5, "The Jewish Attitude," and Chapter 6, "The Arab Attitude." Available online at http://www.mideastweb.org/angloamerican.htm.

The report purports to present the two sides to the Palestine debate in an evenhanded way. Clearly, the committee interviewed many people, official and otherwise. Yet, the debate is filtered through the committee's lens. Even the terms *Jewish* and *Arab* focus the issue in a particular way. What do these terms capture, and what do they miss? How balanced does the report seem? How can you tell? Do you see any signs that the committee favors a particular political outcome? The Committee recommended the immediate acceptance of 100,000 Jewish refugees and the development of a binational state (including Jews and Arabs) under United Nations auspices. (See Map 12.1.) Which groups would have accepted, which opposed, a binational state?

Thinking Historically

It is difficult, if not impossible, to view this debate apart from the knowledge of what later occurred. This report was issued only two years before Israel declared, fought for, and won its independence. Yet one is struck by the lack of unanimity on this issue among the Jews of Palestine as well as the West. Why did some Jews object to Zionism? Are there other arguments from either side that surprise you? Are there any arguments for or against a Jewish state in Palestine that you would expect to find here, but do not? If so, how do you account for the absence of these arguments?

The Jewish Attitude

1. The Committee heard the Jewish case, presented at full length and with voluminous written evidence, in three series of public hearings — in Washington by the American Zionists, in London by the British Zionists, and finally and most massively by the Jewish Agency in Jerusalem. The basic policy advocated was always the same, the so-called Biltmore Program of 1942, with the additional demand that 100,000 certificates for immigration into Palestine should be issued immediately to relieve the distress in Europe. This policy can be summed up in three points: (1) that the Mandatory should hand over control of immigration to the Jewish Agency; (2) that it should abolish restrictions on the sale of land; and (3) that it should proclaim as its ultimate aim the establishment of a Jewish State as soon as a Jewish majority has been achieved. It should be noted that the demand for a Jewish State goes beyond the obligations of either the Balfour Declaration or the Mandate, and was expressly disowned by the Chairman of the Jewish Agency as late as 1932.

2. In all the hearings, although evidence was given by those sections of the Zionist movement which are critical of the Biltmore Program, most

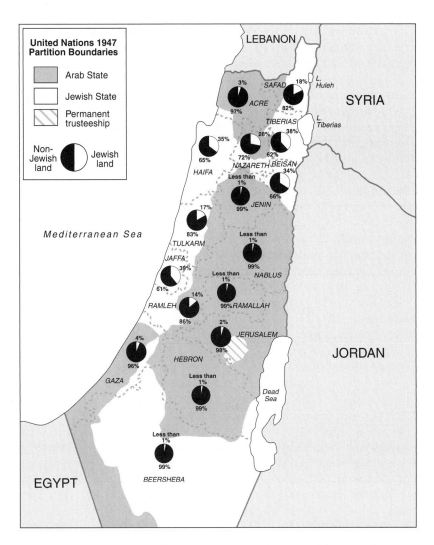

Map 12.1 The 1947 United Nations Partition Plan as a Reflection of Patterns of Land Ownership in Palestine by Subdistrict.

of the witnesses took the official Zionist line. The Committee also heard the Jewish opponents of Zionism: first, the small groups in America and Britain who advocate assimilation as an alternative to Jewish nationalism; second, Agudath Israel, an organization of orthodox Jews which supports unrestricted Jewish immigration into Palestine while objecting to the secular tendencies of Zionism; and third, representatives of important sections of Middle Eastern Jewry, many of whom fear that their friendly relations with the Arabs are being endangered by political Zionism.

3. As the result of the public hearings and of many private conversations, we came to the conclusion that the Biltmore Program has the support of the overwhelming majority of Zionists. Though many Jews have doubts about the wisdom of formulating these ultimate demands, the program has undoubtedly won the support of the Zionist movement as a whole, chiefly because it expresses the policy of Palestinian Jewry which now plays a leading role in the Jewish-Agency.

Whether this almost universal support for the demand for a Jewish State is based on full knowledge of the implications of the policy and of the risks involved in carrying it out is, of course, quite another matter.

4. The position in Palestine itself is somewhat different. Here, where the issue is not the achievement of a remote idea, but is regarded as a matter of life and death for the Jewish nation, the position is naturally more complex. Palestinian Jewry is riddled with party differences. The number of political newspapers and periodicals bears witness to the variety and vitality of this political life, and, apart from pressure exerted on Jews considered to be disloyal to the National Home, we found little evidence to support the rumors that it was dangerous to advocate minority views. Of the major political parties, Mapai (the Labor Party) is far the biggest and largely determines the official line. Opposed to the Agency's policy are two main groups. On the one side stand two small but important parties: the Conservative Aliyah Hadashah (New Settlers), drawn chiefly from colonists of German and western European extraction, and Hashomer Hatzair, a socialist party which, while demanding the right of unrestricted immigration and land settlement, challenges the concept of the Jewish State and particularly emphasizes the need for cooperation with the Arabs. Hashomer Hatzair, though it did not appear before us, published shortly before we left Jerusalem a striking pamphlet in support of bi-nationalism. Very close to Hashomer Hatzair, but without its socialist ideology, stands Dr. Magnes and his small Thud group, whose importance is far greater than its numbers. Taken altogether, these Palestinian critics of the Biltmore Program certainly do not exceed at the moment one quarter of the Jewish population in Palestine. But they represent a constructive minority.

5. On the other side stands the Revisionist Party, numbering some one percent of the Jewish community, and beyond it the various more extreme groups, which call for active resistance to the White Paper[1] and participate in and openly support the present terrorist campaign. This wing of Palestinian Jewry derives its inspiration and its methods from the revolutionary traditions of Poland and eastern Europe. Many of these extremists are boys and girls under twenty, of good education, filled with a political fanaticism as self-sacrificing as it is pernicious.

6. The Biltmore Program can only be fully understood if it is studied against this background of Palestinian life. Like all political platforms, it is a result of conflicting political pressures, an attempt by the leadership to maintain unity without sacrificing principle. The Jew who lives and works in the National Home is deeply aware both of his achievements and of how much more could have been achieved with whole-hearted support by the Mandatory Power. His political outlook is thus a mixture of self-confident pride and bitter frustration: pride that he has turned the desert and the swamp into a land flowing with milk and honey; frustration because he is denied opportunity of settlement in nine-tenths of that Eretz Israel which he considers his own by right; pride that he has disproved the theory that the Jews cannot build a healthy community based on the tilling of the soil; frustration that the Jew is barred entry to the National Home, where that community is now in being; pride that he is taking part in a bold collective experiment; frustration because he feels himself hampered by British officials whom he often regards as less able than himself; pride because in Palestine he feels himself at last a free member of a free community; frustration because he lives, not under a freely elected government, but under an autocratic if humane regime.

7. The main complaint of the Jews of Palestine is that, since the White Paper of 1930, the Mandatory Power has slowed up the development of the National Home in order to placate Arab opposition. The sudden rise of immigration after the Nazi seizure of power had as its direct result the three and a half years of Arab revolt, during which the Jew had to train himself for self-defence, and to accustom himself to the life of a pioneer in an armed stockade. The high barbed wire and the watchtowers, manned by the settlement police day and night, strike the eye of the visitor as he approaches every collective colony. They are an outward symbol of the new attitude to life and politics which developed among the Palestinian Jews between 1936 and 1938. As a Jewish settler said to a member of the Committee: "We are the vanguard of a great army, de-

---

[1]The White Paper of 1939 rescinded British support of the Balfour Declaration. Instead Britain promised to create a Palestinian Arab state and reduce the immigration of Jews. [Ed.]

fending the advanced positions until the reinforcements arrive from Europe."

8. The Jews in Palestine are convinced that Arab violence paid [off]. Throughout the Arab rising, the Jews in the National Home, despite every provocation, obeyed the orders of their leaders and exercised a remarkable self-discipline. They shot, but only in self-defence; they rarely took reprisals on the Arab population. They state bitterly that the reward for this restraint was the Conference and the White Paper of 1939. The Mandatory Power, they argue, yielded to force, cut down immigration, and thus caused the death of thousands of Jews in Hitler's gas chambers. The Arabs, who had recourse to violence, received substantial concessions, while the Jews, who had put their faith in the Mandatory, were compelled to accept what they regard as a violation of the spirit and the letter of the Mandate.

The Arab Attitude

1. The Committee heard a brief presentation of the Arab case in Washington, statements made in London by delegates from the Arab States to the United Nations, a fuller statement from the Secretary General and other representatives of the Arab League in Cairo, and evidence given on behalf of the Arab Higher (committee) and the Arab Office in Jerusalem. In addition, subcommittees visited Baghdad, Riyadh, Damascus, Beirut, and Amman, where they were informed of the views of Government and of unofficial spokesmen.

2. Stripped to the bare essentials, the Arab case is based upon the fact that Palestine is a country which the Arabs have occupied for more than a thousand years, and a denial of the Jewish historical claims to Palestine. In issuing the *Balfour Declaration,* the Arabs maintain, the British Government were giving away something that did not belong to Britain, and they have consistently argued that the Mandate conflicted with the Covenant of the League of Nations from which it derived its authority. The Arabs deny that the part played by the British in freeing them from the Turks gave Great Britain a right to dispose of their country. Indeed, they assert that Turkish was preferable to British rule, if the latter involves their eventual subjection to the Jews. They consider the Mandate a violation of their right of self-determination since it is forcing upon them an immigration which they do not desire and will not tolerate — an invasion of Palestine by the Jews.

3. The Arabs of Palestine point out that all the surrounding Arab States have now been granted independence. They argue that they are just as

advanced as are the citizens of the nearby States, and they demand independence for Palestine now. The promises which have been made to them in the name of Great Britain, and the assurances concerning Palestine given to Arab leaders by Presidents Roosevelt and Truman, have been understood by the Arabs of Palestine as a recognition of the principle that they should enjoy the same rights as those enjoyed by the neighboring countries. Christian Arabs unite with Moslems in all of these contentions. They demand that their independence should be recognized at once, and they would like Palestine, as a self-governing country, to join the Arab League.

4. The Arabs attach the highest importance to the fulfillment of the promises made by the British Government in the White Paper of 1939. King Abdul Aziz ibn Saud, when he spoke with three members of the Committee at Riyadh, made frequent reference both to these promises and to the assurances given him by the late President Roosevelt at their meeting in February, 1945. His Majesty made clear the strain which would be placed upon Arab friendship with Great Britain and the United States by any policy which Arabs regarded as a betrayal of these pledges. The same warning was repeated by an Arab witness in Jerusalem, who said that "Zionism for the Arabs has become a test of Western intentions."

5. The suggestion that self-government should be withheld from Palestine until the Jews have acquired a majority seems outrageous to the Arabs. They wish to be masters in their own house. The Arabs were opposed to the idea of a Jewish National Home even before the Biltmore Program and the demand for a Jewish State. Needless to say, however, their opposition has become more intense and more bitter since that program was adopted.

6. The Arabs maintain that they have never been anti-Semitic; indeed, they are Semites themselves. Arab spokesmen profess the greatest sympathy for the persecuted Jews of Europe, but they point out that they have not been responsible for this persecution and that it is not just that they should be compelled to atone for the sins of Western peoples by accepting into their country hundreds of thousands of victims of European anti-Semitism. Some Arabs even declare that they might be willing to do their share in providing for refugees on a quota basis if the United States, the British Commonwealth, and other Western countries would do the same.

78

ABBA EBAN

The Refugee Problem

The United Nations did not create a binational state as the Anglo-American committee recommended. By 1947 the immigration of Jewish European refugees, many who were survivors of the Nazi holocaust, had increased the Jewish population of Palestine to 600,000, but the Arab population had risen to 1.2 million. A single state would have been two-thirds Arab and one-third Jewish. Zionists wanted a state where Jews were in the majority. With U.S. support, the United Nations passed a resolution in November 1947 that partitioned Palestine into separate Jewish and Arab states, to be established when the British Mandate ended in 1948. (See Map 12.2.) Immediately Palestinian Arabs went on strike in protest. Zionist forces readily took over towns and cities, forcing Arabs to leave. The conflict came to a head in May 1948, when Israel declared its independence and the armies of surrounding Arab states went to war to prevent it. By the time of the armistice in 1949, Israel had increased its territory by 20 percent. Arabs numbering 750,000 had left their homes and become refugees. The conditions of their departure became a matter of contention in future years.

In 1958, Abba Eban, who later became Israeli foreign minister, gave the following explanation in his address to the United Nations. What, according to Eban, were the reasons why so many Palestinian Arabs left their homes in 1948? Who was responsible?

Thinking Historically

Diplomatic speeches before the United Nations rarely contain big surprises, and this is no exception. There may be, however, elements of Abba Eban's address that raise questions. Does he give you a clear idea of how these refugees were created? Could he be clearer about the process? What questions would you want to ask if you were in the audience?

Walter Laqueur and Barry Rubin, eds., *The Israel-Arab Reader* (New York: Penguin Books, 1995), 129–32.

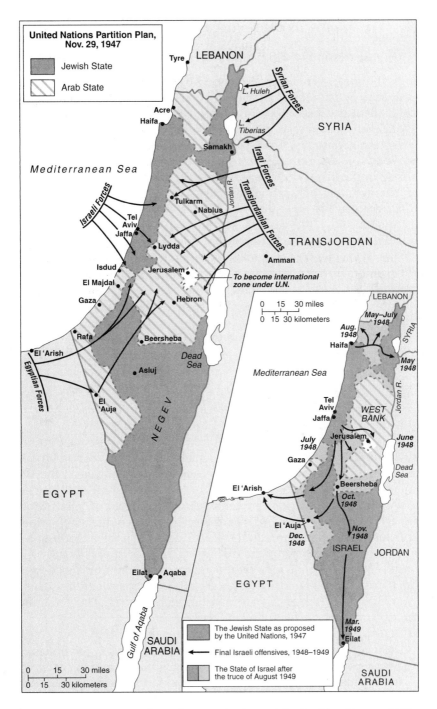

Map 12.2 1948 War and Israeli Expansion beyond the Partition Lines to 1949.

443

How Was the Refugee Problem Caused?

Aggression by Arab States Created Refugee Problem

The Arab refugee problem was caused by a war of aggression, launched by the Arab States against Israel in 1947 and 1948. Let there be no mistake. If there had been no war against Israel, with its consequent harvest of bloodshed, misery, panic, and flight, there would be no problem of Arab refugees today. Once you determine the responsibility for that war, you have determined the responsibility for the refugee problem. Nothing in the history of our generation is clearer or less controversial than the initiative of Arab governments for the conflict out of which the refugee tragedy emerged. The historic origins of that conflict are clearly defined by the confessions of Arab governments themselves: "This will be a war of extermination," declared the Secretary General of the Arab League speaking for the governments of six Arab States; "It will be a momentous massacre to be spoken of like the Mongolian massacre and the Crusades."

Palestine Arabs Urged to Flee by Arab Leaders

The assault began on the last day of November 1947. From then until the expiration of the British Mandate in May 1948 the Arab States, in concert with Palestine Arab leaders, plunged the land into turmoil and chaos. On the day of Israel's Declaration of Independence, on May 14, 1948, the armed forces of Egypt, Jordan, Syria, Lebanon, and Iraq, supported by contingents from Saudi Arabia and the Yemen, crossed their frontiers and marched against Israel. The perils which then confronted our community; the danger which darkened every life and home; the successful repulse of the assault and the emergence of Israel into the life of the world community are all chapters of past history, gone but not forgotten. But the traces of that conflict still remain deeply inscribed upon our region's life. Caught up in the havoc and tension of war; demoralized by the flight of their leaders; urged on by irresponsible promises that they would return to inherit the spoils of Israel's destruction — hundreds of thousands of Arabs sought the shelter of Arab lands. A survey by an international body in 1957 described these violent events in the following terms:

> As early as the first months of 1948 the Arab League issued orders exhorting the people to seek a temporary refuge in neighboring countries, later to return to their abodes in the wake of the victorious Arab armies and obtain their share of abandoned Jewish property (Research Group for European Migration Problems Bulletin, Vol. V, No. 1, 1957, p. 10).

Contemporary statements by Arab leaders fully confirm this version. On 16 August 1948 Msgr. George Hakim, the Greek Catholic Archbishop of Galilee, recalled:

> The refugees had been confident that their absence from Palestine would not last long; that they would return within a few days — within a week or two; their leaders had promised them that the Arab armies would crush the "Zionist gangs" very quickly and that there would be no need for panic or fear of a long exile.

A month later on September 15, 1948, Mr. Emile Ghoury who had been the Secretary of the Arab Higher Committee at the time of the Arab invasion of Israel declared:

> I do not want to impugn anyone but only to help the refugees. The fact that there are these refugees is the direct consequence of the action of the Arab States in opposing partition and the Jewish State. The Arab States agreed upon this policy unanimously and they must share in the solution of the problem.

Misery Is Result of Unlawful Resort to Force by Arabs

No less compelling than these avowals by Arab leaders are the judgments of United Nations organs. In April 1948, when the flight of the refugees was in full swing, the United Nations Palestine Commission inscribed its verdict on the tablets of history:

> Arab opposition to the plan of the Assembly of 29 November 1947 has taken the form of organized efforts by strong Arab elements, both inside and outside Palestine, to prevent its implementation and to thwart its objectives by threats and acts of violence, including repeated armed incursions into Palestine territory. The Commission has had to report to the Security Council that powerful Arab interests, both inside and outside Palestine, are defying the resolution of the General Assembly and are engaged in a deliberate effort to alter by force the settlement envisaged therein.

This is a description of the events between November 1947 and May 1948 when the Arab exodus began. Months later, when the tide of battle rolled away, its consequences of bereavement, devastation and panic were left behind. At the General Assembly meetings in 1948 the United Nations Acting Mediator recorded a grave international judgment:

> The Arab States had forcibly opposed the existence of the Jewish State in Palestine in direct opposition to the wishes of two-thirds of the members of the Assembly. Nevertheless their armed intervention proved useless. The [Mediator's] report was based solely on the fact

that the Arab States had no right to resort to force and that the United Nations should exert its authority to prevent such a use of force.

The significance of the Arab assault upon Israel by five neighboring States had been reflected in a letter addressed by the Secretary General of the United Nations to representatives of the permanent members of the Security Council on 16 May 1948: —

"The Egyptian Government," wrote the Secretary-General, "has declared in a cablegram to the President of the Security Council on 15 May that Egyptian armed forces have entered Palestine and it has engaged in 'armed intervention' in that country. On 16 May I received a cablegram from the Arab League making similar statements on behalf of the Arab States. I consider it my duty to emphasize to you that *this is the first time since the adoption of the Charter that Member States have openly declared that they have engaged in armed intervention outside their own territory.*"

Arab Governments Must Accept Responsibility

These are only a few of the documents which set out the responsibility of the Arab Governments for the warfare of which the refugees are the main surviving victims. Even after a full decade it is difficult to sit here with equanimity and listen to Arab representatives disengaging themselves from any responsibility for the travail and anguish which they caused. I recall this history not for the purpose of recrimination, but because of its direct bearing on the Committee's discussion. Should not the representatives of Arab States, as the authors of this tragedy, come here in a mood of humility and repentance rather than in shrill and negative indignation? Since these governments have, by acts of policy, created this tragic problem, *does it not follow that the world community has an unimpeachable right to claim their full assistance in its solution?* How can governments create a vast humanitarian problem by their action — then wash their hands of all responsibility for its alleviation? The claim of the world community on the cooperation of Arab governments is all the more compelling when we reflect that these States, in their vast lands, command all the resources and conditions which would enable them to liberate the refugees from their plight, in full dignity and freedom.

With this history in mind the Committee should not find it difficult to reject the assertion that the guilt for the refugee problem lies with the United Nations itself. The refugee problem was not created by the General Assembly's recommendation for the establishment of Israel. It was created by the attempts of Arab governments to destroy that recommendation by force. The crisis arose not as Arab spokesmen have said because the United Nations adopted a resolution eleven years ago; it arose because Arab governments attacked that resolution by force. If the United Nations proposal had been peacefully accepted, there would be no refugee problem today hanging as a cloud upon the tense horizons of the Middle East.

The next question is — why has the problem endured?

Why Does the Refugee Problem Endure?

Refugee Problem Cannot Be Solved by Repatriation

In his statement to the Committee on November 10, 1958, the representative of the United States said:

> In our view it is not good enough consciously to perpetuate for over a decade the dependent status of nearly a million refugees.

Other speakers in this debate have echoed a similar sense of frustration.

Apart from the question of its origin, the perpetuation of this refugee problem is an unnatural event, running against the whole course of experience and precedent. Since the end of the Second World War, problems affecting forty million refugees have confronted Governments in various parts of the world. In no case, except that of the Arab refugees, amounting to less than two percent of the whole, has the international community shown constant responsibility and provided lavish aid. In every other case a solution has been found by the integration of refugees into their host countries. Nine million Koreans; 900,000 refugees from the conflict in Viet Nam; 8½ million Hindus and Sikhs leaving Pakistan for India; 6½ million Moslems fleeing India to Pakistan; 700,000 Chinese refugees in Hong Kong; 13 million Germans from the Sudetenland, Poland, and other East European States reaching West and East Germany; thousands of Turkish refugees from Bulgaria; 440,000 Finns separated from their homeland by a change of frontier; 450,000 refugees from Arab lands arrived destitute in Israel; and an equal number converging on Israel from the remnants of the Jewish holocaust in Europe — these form the tragic procession of the world's refugee population in the past two decades. *In every case but that of the Arab refugees now in Arab lands the countries in which the refugees sought shelter have facilitated their integration.* In this case alone has integration been obstructed.

The paradox is the more astonishing when we reflect that the kinship of language, religion, social background and national sentiment existing between the Arab refugees and their Arab host countries has been at least as intimate as those existing between any other host countries and any other refugee groups. It is impossible to escape the conclusion that the integration of Arab refugees into the life of the

Arab world is an objectively feasible process which has been resisted for political reasons.

In a learned study on refugee problems published by the Carnegie Endowment for International Peace in November 1957 under the title "Century of the Homeless Man" Dr. Elfan Rees, Advisor on Refugees to the World Council of Churches, sums up the international experience in the following terms:

> No large scale refugee problem has ever been solved by repatriation, and there are certainly no grounds for believing that this particular problem can be so solved. Nothing can bring it about except wars which in our time would leave nothing to go back to. War has never solved a refugee problem and it is not in the books that a modern war would.

79

ARI SHAVIT

An Interview with Benny Morris

Benny Morris is the leader of the academic Israeli "New History," which has challenged many of the founding myths of Israel and the Zionist movement. His book *The Birth of the Palestinian Refugee Problem* (1987) showed that Palestinian Arabs did not leave voluntarily in 1948, but were terrorized and forced from their villages by militarized Zionists. His upending of some of the sacred Israeli founding myths gave Morris the reputation of a radical anti-Zionist, but in this interview in the Israeli newspaper *Ha'aretz* in January 2004, Morris revealed he was not.

How did Morris's research challenge older Israeli views like that of Abba Eban in the previous selection? How were Morris's conclusions from that research different from what you might expect?

Ari Shavit, "Survival of the Fittest: An Interview with Benny Morris," *Ha'aretz*, 9 (January 2004). Available online at http://www.haaretzdaily.com/hasen/pages/ShArt.jhtml?itemNo= 380986.

Thinking Historically

In this selection, the interviewer, Ari Shavit, cues the surprises for us. They are on both the factual level of Benny Morris's research and the personal level of Morris's response to his research. What do you find surprising or unexpected in this interview? How do those unexpected discoveries deepen your understanding of the conflict?

Benny Morris, in the month ahead the new version of your book on the birth of the Palestinian refugee problem is due to be published. Who will be less pleased with the book — the Israelis or the Palestinians?

"The revised book is a double-edged sword. It is based on many documents that were not available to me when I wrote the original book, most of them from the Israel Defense Forces Archives. What the new material shows is that there were far more Israeli acts of massacre than I had previously thought. To my surprise, there were also many cases of rape. In the months of April-May 1948, units of the Haganah [the pre–state defense force that was the precursor of the IDF] were given operational orders that stated explicitly that they were to uproot the villagers, expel them, and destroy the villages themselves.

"At the same time, it turns out that there was a series of orders issued by the Arab Higher Committee and by the Palestinian intermediate levels to remove children, women, and the elderly from the villages. So that on the one hand, the book reinforces the accusation against the Zionist side, but on the other hand it also proves that many of those who left the villages did so with the encouragement of the Palestinian leadership itself."

According to your new findings, how many cases of Israeli rape were there in 1948?

"About a dozen. In Acre four soldiers raped a girl and murdered her and her father. In Jaffa, soldiers of the Kiryati Brigade raped one girl and tried to rape several more. At Hunin, which is in the Galilee, two girls were raped and then murdered. There were one or two cases of rape at Tantura, south of Haifa. There was one case of rape at Qula, in the center of the country. At the village of Abu Shusha, near Kibbutz Gezer [in the Ramle area] there were four female prisoners, one of whom was raped a number of times. And there were other cases. Usually more than one soldier was involved. Usually there were one or two Palestinian girls. In a large proportion of the cases the event ended with murder. Because neither the victims nor the rapists liked to report these events, we have to assume that the dozen cases of rape that were reported, which I found, are not the whole story. They are just the tip of the iceberg."

According to your findings, how many acts of Israeli massacre were perpetrated in 1948?

"Twenty-four. In some cases four or five people were executed, in others the numbers were 70, 80, 100. There was also a great deal of arbitrary killing. Two old men are spotted walking in a field — they are shot. A woman is found in an abandoned village — she is shot. There are cases such as the village of Dawayima [in the Hebron region], in which a column entered the village with all guns blazing and killed anything that moved.

"The worst cases were Saliha (70–80 killed), Deir Yassin (100–110), Lod (250), Dawayima (hundreds), and perhaps Abu Shusha (70). There is no unequivocal proof of a large-scale massacre at Tantura, but war crimes were perpetrated there. At Jaffa there was a massacre about which nothing had been known until now. The same at Arab al Muwasi, in the north. About half of the acts of massacre were part of Operation Hiram [in the north, in October 1948]: at Safsaf, Saliha, Jish, Eilaboun, Arab al Muwasi, Deir al Asad, Majdal Krum, Sasa. In Operation Hiram there was a unusually high concentration of executions of people against a wall or next to a well in an orderly fashion.

"That can't be chance. It's a pattern. Apparently, various officers who took part in the operation understood that the expulsion order they received permitted them to do these deeds in order to encourage the population to take to the roads. The fact is that no one was punished for these acts of murder. Ben-Gurion silenced the matter. He covered up for the officers who did the massacres."

What you are telling me here, as though by the way, is that in Operation Hiram there was a comprehensive and explicit expulsion order. Is that right?

"Yes. One of the revelations in the book is that on October 31, 1948, the commander of the Northern Front, Moshe Carmel, issued an order in writing to his units to expedite the removal of the Arab population. Carmel took this action immediately after a visit by Ben-Gurion to the Northern Command in Nazareth. There is no doubt in my mind that this order originated with Ben-Gurion. Just as the expulsion order for the city of Lod, which was signed by Yitzhak Rabin, was issued immediately after Ben-Gurion visited the headquarters of Operation Dani [July 1948]."

Are you saying that Ben-Gurion was personally responsible for a deliberate and systematic policy of mass expulsion?

"From April 1948, Ben-Gurion is projecting a message of transfer. There is no explicit order of his in writing, there is no orderly comprehensive policy, but there is an atmosphere of [population] transfer. The transfer idea is in the air. The entire leadership understands that this is the idea. The officer corps understands what is required of them. Under Ben-Gurion, a consensus of transfer is created."

Ben-Gurion was a "transferist"?

"Of course. Ben-Gurion was a transferist. He understood that there could be no Jewish state with a large and hostile Arab minority in its midst. There would be no such state. It would not be able to exist."

I don't hear you condemning him.

"Ben-Gurion was right. If he had not done what he did, a state would not have come into being. That has to be clear. It is impossible to evade it. Without the uprooting of the Palestinians, a Jewish state would not have arisen here."

When Ethnic Cleansing Is Justified

Benny Morris, for decades you have been researching the dark side of Zionism. You are an expert on the atrocities of 1948. In the end, do you in effect justify all this? Are you an advocate of the transfer of 1948?

"There is no justification for acts of rape. There is no justification for acts of massacre. Those are war crimes. But in certain conditions, expulsion is not a war crime. I don't think that the expulsions of 1948 were war crimes. You can't make an omelet without breaking eggs. You have to dirty your hands."

We are talking about the killing of thousands of people, the destruction of an entire society.

"A society that aims to kill you forces you to destroy it. When the choice is between destroying or being destroyed, it's better to destroy."

There is something chilling about the quiet way in which you say that.

"If you expected me to burst into tears, I'm sorry to disappoint you. I will not do that."

So when the commanders of Operation Dani are standing there and observing the long and terrible column of the 50,000 people expelled from Lod walking eastward, you stand there with them? You justify them?

"I definitely understand them. I understand their motives. I don't think they felt any pangs of conscience, and in their place I wouldn't have felt pangs of conscience. Without that act, they would not have won the war and the state would not have come into being."

You do not condemn them morally?

"No."

They perpetrated ethnic cleansing.

"There are circumstances in history that justify ethnic cleansing. I know that this term is completely negative in the discourse of the twenty-first century, but when the choice is between ethnic cleansing and genocide — the annihilation of your people — I prefer ethnic cleansing."

And that was the situation in 1948?

"That was the situation. That is what Zionism faced. A Jewish state would not have come into being without the uprooting of 700,000 Palestinians. Therefore it was necessary to uproot them. There was no choice but to expel that population. It was necessary to cleanse the hinterland and cleanse the border areas and cleanse the main roads. It was necessary to cleanse the villages from which our convoys and our settlements were fired on."

The term "to cleanse" is terrible.

"I know it doesn't sound nice but that's the term they used at the time. I adopted it from all the 1948 documents in which I am immersed."

What you are saying is hard to listen to and hard to digest. You sound hard-hearted.

"I feel sympathy for the Palestinian people, which truly underwent a hard tragedy. I feel sympathy for the refugees themselves. But if the desire to establish a Jewish state here is legitimate, there was no other choice. It was impossible to leave a large fifth column in the country. From the moment the Yishuv [pre-1948 Jewish community in Palestine] was attacked by the Palestinians and afterward by the Arab states, there was no choice but to expel the Palestinian population. To uproot it in the course of war.

"Remember another thing: the Arab people gained a large slice of the planet. Not thanks to its skills or its great virtues, but because it conquered and murdered and forced those it conquered to convert during many generations. But in the end the Arabs have 22 states. The Jewish people did not have even one state. There was no reason in the world why it should not have one state. Therefore, from my point of view, the need to establish this state in this place overcame the injustice that was done to the Palestinians by uprooting them."

And morally speaking, you have no problem with that deed?

"That is correct. Even the great American democracy could not have been created without the annihilation of the Indians. There are cases in which the overall, final good justifies harsh and cruel acts that are committed in the course of history."

And in our case it effectively justifies a population transfer.

"That's what emerges."

And you take that in stride? War crimes? Massacres? The burning fields and the devastated villages of the Nakba? [catastrophe]

"You have to put things in proportion. These are small war crimes. All told, if we take all the massacres and all the executions of 1948, we come to about 800 who were killed. In comparison to the massacres that were perpetrated in Bosnia, that's peanuts. In comparison to the massacres the Russians perpetrated against the Germans at Stalingrad, that's chicken feed. When you take into account that there was a bloody civil war here and that we lost an entire 1 percent of the population, you find that we behaved very well."

The Next Transfer

You went through an interesting process. You went to research Ben-Gurion and the Zionist establishment critically, but in the end you actually identify with them. You are as tough in your words as they were in their deeds.

"You may be right. Because I investigated the conflict in depth, I was forced to cope with the in-depth questions that those people coped with. I understood the problematic character of the situation they faced and maybe I adopted part of their universe of concepts. But I do not identify with Ben-Gurion. I think he made a serious historical mistake in 1948. Even though he understood the demographic issue and the need to establish a Jewish state without a large Arab minority, he got cold feet during the war. In the end, he faltered."

I'm not sure I understand. Are you saying that Ben-Gurion erred in expelling too few Arabs?

"If he was already engaged in expulsion, maybe he should have done a complete job. I know that this stuns the Arabs and the liberals and the politically correct types. But my feeling is that this place would be quieter and know less suffering if the matter had been resolved once and for all. If Ben-Gurion had carried out a large expulsion and cleansed the whole country — the whole Land of Israel, as far as the Jordan River. It may yet turn out that this was his fatal mistake. If he had carried out a full expulsion — rather than a partial one — he would have stabilized the State of Israel for generations."

I find it hard to believe what I am hearing.

"If the end of the story turns out to be a gloomy one for the Jews, it will be because Ben-Gurion did not complete the transfer in 1948. Because he left a large and volatile demographic reserve in the West Bank and Gaza and within Israel itself."

In his place, would you have expelled them all? All the Arabs in the country?

"But I am not a statesman. I do not put myself in his place. But as an historian, I assert that a mistake was made here. Yes. The non-completion of the transfer was a mistake."

And today? Do you advocate a transfer today?

"If you are asking me whether I support the transfer and expulsion of the Arabs from the West Bank, Gaza, and perhaps even from Galilee and the Triangle, I say not at this moment. I am not willing to be a partner to that act. In the present circumstances it is neither moral nor realistic. The world would not allow it, the Arab world would not allow it; it would destroy the Jewish society from within. But I am ready to tell you that in other circumstances, apocalyptic ones, which are liable to be realized in five or ten years, I can see expulsions. If we find ourselves with atomic weapons around us, or if there is a general Arab attack on us and a situation of warfare on the front with Arabs in the rear shooting at convoys on their way to the front, acts of expulsion will be entirely reasonable. They may even be essential."

Including the expulsion of Israeli Arabs?

"The Israeli Arabs are a time bomb. Their slide into complete Palestinization has made them an emissary of the enemy that is among us. They are a potential fifth column. In both demographic and security terms they are liable to undermine the state. So that if Israel again finds itself in a situation of existential threat, as in 1948, it may be forced to act as it did then. If we are attacked by Egypt (after an Islamist revolution in Cairo) and by Syria, and chemical and biological missiles slam into our cities, and at the same time Israeli Palestinians attack us from behind, I can see an expulsion situation. It could happen. If the threat to Israel is existential, expulsion will be justified."

Cultural Dementia

Besides being tough, you are also very gloomy. You weren't always like that, were you?

"My turning point began after 2000. I wasn't a great optimist even before that. True, I always voted Labor or Meretz or Sheli [a dovish party of the late 1970s], and in 1988 I refused to serve in the territories and was jailed for it, but I always doubted the intentions of the Palestinians. The events of Camp David and what followed in their wake turned the doubt into certainty. When the Palestinians rejected the proposal of [prime minister Ehud] Barak in July 2000 and the Clinton proposal in December 2000, I understood that they are unwilling to accept the two-state solution. They want it all. . . .

The situation as you describe it is extremely harsh. You are not entirely convinced that we can survive here, are you?

"The possibility of annihilation exists."

Would you describe yourself as an apocalyptic person?

"The whole Zionist project is apocalyptic. It exists within hostile surroundings and in a certain sense its existence is unreasonable. It wasn't reasonable for it to succeed in 1881 and it wasn't reasonable for it to succeed in 1948 and it's not reasonable that it will succeed now. Nevertheless, it has come this far. In a certain way it is miraculous. I live the events of 1948, and 1948 projects itself on what could happen here. Yes, I think of Armageddon. It's possible. Within the next 20 years there could be an atomic war here."

If Zionism is so dangerous for the Jews and if Zionism makes the Arabs so wretched, maybe it's a mistake?

"No, Zionism was not a mistake. The desire to establish a Jewish state here was a legitimate one, a positive one. But given the character of Islam and given the character of the Arab nation, it was a mistake to think that it would be possible to establish a tranquil state here that lives in harmony with its surroundings."

Which leaves us, nevertheless, with two possibilities: either a cruel, tragic Zionism, or the forgoing of Zionism.

"Yes. That's so. You have pared it down, but that's correct."

Would you agree that this historical reality is intolerable, that there is something inhuman about it?

"Yes. But that's so for the Jewish people, not the Palestinians. A people that suffered for 2,000 years, that went through the Holocaust, arrives at its patrimony but is thrust into a renewed round of bloodshed, that is perhaps the road to annihilation. In terms of cosmic justice, that's terrible. It's far more shocking than what happened in 1948 to a small part of the Arab nation that was then in Palestine."

So what you are telling me is that you live the Palestinian Nakba of the past less than you live the possible Jewish Nakba of the future?

"Yes. Destruction could be the end of this process. It could be the end of the Zionist experiment. And that's what really depresses and scares me."

The title of the book you are now publishing in Hebrew is "Victims." In the end, then, your argument is that of the two victims of this conflict, we are the bigger one.

"Yes. Exactly. We are the greater victims in the course of history and we are also the greater potential victim. Even though we are oppressing the Palestinians, we are the weaker side here. We are a small minority in a large sea of hostile Arabs who want to eliminate us. So it's possible that when their desire is realized, everyone will understand what I am saying to you now. Everyone will understand we are the true victims. But by then it will be too late."

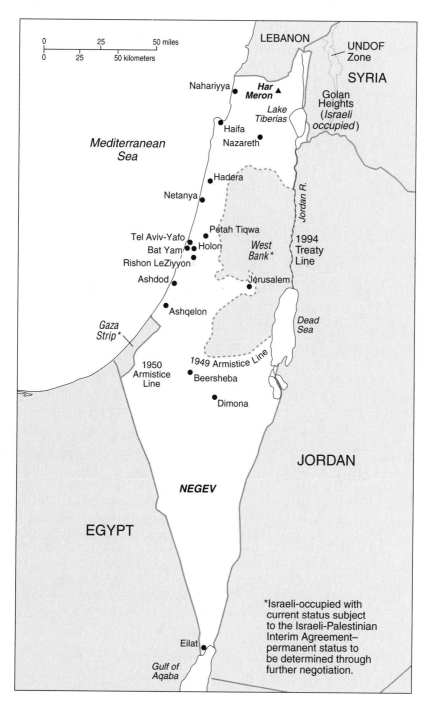

Map 12.3 Israel and Palestine, 2006.

JOHN MEARSHEIMER AND STEPHEN WALT
The Israel Lobby

John Mearsheimer and Stephen Walt are American political scientists, not historians, but in this excerpt from a paper they present a history of U.S. policy toward Israel since 1967 that is different from the more traditional interpretations. What is their argument? How might you dispute it? What do you find convincing?

Thinking Historically

This paper was extremely controversial when it was published in March 2006. Even today you are likely to find the claims the authors make well outside the mainstream of public opinion about Israel and the United States. Which of these claims do you find most surprising? On reflection, are there any which you are prone to dismiss? Which lead you to new ways of thinking about the subject?

For the past several decades, and especially since the Six-Day War in 1967, the centrepiece of U.S. Middle Eastern policy has been its relationship with Israel. The combination of unwavering support for Israel and the related effort to spread "democracy" throughout the region has inflamed Arab and Islamic opinion and jeopardised not only U.S. security but that of much of the rest of the world. This situation has no equal in American political history. Why has the U.S. been willing to set aside its own security and that of many of its allies in order to advance the interests of another state? One might assume that the bond between the two countries was based on shared strategic interests or compelling moral imperatives, but neither explanation can account for the remarkable level of material and diplomatic support that the U.S. provides.

Instead, the thrust of U.S. policy in the region derives almost entirely from domestic politics, and especially the activities of the "Israel Lobby." Other special-interest groups have managed to skew foreign policy, but no lobby has managed to divert it as far from what the na-

John Mearsheimer and Stephen Walt, "The Israel Lobby," *London Review of Books*, 28, no. 6 (March 23, 2006). Available online at http://www.lrb.co.uk/v28/n06/print/mear01_.html. Also available at http://ksgnotes1.harvard.edu/Research/wpaper.nsf/rwp/RWP06-011 as Working Paper Number: RWP06-011. Submitted: March 13, 2006, Harvard University, Kennedy School of Government, Faculty Research Working Paper Series.

tional interest would suggest, while simultaneously convincing Americans that U.S. interests and those of the other country — in this case, Israel — are essentially identical.

Since the October War in 1973, Washington has provided Israel with a level of support dwarfing that given to any other state. It has been the largest annual recipient of direct economic and military assistance since 1976, and is the largest recipient in total since World War Two, to the tune of well over $140 billion (in 2004 dollars). Israel receives about $3 billion in direct assistance each year, roughly one-fifth of the foreign aid budget, and worth about $500 a year for every Israeli. This largesse is especially striking since Israel is now a wealthy industrial state with a per capita income roughly equal to that of South Korea or Spain. . . .

Beginning in the 1990s, and even more after 9/11, U.S. support has been justified by the claim that both states are threatened by terrorist groups originating in the Arab and Muslim world, and by "rogue states" that back these groups and seek weapons of mass destruction. This is taken to mean not only that Washington should give Israel a free hand in dealing with the Palestinians and not press it to make concessions until all Palestinian terrorists are imprisoned or dead, but that the U.S. should go after countries like Iran and Syria. Israel is thus seen as a crucial ally in the war on terror, because its enemies are America's enemies. In fact, Israel is a liability in the war on terror and the broader effort to deal with rogue states.

"Terrorism" is not a single adversary, but a tactic employed by a wide array of political groups. The terrorist organisations that threaten Israel do not threaten the United States, except when it intervenes against them (as in Lebanon in 1982). Moreover, Palestinian terrorism is not random violence directed against Israel or "the West"; it is largely a response to Israel's prolonged campaign to colonise the West Bank and Gaza Strip.

More important, saying that Israel and the U.S. are united by a shared terrorist threat has the causal relationship backwards: The U.S. has a terrorism problem in good part because it is so closely allied with Israel, not the other way around. Support for Israel is not the only source of anti-American terrorism, but it is an important one, and it makes winning the war on terror more difficult. There is no question that many al-Qaida leaders, including Osama bin Laden, are motivated by Israel's presence in Jerusalem and the plight of the Palestinians. Unconditional support for Israel makes it easier for extremists to rally popular support and to attract recruits.

As for so-called rogue states in the Middle East, they are not a dire threat to vital U.S. interests, except inasmuch as they are a threat to Israel. Even if these states acquire nuclear weapons — which is obviously undesirable — neither America nor Israel could be blackmailed, because the blackmailer could not carry out the threat without suffering over-whelming retaliation. The danger of a nuclear handover to terrorists is equally remote, because a rogue state could not be sure the transfer would go undetected or that it would not be blamed and punished after-wards. The relationship with Israel actually makes it harder for the U.S. to deal with these states. Israel's nuclear arsenal is one reason some of its neighbours want nuclear weapons, and threatening them with regime change merely increases that desire.

A final reason to question Israel's strategic value is that it does not behave like a loyal ally. Israeli officials frequently ignore U.S. requests and renege on promises (including pledges to stop building settlements and to refrain from "targeted assassinations" of Palestinian leaders). Is-rael has provided sensitive military technology to potential rivals like China, in what the State Department inspector-general called "a sys-tematic and growing pattern of unauthorised transfers." According to the General Accounting Office, Israel also "conducts the most aggres-sive espionage operations against the U.S. of any ally." In addition to the case of Jonathan Pollard, who gave Israel large quantities of classi-fied material in the early 1980s (which it reportedly passéd on to the Soviet Union in return for more exit visas for Soviet Jews), a new con-troversy erupted in 2004 when it was revealed that a key Pentagon offi-cial called Larry Franklin had passed classified information to an Israeli diplomat. Israel is hardly the only country that spies on the U.S., but its willingness to spy on its principal patron casts further doubt on its strategic value.

Israel's strategic value isn't the only issue. Its backers also argue that it deserves unqualified support because it is weak and surrounded by enemies; it is a democracy; the Jewish people have suffered from past crimes and therefore deserve special treatment; and Israel's con-duct has been morally superior to that of its adversaries. On close in-spection, none of these arguments is persuasive. There is a strong moral case for supporting Israel's existence, but that is not in jeopardy. Viewed objectively, its past and present conduct offers no moral basis for privileging it over the Palestinians.

Israel is often portrayed as David confronted by Goliath, but the converse is closer to the truth. Contrary to popular belief, the Zionists had larger, better equipped, and better led forces during the 1947–49 War of Independence, and the Israel Defence Forces won quick and easy victories against Egypt in 1956 and against Egypt, Jordan, and Syria in 1967 — all of this before large-scale U.S. aid began flowing. Today, Israel is the strongest military power in the Middle East. Its conventional forces are far superior to those of its neighbours and it is the only state in the region with nuclear weapons. Egypt and Jordan have signed peace treaties with it, and Saudi Arabia has offered to do so. Syria has lost its Soviet patron, Iraq has been devastated by three disastrous wars, and Iran is hundreds of miles away. The Palestinians barely have an effective police force, let alone an army that could pose a threat to Israel. According to a 2005 assessment by Tel Aviv University's Jaffee Centre for Strategic Studies, "the strategic balance decidedly favours Israel, which has continued to widen the qualitative gap between its own military capability and deterrence powers and those of its neighbours." If backing the underdog were a compelling motive, the United States would be supporting Israel's opponents.

That Israel is a fellow democracy surrounded by hostile dictatorships cannot account for the current level of aid: there are many democracies around the world, but none receives the same lavish support. The U.S. has overthrown democratic governments in the past and supported dictators when this was thought to advance its interests — it has good relations with a number of dictatorships today.

Some aspects of Israeli democracy are at odds with core American values. Unlike the U.S., where people are supposed to enjoy equal rights irrespective of race, religion, or ethnicity, Israel was explicitly founded as a Jewish state and citizenship is based on the principle of blood kinship. Given this, it is not surprising that its 1.3 million Arabs are treated as second-class citizens, or that a recent Israeli government commission found that Israel behaves in a "neglectful and discriminatory" manner towards them. Its democratic status is also undermined by its refusal to grant the Palestinians a viable state of their own or full political rights.

A third justification is the history of Jewish suffering in the Christian West, especially during the Holocaust. Because Jews were persecuted for centuries and could feel safe only in a Jewish homeland, many people now believe that Israel deserves special treatment from the United States. The country's creation was undoubtedly an appropriate response to the long record of crimes against Jews, but it also brought about fresh crimes against a largely innocent third party: the Palestinians.

This was well understood by Israel's early leaders. David Ben-Gurion told Nahum Goldmann, the president of the World Jewish Congress:

> If I were an Arab leader I would never make terms with Israel. That is natural: we have taken their country . . . We come from Israel, but two thousand years ago, and what is that to them? There has been anti-semitism, the Nazis, Hitler, Auschwitz, but was that their fault? They only see one thing: we have come here and stolen their country. Why should they accept that?

Since then, Israeli leaders have repeatedly sought to deny the Palestinians' national ambitions. When she was prime minister, Golda Meir famously remarked that "there is no such thing as a Palestinian." Pressure from extremist violence and Palestinian population growth has forced subsequent Israeli leaders to disengage from the Gaza Strip and consider other territorial compromises, but not even Yitzhak Rabin was willing to offer the Palestinians a viable state. Ehud Barak's purportedly generous offer at Camp David would have given them only a disarmed set of Bantustans under de facto Israeli control. The tragic history of the Jewish people does not obligate the U.S. to help Israel today no matter what it does.

Israel's backers also portray it as a country that has sought peace at every turn and shown great restraint even when provoked. The Arabs, by contrast, are said to have acted with great wickedness. Yet on the ground, Israel's record is not distinguishable from that of its opponents. Ben-Gurion acknowledged that the early Zionists were far from benevolent towards the Palestinian Arabs, who resisted their encroachments — which is hardly surprising, given that the Zionists were trying to create their own state on Arab land. In the same way, the creation of Israel in 1947–48 involved acts of ethnic cleansing, including executions, massacres, and rapes by Jews, and Israel's subsequent conduct has often been brutal, belying any claim to moral superiority. Between 1949 and 1956, for example, Israeli security forces killed between 2700 and 5000 Arab infiltrators, the overwhelming majority of them unarmed. The IDF murdered hundreds of Egyptian prisoners of war in both the 1956 and 1967 wars, while in 1967, it expelled between 100,000 and 260,000 Palestinians from the newly conquered West Bank, and drove 80,000 Syrians from the Golan Heights.

During the first intifada, the IDF distributed truncheons to its troops and encouraged them to break the bones of Palestinian protesters. The Swedish branch of Save the Children estimated that "23,600 to 29,900 children required medical treatment for their beating injuries in the first two years of the intifada." Nearly a third of them were aged ten or under. The response to the second intifada has been even more violent, leading *Ha'aretz* to declare that "the IDF . . . is turning into a killing machine whose efficiency is awe-inspiring, yet shocking." The IDF fired one million bullets in the first days of the uprising. Since then, for every Israeli lost, Israel has killed 3.4 Palestinians, the majority of whom have been innocent bystanders; the ratio of Palestinian to Israeli children killed is even higher (5.7:1). It is also worth bearing in mind that the Zionists relied on terrorist bombs to drive the British from Palestine, and that Yitzhak Shamir, once a terrorist and later prime minister, declared that "neither Jewish ethics nor Jewish tradition can disqualify terrorism as a means of combat."

The Palestinian resort to terrorism is wrong but it isn't surprising. The Palestinians believe they have no other way to force Israeli concessions. As Ehud Barak once admitted, had he been born a Palestinian, he "would have joined a terrorist organisation."

So if neither strategic nor moral arguments can account for America's support for Israel, how are we to explain it?

The explanation is the unmatched power of the Israel Lobby. We use "the Lobby" as shorthand for the loose coalition of individuals and organisations who actively work to steer U.S. foreign policy in a pro-Israel direction. This is not meant to suggest that "the Lobby" is a unified movement with a central leadership, or that individuals within it do not disagree on certain issues. Not all Jewish Americans are part of the Lobby, because Israel is not a salient issue for many of them. In a 2004 survey, for example, roughly 36 per cent of American Jews said they were either "not very" or "not at all" emotionally attached to Israel.

Jewish Americans also differ on specific Israeli policies. Many of the key organisations in the Lobby, such as the American-Israel Public Affairs Committee (AIPAC) and the Conference of Presidents of Major Jewish Organisations, are run by hardliners who generally support the Likud Party's expansionist policies, including its hostility to the Oslo peace process. The bulk of U.S. Jewry, meanwhile, is more inclined to make concessions to the Palestinians, and a few groups — such as Jewish Voice for Peace — strongly advocate such steps. Despite these differences, moderates and hardliners both favour giving steadfast support to Israel. . . .

In its basic operations, the Israel Lobby is no different from the farm lobby, steel or textile workers' unions, or other ethnic lobbies. There is nothing improper about American Jews and their Christian allies attempting to sway U.S. policy: the Lobby's activities are not a conspiracy of the sort depicted in tracts like the *Protocols of the Elders of Zion*. For the most part, the individuals and groups that comprise it are only doing what other special interest groups do, but doing it very much better. By contrast, pro-Arab interest groups, in so far as they exist at all, are weak, which makes the Israel Lobby's task even easier.

The Lobby pursues two broad strategies. First, it wields its significant influence in Washington, pressuring both Congress and the executive branch. Whatever an individual lawmaker or policymaker's own views may be, the Lobby tries to make supporting Israel the "smart" choice. Second, it strives to ensure that public discourse portrays Israel in a positive light, by repeating myths about its founding and by promoting its point of view in policy debates. The goal is to prevent critical comments from getting a fair hearing in the political arena. Controlling the debate is essential to guaranteeing U.S. support, because a candid discussion of U.S.-Israeli relations might lead Americans to favour a different policy.

A key pillar of the Lobby's effectiveness is its influence in Congress, where Israel is virtually immune from criticism. This in itself is remarkable, because Congress rarely shies away from contentious issues.

Where Israel is concerned, however, potential critics fall silent. One reason is that some key members are Christian Zionists like Dick Armey, who said in September 2002: "My No. 1 priority in foreign policy is to protect Israel." One might think that the No. 1 priority for any congressman would be to protect America. There are also Jewish senators and congressmen who work to ensure that U.S. foreign policy supports Israel's interests. . . .

The bottom line is that AIPAC, a de facto agent for a foreign government, has a stranglehold on Congress, with the result that U.S. policy towards Israel is not debated there, even though that policy has important consequences for the entire world. In other words, one of the three main branches of the government is firmly committed to supporting Israel. As one former Democratic senator, Ernest Hollings, noted on leaving office, "you can't have an Israeli policy other than what AIPAC gives you around here." Or as Ariel Sharon once told an American audience, "when people ask me how they can help Israel, I tell them: 'Help AIPAC.'"

Thanks in part to the influence Jewish voters have on presidential elections, the Lobby also has significant leverage over the executive branch. Although they make up fewer than 3 per cent of the population, they make large campaign donations to candidates from both parties. The *Washington Post* once estimated that Democratic presidential candidates "depend on Jewish supporters to supply as much as 60 per cent of the money." And because Jewish voters have high turn-out rates and are concentrated in key states like California, Florida, Illinois, New York, and Pennsylvania, presidential candidates go to great lengths not to antagonise them. . . .

During the Clinton administration, Middle Eastern policy was largely shaped by officials with close ties to Israel or to prominent pro-Israel organisations; among them, Martin Indyk, the former deputy director of research at AIPAC and co-founder of the pro-Israel Washington Institute for Near East Policy (WINEP); Dennis Ross, who joined WINEP after leaving government in 2001; and Aaron Miller, who has lived in Israel and often visits the country. These men were among Clinton's closest advisers at the Camp David summit in July 2000. Although all three supported the Oslo peace process and favoured the creation of a Palestinian state, they did so only within the limits of what would be acceptable to Israel. The American delegation took its cues from Ehud Barak, coordinated its negotiating positions with Israel in advance, and did not offer independent proposals. Not surprisingly, Palestinian negotiators complained that they were "negotiating with two Israeli teams — one displaying an Israeli flag, and one an American flag."

The situation is even more pronounced in the Bush administration, whose ranks have included such fervent advocates of the Israeli cause as Elliot Abrams, John Bolton, Douglas Feith, I. Lewis ("Scooter") Libby, Richard Perle, Paul Wolfowitz, and David Wurmser. As we shall see, these officials have consistently pushed for policies favoured by Israel and backed by organisations in the Lobby.

The Lobby doesn't want an open debate, of course, because that might lead Americans to question the level of support they provide. Accordingly, pro-Israel organisations work hard to influence the institutions that do most to shape popular opinion.

The Lobby's perspective prevails in the mainstream media: the debate among Middle East pundits, the journalist Eric Alterman writes, is "dominated by people who cannot imagine criticising Israel." He lists 61 "columnists and commentators who can be counted on to support Israel reflexively and without qualification." Conversely, he found just five pundits who consistently criticise Israeli actions or endorse Arab positions. Newspapers occasionally publish guest op-eds challenging Israeli policy, but the balance of opinion clearly favours the other side. It is hard to imagine any mainstream media outlet in the United States publishing a piece like this one. . . .

No discussion of the Lobby would be complete without an examination of one of its most powerful weapons: the charge of anti-semitism. Anyone who criticises Israel's actions or argues that pro-Israel groups have significant influence over U.S. Middle Eastern policy — an influence AIPAC celebrates — stands a good chance of being labelled an anti-semite. Indeed, anyone who merely claims that there *is* an Israel Lobby runs the risk of being charged with anti-semitism, even though the Israeli media refer to America's "Jewish Lobby." In other words, the Lobby first boasts of its influence and then attacks anyone who calls attention to it. It's a very effective tactic: anti-semitism is something no one wants to be accused of. . . .

Critics are also accused of holding Israel to an unfair standard or questioning its right to exist. But these are bogus charges too. Western critics of Israel hardly ever question its right to exist: they question its behaviour towards the Palestinians, as do Israelis themselves. Nor is Israel being judged unfairly. Israeli treatment of the Palestinians elicits criticism because it is contrary to widely accepted notions of human rights, to international law, and to the principle of national self-determination. And it is hardly the only state that has faced sharp criticism on these grounds.

In the autumn of 2001, and especially in the spring of 2002, the Bush administration tried to reduce anti-American sentiment in the Arab world and undermine support for terrorist groups like al-Qaida by halting Israel's expansionist policies in the Occupied Territories and advocating the creation of a Palestinian state. Bush had very significant means of persuasion at his disposal. He could have threatened to reduce economic and diplomatic support for Israel, and the American people would almost certainly have supported him. A May 2003 poll reported that more than 60 per cent of Americans were willing to withhold aid if Israel resisted U.S. pressure to settle the conflict, and that number rose to 70 per cent among the "politically active." Indeed, 73 per cent said that the United States should not favour either side.

Yet the administration failed to change Israeli policy, and Washington ended up backing it. Over time, the administration also adopted Israel's own justifications of its position, so that U.S. rhetoric began to mimic Israeli rhetoric. By February 2003, a *Washington Post* headline summarised the situation: "Bush and Sharon Nearly Identical on Mideast Policy." The main reason for this switch was the Lobby. . . .

Maintaining U.S. support for Israel's policies against the Palestinians is essential as far as the Lobby is concerned, but its ambitions do not stop there. It also wants America to help Israel remain the dominant regional power. The Israeli government and pro-Israel groups in the United States have worked together to shape the administration's policy towards Iraq, Syria, and Iran, as well as its grand scheme for reordering the Middle East.

Pressure from Israel and the Lobby was not the only factor behind the decision to attack Iraq in March 2003, but it was critical. Some Americans believe that this was a war for oil, but there is hardly any direct evidence to support this claim. Instead, the war was motivated in good part by a desire to make Israel more secure. According to Philip Zelikow, a former member of the president's Foreign Intelligence Advisory Board, the executive director of the 9/11 Commission, and now a counsellor to Condoleezza Rice, the "real threat" from Iraq was not a threat to the United States. The "unstated threat" was the "threat against Israel," Zelikow told an audience at the University of Virginia in September 2002. "The American government," he added, "doesn't want to lean too hard on it rhetorically, because it is not a popular sell." . . .

Within the U.S., the main driving force behind the war was a small band of neo-conservatives, many with ties to Likud. But leaders of the Lobby's major organisations lent their voices to the campaign. "As President Bush attempted to sell the . . . war in Iraq," the *Forward* reported, "America's most important Jewish organisations rallied as one to his defence. In statement after statement community leaders stressed the need to rid the world of Saddam Hussein and his weapons of mass destruction." The editorial goes on to say that "concern for Israel's safety rightfully factored into the deliberations of the main Jewish groups."

Although neo-conservatives and other Lobby leaders were eager to invade Iraq, the broader American Jewish community was not. Just after the war started, Samuel Freedman reported that "a compilation of nationwide opinion polls by the Pew Research Center shows that Jews are less supportive of the Iraq war than the population at large, 52 per cent to 62 per cent." Clearly, it would be wrong to blame the war in Iraq on "Jewish influence." Rather, it was due in large part to the Lobby's influence, especially that of the neo-conservatives within it. . . .

Given the neo-conservatives' devotion to Israel, their obsession with Iraq, and their influence in the Bush administration, it isn't surprising that many Americans suspected that the war was designed to further Israeli interests. Last March, Barry Jacobs of the American Jewish Committee acknowledged that the belief that Israel and the neo-conservatives had conspired to get the U.S. into a war in Iraq was "pervasive" in the intelligence community. Yet few people would say so publicly, and most of those who did — including Senator Ernest Hollings and Representative James Moran — were condemned for raising the issue. Michael Kinsley wrote in late 2002 that "the lack of public discussion about the role of Israel . . . is the proverbial elephant in the room." The reason for the reluctance to talk about it, he observed, was fear of being labelled an anti-semite. There is little doubt that Israel and the Lobby were key factors in the decision to go to war. It's a decision the U.S. would have been far less likely to take without their efforts. And the war itself was intended to be only the first step. A front-page headline in the *Wall Street Journal* shortly after the war began says it all: "President's Dream: Changing Not Just Regime but a Region: A Pro-US, Democratic Area Is a Goal That Has Israeli and Neo-Conservative Roots."

REFLECTIONS

We began the chapter by asking how representative the Israel/Palestine conflict was of other conflicts over religion and politics at the end of the twentieth century. It is almost commonplace today to describe the conflict between Israel and Palestine as an eternal struggle between two implacably opposed religions: Judaism and Islam. We do this with other contemporary conflicts where religion plays a role: We call the conflict in Northern Ireland one between Catholics and Protestants, that of India and Pakistan a conflict between Hindus and Muslims. But in all of these cases, religion is only part of the story. There is also a conflict over land, ethnic and class differences, and political alliances that have nothing to do with religion (Pakistan and China, for instance), and often secular military leaders play a major role.

One of the greatest surprises in our investigation of the background of the conflict between Israel and Palestine might be how unimportant religion was at many stages. For Herzl and the early Zionists, religion as nationality was important, but most Jews were more intent on assimilating into their European or American cultures. David Fromkin notes that before World War I only about 1 percent of the world's Jews were Zionists, a proportion also roughly true for Jews in the United States. After the Balfour Declaration, and far more after World War II and the Holocaust, the number of Jews who chose to emigrate to Israel increased considerably, as did those who supported Israel.

Many Jewish immigrants to Israel, however, were secular in culture and belief. Herzl imagined a flag with seven stars not to evoke the days of creation and the Sabbath day of rest but to symbolise the hope of Jewish socialists for a seven-hour day. The model form of early Jewish colonization was the communal settlement or *kibbutz*. European and Russian refugees came to Israel for land and political autonomy, many from communities which were not religious. Even today many Israelis describe themselves as secular Jews.

Similarly on the Palestinian side, we read complaints in the documents of Jewish immigrants buying and taking Arab land and of changing the character of Palestine, but not of animosity to Judaism as a faith or practice. In fact, one of the central Palestinian fears from 1917 to 1948 was that the creation of a Jewish state — as opposed to a binational state — would make Palestinians unwelcome in their own land. There appears to be little conflict between the faiths of Judaism and Islam in these documents. Jews and the international inquiries speak of Arabs, not Muslims. From 1948 until 2000 the dominant parties of the Palestinian resistance movement were all rigorously secular. Hamas and Muslim fundamentalist or Islamicist groups gained popular support only after the failure of the secular movement sensed in the collapse of the Camp David peace talks in 2000 and the death of Yassir Arafat and defeat of his Fatah party shortly thereafter. Notice how deeply disillusioned Benny Morris became after 2000.

Recent years have witnessed increased religious motivation and more widespread religious fundamentalism on the part of Jews and Christians as well as Muslims. Hamas fundamentalists have their counterparts in Israeli settlers who believe God calls them to claim all of Biblical Israel regardless of current state boundaries and Christian evangelicals who foment strife in Israel to realize Armageddon.

The last reading, however, suggests that the religious fervor of Jews and Christians has been exploited and channeled by more political interests in the United States and Israel. If our analysis is correct, the local and global political powers play a dangerous game manipulating popular religious extremism to temporary advantages. When the great powers of 1914 used nationalist extremists in the same way, the disastrous consequences were felt globally and lasted for generations.

Women's World

1950 to the Present

HISTORICAL CONTEXT

Today, historians both male and female try not to restrict their work to the activities or testimonies of men. Yet, because men dominated politics, war, and industry for many years, oftentimes important historical studies have ignored women. Historians now attempt to research and write more complete, balanced historical accounts, addressing topics in which women have played important roles. Such topics include the history of the family, sexuality, privacy, popular culture, domesticity, and work, among others. In recent years, women's history and women's studies have become vibrant fields of specialization and discovery.

This chapter offers readings that, taken together, constitute a history of women since 1950. We will read women's accounts from various parts of the world, as they describe aspects of their lives and those of other women. We begin, however, with the Chinese Marriage Law of 1950 so we might consider the new legal baseline for one-fifth of the world's population. (This law was replicated in many other countries as well.) We then turn to the emerging women's movement in the United States, spearheaded by a far-reaching book, *The Feminine Mystique* (1963). Next, an Algerian novelist reflects on youth, adolescence, and family. Then an unemployed Brazilian talks about her life. Finally, we move from the personal to the political, with letters from Aung San Suu Kyi of Burma, a U.N. document on women in politics, and an unusual news story.

All of the women featured in this chapter are articulate, literate, self-conscious writers. Their eloquence allows us to reflect on the power of words for women, as well as for men.

THINKING HISTORICALLY
Constructing Theory

The notion of "constructing theory" may seem much more demanding than it is. It is little more than bringing together ideas that explain phenomena in history. Put simply, a theory offers a possible answer to a question or an explanation of a problem. Theories are not necessarily true; they are guesses, called hypotheses, and have to be tested and supported with evidence. Theories might come to us from reading either primary or secondary sources, but ultimately a theory must make sense of the primary sources, the raw experience of history. A theory organizes experience in a way that makes it more comprehensible. It seeks patterns or an explanation of patterns: causes, consequences, connections, relationships, reasons.

Ultimately, of course, a theory must be tested with new evidence. A good theory will interpret or incorporate new evidence without needing much change. In this chapter, you are asked only to focus on constructing theory. Occasionally, you will be reminded of the limitations of the sources included here, but our emphasis will be on conceiving and expressing theories that give meaning to the material at hand.

As you read these selections, try to construct a theory about the history of women over the last fifty or sixty years. You might begin with the very basic question: Did the lives of women improve during this period? If you think they have, or have not, you might develop a theory as to why. It could be more modest than that. You might, for instance, develop a theory about why women's lives improved in a particular kind of society, but not in some other type of society. It might be something unrelated to the larger question of improvements for women. You might have a theory about particular kinds of women, or gender relations somewhere, or voting for women, or whatever springs from the readings and answers some question that the readings pose for you.

81

The Marriage Law of the
People's Republic of China

Chinese revolutionaries in the twentieth century frequently called for women's rights and equality. The "women question" was at the forefront of the Nationalist revolution of 1911 and, again, of the Communist revolution of 1949. Women who had been active in the revolution of 1911 sought women's suffrage and an end to such patriarchal practices as foot-binding, the concubine system, child marriage, and prostitution. But the visions of Chinese revolutionaries often remained promises in word only.

The government of Chiang Kai-shek passed major resolutions in 1924 and 1926 to enact laws that would codify many of the aspirations of the women's movement: legal equality, right to own property, freely entered marriage, right to divorce, even equal pay for equal work. But in 1927, Chiang's Nationalist party broke its alliance with the communists and identified them with women's issues to smear them. In fact, many of the founders of the Communist party, including Mao Zedong, were proponents of family reform (free marriage and free love) before they were Marxists. Despite this, as they sought supporters and volunteers throughout China after 1927, especially in the more traditional and male-dominated countryside, they quickly dropped their calls for reform of the marriage and family laws.

When the Communists came to power in China in 1949, marriage reform again surfaced as a high priority in constructing a new society. The 1950 Marriage Law, excerpted here, led to a widespread debate on the role of women in Chinese communist society. What practices did the Chinese Communists seek to curb with this law?

Thinking Historically

Construct a theory about how different groups of people in China might respond to this law. Among the groups you might consider are rich men, poor men, rich women, poor women, young and old, city and country people.

The Marriage Law of the People's Republic of China (Peking: Foreign Languages Press, 1959).

Chapter I. General Principles

Article 1. The arbitrary and compulsory feudal marriage system, which is based on the superiority of man over woman and which ignores the children's interests, shall be abolished.

The new democratic marriage system, which is based on free choice of partners, on monogamy, on equal rights for both sexes, and on protection of the lawful interests of women and children, shall be put into effect.

Article 2. Bigamy, concubinage, child betrothal, interference with the remarriage of widows, and the exaction of money or gifts in connection with marriage shall be prohibited. . . .

Chapter III. Rights and Duties of Husband and Wife

Article 7. Husband and wife are companions living together and shall enjoy equal status in the home.

Article 8. Husband and wife are in duty bound to love, respect, assist, and look after each other, to live in harmony, to engage in production, to care for the children, and to strive jointly for the welfare of the family and for the building up of a new society.

Article 9. Both husband and wife shall have the right to free choice of occupation and free participation in work or in social activities.

Article 10. Both husband and wife shall have equal right in the possession and management of family property.

82

BETTY FRIEDAN

From The Feminine Mystique

This book elicited an enormous response from women in the United
States and around the world when it was published in 1963. What
Friedan* called "the problem that has no name" was immediately understood and widely discussed. What name would you give to the
problem? What were its causes? Do women still feel it today?

Thinking Historically

In what ways were the needs of American women after World War II
like those of Chinese women? In what ways were they different?
Which do you find more striking, the similarities or the differences?
What theories would explain why Chinese and American women had
different problems in the 1950s and 1960s?

The problem lay buried, unspoken, for many years in the minds of
American women. It was a strange stirring, a sense of dissatisfaction, a
yearning that women suffered in the middle of the twentieth century in
the United States. Each suburban wife struggled with it alone. As she
made the beds, shopped for groceries, matched slipcover material, ate
peanut butter sandwiches with her children, chauffeured Cub Scouts
and Brownies, lay beside her husband at night — she was afraid to ask
even of herself the silent question — "Is this all?"

For over fifteen years there was no word of this yearning in the millions of words written about women, for women, in all the columns,
books, and articles by experts telling women their role was to seek fulfillment as wives and mothers. Over and over women heard in voices of
tradition and of Freudian sophistication that they could desire no
greater destiny than to glory in their own femininity. Experts told them
how to catch a man and keep him, how to breastfeed children and
handle their toilet training, how to cope with sibling rivalry and adolescent rebellion; how to buy a dishwasher, bake bread, cook gourmet
snails, and build a swimming pool with their own hands; how to dress,
look, and act more feminine and make marriage more exciting; how to

*free DAN

Betty Friedan, *The Feminine Mystique* (New York: Dell, 1963), 11–12, 14, 15–16, 27.

keep their husbands from dying young and their sons from growing into delinquents. They were taught to pity the neurotic, unfeminine, unhappy women who wanted to be poets or physicists or presidents. They learned that truly feminine women do not want careers, higher education, political rights — the independence and the opportunities that the old-fashioned feminists fought for. Some women, in their forties and fifties, still remembered painfully giving up those dreams, but most of the younger women no longer even thought about them. A thousand expert voices applauded their femininity, their adjustment, their new maturity. All they had to do was devote their lives from earliest girlhood to finding a husband and bearing children. . . .

In the fifteen years after World War II, this mystique of feminine fulfillment became the cherished and self-perpetuating core of contemporary American culture. Millions of women lived their lives in the image of those pretty pictures of the American suburban housewife, kissing their husbands goodbye in front of the picture window, depositing their stationwagonsful of children at school, and smiling as they ran the new electric waxer over the spotless kitchen floor. They baked their own bread, sewed their own and their children's clothes, kept their new washing machines and dryers running all day. They changed the sheets on the beds twice a week instead of once, took the rug-hooking class in adult education, and pitied their poor frustrated mothers, who had dreamed of having a career. Their only dream was to be perfect wives and mothers; their highest ambition to have five children and a beautiful house, their only fight to get and keep their husbands. They had no thought for the unfeminine problems of the world outside the home; they wanted the men to make the major decisions. They gloried in their role as women, and wrote proudly on the census blank: "Occupation: housewife." . . .

If a woman had a problem in the 1950s and 1960s, she knew that something must be wrong with her marriage, or with herself. Other women were satisfied with their lives, she thought. What kind of a woman was she if she did not feel this mysterious fulfillment waxing the kitchen floor? She was so ashamed to admit her dissatisfaction that she never knew how many other women shared it. If she tried to tell her husband, he didn't understand what she was talking about. She did not really understand it herself. For over fifteen years women in America found it harder to talk about this problem than about sex. Even the psychoanalysts had no name for it. When a woman went to a psychiatrist for help, as many women did, she would say, "I'm so ashamed," or "I must be hopelessly neurotic." "I don't know what's wrong with women today," a suburban psychiatrist said uneasily. "I only know something is wrong because most of my patients happen to be women. And their problem isn't sexual." Most women with this problem did not go to see a psychoanalyst, however. "There's nothing wrong really," they kept telling themselves. "There isn't any problem."

But on an April morning in 1959, I heard a mother of four, having coffee with four other mothers in a suburban development fifteen miles from New York, say in a tone of quiet desperation, "the problem." And the others knew, without words, that she was not talking about a problem with her husband, or her children, or her home. Suddenly they realized they all shared the same problem, the problem that has no name. They began, hesitantly, to talk about it. Later, after they had picked up their children at nursery school and taken them home to nap, two of the women cried, in sheer relief, just to know they were not alone.

Gradually I came to realize that the problem that has no name was shared by countless women in America. As a magazine writer I often interviewed women about problems with their children, or their marriages, or their houses, or their communities. But after a while I began to recognize the telltale signs of this other problem. I saw the same signs in suburban ranch houses and split-levels on Long Island and in New Jersey and Westchester County; in colonial houses in a small Massachusetts town; on patios in Memphis; in suburban and city apartments; in living rooms in the Midwest. Sometimes I sensed the problem, not as a reporter, but as a suburban housewife, for during this time I was also bringing up my own three children in Rockland County, New York. I heard echoes of the problem in college dormitories and semi-private maternity wards, at PTA meetings and luncheons of the League of Women Voters, at suburban cocktail parties, in station wagons waiting for trains, and in snatches of conversation overheard at Schrafft's.[1] The groping words I heard from other women, on quiet afternoons when children were at school or on quiet evenings when husbands worked late, I think I understood first as a woman long before I understood their larger social and psychological implications.

Just what was this problem that has no name? What were the words women used when they tried to express it? Sometimes a woman would say "I feel empty somehow . . . incomplete." Or she would say, "I feel as if I don't exist." Sometimes she blotted out the feeling with a tranquilizer. Sometimes she thought the problem was with her husband, or her children, or that what she really needed was to redecorate her house, or move to a better neighborhood, or have an affair, or another baby. Sometimes, she went to a doctor with symptoms she could hardly describe: "A tired feeling . . . I get so angry with the children it

---

[1] A popular restaurant. [Ed.]

scares me . . . I feel like crying without any reason." (A Cleveland doctor called it "the housewife's syndrome.") A number of women told me about great bleeding blisters that break out on their hands and arms. "I call it the housewife's blight," said a family doctor in Pennsylvania. "I see it so often lately in these young women with four, five, and six children who bury themselves in their dishpans. But it isn't caused by detergent and it isn't cured by cortisone." . . .

If I am right, the problem that has no name stirring in the minds of so many American women today is not a matter of loss of femininity or too much education, or the demands of domesticity. It is far more important than anyone recognizes. It is the key to these other new and old problems which have been torturing women and their husbands and children, and puzzling their doctors and educators for years. It may well be the key to our future as a nation and a culture. We can no longer ignore that voice within women that says: "I want something more than my husband and my children and my home."

83

ASSIA DJEBAR

Growing Up in Algeria

Excerpted from a novel by Algerian author Assia Djebar*, this selection is about growing up in Algeria just before the revolution for independence from France, which began in 1954. To the extent to which her account is autobiographical, what do you think it was like to grow up in Algeria as a young teenage girl around 1950? How typical do you think this girl's life and concerns were?

The author discusses how her experiences in the French and Koranic religious school pulled her in different directions. What were they? Writing and reading were very important to her, but they both meant different things in Arabic Muslim culture and French culture. In the Koranic schools, young people learn the Koran by reciting and memorizing it (just as Mohammed did). What was the meaning of reading in French

*AHS yuh   jeh BAHR

Assia Djebar, "Growing Up in Algeria," in *Fantasia: An Algerian Cavalcade*, trans. Dorothy S. Blair (Portsmouth, N.H.: Heinemann, 1993), 179–85.

for the author? What were the different meanings of writing for her? Do you think this exposure to both languages was making her more Arabic or French? Which identity was more real for her?

In what ways were the needs and interests of this teenage girl similar to, or different from, those of an American teenage girl in the same period? Do you think their lives have become more alike since then?

Thinking Historically

Construct a theory that answers one of the questions posed above. Keep in mind that a theory is not an answer — it is a guiding principle for an answer. So, for instance, if you choose to consider the question, "Which identity was more real for her?" an answer might be "Arabic," and a theory could be that "a person's mother tongue determines who she is." A theory is a general principle supported by evidence. (For example, you could interview bilingual people to find out if their first language played a greater role than their second in shaping their identities.) Keep in mind that many different theories are possible in answer to each question.

At the age when I should be veiled already, I can still move about freely thanks to the French school: Every Monday the village bus takes me to the boarding school in the nearby town, and brings me back on Saturday to my parents' home.

I have a friend who is half Italian and who goes home every weekend to a fishing port on the coast; we go together to catch our respective buses and are tempted by all sorts of escapades ... With beating hearts we make our way into the centre of the town; to enter a smart cake-shop, wander along the edge of the park, stroll along the boulevard, which only runs alongside common barracks, seems the acme of freedom, after a week of boarding school! Excited by the proximity of forbidden pleasures, we eventually each catch our bus; the thrill lay in the risk of missing it!

As a young teenager I enjoy the exhilarating hours spent every Thursday in training on the sports field. I only have one worry: fear that my father might come to visit me! How can I tell him that it's compulsory for me to wear shorts, in other words, I have to show my legs? I keep this fear a secret, unable to confide in any of my schoolfriends; unlike me, they haven't got cousins who do not show their ankles or their arms, who do not even expose their faces. My panic is also compounded by an Arab woman's "shame." The French girls whirl around me; they do not suspect that my body is caught in invisible snares.

"Doesn't your daughter wear a veil yet?" asks one or other of the matrons, gazing questioningly at my mother with suspicious kohl-rimmed eyes, on the occasion of one of the summer weddings. I must be thirteen, or possibly fourteen.

"She reads!" my mother replies stiffly.

Everyone is swallowed up in the embarrassed silence that ensues. And in my own silence.

"She reads," that is to say in Arabic, "she studies." I think now that this command "to read" was not just casually included in the Quranic revelation made by the Angel Gabriel in the cave . . . "She reads" is tantamount to saying that writing to be read, including that of the unbelievers, is always a source of revelation: in my case of the mobility of my body, and so of my future freedom.

When I am growing up — shortly before my native land throws off the colonial yoke — while the man still has the right to four legitimate wives, we girls, big and little, have at our command four languages to express desire before all that is left for us is sighs and moans: French for secret missives; Arabic for our stifled aspirations towards God-the-Father, the God of the religions of the Book; Lybico-Berber which takes us back to the pagan idols — mother-gods — of pre-Islamic Mecca. The fourth language, for all females, young or old, cloistered or half-emancipated, remains that of the body: the body which male neighbours' and cousins' eyes require to be deaf and blind, since they cannot completely incarcerate it; the body which, in trances, dances or vociferations, in fits of hope or despair, rebels, and unable to read or write, seeks some unknown shore as destination for its message of love.

In our towns, the first woman-reality is the voice, a dart which flies off into space, an arrow which slowly falls to earth; next comes writing with the scratching pointed quill forming amorous snares with its liana letters. By way of compensation, the need is felt to blot out women's bodies and they must be muffled up, tightly swathed, swaddled like infants or shrouded like corpses. Exposed, a woman's body would offend every eye, be an assault on the dimmest of desires, emphasize every separation. The voice, on the other hand, acts like a perfume, a draft of fresh water for the dry throat; and when it is savoured, it can be enjoyed by several simultaneously; a secret, polygamous pleasure . . .

When the hand writes, slow positioning of the arm, carefully bending forward or leaning to one side, crouching, swaying to and fro, as in an act of love. When reading, the eyes take their time, delight in caressing the curves, while the calligraphy suggests the rhythm of the scansion: as if the writing marked the beginning and the end of possession.

Writing: Everywhere, a wealth of burnished gold and in its vicinity there is no place for other imagery from either animal or vegetable kingdom; it looks in the mirror of its scrolls and curlicues and sees itself as woman, not the reflection of a voice. It emphasizes by its presence alone where to begin and where to retreat; it suggests, by the song that smoulders in its heart, the dance floor for rejoicing and hair-shirt for the ascetic; I speak of the Arabic script; to be separated from it is to be separated from a great love. This script, which I mastered only to write the sacred words, I see now spread out before me cloaked in innocence and whispering arabesques — and ever since, all other scripts (French, English, Greek) seem only to babble, are never cathartic; they may contain truth, indeed, but a blemished truth.

Just as the pentathlon runner of old needed the starter, so, as soon as I learned the foreign script, my body began to move as if by instinct.

As if the French language suddenly had eyes, and lent them me to see into liberty; as if the French language blinded the peeping-toms of my clan and, at this price, I could move freely, run headlong down every street, annex the outdoors for my cloistered companions, for the matriarchs of my family who endured a living death. As if . . . Derision! I know that every language is a dark depository for piled-up corpses, refuse, sewage, but faced with the language of the former conquerer, which offers me its ornaments, its jewels, its flowers, I find they are the flowers of death — chrysanthemums on tombs!

Its script is a public unveiling in front of sniggering onlookers . . . A queen walks down the street, white, anonymous, draped, but when the shroud of rough wool is torn away and drops sudddenly at her feet, which a moment ago were hidden, she becomes a beggar again, squatting in the dust, to be spat at, the target of cruel comments.

In my earliest childhood — from the age of five to ten — I attended the French school in the village, and every day after lessons there I went on to the Quranic school.

Classes were held in a back room lent by a grocer, one of the village notables. I can recall the place, and its dim light: Was it because the time for the lessons was just before dark, or because the lighting of the room was so parsimonious? . . .

The master's image has remained singularly clear: delicate features, pale complexion, a scholar's sunken cheeks; about forty families supported him. I was struck by the elegance of his bearing and his traditional attire: A spotless light muslin was wrapped around his headdress and floated behind his neck; his serge tunic was dazzling white. I never saw this man except sitting.

In comparison, the horde of misbehaving little urchins squatting on straw mats — sons of *fellaheen* [peasants] for the most part — seemed crude riffraff, from whom I kept my distance.

We were only four or five little girls. I suppose that our sex kept us apart, rather than my supercilious amazement at their behaviour. In spite of his aristocratic bearing, the *taleb* [teacher] did not hesitate to lift his cane and bring it down on the fingers of a recalcitrant or slow-witted lad. (I can still hear it whistle through the air.) We girls were spared this regular punishment.

I can remember the little impromptu parties my mother devised in our flat when I brought home (as later my brother was to do) the walnut table decorated with arabesques. This was the master's reward when we had learnt a long *sura* by heart. My mother and our village nanny, who was a second mother to us, then let out that semi-barbaric "you-you." That prolonged, irregular, spasmodic cooing, which in our building reserved for teachers' families — all European except for ours — must have appeared incongruous, a truly primitive cry. My mother considered the circumstances (the study of the Quran undertaken by her children) sufficiently important for her to let out this ancestral cry of jubilation in the middle of the village where she nevertheless felt herself an exile.

At every prize-giving ceremony at the French school, every prize I obtained strengthened my solidarity with my own family; but I felt there was more glory in this ostentatious clamour. The Quranic school, that dim cavern in which the haughty figure of the Sheikh was enthroned above the poor village children, this school became, thanks to the joy my mother demonstrated in this way, an island of bliss — Paradise regained.

Back in my native city, I learned that another Arab school was being opened, also funded by private contributions. One of my cousins attended it; she took me there. I was disappointed. The buildings, the timetable, the modern appearance of the masters, made it no different from a common-or-garden French school . . .

I understood later that in the village I had participated in the last of popular, secular teaching. In the city, thanks to the Nationalist movement of "Modernist Muslims," a new generation of Arab culture was being forged.

Since then these *medrasas* have sprung up everywhere. If I had attended one of them (if I'd grown up in the town where I was born) I would have found it quite natural to swathe my head in a turban, to hide my hair, to cover my arms and calves, in a word to move about out of doors like a Muslim nun!

After the age of ten or eleven, shortly before puberty, I was no longer allowed to attend the Quranic school. At this age, boys are suddenly excluded from the women's Turkish bath — that emollient world of naked bodies stifling in a whirl of scalding steam . . . The same thing happened to my companions, the little village girls, one of whom I would like to describe here.

The daughter of the Kabyle baker must, like me, have attended the French school simultaneously with the Quranic school. But I can only recall her presence squatting at my side in front of the Sheikh: side by side, half smiling to each other, both already finding it uncomfortable to sit cross-legged! . . . My legs must have been too long, because of my height: It wasn't easy for me to hide them under my skirt.

For this reason alone I think that I would in any case have been weaned from Quranic instruction at this age: There is no doubt that it's easier to sit cross-legged when wearing a *seroual*; a young girl's body that is beginning to develop more easily conceals its form under the ample folds of the traditional costume. But my skirts, justified by my attendance at the French school, were ill adapted to such a posture.

When I was eleven I started secondary school and became a boarder. What happened to the baker's daughter? Certainly veiled, withdrawn overnight from school: betrayed by her figure. Her swelling breasts, her slender legs, in a word, the emergence of her woman's personality transformed her into an incarcerated body!

I remember how much this Quranic learning, as it is progressively acquired, is linked to the body.

The portion of the sacred verse, inscribed on both sides of the walnut tablet, had to be wiped off at least once a week, after we had shown that we could recite it off by heart. We scrubbed the piece of wood thoroughly, just like other people wash their clothes: The time it took to dry seemed to ensure the interval that the memory needed to digest what it had swallowed . . .

The learning was absorbed by the fingers, the arms, through the physical effort. The act of cleaning the tablet seemed like ingesting a portion of the Quranic text. The writing — itself a copy of writing which is considered immutable — could only continue to unfold before us if it relied, clause by clause, on this osmosis . . .

As the hand traces the liana-script, the mouth opens to repeat the words, obedient to their rhythm, partly to memorize, partly to relieve the muscular tension . . . The shrill voices of the drowsy children rise up in a monotonous, sing-song chorus.

Stumbling on, swaying from side to side, care taken to observe the tonic accents, to differentiate between long and short vowels, attentive to the rhythm of the chant; muscles of the larynx as well as the torso moving in harmony. Controlling the breath to allow the correct emission of the voice, and letting the understanding advance precariously along its tight-rope. Respecting the grammar by speaking it aloud, making it part of the chant.

This language which I learn demands the correct posture for the body, on which the memory rests for its support. The childish hand, spurred on — as in training for some sport — by willpower worthy of an adult, begins to write. "Read!" The fingers labouring on the tablet send back the signs to the body, which is simultaneously reader and servant. The lips having finished their muttering, the hand will once more do the washing, proceeding to wipe out what is written on the tablet: This is the moment of absolution, like touching the hem of death's garment. Again, it is the turn of writing, and the circle is completed.

And when I sit curled up like this to study my native language it is as though my body reproduces the architecture of my native city: the *medinas* with their tortuous alleyways closed off to the outside world, living their secret life. When I write and read the foreign language, my body travels far in subversive space, in spite of the neighbours and suspicious matrons; it would not need much for it to take wing and fly away!

As I approach a marriageable age, these two different apprenticeships, undertaken simultaneously, land me in a dichotomy of location. My father's preference will decide for me: light rather than darkness. I do not realize that an irrevocable choice is being made: the outdoors and the risk, instead of the prison of my peers. This stroke of luck brings me to the verge of breakdown.

I write and speak French outside: The words I use convey no flesh-and-blood reality. I learn the names of birds I've never seen, trees I shall take ten years or more to identify, lists of flowers and plants that I shall never smell until I travel north of the Mediterranean. In this respect, all vocabulary expresses what is missing in my life, exoticism without mystery, causing a kind of visual humiliation that it is not seemly to admit to . . . Settings and episodes in children's books are nothing but theoretical concepts; in the French family the mother comes to fetch her daughter or son from school; in the French street, the parents walk quite naturally side by side . . . So, the world of the school is expunged from the daily life of my native city, as it is from the life of my family. The latter is refused any referential rôle.

My conscious mind is here, huddled against my mother's knees, in the darkest corners of the flat which she never leaves. The ambit of the school is elsewhere: My search, my eyes are fixed on other regions. I do not realize, no-one around me realizes, that, in the conflict between these two worlds, lies an incipient vertigo.

84

CAROLINA MARIA DE JESUS

From Child of the Dark:
The Diary of Carolina Maria de Jesus

This selection is from the diary of a common — and extraordinary — woman in Brazil in 1958. Carolina Maria de Jesus* was born in 1913 in a small town in the interior of Brazil. Her mother, unmarried and unemployed, insisted that Carolina attend school, which she hated until the day she learned to read. She remembers reading out loud every sign and label she could find. It was the beginning of a lifetime fascination with words, but she was forced to leave school after the second grade.

When Carolina was sixteen, her mother moved to the suburbs of São Paulo.† Carolina worked in a hospital, ran away to sing in a circus, and was employed in a long succession of jobs as cleaning woman and maid when, in 1947, she became pregnant. Her lover had abandoned her, and the family she worked for refused to let her into their house. Desperate, she moved into a *favela*‡ (slum) in São Paulo, building her own shack with cardboard and cans taken from a Church construction site. In the next ten years she had two more children. In order to keep from thinking of her troubles, she wrote. Poems, plays, novels, "anything and everything, for when I was writing I was in a golden palace, with crystal windows and silver chandeliers." She also kept a diary that reveals the actual details of her daily life. It is a life still lived by many women in the *favelas* of Brazil.

What does the diary tell you about the lives of the poor in Brazil?

Thinking Historically

Carolina Maria de Jesus is an articulate and thoughtful woman whose writing has helped her shape her own ideas. If you asked her what caused such poverty in her country, what might she say? Does she offer any theories about this? What is your theory for the existence of such poverty? How do you think she would respond to *The Feminine Mystique*? Do you have a theory about that?

*kah rol LEE nah   mah REE ah   duh jay SOOS
†sown   POW loh
‡fah VEL uh

Carolina Maria de Jesus, *Child of the Dark: The Diary of Carolina Maria de Jesus*, trans. David St. Clair (New York: NAL Penguin, 1962), 32–34, 42–47.

May 2, 1958 I'm not lazy. There are times when I try to keep up my diary. But then I think it's not worth it and figure I'm wasting my time.

I've made a promise to myself. I want to treat people that I know with more consideration. I want to have a pleasant smile for children and the employed.

I received a summons to appear at 8 P.M. at police station number 12. I spent the day looking for paper. At night my feet pained me so I couldn't walk. It started to rain. I went to the station and took José Carlos with me. The summons was for him. José Carlos is nine years old.

May 3 I went to the market at Carlos de Campos Street looking for any old thing. I got a lot of greens. But it didn't help much, for I've got no cooking fat. The children are upset because there's nothing to eat.

May 6 In the morning I went for water. I made João carry it. I was happy, then I received another summons. I was inspired yesterday and my verses were so pretty, I forgot to go to the station. It was 11:00 when I remembered the invitation from the illustrious lieutenant of the 12th precinct.

My advice to would-be politicians is that people do not tolerate hunger. It's necessary to know hunger to know how to describe it.

They are putting up a circus here at Araguaia Street. The Nilo Circus Theater.

May 9 I looked for paper but I didn't like it. Then I thought: I'll pretend that I'm dreaming.

May 10 I went to the police station and talked to the lieutenant. What a pleasant man! If I had known he was going to be so pleasant, I'd have gone on the first summons. The lieutenant was interested in my boys' education. He said the *favelas* have an unhealthy atmosphere where the people have more chance to go wrong than to become useful to state and country. I thought: If he knows this why doesn't he make a report and send it to the politicians? . . . Now he tells me this, I a poor garbage collector. I can't even solve my own problems.

Brazil needs to be led by a person who has known hunger. Hunger is also a teacher.

Who has gone hungry learns to think of the future and of the children.

May 11 Today is Mother's Day. The sky is blue and white. It seems that even nature wants to pay homage to the mothers who feel unhappy because they can't realize the desires of their children.

The sun keeps climbing. Today it's not going to rain. Today is our day.

Dona Teresinha came to visit me. She gave me 15 *cruzeiros* and said it was for Vera to go to the circus. But I'm going to use the money to buy bread tomorrow because I only have four *cruzeiros*.

Yesterday I got half a pig's head at the slaughterhouse. We ate the meat and saved the bones. Today I put the bones on to boil and into the broth I put some potatoes. My children are always hungry. When they are starving they aren't so fussy about what they eat.

Night came. The stars are hidden. The shack is filled with mosquitoes. I lit a page from a newspaper and ran it over the walls. This is the way the *favela* dwellers kill mosquitoes.

May 13 At dawn it was raining. Today is a nice day for me, it's the anniversary of the Abolition. The day we celebrate the freeing of the slaves. In the jails the Negroes were the scapegoats. But now the whites are more educated and don't treat us any more with contempt. May God enlighten the whites so that the Negroes may have a happier life.

It continued to rain and I only have beans and salt. The rain is strong but even so I sent the boys to school. I'm writing until the rain goes away so I can go to Senhor Manuel and sell scrap. With that money I'm going to buy rice and sausage. The rain has stopped for a while. I'm going out.

I feel so sorry for my children. When they see the things to eat that I come home with they shout:

"Viva Mama!"

Their outbursts please me. I've lost the habit of smiling. Ten minutes later they want more food. I sent João to ask Dona Ida for a little pork fat. She didn't have any. I sent her a note:

"Dona Ida, I beg you to help me get a little pork fat, so I can make soup for the children. Today it's raining and I can't go looking for paper. Thank you, Carolina."

It rained and got colder. Winter had arrived and in winter people eat more. Vera asked for food, and I didn't have any. It was the same old show. I had two *cruzeiros* and wanted to buy a little flour to make a *virado*.[1] I went to ask Dona Alice for a little pork. She gave me pork and rice. It was 9 at night when we ate.

And that is the way on May 13, 1958, I fought against the real slavery — hunger!

May 15 On the nights they have a party they don't let anybody sleep. The neighbors in the brick houses near by have signed a petition to get rid of the *favelados*. But they won't get their way. The neighbors in the brick houses say:

"The politicians protect the *favelados*."

Who protects us are the public and the Order of St. Vincent Church. The politicians only show up here during election campaigns. Senhor Candido Sampaio, when he was city councilman in 1953, spent his Sundays here in the *favela*. He was so nice. He drank our coffee, drinking right out of our cups. He made us laugh with his jokes. He played with our children. He left a good impression here

---

[1] A dish of black beans, manioc flour, pork, and eggs.

and when he was candidate for state deputy, he won. But the Chamber of Deputies didn't do one thing for the *favelados*. He doesn't visit us any more. . . .

May 22 Today I'm sad. I'm nervous. I don't know if I should start crying or start running until I fall unconscious. At dawn it was raining. I couldn't go out to get any money. I spent the day writing. I cooked the macaroni and I'll warm it up again for the children. I cooked the potatoes and they ate them. I have a few tin cans and a little scrap that I'm going to sell to Senhor Manuel. When João came home from school I sent him to sell the scrap. He got 13 *cruzeiros*. He bought a glass of mineral water: two *cruzeiros*. I was furious with him. Where had he seen a *favelado* with such highborn tastes?

The children eat a lot of bread. They like soft bread but when they don't have it, they eat hard bread.

Hard is the bread that we eat. Hard is the bed on which we sleep. Hard is the life of the *favelado*.

Oh, São Paulo! A queen that vainly shows her skyscrapers that are her crown of gold. All dressed up in velvet and silk but with cheap stockings underneath — the *favela*.

The money didn't stretch far enough to buy meat, so I cooked macaroni with a carrot. I didn't have any grease, it was horrible. Vera was the only one who complained yet asked for more.

"Mama, sell me to Dona Julita, because she has delicious food."

I know that there exist Brazilians here inside São Paulo who suffer more than I do. In June of '57 I felt sick and passed through the offices of the Social Service. I had carried a lot of scrap iron and got pains in my kidneys. So as not to see my children hungry I asked for help from the famous Social Service. It was there that I saw the tears slipping from the eyes of the poor. How painful it is to see the dramas that are played out there. The coldness in which they treat the poor. The only things they want to know about them is their name and address.

I went to the Governor's Palace.[2] The Palace sent me to an office at Brigadeiro Luis Antonio Avenue. They in turn sent me to the Social Service at the Santa Casa charity hospital. There I talked with Dona Maria Aparecida, who listened to me, said many things yet said nothing. I decided to go back to the Palace. I talked with Senhor Alcides. He is not Japanese yet is as yellow as rotten butter. I said to Senhor Alcides:

"I came here to ask for help because I'm ill. You sent me to Brigadeiro Luis Antonio Avenue, and I went. There they sent me to the Santa Casa. And I spent all the money I have on transportation."

"Take her!"

---

[2]Like most Brazilians, Carolina believes in going straight to the top to make her complaints.

They wouldn't let me leave. A soldier put his bayonet at my chest. I looked the soldier in the eyes and saw that he had pity on me. I told him:

"I am poor. That's why I came here."

Dr. Osvaldo de Barros entered, a false philanthropist in São Paulo who is masquerading as St. Vincent de Paul. He said:

"Call a squad car!"

The policeman took me back to the *favela* and warned me that the next time I made a scene at the welfare agency I would be locked up.

Welfare agency! Welfare for whom? . . .

May 27 It seems that the slaughterhouse threw kerosene on their garbage dump so the *favelados* would not look for meat to eat. I didn't have any breakfast and walked around half dizzy. The daze of hunger is worse than that of alcohol. The daze of alcohol makes us sing, but the one of hunger makes us shake. I know how horrible it is to only have air in the stomach.

I began to have a bitter taste in my mouth. I thought: Is there no end to the bitterness of life? I think that when I was born I was marked by fate to go hungry. I filled one sack of paper. When I entered Paulo Guimarães Street, a woman gave me some newspapers. They were clean and I went to the junk yard picking up everything that I found. Steel, tin, coal, everything serves the *favelado*. Leon weighed the paper and I got six *cruzeiros*.

I wanted to save the money to buy beans but I couldn't because my stomach was screaming and torturing me.

I decided to do something about it and bought a bread roll. What a surprising effect food has on our organisms. Before I ate, I saw the sky, the trees, and the birds all yellow, but after I ate, everything was normal to my eyes.

Food in the stomach is like fuel in machines. I was able to work better. My body stopped weighing me down. I started to walk faster. I had the feeling that I was gliding in space. I started to smile as if I was witnessing a beautiful play. And will there ever be a drama more beautiful than that of eating? I felt that I was eating for the first time in my life.

The Radio Patrol arrived. They came to take the two Negro boys who had broken into the power station. Four and six years old. It's easy to see that they are of the *favela*. *Favela* children are the most ragged children in the city. What they can find in the streets they eat. Banana peels, melon rind, and even pineapple husks. Anything that is too tough to chew, they grind. These boys had their pockets filled with aluminum coins, that new money in circulation.

May 28 It dawned raining. I only have three *cruzeiros* because I loaned Leila five so she could get her daughter in the hospital. I'm confused and don't know where to begin. I want to write, I want to work, I want to wash clothes. I'm cold and I don't have any shoes to wear. The children's shoes are worn out.

The worst thing in the *favela* is that there are children here. All the children of the *favela* know what a woman's body looks like. Because when the couples that are drunk fight, the woman, so as not to get a beating, runs naked into the street. When the fights start the *favelados* leave whatever they are doing to be present at the battle. So that when the woman goes running naked it's a real show for Joe Citizen. Afterward the comments begin among the children:

"Fernanda ran out nude when Armin was hitting her."

"Oh, I didn't see it. Damn!"

"What does a naked woman look like?"

And then the other, in order to tell him, puts his mouth near his ear. And the loud laughter echoes. Everything that is obscene or pornographic the *favelado* learns quickly.

There are some shacks where prostitutes play their love scenes right in front of the children.

The rich neighbors in the brick houses say we are protected by the politicians. They're wrong. The politicians only show up here in the Garbage Dump at election time. This year we had a visit from a candidate for deputy, Dr. Paulo de Campos Moura, who gave us beans and some wonderful blankets. He came at an opportune moment, before it got cold.

What I want to clear up about the people who live in the *favela* is the following: The only ones who really survive here are the *nordestinos*.[3] They work and don't squander. They buy a house or go back up north.

Here in the *favela* there are those who build shacks to live in and those who build them to rent. And the rents are from 500 to 700 *cruzeiros*. Those who make shacks to sell spend 4,000 *cruzeiros* and sell them for 11,000. Who made a lot of shacks to sell was Tiburcio.

May 29 It finally stopped raining. The clouds glided toward the horizon. Only the cold attacked us. Many people in the *favela* don't have warm clothing. When one has shoes he won't have a coat. I choke up watching the children walk in the mud. It seems that some new people have arrived in the *favela*. They are ragged with undernourished faces. They improvised a shack. It hurts me to see so much pain, reserved for the working class. I stared at my new companion in misfortune. She looked at the *favela* with its mud and sickly children. It was the saddest look I'd ever seen. Perhaps she has no more illusions. She had given her life over to misery.

---

[3]Forced by land-parching droughts and almost no industry, the poor of the north swarm into cities like São Paulo and Rio looking for work. Needing a place to live, they choose the *favelas* and end up worse off than they were before.

There will be those who reading what I write will say — this is untrue. But misery is real.

What I revolt against is the greed of men who squeeze other men as if they were squeezing oranges.

AUNG SAN SUU KYI*

From Letters from Burma

The author of these letters heads the democratic political party that won election in Burma in 1980. In consequence, she was placed under house arrest by the brutal military junta (SLORC, for State Law and Order Restoration Council), which has continued to rule. Despite her receipt of the Nobel Prize in 1991 and continued devotional support from the Burmese people, the generals have refused to let this daughter of Aung San — Burma's national hero who was assassinated in 1947 just before Burma achieved independence — take office and sometimes even leave her house.

In these letters, written to a Japanese newspaper in 1996, Suu Kyi reveals an unusual combination of the personal and political, some might say the patriotic without the patriarchal. Is this a view of politics that a male politician would be unlikely to hold?

Thinking Historically

Is there such a thing as women's politics? Do women vote differently than men? If so, what is that difference? Construct a theory that explains it.

Some people have pointed to the relatively large number of women presidents and prime ministers in South Asia in recent years. Women have been elected to govern India, Pakistan, Sri Lanka, as well as Burma. Can you formulate a theory that might explain this?

Many would say that particular women who have governed South Asia — Indira Gandhi of India, Benazir Bhutto of Pakistan, Sirimavo Bandaranaike of Sri Lanka — have not governed any differently from

*ong sahn   soo KYEE

Aung San Suu Kyi, *Letters from Burma* (New York: Penguin, 1996), 19–21, 55–57.

men. Perhaps politics has more to do with social background, interests, wealth, and class than it does with gender. Try to formulate a theory about women in politics that is based on the readings of this chapter.

The Peacock and the Dragon

The tenth day of the waning moon of the month of Tazaungdine marks National Day in Burma. It is the anniversary of the boycott against the 1920 Rangoon University Act which was seen by the Burmese as a move to restrict higher education to a privileged few. This boycott, which was initiated by university students, gained widespread support and could be said to have been the first step in the movement for an independent Burma. National Day is thus a symbol of the intimate and indissoluble link between political and intellectual freedom and of the vital role that students have played in the politics of Burma.

This year the seventy-fifth anniversary of National Day fell on 16 November. A committee headed by elder politicians and prominent men of letters was formed to plan the commemoration ceremony. It was decided that the celebrations should be on a modest scale in keeping with our financial resources and the economic situation of the country. The programme was very simple: some speeches, the presentation of prizes to those who had taken part in essay competitions organized by the National League for Democracy, and the playing of songs dating back to the days of the independence struggle. There was also a small exhibition of photographs, old books, and magazines.

An unseasonable rain had been falling for several days before the sixteenth but on the morning of National Day itself the weather turned out to be fine and dry. Many of the guests came clad in *pinni*, a hand-woven cotton cloth that ranges in colour from a flaxen beige through varying shades of apricot and orange to burnt umber. During the independence struggle *pinni* had acquired the same significance in Burma as *khaddi* in India, a symbol of patriotism and a practical sign of support for native goods.

Since 1988 it has also become the symbol of the movement for democracy. A *pinni* jacket worn with a white collarless shirt and a Kachin sarong (a tartan pattern in purple, black, and green) is the unofficial uniform for "democracy men." The dress for "democracy women" is a *pinni aingyi* (Burmese style blouse) with a traditional hand-woven sarong. During my campaign trip to the state of Kachin in 1989 I once drove through an area considered unsafe because it was within a zone where insurgents were known to be active. For mile upon mile men clad in *pinni* jackets on which the red badge of NLD [National League for Democracy] gleamed bravely stood as a "guard of honour" along the route, entirely unarmed. It was a proud and joyous sight.

The seventy-fifth anniversary of National Day brought a proud and joyous sight too. The guests were not all clad in *pinni* but there was about them a brightness that was pleasing to both the eye and the heart. The younger people were full of quiet enthusiasm and the older ones seemed rejuvenated. A well-known student politician of the 1930s who had become notorious in his mature years for the shapeless shirt, shabby denim trousers, scuffed shoes (gum boots during the monsoons), and battered hat in which he would tramp around town was suddenly transformed into a dapper gentleman in full Burmese national costume. All who knew him were stunned by the sudden picture of elegance he presented and our photographer hastened to record such an extraordinary vision.

The large bamboo and thatch pavilion that had been put up to receive the thousand guests was decorated with white banners on which were printed the green figure of a dancing peacock. As a backdrop to the stage there was a large dancing peacock, delicately executed on a white disc. This bird is the symbol of the students who first awoke the political consciousness of the people of Burma. It represents a national movement that culminated triumphantly with the independence of the country.

The orchestra had arrived a little late as there had been an attempt to try to "persuade" the musicians not to perform at our celebration. But their spirits were not dampened. They stayed on after the end of the official ceremony to play and sing nationalist songs from the old days. The most popular of these was *Nagani*, "Red Dragon." *Nagani* was the name of a book club founded by a group of young politicians in 1937 with the intention of making works on politics, economics, history, and literature accessible to the people of Burma. The name of the club became closely identified with patriotism and a song was written about the prosperity that would come to the country through the power of the Red Dragon.

Nagani was sung by a young man with a strong, beautiful voice and we all joined in the chorus while some of the guests went up on stage and performed Burmese dances. But beneath the light-hearted merriment ran a current of serious intent. The work of our national movement remains unfinished. We have still to achieve the prosperity promised by the dragon. It is not yet time for the triumphant dance of the peacock. . . .

A Baby in the Family

A couple of weeks ago some friends of mine became grandparents for the first time when their daughter gave birth to a little girl. The husband accepted his new status as grandfather with customary joviality, while the wife, too young-looking and pretty to get into the conventional idea of a cosily aged grandmother, found it a somewhat startling experience. The baby was the first grandchild for the "boy's side" as well, so she was truly a novel addition to the family circle, the subject of much adoring attention. I was told the paternal grandfather was especially pleased because the baby had been born in the Burmese month of *Pyatho* — an auspicious time for the birth of a girl child.

In societies where the birth of a girl is considered a disaster, the atmosphere of excitement and pride surrounding my friends' granddaughter would have caused astonishment. In Burma there is no prejudice against girl babies. In fact, there is a general belief that daughters are more dutiful and loving than sons and many Burmese parents welcome the birth of a daughter as an assurance that they will have somebody to take care of them in their old age.

My friends' granddaughter was only twelve days old when I went to admire her. She lay swaddled in pristine white on a comfortable pile of blankets and sheets spread on the wooden floor of my friends' bungalow, a small dome of mosquito netting arched prettily over her. It had been a long time since I had seen such a tiny baby and I was struck by its miniature perfection. I do not subscribe to the Wodehousian view that all babies look like poached eggs. Even if they do not have clearly defined features, babies have distinct expressions that mark them off as individuals from birth. And they certainly have individual cries, a fact I learned soon after the birth of my first son. It took me a few hours to realize that the yells of each tiny vociferous inmate of the maternity hospital had its own unique pitch, cadence, range, and grace-notes.

My friends' grandchild, however, did not provide me with a chance to familiarize myself with her particular milk call. Throughout my visit she remained as inanimate and still as a carved papoose on display in a museum, oblivious of the fuss and chatter around her. At one time her eyelids fluttered slightly and she showed signs of stirring but it was a false alarm. She remained resolutely asleep even when I picked her up and we all clustered around to have our photograph taken with the new star in our firmament.

Babies, I have read somewhere, are specially constructed to present an appealingly vulnerable appearance aimed at arousing tender, protective instincts: only then can tough adults be induced to act as willing slaves to demanding little beings utterly incapable of doing anything for themselves. It is claimed that there is something about the natural smell of a baby's skin that invites cuddles and kisses. Certainly I like both the shape and smell of babies, but I wonder whether their attraction does not lie in something more than merely physical attributes. Is it not the thought of a life stretching out like a shining clean slate on which might one day be written the most beautiful prose and poetry of existence that engenders such joy in the hearts of the parents and grandparents of a newly born child? The birth of a baby is an occasion for weaving hopeful dreams about the future.

However, in some families parents are not able to indulge in long dreams over their children. The infant mortality rate in Burma is 94 per 1000 live births, the fourth highest among the nations of the East Asia and Pacific Region. The mortality rate for those under the age of five too is the fourth highest in the region, 147 per 1000. And the maternal mortality rate is the third highest in the region at the official rate of 123 per 100 000 live births. (United Nations agencies surmise that the actual maternal mortality rate is in fact higher, 140 or more per 100 000.)

The reasons for these high mortality rates are malnutrition, lack of access to safe water and sanitation, lack of access to health services, and lack of caring capacity, which includes programmes for childhood development, primary education, and health education. In summary, there is a strong need in Burma for greater investment in health and education. Yet government expenditure in both sectors, as a proportion of the budget, has been falling steadily. Education accounted for 5.9 per cent of the budget in 1992–3, 5.2 per cent in 1993–4, and 5 per cent in 1994–5. Similarly, government spending on health care has dropped from 2.6 per cent in 1992–3, to 1.8 per cent in 1993–4, and 1.6 per cent in 1994–5.

Some of the best indicators of a country developing along the right lines are healthy mothers giving birth to healthy children who are assured of good care and a sound education that will enable them to face the challenges of a changing world. Our dreams for the future of the children of Burma have to be woven firmly around a commitment to better health care and better education.

UNFPA

Gender Inequality in National Parliaments

The United Nations Population Fund known by the acronym UNFPA (because it was established in 1969 as the United Nations Fund for Population Activities) works with governments and nongovernmental organizations in over 140 countries. As the largest international source for funding of population and reproductive health programs, the Fund is particularly concerned with the lives and needs of women. This reading is drawn from UNFPA's *State of the World 2005 Fact Sheet*, which summarizes the global dimensions of women's health, employment, education, and, in this particular selection, political participation. What do these charts and accompanying explanations tell you about women's political power in the governments of our contemporary world?

Thinking Historically

Theory construction almost always begins with questions. Look over the numbers in the two charts (Tables 13.1 and 13.2) in this selection and see what questions these numbers raise in your mind. Construct a theory based on the numbers in one or both of the charts. Notice how the accompanying explanations to the charts pose or answer questions. What theories do these explanations offer? How is your theory similar or different from those suggested by the explanations? What other types of sources (aside from this fact sheet and tables) would you look to to reinforce your theory?

Gender Inequality in National Parliaments

The number of women in national parliaments continues to increase, but no country in the world has yet reached gender parity.

A number of factors continue to present challenges to women's parliamentary representation:

- The type of electoral system in place in a country
- The role and discipline of political parties

United Nations Population Fund, Gender Equality Fact Sheet UNFPA, in *State of the World 2005 Fact Sheet*. Available on-line at http://www.unfpa.org/swp/2005/presskit/factsheets/facts_gender.htm.

- Women's social and economic status
- Socio-cultural traditions and beliefs about a woman's place in the family and society.
- Women's double burden of work and family responsibilities.

Since the early 1990s, women's share of *seats in parliament* has steadily increased. Nevertheless, women still hold only 16 per cent of seats worldwide.

Share of Women in Single or Lower Houses of Parliament, 1990–2005[1]

Table 13.1 Percentage of Parliamentary Seats Held by Women (single or lower house only),* 1990–2005

Regions	1990	1997	2005
World	12.4	11.4	15.9
Developed regions	15.4	15.6	20.9
Commonwealth of Independent States	—	6.2	10.5
Commonwealth of Independent States, Asia	—	7.0	11.5
Commonwealth of Independent States, Europe	—	5.4	10.5
Developing regions	10.4	10.1	14.3
Northern Africa	2.6	1.8	8.5
Sub-Saharan Africa	7.2	9.0	14.2
Latin America and the Caribbean	11.9	12.4	19.0
Eastern Asia	20.2	19.3	19.4
Southern Asia	5.7	5.9	8.3
South-Eastern Asia	10.4	10.8	15.5
Western Asia	4.6	3.0	5.0
Oceania	1.2	1.6	3.0
Least developed countries	7.3	7.3	12.7
Landlocked developing countries	14.0	6.6	13.2
Small island developing states	14.4	11.0	17.3

*Data refer to 1 January of each year.

Source: United Nations Statistics Division, "World and Regional Trends," Millennium Indicators Database, http://millenniumindicators.un.org (accessed June 2005) based on data provided by the Inter-Parliamentary Union.

The largest relative increases in the proportion of women in parliament have been in Northern Africa — where the percentage of women in parliaments tripled since 1990 — followed by Latin America and the Caribbean and sub-Saharan Africa.

---

[1]Statistics and charts are based on Department of Economic and Social Affairs. Statistics Division. Progress towards the Millennium Development Goals, 1990–2005. Available on-line at http://unstats.un.org/unsd/mi/goals_2005/goal_3.pdf. [Ed.]

There was significant progress also in the developed regions and in Southern and South-Eastern Asia.

In moving towards multiparty democracies, countries in the CIS (former Soviet Union) saw a significant decrease in the number of women in the political arena in the early 1990s. Previously, women's political participation was guaranteed, and their representation was frequently over 30 per cent.

Nordic countries have experienced a sustained and exceptionally high level of women's participation in the political arena, with the percentage of women in parliament well above 30 per cent.

Strategies for Increased Political Participation of Women

Many post-conflict countries have recognized the importance of including women in peace-building and reconstruction and have instituted measures to ensure women's participation in new democratic institutions.

- The national constitutions of Rwanda and Burundi now include provisions to reserve seats for women.
- In 2003, elections in Rwanda saw the greatest proportion of women elected to any parliament in history. These elections were the first since the internal conflict of 1994.
- The Rwandan parliament has come closest to reaching an equal number of men and women in parliament.
- In South Africa and Mozambique, the introduction of quota mechanisms by political parties meant that, in 2004, post-conflict and post-crisis countries ranked among the highest in the world in terms of women's representation.
- In Eritrea, Mozambique, and South Africa women comprise between 22 per cent to 35 per cent of the legislature.

The increase in women's parliamentary representation in Latin America and the Caribbean is also attributable to the introduction of affirmative action measures. Various quotas for women's political participation exist in 17 countries in this region. Similar efforts have been made in the Arab world.

In Morocco, the electoral law was amended prior to the 2002 parliamentary elections to reserve 30 seats for women. Thirty-five women were subsequently elected. In Tunisia, the President's party allocated 25 per cent of positions on its electoral list for women, winning them 22.7 per cent of the seats in the Chamber of Deputies in 2004. Consequently, Tunisia leads the regional ranking for women in Arab parliaments. See http://unstats.un.org/unsd/mi/goals_2005/goal_3.pdf.

Table 13.2 Countries That Have Reached 30 Per Cent Representation by Women in Parliament, as of 1 January 2005

	Percentage of seats held by women	Number of seats held by women	Total number of seats
Rwanda	48.8	39	80
Sweden	45.3	158	349
Norway	38.2	63	165
Denmark	38.0	68	179
Finland	37.5	75	200
Netherlands	36.7	55	150
Cuba	36.0	219	609
Spain	36.0	126	350
Costa Rica	35.1	20	57
Mozambique	34.8	87	250
Belgium	34.7	52	150
Austria	33.9	62	183
Argentina	33.7	86	255
Germany	32.8	197	601
South Africa	32.8	131	400
Guyana	30.8	20	65
Iceland	30.2	19	63

Source: United Nations Statistics Division, "World and Regional Trends," Millennium Indicators Database, http://millenniumindicators.un.org (accessed June 2005), based on data provided by the Inter-Parliamentary Union.

DIANE DIXON

Michelle, Top Woman in a Macho World

On March 11, 2005, Michelle Bachelet* became the first woman president of Chile, a victory made even more impressive by the fact that she was a socialist, an agnostic, and an unwed mother in a traditionally Catholic conservative country. Nor was she the daughter or widow of a previous president. In fact, she had been imprisoned and tortured by the Pinochet government that toppled the socialist

*bah chel LEHT

Diane Dixon, "Michelle, Top Woman in a Macho World," *The Observer*, April 2, 2006, n.p. Also available on-line at http://observer.guardian.co.uk/world/story/0,,1744947,00.html.

Salvador Allende* in 1973. Like Allende, she is also a medical doctor. This selection is drawn from *The Observer,* the Sunday magazine, from the British newspaper *The Guardian.* How would you explain Michelle Bachelet's popularity and political success? Is there a pattern in the success of the twelve heads of state profiled here?

Thinking Historically

This selection presents the stories of Michelle Bachelet and those of the eleven other women recently elected heads of state. Collectively they suggest various theories about a wide range of issues. We might ask how women attain such an office, what conditions or cultures make the success of women more or less likely, whether women in office pursue significantly different policies than men, whether women officials significantly improve the lives of women, and many other questions. Choose one of these questions, or ask another, and then suggest a theory to answer it. How would you try to find out if your theory was accurate or mistaken?

Michelle Bachelet remembers the day of her inauguration as Chile's first woman leader with pride: "They were very beautiful moments. I remember the feeling of joy. In the streets, thousands of women and children put on presidential sashes. It meant everyone was going to La Moneda [the Presidential Palace] together with me."

With that bright display of solidarity on a warm March day three weeks ago Bachelet became the world's 11th female elected leader. On Thursday the inauguration of Portia Simpson-Miller in Jamaica made her the 12th, and just over 6 per cent of countries are led by women. Discounting the crowned heads of the past, it is a small but unprecedented number.

What these dozen women have in common — with the exception perhaps of Bangladesh's Begum Khaleda Zia, who was projected into premiership by her husband's death — is beating intensely male-dominated odds to achieve power in some fairly conservative societies. As Bachelet said in her victory speech: "Who would have thought, friends . . . 20, 10, or five years ago, that Chile would elect a woman as president?"

And who would have thought that a Catholic country that only legalised divorce a few years ago would elect an agnostic, single mother who promised equality — exactly half of her cabinet appointees are women.

It is an undoubted phenomenon that this immensely popular multilingual mother-of-three was able to slash through the bonds of male

*ah YEHN day

political party politics to become Minister of Health and, subsequently, South America's first woman Minister of Defence. But, in an exclusive interview with *The Observer*, Bachelet said she believes the credit does not go so much to the willing patronage of her male politicians as to that of the Chilean people, who commonly call their president by her first name and sing the Beatles tune of the same name to her.

"It was said that Chile was not ready to vote for a woman, it was traditionally a sexist country. In the end, the reverse happened: The fact of being a woman became a symbol of the process of cultural change the country was undergoing. Men voted for me in their majority, but, for the first time, the Concertación [the Centre Left Coalition of which Bachelet was the candidate] also won extensively among women."

"The possibility of my presidential candidacy emerged spontaneously in public opinion polls. For my part, I noticed people's affection when I was doing work on the ground. I think the important thing is that my candidacy was born from citizens themselves, driven by the people and which the parties picked up favourably."

She is the daughter of an air force general, Alberto Bachelet, who, because he remained loyal to Salvador Allende, was killed by his own comrades after the coup that brought Augusto Pinochet to power in September 1973. She herself was a victim, along with her archaeologist mother, Angela Jeria, of the worst abuses of the Pinochet dictatorship, jailed and tortured and exiled first to Australia and then to Germany. Her only brother, Alberto, died in 2001.

In difficult circumstances under the dictatorship, she qualified as a doctor and paediatrician, going on to work with child victims of human rights abuses. But politics were always close to her. Bachelet joined Chile's Young Socialists in her teens, rising through the ranks and campaigning for the return to democracy in Chile, which was achieved in the 1988 plebiscite that ousted the Pinochet regime. When the opposition lambasted Bachelet for being overweight in the physical sense and lightweight in the political, her mother's retort was: "Have they ever looked at her CV!"

Bachelet the girl was renowned for her insistence on having her views heard and, according to Jeria, "was very firm and defended her ideas forcefully. She never accepted being told that no you can't do that. She always demanded an explanation. But at the same time she was a sweet child whose intelligence was noticeable in thousands of details."

And it was in her youth, Bachelet says, that "her most intense moments" came. "Having experienced personally and through my family the tragedy of Chile is something always present in my memory. I do not want events of that nature ever to happen again, and I have dedicated an important part of my life to ensuring that and to the reunion of all Chileans."

By the mid-1990s, she was established as an adviser in the Ministry of Health and started studies in military strategy at Chile's National

Academy for Political and Military Strategy on a course normally the reserve of military commanders. Having graduated, she was awarded a presidential grant of honour which took her to Washington to take an elite course at the Inter-American Defence College, where once again she came first.

"During the transition to democracy, I felt there was a necessity to unite two worlds, the military and the civic. I felt political leaders didn't know or understand the military world and that it was fundamentally important that political leaders got inside the world of defence to establish a bridge between the two worlds. Given political history in Chile, it seemed to me that there was a critical task of consolidating a democracy and creating healthy civic-military and political-military relationships."

In 2000, Bachelet was made minister of health by President Ricardo Lagos and handed the task of ending within three months the queues for appointments in health centres: "It was about giving a very clear signal of making people the central focus of state services. The state is at the service of people, not the opposite. My impression is that people understood the message very well, they realised the effort that we made."

In January 2002 came another challenge. Lagos took the bold step in macho Latin America of naming her minister of defence: "The truth is that I confronted it with a great deal of calm. My relationship with the armed forces was proper and normal from the beginning, despite the fact I was a woman, a socialist, and a victim of human rights abuses. But I must be honest: There was never any improper attitude towards me in the armed forces for these reasons, quite the contrary. I believe it is important to highlight this.

"In respect of political achievements, the most important thing for me is to have contributed to the consolidation of the first process of reunion between the Armed Forces and society in Chile's modern history. For many decades the military had aligned themselves to an ideology that was not shared by the whole country. Today, the Chilean military have embraced a democratic vision of their profession and are committed to a democratic state of law. I am pleased to have contributed to this process."

Having made the appointment, Lagos asked a close collaborator of Bachelet's, Carlos Ominami, if he thought she would do well. The response was: "If only we had 20 like Michelle."

Bachelet is also the mother of three children, Sebastián, Francisca, and Sofía, the youngest, who is 12. Two are by her former husband, architect Jorge Davalos, one by a subsequent boyfriend, Dr. Anibal Henriquez. Her mother gave up her own political activities to help with the grandchildren and has become a celebrity in her own right. "Once it took me five minutes to go to the supermarket," she told *The Observer*. "Now everyone wants to chat and it takes five times that."

And Bachelet recognises the support: "It is undeniable that my current responsibilities demand some changes in my life, but I aspire to maintaining the most normal family life possible. I hope that not much changes now that I am president. I would like Chileans to remember me as a transparent woman, who always said what she thought and did what she said."

Other Female Leaders

The Philippines: Undaunted Coup Survivor

The President of the Philippines may be on the *Forbes* list as the fourth most powerful woman in the world, but Gloria Arroyo, 58, is fighting calls for her resignation after narrowly escaping impeachment for allegedly rigging last year's presidential election, in which she defeated a popular film star, Fernando Poe. During her first term, she overcame a coup attempt and a Senate investigation of her lawyer husband, Jose Miguel, into alleged money laundering and keeping excess campaign funds. Arroyo, the daughter of former president Diosdado Macapagal and a trained economist, was elected to the Senate in 1992. She came to power in the rollercoaster world of Philippines politics when former film star President Joseph Estrada was toppled in a "people's revolution."

Germany: East Berlin's "Thatcher"

Often described as the German Margaret Thatcher, Angela Merkel* is the first female Chancellor of Germany. She is also the first former citizen of the old communist East Germany to head the reunited country. Fluent in Russian and English, she grew up in the countryside north of Berlin. She became involved in the pro-democracy movements that helped bring down the Berlin wall in 1989 and then entered national German politics after reunification. Her old East German party merged with the conservative CDU. She became Chancellor by defeating Gerhard Schroeder in 2005's narrow elections. After a shaky start, one poll in January showed that Merkel's popularity ratings were the highest for any German chancellor since 1949. But it has been a long hard struggle all the way for the woman whose childlessness became an election issue for her when critics attacked her for being "incomplete."

Liberia: After Exile and Prison,
the Chance to Rebuild a Nation

Liberia's new 68-year-old female president faces one of the biggest tasks of any world leader: rebuilding her shattered homeland after

*AHN gel ah   MAYR kuhl

decades of civil war. Ellen Johnson Sirleaf has said the problems are so great that even just restoring electricity to the capital Monrovia will be an achievement. She also faces a country deeply divided ethnically, flooded with guns and traumatised child soldiers.

Sirleaf has a German grandfather who married a Liberian market-woman from a rural village. She went to college in Liberia and then studied in America, including Harvard. She entered Liberian politics in 1979 and became an assistant minister of finance. During the country's multiple civil wars in the 1980s and 1990s Sirleaf spent time in jail, was exiled to Kenya, and ended up working for the World Bank. She returned with the overthrow of warlord Charles Taylor and won countrywide elections last year, defeating footballer George Weah. She was inaugurated in January.

Jamaica: "Sista P" Breaks Male Monopoly as She Guns for the Drug Gangs

Portia Simpson Miller, 60, who was sworn in as Jamaica's new Prime Minister last Thursday, has become the first female leader of a nation with a very male political culture. She launched her bid to head first the People's National Party and then the country by ignoring her critics. She was ridiculed in some parts of the island nation's media as a "serial kisser" at rallies and an intellectual lightweight. Yet Miller confounded the nay-sayers, and her genuine popularity at the grassroots level of politics saw her swept into office.

Known to many as "Sista P," Miller is seen as someone who can crack down on crime, especially the drugs trade, and bring greater economic development to a country still mired in poverty and drug violence. She has promised to enlist her friend, star athlete Asafa Powell, in the quest to end drug-related killings, especially in the slums of the capital, Kingston.

Miller first entered parliament in 1976. In a male-dominated culture she fought her way to the top, earning several ministerial portfolios including labour, welfare, and sports. She is married to Errald Miller, a former chief executive of the Jamaica arm of Cable and Wireless. She is a keen fan of boxing and golf.

Miller has criticised some aspects of Jamaica's tourist industry, saying the behaviour of some visitors clashes with the island's traditional morals.

Finland: Radical Leftist Goes on with 90 Per Cent Approval

Finland's president Tarja Halonen, 61, has just begun her second term in office. When it expires in 2012, she will have been the Scandinavian nation's head of state for 12 years. Raised in a working-class area of

Helsinki, she represents a radical leftist strand of Finnish politics. She was an unmarried mother — although has since wed her partner.

Her time in office has put a strong emphasis on pacifism, human rights, and international co-operation. Despite initially coming to office after a narrow election victory, she has become extremely popular with Finns of every political persuasion, regularly enjoying approval ratings in excess of 90 per cent. In 2004 she was the only living person to be placed in the top 10 of a television programme dedicated to the country's greatest public and historic figures.

Bangladesh: Widow Who Inherited the Mantle of Leadership

As the widow of assassinated president Ziaur Rahman, Bangladesh's first woman Prime Minister, Khaleda Zia is among the women who have had leadership foisted on them because of their marriage and subsequent widowhood. She was premier from 1991 to 1996 and again from 2001 to the present. Until her husband's death in a 1981 attempted military coup, Zia had little role in politics. But afterwards she became a senior figure in her husband's old party, the Bangladesh Nationalist Party. She has made education for girls, particularly those from poor rural families, one of her government's top priorities.

Others

Vaira Vike-Freiberga, aged 68, President of Latvia. Has been in power since 1999.

Mary McAleese, 54, President of Ireland since 1997.

Luisa Diogo, 47, Prime Minister of Mozambique since 2004.

Helen Clark, 55, Prime Minister of New Zealand since 1999.

Chandrika Kumaratunga, 60, President of Sri Lanka, in power since 1994.

Women on the Verge

Hillary Clinton, 59, hopes to run as Democratic party candidate in America's 2008 presidential race.

Ségolène Royal, 52, front runner to be chosen as the Socialist candidate to fight France's presidential elections next year.

Yulia Tymoshenko, 45, was dismissed as Prime Minister of Ukraine last September. But the results of last month's parliamentary elections, which brought her success, have brought pressure on President Viktor Yushchenko to reinstate her in a coalition government. He needs her support after suffering a setback.

REFLECTIONS

Can there be a history of women, even a history of women during the last half of the twentieth century? Or are the lives of women too diverse — globally, economically, politically, culturally — to make a single, coherent story? Is the history of women during the last fifty years markedly different from the history of men or the history of humanity?

This chapter gives only a hint of the diversity of women's lives. We included China's hopeful marriage law at the beginning of the chapter but nothing about the failures to observe it, or about women who were forced out of work to make room for men, or about girls who were sold into virtual slavery, or about young women forced to work long hours in sweatshops. Nor did we include any discussion of glamorous models in Shanghai, rich capitalists and poor sex workers in Hong Kong, or ordinary mothers, wives, and workers for whom the law of 1950 *did* make a difference.

While Betty Friedan verbalized the feelings of many American women in 1963, how many women today, exhausted by working long hours that barely cover the costs of child care and commuting, would consider returning to a fifties world of motherhood and housework? How important are national differences? In what sense, if any, does an Algerian woman who is Muslim speak for a Muslim woman in Egypt or Iran or Pakistan, or for a Christian woman in Algeria? We have not even considered women from the Middle East, India, Russia, and Europe. These questions are intended to point to the enormous variety of women's experiences. Of course, the historian is forever seeking patterns and process, but finding even the general direction of change is not as simple as it might seem.

Have the lives of women improved over the course of the last hundred or the last fifty years? It is commonly thought that the twentieth century was extremely important in freeing women from the bonds of patriarchal limitations. Often, this process is divided into two stages, the first consisting of gaining the vote in the early decades of the century in Europe and America, and the second, the successes of the women's movement since 1960. This second wave broadened the feminist critique from concerns about elections to issues of equality in the workplace and patriarchy as a social and cultural force, ultimately resulting in a cohesive movement, improved public awareness, and specific legislation regarding women's rights. In this way, the movement of the sixties became public policy.

Patriarchies continue to oppress women in many parts of the world. Women in Africa, Asia, and Latin America suffer from higher rates of illiteracy, child marriage, spousal abuse, and mortality in child birth than women in the developed world, but recent increases in parliamentary representation by women in the developing world must inevitably redress these imbalances. If the campaign for women's political rights came first to the developed world, some of the countries in the developing world have left Europe and North America far behind. Nor is the second wave or "cultural revolution" for women limited to the rich countries of the West. The success of women like Aung San Suu Kyi in Burma and Michelle Bachelet in Chile suggest that the United States and Europe might still have far to go in achieving true social and political equality for women.

For most women today, the world has been shaped less by political struggles and more by the expanding global market. Poor women in Brazil, Indonesia, China, and the Philippines have seized the opportunity to escape the authority of fathers and village elders to work in modern factories that pay far more than they ever imagined, but barely enough to survive in distant cities after sending money home. The victory of market forces in former "command economies," like Russia, Poland, and Lithuania (countries where most doctors were women), has been accompanied by drastic declines in the employment of women and men, as well as declines in the percentage of professional women.

If there is not a single history of women that is different from a single history of humanity, there are millions, indeed billions, of histories of women, women's acts, women's worlds. The selections in this chapter hint at just a few of those histories. Perhaps the most useful service our brief discussions here can serve is to encourage you to explore women's stories further.

Globalization
and Planetary Health

1960 to the Present

HISTORICAL CONTEXT

Globalization is a term used by historians, economists, politicians, religious leaders, social reformers, business people, and average citizens to describe large-scale changes and trends in the world today. It is often defined as a complex phenomenon whereby individuals, nations, and regions of the world become increasingly integrated and interdependent, and national and traditional identities are diminished. Although it is a widely used term, globalization is also a controversial and widely debated topic. Is globalization really a new phenomenon or is it a continuation of earlier trends? Is it driven by technological forces or economic forces, or both? Does it enrich or impoverish? Is it democratizing or antidemocratic? Is it generally a positive or negative thing?

Some limit the definition of globalization to the global integration driven by the development of the international market economy in the last twenty to forty years. Worldwide integration dates back much further, however, and has important technological, cultural, and political causes as well. In fact, all of human history can be understood as the story of increased interaction on a limited planet. Ancient empires brought diverse peoples from vast regions of the world together under single administrations. These empires, connected by land or maritime routes, interacted with each other through trade and exploration, exchanging goods as well as ideas. The unification of the Eastern and Western hemispheres after 1492 was a major step in the globalization of crops, peoples, cultures, and diseases. The industrial revolution joined countries and continents in ever vaster and faster transportation and communication networks. The great colonial empires that developed during the eighteenth and nineteenth centuries integrated the populations of far-flung areas of the world. The commercial aspects of these developments cannot be divorced from religious zeal, technological innovations, and political motives, which were often driving factors.

The current era of economic globalization is largely a product of the industrial capitalist world, roughly dating back to the middle of the nineteenth century. We might call the period between 1850 and 1914 the first great age of globalization in the modern sense. It was the age of ocean liners, mass migrations, undersea telegraph cables, transcontinental railroads, refrigeration, and preserved canned foods, when huge European empires dramatically reduced the number of sovereign states in the world. The period ended with World War I, which not only dug trenches between nations and wiped out a generation of future migrants and visitors, but also planted seeds of animosity that festered for decades, strangling the growth of international trade, interaction, and immigration.

Since the conclusion of World War II in 1945, and increasingly since the end of the Cold War in 1989, political and technological developments have enabled economic globalization on a wider scale and at a faster pace than occurred during the previous age of steamships and telegraphs. The collapse of the Soviet Union and international communism unleashed the forces of market capitalism as never before. Jet travel, satellite technology, mobile phones, and the World Wide Web have revived global integration and enabled the global marketplace. The United States, the World Bank, and the International Monetary Fund led in the creation of regional and international free-trade agreements, the reduction of tariffs, and the removal of national trade barriers, touting these changes as agents of material progress and democratic transformation. Yet these changes have also elicited wide-ranging resistance in peaceful protests, especially against the West's economic dominance, and violent ones against the West's political and cultural domination, protest that has taken the form of terrorist attacks like those of September 11, 2001.

Multinational companies are now able to generate great wealth by moving capital, labor, raw materials, and finished products through international markets at increasing speeds and with lasting impact. This economic globalization has profound cultural ramifications; increasingly the peoples of the world are watching the same films and television programs, speaking the same languages, wearing the same clothes, enjoying the same amusements, and listening to the same music. Whether free-market capitalism lifts all boats, or only yachts, is a hotly debated issue today.

Global health may or may not benefit from globalization, but recent developments suggest the well-being of the planet and the welfare of its inhabitants may be in jeopardy. The very integration of the world makes it possible for a virus, whether organic or cyber, to travel fast and infect the most distant areas of the planet. The uniformity of modern life makes it possible to share our dreams and inventions but also our nightmares and mistakes, and with a global and instantaneous effect as September 11th and subsequent terrorist attacks made abundantly clear. The technology of nuclear energy and war and the impact of our fossil fuel binge on the very atmosphere that supports us are causes of great concern, as are the perceived political and cultural dominance of the West.

THINKING HISTORICALLY
Understanding Process

What are the most important ways in which the world is changing? What are the most significant and powerful forces of change? What is the engine that is driving our world? These are the big questions raised at the end of historical investigation. They also arise at the beginning, as the assumptions that shape our specific investigations. Globalization is one of the words most frequently used to describe the big changes that are occurring in our world. All of the readings in this chapter assume or describe some kind of global integration as a dominant driver of the world in which we live. This chapter asks you to think about large-scale historical processes. It asks you to examine globalization as one of the most important of these processes. It asks you to reflect on what globalization means, and what causes it. How does each of these authors use the term? Do the authors see this process as primarily commercial and market-driven, or do they view it as a matter of culture or politics? Does globalization come from one place or many, from a center outwards, from one kind of society to another? Is globalization linear or unidirectional, or does it have differing, even opposite effects? What do these writers, thinkers, and activists believe about the most important changes transforming our world? And what do you think?

88

SHERIF HETATA

Dollarization

Sherif Hetata is an Egyptian intellectual, novelist, and activist who
was originally trained as a medical doctor. He and his wife, the
prominent feminist writer Nawal El-Saadawi, have worked together
to promote reform in Egypt and the larger Arab world. In the following address Hetata outlines the global economy's homogenizing effects on culture. Through what historic lens does Hetata view globalization? What links does he make between globalization and
imperialism? What do you think of his argument?

Thinking Historically

What, according to Hetata, is the main process that is changing the
world? Does he think the engine of world change is primarily technological, commercial, or cultural?

As a young medical student, born and brought up in a colony, like
many other people in my country, Egypt, I quickly learned to make the
link between politics, economics, culture, and religion. Educated in an
English school, I discovered that my English teachers looked down on
us. We learned Rudyard Kipling by heart, praised the glories of the
British Empire, followed the adventures of Kim in India, imbibed the
culture of British supremacy, and sang carols on Christmas night.

At the medical school in university, when students demonstrated
against occupation by British troops it was the Moslem Brothers who
beat them up, using iron chains and long curved knives, and it was
the governments supported by the king that shot at them or locked
them up.

When I graduated in 1946, the hospital wards taught me how
poverty and health are linked. I needed only another step to know
that poverty had something to do with colonial rule, with the king who
supported it, with class and race, with what was called imperialism at the
time, with cotton prices falling on the market, with the seizure of land by
foreign banks. These things were common talk in family gatherings,

Sherif Hetata, "Dollarization, Fragmentation, and God," in *The Cultures of Globalization*,
ed. Fredric Jameson and Masao Miyoshi (Durham, N.C.: Duke University Press, 1998),
273–74, 276–80.

expressed in a simple, colorful language without frills. They were the facts of everyday life. We did not need to read books to make the links: They were there for us to see and grasp. And every time we made a link, someone told us it was time to stop, someone in authority whom we did not like: a ruler or a father, a policeman or a teacher, a landowner, a *maulana* (religious leader or teacher), a Jesuit, or a God.

And if we went on making these links, they locked us up.

For me, therefore, coming from this background, cultural studies and globalization open up a vast horizon, one of global links in a world where things are changing quickly. It is a chance to learn and probe how the economics, the politics, the culture, the philosophical thought of our days connect or disconnect, harmonize or contradict.

Of course, I will not even try to deal with all of that. I just want to raise a few points to discuss under the title of my talk, "Dollarization, Fragmentation, and God." Because I come from Egypt, my vantage point will be that of someone looking at the globe from the part we now call South, rather than "third world" or something else.

A New Economic Order: Gazing North at the Global Few

Never before in the history of the world has there been such a concentration and centralization of capital in so few nations and in the hands of so few people. The countries that form the Group of Seven, with their 800 million inhabitants, control more technological, economic, informatics, and military power than the rest of the approximately 430 billion who live in Asia, Africa, Eastern Europe, and Latin America.

Five hundred multinational corporations account for 80 percent of world trade and 75 percent of investment. Half of all the multinational corporations are based in the United States, Germany, Japan, and Switzerland. The OECD (Organization for Economic Cooperation and Development) group of countries contributes 80 percent of world production. . . .

A Global Culture for a Global Market

To expand the world market, to globalize it, to maintain the New Economic Order, the multinational corporations use economic power and control politics and the armed forces. But this is not so easy. People will always resist being exploited, resist injustice, struggle for their freedom, their needs, security, a better life, peace.

However, it becomes easier if they can be convinced to do what the masters of the global economy want them to do. This is where the issue of culture comes in. Culture can serve in different ways to help the global economy reach out all over the world and expand its markets to the most distant regions. Culture can also serve to reduce or destroy or prevent or divide or outflank the resistance of people who do not like what is happening to them, or have their doubts about it, or want to think. Culture can be like cocaine, which is going global these days: from Kali in Colombia to Texas, to Madrid, to the Italian mafiosi in southern Italy, to Moscow, Burma, and Thailand, a worldwide network uses the methods and the cover of big business, with a total trade of $5 billion a year, midway between oil and the arms trade.

At the disposal of global culture today are powerful means that function across the whole world: the media, which, like the economy, have made it one world, a bipolar North/South world. If genetic engineering gives scientists the possibility of programming embryos before children are born, children, youth, and adults are now being programmed after they are born in the culture they imbibe mainly through the media, but also in the family, in school, at the university, and elsewhere. Is this an exaggeration? an excessively gloomy picture of the world?

To expand the global market, increase the number of consumers, make sure that they buy what is sold, develop needs that conform to what is produced, and develop the fever of consumerism, culture must play a role in developing certain values, patterns of behavior, visions of what is happiness and success in the world, attitudes toward sex and love. Culture must model a global consumer.

In some ways, I was a "conservative radical." I went to jail, but I always dressed in a classical, subdued way. When my son started wearing blue jeans and New Balance shoes, I shivered with horror. He's going to become like some of those crazy kids abroad, the disco generation, I thought! Until the age of twenty-five he adamantly refused to smoke. Now he smokes two packs of Marlboros a day (the ones that the macho cowboy smokes). That does not prevent him from being a talented film director. But in the third-world, films, TV, and other media have increased the percentage of smokers. I saw half-starved kids in a marketplace in Mali buying single imported Benson & Hedges cigarettes and smoking.

But worse was still to come. Something happened that to me seemed impossible at one time, more difficult than adhering to a left-wing movement. At the age of seventy-one, I have taken to wearing blue jeans and Nike shoes. I listen to rock and reggae and sometimes rap. I like to go to discos and I sometimes have other cravings, which so far I have successfully fought! And I know these things have crept into our lives through the media, through TV, films, radio, advertisements, newspapers, and even novels, music, and poetry. It's a culture and it's reaching out, becoming global.

In my village, I have a friend. He is a peasant and we are very close. He lives in a big mud hut, and the animals (buffalo, sheep, cows, and donkeys) live in the house with him. Altogether, in the household, with the wife and children of his brother, his uncle, the mother, and his own family, there are thirty people. He wears a long *galabeya* (robe), works in the fields for long hours, and eats food cooked in the mud oven.

But when he married, he rode around the village in a hired Peugeot car with his bride. She wore a white wedding dress, her face was made up like a film star, her hair curled at the hairdresser's of the provincial town, her finger and toe nails manicured and polished, and her body bathed with special soap and perfumed. At the marriage ceremony, they had a wedding cake, which she cut with her husband's hand over hers. Very different from the customary rural marriage ceremony of his father. And all this change in the notion of beauty, of femininity, of celebration, of happiness, of prestige, of progress happened to my peasant friend and his bride in one generation.

The culprit, or the benevolent agent, depending on how you see it, was television.

In the past years, television has been the subject of numerous studies. In France, such studies have shown that before the age of twelve a child will have been exposed to an average 100,000 TV advertisements. Through these TV advertisements, the young boy or girl will have assimilated a whole set of values and behavioral patterns, of which he or she is not aware, of course. They become a part of his or her psychological (emotional and mental) makeup. Linked to these values are the norms and ways in which we see good and evil, beauty and ugliness, justice and injustice, truth and falseness, and which are being propagated at the same time. In other words, the fundamental values that form our aesthetic and moral vision of things are being inculcated, even hammered home, at this early stage, and they remain almost unchanged throughout life.

The commercial media no longer worry about the truthfulness or falsity of what they portray. Their role is to sell: beauty products, for example, to propagate the "beauty myth" and a "beauty culture" for both females and males alike and ensure that it reaches the farthest corners of the earth, including my village in the Delta of the Nile. Many of these beauty products are harmful to the health, can cause allergic disorders or skin infections or even worse. They cost money, work on the sex drives, and transform women and men, but especially women, into sex objects. They hide the real person, the natural beauty, the process of time, the stages of life, and instill false values about who we are, can be, or should become.

Advertisements do not depend on verifiable information or even rational thinking. They depend for their effect on images, colors, smart technical production, associations, and hidden drives. For them, attracting the opposite sex or social success or professional achievement and promotion or happiness do not depend on truthfulness or hard work or character, but rather on seduction, having a powerful car, buying things or people. . . .

Thus the media produce and reproduce the culture of consumption, of violence and sex to ensure that the global economic powers, the multinational corporations can promote a global market for themselves and protect it. And when everything is being bought or sold everyday and at all times in this vast supermarket, including culture, art, science, and thought, prostitution can become a way of life, for everything is priced. The search for the immediate need, the fleeting pleasure, the quick enjoyment, the commodity to buy, excess, pornography, drugs keeps this global economy rolling, for to stop is suicide.

89

PHILIPPE LEGRAIN

Cultural Globalization Is Not Americanization

Philippe Legrain, an economist, journalist, and former advisor to the World Trade Organization, takes aim at what he calls the myths of globalization in the following article. He argues that globalization brings cultural enrichment, not monotonous conformity, and that the intermixing of cultures is an old story with many happy results. What do you think of his argument? How might Sherif Hetata respond to it?

Thinking Historically

Does the author believe the driving force of globalization is economic or cultural? How important does he think globalization is? How, according to the author, is globalization changing the world? What examples does he cite? How does Legrain's view of America differ from Hetata's?

Philippe Legrain, "Cultural Globalization Is Not Americanization," *The Chronicle of Higher Education*, 49, no. 35 (May 9, 2003): B7.

Fears that globalization is imposing a deadening cultural uniformity are as ubiquitous as Coca-Cola, McDonald's, and Mickey Mouse. Europeans and Latin Americans, left-wingers and right, rich and poor — all of them dread that local cultures and national identities are dissolving into a crass All-American consumerism. That cultural imperialism is said to impose American values as well as products, promote the commercial at the expense of the authentic, and substitute shallow gratification for deeper satisfaction.

. . . If critics of globalization were less obsessed with "Coca-colonization," they might notice a rich feast of cultural mixing that belies fears about Americanized uniformity. Algerians in Paris practice Thai boxing; Asian rappers in London snack on Turkish pizza; Salman Rushdie delights readers everywhere with his Anglo-Indian tales. Although — as with any change — there can be downsides to cultural globalization, this cross-fertilization is overwhelmingly a force for good.

The beauty of globalization is that it can free people from the tyranny of geography. Just because someone was born in France does not mean they can only aspire to speak French, eat French food, read French books, visit museums in France, and so on. A Frenchman — or an American, for that matter — can take holidays in Spain or Florida, eat sushi or spaghetti for dinner, drink Coke or Chilean wine, watch a Hollywood blockbuster or an Almodóvar, listen to bhangra or rap, practice yoga or kickboxing, read *Elle* or *The Economist*, and have friends from around the world. That we are increasingly free to choose our cultural experiences enriches our lives immeasurably. We could not always enjoy the best the world has to offer.

Globalization not only increases individual freedom, but also revitalizes cultures and cultural artifacts through foreign influences, technologies, and markets. Thriving cultures are not set in stone. They are forever changing from within and without. Each generation challenges the previous one; science and technology alter the way we see ourselves and the world; fashions come and go; experience and events influence our beliefs; outsiders affect us for good and ill.

Many of the best things come from cultures mixing: V. S. Naipaul's Anglo-Indo-Caribbean writing, Paul Gauguin painting in Polynesia, or the African rhythms in rock 'n' roll. Behold the great British curry. Admire the many-colored faces of France's World Cup–winning soccer team, the ferment of ideas that came from Eastern Europe's Jewish diaspora, and the cosmopolitan cities of London and New York. Western numbers are actually Arabic; zero comes most recently from India; Icelandic, French, and Sanskrit stem from a common root.

John Stuart Mill was right: "The economical benefits of commerce are surpassed in importance by those of its effects which are intellectual and moral. It is hardly possible to overrate the value, for the improvement of human beings, of things which bring them into contact with persons dissimilar to themselves, and with modes of thought and action unlike those with which they are familiar. . . . It is indispensable to be perpetually comparing [one's] own notions and customs with the experience and example of persons in different circumstances. . . . There is no nation which does not need to borrow from others."

It is a myth that globalization involves the imposition of Americanized uniformity, rather than an explosion of cultural exchange. For a start, many archetypal "American" products are not as all-American as they seem. Levi Strauss, a German immigrant, invented jeans by combining denim cloth (or "serge de Nîmes," because it was traditionally woven in the French town) with Genes, a style of trousers worn by Genoese sailors. So Levi's jeans are in fact an American twist on a European hybrid. Even quintessentially American exports are often tailored to local tastes. MTV in Asia promotes Thai pop stars and plays rock music sung in Mandarin. CNN en Español offers a Latin American take on world news. McDonald's sells beer in France, lamb in India, and chili in Mexico.

In some ways, America is an outlier, not a global leader. Most of the world has adopted the metric system born from the French Revolution; America persists with antiquated measurements inherited from its British-colonial past. Most developed countries have become intensely secular, but many Americans burn with fundamentalist fervor — like Muslims in the Middle East. Where else in the developed world could there be a serious debate about teaching kids Bible-inspired "creationism" instead of Darwinist evolution?

America's tastes in sports are often idiosyncratic, too. Baseball and American football have not traveled well, although basketball has fared rather better. Many of the world's most popular sports, notably soccer, came by way of Britain. Asian martial arts — judo, karate, kickboxing — and pastimes like yoga have also swept the world.

People are not only guzzling hamburgers and Coke. Despite Coke's ambition of displacing water as the world's drink of choice, it accounts for less than 2 of the 64 fluid ounces that the typical person drinks a day. Britain's favorite takeaway is a curry, not a burger: Indian restaurants there outnumber McDonald's six to one. For all the concerns about American fast food trashing France's culinary traditions, France imported a mere $620 million in food from the United States in 2000, while exporting to America three times that. Nor is plonk[1] from America's Gallo displacing Europe's finest: Italy and France together account for three-fifths of global wine exports, the United States for only a twentieth. Worldwide, pizzas are more popular than burgers, Chinese

---

[1]British slang for cheap, low-quality alcohol. [Ed.]

restaurants seem to sprout up everywhere, and sushi is spreading fast. By far the biggest purveyor of alcoholic drinks is Britain's Diageo, which sells the world's best-selling whiskey (Johnnie Walker), gin (Gordon's), vodka (Smirnoff), and liqueur (Baileys).

In fashion, the ne plus ultra is Italian or French. Trendy Americans wear Gucci, Armani, Versace, Chanel, and Hermès. On the high street and in the mall, Sweden's Hennes & Mauritz (H&M) and Spain's Zara vie with America's Gap to dress the global masses. Nike shoes are given a run for their money by Germany's Adidas, Britain's Reebok, and Italy's Fila.

In pop music, American crooners do not have the stage to themselves. The three artists who were featured most widely in national Top Ten album charts in 2000 were America's Britney Spears, closely followed by Mexico's Carlos Santana and the British Beatles. Even tiny Iceland has produced a global star: Björk. Popular opera's biggest singers are Italy's Luciano Pavarotti, Spain's José Carreras, and the Spanish-Mexican Placido Domingo. Latin American salsa, Brazilian lambada, and African music have all carved out global niches for themselves. In most countries, local artists still top the charts. According to the IFPI, the record-industry bible, local acts accounted for 68 percent of music sales in 2000, up from 58 percent in 1991.

One of the most famous living writers is a Colombian, Gabriel García Márquez, author of *One Hundred Years of Solitude*. Paulo Coelho, another writer who has notched up tens of millions of global sales with *The Alchemist* and other books, is Brazilian. More than 200 million Harlequin romance novels, a Canadian export, were sold in 1990; they account for two-fifths of mass-market paperback sales in the United States. The biggest publisher in the English-speaking world is Germany's Bertelsmann, which gobbled up America's largest, Random House, in 1998.

Local fare glues more eyeballs to TV screens than American programs. Although nearly three-quarters of television drama exported worldwide comes from the United States, most countries' favorite shows are homegrown.

Nor are Americans the only players in the global media industry. Of the seven market leaders that have their fingers in nearly every pie, four are American (AOL Time Warner, Disney, Viacom, and News Corporation), one is German (Bertelsmann), one is French (Vivendi), and one Japanese (Sony). What they distribute comes from all quarters: Bertelsmann publishes books by American writers; News Corporation broadcasts Asian news; Sony sells Brazilian music.

The evidence is overwhelming. Fears about an Americanized uniformity are over-blown: American cultural products are not uniquely dominant; local ones are alive and well.

90

MIRIAM CHING YOON LOUIE

From Sweatshop Warriors: Immigrant Women Workers Take On the Global Factory

Sherif Hetata and Philippe Legrain highlight the impact of globaliza-tion on consumers, but it is also important to examine how it affects workers. Free-trade policies have removed barriers to international trade, with global consequences. An example of such change can be witnessed along the border between Mexico and the United States, es-pecially in the export factories, or *maquiladoras*,* that are run by in-ternational corporations on both the U.S. and Mexican side of the border. In the following excerpt, Miriam Ching Yoon Louie, a writer and activist, interviews Mexican women who work in these factories and explores both the challenges they face and the strength they show in overcoming these challenges. What is the impact of liberalized trade laws on women who work in the *maquiladoras*? What is neoliberal-ism and how is it tied to globalization? Why are women particularly vulnerable to these policies?

Thinking Historically

According to Louie, how far back do neoliberalism and economic globalization date? How does Louie's assessment of economic global-ization differ from the views expressed by Legrain? How might they both be right?

M any of today's *nuevas revolucionarias* started working on the global assembly line as young women in northern Mexico for foreign transna-tional corporations. Some women worked on the U.S. side as "com-muters" before they moved across the border with their families. Their stories reveal the length, complexity, and interpenetration of the U.S. and Mexican economies, labor markets, histories, cultures, and race re-lations. The women talk about the devastating impact of globalization, including massive layoffs and the spread of sweatshops on both sides of

*mah kee lah DOH rahs

Miriam Ching Yoon Louie, *Sweatshop Warriors: Immigrant Women Workers Take On the Global Factory* (Cambridge, Mass.: South End Press, 2001), 65–71, 87–89.

the border. *Las mujeres* recount what drove them to join and lead movements for economic, racial, and gender justice, as well as the challenges they faced within their families and communities to assert their basic human rights. . . .

Growing Up Female and Poor

Mexican women and girls were traditionally expected to do all the cooking, cleaning, and serving for their husbands, brothers, and sons. For girls from poor families, shouldering these domestic responsibilities proved doubly difficult because they also performed farm, sweatshop, or domestic service work simultaneously. . . .

Petra Mata, a former seamstress for Levi's whose mother died shortly after childbirth, recalls the heavy housework she did as the only daughter:

> Aiyeee, let me tell you! It was very hard. In those times in Mexico, I was raised with the ideal that you have to learn to do everything — cook, make tortillas, wash your clothes, and clean the house — just the way they wanted you to. My grandparents were very strict. I always had to ask their permission and then let them tell me what to do. I was not a free woman. Life was hard for me. I didn't have much of a childhood; I started working when I was 12 or 13 years old.

Neoliberalism and Creeping Maquiladorization

These women came of age during a period of major change in the relationship between the Mexican and U.S. economies. Like Puerto Rico, Hong Kong, South Korea, Taiwan, Malaysia, Singapore, and the Philippines, northern Mexico served as one of the first stations of the global assembly line tapping young women's labor. In 1965 the Mexican government initiated the Border Industrialization Program (BIP) that set up export plants, called *maquiladoras* or *maquilas*, which were either the direct subsidiaries or subcontractors of transnational corporations. Mexican government incentives to U.S. and other foreign investors included low wages and high productivity; infrastructure; proximity to U.S. markets, facilities, and lifestyles; tariff loopholes; and pliant, pro-government unions. . . .

Describing her quarter-century-long sewing career in Mexico, Celeste Jiménez ticks off the names of famous U.S. manufacturers who hopped over the border to take advantage of cheap wages:

> I sewed for twenty-four years when I lived in Chihuahua in big name factories like Billy the Kid, Levi Strauss, and Lee *maquiladoras*. Every-

one was down there. Here a company might sell under the brand name of Lee; there in Mexico it would be called Blanca García.

Transnational exploitation of women's labor was part of a broader set of policies that critical opposition movements in the Third World have dubbed "neoliberalism," i.e., the new version of the British Liberal Party's program of laissez faire capitalism espoused by the rising European and U.S. colonial powers during the late eighteenth and nineteenth centuries. The Western powers, Japan, and international financial institutions like the World Bank and International Monetary Fund have aggressively promoted neoliberal policies since the 1970s. Mexico served as an early testing ground for such standard neoliberal policies as erection of free trade zones; commercialization of agriculture; currency devaluation; deregulation; privatization; outsourcing; cuts in wages and social programs; suppression of workers', women's, and indigenous people's rights; free trade; militarization; and promotion of neoconservative ideology.

Neoliberalism intersects with gender and national oppression. Third World women constitute the majority of migrants seeking jobs as maids, vendors, maquila operatives, and service industry workers. Women also pay the highest price for cuts in education, health and housing programs, and food and energy subsidies and increases in their unpaid labor. . . .

The deepening of the economic crisis in Mexico, especially under the International Monetary Fund's pressure to devaluate the peso in 1976, 1982, and 1994, forced many women to work in both the formal and informal economy to survive and meet their childbearing and household responsibilities. María Antonia Flores was forced to work two jobs after her husband abandoned the family, leaving her with three children to support. She had no choice but to leave her children home alone, *solitos*, to look after themselves. Refugio Arrieta straddled the formal and informal economy because her job in an auto parts assembly *maquiladora* failed to bring in sufficient income. To compensate for the shortfall, she worked longer hours at her *maquila* job and "moonlighted" elsewhere:

> We made chassis for cars and for the headlights. I worked lots! I worked 12 hours more or less because they paid us so little that if you worked more, you got more money. I did this because the schools in Mexico don't provide everything. You have to buy the books, notebooks, *todos, todos* [everything]. And I had five kids. It's very expensive. I also worked out of my house and sold ceramics. I did many things to get more money for my kids.

In the three decades following its humble beginnings in the mid-1960s, the *maquila* sector swelled to more than 2,000 plants employing an estimated 776,000 people, over 10 percent of Mexico's labor force. In 1985, *maquiladoras* overtook tourism as the largest source of foreign exchange. In 1996, this sector trailed only petroleum-related industries in economic importance and accounted for over U.S. $29 billion in export earnings annually. The *maquila* system has also penetrated the interior of the country, as in the case of Guadalajara's electronics assembly industry and Tehuacán's jeans production zones. Although the proportion of male *maquila* workers has increased since 1983, especially in auto-transport equipment assembly, almost 70 percent of the workers continue to be women.

As part of a delegation of labor and human rights activists, this author met some of Mexico's newest proletarians — young indigenous women migrant workers from the Sierra Negra to Tehuacán, a town famous for its refreshing mineral water springs in the state of Puebla, just southeast of Mexico City. Standing packed like cattle in the back of the trucks each morning the women headed for jobs sewing for name brand manufacturers like Guess?, VF Corporation (producing Lee brand clothing), Gap, Sun Apparel (producing brands such as Polo, Arizona, and Express), Cherokee, Ditto Apparel of California, Levi's, and others. The workers told U.S. delegation members that their wages averaged U.S. $30 to $50 a week for 12-hour work days, six days a week. Some workers reported having to do *veladas* [all-nighters] once or twice a week. Employees often stayed longer without pay if they did not finish high production goals.

Girls as young as 12 and 13 worked in the factories. Workers were searched when they left for lunch and again at the end of the day to check that they weren't stealing materials. Women were routinely given urine tests when hired and those found to be pregnant were promptly fired, in violation of Mexican labor law. Although the workers had organized an independent union several years earlier, Tehuacán's Human Rights Commission members told us that it had collapsed after one of its leaders was assassinated.

Carmen Valadez and Reyna Montero, long-time activists in the women's and social justice movements, helped found Casa de La Mujer Factor X in 1977, a workers' center in Tijuana that organizes around women's workplace, reproductive, and health rights, and against domestic violence. Valadez and Montero say that the low wages and dangerous working conditions characteristic of the *maquiladoras* on the Mexico-U.S. border are being "extended to all areas of the country and to Central America and the Caribbean. NAFTA represents nothing but the '*maquiladorization*' of the region."

Elizabeth "Beti" Robles Ortega, who began working in the *maquilas* at the age of fourteen and was blacklisted after participating in independent union organizing drives on Mexico's northern border, now works as an organizer for the Servicio, Desarrollo y Paz, AC

(SEDEPAC) [Service, Development and Peace organization]. Robles described the erosion of workers' rights and women's health under NAFTA:

> NAFTA has led to an increase in the workforce, as foreign industry has grown. They are reforming labor laws and our constitution to favor even more foreign investment, which is unfair against our labor rights. For example, they are now trying to take away from us free organization which was guaranteed by Mexican law. Because foreign capital is investing in Mexico and is dominating, we must have guarantees. The government is just there with its hands held out; it's always had them out but now even more shamelessly. . . . Ecological problems are increasing. A majority of women are coming down with cancer — skin and breast cancer, leukemia, and lung and heart problems. There are daily deaths of worker women. You can see and feel the contamination of the water and the air. As soon as you arrive and start breathing the air in Acuña and Piedras Negras [border cities between the states of Coahuila and Texas], you sense the heavy air, making you feel like vomiting.

. . .

Joining the Movement

Much of the education and leadership training the women received took place "on the job." The women talked about how much their participation in the movement had changed them. They learned how to analyze working conditions and social problems, who was responsible for these conditions, and what workers could do to get justice. They learned to speak truth to power, whether this was to government representatives, corporate management, the media, unions, or co-ethnic gatekeepers. They built relations with different kinds of sectors and groups and organized a wide variety of educational activities and actions. Their activism expanded their world view beyond that of their immediate families to seeing themselves as part of peoples' movements fighting for justice. . . .

. . . Through her participation in the movement, [María del Carmen Domínguez] developed her skills, leadership, and awareness:

> When I stayed at work in the factory, I was only thinking of myself and how am I going to support my family — nothing more, nothing less. And I served my husband and my son, my girl. But when I started working with La Mujer Obrera I thought, "I need more respect for myself. We need more respect for ourselves." (laughs) . . .
>
> . . . I learned about the law and I learned how to organize classes with people, whether they were men or women like me.

91

BENJAMIN BARBER

From Jihad vs. McWorld

Not everyone views the world as coming together, for better or worse, under the umbrella of globalization. Benjamin Barber, a political scientist, uses the terms *Jihad* and *McWorld* to refer to what he sees as the two poles of the modern global system. *McWorld* is the force of Hollywood, fast-food outlets, jeans, and Americanization. *Jihad* (the Arab word for "struggle") is used to symbolize all the nationalist, fundamentalist, ethnocentric, and tribal rejections of McWorld. Barber's argument is that these forces have largely shaped modern culture and that despite their opposition to each other, they both prevent the development of civic society and democracy: Jihad by terrorist opposition to discussion and debate, and McWorld by turning everyone into complacent, unthinking robots. What do you think of his argument? Is it persuasive? What sort of future does he predict?

Thinking Historically

Barber argues that Jihad originated in opposition to McWorld and that the two play off each other in a way that gives them both substance and support. Jihad thrives on the insensitivity, blandness, and oppression of McWorld; McWorld needs ethnic realities to give substance and soul to its theme parks and entertainments. Thus, according to Barber, they make each other stronger by struggling against each other. The gains of these two extreme positions come at the expense of a genuine, democratic civic culture. How useful is Barber's model for understanding how the world has changed?

History is not over. Nor are we arrived in the wondrous land of techné[1] promised by the futurologists. The collapse of state communism has not delivered people to a safe democratic haven, and the past, fratricide and civil discord perduring, still clouds the horizon just behind us. Those who look back see all of the horrors of the ancient slaughterbench reenacted in disintegral nations like Bosnia, Sri Lanka,

---

[1]Technology.

Benjamin Barber, *Jihad vs. McWorld: How Globalism and Tribalism Are Reshaping the World* (New York: Ballantine, 1995), 3–8.

Ossetia, and Rwanda and they declare that nothing has changed. Those who look forward prophesize commercial and technological interdependence — a virtual paradise made possible by spreading markets and global technology — and they proclaim that everything is or soon will be different. The rival observers seem to consult different almanacs drawn from the libraries of contrarian planets.

Yet anyone who reads the daily papers carefully, taking in the front page accounts of civil carnage as well as the business page stories on the mechanics of the information superhighway and the economics of communication mergers, anyone who turns deliberately to take in the whole 360-degree horizon, knows that our world and our lives are caught between what [Irish poet] William Butler Yeats called the two eternities of race and soul: that of race reflecting the tribal past, that of soul anticipating the cosmopolitan future. Our secular eternities are corrupted, however, race reduced to an insignia of resentment, and soul sized down to fit the demanding body by which it now measures its needs. Neither race nor soul offers us a future that is other than bleak, neither promises a polity that is remotely democratic.

The first scenario rooted in race holds out the grim prospect of a retribalization of large swaths of humankind by war and bloodshed: a threatened balkanization of nation-states in which culture is pitted against culture, people against people, tribe against tribe, a Jihad in the name of a hundred narrowly conceived faiths against every kind of interdependence, every kind of artificial social cooperation and mutuality: against technology, against pop culture, and against integrated markets; against modernity itself as well as the future in which modernity issues. The second paints that future in shimmering pastels, a busy portrait of onrushing economic, technological, and ecological forces that demand integration and uniformity and that mesmerize peoples everywhere with fast music, fast computers, and fast food — MTV, Macintosh, and McDonald's — pressing nations into one homogenous global theme park, one McWorld tied together by communications, information, entertainment, and commerce. Caught between Babel and Disneyland, the planet is falling precipitously apart and coming reluctantly together at the very same moment.

Some stunned observers notice only Babel, complaining about the thousand newly sundered "peoples" who prefer to address their neighbors with sniper rifles and mortars; others — zealots in Disneyland — seize on futurological platitudes and the promise of virtuality, exclaiming "It's a small world after all!" Both are right, but how can that be?

We are compelled to choose between what passes as "the twilight of sovereignty" and an entropic end of all history, or a return to the past's most fractious and demoralizing discord; to "the menace of global anarchy," to [John] Milton's capital of hell, Pandaemonium; to a world totally "out of control."

The apparent truth, which speaks to the paradox at the core of this book, is that the tendencies of both Jihad *and* McWorld are at work, both visible sometimes in the same country at the very same instant. Iranian zealots keep one ear tuned to the mullahs urging holy war and the other cocked to [Australian media mogul] Rupert Murdoch's Star television beaming in *Dynasty, Donahue,* and *The Simpsons* from hovering satellites. Chinese entrepreneurs vie for the attention of party cadres in Beijing and simultaneously pursue KFC franchises in cities like Nanjing, Hangzhou, and Xian where twenty-eight outlets serve over 100,000 customers a day. The Russian Orthodox church, even as it struggles to renew the ancient faith, has entered a joint venture with California businessmen to bottle and sell natural waters under the rubric Saint Springs Water Company. Serbian assassins wear Adidas sneakers and listen to Madonna on Walkman headphones as they take aim through their gunscopes at scurrying Sarajevo civilians looking to fill family watercans. Orthodox Hasids and brooding neo-Nazis have both turned to rock music to get their traditional messages out to the new generation, while fundamentalists plot virtual conspiracies on the Internet.

Now neither Jihad nor McWorld is in itself novel. History ending in the triumph of science and reason or some monstrous perversion thereof (Mary Shelley's Doctor Frankenstein) has been the leitmotiv of every philosopher and poet who has regretted the Age of Reason since the Enlightenment. [W. B.] Yeats lamented "the center will not hold, mere anarchy is loosed upon the world," and observers of Jihad today have little but historical detail to add. The Christian parable of the Fall and of the possibilities of redemption that it makes possible captures the eighteenth-century ambivalence — and our own — about past and future. I want, however, to do more than dress up the central paradox of human history in modern clothes. It is not Jihad and McWorld but the relationship between them that most interests me. For, squeezed between their opposing forces, the world has been sent spinning out of control. Can it be that what Jihad and McWorld have in common is anarchy: the absence of common will and that conscious and collective human control under the guidance of law we call democracy?

Progress moves in steps that sometimes lurch backwards; in history's twisting maze, Jihad not only revolts against but abets McWorld, while McWorld not only imperils but re-creates and reinforces Jihad. They produce their contraries and need one another. My object here then is not simply to offer sequential portraits of McWorld and Jihad, but while examining McWorld, to keep Jihad in my field of vision, and while dissecting Jihad, never to forget the context of McWorld. Call it a dialectic of McWorld: a study in the cunning of reason that does honor to the radical differences that distinguish Jihad and McWorld yet that acknowledges their powerful and paradoxical interdependence.

There is a crucial difference, however, between my modest attempt at dialectic and that of the masters of the nineteenth century. Still seduced by the Enlightenment's faith in progress, both [G. W. F.] Hegel and [Karl] Marx believed reason's cunning was on the side of progress. But it is harder to believe that the clash of Jihad and McWorld will issue in some overriding good. The outcome seems more likely to pervert than to nurture human liberty. The two may, in opposing each other, work to the same ends, work in apparent tension yet in covert harmony, but democracy is not their beneficiary. In East Berlin, tribal communism has yielded to capitalism. In Marx-Engelsplatz, the stolid, overbearing statues of Marx and [Friedrich] Engels face east, as if seeking distant solace from Moscow: but now, circling them along the streets that surround the park that is their prison are chain eateries like T.G.I. Friday's, international hotels like the Radisson, and a circle of neon billboards mocking them with brand names like Panasonic, Coke, and GoldStar. New gods, yes, but more liberty?

What then does it mean in concrete terms to view Jihad and McWorld dialectically when the tendencies of the two sets of forces initially appear so intractably antithetical? After all, Jihad and McWorld operate with equal strength in opposite directions, the one driven by parochial hatreds, the other by universalizing markets, the one re-creating ancient subnational and ethnic borders from within, the other making national borders porous from without. Yet Jihad and McWorld have this in common: They both make war on the sovereign nation-state and thus undermine the nation-state's democratic institutions. Each eschews civil society and belittles democratic citizenship, neither seeks alternative democratic institutions. Their common thread is indifference to civil liberty. Jihad forges communities of blood rooted in exclusion and hatred, communities that slight democracy in favor of tyrannical paternalism or consensual tribalism. McWorld forges global markets rooted in consumption and profit, leaving to an untrustworthy, if not altogether fictitious, invisible hand issues of public interest and common good that once might have been nurtured by democratic citizenries and their watchful governments. Such governments, intimidated by market ideology, are actually pulling back at the very moment they ought to be aggressively intervening. What was once understood as protecting the public interest is now excoriated as heavy-handed regulatory browbeating. Justice yields to markets, even though, as [New York banker] Felix Rohatyn has bluntly confessed, "there is a brutal Darwinian logic to these markets. They are nervous and greedy. They look for stability and transparency, but what they reward is not always our preferred form of democracy." If the traditional conservators of freedom were democratic constitutions and Bills of Rights, "the new temples to liberty," [literary critic and philosopher] George Steiner suggests, "will be McDonald's and Kentucky Fried Chicken."

In being reduced to a choice between the market's universal church and a retribalizing politics of particularist identities, peoples around the globe are threatened with an atavistic return to medieval politics where local tribes and ambitious emperors together ruled the world entire, women and men united by the universal abstraction of Christianity even as they lived out isolated lives in warring fiefdoms defined by involuntary (ascriptive) forms of identity. This was a world in which princes and kings had little real power until they conceived the ideology of nationalism. Nationalism established government on a scale greater than the tribe yet less cosmopolitan than the universal church and in time gave birth to those intermediate, gradually more democratic institutions that would come to constitute the nation-state. Today, at the far end of this history, we seem intent on re-creating a world in which our only choices are the secular universalism of the cosmopolitan market and the everyday particularism of the fractious tribe.

In the tumult of the confrontation between global commerce and parochial ethnicity, the virtues of the democratic nation are lost and the instrumentalities by which it permitted peoples to transform themselves into nations and seize sovereign power in the name of liberty and the commonweal are put at risk. Neither Jihad nor McWorld aspires to resecure the civic virtues undermined by its denationalizing practices; neither global markets nor blood communities service public goods or pursue equality and justice. Impartial judiciaries and deliberate assemblies play no role in the roving killer bands that speak on behalf of newly liberated "peoples," and such democratic institutions have at best only marginal influence on the roving multinational corporations that speak on behalf of newly liberated markets. Jihad pursues a bloody politics of identity, McWorld a bloodless economics of profit. Belonging by default to McWorld, everyone is a consumer; seeking a repository for identity, everyone belongs to some tribe. But no one is a citizen. Without citizens, how can there be democracy?

92

Global Snapshots

Cartogram of Global Warming

The Earth at Night

Population Density of the World, 2004

GDP per Capita Growth, 1990–2001

At the heart of many debates surrounding globalization is the natural environment. It is difficult to ignore the vast problems endangering the planet — global warming, acid rain, species extinction, rainforest depletion. These environmental issues require global cooperation to be solved, and they also require a certain global consciousness, or understanding, that all people are part of a global community and that what people do in one part of the world affects those in another part.

These four images provide a graphic measure of the integration and imbalances of the world today. Specifically, they show how the consumption of energy resources — heat and light — is distributed throughout the world, population density across the planet, and natural differences in economic growth, or GDP.

Figure 14.1 is a cartogram, which is a stylized map in which countries are not represented to scale, but are sized to reflect a specific measurement. This cartogram measures relative emissions of greenhouse gases by country, so the largest countries on the map emit the most gases, and the smallest emit the fewest. Which countries produce the most greenhouse gases? Which countries produce the least? What accounts for these differences?

Figure 14.2, a satellite photograph of the Earth at night, shows that energy use is no more uniform within countries than it is from one country to another. What areas of countries use the most light? Why? Does the photograph correspond to the cartogram in every respect? What does the photograph tell you about the relationship between energy use, transportation routes, urban centers, and general population density? What else can you deduce about global energy use from the photograph?

Figure 14.1 Cartogram of Global Warming. Emissions of carbon dioxide, one of the main greenhouse gases.
Source: Courtesy Mark Newman.

Figure 14.2 Satellite Photo of the Earth at Night.
Source: NASA.

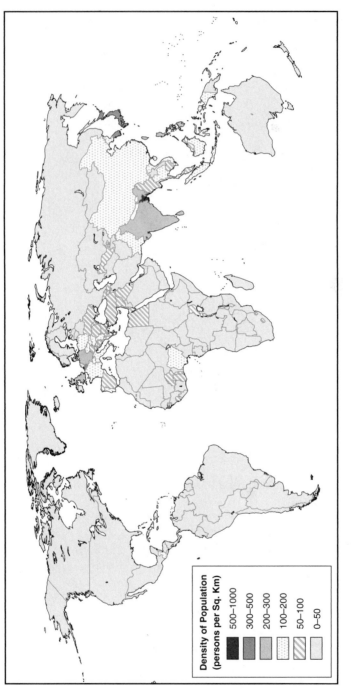

Map 14.1 Population Density of the World, 2004.
Source: © 2004 Compare Infobase Pvt. Ltd.

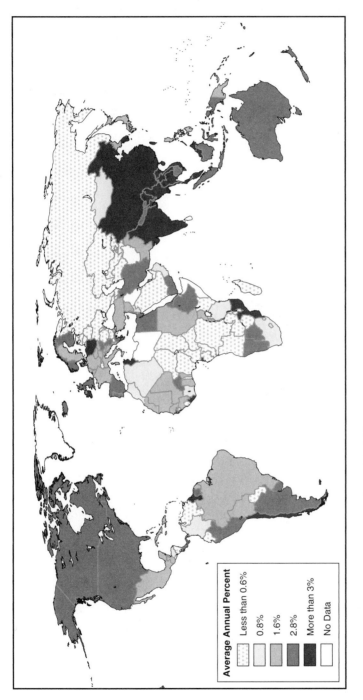

Map 14.2 GDP per Capita Growth, 1990–2001.

Source: © 2003–2004 Compare Infobase Pvt. Ltd.

Average Annual Percent

Less than 0.6%
0.8%
1.6%
2.8%
More than 3%
No Data

Thinking Historically

A snapshot is hardly the proper format to display change since it captures only a moment in time. Nevertheless, what long-term global trends can you extrapolate from these images? Can you see evidence of any of the historical processes discussed in this chapter? What historical processes do these snapshots capture most dramatically? Compare the maps of population density and of GDP with the cartogram and the satellite photo and with each other. Is there a correlation between energy use and population? Between density of population and wealth? What conclusions might you draw from comparing these maps with each other, and with previous images?

JOHN ROACH

By 2050 Warming to Doom Million Species, Study Says

Global warming looms as perhaps the most serious threat to planetary health ever. What according to this article are the likely consequences of global warming? What are its causes?

What does the cartogram in the previous selection (Figure 14.1) suggest about the causes of global warming? What is the relationship between the places most responsible for global warming and the places where the most species are disappearing?

Thinking Historically

According to the author, some scientists think that the loss of 15–35 percent of the earth's species by the year 2050 may be optimistic. They say that global warming sets in motion other processes — habitat destruction, invasive species, and the buildup of carbon dioxide in the landscape — that further increase global warming. How might these different processes be related?

John Roach, "By 2050 Warming to Doom Million Species, Study Says," *National Geographic News* (July 12, 2004), http://nationalgeographic.com/news/2004/01/0107_040107_extinction.html.

By 2050, rising temperatures exacerbated by human-induced belches of carbon dioxide and other greenhouse gases could send more than a million of Earth's land-dwelling plants and animals down the road to extinction, according to a recent study.

"Climate change now represents at least as great a threat to the number of species surviving on Earth as habitat-destruction and modification," said Chris Thomas, a conservation biologist at the University of Leeds in the United Kingdom.

Thomas is the lead author of the study published earlier this year in the science journal *Nature*. His co-authors included 18 scientists from around the world, making this the largest collaboration of its type.

Townsend Peterson, an evolutionary biologist at the University of Kansas in Lawrence and one of the study's co-authors, said the paper allows scientists for the first time to "get a grip" on the impact of climate change as far as natural systems are concerned. "A lot of us are in this to start to get a handle on what we are talking about," he said. "When we talk about the difference between half a percent and one percent of carbon dioxide emissions what does that mean?"

The researchers worked independently in six biodiversity-rich regions around the world, from Australia to South Africa, plugging field data on species distribution and regional climate into computer models that simulated the ways species' ranges are expected to move in response to temperature and climate changes. "We later met and decided to pool results to produce a more globally relevant look at the issue," said Lee Hannah, a climate change biologist with Conservation International's Center for Applied Biodiversity Science in Washington, D.C.

Study Results

According to the researchers' collective results, the predicted range of climate change by 2050 will place 15 to 35 percent of the 1,103 species studied at risk of extinction. The numbers are expected to hold up when extrapolated globally, potentially dooming more than a million species. "These are first-pass estimates, but they put the problem in the right ballpark . . . I expect more detailed studies to refine these numbers and to add data for additional regions, but not to change the general import of these findings," said Hannah.

Writing in an accompanying commentary to the study in *Nature*, J. Alan Pounds of the Monteverde Cloud Forest Reserve in Costa Rica, and Robert Puschendorf, a biologist at the University of Costa Rica, say these estimates "might be optimistic." As global warming interacts with other factors such as habitat-destruction, invasive species, and the build up of carbon dioxide in the landscape, the risk of extinction increases even further, they say.

In agreement with the study authors, Pounds and Puschendorf say taking immediate steps to reduce greenhouse gas emissions is imperative to constrain global warming to the minimum predicted levels and thus prevent many of the extinctions from occurring. "The threat to life on Earth is not just a problem for the future. It is part of the here and now," they write.

Climate Scenarios

The researchers based their study on minimum, mid-range, and maximum future climate scenarios based on information released by the United Nations Intergovernmental Panel on Climate Change (IPCC) in 2001.

According to the IPCC, temperatures are expected to rise from somewhere between 1.5 and more than 4 degrees Fahrenheit (0.8 and more than 2 degrees Celsius) by the year 2050. "Few climate scientists around the world think that 2050 temperatures will fall outside those bounds," said Thomas. "In some respects, we have been conservative because almost all future climate projections expect more warming and hence more extinction between 2050 and 2100."

In addition, the researchers accounted for the ability of species to disperse or successfully move to a new area, thus preventing climate change-induced extinction. They used two alternatives: one where species couldn't move at all, the other assuming unlimited abilities for movement. "We are trying to bracket the truth," said Peterson. "If you bracket the truth and look at the two endpoints and they give the same general message, then you can start to believe it."

Outside of the small group of researchers working directly on the impacts of climate change to species diversity, "the numbers will come as a huge shock," said Thomas.

Extinction Prevention

The researchers point out that there is a significant gap between the low and high ends of the species predicted to be on the road to extinction by 2050. Taking action to ensure the climate ends up on the low end of the range is vital to prevent catastrophic extinctions. "We need to start thinking about the fullest of costs involved with our activities, the real costs of what we do in modern society," said Peterson.

Thomas said that since there may be a large time lag between the climate changing and the last individual of a doomed species dying off, rapid reductions of greenhouse gas emissions may allow some of these species to hang on. "The only conservation action that really makes sense, at a global scale, is for the international community to minimize warming through reduced emissions and the potential establishment of carbon-sequestration programs," he said.

ANDREW C. REVKIN

Climate Data Hint at Irreversible Rise in Seas

This is another news story on global warming, reporting another set of scientific studies. But the danger presented here is rising sea levels rather than the extinction of species. What according to the author are the threats to coastal areas from the kind of global warming projected over the next one hundred years? In what ways are these conclusions similar to that of the previous article?

Thinking Historically

We might add rising sea levels to the list of factors that would interact to cause the depletion of species. Studies of global warming show us the extent of interrelationship among natural processes. This selection also warns us that natural processes can suddenly speed up or reach a tipping point of no return. Yet both of these studies suggest a fairly obvious remedy: reducing the carbon dioxide and other greenhouse gases produced by humans. What should be done? If humans can cause long-term changes in nature, can humans also prevent them?

Within the next 100 years, the growing human influence on Earth's climate could lead to a long and irreversible rise in sea levels by eroding the planet's vast polar ice sheets, according to new observations and analysis by several teams of scientists.

One team, using computer models of climate and ice, found that by about 2100, average temperatures could be four degrees higher than today and that over the coming centuries, the oceans could rise 13 to

Andrew C. Revkin, "Climate Data Hint at Irreversible Rise in Seas," *New York Times*, March 24, 2006, p. A-12.

20 feet — conditions last seen 129,000 years ago, between the last two ice ages. The findings, being reported today in the journal *Science,* are consistent with other recent studies of melting and erosion at the poles. Many experts say there are still uncertainties about timing, extent, and causes.

But Jonathan T. Overpeck of the University of Arizona, a lead author of one of the studies, said the new findings made a strong case for the danger of failing to curb emissions of carbon dioxide and other gases that trap heat in a greenhouselike effect. "If we don't like the idea of flooding out New Orleans, major portions of South Florida, and many other valued parts of the coastal U.S.," Dr. Overpeck said, "we will have to commit soon to a major effort to stop most emissions of carbon to the atmosphere."

According to the computer simulations, the global nature of the warming from greenhouse gases, which diffuse around the atmosphere, could amplify the melting around Antarctica beyond that of the last warm period, which was driven mainly by extra sunlight reaching the Northern Hemisphere.

The researchers also said that stains from dark soot drifting from power plants and vehicles could hasten melting in the Arctic by increasing the amount of solar energy absorbed by ice. The rise in sea levels, driven by loss of ice from Greenland and West Antarctica, would occur over many centuries and be largely irreversible, but could be delayed by curbing emissions of the greenhouse gases, said Dr. Overpeck and his fellow lead author, Bette L. Otto-Bliesner of the National Center for Atmospheric Research in Boulder, Colo.

In a second article in *Science,* researchers say they have detected a rising frequency of earthquakelike rumblings in the bedrock beneath Greenland's two-mile-thick ice cap in late summer since 1993. They say there is no obvious explanation other than abrupt movements of the overlying ice caused by surface melting. The jostling of that giant ice-cloaked island is five times more frequent in summer than in winter, and has greatly intensified since 2002, the researchers found. The data mesh with recent satellite readings showing that the ice can lurch toward the sea during the melting season. The analysis was led by Goran Ekstrom of Harvard and Meredith Nettles of the Lamont-Doherty Earth Observatory in Palisades, N.Y., part of Columbia University.

H. Jay Zwally, a NASA scientist studying the polar ice sheets with satellites, said the seismic signals from ice movement were consistent with his discovery in 2002 that summer melting on the surface of Greenland's ice sheets could almost immediately spur them to shift measurably. The meltwater apparently trickles through fissures and lubricates the interface between ice and underlying rock. "Models are important, but measurements tell the real story," Dr. Zwally said. "During the last 10 years, we have seen only about 10 percent of the greenhouse warming expected during the next 100 years, but already the polar ice sheets are responding in ways we didn't even know about only a few years ago."

In both Antarctica and Greenland, it appears that warming waters are also at work, melting the protruding tongues of ice where glaciers flow into the sea or intruding beneath ice sheets, like those in western Antarctica, that lie mostly below sea level. Both processes can cause the ice to flow more readily, scientists say. Many experts on climate and the poles, citing evidence from past natural warm periods, agreed with the general notion that a world much warmer than today's, regardless of the cause of warming, will have higher sea levels.

But significant disagreements remain over whether recent changes in sea level and ice conditions cited in the new studies could be attributed to rising concentrations of the greenhouse gases and temperatures linked by most experts to human activities.

Sea levels have been rising for thousands of years as an aftereffect of the warming and polar melting that followed the last ice age, which ended about 10,000 years ago. Discriminating between that residual effect and any new influence from human actions remains impossible for the moment, many experts say.

Satellites and tide gauges show that seas rose about eight inches over the last century and the pace has picked up markedly since the 1990's. Dr. Overpeck, the co-author of the paper on rising sea levels, acknowledged the uncertainties about the causes. But he said that in a world in which humans, rich and poor, increasingly clustered on coasts, the risks were great enough to justify prompt action.

"People driving big old S.U.V.'s to their favorite beach or coastal golf course," he said, should "start to think twice about what they might be doing."

LARRY ROHTER

With Big Boost from Sugar Cane, Brazil Is Satisfying Its Fuel Needs

Because modern industrial technologies bear so much responsibility for global warming, pessimists often blame technology itself or even Man the Toolmaker. Optimists, on the other hand, see hope in green technologies, which they expect to be developed by the cutting-edge, science-based, rich, competitive economies. This article gives reason to question both those who envision no technological solutions and those who look for the contemporary masters of the industrial world to go green.

How has Brazil been able to do something as important as this? What can the United States learn from Brazil?

Thinking Historically

This is a story about human, not natural, processes. Human processes frequently involve various political and economic motivations and decisions. What are some of the political and economic decisions that Brazil and the United States made in their different responses to the need for renewable energy? Why did the two countries go different ways?

At the dawn of the automobile age, Henry Ford predicted that "ethyl alcohol is the fuel of the future." With petroleum about $65 a barrel, President Bush has now embraced that view, too. But Brazil is already there. . . .

This country expects to become energy self-sufficient this year, meeting its growing demand for fuel by increasing production from petroleum and ethanol. Already the use of ethanol, derived in Brazil from sugar cane, is so widespread that some gas stations have two sets of pumps, marked A for alcohol and G for gas.

In his State of the Union address in January, Mr. Bush backed financing for "cutting-edge methods of producing ethanol, not just from corn but wood chips and stalks or switch grass" with the goal of making ethanol competitive in six years.

Larry Rohter, "With Big Boost from Sugar Cane, Brazil Is Satisfying Its Fuel Needs," *New York Times*, April 10, 2006, p. 1.

But Brazil's path has taken 30 years of effort, required several billion dollars in incentives and involved many missteps. While not always easy, it provides clues to the real challenges facing the United States' ambitions.

Brazilian officials and scientists say that, in their country at least, the main barriers to the broader use of ethanol today come from outside. Brazil's ethanol yields nearly eight times as much energy as corn-based options, according to scientific data. Yet heavy import duties on the Brazilian product have limited its entry into the United States and Europe.

Brazilian officials and scientists say sugar cane yields are likely to increase because of recent research.

"Renewable fuel has been a fantastic solution for us," Brazil's minister of agriculture, Roberto Rodrigues, said in a recent interview in São Paulo, the capital of São Paulo State, which accounts for 60 percent of sugar production in Brazil. "And it offers a way out of the fossil fuel trap for others as well."

Here, where Brazil has cultivated sugar cane since the 16th century, green fields of cane, stalks rippling gently in the tropical breeze, stretch to the horizon, producing a crop that is destined to be consumed not just as candy and soft drinks but also in the tanks of millions of cars.

The use of ethanol in Brazil was greatly accelerated in the last three years with the introduction of "flex fuel" engines, designed to run on ethanol, gasoline, or any mixture of the two. (The gasoline sold in Brazil contains about 25 percent alcohol, a practice that has accelerated Brazil's shift from imported oil.)

But Brazilian officials and business executives say the ethanol industry would develop even faster if the United States did not levy a tax of 54 cents a gallon on all imports of Brazilian cane-based ethanol.

With demand for ethanol soaring in Brazil, sugar producers recognize that it is unrealistic to think of exports to the United States now. But Brazilian leaders complain that Washington's restrictions have inhibited foreign investment, particularly by Americans.

As a result, ethanol development has been led by Brazilian companies with limited capital. But with oil prices soaring, the four international giants that control much of the world's agribusiness — Archer Daniels Midland, Bunge and Born, Cargill, and Louis Dreyfus — have recently begun showing interest.

Brazil says those and other outsiders are welcome. Aware that the United States and other industrialized countries are reluctant to trade their longstanding dependence on oil for a new dependence on renewable fuels, government and industry officials say they are willing to share technology with those interested in following Brazil's example.

"We are not interested in becoming the Saudi Arabia of ethanol," said Eduardo Carvalho, director of the National Sugarcane Agro-Industry

Union, a producer's group. "It's not our strategy because it doesn't produce results. As a large producer and user, I need to have other big buyers and sellers in the international market if ethanol is to become a commodity, which is our real goal."

The ethanol boom in Brazil, which took off at the start of the decade after a long slump, is not the first. The government introduced its original "Pro-Alcohol" program in 1975, after the first global energy crisis, and by the mid-1980's, more than three quarters of the 800,000 cars made in Brazil each year could run on cane-based ethanol.

But when sugar prices rose sharply in 1989, mill owners stopped making cane available for processing into alcohol, preferring to profit from the hard currency that premium international markets were paying.

Brazilian motorists were left in the lurch, as were the automakers who had retooled their production lines to make alcohol-powered cars. Ethanol fell into discredit, for economic rather than technical reasons.

Consumers' suspicions remained high through the 1990's and were overcome only in 2003, when automakers, beginning with Volkswagen, introduced the "flex fuel" motor in Brazil. Those engines gave consumers the autonomy to buy the cheapest fuel, freeing them from any potential shortages in ethanol's supply. Also, ethanol-only engines can be slower to start when cold, a problem the flex fuel owners can bypass.

"Motorists liked the flex-fuel system from the start because it permits them free choice and puts them in control," said Vicente Lourenço, technical director at General Motors do Brasil.

Today, less than three years after the technology was introduced, more than 70 percent of the automobiles sold in Brazil, expected to reach 1.1 million this year, have flex fuel engines, which have entered the market generally without price increases.

"The rate at which this technology has been adopted is remarkable, the fastest I have ever seen in the motor sector, faster even than the airbag, automatic transmission or electric windows," said Barry Engle, president of Ford do Brasil. "From the consumer standpoint, it's wonderful, because you get flexibility and you don't have to pay for it."

Yet the ethanol boom has also brought the prospect of distortions that may not be as easy to resolve. The expansion of sugar production, for example, has come largely at the expense of pasture land, leading to worries that the grazing of cattle, another booming export product, could be shifted to the Amazon, encouraging greater deforestation.

Industry and government officials say such concerns are unwarranted. Sugar cane's expanding frontier is, they argue, an environmental plus, because it is putting largely abandoned or degraded pasture land back into production. And of course, ethanol burns far cleaner than fossil fuels.

Human rights and worker advocacy groups also complain that the boom has led to more hardships for the peasants who cut sugar cane. "You used to have to cut 4 tons a day, but now they want 8 or 10, and if you can't make the quota, you'll be fired," said Silvio Donizetti Palvequeres, president of the farmworkers union in Ribeirão Preto, an important cane area north of here. "We have to work a lot harder than we did 10 years ago, and the working conditions continue to be tough."

Producers say that problem will be eliminated in the next decade by greater mechanization. A much more serious long-term worry, they say, is Brazil's lack of infrastructure, particularly its limited and poorly maintained highways.

Ethanol can be made through the fermentation of many natural substances, but sugar cane offers advantages over others, like corn. For each unit of energy expended to turn cane into ethanol, 8.3 times as much energy is created, compared with a maximum of 1.3 times for corn, according to scientists at the Center for Sugarcane Technology here and other Brazilian research institutes.

"There's no reason why we shouldn't be able to improve that ratio to 10 to 1," said Suani Teixeira Coelho, director of the National Center for Biomass at the University of São Paulo. "It's no miracle. Our energy balance is so favorable not just because we have high yields, but also because we don't use any fossil fuels to process the cane, which is not the case with corn."

Brazilian producers estimate that they have an edge over gasoline as long as oil prices do not drop below $30 a barrel. But they have already embarked on technical improvements that promise to lift yields and cut costs even more.

In the past, the residue left when cane stalks are compressed to squeeze out juice was discarded. Today, Brazilian sugar mills use that residue to generate the electricity to process cane into ethanol, and use other byproducts to fertilize the fields where cane is planted.

Some mills are now producing so much electricity that they sell their excess to the national grid. In addition, Brazilian scientists, with money from São Paulo State, have mapped the sugar cane genome. That opens the prospect of planting genetically modified sugar, if the government allows, that could be made into ethanol even more efficiently.

"There is so much biological potential yet to be developed, including varieties of cane that are resistant to pesticides and pests and even drought," said Tadeu Andrade, director of the Center for Sugarcane Technology. "We've already had several qualitative leaps without that, and we are convinced there is no ceiling on productivity, at least theoretically."

REFLECTIONS

Understanding the process of change is the most useful "habit of mind" we gain from studying the past. Although the facts are many and the details overwhelming, process only appears through the study of the specific. And we must continually check our theories of change with the facts, and revise them to conform to new information.

More important, understanding change does not necessarily mean that we must submit to it. Of the processes of globalization discussed in this chapter — trade and technological transfers, cultural homogenization and competition, commercialization, and market expansion — some may seem inevitable, some merely strong, some even reversible. Intelligent action requires an appreciation of the possible as well as the identification of the improbable.

The process of global warming poses the threat of a far greater catastrophe than globalization. For the first time, humans threaten to permanently unbalance nature. We do not know when human action will push nature to a tipping point that is irreversible. The results for hundreds of millions of people living in coastal zones, the extinction of species, and the unleashing of violent weather patterns would constitute the greatest multiple disasters of human history. We would have only ourselves to blame.

History is not an exact science. Fortunately, human beings are creators, as well as subjects, of change. Even winds that cannot be stopped can be deflected and harnessed. Which way is the world moving? What are we becoming? What can we do? What kind of world can we create? These are questions that can only be answered by studying the past, both distant and recent, and trying to understand the overarching changes that are shaping our world. Worlds of history converge upon us, but only one world will emerge from our wishes, our wisdom, and our will.

Acknowledgments

Chinua Achebe. "An Image of Africa: Racism in Conrad's *Heart of Darkness*." First published in *Massachusetts Review* 18 (1977): 782–94. Copyright © by Chinua Achebe. Reprinted by permission of David Higham Associates, Limited.

"Aztec Account of the Conquest." From *The Broken Spears: The Atzec Account of the Conquest of Mexico*, by Miguel Leon-Portilla. Copyright © 1962, 1990 by Miguel Leon-Portilla. Expanded and Updated Edition © 1992 by Miguel Leon-Portilla. Reprinted by permission of Beacon Press, Boston.

Benjamin Barber. Excerpt from *Jihad vs. McWorld: How Globalism and Tribalism Are Reshaping the World*. Copyright © 1995 by Benjamin R. Barber. Used by permission of Times Books, a division of Random House, Inc.

Franklin Le Van Baumer. "The Scientific Revolution in the West." From *Main Currents of Western Thought*, edited by Franklin Le Van Baumer. Copyright © 1978 by Franklin Le Van Baumer. Reprinted by permission of Yale University Press.

Anna Bijns. "Unyoked Is Best! Happy Is the Woman without a Man." From *Women Writers of the Renaissance and Reformation*, edited by Katharina M. Wilson. Copyright 1987 by The University of Georgia Press. Reprinted by permission of The University of Georgia Press.

David Cannadine. Excerpt from *Ornamentalism: How the British Saw Their Empire*. Copyright © 2005. Reprinted by permission of Oxford University Press.

Iris Chang. Excerpt from *The Rape of Nanking: The Forgotten Holocaust of World War II*. Copyright © 1997 by Iris Chang. Reprinted with the permission of Basic Books, a member of Perseus Books, LLC.

John H. Coatsworth. "Economic Trajectories in Nineteenth-Century Latin America." From *Latin America and the World Economy since 1800*, edited by John H. Coatsworth and Alan M. Taylor. Copyright © 1998 by Harvard University Press. Reprinted by permission.

Natalie Zemon Davis. Excerpted text from *Women on the Margins: Three Seventeenth-Century Lives* by Natalie Zemon Davis. The Belknap Press of Harvard University Press. Copyright © 1995 by the President and Fellows of Harvard College. Reprinted by permission of the publisher.

Carolina Maria de Jesus. Excerpts from *Child of the Dark: The Diary of Carolina Maria de Jesus* by Carolina Maria de Jesus, translated by David St. Clair. Translation copyright © 1962 by E. P. Dutton & Co., Inc., New York and Souvenier Press Ltd., London. Used by permission of Dutton, a division of Penguin Group (USA) Inc.

Bernal Díaz. Excerpt from *The Conquest of New Spain* by Bernal Díaz. Translated by J. M. Cohen (Penguin Classics, 1963). Copyright © J. M. Cohen, 1963. Reprinted by permission of Penguin Group, UK.

Diane Dixon. "Michelle, Top Woman in a Macho World." From *The Observer*, Sunday, April 2, 2006. Copyright © Guardian Newspapers Limited, 2006. Reprinted with permission.

Bartolomeo de Las Casas. Excerpt from *Bartolomeo de Las Casas: A Selection of His Writings* by Bartolomeo de Las Casas, translated by George Sanderlin. Copyright © 1971 by Alfred A. Knopf, a division of Random House, Inc. Used by permission of Alfred A. Knopf, a division of Random House, Inc.

Assia Djebar. "Growing Up in Algeria." From *Fantasia: An Algerian Cavalcade*, translated by Dorothy S. Blair. Copyright © 1993 Dorothy S. Blair. Reprinted by permission of Heinemann (Portsmouth, NH).

Jawaharlal Nehru. "Gandhi." From *Toward Freedom: The Autobiography of Jawaharlal Nehru.* Reprinted by permission of the Jawaharlal Nehru Memorial Fund.

George Orwell. Excerpt from *Burmese Days* by George Orwell. Copyright © by George Orwell and renewed 1962 by Sonia Pitt-Rivers. Reprinted by permission of Harcourt, Inc. and Bill Hamilton as the Literary Executor of the Estate of the Late Sonia Brownell Orwell and Seeker & Warburg, Ltd.

Jurgen Osterhammel. Excerpt from *Colonialism*, translated by Shelly Frisch. Copyright © 1997 by Shelly L. Frisch. Reprinted with the permission of Markus Weiner Publishers.

Arnold Pacey. "Asia and the Industrial Revolution." From *Technology in World Civilizations: A Thousand Year History.* Copyright 1990. Reprinted by permission of MIT Press, Cambridge, Mass.

Kenneth Pomeranz. "How the Other Side Traded." From *The World That Trade Created: Society, Culture, and the World Economy, 1400 to the Present*, 2nd edition by Kenneth Pomeranz and Steven Topik. Copyright © 2006 by M. E. Sharpe, Inc. Reprinted with permission.

Donald Quataert. Excerpts from *The Ottoman Empire, 1700–1922.* Copyright © 2000 by Donald Quataert. Reprinted with the permission of Cambridge University Press.

Erich Maria Remarque. Excerpt from *All Quiet on the Western Front* by Erich Maria Remarque. "Im Western Nichts Neues." Copyright 1928 by Ullstein A. G.; Copyright renewed © 1956 by Erich Maria Remarque. "All Quiet on The Western Front." Copyright 1929, 1930 by Little, Brown and Company. Copyright renewed © 1957, 1958 by Erich Maria Remarque. All rights reserved. Reprinted by permission of Pryor Cashman Sherman and Flynn LLP.

Andrew C. Revkin. "Climate Data Hint at Irreversible Rise in Seas." From *The New York Times*, March 24, 2006. Copyright © 2006 by The New York Times Company. Reprinted with permission.

Matteo Ricci. "Jesuit Missionaries in Ming China." From *China in the Sixteenth Century* by Matteo Ricci, translated by Louis J. Gallagher. Copyright © 1942, 1953 and renewed 1970 by Louis J. Gallagher, S.J. Used by permission of Random House, Inc.

John Roach. "By 2050 Warming to Doom Million Species, Study Says." From *National Geographic News*, July 12, 2004. Copyright © 2004 by National Geographic Society. Reprinted with permission.

Larry Rohter. "With Big Boost from Sugar Cane, Brazil Is Satisfying Its Fuel Needs." From *The New York Times*, April 10, 2006. Copyright © 2006 by The New York Times Company. Reprinted with permission.

Kirkpatrick Sale. Excerpt from *The Conquest of Paradise.* Copyright © 1990 Kirkpatrick Sale. Used by permission of Alfred A. Knopf, a division of Random House, Inc.

Lynda Norene Shaffer. "China, Technology and Change." From *World History Bulletin* 4, no. 1 (Fall/Winter, 1986–87): 1–6. Copyright © 1987. Reprinted with permission.

Ari Shavit. "An Interview with Benny Morris." From *Ha'aretz*, January 9, 2004. Copyright © 2004 by Ari Shavit. Reprinted with permission of Ha'aretz Syndication Service.

Jonathan Spence. "The Late Ming Empire." From *The Search for Modern China.* Copyright © 1990 by Jonathan Spence. Used by permission of W. W. Norton & Company, Inc. Includes Tang Xianzu, excerpts from *The Peony Pavilion*, translated by Cyril Birch. Copyright © 1980 by Indiana University Press. Reprinted with the permission of the publishers.

Luther Standing Bear. Excerpt from *Land of the Spotted Eagle* by Luther Standing Bear. Copyright © 1933 by Luther Standing Bear. Renewal Copyright 1960 by May Jones. Reprinted by permission of the University of Nebraska Press.

Peter N. Stearns. "The Industrial Revolution Outside the West." From *Industrial Revolution in World History* by Peter N. Stearns. Copyright © 1998 by Westview Press. Reprinted by permission of Westview Press, a member of Perseus Books, LLC.

Jean-François Steiner. Excerpt from *Treblinka.* English translation copyright © 1967 by Simon & Schuster, Inc. Reprinted with the permission of Simon & Schuster Adult Publishing Group.

Theodore von Laue. Excerpt from *The World Revolution of Westernization: The Twentieth Century in Global Perspective.* Copyright 1987 by Oxford University Press, Inc. Used by permission of Oxford University Press, Inc.

John E. Wills Jr. "Sor Juana Inés de la Cruz." From *1688: A Global History.* Copyright © 2001 John E. Wills Jr. Used by permission of W. W. Norton & Company, Inc.

Iwasaki Yataro. "Letter to Employees of the Mitsubishi Company." From *Sources of Japanese History*, Volume II, by David Lu, ed. Copyright © 1974 (McGraw-Hill). Reprinted by permission of David Lu.

Fukuzawa Yukichi. "Datsu-a Ron (On Saying Good-bye to Asia)." From *Japan: A Documentary History*, Vol II: *The Late Tokugawa Period to the Present* by David J. Lu, ed. Translation copyright © 1997 by David J. Lu. Reprinted by permission of M. E. Sharpe, Inc.

Zheng He. "Inscription to the Goddess." From *China and Africa in the Middle Ages*, ed. Teobaldo Filesi, translated and inscribed by David Morrison. Copyright © 1972 by David Morrison. Reprinted with permission of the publisher.

Selected World History Titles in the *Bedford Series in History and Culture*

SPARTACUS AND THE SLAVE WARS
A Brief History with Documents
Translated, Edited, and with an Introduction by Brent D. Shaw, *University of Pennsylvania*

THE BLACK DEATH: THE GREAT MORTALITY OF 1348–1350
A Brief History with Documents
John Aberth, *Castleton State College*

CHRISTOPHER COLUMBUS AND THE ENTERPRISE OF THE INDIES
A Brief History with Documents
Geoffrey Symcox, *University of California, Los Angeles*, and Blair Sullivan, *University of California, Los Angeles*

VICTORS AND VANQUISHED
Spanish and Nahua Views of the Conquest of Mexico
Edited with an Introduction by Stuart B. Schwartz, *Yale University*

THE INTERESTING NARRATIVE OF THE LIFE OF OLAUDAH EQUIANO, **Written by Himself, With Related Documents, Second Edition**
Edited with an Introduction by Robert J. Allison, *Suffolk University*

SLAVE REVOLUTION IN THE CARIBBEAN, 1789–1804
A Brief History with Documents
Laurent Dubois, *Michigan State University,* and John D. Garrigus, *Jacksonville University*

SLAVERY, FREEDOM, AND THE LAW IN THE ATLANTIC WORLD
A Brief History with Documents
Sue Peabody, *Washington State University Vancouver,* and Keila Grinberg, *Universidade Federal do Estado do Rio de Janeiro / Universidade Candido Mendes*

MAO ZEDONG AND CHINA'S REVOLUTIONS
A Brief History with Documents
Timothy Cheek, *University of British Columbia*

For a complete list of titles in the Bedford Series in History and Culture, please visit bedfordstmartins.com/history.

TradeUp

Package any title from our sister companies at Holtzbrinck Publishers — at a discount of 50% off the regular price. To see a complete list of trade titles available for packaging, go to bedfordstmartins.com/tradeup.

 PICADOR palgrave macmillan